Global Leadership Perspectives on Industry, Society, and Government in an Era of Uncertainty

Ataus Samad
Western Sydney University, Australia

Ezaz Ahmed
Columbia College, USA

Nitin Arora
Amity International Business School, Amity University, India

A volume in the Advances in Logistics, Operations, and Management Science (ALOMS) Book Series

Published in the United States of America by
IGI Global
Business Science Reference (an imprint of IGI Global)
701 E. Chocolate Avenue
Hershey PA, USA 17033
Tel: 717-533-8845
Fax: 717-533-8661
E-mail: cust@igi-global.com
Web site: http://www.igi-global.com

Copyright © 2023 by IGI Global. All rights reserved. No part of this publication may be reproduced, stored or distributed in any form or by any means, electronic or mechanical, including photocopying, without written permission from the publisher. Product or company names used in this set are for identification purposes only. Inclusion of the names of the products or companies does not indicate a claim of ownership by IGI Global of the trademark or registered trademark.
Library of Congress Cataloging-in-Publication Data

Names: Samad, Ataus, 1966- editor. | Ahmed, Ezaz, 1975- editor. | Arora, Nitin, 1979- editor. | Sharif, Taimur, 1972- editor.
Title: Global leadership perspectives on industry, society, and government in an era of uncertainty / edited by Ataus Samad, Ezaz Ahmed, Nitin Arora, Taimur Sharif.
Description: Hershey, PA : Business Science Reference, [2023] | Includes bibliographical references and index. | Summary: "The objective of this book is to examine how leaders from industry, society, and government respond to and manage crisis such as COVID-19 pandemic in a variety of cultural and national contexts. The proposed book 'Global Leadership Perspectives on Industry, Society, and Government in an Era of Uncertainty' is poised to address the contemporary leadership issues besides addressing the fundamental issues such as its definition, evolution of leadership theories, its distinction from management, and implication for gender, culture and different fields of knowledge will focus on contemporary global issues such as changes in the business environment, rapidly changing technological advancement, climate change , natural disaster and pandemic such as COVID 19 that may affect leadership"-- Provided by publisher.
Identifiers: LCCN 2023003360 (print) | LCCN 2023003361 (ebook) | ISBN 9781668482575 (hardcover) | ISBN 9781668482582 (paperback) | ISBN 9781668482599 (ebook)
Subjects: LCSH: Leadership. | Crisis management.
Classification: LCC HD57.7 .G6525 2023 (print) | LCC HD57.7 (ebook) | DDC 658.4/092--dc23/eng/20230310
LC record available at https://lccn.loc.gov/2023003360
LC ebook record available at https://lccn.loc.gov/2023003361

This book is published in the IGI Global book series Advances in Logistics, Operations, and Management Science (ALOMS) (ISSN: 2327-350X; eISSN: 2327-3518)

British Cataloguing in Publication Data
A Cataloguing in Publication record for this book is available from the British Library.

All work contributed to this book is new, previously-unpublished material. The views expressed in this book are those of the authors, but not necessarily of the publisher.

For electronic access to this publication, please contact: eresources@igi-global.com.

Advances in Logistics, Operations, and Management Science (ALOMS) Book Series

John Wang
Montclair State University, USA

ISSN:2327-350X
EISSN:2327-3518

Mission

Operations research and management science continue to influence business processes, administration, and management information systems, particularly in covering the application methods for decision-making processes. New case studies and applications on management science, operations management, social sciences, and other behavioral sciences have been incorporated into business and organizations real-world objectives.

The **Advances in Logistics, Operations, and Management Science** (ALOMS) Book Series provides a collection of reference publications on the current trends, applications, theories, and practices in the management science field. Providing relevant and current research, this series and its individual publications would be useful for academics, researchers, scholars, and practitioners interested in improving decision making models and business functions.

Coverage

- Networks
- Risk Management
- Finance
- Organizational Behavior
- Political Science
- Marketing engineering
- Computing and information technologies
- Services management
- Decision analysis and decision support
- Operations Management

IGI Global is currently accepting manuscripts for publication within this series. To submit a proposal for a volume in this series, please contact our Acquisition Editors at Acquisitions@igi-global.com or visit: http://www.igi-global.com/publish/.

The Advances in Logistics, Operations, and Management Science (ALOMS) Book Series (ISSN 2327-350X) is published by IGI Global, 701 E. Chocolate Avenue, Hershey, PA 17033-1240, USA, www.igi-global.com. This series is composed of titles available for purchase individually; each title is edited to be contextually exclusive from any other title within the series. For pricing and ordering information please visit http://www.igi-global.com/book-series/advances-logistics-operations-management-science/37170. Postmaster: Send all address changes to above address. Copyright © 2023 IGI Global. All rights, including translation in other languages reserved by the publisher. No part of this series may be reproduced or used in any form or by any means – graphics, electronic, or mechanical, including photocopying, recording, taping, or information and retrieval systems – without written permission from the publisher, except for non commercial, educational use, including classroom teaching purposes. The views expressed in this series are those of the authors, but not necessarily of IGI Global.

Titles in this Series

For a list of additional titles in this series, please visit: www.igi-global.com/book-series/advances-logistics-operations-management-science/37170

Digital Supply Chain, Disruptive Environments, and the Impact on Retailers
Ehap Sabri (University of Texas at Dallas, USA)
Business Science Reference • © 2023 • 373pp • H/C (ISBN: 9781668472989) • US $250.00

Digital Entrepreneurship and Co-Creating Value Through Digital Encounters
Farag Edghiem (Manchester Metropolitan University, UK) Mohammed Ali (University of Salford, UK) and Robert Wood (University of Manchester, UK)
Business Science Reference • © 2023 • 312pp • H/C (ISBN: 9781668474167) • US $250.00

Principles of External Business Environment Analyzability in an Organizational Context
Bruno F. Abrantes (Niels Brock Copenhagen Business College, Denmark)
Business Science Reference • © 2023 • 318pp • H/C (ISBN: 9781668455432) • US $215.00

Change Management During Unprecedented Times
Kyla Latrice Tennin (College of Doctoral Studies, University of Phoenix, USA & Forbes School of Business, USA & World Business Angels Investment Forum (WBAF)-G20, USA & Lady Mirage Global, Inc., USA)
Business Science Reference • © 2023 • 413pp • H/C (ISBN: 9781668475096) • US $250.00

Handbook of Research on Blockchain Technology and the Digitalization of the Supply Chain
Tharwa Najar (Gafsa University, Tunisia) Yousra Najar (Manar University, Tunisia) and Adel Aloui (EM Normandie Business School, France)
Business Science Reference • © 2023 • 520pp • H/C (ISBN: 9781668474556) • US $295.00

Perspectives on Women in Management and the Global Labor Market
Elisabete S. Vieira (GOVCOPP, University of Aveiro, Portugal) Mara Madaleno (GOVCOPP, University of Aveiro, Portugal) and João Teodósio (Polytechnic Institute of Santarém, Portugal)
Business Science Reference • © 2023 • 382pp • H/C (ISBN: 9781668459812) • US $240.00

Perspectives and Strategies of Family Business Resiliency in Unprecedented Times
Hotniar Siringoringo (Gunadarma University, Indonesia) and Ravindra Hewa Kuruppuge (University of Peradeniya, Sri Lanka)
Business Science Reference • © 2023 • 322pp • H/C (ISBN: 9781668473948) • US $240.00

701 East Chocolate Avenue, Hershey, PA 17033, USA
Tel: 717-533-8845 x100 • Fax: 717-533-8661
E-Mail: cust@igi-global.com • www.igi-global.com

Dedicated to the invisible leaders, the unseen architects of change, who lead without ceremony, inspire without publicity, and shape the future of society. This book carries your legacy.

Editorial Advisory Board

Kristine Barnett, *Columbia College, Columbia, USA*
Stephen Boyle, *James Cook University, Australia*
Roopak Kumar Gupta, *Indian Institute of Management, Kozhikode, India*
Yvonne Howie, *Chancellor Institute, Australia*
Raman K. Jha, *ICFAI Jharkhand, India*
Amir Mahmood, *Western Sydney University, Australia*
Shamira Soren Malekar, *Borough of Manhattan Community College, City University of New York, USA*
Kristin Martin, *University in Columbus, USA*
Priyadarshi Patnaik, *Indian Institute of Technology, Kharagpur, India*
Francis Schodowski, *Presbyterian College, Clinton, USA*
Meg Smith, *School of Business, Western Sydney University, Australia*

Table of Contents

Foreword *by Amir Mahmood* xx

Foreword *by Francis G. Schodowski* xxii

Foreword *by Gurinder Singh* xxiv

Foreword *by Meg Smith* xxvi

Foreword *by Kristine Barnett* xxviii

Preface xxx

Acknowledgment xxxiii

Section 1
Concept of Leadership

Chapter 1
Managerialism and Leadership 1
    Thomas Klikauer, Western Sydney University, Australia

Chapter 2
Positive Leadership and the Quiet Quitting Movement in Organizations 19
    Ana Filipa Vieira Lopes Joaquim, Faculdade de Ciências Sociais e Humanas, Portugal
    Paula Cristina Nunes Figueiredo, Universidade Lusófona, Portugal
    Vasco Rafael Costa Silva, Instituto Politécnico de Gestão e Tecnologia, Portugal
    Cristina Nogueira da Fonseca, Instituto Politécnico de Gestão e Tecnologia, Portugal

Section 2
Leadership and Gender

Chapter 3
Indigenous Women in Academia: Reflections on Leadership 36
    Bronwyn Fredericks, The University of Queensland, Australia
    Tracey Bunda, The University of Queensland, Australia
    Abraham Bradfield, The University of Queensland, Australia

Chapter 4
Emerging Issues in Gender and Leadership: Succession Planning and Gender Equality in Australian Universities 55
    Sheree Gregory, Western Sydney University, Australia

Section 3
Leadership in an Organisational Context

Chapter 5
Women in School Leadership in India and the United States: Realities, Complexities, and Future Directions 69
    Adity Saxena, Woxsen University, India
    Monique Darrisaw Akil, Uniondale Union Free School District, USA
    Pavani Ayinampudi, Telangana Social Welfare Residential Educational Institutions Society, India

Chapter 6
An Integrated Framework for Leadership: The Case of Higher Education 92
    Narayan Tiwari, Crown Institute of Higher Education, Australia
    Wayne Fallon, Western Sydney University, Australia
    Jayne Bye, Western Sydney University, Australia

Chapter 7
Trade Union Leadership and Sustainability in the Contemporary World of Work............................ 110
    Adekunle Tinuoye, Micheal Imoudu National Institute for Labour Studies, Nigeria

Section 4
Leadership, Work-Life Conflict, Wellbeing, and Happiness

Chapter 8
Leading With Happiness: The Institutional Happiness Framework for Higher Education Leaders... 132
    Palak Verma, Amity University, Noida, India
    Nitin Arora, Amity University, Noida, India
    Ezaz Ahmed, Columbia College, USA

Chapter 9
Ethical Leadership and Its Impact on Employee Well-Being: A Study Based in Manufacturing Firms 148
    Reshma Shrivastava, Amity University, Raipur, India
    Imran Nadeem Siddiqui, Amity University, Raipur, India
    Gazala Yasmin Ashraf, Amity University, Raipur, India

Chapter 10
The Basic Strategy of Leadership Landscape: Employee Retention and Work-Life Balance 163
    Sonali Malewar, Marketing Department, Sri Balaji University, Pune, India
    Shilpi Gupta, Amity Business School, Amity University, Raipur, India

Section 5
Dark Side of Leadership

Chapter 11
The Dark Side of Leadership 176
Bhawna Gaur, Amity University, Dubai, UAE

Chapter 12
Positive Impact of Leaders' Dark Triad Personality Traits in Uncertain Times 202
Gunjan Mishra, ITM University, Raipur, India
Shaivi Shrivastava, Amity University, Raipur, India
Mrityunjay Bandhopadhyay, Amity University, Raipur, India
Navisha Bajaj, Amity University, Raipur, India
Sakshi Mishra, Institute of Public Health, India
Tarannum Sarwar Dani, Jain University (Deemed), India

Section 6
Emerging Leadership Concepts

Chapter 13
Leadership in a VUCA World 217
Bhavika Bindra, Amity University, Noida, India
Shikha Kapoor, Amity University, Noida, India

Chapter 14
Future of Leadership: A Study on Small and Medium Sized Enterprises 235
Mansi Dudeja, Amity University, Noida, India
Shikha Kapoor, Amity University, Noida, India

Chapter 15
E-Leadership Concepts, Competencies, and Challenges 248
Siyu Liu, Swinburne University of Technology, Australia
Diana Rajendran, Swinburne University of Technology, Australia

Chapter 16
Undergraduate Business Students' Perceptions About Virtual and Remote-Work Leadership Skills 272
Anas Al-Fattal, University of Minnesota, Crookston, USA
Eddie G. Walker II, University of Minnesota, Crookston, USA
Rachel Lundbohm, University of Minnesota, Crookston, USA

Chapter 17
Anglophone Shattered Hopes and Lost Illusions: Post-Pandemic Political Leadership 289
Sureyya Yigit, New Vision University, Georgia

Compilation of References 313

About the Contributors 370

Index 376

Detailed Table of Contents

Foreword by Amir Mahmood xx

Foreword by Francis G. Schodowski.. xxii

Foreword by Gurinder Singh xxiv

Foreword by Meg Smith xxvi

Foreword by Kristine Barnett xxviii

Preface... xxx

Acknowledgment xxxiii

Section 1
Concept of Leadership

These chapters deal with the basic issues related to leadership such as leadership, management, and styles of leadership. The first chapter explains key models of managerialism and links them to managerial leadership by discussing its impact on workers, on organizations, and the environment. The next chapter highlights the importance of positive leadership in mitigating the quiet quitting movement or intention to leave through developing an organizational culture of promoting employee engagement.

Chapter 1
Managerialism and Leadership 1
  Thomas Klikauer, Western Sydney University, Australia

The term managerialism has been used for a long time. Yet, managerialism lacks theory development and models explaining how it spreads through organizations and how it is linked to management leadership. In recent years, several conceptual frameworks of managerialism have been constructed. These enable the building of managerialism models and connecting them to managerial leadership. Three key models of managerialism have been developed: (1) organizational model, (2) global model, and (3) trident model. This chapter explains these models and links them to managerial leadership. Developing a conceptual model of managerialism might allow us to ascertain the impact of managerialism on organizations, workers, and the environment. They may provide preliminary elements in the development of a theory of managerialism. The link between these models and managerial leadership is discussed by highlighting two versions of managerial leaders: corporate apparatchiks and the apostles of managerialism. This is applied to managerial leadership working in two distinctly different spheres.

Chapter 2
Positive Leadership and the Quiet Quitting Movement in Organizations... 19
    Ana Filipa Vieira Lopes Joaquim, Faculdade de Ciências Sociais e Humanas, Portugal
    Paula Cristina Nunes Figueiredo, Universidade Lusófona, Portugal
    Vasco Rafael Costa Silva, Instituto Politécnico de Gestão e Tecnologia, Portugal
    Cristina Nogueira da Fonseca, Instituto Politécnico de Gestão e Tecnologia, Portugal

This chapter seeks to highlight the importance of positive leadership in combating the phenomenon of quiet quitting. This phenomenon is not new, but it has gone viral with the COVID-19 pandemic, being more 'visible' in the organizational context. Thus, the objective of this research is to identify the main advantages of positive leadership in mitigating the quiet quitting movement. The research methodology is qualitative and starts by conceptualizing and identifying the main causes and consequences of the quiet quitting movement. Afterwards, the advantages of positive leadership are identified and, finally, this leadership style is systematized in relation to happiness and well-being at work. This research thus integrates the positive leadership approach with practices to improve employee engagement and organizational culture, highlighting the importance of human resource management practices to attract, integrate and manage talent in companies.

Section 2
Leadership and Gender

Significant changes have occurred over the last few decades in terms of female participation including female leadership in organizations and social scientists, management consultants, and others have highlighted the aspect of gender and leadership in different organisational setting. The first chapter in this section reflects upon the barriers Indigenous women academics face in achieving senior leadership positions in the higher education sector and how leadership is intertwined with resistance and cultural safety. The next chapter discusses succession planning and gender equality in Australian universities. The author advocated for a longer-term focus on diversity, equality, and inclusion of women in leadership succession planning within the higher education sector and prioritizing intersectional practices and approaches to diminish barriers of female leadership for facilitating a more equitable workplace in the future.

Chapter 3
Indigenous Women in Academia: Reflections on Leadership 36
    Bronwyn Fredericks, The University of Queensland, Australia
    Tracey Bunda, The University of Queensland, Australia
    Abraham Bradfield, The University of Queensland, Australia

Despite increasing numbers of Indigenous women within Australian universities, Indigenous academics continue to face barriers that obstruct promotions to senior leadership positions. Reflecting on a capacity-building program run by and for Indigenous women, the authors explore Indigenous peoples' responses to institutional racism. The authors consider how leadership is synonymous with resistance and misguided characterisations of Indigenous people and scholarship. They demonstrate that leadership emerges out of culturally safe spaces conducive to communal and reciprocal learning. Providing participants with the tools and mentorship needed to progress within the academy, they can acquire the support and confidence needed to push back to oppressive structures. Indigenous academics continue to engage their sovereignty and forge their own spaces. The authors argue that greater leadership is needed by universities whose policies and governance structures have the ability and power to further promote Indigenous peoples to leadership positions and build capacity amongst emerging leaders.

Chapter 4
Emerging Issues in Gender and Leadership: Succession Planning and Gender Equality in
Australian Universities.. 55
Sheree Gregory, Western Sydney University, Australia

Diversity, equality, and inclusion in leadership are critical for innovation and Australia's future. Despite considerable changes to the position of women in public life in advanced economies since second wave feminism, the invisibility of women in leadership has persisted. The under-representation of women in senior leadership, including women from culturally diverse backgrounds, remains a major challenge. This chapter presents a qualitative study of succession planning in relation to gender in Australian universities. The author argues for a longer-term focus on diversity, equality, and inclusion in leadership, and non-traditional leadership, in succession planning, to negotiate the glass ceiling and move towards a more equitable future of work in Australian universities. The author discusses prioritising intersectional approaches and practices of inclusion in leadership succession planning and management, to reveal how barriers to career progression in the neoliberal university, for non-traditional leaders can be dismantled and more equitable futures of work can be reimagined.

Section 3
Leadership in an Organisational Context

While identification and development of effective leaders is of prime concern in contemporary organizations, context is an important factor that influences leadership styles and leader effectiveness. This section discusses leadership in the organisational context. Linking the issues of gender that is discussed in the previous chapter, the first chapter examines the underrepresentation of women in school leadership positions in India and the United States. The next chapter explored integrated framework for leadership in higher education in Australia, incorporating three major domains, e.g., behaviors, mindsets, and skills. The next chapter discusses the challenges faced by trade unions in the contemporary work environment and emphasized the importance of cohesion, unity, and solidarity, supported by pragmatic, and ethical leadership.

Chapter 5
Women in School Leadership in India and the United States: Realities, Complexities, and Future
Directions... 69
Adity Saxena, Woxsen University, India
Monique Darrisaw Akil, Uniondale Union Free School District, USA
Pavani Ayinampudi, Telangana Social Welfare Residential Educational Institutions Society, India

Women's representation in school leadership positions in India, and of Black women in the United States, remains unexplored. This chapter addresses the realities and complexities of women leaders in school education and develops a narrative based on current trends and anticipated challenges for the future. Existing research in educational leadership in schools, case studies, and interviews tend to focus on developing a coherent understanding of the topic. The representation of women in the school, from teachers to leaders, is an inverted pyramid. This chapter aims to provide an overview of how women school leaders from India and the USA manage crises, navigate politics, establish policies and budgets, and where the constraints lie at the school board and family level. Finally, using the grounded theory framework, the authors will present a pattern of women's leadership similarities, differences, and uniqueness in the context of both countries.

Chapter 6
An Integrated Framework for Leadership: The Case of Higher Education 92
  Narayan Tiwari, Crown Institute of Higher Education, Australia
  Wayne Fallon, Western Sydney University, Australia
  Jayne Bye, Western Sydney University, Australia

In the turbulent and volatile operating environment of Australia's higher education sector, leadership is critical in responding to institutional challenges. This chapter presents a dynamic integrated framework for leadership that can support leaders in these institutions and, potentially, other organisations as well. The chapter describes the outcomes of a Delphi study that sought to uncover areas of consensus about leadership, among leaders and academics across the sector. The study revealed 15 distinct elements of leadership, and these were found to fall into three separate but interrelated groups or domains of leadership: behaviours, mindsets, and skills. Together, these domains are claimed to provide an appropriate and practical representation of effective leadership in higher education. The dynamic integration of these domains and elements of leadership into an interrelated tripartite arrangement, a framework for leadership, is argued to represent a new approach to understanding the leadership phenomenon.

Chapter 7
Trade Union Leadership and Sustainability in the Contemporary World of Work 110
  Adekunle Tinuoye, Micheal Imoudu National Institute for Labour Studies, Nigeria

The industrial revolution resulted in a conflict of interest between the employer and employee and the emergence of trade unions. By contributing to harmonizing workplace interests, formulating rules governing workplace relations, and protecting workers' rights and welfare, the imprimatur of trade unions are manifest in every facet of global socio-economic and political progress. However, certain developments, practices, and trends have served to weaken the labor movement and brought to the fore germane questions about the utility of trade unions; and it is against this background, that the ethos of unity, cohesion, and solidarity and backed by sound, pragmatic, and ethical leadership should be utilized in their quest to continue to organize, mobilize, and strategize to champion the cause of the working class. Therefore, this chapter would focus on the above themes and proffer leadership strategies for the continued relevance of trade unions as institutions for servicing worker needs in eras of uncertainty.

Section 4
Leadership, Work-Life Conflict, Wellbeing, and Happiness

In today's volatile, uncertain, complex, and ambiguous global environment, organisations are increasingly recognising the importance of employee well-being and, their work-life conflict and happiness and the effect of leadership on these issues. The first chapter in this section examines the factors contributing to happiness of academics and proposes a framework for institutional happiness for building sustainable universities. The next chapter explores the effect of ethical leadership on employee well-being in an organisational context. And the third chapter examined the role of effective leadership in enhancing employee performance and retention while promoting employee work-life balance.

Chapter 8
Leading With Happiness: The Institutional Happiness Framework for Higher Education Leaders... 132
    Palak Verma, Amity University, Noida, India
    Nitin Arora, Amity University, Noida, India
    Ezaz Ahmed, Columbia College, USA

This study investigates the changes in leaders' perspectives towards framing new educational policies supporting sustainable empowerment of academicians via focusing on happiness and well-being. The objectives of this study are (1) to explore various factors influencing academicians' happiness post-pandemic, (2) to propose various guidelines for educational leaders to support future policy formulation, and (3) to develop an institutional happiness framework for building sustainable universities. Based on interviews with university professors, a qualitative methodology is being utilized where themes are extracted using NVIVO. The study highlights various factors contributing towards enhancing academicians' happiness (i.e., academic freedom, work-life balance, workload management, annual academic retreats, ex-student appreciation rewards, mindfulness in research). The proposed institutional happiness model can be used to enhance research practices, teaching patterns, community service awareness, and innovation, which positively contribute towards achieving SDG 3, SDG 4, and SDG 9.

Chapter 9
Ethical Leadership and Its Impact on Employee Well-Being: A Study Based in Manufacturing Firms 148
    Reshma Shrivastava, Amity University, Raipur, India
    Imran Nadeem Siddiqui, Amity University, Raipur, India
    Gazala Yasmin Ashraf, Amity University, Raipur, India

Though ethical leadership and the well-being of employees have been important topics of discussion for research in recent years, just a few studies have looked at the impact of ethical leadership on employee well-being. This chapter aims to examine the effect of ethical leadership on the well-being of employees in the manufacturing firm and to examine the mediating role of employee engagement. The purposive sampling method was used to collect the data through a structured questionnaire, and a total of 264 responses were collected, which were analyzed on Smart PLS version 3.3.2. The findings suggest that there exists a strong correlation between EL and EWB. Also, there is a strong mediation of EE on the relationship between EE and EWB. The theory builds upon and suggests a strong mediating relationship between EL and EWB when EE acts as a mediator. The finding also suggests that the employees can be engaged in an organization to improve performance through EL.

Chapter 10
The Basic Strategy of Leadership Landscape: Employee Retention and Work-Life Balance 163
    Sonali Malewar, Marketing Department, Sri Balaji University, Pune, India
    Shilpi Gupta, Amity Business School, Amity University, Raipur, India

Leadership comportment has a substantial influence on employee behavior, performance, and welfare. The existing theory and research on leadership performance has mainly focused on employee performance, but both terminologies have expanded a lot of magnitude in the present era of the business world. The leaders of the team construct and communicate a vision or an aim that they want the team to accomplish, and the leaders motivate the team to accomplish that goal by explaining the benefits of doing so. The leaders provide their team members with assistance and guidance so that they may make progress toward completing their duties. The present study explains in a theoretical but very interactive way how effective leadership can help boost the performance of employees and sequentially helps the organization recognize its quality employees and tap their efficiencies for the long term through employee retention. Previous research has discovered the influence of several factors on employee well-being to inform the practice to enhance workplace results for both employees and employers.

Section 5
Dark Side of Leadership

While traditional leadership literature looked at leadership in terms of a positive virtue and charismatic attributes among leaders, the contemporary leadership literature also examines the negative aspects of different leadership styles and attributes. The first chapter in this section provides solutions for reducing toxicity in the work environment while introducing the concept of destructive leadership styles associated with personality disorders. The next chapter examined the relationship between dark triad personality traits such as narcissism, psychopathy, and Machiavellianism and their impact on effective leadership outcomes. The authors argued that dark leadership traits positively correlate with capabilities in leaders during crisis.

Chapter 11
The Dark Side of Leadership 176
    Bhawna Gaur, Amity University, Dubai, UAE

Personality traits favored by situational factors may lead to destructive tendencies in a good leader. For example, CEOs such as Larry Page of Google, Lloyd Blankfein of Goldman Sachs, Mark Zuckerberg of Facebook, and Elon Musk of Tesla have exhibited a shift from constructive to destructive leadership style due to situational or environmental factors. Destructive or dark leadership style is associated with personality traits such as narcissism, Machiavellianism, and psychopathy. This chapter introduces the concept of personality disorders that might threaten the effectiveness of an individual as a leader. It will further discuss the factors that contribute to the development of destructive personalities and different types of destructive personalities. This chapter will identify the role of followers and environment that provide legitimacy for immoral actions. It will provide solutions to improve leadership practices to reduce toxicity in the work environment and create a positive workplace.

Chapter 12
Positive Impact of Leaders' Dark Triad Personality Traits in Uncertain Times 202
    Gunjan Mishra, ITM University, Raipur, India
    Shaivi Shrivastava, Amity University, Raipur, India
    Mrityunjay Bandhopadhyay, Amity University, Raipur, India
    Navisha Bajaj, Amity University, Raipur, India
    Sakshi Mishra, Institute of Public Health, India
    Tarannum Sarwar Dani, Jain University (Deemed), India

The effectiveness of a leader is determined by their leadership skills. Although each leader has their own distinct style, there are a few commonly known forms of leadership, including transformational, transactional, democratic, servant, and charismatic authority leadership. Contrarily, the dark triad, which includes the personality traits of narcissism, psychopathy, and Machiavellianism, is a dark personality trait. Even though these characteristics of dark triad can cause personality disorders, they somehow improve a leader's ability in a crisis. Secondary data have been gathered through a variety of techniques to support the former mentioned statement. According to the findings, dark traits are positively correlated with effective leadership outcomes and crisis management and decision making, in whole or in part.

Section 6
Emerging Leadership Concepts

The recent COVID-19 pandemic environment revealed the importance of leadership in leading organisations in uncertain and volatile environment. Furthermore, in the face of the organizational challenges brought by the digital revolution, globalisation, and other socioeconomic changes in the word undoubtedly affected future leadership. Hence the first topic in this section explores the challenges of leading in a volatile, uncertain, complex, and ambiguous global environment, while the second discusses the impact of digitization on leadership in small and medium enterprises (SMEs), followed by a chapter examining e-leadership concepts, competencies, and challenges in the era of digital transformation and remote work. The next chapter would investigate business students' understanding of the challenges and preferences in virtual and remote work settings and their perceptions of virtual leadership skills. The last chapter of this section analyses transformational and transactional leadership styles among leaders during the COVID-19 pandemic.

Chapter 13
Leadership in a VUCA World.. 217
    Bhavika Bindra, Amity University, Noida, India
    Shikha Kapoor, Amity University, Noida, India

This chapter expands on all of the preceding material by focusing on a leader's capacity to formulate and convey leadership in uncertain times. As the world has become "VUCA"—volatile, unpredictable, complex, and ambiguous—there are no hard and fast rules for operating enterprises in the 2020s. The hierarchical organization paradigm is dead in the VUCA environment, and other models are developing, but there is no dominant model that works for everyone. New times necessitate new regulations, but there is no universal norm that applies to every sector and scenario. Leaders have been walking a tightrope for the last two years, attempting to maintain stability while coping with a disruptive and unpredictable pandemic, failing to hire despite a 15-year high in talent shortages, and revising policies to suit employee expectations for more flexibility at work. Multiple waves of coronavirus variations have put executives in a difficult position: trying to comfort and focus people in the face of ongoing uncertainty while having no idea what will happen next.

Chapter 14
Future of Leadership: A Study on Small and Medium Sized Enterprises 235
    Mansi Dudeja, Amity University, Noida, India
    Shikha Kapoor, Amity University, Noida, India

This chapter discusses how digitization has changed leadership and what it means for leaders. Digitalization has been heralding changes for years, including an increase in remote leadership and the usage of digital communication tools. Small and medium-sized businesses (SMEs) are now faced with the challenge of adjusting to these developments and must deal with significant uncertainties: the key trends that leaders in SMEs should consider, the changes that will affect leadership and how they will alter the behaviours that are essential for success. The experts' predictions for trends include adjustments to organizational structures and workplace practices. Organizationally, businesses will become more flexible and diversified with less emphasis on hierarchies, and they will work more closely together. Big data will have a bigger impact on work, and many jobs will be automated or made simpler by technology.

Chapter 15
E-Leadership Concepts, Competencies, and Challenges 248
    Siyu Liu, Swinburne University of Technology, Australia
    Diana Rajendran, Swinburne University of Technology, Australia

The information technology industry is transforming organisations in unprecedented ways. The COVID-19 pandemic has resulted in most organisations having to convert to virtual offices. This transformation has promoted e-leadership in organisations as a means and style of management. To explore e-leadership, this chapter focuses on its concepts, competencies, and challenges. A systematic literature review was conducted involving 331 journal articles, of which 21 were explored in greater depth. The chapter provides a valuable insight into e-leadership practice. It argues that new e-leadership challenges arising from modern ICTs urgently require further research, especially in e-trust, work-life balance, and psychological contracts between management and workers. E-competencies need to be developed together with the ability to manage emotions to overcome challenges in virtual environments that did not exist in the 'face-to-face' world.

Chapter 16
Undergraduate Business Students' Perceptions About Virtual and Remote-Work Leadership Skills 272
    Anas Al-Fattal, University of Minnesota, Crookston, USA
    Eddie G. Walker II, University of Minnesota, Crookston, USA
    Rachel Lundbohm, University of Minnesota, Crookston, USA

With changes introduced to the work environment since the COVID-19 pandemic, an ever-increasing amount of interest has been focused on virtual leadership. This chapter researches the topic of virtual leadership and focuses on investigating business students' perceptions of skills relevant to virtual leadership positions. The chapter presents an empirical exploratory research study conducted through four focus groups with 20 undergraduate business students. The findings reveal business students have a relevant understanding of the differences between traditional and virtual work environments. Socialization and isolation are among the most dominant themes regarding the differences in work modes. The findings also show that business students understand the challenges associated with leading in virtual and remote work settings, and they prefer traditional future leadership positions to avoid such challenges. The study highlights several relevant leadership skills needed according to business students such as communication, the ability to engage, and technological competencies.

Chapter 17
Anglophone Shattered Hopes and Lost Illusions: Post-Pandemic Political Leadership 289
    Sureyya Yigit, New Vision University, Georgia

This chapter investigates within the realm of political communication transformational and transactional leadership during and after the COVID-19 pandemic. It attempts to identify which qualities and styles political leaders need to incorporate in the face of such challenges such as the COVID-19 pandemic. It focuses on the actions taken by Trump, Johnson, Marin, and Ardern within the fields of public health strategies, education, and employment to draw a clear and contrasting portrait of the political landscape regarding trustworthy and resilient leadership.

Compilation of References 313

About the Contributors 370

Index 376

Foreword

The call for extraordinary leadership has never been more urgent in a world shaken to its core by the COVID-19 pandemic. It is impossible to exaggerate the significance of visionary, adaptable, and compassionate leadership as we navigate the uncharted waters of these turbulent times. *Global Leadership Perspectives on Industry, Society, and Government in an Era of Uncertainty* is a ground-breaking and timely compilation that sheds light on the complexities and difficulties of leadership in our swiftly changing world.

This book explores the kaleidoscope of leadership topics, revealing contemporary dilemmas and the guiding principles that have shaped the field throughout history. The breadth of the topics covered in "Global Leadership Perspectives" is remarkable. This book provides a valuable window on how to keep good employees to develop their leadership abilities to the rise of successful female business owners and more. Readers will embark on an exciting journey through chapters that examine, among other topics, ethical leadership, the influence of digitalization on small and medium-sized businesses, the challenges faced by Indigenous women in academia, and the complexities of leading in remote and virtual work environments.

Diverse contributors contribute their voices and expertise, revealing a treasury of perspectives and disciplines woven into a rich tapestry of leadership insights. The authors' wealth of knowledge and experience illuminates the multidimensional leadership landscape in an uncertain era and equips readers with the tools to navigate confidently and resiliently. *Global Leadership Perspectives on Industry, Society, and Government in an Era of Uncertainty* is a must-read for anyone seeking to comprehend the critical role of leadership in times of difficulty.

As the world continues to grapple with the lingering effects of the COVID-19 pandemic and the changes it has created in our social, economic, and political spheres, this book serves as a beacon for those who wish to learn from the past and forge a brighter, more adaptive, and more compassionate future. This book will serve as a compass for leaders, managers, executives, policymakers, human resource managers, entrepreneurs, students, higher education instructors, researchers, and academics by presenting an array of perspectives and analyses. I enthusiastically recommend this book to anyone seeking to understand leadership's mysteries and its impact on our world in these challenging and uncertain times. The authors' diverse perspectives and insightful analyses will captivate and enlighten readers, nurturing a profound appreciation for leadership's pivotal role in determining our collective destiny.

Amir Mahmood
School of Business, Western Sydney University, Australia

Foreword

Amir Mahmood *is the Dean of Western Sydney University, School of Business. He holds a Master and a PhD in Economics from the University of Manitoba, Canada. Before joining Western Sydney University, he was the Pro Vice-Chancellor of the University of Newcastle (UON) in Singapore and the Chief Executive Officer of UON Singapore. He also held a number of senior academic leadership positions at UON, including the interim Pro Vice-Chancellor (Business & Law), Deputy Head of Faculty (Business & Law), Interim Pro Vice-Chancellor (International & Advancement), Assistant Dean International, Director Executive and Corporate Programs, Deputy and interim Head of Newcastle Graduate School of Business. With extensive experience in Australian and international higher education systems, Professor Mahmood is an established leader in the area of internationalisation of higher education. Over the years, he has successfully negotiated, implemented, and managed international collaborative initiatives across a range of cultural, linguistic, political and economic contexts in the Asia Pacific region. A recipient of the Australian Government Endeavour Malaysia Research Fellowship, Professor Mahmood has an active research track record in the field of economics, business and management. Professor Mahmood has also worked on projects funded by international and national organisations such as the World Bank, Agriculture Canada/Canadian International Development Agency (CIDA), the Department for International Development (DFID, UK), and the Workplace Safety and Health (WSH) Institute, Singapore.*

Foreword

Leadership is not only a topic of research for the academy, it is a topic that permeates all aspects of life- personally and professionally. The topic is often brought to light when there is significance in the accomplishments of an individual in a role, or when there is an individual who has fallen from grace. What it is that got a person to the spot of leadership; and what will assist others in what is a perceived ascent are often at the heart of such conversation. Leadership needs to be reviewed from a broad and worldly lens, particularly in a world that intersects personal and professional, in a sociologically, economically, and demographically diverse and enriched global environment of business, education, and societal perspectives. The world has been challenged to adapt, change, and grow through the ever-present unknowns that exist. Outbreaks of war, inflationary pressures, global pandemics, shifts in demographics, and technological breakthroughs are cause for shifts in perspective on leadership during times of uncertainty.

The authors of each chapter of *Global Leadership Perspectives on Industry, Society, and Government in an Era of Uncertainty* reach deep into the various areas around which leadership impact. This book digs into aspects of the topic that will provide meaning and impact for those who are engaged in components of leadership with an understanding that can be central to their lives and their work. Beyond a narrow lens, the editors and authors touch on the reality of leadership that is relevant in the day-to-day of a world that is diverse, embracing each chapter with a look at leadership on a topic that presents relevance and understanding. A key strength demonstrated is the diverse range of perspectives it presents. The authors, from various academic disciplines provide a multi-faceted view of leadership.

This book serves as a valuable resource for those who are within the academy, and those who seek to learn from and become engaged in a study of true global leadership – leadership that spans so many areas. From looking at employees to others impacted by leadership and from education to workplace. Leadership continues to develop and grow as society adjusts to the fluidity that has been brought forth through a shrinking world exacerbated by the pandemic and the sharing of information.

Dr. Ezaz Ahmed and Ataus Samad, along with Professor Nitin Arora, lend their expertise, global perspective, and scholarly purview to compiling and editing a book that elevates the importance of all aspects of leadership in an eloquent academic perspective. For anyone who is looking to better understand leadership that reaches all people, this is a book that brings together the many aspects that will impact shaping their personal and professional lives.

Francis G. Schodowski
Presbyterian College, USA

Foreword

Francis G. Schodowski *is a leader within American higher education serving in the areas of enrollment management, advancement and fundraising, athletics, and strategic planning. He has been a presidential advisor and worked with members of Board of Trustees and governing bodies to be engaged as key leaders across institutions. He received his Bachelor's degree from Elizabethtown College (PA) in business administration/marketing, his Master's in Business Administration from Alvernia University (PA) in non-profit and community service, and his Doctor of Education from Northeastern University (MA). His doctoral study was on the recruitment and onboarding of the Board of Trustees. Mr. Schodowski has served higher education in leadership roles for more than 25 years, most recently as the Vice President for Advancement at Presbyterian College (SC).*

Foreword

It is my great pleasure to introduce the exceptional publication *Global Leadership Perspectives on Industry, Society, and Government in the Era of Uncertainty*. This book, meticulously curated by esteemed academicians, researchers, and leadership experts, provides invaluable insights into the dynamic landscape of leadership in today's world.

In an era characterized by unprecedented challenges and constant change, effective leadership has become more crucial than ever. The contributors to this book have delved deep into the complexities of leadership, offering diverse perspectives that illuminate its multifaceted nature. Through their collective wisdom and experiences, readers gain a comprehensive understanding of the intricacies and demands faced by leaders across industries, societies, and governments.

Within the pages of this book, readers embark on a transformative journey, exploring critical topics such as leadership and employee well-being, the legacy of leadership, contemporary leadership issues, leadership and organizational change, and the influence of culture. Each chapter presents innovative approaches, practical strategies, and thought-provoking analyses that enrich the understanding of aspiring and seasoned leaders alike.

I commend the contributors for their remarkable expertise and dedication, as their profound knowledge and passion for leadership have culminated in a collection of research insights that inspire, challenge, and empower readers from all walks of life.

With over 28 years of experience in institutional building, teaching, consultancy, research, and industry, I have had the privilege of witnessing firsthand the transformative power of effective leadership. Through my interactions with renowned scholars, academics, and industry leaders, I have developed a deep appreciation for the significance of leadership in shaping the trajectory of organizations and societies.

As you embark on this intellectual expedition, I encourage you to immerse yourself in the profound wisdom presented in this book. May the insights shared by the contributors guide and inspire leaders to navigate the challenges of our uncertain world with resilience, empathy, and visionary thinking.

I extend my heartfelt congratulations to the authors, editors, and the IGI publisher for their remarkable efforts in bringing forth this exceptional publication. May it serve as a beacon of knowledge and inspiration, fostering a new generation of global leaders committed to shaping a brighter and more prosperous future.

Gurinder Singh
Amity University, India

Foreword

Gurinder Singh, *Group Vice Chancellor, Amity Universities, Director General, Amity Group of Institutions and Vice Chairman, Global Foundation for Learning Excellence, has an extensive experience of more than 28 years in Institutional Building, Teaching, Consultancy, Research &Industry. A renowned scholar & academician in the area of International Business, he holds a prestigious Doctorate in the area along with a Post Graduate degree from Indian Institute of Foreign Trade where he illustriously topped with 7 merits. He holds the distinction of being the youngest Founder Pro Vice Chancellor of Amity University for two terms, the Founder Director General of Amity International Business School and the Founder CEO of Association of International Business School, London. He has been instrumental in establishing various Amity campuses abroad including at London, USA, Singapore, Mauritius, Australia, Tashkent & other parts of the world. He has spoken at various international forums which includes, prestigious Million Dollar Round Table Conference at Harvard Business School, New York University, Massachusetts Institute of Technology, Thunderbird Business School, University of Leeds, Loughbrough Business School, Coventry Business School, Rennes Business School, Essex University, University of Berkeley, California State University, NUS, MIT, UMAS Lowell, Brunel, Northampton, RMIT, Swinburne, Eduniversal Conference, Addis Ababa, QS Apple Conference, Teeside, Northumbria, Middlesex, Birmingham, Gannon, Deakin, Canberra, Cincinnati, Curtin, Queensland, Queens Mary, Babson, NTU, NTHU Taiwan and many more. He has received more than 25 International & National awards and has graced a host of talk shows on various TV channels. He is a mesmerizing orator and has the rare ability of touching the human soul. He is internationally recognized as a known Professor in the area of Management and is known in the field of academics as an institution builder, a writer, professor, distinguished academician, a top-class trainer, International Business Expert & the Champion of the Hearts of Students.*

Foreword

It is an opportune time to be renewing our research focus on leadership. The global community has endured an unprecedented pandemic and it is premature to suggest that the community has decisively entered a post-COVID-19 phase. In an era of uncertainty, what is clear is that nation-states, organisations and communities have been significantly disrupted.

A wide range of communities—national, organisation, and local—looked to leadership. Expectantly yes, but often equivocally. How have leaders responded? What have we learned about leadership? Are our ways of 'knowing' leadership sufficient to analyze leadership in an era of uncertainty? Herein lies the challenge and research focus of this edited volume. This focus resides within an evolving leadership scholarship, a foundation that is more diverse and reflective than that which informed previous assessments of leadership in times of crises.

We have witnessed a welcome and overdue turn in leadership scholarship. The increased theoretical and empirical heterogeneity in leadership scholarship is to be celebrated. There is more significant weight and attention to different styles, perspectives, and concepts of leadership. Expanded models of leadership reflect an increasingly diverse and global world. More acutely, leadership scholarship has looked to the capacity of increased diversity in leadership to address endemic inequalities in social relations. Stereotypes of leadership have been challenged, most prominently through the lens of gendered difference. Through this discourse, the practices of inclusion and exclusion have been examined. From this critique, the basis upon which leadership is evaluated has widened, accompanied by a reassessment of the goals and objectives of effective leadership.

In this time of uncertainty and crises and utilizing a more discursive corpus of leadership scholarship, this volume presents key observations about leadership practice. What guiding principles and ethical precepts are evident? Recognizing that the pandemic has exercised disparate impacts by income and employment, how has leadership addressed the requirements of decent and secure work, equality, diversity, and inclusion. In an organisational context, have these objectives been prioritized alongside those of resilience and agility, strategic innovation and collaboration, organisational development, and knowledge creation.

Editors Ataus Samad, Ezaz Ahmed, and Nitin Arora are to be congratulated for curating this timely contribution to leadership scholarship. Drawing on studies from a variety of contexts, including Australia, India and the United States, the volume self-evidently recognizes spatial and cultural differences. The studies offer both granular insights about leadership practice through the pandemic but also the capacity of current theorizations to critically examine leadership in times of crises and uncertainty. The collection also continues a searching examination of leadership shibboleths, forever a worthy objective deserving of our attention.

Foreword

Meg Smith
School of Business, Western Sydney University, Australia

Meg Smith *is the Deputy Dean at the School of Business of Western Sydney University. Professor Meg has an extensive research record in the area of gender equity, a key prerequisite to sustainable employment outcomes. Her expertise in pay equity investigations and institutional explanations for the undervaluation of feminised work has been the basis of international and domestic journal articles, research consultancy, expert opinion and submissions to parliamentary inquiries. Meg's scholarship has focused in contrasting and complimentary approaches to gender equity evaluation and regulation. These include equal rights discourses in industrial and discrimination-based legislation, and also gender equity auditing and reporting. Professor Meg Smith's expertise in the concept of gender undervaluation was reflected in her appointment by the FWC to complete a research-based independent report to assist parties to the proceedings under Part 2 – 7 of the Fair Work Act 2009 (Cth) (together with Professor Andrew Stewart and Dr Robyn Layton). She has previously undertaken research case studies, highlighting undervaluation, that were the basis of examination in the NSW Pay Equity Inquiry. Most recently (September 2020) she co-edited a special issue of the Journal of Industrial Relations assessing the application of the principle of equal pay for work of equal value, as expressed in the International Labour Organization (ILO) Equal Remuneration Convention (No.100) of 1951.*

Foreword

In today's interconnected world, effective leadership on a global scale has become more important than ever before. Leaders must quickly navigate complex challenges that span borders, cultures, and systems. Leaders are routinely called to make decisions that impact not only their own organizations, but also the broader society and the planet. Rapid technological advancements, political, societal, and ecological evolution, and economic uncertainty contribute to the context in which leaders must act. No matter the office, country, or continent, leaders in all industries and disciplines can affirm two certainties: (a) change is inevitable; (b) to manage this change, leaders must be adaptable, nimble, and informed. *Global Leadership Perspectives on Industry, Society, and Government in an Era of Uncertainty* is an indispensable resource in enlightening emerging and experienced leaders to the theories, practical strategies, and real-world examples that will help them harness the winds of change.

Threaded through each chapter is the reminder that at the core of leadership is the power of people. I truly believe that organizations will thrive if they follow the principle that there is a leader in every seat. Each individual can be prepared and empowered to lean in to leadership, knowing when to lead and when to follow, at scale, to solve problems, address issues, and refine strategies that support forward movement. The most impactful organizations are those that support leaders who are not only knowledgeable, but also innovative and empathetic. A leader in every seat ensures that myriad voices and perspectives are heard and are recognized as important contributors at every level of an organization.

This book takes a unique approach to the topic of global leadership and provides readers with a comprehensive understanding of what it takes to be a successful global leader in the 21st century.

Readers will appreciate the wide range of topics, from understanding organization and cultural nuances to managing diverse teams, from developing a global mindset to building sustainable and inclusive organizations. From the challenges of leading diverse teams to the importance of ethical leadership, this book covers an array of issues that are essential for aspiring and current leaders alike.

Professor Ezaz Ahmed, Dr. Ataus Samad, and Professor Nitin Arora's collective wisdom has cultivated a text that draws on the expertise of global leaders from different sectors and regions to provide a truly diverse and insightful perspective on leadership. Through case studies, expert insights, and practical tools, this book equips leaders with the knowledge and skills to effectively navigate the complexities inherent in global leadership. Whether you're leading a multinational corporation, a non-profit organization, or a government agency, this book will help you to become a more effective and impactful global leader who can in turn inspire a leader in every seat.

Kristine Barnett
Columbia College, USA

Foreword

Kristine Barnett *has been an academic leader and practitioner in academia for nearly 30 years, spending much of her career focusing on operations and academic growth at small, private women's colleges in the US. She holds a doctorate in Higher Education Leadership and currently serves as the Provost at Columbia College in Columbia, South Carolina. In addition to other publications, she is author of the vlog, "The Provost's Window" and is a frequent presenter and coach specializing in academic leadership.*

Preface

In a world characterized by uncertainty and constant change, leadership is paramount in navigating crises and guiding communities, organizations, and nations through turbulent times. The COVID-19 pandemic has emphasized the significance of effective leadership in addressing the complex challenges that emerge in such situations. As we confront an increasingly uncertain and interconnected world, *Global Leadership Perspectives on Industry, Society, and Government in an Era of Uncertainty* offers an in-depth analysis of how leaders from diverse cultural and national contexts respond to crises and manage change in the face of adversity.

The book delivers a timely and indispensable guide to understanding the intricacies of leadership and the crucial role that effective leaders play in forging a more resilient and prosperous future for all.

This edited volume assembles a wide variety of topics, delving into the evolving nature of leadership, the impact of digitization on leadership styles, the importance of ethics in leadership, and the specific challenges and opportunities encountered by leaders in sectors such as higher education, political communication, and business. Through these chapters, readers will acquire a deeper understanding of the essential leadership skills needed to navigate an ever-changing world and the strategies that leaders can implement to promote resilience and growth.

The contributors to this volume come from an extensive range of academic disciplines and professional backgrounds, presenting a comprehensive and multidisciplinary view of leadership in this era of uncertainty. Opinions presented in the book chapters are reflection of respective authors on that issue based on their analysis of the topic and knowledge in that field, hence not necessarily the views of the editors. By examining the experiences of leaders who have successfully navigated crises and change, this volume serves as an invaluable resource for current and aspiring leaders, managers, executives, investors, economic analysts, policymakers, human resource managers, entrepreneurs, students and educators of higher education, researchers, and academicians.

This edited book features a diverse range of chapters addressing various aspects of leadership, from theoretical frameworks to practical applications, in various organizational contexts.

1. **Managerialism and Leadership** explains three key models of managerialism and links them to managerial leadership, discussing the impact on organizations, workers, and the environment.
2. **Positive Leadership and the Quiet Quitting Movement in Organizations** highlights the importance of positive leadership in mitigating the quiet quitting movement and promoting employee engagement and organizational culture.

Preface

3. **Indigenous Women in Academia: Reflections on Leadership** highlights the barriers Indigenous women academics face in achieving senior leadership positions and how leadership is intertwined with resistance and cultural safety.
4. **Emerging Issues in Gender and Leadership: Succession Planning and Gender Equality in Australian Universities** presents a qualitative study on succession planning and gender in Australian universities, highlighting the persistent underrepresentation of women in senior leadership. The author advocates for a longer-term focus on diversity, equality, and inclusion in leadership succession planning and management, prioritizing intersectional approaches and practices of inclusion to dismantle barriers and reimagine more equitable futures of work.
5. **Women in School Leadership in India and the United States** investigates the underrepresentation of women in school leadership positions in India and Black women in the United States. It examines how women school leaders from both countries manage crises, navigate politics, establish policies and budgets, and confront constraints at the school board and family levels.
6. **An Integrated Framework for Leadership** presents a dynamic integrated Framework for Leadership in higher education, derived from a Delphi study that identified 15 elements falling into three domains: behaviors, mindsets, and skills.
7. **Trade Union Leadership and Sustainability in the Contemporary World of Work** discusses the challenges faced by trade unions in the modern world and proposes leadership strategies for their continued relevance. The author emphasizes the importance of unity, cohesion, and solidarity, backed by sound, pragmatic, and ethical leadership, in organizing, mobilizing, and strategizing to champion workers' rights in uncertain times.
8. **Leading With Happiness** investigates the factors contributing to academicians' happiness and proposes an institutional Happiness Framework for building sustainable universities.
9. **Ethical Leadership and Its Impact on Employee Well-Being** explores the effect of ethical leadership on employee well-being in manufacturing firms and the mediating role of employee engagement.
10. **The Basic Strategy of Leadership Landscape** discusses the role of effective leadership in enhancing employee performance and promoting employee retention and work-life balance.
11. **The Dark Side of Leadership** introduces the concept of destructive leadership styles associated with personality disorders and provides solutions for reducing toxicity in the work environment.
12. **Positive Impact of Leaders' Dark Triad Personality Traits in Uncertain Times** explores the relationship between dark triad personality traits (narcissism, psychopathy, and Machiavellianism) and effective leadership outcomes. Despite the potential negative impact of these traits, the findings suggest that dark traits can positively correlate with crisis management and decision-making capabilities in leaders.
13. **Leadership in a VUCA World** explores the challenges of leading in a volatile, uncertain, complex, and ambiguous world, with a focus on adaptability and navigating change.
14. **Future of Leadership: A Study on Small and Medium Sized Enterprises** discusses the impact of digitization on leadership in SMEs, touching on organizational structure, workplace practices, and the role of technology.
15. **E-Leadership Concepts, Competencies and Challenges** examines e-leadership concepts, competencies, and challenges in the era of digital transformation and remote work. The authors argue that new e-leadership challenges arising from modern ICTs urgently require further research, especially in areas such as e-trust, work-life balance, and psychological contracts between management and

workers. The chapter underscores the need for developing e-competencies and managing emotions to overcome challenges in virtual environments.
16. **Undergraduate Business Students' Perceptions About Virtual and Remote-Work Leadership Skills** investigates business students' perceptions of virtual leadership skills and their understanding of the challenges and preferences in virtual and remote work settings.
17. **Anglophone Shattered Hopes and Lost Illusions** examines the transformational and transactional leadership styles of political leaders during and after the COVID-19 pandemic, focusing on Trump, Johnson, Marin, and Ardern.

Throughout the book, readers will discover a rich array of leadership perspectives and practices that can inform and inspire action in various contexts. This would be a useful for both undergraduate and postgraduate level students as the contents will provide a kaleidoscope of leadership topics, revealing contemporary issues and the guiding principles that have shaped the field of leadership. Furthermore, we hope, academicians, researchers, and practitioners in management, human resource management, organizational development, entrepreneurship, sociology, corporate psychology, and information technology will benefit from the research presented in this publication.

Sincerely,

Ataus Samad
Western Sydney University, Australia

Ezaz Ahmed
Columbia College, USA

Nitin Arora
Amity International Business School, Amity University, India

Acknowledgment

The editors would like to acknowledge the support of everybody involved in this project and, more specifically, the authors, who made intellectual contributions using their valuable time, knowledge and efforts and reviewers who contributed to improving the quality, coherence, and content presentation of the chapters. We acknowledge that several authors also served as reviewers and hence appreciate their valuable contribution as reviewers. We gratefully acknowledge the Editorial Advisory Board members for their advice and involvement in the project. Finally, we sincerely thank our institutional colleagues at Western Sydney University, Columbia College, and Amity University, who actively encouraged and supported us in publishing this book.

Section 1
Concept of Leadership

These chapters deal with the basic issues related to leadership such as leadership, management, and styles of leadership. The first chapter explains key models of managerialism and links them to managerial leadership by discussing its impact on workers, on organizations, and the environment. The next chapter highlights the importance of positive leadership in mitigating the quiet quitting movement or intention to leave through developing an organizational culture of promoting employee engagement.

Chapter 1
Managerialism and Leadership

Thomas Klikauer
Western Sydney University, Australia

ABSTRACT

The term managerialism has been used for a long time. Yet, managerialism lacks theory development and models explaining how it spreads through organizations and how it is linked to management leadership. In recent years, several conceptual frameworks of managerialism have been constructed. These enable the building of managerialism models and connecting them to managerial leadership. Three key models of managerialism have been developed: (1) organizational model, (2) global model, and (3) trident model. This chapter explains these models and links them to managerial leadership. Developing a conceptual model of managerialism might allow us to ascertain the impact of managerialism on organizations, workers, and the environment. They may provide preliminary elements in the development of a theory of managerialism. The link between these models and managerial leadership is discussed by highlighting two versions of managerial leaders: corporate apparatchiks and the apostles of managerialism. This is applied to managerial leadership working in two distinctly different spheres.

INTRODUCTION

The concept of managerialism is the combination of management knowledge and ideology (Klikauer & Tannò 2022). Managerialism establishes itself systemically in organizations and society while depriving owners, employees (organizational-economical), and civil society (social-political) of all decision-making powers. By contrast, managerialism (Klikauer 2019) justifies the application of managerial techniques to all areas of society on the grounds of, not just any ideology, but "superior" ideology (Doran 2016). The belief into ideological "superiority" shapes expert training, the exclusive possession of managerial knowledge necessary, and the claim to efficiently run corporations and societies (Klikauer 2013:2). But managerialism has become something that transcends management, mutating a full-fledged ideology under the formula:

DOI: 10.4018/978-1-6684-8257-5.ch001

MANAGERIALISM = MANAGEMENT + IDEOLOGY + EXPANSION

This formula (M_A=MIE) signifies managerialism's origins to which it added ideology as the second ingredient (Klikauer 2013:3; Shepherd 2018:1672; Micocci & Di Mario 2018:54). Its third ingredient is its drive to spread managerial techniques 'across space and time' (Eagleton-Pierce & Knafo 2020:767), far beyond the realms of managerial organizations into the *lifeworld* (Chauvière & Mick 2013; Ion 2015). Managerialism also claims that technology is value-neutral. Still, technology remains deeply ideological (Klikauer 2007:151). In other words, ideology remains a key aspect of managerialism. Yet, this also means that such an ideology (Klikauer 2018) serves three key functions (Klikauer 2019:424):

1. Ideologies like managerialism and managerial leadership need to camouflage the inexorable contradictions that plague capitalism like, for example, the contradiction between workers' quest for high wages while an individual capitalist company has an interest in low wages. Simultaneously, capitalism as a system – the assembly of many companies and corporations needs high wages to sustain consumer capitalism. This creates an unsolvable contradiction.
2. An ideology also needs to sustain domination (DeMarrais, et al. 1996:16), as all capitalist societies are defined by domination from the school's headmaster to the corporate leader, etc. (Seeck, et al. 2020:15).
3. Finally, all ideologies need to prevent emancipation from these structures of domination – by those deemed followers (Zhu, et al. 2009) of those who rule over them – managerial leaders – under what Selin Metin Camgöz & Özge Tayfur Ekmekci have recently called *dark and destructive leadership* (Camgöz & Ekmekci 2021). An ideology needs to prevent those oppressed – followers (Kark & Van Dijk. 2019) – from two things: (i) an ideology needs to prevent them from realizing that they live in oppressive structures (Alemán 2014) – the often enforced top-down structure of managerial leadership (Scott & Scott 2016); (ii) an ideology needs to prevent followers (Plachy & Smunt 2022) from realizing that there is ideology, so that ideology can assure the following, *"immovably, they insist on the very ideology which enslaves them"* as German philosopher Adorno (Adorno & Horkheimer 1944) once said.

Based on the definition of managerialism, one might likely to realize that managerialism is *not* the same as management. While 'management, to put it plainly, is boring' (Scott, W. G. & Hart, D. K. 1991:39), perhaps managerialism isn't much better. Yet, at its most basic level, management might be narrowed down to a hierarchy of controlling people and things (Fayol 1916). In short, Management runs a business while managerialism supplies ideological legitimacy creating a positive pro-business atmosphere (Doran 2016:81). Secondly, management is a hierarchy of controlling (Magretta 2012) 'people and things' (Parker 2019:497) while managerialism (Lynn 2017; Wren, et al. 2002) is less practical and more illusive – perhaps even evasive (Doran 2016). When viewed from the famous – some might say "infamous" – 80/20 rule (Egghe 1986; Aljukhadar & Senecal 2022), one might argue that management occurs when managers spend about 80% of their time with actually running a business organization, and 20% of their time on the ideological legitimation of management. Meanwhile, managerialism reverses this. Here, managerialists spend about 80% of their time with inventing and perpetrating ideology (Al Mahameed et al. 2023), while only 20% of their time is spent on the actual managing of companies and corporations.

THE HISTORICAL DEVELOPMENT OF MANAGERIALISM

Managerialism is the latest development in the history of management that began as factory administrations during the rise of industrial capitalism. With the end of feudalism and serfdom – throughout the 18th and 19th centuries – workers found industrial employment in a process that first started in England and soon caught on in continental Europe. By the early 20th century, Frederic Taylor (Lepore 2009), Henri Fayol (Hatchuel & Segrestin 2019), and Henry Ford had changed capitalism, its factories, and the way management was understood. Simultaneously, Fayol and Ford had legitimized what is today known as *management*. By the late 20th century, a new term started to emerge – *managerialism* (Locke 1996).

The first academic book to carry the term *managerialism* in its title appears to be Benjamin S. Prasad's *managerialism in India*. (Prasad 1968). A few decades later, Prasad's work was followed up by Pollitt's *managerialism and the Public Services* (Pollitt, C. 1990) and Enteman's seminal work on *managerialism* (Enteman 1993). It took another one and a half decades for Locke and Spender's *Confronting managerialism* (Locke & Spender 2011), and Klikauer's *managerialism* (Klikauer 2013) to develop the concept of managerialism further.

Based on these initial studies, it became clear that managerialism drives towards expansion into a number of previously non-managerial fields. The term *new public management* – albeit somewhat synonymous to managerialism – became used in what might be called as *as-if* organizations (Miller 2008). These are public non-profit organizations often run *as if* these were for-profit organizations. This entry addresses the need for a model of managerialism by investigating today's three most advanced versions.

THE ORGANIZATIONAL MODEL OF MANAGERIALISM

The organizational model of managerialism links two British models to an Italian model. The first framework is by Sue Shepherd (2018), the second is by Mike Dent and Jim Barry (Dent & Barry (2014:8), and the third is suggested by Flavio Di Mario (Micocci & Di Mario 2018). These three frameworks show significant overlaps. Most importantly, all three models focus on the organizational existence of managerialism. Yet, these three frameworks can be combined to create one consistent model (see Figure 1). By combining the three frameworks, five key elements of managerialism emerge.

1) **Private sector methods are superior:** The organizational model of managerialism starts with widely accepted aspect of managerialism, namely, an ideology. The first ideology tells us that private sector methods are superior to public administration.
2) **Management is good:** The second ingredient is the belief that management is inherently good, focusing on practical hands-on methods derived from what is called 'the real world'. Management is also optimistic about the future – a future that can be managed (Wallace-Wells 2017). Such optimism is shared by managerialism.
3) **Management is a discrete function:** The third element of the organizational model of managerialism addresses management as the sole institution administering companies and corporations on behalf of their owners. This further legitimized management's self-invented *right to manage*.
4) **Management is rational:** The fourth element is the belief that management is rational, value-neutral, generic, and universally applicable.

5) **Organizational behavior:** Finally, managerialism seeks to convert organizational behavior into measurable and monetized elements. Combining all these elements results in the following model:

Figure 1. The Organizational Model of managerialism

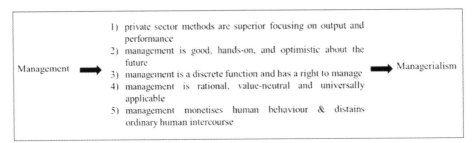

In line with the above-noted definition of managerialism, the organizational model suggests that managerialism has a number of generic ideologies applicable to a wide range of both for-profit and not-for-profit business organizations. The taking on of elements from commercial management also applies to the next model but places a strong focus on the external affairs of organizations.

The Global Model of managerialism

The global model examines managerialism across the boundaries of public or private organizations from an economic and sociological angle. As with the organizational model, profit is assumed to be the motive that drives companies. Further to the organizational model, however, in the global model, profit also acts as a driver of the overall capitalist system.

1) **Profits:** Ever since the emergence of capitalism, the profit imperative remains the ultimate measure of management performance. This applies to both management and managerialism. Adam Smith's 'profit making' takes precedence over many other managerial considerations.
2) **Ideology:** Closely following is ideology. One might argue that 'managerialism is *the* organizational ideology' of today (Alemán 2014:116, emphasis in original) supplying a 'general management ideology' (McCann 2017:492).
3) **Growth:** managerialism lives through supporting corporate growth. Managerialism is fully aware that growth depends on good relationships with investors, stock markets, banks, as well as the ability to influence and ultimately manipulate public perceptions via Public Relations (Miller 2008). Corporate PR helps, for example, to legitimize the idea of endless growth by accepting to exploit scarce resources for it. Much of this is driven by the ideological belief in free market competition.
4) **The free market:** Ever since the days of Adam Smith (18th century) and Karl Marx (19th century), the unchallenged purpose of any business organization is to engage in competition through the so-called *free market*. It is here where managerialism provides an overall ideology that legitimizes the *competition-is-good* mantra. Simultaneously, managerialism supports the seeking of monopolies while claiming there is a monopoly-ridden public sector. Such organizational hypocrisies may collide with managerialism's amorality.

5) **Amorality:** Since managerialism isn't human, it does not have human morals. Lacking morality, many Managerialist decisions are non-ethical. Often, decisions damaging to human beings, local communities and the environmental health of our planet are made without any misgivings (Wallace-Wells 2019). To divert attention away from its amorality, managerialism refers to concepts of business ethics and corporate social responsibility. Simultaneously, it also praises objectivity, evidence-based decision-making, techno-engineering, science orientation and non-emotional decision making (Simon 1960). Finally, managerialism has serious problems with democratic decision-making.

6) **Democracy:** There certainly is 'a lineage associating managerialism with totalitarianism [and there is also the fact that managerialism] is certainly not democratic' (Doran 2016:88f.). Necessarily, managerialism needs to divert attention away from inclination directed towards democracy. One way in which the devotees of managerialism achieve this is by focusing on *leadership*. Leadership implies formal or informal top-down hierarchies (ABC 2023), as well as Fayol's infamous 'unity of command' (Wren, et al. 2002:912). Particularly the highly militaristic (Gaskell 2017) and deeply anti-democratic 'unity of command' ideology is sold as pretty much the only way in which companies and corporations can "objectively" be organized (Denning 2020).

7) **Objectivity in numbers:** Management and managerialism live with numbers. Both use numbers to justify managerial decisions as they supply an aura of neutrality and rationality. To deal with subjective information, managerialism relies on two strategies: firstly, it translates subjective information into an objective form of numbers. Secondly, when this is not possible, subjective information is excluded. Managerialism is convinced that if *you can manipulate numbers - you can control events*, never mind the dehumanizing impact of transforming human beings into numbers.

8) **Dehumanization:** Under managerialism, dehumanization is found when employees are viewed as cryptograms – as numbers and figures on an *Excel* spread sheet. Human Resources Management converts human beings into *objects of power (*Bauman 1989).

9) **Exploitation:** managerialism not only justifies dehumanization; it also defends exploitation. This includes the exploitation of human labor as well as the environment. To camouflage human exploitation, managerialism argues that this is a fair exchange. Workers produce valuable resources, and they still get paid in one way or the other. In an ever-accelerating process, the surplus profits which the workers produce, are technically reinvested to provide more surplus. Capital enforces a relentless speeding up of this process. Undeterred, managerialism remains focused on short-term gains.

10) **Short-termism:** managerialism pretends that management exists beyond time and space (Cooke 1999). Many companies and corporations will never die a natural death. Instead, they will – and actually have – outlive their creator. Henry Ford's *Ford Motor Company* is a point in case. Often, such companies continue to exist even though their managers never focused on the long-term.

managerialism disguises the contradictory pair of strategic management dedicated to long-term planning vis-*à-v*is management's drive towards short-term gains. Corporate short-termism can also result in value-destructive ways for market participants and discourages long-term values often found in human beings, local communities, sustainability, and the environment (Grinyer, J. et al., 1998).

11) **The environment:** managerialism's task is to provide ideological support to those business entities that are intrinsically committed to intervening in, altering of, transforming, and in some cases even

destroying nature (Klikauer & Young 2021). Managerialism also provides ideological support for the so-called *resource corporations* engaged in commodity manufacturing and resource extraction. Humans encounter this environmental destruction semi-consciously. Above all, managerialism is interested in humans as homogeneous consumers.

12) **Homogenization:** Neoliberalism's rhetoric claims that consumerism and consumer society deliver a greater choice and greater diversity than any previous society. The mantra is: *freely choose what you buy, your profession, university degree and career*. Managerialism includes neoliberalism's concept of rational choice (Micocci & Di Mario 2018:52). In fact, managerialism has been seen as 'the organizational arm of neoliberalism' (Jaros 2018:3). The one delivers *organizational* choice while the other delivers *consumer* choice.

Neoliberalism and managerialism work hard to maintain the illusion of individualism by furnishing people with attitudes and values appropriate to corporate goals. In the end, Neoliberalism and managerialism foster a homogeneous global society. Everyone is to know Google and Coca Cola. The homogenization of a global society is the twelfth element that defines managerialism. When these twelve elements are combined, a global model of managerialism emerges (Fig. 2):

Figure 2. The global model of managerialism

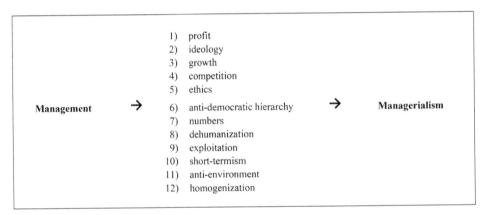

Unlike the organizational model of managerialism (Figure 1), the global model of managerialism (Figure 2) reaches beyond the confinements of public or private organizations. The organizational model of managerialism focuses on micro-economic aspects while the global model of managerialism focuses on macro-economic aspects. Still, there are several commonalities between the organizational model and the global model. For one, both operate under capitalism's guiding profit maxim. For both, ideology remains an essential ingredient. Both seek expansion – M_A=MEI. Both pretend to be ethical while fostering top-down hierarchies and both are anti-democratic. In addition, both cultivate dehumanization while relying on numbers and quantification.

There are also significant differences. In the global model of managerialism (Figure. 2), growth is not directed towards business growth; managerialism promotes it as an economic concept enshrined in the belief that increases in GDP are inherently good. More than the organizational model, the global model reaches beyond organizational boundaries. Ultimately, exploitation is no longer just the exploitation of workers inside a for-profit organization, now managerialism increasingly legitimizes global exploitation. The same goes for short-termism and managerialism's anti-environmental stance.

Finally, there is a global homogenization: While managerialism believes that its ideology and techniques are universally applicable, it also believes that there is a global consumer society with mass taste. Next to the global and the organizational models of managerialism, the final model offers three different perspectives on managerialism.

THE TRIDENT MODEL OF MANAGERIALISM

A trident is a three-pronged fishing spear used by Poseidon (Greek) and Neptune (Latin) indicating the three spikes of the spear which identifies, in this case, the three aspects of the trident model of managerialism and its three essential parts are:

1. neo-Taylorist managerialism;
2. entrepreneurial managerialism; and finally,
3. cultural managerialism.

Originally, these three parts were proposed by Eric Hoyle and Mike Wallace (Hoyle & Wallace 2005). Neo-Taylorist managerialism argues that Taylorism has experienced a significant upgrading through new work techniques (intensification) and new managerial techniques (performance management). Neo-Taylorism's emphasis on control has also been on the increase. Largely, through the use of information technology allowing the constant monitoring of workers through a digital *panopticon*. The second part is entrepreneurial managerialism, which places emphasis on the self-driving symbolic figure of the entrepreneur. The last part – cultural managerialism – places emphasis on organizational culture. Shown as a model, the following picture emerges (Fig. 3):

Figure 3. The trident model of managerialism

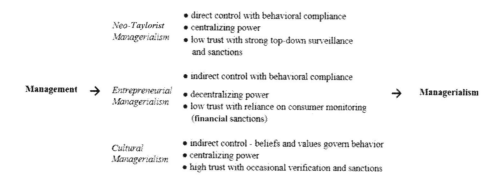

The trident model of managerialism depicts three versions of managerialism. The issue of control might exemplify the difference between the three variants (Figure 3). When viewed from Edwards' three versions of control (Edwards 1979), the following picture emerges: Neo-Taylorism (1) focuses on

Edward's direct and technical control while entrepreneurial (2) and cultural (3) managerialism focus on bureaucratic and increasingly on ideological control. Beyond that, there are also other differences:

1. Neo-Taylorist Managerialism

Neo-Taylorist managerialism achieves its goals through target-setting, the identification of key performance indicators (KPIs), and task-based training regimes. Neo-Taylorist managerialism sets up high targets – so-called *high-performance work systems (*Ramsay, et al. 2000) – for the performance of employees.

2. Entrepreneurial Managerialism

Entrepreneurial managerialism focuses on the individual and its assumed capacity for self-control (Van Gelderen, et al. 2015). Entrepreneurial managerialism controls through the setting up of financial inducements. It places decision making powers onto employees. Control is no longer achieved through surveillance but through financial incentives for the individual.

3. Cultural Managerialism

Cultural managerialism sees employees as contributors to the formulation of organizational goals. In cultural managerialism, trust plays a much more significant role when compared to neo-Taylorist managerialism and entrepreneurial managerialism.

Cultural managerialism expects the CEO and its top-managerial team to develop an organizational vision that is shared by those down the chain of command (McCann 2017). Cultural managerialism relies less on direct disciplining (e.g. neo-Taylorist managerialism) and financial penalties (e.g. entrepreneurial managerialism).

The term managerialism has been used for several decades. What started as a rather vague idea has become a concept with a definition. Despite these developments, a theory of managerialism is still missing. The three models of managerialism outlined above show commonalities. They are aligned to the definition of managerialism. For all three models, managerialism cannot exist without management. All three models also agree that managerialism has an inherent drive towards expansion. Finally, all three models also agree that managerialism is an ideological affair. Common to all three models is also the fact that these three models are not in competition with one another but places a different emphasis on core aspects of managerialism.

These three models are useful to ascertain when managerialism exists. They also explain how managerialism operates and what the consequences of managerialism are. They can also provide a starting point for the development of a complete theory of managerialism. Beyond that, they do not just enable us to understand managerialism but also how those who push managerialism operate. Those who push the ideology – the ideological leaders of managerialism – can be divided into two basic groups.

MANAGERIAL LEADERS: APPARATCHIKS AND APOSTLES

Just like management and managerialism, ideology is a top-down issue in which some create ideologies (leaders) and some follow ideologies (followers). Yet, the leaders of ideology can be divided into two basic groups: a) the *corporate apparatchiks* who create and apply managerial ideologies in companies and corporations and b) those that might be called the *apostles of the ideology of managerialism* who are employed in external agencies.

Any sensible theory of the ideology of managerialism would distinguish between simple management (Locke, R. R. 1996) and managerial leaders of organizational practicalities (Fayol, Taylor, Ford, etc.) and the more ideological leaders of managerialism. These are based on two sets of ideas: management and managerial leaders; and managerialism and its ideological leaders. At the same time, these two sets of ideas also contain two different kinds of managerial leaders. In any case, there is a difference between traditional managerial leaders running a business organization and today's more ideological managerialist leaders who – are even more than the simple managerial leaders – occupied with the invention, production, and dissemination of an ideology – the ideology of managerialism. The original managerial leaders had – and still have – to fulfill three aspects:

- firstly, managerial leaders are a social resource. In other words, managerial leaders are a socio-economical resource; secondly, managerial leaders are social class. Managers are mostly found in what sociology calls "the middle class" (e.g. business class) preferring Hirschman's loyalty – as in corporate loyalty (Ewin 1993; Trofimov et al. 2019. – and voice rather than exit option (Hirschman 1970); and finally, managerial leaders represent a system of authority – leaders over followers. Managerial leaders have corporate authority representing the domination over others – those called: workers, subordinates, and followers. This is enshrined in the managerial leaders' self-assigned *right to manage* (Clarke & Newman 1993; Koliousi & Miaouli 2018).

Seen from the aforementioned and rather crude 80/20 rule (Koch 2011), one might even say that managerial leaders are 80% of their time occupied with managing, organizing, and controlling a business organization while spending 20% on the ideology of managerialism that ideologically sustains companies and corporations. Under managerialism, this rough rule is reversed. Corporate apparatchiks (internal) and the apostles of the ideology of managerialism (external) dedicate 80% of their time and effort on ideology, while the true ideologues of managerialism think with just 20% of their time about managing, organizing, and controlling a business.

In any case, the latter group of managerialist leaders might better be called *corporate apparatchiks* as they depict a core element that turns a manager into an ideologically driven apparatchik. An apparatchik [Russian: *аппара́тчик* [ɐpɐˈratɕːɪk]) was a full-time, professional functionary of the Soviet government apparatus holding a position with bureaucratic and political-ideological responsibilities. Similarly, corporate apparatchiks are full-time functionaries of the managerialist apparatus. For corporate apparatchiks in middle-management, for example, adhering, fostering, and propagating the ideology of managerialism can easily mean moving from their position of being a managerial leader in middle-management to becoming a managerial leader in top-management.

As a consequence, and as an outcome of this process, truly ideology-driven corporate apparatchiks can be found mostly in top-management and less so in middle-management. Yet, corporate apparatchiks' function inside a corporate apparatus seek to stabilize the managerialist-corporate apparatus. Corporate apparatchiks too, have bureaucratic and administrative – also called organizational and managerial – as well as ideological responsibilities.

One might indeed argue that Soviet apparatchiks and the corporate apparatchiks of managerialism share many similarities. Like the original apparatchiks, corporate apparatchiks too, are people who 'issue instructions and rules' (Gregory 1991:1) Corporate apparatchiks also *occupy a responsible position in a functional unit*. And their work involves *technical documentation and norm setting*. Furthermore, the effect of the corporate apparatchik's work *on economic outcomes is difficult to establish*. Like the Soviet apparatchik, the modern-day corporate apparatchik's work can be called: *paper output (bumazhny val)*.

As leaders, the corporate apparatchiks of managerialism also occupy a *privileged position* and – this is one of the most important aspects for both – *their prime concern was to keep their positions*. Both – the Soviet apparatchiks, as well as today's corporate apparatchiks are dedicated to the apparatus. One was dedicated to the Soviet apparatus while the other is dedicated to the corporate apparatus – the apparatus of management or the body of management run by the 'managerial elite' (Davis, A. 2017).

The second important aspect is: *to keep their positions, apparatchiks had to be willing to carry out any task no matter how impossible or senseless*. There is next to no better description of the modern-day corporate apparatchiks than that. This is what corporate apparatchiks are willing to do at any time. Today, elements of this are called 'managerial opportunism' (Noe & Rebello 1996; Bushee et al. 2020) and 'careerism' (Feldman & Weitz 1991; Jain & Sullivan 2019). Both reflect the traditional 'apparatchik's career commitment' (Brzezinski & Huntington 1963:57).

Like the Soviet 'apparatchik' (Brzezinski & Huntington 1963:59), the corporate apparatchik too, *survives and gets ahead by saying, "yes, it will be done" (budet sdelano)*. Soviet, as well as corporate apparatchiks are also *willing to support any hare-brained schemes simply because this would look good on their records*. Yet, they also *set the rules of game* and of course, a corporate apparatchik is *a less-than-honest broker of information* (Klikauer 2023). Much of this – if not most – also reflects on corporate growth from which corporate apparatchiks always gain since the 'growth of the apparatus [keeps] pace with the growth' of the corporate apparatchiks or as one might say 'true establishment men' (Brzezinski & Huntington 1963:66). These true establishment men or managerial leaders come in two variants:

1. **Internal:** managerial leaders who function as corporate apparatchiks and are employed by companies and corporations; and

External: managerial leaders who function as the apostles of the ideology of managerialism. These are the pure ideologues of managerialism propagating the ideology of managerialism with the quasi-religious zeal – just like an apostle (Marguerat 2002; Fiorenza 1986). They always work outside of companies and corporations. Instead of working inside a firm, these ideology-creating leaders are employed by five main institutions: (i) business schools (Juusola 2023); (ii) think tanks; (iii) corporate lobbying organizations; (iv) the pro-business press, and finally, (v) corporate consultancy firms.

i. **business schools**: Stanford Graduate School of Business, Harvard Business School, Penn (Wharton), HEC Paris, MIT (Sloan), London Business School, IE Business School, INSEAD, etc.
ii. **think tanks**: RAND, Cato, Heritage Foundation, The Bow Group (UK), American Enterprise Institute, Aspen Institute, Mises Institute, etc.
iii. **corporate lobbying** and corporate public relations organizations: Brownstein Hyatt Farber Schreck, Akin Gump Strauss Hauer, BGR Government Affairs, Cornerstone Government Affairs, Invariant, Forbes Tate, Edelman, Weber Shandwick, BCW, FleishmanHillard, Ketchum, MSL, Hill+Knowlton Strategies, Ogilvy, etc.
iv. **pro-business press**: Wall Street Journal, The Economist, Business Insider, Harvard Business Review, Financial Times, Australian Financial Review, Forbes, Reuter, Bloomberg,

v. **corporate consultancy** firms: McKinsey & Company, Boston Consulting Group, Bain & Company, EY-Parthenon, Roland Berger, Accenture, Deloitte Consulting, etc.

How both groups – managerial leaders as corporate apparatchiks and managerial leaders as apostles of the ideology of managerialism (including the five sub-groups (i-v) – relate to each other and work together to sustain the ideology of managerialism is shown in Figure 4 below:

Figure 4. Managerial leaders as corporate apparatchiks and ideological apostles

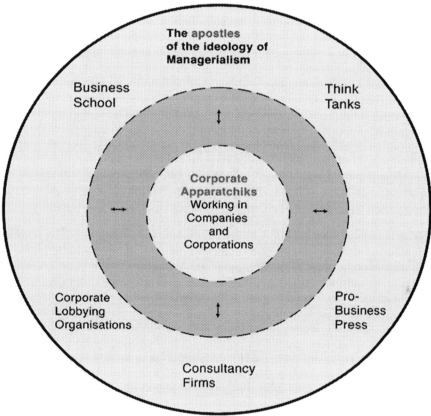

Figure 4 shows the corporate apparatchiks at the center of the disk. This includes the place where they can be found: companies and corporations. Corporate apparatchiks are linked to the apostles of managerialism of the outer ring through [↔] because members of both groups – a) corporate apparatchiks, and b) the apostles of the ideology of managerialism – move back and forth and have – at times – intimate connections to one another. Yet at the same time, this semi-openness between a) and b) as indicated through a broken line [- - -] as both groups are not sealed off from each other. Rather, both groups of managerial leaders, as well as individuals in both groups work closely when it comes to the ideology of managerialism. Both leadership groups have, what might be called as, an 'interest symbiosis' (Klikauer 2013:211) when it comes to the ideology of managerialism. Both groups of managerial-ideological leadership are interested in sustaining companies and corporations ideologically (corporate apparatchiks)

and corporate capitalism (the apostles of the ideology of managerialism) (Herman & McChesney 1997; Gupta 2002; Gagnon 2021.

In terms of the creation of ideology, the outer ring is the dominant location as most ideologies linked to managerialism are generated by managerial-ideological leaders employed in organizations and institutions of the outer ring (business schools, consultancies, corporate lobbying, think tanks, and the pro-business press (Klikauer 2022; Ali 2022.) rather than the inner ring of corporate apparatchiks who are more often than not, apply the ideology of managerialism. In terms of their companies and corporations, the inner ring is the most important when it comes to the actual application of the ideology of managerialism – mostly for corporate-internal affairs, such as, for example, when shaping and manipulating organizational culture, organizational restructuring, etc. Meanwhile, the outer ring is the more important locale for ideologies that support the entire system of managerialism and its place within managerial capitalism (Chandler 1984; Sood 2021).

Beyond all that, managerial-ideological leaders – internal corporate apparatchiks and the external apostles of the ideology of managerialism (Fig. 4) depict many of the traces found in the original apparatchiks of the Soviet regime. Both managerial-ideological leaders are fulltime operatives who function to stabilize an apparatus – a political regime or a managerial regime. Both occupy a responsible position furnished with the ability to issue instruction and to rule based on an overall ideology – the ideology of managerialism. Both are also primarily concerned with keeping their leadership position inside the corporate apparatus. Both are also willing to g*et ahead* by being dedicated to the saying, *yes, it will be done*. And both are willing to follow it through. Finally, both are also willing to support any – even the most bizarre, absurd, and wacky – schemes simply because it makes them look good (Gardner & Martinko 1988; Rosenfeld et al. 1995; Ai, et al. 2022) while enhancing their CVs and leadership careers (Allred et al. 1996). As a consequence, modern day managerial-ideological leaders depict most – if not all – the trimmings that Soviet apparatchiks had shown during the 20th century. Beyond that, managerial-ideological leaders are a well-established 'professional-managerial class' ready to enforce managerialism (Graeber, D. 2014:73).

CONCLUSION: FROM MANAGEMENT LEADER TO MANAGERIAL-IDEOLOGICAL LEADER

Just as management and managerialism are not the same, management leaders and managerial-ideological leaders are also not the same. While the simple management of Fayol, Taylor, Ford, etc. is dedicated to running a business organization, managerialism is dedicated to ideology. As an ideology, the ideology of managerialism serves three functions: camouflage contradictions; sustain domination like the domination of the managerial leader over followers; and prevent emancipation like the emancipation of those ideologically kept in the confinements of being a follower, a subordinate, a tool, an asset, a chattel, and a human resource. Since most, if not all, ideologies function in a top-down manner and management – including managerial leadership – as a hierarchical top-down affair, it is highly likely to suspect that the process of ideology-making involves managerial leaders located at the top of the managerial hierarchy. Once tasked with ideology-making, these managerial leaders mutate from simply managing a business organization into ideology-makers becoming managerial-ideological leaders.

As such, these managerial-ideological leaders carry strong connotations to Soviet-style apparatchiks interested in sustaining their position within the managerial hierarchy. For the managerial-ideological leader, it is less the physical nature of a firm (the apparatus), but by far more the body of ideological knowledge, i.e. the ideology of managerialism, that needs to be sustained. For the ideology of managerialism, these are just the material manifestations of a locale at which ideology is generated. What counts is not the locale but the ideology. It is the securing of the ideology of managerialism – rather than a survival of an individual business – that underwrites and secures their position as managerial leaders. For example, it is the support of the ideology of managerialism that gets you your next job higher up the ladder – not the support of some business. In other words, the managerial apparatus and even more so, the ideological support for it, is the key element that secures the existence of managerial-ideological leaders.

As a consequence, managerial-ideological leaders in the form of corporate apparatchiks (internal) and the apostles of the ideology of managerialism (external) have become dependent on a functional ideology – the ideology of managerialism. As long as the ideology of managerialism sustains both groups, the position of managerial leaders is secured. To secure managerial leadership as well as companies, corporations, and corporate capitalism, the ideology of managerialism needs to eliminate contradictions such as, for example, those contradiction between a corporate leader's interest vs. a follower's, i.e. a worker's interests (corporate profits vs. high wages; long working hours vs. short working hours, etc.). Secondly, managerial-ideological leaders also depend on the ability of the ideology of managerialism to mask domination – the domination of managerial leaders over workers. Thirdly, and finally, their ideology must be capable of preventing those framed as followers, i.e. workers, from realizing that management's communication in *The Age of managerialism* is about ideology and the ideological entrapment. It is also about *interpellation* as the French philosopher Althusser calls it. It ideologically *interpells* or *hails* followers and workers to follow the ideological pathway set out by managerial leaders. In the end, managerial leadership's *raison d'être* is ideology, the ideology of managerialism.

REFERENCES

ABC. (2023). *Managerialism and our obsession with hierarchy*. ABC News. https://www.abc.net.au/radionational/programs/futuretense/managerialism-and-our-obsession-with-hierarchy/101919764.

Adorno, T., & Horkheimer, M. (1944). *The Culture Industry: Enlightenment as Mass Deception* https://www.marxists.org/reference/archive/adorno/1944/culture-industry.htm.

Ai, W., Cunningham, W. A., & Lai, M. C. (2022). Reconsidering autistic 'camouflaging' as transactional impression management. *Trends in Cognitive Sciences*, 26(8), 631–645. doi:10.1016/j.tics.2022.05.002 PMID:35641372

Al Mahameed, M., Yates, D., & Gebreiter, F. (2023). Management as Ideology: 'new' managerialism and the corporate university in the period of COVID-19. *Financial Accountability & Management* (https://research.birmingham.ac.uk/en/publications/management-as-ideology-new-managerialism-and-the-corporate-univer.

Alemán, A. M. M. (2014). Managerialism as the "new" discursive masculinity in the university. *Feminist Formations*, 26(2), 107–134. doi:10.1353/ff.2014.0017

Ali, C. (2022). Book Review: Media Capitalism. *TripleC*, *2*(20), 143–146. doi:10.31269/triplec.v20i2.1344

Aljukhadar, M. & Senecal, S. (2022). Targeting the very important buyers VIB: A cluster analysis approach. *Cogent Business & Management, 9*(1).

Allred, B. B., Snow, C. C., & Miles, R. E. (1996). Characteristics of managerial careers in the 21st century. *The Academy of Management Perspectives*, *10*(4), 17–27. doi:10.5465/ame.1996.3145316

Bauman, Z. (1989). *Modernity and the Holocaust*. Blackwell.

Brzezinski, Z., & Huntington, S. P. (1963). Cincinnatus and the Apparatchik. *World Politics*, *16*(1), 52–78. doi:10.2307/2009251

Bushee, B., Taylor, D. J., & Zhu, C. 2020. The dark side of investor conferences: Evidence of managerial opportunism. *The Accounting Review* (https://meridian.allenpress.com/accounting-review/article-abstract/doi/10.2308/TAR-2020-0624/487384/The-Dark-Side-of-Investor-Conferences-Evidence-of,

Camgöz, S. M., & Ekmekci, Ö. T. (2021). *Destructive Leadership and Management Hypocrisy: Advances in Theory and Practice*. Emerald Publishing Limited. doi:10.1108/9781800431805

Chandler, A. D. Jr. (1984). The emergence of managerial capitalism. *Business History Review*, *58*(4), 473–503. doi:10.2307/3114162

Chauvière, M., & Mick, S. S. (2013). The French Sociological Critique of managerialism: Themes and Frameworks. *Critical Sociology*, *39*(1), 139. doi:10.1177/0896920511431501

Clarke, J., & Newman, J. (1993). The right to manage: A second managerial revolution? *Cultural Studies*, *7*(3), 427–441. doi:10.1080/09502389300490291

Cooke, B. (1999). Writing the left out of management theory: The historiography of the management of change. *Organization*, *6*(1), 81–105. doi:10.1177/135050849961004

Davis, A. (2017). Sustaining corporate class consciousness across the new liquid managerial elite in Britain. *The British Journal of Sociology*, *68*(2), 234–253. doi:10.1111/1468-4446.12257 PMID:28369838

DeMarrais, E., Castillo, L. J., & Earle, T. (1996). Ideology, materialization, and power strategies. *Current Anthropology*, *37*(1), 15–31. doi:10.1086/204472

Denning, S. (2020). The quest for genuine business agility. *Strategy and Leadership*, *48*(1), 21–28. doi:10.1108/SL-11-2019-0166

Dent, M., & Barry, J. (2014). New Public Management and the Professions in the UK. In M. Dent, J. Chandler, & J. Barry (Eds.), *Questioning the New Public Management* (p. 8). Routledge.

Doran, C. (2016). Managerialism: An Ideology and its Evolution. *International Journal of Management. Knowledge and Learning*, *5*(1), 81–97.

Eagleton-Pierce, M., & Knafo, S. (2020). Introduction: The political economy of managerialism. *Review of International Political Economy*, *27*(4), 763–779. doi:10.1080/09692290.2020.1735478

Edwards, R. (1979). *Contested Terrain*. Heinemann.

Egghe, L. (1986). On the 80/20 rule. *Scientometrics*, *10*(1-2), 55–68. doi:10.1007/BF02016860

Enteman, W. F. (1993). Managerialism: the Emergence of a New Ideology. University of Wisconsin Press.

Ewin, R. E. (1993). Corporate loyalty: Its objects and its grounds. *Journal of Business Ethics*, *12*(5), 387–396. doi:10.1007/BF00882029

Fayol, H. (1916). *Managerialism Industrielle et Generale [Industrial and General managerialism]*. London: Sir I. Pitman & Sons, ltd.

Feldman, D. C., & Weitz, B. A. (1991). From the invisible hand to the gladhand: Understanding a careerist orientation to work. *Human Resource Management*, *30*(2), 237–257. doi:10.1002/hrm.3930300206

Fiorenza, E. S. (1986). Missionaries, Apostles, Coworkers: Romans 16 and the Reconstruction of Women's Early Christian History. *Word & World*, *6*(4), 420–433.

Gagnon, M. A. (2021). Ghost management as a central feature of accumulation in corporate capitalism: the case of the global pharmaceutical sector. In M. Benquet & T. Bourgeron (Eds.), *Accumulating Capital Today - Contemporary Strategies of Profit and Dispossessive Policies* (pp. 163–177). Routledge. doi:10.4324/9781003089513-15

Gardner, W. L., & Martinko, M. J. (1988). Impression management in organizations. *Journal of Management*, *14*(2), 321–338. doi:10.1177/014920638801400210

Gaskell, K. (2017). *Inspired leadership: how you can achieve extraordinary results in business*. John Wiley & Sons.

Graeber, D. (2014). Anthropology and the rise of the professional-managerial class. *HAU*, *4*(3), 73–88. doi:10.14318/hau4.3.007

Gregory, P. R. 1991. *Soviet Bureaucratic Behavior*. University of Houston. https://www.ucis.pitt.edu/nceeer/1991-804-13-Gregory.pdf

Grinyer, J., Russell, A., & Collison, D. (1998). Evidence of Managerial Short-termism in the UK. *British Journal of Management*, *9*(1), 13–22. doi:10.1111/1467-8551.00072

Gupta, S. (2002). *Corporate capitalism and political philosophy*. Pluto Press.

Hatchuel, A., & Segrestin, B. (2019). A century old and still visionary: Fayol's innovative theory of management. *European Management Review*, *16*(2), 399–412. doi:10.1111/emre.12292

Herman, E. S., & McChesney, R. W. (1997). *The global media: The new missionaries of corporate capitalism*. Cassell.

Hirschman, A. (1970). *Exit, Voice, and Loyalty: responses to decline in firms, organizations, and states*. Harvard University Press.

Hoyle, E., & Wallace, M. (2005). *Educational Leadership – Ambiguity, Professionals & managerialism*. Sage. doi:10.4135/9781446220078

Ion, C. G. (2015). Husserl, Habermas, and the Lifeworld as the Overall Horizon within Which Individuals Act. *Linguistic and Philosophical Investigations*, (14), 115–120.

Jain, A. K., & Sullivan, S. (2019). An examination of the relationship between careerism and organizational commitment, satisfaction, and performance. *Personnel Review*, *49*(9), 1553–1571. doi:10.1108/PR-05-2019-0280

Jaros, S. (2018). Expansive and Focused Concepts of managerialism in CMS. *Tamara, 16*(1-2):1-12.

Juusola, K. (2023). Coping with managerialism: Academics' responses to conflicting institutional logics in business schools. *International Journal of Management Education*, *17*(1), 89–107.

Kark, R., & Van Dijk, D. (2019). Keep your head in the clouds and your feet on the ground: A multifocal review of leadership–followership self-regulatory focus. *The Academy of Management Annals*, *13*(2), 509–546. doi:10.5465/annals.2017.0134

Klikauer, T. (2007). *Communication and Management at Work*. Palgrave. doi:10.1057/9780230210899

Klikauer, T. (2013). Managerialism – Critique of an Ideology. Palgrave.

Klikauer, T. 2018. Adorno on ideology: ideology critique and mass consumerism, in: Coban. S. (eds), Media, Ideology and Hegemony. Leiden: Brill. doi:10.1163/9789004364417_006

Klikauer, T. (2019). A preliminary theory of managerialism as an ideology. *Journal for the Theory of Social Behaviour*, *49*(4), 421–442. doi:10.1111/jtsb.12220

Klikauer, T. (2022). *Media Capitalism*. Palgrave.

Klikauer, T. (2023). *The Language of managerialism*. Palgrave/Springer. doi:10.1007/978-3-031-16379-1

Klikauer, T., & Tannò, A. (2022). Managerialism. In K. Schedler (Ed.), Elgar Encyclopaedia of Public Management (pp. 340–345). Edward Elgar. doi:10.4337/9781800375499.managerialism

Klikauer, T., & Young, M. (2021). Global Warming's Walking Dead. *Counterpunch*. https://www.counterpunch.org/2021/08/23/global-warmings-walking-dead/

Koch, R. (2011). *The 80/20 Principle: The Secret of Achieving More with Less: Updated 20th anniversary edition of the productivity and business classic*. Hachette.

Koliousi, P., & Miaouli, N. 2018. *Efficient bargaining versus Right to manage in the era of liberalization*. School of Economic Sciences, Athens University of Economics and Business. https://www.dept.aueb.gr/sites/default/files/wp04-2018-Koliousi-Miaouli-JULY-27.pdf.

Lepore, J. (2009). Not So Fast - Scientific management started as a way to work. How did it become a way of life? *The New Yorker* (www.newyorker.com).

Locke, R. R. (1996). *The Collapse of the American Management Mystique*. Oxford University Press. doi:10.1093/acprof:oso/9780198774068.001.0001

Locke, R. R., & Spender, J. C. (2011). *Confronting managerialism: how the Business Elite and their Schools threw our Lives out of Balance*. Zed Books. doi:10.5040/9781350219304

Lynn, A. (2017). MacIntyre, managerialism, and Metatheory: Organizational Theory as an Ideology of Control. *Journal of Critical Realism, 16*(2), 143–162. doi:10.1080/14767430.2017.1282299Magretta, J. (2012). *What Management Is: How it works and why it's everyone's business.* Profile.

Marguerat, D. (2002). *The first Christian historian: Writing the'Acts of the Apostles.* Cambridge University Press. doi:10.1017/CBO9780511488061

McCann, L. (2017). Killing is our business and business is good: The evolution of war managerialism from body counts to counterinsurgency. *Organization, 24*(4), 491–515. doi:10.1177/1350508417693852

Micocci, A., & Di Mario, F. (2018). *The fascist nature of neoliberalism.* Routledge.

Miller, D. (2008). *A century of spin: how public relations became the cutting edge of corporate power.* Pluto Press.

Noe, T. H., & Rebello, M. J. (1996). Asymmetric information, managerial opportunism, financing, and payout policies. *The Journal of Finance, 51*(2), 637–660. doi:10.1111/j.1540-6261.1996.tb02697.x

Parker, M. (2019). Alternatives to Management Ideas. In A. Sturdy, (Eds.), *Oxford Handbook of Management Ideas* (p. 497). Oxford University Press.

Plachy, R. J., & Smunt, T. L. (2022). Rethinking managership, leadership, followership, and partnership. *Business Horizons, 65*(4), 401–411. doi:10.1016/j.bushor.2021.04.004

Pollitt, C. (1990). Managerialism and the public services: the Anglo-American experience. Basil Blackwell.

Prasad, S. B. (Ed.). (1968). Managerialism for economic development: essays on India. Martinus Nijhoff. doi:10.1007/978-94-011-7499-2

Ramsay, H., Scholarios, D., & Harley, B. (2000). Employees and high-performance work systems: Testing inside the black box. *British Journal of Industrial Relations, 38*(4), 501–531. doi:10.1111/1467-8543.00178

Rosenfeld, P. (1995). *Impression Management in Organisations – Theory, Measures, Practice.* Routledge.

Scott, D. E., & Scott, S. (2016). Leadership for quality university teaching: How bottom-up academic insights can inform top-down leadership. *Educational Management Administration & Leadership, 44*(3), 511–531. doi:10.1177/1741143214549970

Scott, W. G., & Hart, D. K. (1991). The Exhaustion of managerialism. *Society, 28*(3), 39–48. doi:10.1007/BF02695594

Seeck, H., Sturdy, A., Boncori, A. L., & Fougère, M. (2020). Ideology in management studies. *International Journal of Management Reviews, 22*(1), 57. doi:10.1111/ijmr.12215

Shepherd, S. (2018). Managerialism: An ideal type. *Studies in Higher Education, 43*(9), 1668–1678. doi:10.1080/03075079.2017.1281239

Simon, H. A. (1960). *The new science of management decision.* Harper. doi:10.1037/13978-000

Sood, B. (2021). The Emergence of Managerial Capitalism in Europe, *International Journal of Research in Engineering. Science and Management, 4*(11), 169–177.

Trofimov, A., Matviienko, L., Emishyants, O., Tretiakova, Y., Zelenin, V., Andrushchenko, T., & Kotsiuba, H. (2019). Socio-psychological factors of corporate loyalty. *International Journal of Scientific and Technology Research*, *8*(11), 3439–3442.

Van Gelderen, M., Kautonen, T., & Fink, M. (2015). From entrepreneurial intentions to actions: Self-control and action-related doubt, fear, and aversion. *Journal of Business Venturing*, *30*(5), 655–673. doi:10.1016/j.jbusvent.2015.01.003

Wallace-Wells, D. (2017). The Uninhabitable Earth. *NY Mag*. https://nymag.com/.

Wallace-Wells, D. (2019). *The Uninhabitable Earth: life after warming*. Tim Duggan Books.

Wren, D. A., Bedeian, A. G., & Breeze, J. D. (2002). The foundations of Henri Fayol's administrative theory. *Management Decision*, *40*(9), 906–918. doi:10.1108/00251740210441108

Zhu, W., Avolio, B. J., & Walumbwa, F. O. (2009). Moderating role of follower characteristics with transformational leadership and follower work engagement. *Group & Organization Management*, *34*(5), 590–619. doi:10.1177/1059601108331242

Chapter 2
Positive Leadership and the Quiet Quitting Movement in Organizations

Ana Filipa Vieira Lopes Joaquim
Faculdade de Ciências Sociais e Humanas, Portugal

Paula Cristina Nunes Figueiredo
Universidade Lusófona, Portugal

Vasco Rafael Costa Silva
Instituto Politécnico de Gestão e Tecnologia, Portugal

Cristina Nogueira da Fonseca
Instituto Politécnico de Gestão e Tecnologia, Portugal

ABSTRACT

This chapter seeks to highlight the importance of positive leadership in combating the phenomenon of quiet quitting. This phenomenon is not new, but it has gone viral with the COVID-19 pandemic, being more 'visible' in the organizational context. Thus, the objective of this research is to identify the main advantages of positive leadership in mitigating the quiet quitting movement. The research methodology is qualitative and starts by conceptualizing and identifying the main causes and consequences of the quiet quitting movement. Afterwards, the advantages of positive leadership are identified and, finally, this leadership style is systematized in relation to happiness and well-being at work. This research thus integrates the positive leadership approach with practices to improve employee engagement and organizational culture, highlighting the importance of human resource management practices to attract, integrate and manage talent in companies.

INTRODUCTION

There is a dearth of scientific studies on the Quiet Quitting movement, not only because it is a new

DOI: 10.4018/978-1-6684-8257-5.ch002

term for workers who want to get their work tasks done but because the movement began with this new nomenclature in the summer of 2022 by Tik Tok Influencer, such as Khaby Lame, Charli d' Amelio or Addison Rae, just to name a few.

This phenomenon has gone viral; however, it is essential to emphasize that this behavior of workers is not new, as there have always been unmotivated workers (Aydın & Azizoglu, 2022). More than a productivity reduction problem, the frustrations that lead to quiet quitting are increasingly mental health issues that leaders and organizations must be aware of (Singh et al., 2022; Singh et al., 2022)

People tend to have mixed feelings about their jobs, not only due to the intergenerational co-worker's reality (Figueiredo & Joaquim, 2022) but also because the expectations and the goals achievements are different from one individual. However, nowadays, competitiveness on the business level is exceptionally high, and workers spend several hours per day in their workplaces (OECD.Stat, 2021).

Until 2020, employees had not fully realized their working hours, not only because they had traditional methods and established schedules, but they had an office to attend to, so their perception about work and personal life were two different matters that were explicitly divided on their lives (De Smet et al., 2021; Stahl, 2022). Nevertheless, all that changed in the year mentioned because of COVID-19 lockdown measures worldwide.

Workers were forced to adapt their working procedures to remote work or telecommuting during this period, blurring the distinction between professional and personal life. As a result, according to Schmidt (2010), individuals felt overwhelmed, and burnout became a real and concerning mental health issue.

Workers started to realize that their daily tasks were beyond their job description; consequently, their personal life was neglected in favor of their professional life, resulting in lower engagement feelings about work (Aydın & Azizoglu, 2022; Thompson, 2022).

Happiness at work has become a natural feeling to improve efficiency and productivity (Sohail Butt et al., 2020). According to Maenapothi (2007) (referred in Chaiprasit & Santidhiraku, 2011), "happiness at the workplace means a situation at the workplace when personnel is happy working and not feeling like it is work, are efficient and achieve targeted goals, both at the personnel and organizational levels" (2011, p. 191).

Regarding Windham-Bradstock (2022), there are three solutions to mitigate quiet quitting: communication, setting expectations, and cultivating trust. These are also significant assumptions for positive leadership. This leadership style emerged at the beginning of the 21st century, integrating leadership theories and the positive psychology approach. Although positive leadership is not univocally defined, evidence shows that positive leadership theories are based on positive psychology (Gauthier, 2015; Stander & Coxen, 2017).

Evidence has shown positive effects of positive psychology on improving work outcomes (Donaldson et al., 2019; Rudolph et al., 2017). In addition, positive leadership stimulates individuals' potential since leaders encourage exceptional performance by focusing on virtue and eudemonism.

In this research, the authors aim to understand the importance of positive leadership in combating the phenomenon of quiet quitting. The main question relies on the following:

- **What are the key advantages of positive leadership for organizations to mitigate the quiet quitting movement?**

The objectives of this research rely on the following:

O1 – Conceptualize and identify the leading causes and consequences of the quiet quitting movement.
O2 – Identify and conceptualize the critical advantages of positive leadership for organizations to mitigate the quiet quitting movement.
O3 - Systematize positive leadership regarding happiness in the workplace.

The structure of the chapter is based on three main sections, first, quiet quitting: the new trend where the causes and consequences of this phenomenon will be exposed; the second section intends to conceptualize and systematize corporate happiness theories; and the last section discusses issues regarding the integration of positive leadership in companies to improve the engagement between workers and business culture.

METHODS

The research method of the chapter is based on a qualitative overview of the literature review of academic articles, HRM studies, and opinion articles by HRM experts in internationally renowned online magazines and newspapers and transnational organizations' websites.

A comprehensive search was conducted in the dominant databases, namely Scopus, SAGE, Emeralds, Science Direct, and EBSCOhost, following the keywords for article selection presented in Table 1. In addition, studies and reports on this theme developed by private entities were also considered.

Table 1. Keywords criteria used to select research

Quiet Quitting	Corporate Happiness	Positive Leadership
Engagement with business culture	Well-being The balance between professional and personal life	Leadership Leadership style

The lack of academic literature forced to open the research spectrum to studies carried out in the labor market by transnational and private organizations and opinion articles by HRM experts in internationally renowned online magazines. Also, newspapers were considered to integrate multi-disciplinary subjects better.

Our main goal was to systematize the critical advantages of positive leadership for organizations to mitigate the quiet quitting movement. The next step in the study was to define the objectives and chapter approach to the literature researched.

Methodological quality and quantity of evidence were based on several case studies where the quiet quitting movement became a trend.

To understand the causes and consequences of this phenomenon, it was necessary to correlate it with the effects of positive leadership.

During the research, the authors identified, read, and analyzed over ninety academic articles (95) regarding positive leadership and corporate happiness, twenty opinion articles by HRM experts (20), and ten (10) databases of international organizations regarding the quiet quitting movement versus employee engagement. In addition, the authors decided to exclude ten (10) opinion daily newspaper articles from their research that were not based on practical or academic research.

The multiplicity of research methods aims to be the first approach to investigating the advantages of practicing positive leadership to improve corporate happiness and lessen negative feelings about corporate cultures. Far from being a closed analysis, it is intended to be the trigger for understanding the emotional importance of positive leadership on employees.

QUIET QUITTING: THE NEW TREND

Quiet quitting has become a new trend, according to Aydın & Azizoglu (2022), "More than 19 million US workers—and counting—have quit their jobs since April 2021" (De Smet et al., 2021, p. 1), but this is a worldwide movement that has become a tremendous problem at the business level.

Although for Thompson (2022), this is a trend that has been studied by Gallup (2022) since 2010, and the data indicate that 26% of United States (US) workers felt disengaged from their work in 2010. In 2018, there were 34%.

Despite all the buzziness in social media, the author believes that quiet quitting is not a real trend.

Aydın & Azizoglu (2022) also reiterate that "Quiet Quitting has been conceptualized under different names in the field of organizational behavior for decades" (2022, p. 287).

This movement started in the summer of 2022, after COVID-19 lockdown measures worldwide, with Tik Tok influencers defending that it is possible to have a job without it taking over their lives (Thompson, 2022) and media widely disseminated the concept (Aydın & Azizoglu, 2022).

It is essential to understand the real meaning of this phenomenon.

Quiet quitting is not about workers leaving their jobs regarding mass layoffs but about balancing working and social life. According to Stahl (2022), "workers are no longer willing to go above and beyond the scope of their job descriptions if it means sacrificing their mental health, and instead, they are staying within the limits of their job description"(2022). Employees realized they felt overwhelmed during the COVID-19 pandemic when they were obliged to manage their tasks through remote work. As a result, the disengagement between workers and their jobs in the United States grew to 36% in 2020 (Gallup, 2022).

Thompson (2022) minimizes this movement, saying that quiet quitting is not more than "in previous decades, simply known as "having a job" and "the term has taken off in part because burned-out or bored workers are simply desperate for a fresh vocabulary to describe their feelings" (2022, p. 1). Despite this argument, the truth is that "people are switching jobs and industries, moving from traditional to nontraditional roles, retiring early, or starting their businesses. They are taking time to tend to their personal lives or embarking on sabbaticals" (De Smet et al., 2021).

To understand the Quiet Quitting phenomenon, it is essential to identify its causes. During 2020 the world experienced a new type of global pandemic, COVID-19, and nations worldwide applied lockdown measures to mitigate the spread of the virus. As a result, companies and employees had to adjust their working habits and procedures to a remote work model in their homes (Aydın & Azizoglu, 2022).

The internet had become the *Holy Grail* of their lives, and the balance between their personal and professional life was measured through a fine line that some workers could not differentiate (Figueiredo & Joaquim, 2022). As a result, mental health becomes an important issue to maintain because of the loneliness and the lack of physical connections with the companies and other co-workers. (Schmidt, 2010; Vieira De Faria & Zanotelli De Alvarenga, 2021).

Individuals tend to need "interactions, not just transactions" (De Smet et al., 2021) because they feel that they have lost the "sense of shared identity" (De Smet et al., 2021).

Despite most studies and articles being related to the US working class reality (De Smet et al., 2022; Harter, 2022; Stahl, 2022), Quiet Quitting has become a worldwide movement, primarily thanks to the advent of new technologies, particularly social networking platforms (Graham, 2022).

In Portugal, Afonso (2022) exposes his concern regarding predicting an economic recession that will be experienced nationally.[1], expressing concerns that people publishing on social media live their position about Quiet quitting may be the first ones companies will lay off.

As noticed before, the lack of engagement with business culture is not the principal cause of this movement., In Afonso's (2022) words, the causes also relied on the "permanent environment of stress at work, fostered by the pressure of absurdly short deadlines and the quick achievement of results. For many companies, man is now treated as a mere production instrument" (2022, p. 2).

Schindler (2022) alludes that this company behavior is caused by extreme globalization; in other words, competition on the business level extrapolated the demand for revenues through a working process that relies on full availability from the workers.

FlexJobs (2022), between July 13 and July 31, 2022, surveyed over 2,000 employed professionals to get their insight on important topics surrounding the current work landscape. The report explored how workers think about engagement, job satisfaction, flexibility, and return-to-office plans. Regarding engagement, "the slight majority (51%) of workers say they are only "somewhat" engaged (42%) or "not at all" engaged (9%) at work," and only 15% are highly engaged. Regarding how workers feel in their job, the majority answered "okay," with 40% (Howington, 2022).

The *more or less* feeling must be a red flag to employers because "workers are tired of being asked to do more without the compensation to back their responsibility level" (Stahl, 2022). Although despite understanding the reasons for this, most companies tend to give material benefits to their employees without success (De Smet et al., 2021). "Employers should understand the common themes that reveal what people most value or most dislike about a job" (De Smet et al., 2022, p. 5).

Nowadays, workers need to feel involved and engaged with their work and balance their professional and personal life (Rudolph et al., 2017; Sohail Butt et al., 2020).

According to Aydın & Azizoglu (2022), Generation Z whore the leading group that "raised their voice" against excessive tasks and working hours (2022, p. 286). This generation is characterized by their pioneer skills and behavior (Figueiredo & Joaquim, 2022).

Today, organizations are not in a position to guarantee jobs but only to offer employability and further training to employees (De Smet et al., 2021, 2022). Therefore, one of the significant challenges that companies face is to create a learning and development culture that starts at the leadership level and spreads to the remaining employees. So "21st-century leaders recognize that creating the leadership potential in their organizations will be the biggest differentiator for success to come" (Kets de Vries & Korotov, 2012, p. 6).

Since 2020, companies worldwide have faced structural changes because of the lockdown measures regarding the COVID-19 pandemic; workers were forced to adapt their working procedures to remote work. However, despite all the constraints, most employees have understood that the traditional way of doing their work affects their balance between professional and personal life (De Smet et al., 2022; Figueiredo & Joaquim, 2022).

By constraints, the literature acknowledges that the lack of digital literacy and working feelings and behavior between generations are the main issues in telecommuting work (Figueiredo & Fonseca, 2022; Figueiredo & Joaquim, 2022; Scott, 2018).

After the easing of measures, employees were called to return to their offices. They realized they were no longer happy in their working place because they felt overwhelmed, stressed, and disconnected from their jobs, colleagues, and corporate culture (De Smet et al., 2022).

"Employees are tired, and many are grieving. They want a renewed and revised sense of purpose in their work. They want social and interpersonal connections with their colleagues and managers" (2022, p. 1).

If in previous generations, engagement with work was not a problem (e.g., baby boomers), but for the new generations (e.g., millennials and generation x), being emotionally involved is one of the most essential items to be considered in a job (Figueiredo & Joaquim, 2022).

Robison (2021) wrote that in 2021, about 75% of some millennials were engaged at work, despite 35% of the national average, in 2019, in the US. Because they can have remote work (*i*), a plan of action (*ii*), academic preparation and digital skills (*iii*), managers that provide information (*iv*), and well-being concerns (*v*) in opposition to the previous generations (Figueiredo & Joaquim, 2022).

Figueiredo & Joaquim (2022) realize that millennials[2] are.

(…) *career-oriented, team-oriented, confident, and optimistic with a strong demand balance to ensure between social and professional life, true to be told, despite that they are a hard work generation with gold achievement but require recognition and detailed feedback in the workplace* (2022, p. 76).

However, Harter (2022) and Aydın & Azizoglu (2022), despite the high level of engagement, are the generation that embraced the quiet quitting, with a particular focus on those born between 1990 and 2010, called Generation Z because, as mentioned before, they need to have purpose and meaning in their work task and, also, a more vital delimited balance with personal and professional life.

Rescuing the variables of engagement with work by millennials, Robison (2021) alludes that being able to have remote work (i) is one of the essential features to have the engagement feeling with work because it provides "flexibility and greater work-life balance ."Regarding having a plan of action (ii), about 56% of the data sample had identified this feature as a purpose in work because knowing their tasks, objectives, and goals (iii) allowed them to have more control over time and task planning (iv). Well-being (v) is not only about health; it "is a combination of social, community, financial, career and physical elements that affect each other" (Robison, 2021).

THE WORKPLACE SHOULD BE A HAPPY PLACE

According to the OECD. Stat (2021), the *average annual hours worked per worker* was the OECD workers, in 2020, 1668 hours, but in 2021 this number had increased to 1716. Regarding this data, the workers spent 33 hours weekly on their jobs. Although more hours in the workplace does not mean more productivity, to improve efficiency is essential that the employees engage with organizational culture.

The definitions of organizational culture are inconclusive, as the various cultures have different specificities that may or may not provide a better response to market stimuli due to globalization. Nevertheless, they can always be considered changeable and adaptable; therefore, Zheng et al. (2009) state that the extent "of definitions of the cultural organization also represents the range of assumptions, approaches, purposes and even paradigms in the study of what organizational culture is" (2009, p. 154).

Regardless of the various definitions, the authors conceptualize organizational culture as "composed of a set of shared assumptions, values, behavioral norms and artifacts that end up differentiating the groups" (2009, p. 154).

However, despite all the theories and models studied to explain better different cultures prevailing in organizations, there are still several aspects, according to Zheng et al. (2009), that raise some doubts, which are related to the fact that the existing studies have a static view on the term of organizational culture. In addition, organizations face different challenges that can develop culture through its nature, the competitive market, and the survival instinct needed.

Leaders play a crucial role in organizational culture change by promoting subcultures and adopting new technologies regarding mechanisms, mergers, acquisitions, or company reorganization (Zheng et al., 2009).

According to Unnu (2019), leaders must boost positivity and performance to create a productive and pleasing organizational climate between workers.

It is also very important to refer to the organizational climate as how the members of an organization perceive what surrounds them, and through how they see their environment and experience the different stimuli to which they are subject within the organization, it is more practical to be able to define the culture in which they are inserted and to be able to implement any change and perceive its impact since it will be automatically reflected in the environment experienced by all (Schneider & Barbera, 2014).

So, the importance of being happy in the workplace has become a massive issue for companies and employees because happy individuals tend to be more engaged with the organizational culture of the companies, and, consequently, more productive.

Niu (2021) understands that happiness is linked to positive feelings and pleasures thru individual tasks and activities that maintain the subjects in a state of commitment with their positive characteristics. The author identified pleasure, commitment, and meaning as the basis for happiness.

Unnu (2019) also reinforces that meaning is characterized by "positivity feelings" and how the individual can connect to them through a sense of belonging to serve something greater than them, such as a community, a religion, or a social group.

According to Fisher (2010), workplace happiness aggregates many constructs that have been the subject of further investigation in recent times. However, all are related to happiness in organizations by representing positive attitudes and pleasant experiences such as positive feelings, mood, emotions, and the involvement or flow individuals feel in the workplace (Niu, 2021; Redín et al., 2023).

The Covid-19 lockdown measures and telecommuting brought negative feelings to workers (P. Singh et al., 2022); as mentioned before, insecurity and anxiety were extrapolated (Niu, 2021). Therefore, positive psychology and leadership have become crucial issues in Human Resources Management (HRM).

Positive psychology was "first put forward by American psychologist Martin Seligman, who advocated that psychological research should focus on people's actual potential, constructive power, and virtue" (Niu, 2021, p. 212). On the other hand, there has yet to be a consensus in the literature regarding positive leadership. However, in the words of Redín et al. (2023), "the positive leader automatically provides followers with a vision of the end towards the common good and achieves to set his/her organization on a pathway towards excellence" (2023, p. 1).

Robertson & Cooper (2011) allude to the importance of positive psychology and psychological capital allied with the happiness felt by employees. For them, the building of psychological capital may be at the center of the results obtained by organizations that foster the happiness and well-being of their members.

People with elevated levels of well-being have better psychological resources for dealing with problems because they are more optimistic, more resilient, and have an unshakeable belief in their ability.

For companies to provide corporate happiness, which should be a change in leadership bias; in other words, to mitigate the quiet quitting movement, corporations must improve their leadership skills to a positive ideology to reconnect with their workers.

POSITIVE LEADERSHIP: A TOPIC THAT SHOULD BE A TREND

Positive leadership emerged at the beginning of the 21st century, integrating leadership theories and the positive psychology approach (Cameron, 2012; Seligman & Csikszentmihaly, 2000). Although positive leadership is not univocally defined, evidence shows that positive leadership theories are based on positive psychology (Cameron, 2012; Gauthier, 2015; Klug et al., 2022; Olckers et al., 2017; Unnu, 2019). Therefore, studies have been carried out to conceptualize this leadership style, more specifically, its nature, antecedents, and consequences (Cameron, 2012; Figueiredo & Fonseca, 2022; Gauthier, 2015; Redín et al., 2023; Stander & Coxen, 2017) and the search for positive leadership models (Gauthier, 2015).

Cameron (2012) established four fundamental principles underlying the development of the concept of positive leadership: (i) positive climate; (ii) positive relationships; (iii) positive communication, and (iv) positive purpose, as well as the practices associated with each one.

Thus, the optimistic leader fosters a positive work climate (i), identifying positive motivational elements tasks and the recognition and support of teams (ii); they promote positive communication (iii) based on affirmative and supportive language to the detriment of negative and critical language (iv); the leader does not fail to address negative aspects, but does so through a positive and constructive approach; the positive leader promotes positive relationships among members, fostering positive energy, diagnosing and building positive energy networks.

This type of leader ensures that work is associated with a positive purpose that keeps everyone focused and motivated on meaningful goals (Fisher, 2010).

A recent study demonstrated a positive relationship between high-performance human resource management practices, employee engagement, and effective leadership (Goswami et al., 2019).

A good leader must have certain qualities such as (i) the ability to inspire and empower his team members to achieve their full potential; (ii) the ability to provide clear direction; (iii) interpersonal, communication, team building, and motivational skills, and (iv) the ability to develop other leaders (Kets de Vries & Korotov, 2012). A leader guided by ethical values, authenticity, altruism, honesty, and fairness presents a unique environment of trust. Their subordinates react the same way, which gives rise to a stronger bond between both parties, arousing positive attitudes in employees, such as satisfaction, commitment, and motivation in their workplace (A. Singh et al., 2022). The ability of leaders to demonstrate optimism, calm, empathy, trust, resilience, and make informed decisions are characteristics of positive leadership (Figueiredo & Fonseca, 2022).

Positive leaders who are optimistic and hopeful about the future positively impact leadership outcomes, such as greater employee engagement and increased employee productivity (Donaldson et al., 2019; Klug et al., 2022; Unnu, 2019).

Considering the flexibility, instability, and unpredictability that characterize today's organizations (Oleksa-Marewska & Tokar, 2022; Unnu, 2019), the importance of the presence of a positive, strategic leader is recognized (Figueiredo & Fonseca, 2022; Stander & Coxen, 2017), whose values are guided by participative leadership that induces others to be leaders themselves, thus favoring self-leadership; by the emphasis placed on teams, which translates into their valorization, so-called leader with coaching skills(Berg & Karlsen, 2016; Unnu, 2019).

This type of performance positively affects team performance and employees' attitudes and behaviors that are reflected in organizational terms (Berg & Karlsen, 2016; Unnu, 2019).

Osula & Ng (2014) argued that leadership strategies cannot be understood as a series of activities but as decision-making and vision. In this context, leadership development necessarily involves action and reflection, and both are necessary to enhance critical skills such as analysis, strategic planning, and critical awareness (Kets de Vries & Korotov, 2012).

Importantly, studies on the outcome of effective leadership on employee retention, performance, and well-being attend to two primary constructs: satisfaction with activities performed and affective organizational commitment (Cameron, 2012; Donaldson et al., 2019; Goswami et al., 2019).

Affective organizational commitment is a positive emotional effect that fosters an individual's involvement in the organization where he or she works (Olckers et al., 2017) positive leader.

In all types of organizations, whether for-profit or non-profit, organizational affective commitment has proven to be strongly related to the internalization of organizational values, dedication, and loyalty, as well as by alignment with the organization's goals. At the same time, it needs leadership capable of inspiring employees to perform tasks for the overall good of the organization (Cameron, 2012; Fisher, 2010; Gauthier, 2015).

Positive leadership thus leads to positive emotions (Olckers et al., 2017; Stander & Coxen, 2017), increased social well-being, improved organizational citizenship behavior, and individual and organizational performance (Gauthier, 2015).

Literature has revealed that the leader's actions can dramatically affect how an individual feels about work and self, both good and evil (Gauthier, 2015; Klug et al., 2022; Seligman & Csikszentmihalyi, 2000). Thus, leaders can have a toxic influence on organizations by potentiating emotional exhaustion in their employees (Kets de Vries & Korotov, 2012). Furthermore, since emotional exhaustion leads to burnout in the workplace (Donaldson et al., 2019), it can harm both employees and their employers (Klug et al., 2022).

Evidence has shown that emotional exhaustion correlates positively with poor health and well-being, lower job satisfaction and commitment, higher turnover rates, and lower performance(Donaldson et al., 2019; Kets de Vries & Korotov, 2012; Klug et al., 2022). In contrast, job satisfaction, the result of a high level of commitment and positive trust in the leader, contributed to higher worker engagement associated with feelings of enthusiasm, inspiration, pride, meaning, and challenge (Fairlie, 2011; Gauthier, 2015; Kets de Vries & Korotov, 2012). In addition, evidence has revealed that job satisfaction can offer valuable outcomes: i) greater vigor, dedication, and absorption (Fairlie, 2011); ii) more excellent health and well-being (Klug et al., 2022; Olckers et al., 2017) and lower rates of absenteeism (Cameron, 2012; Olckers et al., 2017).

Happiness at work is undoubtedly essential for higher productivity rates in organizations (Sohail Butt et al., 2020). Satisfied employees work harder and are more productive since they feel motivation and confidence are indispensable to work performance, which increases engagement and commitment, perhaps mitigating the quiet quitting movement (Windham-Bradstock, 2022).

A positive leader builds favorable structures by appointing the right talent, sharing their vision and goals, and focusing on organizational effectiveness (Gauthier, 2015). In addition, this type of leader seeks to assess patterns and trends in employee performance, create awareness through continuous feedback, provide learning experiences, allow opportunities for reflection, and collaborate in planning actions and identifying critical steps to achieve goals (Cameron, 2012; Figueiredo & Fonseca, 2022; Seligman & Csikszentmihaly, 2000).

According to Goleman (2000), emotional intelligence is far more critical them other subjects regarding individuals in their work. However, the author still needs to remove the importance of physical and academic skills. He understands that workers more attached to their feelings and emotions are more effective and productive than others.

As mentioned before, this is a collaborative procedure, not only because it should be implemented through positive leadership, as should be fostered, and continued work in the companies.

Nowadays, professional qualifications and physical profiles have changed a lot. After all, they are relegated to an almost secondary role because companies are looking for other skills in their job candidates (De Smet et al., 2022). Regardless, positive leadership must be present to create and maintain well-being and job satisfaction in their workers. So, looking for social, emotional, or engagement skills and commitment are not a one-way path. It should be conquered and applied through positive leadership and corporate happiness.

In short, positive leadership can contribute decisively to job satisfaction, which leads to happiness in the workplace, which contributes to improved performance and employee productivity (Cameron, 2012) and mitigates the feeling of disengagement that consequently tends to be part of the quiet quitting movement (Graham, 2022).

CONCLUSION AND IMPLICATIONS

Conceptualize and identify the leading causes and consequences of the quiet quitting movement.

The leading causes of the quiet quitting movement rely on an absence of engagement between the organization's culture and the workers, not only because of the worker's lack of work/life balance but because they understood the remote work forced by the lockdown measures to mitigate the spread of the COVID-19 virus, that they felt overwhelmed with their job tasks.

The meaning of quiet quitting movement is not a layoff mass movement; instead, it relies on employees doing strictly what is their job description.

Workers do not feel happy in their workplace; according to the FlexJobs survey, most of the workers (40%) felt okay on their jobs (2022), as a consequence of this, they felt disengaged with the company values and consequentially, their productiveness suffer a decrease (Sohail Butt et al., 2020).

Employers should understand what their workers most value in their work. Then, regardless of offering material benefits, they should create a productive system based on communication, path, purpose, and flexibility that allows workers to create a positive balance between professional/social life bias.

Goleman (2000) believes workers who understand their emotional intelligence are more engaged with their job tasks. Hence, the probability of quitting their jobs becomes lower than the disengaged individuals. For this achievement, the leadership model must be changed to a positive one.

Identify and conceptualize the critical advantages of positive leadership for organizations to mitigate the quiet quitting movement.

Workers tend to be more productive when they are happy and when the organizational environment is based on interpersonal relationships and the purpose of their job tasks. That does not mean that leaders should let their workers do whatever they please, but through open communication and structure, companies will realize their workers' values, goals, and expectations (Fairlie, 2011). So "many senior executives will be challenged to reimagine how they lead" (De Smet et al., 2022, p. 2)

An environment based on trust is more profitable than a negative one (Windham-Bradstock, 2022). The key advantages of positive leadership for organizations to mitigate the quiet quitting movement are based on three essential factors, according to Windham-Bradstock (2022) communication, setting expectations, and cultivating trust.

De Smet et al. (2022) identifies twelve reasons for people to quit their traditional job. However, for this chapter, the authors identified the three most important for the author and data sample based on his surveys: career development and advancement, adequate total compensation, meaningful work, and workplace flexibility.

Positive leadership embraces the Windham-Bradstock (2022) theory. Although, as mentioned before, positive leadership is not univocally defined; evidence shows that positive leadership theories are based on positive psychology (Cameron, 2012; Gauthier, 2015; Klug et al., 2022; Olckers et al., 2017; Unnu, 2019). However, Cameron (2012) established four fundamental principles underlying the development of the concept of leadership: i) positive climate; ii) positive relationships; iii) positive communication, and iv) positive purpose, as well as the practices associated with each one.

In conclusion, the key advantages of positive leadership are responding to employees' needs to attend to happiness in their workplace and renouncing the quiet quitting phenomenon.

Systematize positive leadership regarding happiness at the workplace.

According to Zheng et al. (2009), leaders have a privileged role in organizational culture because they can change that.

Leaders are the primary tools for changing and promoting and healthy and positive environment in the workplace; they are obliged to create a safe space to improve the happiness of their workers.

Gauthier (2015) alludes that a positive leader can build a cohesive, productive team by appointing the right talent, sharing their vision and goals, and focusing on organizational effectiveness. Figueiredo & Fonseca (2022) reiterates by exposing that a leader should create awareness through continuous feedback, provide learning experiences, allow opportunities for reflection, and collaborate in planning actions and identifying critical steps to help their workers achieve goals. This is only possible when the employees feel safe, validated, recognized, and happy in their workplace.

The implications of the research on human resource management and leadership are highlighted. As for HRM, there is a need to listen to the teams and adopt the best hiring, integration, and talent management practices, as they are essential to keep companies competitive and attractive to professionals. It is also important to know the reasons for demotivation and what leads to the quiet quitting of a worker, which can quickly spread to other workers. Regarding the implications at the leadership level, emphasis is placed on the need for more significant concern with burnout and mental health situations. The leader must take on a more active role, speaking openly about the issue and internally promoting a mental health strategy. This type of leader is essential to find direct impacts in terms of productivity and results of companies. In today's context of intergenerational differences, leaders still need to pay more attention to how they attract and include multiple generations in the workplace.

LIMITATIONS AND RECOMMENDATIONS FOR FUTURE RESEARCH

This research is intended to become a first-line investigation concerning the quiet quitting movement phenomenon and positive leadership.

According to the literature review, several topics represent the phenomenon's cause, so this research's theme is still ongoing. However, the importance of the theme is understood when there is a gap in the correlation between quiet quitting and leadership *per se*.

It is vital to research individuals' feelings regarding their jobs so they do not feel the need to quit. Nevertheless, this research is far from over and must be knowledge as one of the most critical subjects in Human Resource Management.

Until 2020, the lack of engagement was decreasing among American workers, according to Gallup (2022). However, when workers had remote or hybrid work models, the absence of human contact already demonstrated workers' perception of being overwhelmed in their work. During that period, according to Aydın & Azizoglu (2022) and Oleksa-Marewska & Tokar (2022), individuals forgot to create and establish boundaries on their working schedules, as well as their employers, so they became overwhelmed, and mental health was a big issue (Haciyakupoglu et al., 2018).

There was a step-learning process during COVID-19 lockdown measures, and no one knew how to react. Companies and leaders acted the same way as they acted before in a traditional company environment, with the aggravating factor that workers were alone in their houses trying to manage family, work, and several other's obligations away from the business environment.

In 2021, workers were called to return to their offices to reestablish the traditional way of their tasks and schedules. Although according to FlexJobs (2022), about 26% and 22% are allowed to maintain the hybrid and remote work system, respectively, because they assumed that it is easier to balance life and work.

In the same survey, 37% had to return to the office full-time, but 51% felt "somewhat" engaged with their work and company. The number of disengaged workers with the company culture grew after COVID-19 lockdown measures.

Schindler (2022) claims that " a leader must take a long hard look not only at the employee but also at themselves as a manager and the corporate culture that may be demotivating employees."

This literature review intended to fill the gap in the academic literature regarding the quiet quitting movement and positive leadership through a catch-all overview of the major themes about these topics.

The authors' contribution is related to identifying different variables that needed more clarity in academia.

REFERENCES

Afonso, P. (2022). A demissão silenciosa (quiet quitting) vai acabar mal. *Observador Jornal Online*. https://observador.pt/opiniao/a-demissao-silenciosa-quiet-quitting-vai-acabar-mal/

Aydın, E., & Azizoglu, O. (2022). *A new term for an existing concept: Quiet Quitting - A self-determination perspective*. V International Congress on Critical Debates in Social Sciences (ICCDSS). https://www.researchgate.net/publication/366530514

Banco de Portugal. (2022). *Taxa de inflação*. Bpstat. https://bpstat.bportugal.pt/conteudos/noticias/1299

Berg, M. E., & Karlsen, J. T. (2016). A study of coaching leadership style practice in projects. *Management Research Review*, *39*(9), 1122–1142. doi:10.1108/MRR-07-2015-0157

Cameron, K. (2012). *Positive Leadership: Strategies for Extraordinary Performance*. Berrett-Koehler Publishers.

Chaiprasit, K., & Santidhiraku, O. (2011). Happiness at Work of Employees in Small and Medium-sized Enterprises, Thailand. *Procedia: Social and Behavioral Sciences*, *25*, 189–200. doi:10.1016/j.sbspro.2011.10.540

De Smet, A., Dowling, B., Hancock, B., & Schaninger, B. (2022). The Great Attrition is making hiring harder. Are you searching the right talent pools ? *McKinsey Quarterly, July*.

De Smet, A., Dowling, B., Mugayar-Baldocchi, M., & Schaninger, B. (2021). "Great Attraction" or "Great Attrition"? The choice is yours. *The McKinsey Quarterly*, (September), 1–8. https://www.mckinsey.com/business-functions/people-and-organizational-performance/our-insights/great-attrition-or-great-attraction-the-choice-is-yours

Donaldson, S. I., Lee, J. Y., & Donaldson, S. I. (2019). Evaluating Positive Psychology Interventions at Work: A Systematic Review and Meta-Analysis. *International Journal of Applied Positive Psychology*, *4*(3), 113–134. doi:10.100741042-019-00021-8

Fairlie, P. (2011). Meaningful work, employee engagement, and other key employee outcomes: Implications for human resource development. *Advances in Developing Human Resources*, *13*(4), 508–525. doi:10.1177/1523422311431679

Figueiredo, P., & Fonseca, C. (2022). Leadership and Followership in an Organizational Change Context: Positive leader development: Theoretical model proposal, 161–196.

Figueiredo, P., & Joaquim, A. F. (2022). The impact of artificial intelligence and intergenerational diversity. In F. Ince (Ed.), *Leadership Perspectives on Effective Intergenerational Communication and Management* (p. 28). IGI Global.

Fisher, C. D. (2010). Happiness at Work. *International Journal of Management Reviews*, *12*(4), 384–412. doi:10.1111/j.1468-2370.2009.00270.x

Gauthier, H. (2015). A Multi-Dimensional Model for Positive Leadership. *Strategic Leadership Review, 5*(1), 6–16. https://slr.scholasticahq.com/article/9-a-multi-dimensional-model-for-positive-leadership

Goleman, D. (2000). *Emotional Intelligence & Working With Emotional Intelligence*. Bantam; Reprint edition.

Goswami, B. K., Singh, J., & Goswami, A. (2019). Impact Of High Performance Human Resource Management Practices On Employee Engagement With The Moderating Role Of Ethical Leadership. *International Journal of Advanced Science and Technology, 28*(19), 331–334. http://sersc.org/journals/index.php/IJAST/article/view/2538

Graham, J. T. (2022). The Quiet Quitting Movement. *Sage HR Blog*. https://blog.sage.hr/the-quiet-quitting-movement/

Haciyakupoglu, G., Hui, J. Y., Suguna, V. S., Leong, D., Bin, M. F., & Rahman, A. (2018). *Countering Fake News A Survey Of Recent Global Initiatives*. S. Rajaratnam School of International Studies. https://think-asia.org/handle/11540/8063

Harter, J. (2022). *Is Quiet Quitting Real?* Gallup. https://www.gallup.com/workplace/398306/quiet-quitting-real.aspx

Howington, J. (2022). *Employee Engagement Report: Job Satisfaction and Work Flexibility*. FlexJobs for Employers. https://www.flexjobs.com/employer-blog/employee-engagement-report-job-satisfaction-work-flexibility/

Incentive Research Foundation. (2015). Generations in the Workforce & Marketplace : Preferences in Rewards. *Recognition & Incentives*, (January), 2018.

Kets de Vries, M. F. R., & Korotov, K. (2012). Developing Leaders and Leadership Development. *SSRN Electronic Journal*. doi:10.2139/ssrn.1684001

Klug, K., Felfe, J., & Krick, A. (2022). Does Self-Care Make You a Better Leader? A Multisource Study Linking Leader Self-Care to Health-Oriented Leadership, Employee Self-Care, and Health. *International Journal of Environmental Research and Public Health, 19*(11), 6733. doi:10.3390/ijerph19116733 PMID:35682319

Niu, Y. (2021). Enlightenment of Positive Psychology on Human Resource Management. *Modern Management Forum, 5*(1), 30. 10.18686/mmf.v5i1.3169

OECD. Stat. (2021). *Average annual hours actually worked per worker*. Labour Force Statistics. https://stats.oecd.org/index.aspx?DataSetCode=ANHRS

Olckers, C., van Zyl, L., & van der Vaart, L. (2017). *Theoretical Orientations and Practical Applications of Psychological Ownership*, 1–332. doi:10.1007/978-3-319-70247-6

Oleksa-Marewska, K., & Tokar, J. (2022). Facing the Post-Pandemic Challenges: The Role of Leadership Effectiveness in Shaping the Affective Well-Being of Healthcare Providers Working in a Hybrid Work Mode. *International Journal of Environmental Research and Public Health, 19*(21), 14388. doi:10.3390/ijerph192114388 PMID:36361264

Osula, B., & Ng, E. C. W. (2014). Toward a Collaborative, Transformative Model of Non-Profit Leadership: Some Conceptual Building Blocks. *Administrative Sciences, 4*(2), 87–104. doi:10.3390/admsci4020087

Redín, D. M., Meyer, M., & Rego, A. (2023). Positive leadership action framework: Simply doing good and doing well. *Frontiers in Psychology, 13*(January), 1–14. doi:10.3389/fpsyg.2022.977750 PMID:36687856

Robertson, I., & Cooper, C. (2011). *Well-being Productivity and Happiness at Work*. Palgrave Macmillan London. doi.org/10.1057/9780230306738

Robison, J. (2021). *What Disruption Reveals About Engaging Millennial Employees*. Gallup. https://www.gallup.com/workplace/328121/disruption-reveals-engaging-millennial-employees.aspx

Rudolph, C. W., Katz, I. M., Lavigne, K. N., & Zacher, H. (2017). Job crafting: A meta-analysis of relationships with individual differences, job characteristics, and work outcomes. *Journal of Vocational Behavior, 102*(314), 112–138. doi:10.1016/j.jvb.2017.05.008

Schindler, J. (2022). *How To Identify And Manage Quiet Quitting*. *Forbes*. https://www.forbes.com/sites/forbescoachescouncil/2022/10/28/how-to-identify-and-manage-quiet-quitting/?sh=3f1d95c24c4f

Schmidt, M. (2010). Trabalho e saúde mental na visão da OIT. *Revista Do Tribunal Regional Do Trabalho, 51*(81), 489–526.

Scott, A. (2018). *How Artificial Intelligence and Intergenerational Diversity Are Creating Anxiety in The Workplace*. Institute for Public Relations. https://instituteforpr.org/how-artificial-intelligence-and-intergenerational-diversity-is-creating-anxiety-in-the-workplace/

Seligman, M. E., & Csikszentmihaly, M. (2000). Positive Psychology. In American Psychologist Asociation, 55(1), 5–14.

Singh, A., Jha, S., Srivastava, D. K., & Somarajan, A. (2022). Future of work: A systematic literature review and evolution of themes. *Foresight, 24*(1), 99–125. doi:10.1108/FS-09-2020-0093

Singh, P., Bala, H., Dey, B. L., & Filieri, R. (2022). Enforced remote working: The impact of digital platform-induced stress and remote working experience on technology exhaustion and subjective well-being. *Journal of Business Research, 151*(August 2021), 269–286. doi:10.1016/j.jbusres.2022.07.002

Sohail Butt, R., Wen, X., & Yassir Hussain, R. (2020). Mediated Effect of Employee Job Satisfaction on Employees' Happiness at Work and Analysis of Motivational Factors: Evidence from Telecommunication Sector. *Asian Business Research Journal, 5*(September), 19–27. doi:10.20448/journal.518.2020.5.19.27

Spiro, C. (2006). Generation Y in the Workplace. *Defense AT, L*(November- December), 16–19.

Stahl, A. (2022). What's Really Happening With Quiet Quitting? *Forbes*. https://www.forbes.com/sites/ashleystahl/2022/11/02/whats-really-happening-with-quiet-quitting/?sh=3d6f676c2ab1

Stander, M. W., & Coxen, L. (2017). A Review of the Relationship Between Positive Leadership Styles and Psychological Ownership. In *Theoretical Orientations and Practical Applications of Psychological Ownership*. Springer International Publishing. doi:10.1007/978-3-319-70247-6_3

Thompson, D. (2022). Quiet Quitting Is a Fake Trend. Why Does It Feel Real? *The Atlantic*. https://www.theatlantic.com/newsletters/archive/2022/09/quiet-quitting-trend-employee-disengagement/671436/

Unnu, N. A. A. (2019). Boosting positivity and performance: A case study of organizational coaching. Handbook of Research on Positive Organizational Behavior for Improved Workplace Performance, 34–54. doi:10.4018/978-1-7998-0058-3.ch003

Vieira De Faria, R., & Zanotelli De Alvarenga, R. (2021). A Convenção 190 Da Oit E a Proteção À Saúde Mental Dos Trabalhadores. *Ano, 7*, 1257–1285.

Windham-Bradstock, C. (2022). Three Solutions To Quiet Quitting. *Forbes*. https://www.forbes.com/sites/forbeshumanresourcescouncil/2022/10/12/three-solutions-to-quiet-quitting/?sh=64327b435f1b

Zheng, W., Qu, Q., & Yang, B. (2009). *Toward a theory of Organizational Culture Evolution*. Human Resource Development Review. https://www.semanticscholar.org/paper/Toward-a-Theory-of-Organizational-Cultural-Zheng-Qu/ef7901609c74b998aee4c6bcfea3376221c4d554

ENDNOTES

[1] In 2020, in Portugal, the Inflation Rate had grown to 10%. However, nominal wages do not keep up with similar increases, reducing the purchasing power of families and, consequently, national economic growth (Banco de Portugal, 2022).

[2] "Some authors allude that Millennials are the generation that comes after X, a macro group that includes Generation Y, Digital Generation, and Echo Boomers (Incentive Research Foundation, 2015), but it is important for this Chapter to subdivide this macro generation into two main generations, the first one was born between 1981 and 1993 (Spiro, 2006), so-called Generation Y and the other is known as the Millennials generation who had been born until 2000" (Figueiredo & Joaquim, 2022).

Section 2
Leadership and Gender

Significant changes have occurred over the last few decades in terms of female participation including female leadership in organizations and social scientists, management consultants, and others have highlighted the aspect of gender and leadership in different organisational setting. The first chapter in this section reflects upon the barriers Indigenous women academics face in achieving senior leadership positions in the higher education sector and how leadership is intertwined with resistance and cultural safety. The next chapter discusses succession planning and gender equality in Australian universities. The author advocated for a longer-term focus on diversity, equality, and inclusion of women in leadership succession planning within the higher education sector and prioritizing intersectional practices and approaches to diminish barriers of female leadership for facilitating a more equitable workplace in the future.

Chapter 3
Indigenous Women in Academia:
Reflections on Leadership

Bronwyn Fredericks
https://orcid.org/0000-0001-8120-6470
The University of Queensland, Australia

Tracey Bunda
https://orcid.org/0000-0001-6824-8713
The University of Queensland, Australia

Abraham Bradfield
https://orcid.org/0000-0002-3968-0934
The University of Queensland, Australia

ABSTRACT

Despite increasing numbers of Indigenous women within Australian universities, Indigenous academics continue to face barriers that obstruct promotions to senior leadership positions. Reflecting on a capacity-building program run by and for Indigenous women, the authors explore Indigenous peoples' responses to institutional racism. The authors consider how leadership is synonymous with resistance and misguided characterisations of Indigenous people and scholarship. They demonstrate that leadership emerges out of culturally safe spaces conducive to communal and reciprocal learning. Providing participants with the tools and mentorship needed to progress within the academy, they can acquire the support and confidence needed to push back to oppressive structures. Indigenous academics continue to engage their sovereignty and forge their own spaces. The authors argue that greater leadership is needed by universities whose policies and governance structures have the ability and power to further promote Indigenous peoples to leadership positions and build capacity amongst emerging leaders.

DOI: 10.4018/978-1-6684-8257-5.ch003

INTRODUCTION

Indigenous women employed or studying in universities face many challenges that can impede on their success or prospects for promotion in their professions and/or educational pathways. Structural institutional racism, paternalism, a lack of opportunities for career development or promotion, amongst other factors, are common experiences amongst Aboriginal and Torres Strait Islander academics (Deloria Jr, 2004; Fredericks and White, 2018; Locke et al., 2023a). Despite institutional constraints, Indigenous women continue to demonstrate their tenacity and solidify their role as leaders for Indigenous people and Indigenous and non-Indigenous communities more broadly (regardless of whether this is recognised or not). Through their collective experience, female Indigenous academics share strong and enduring bonds of kinship and friendship, reflected by the term *tiddas* – roughly translating to sisters. For Indigenous women who have succeeded in the academy, establishing themselves as leading scholars in their disciplines, leadership is partly characterised by a moral responsibility to demonstrate to other Indigenous women, especially early-career and emerging scholars, that the prospect of occupying high-level leadership positions and achieving personal and collective goals is not beyond the realm of possibilities, despite the hardships faced.

In this Chapter, we reflect on leadership within Australian universities and discuss what characterises leadership for Aboriginal and Torres Strait Islander people within academia. We consider how institutional structures can hinder Indigenous women's progression to senior leadership positions. Drawing on the outcomes of a capacity-building program entitled *Tiddas showin' up, talkin' up, and puttin' up,* which was targeted towards Indigenous women who work in Australian universities, we highlight how women empower one another by creating safe spaces where experiences within the academy can be shared and the skills, networks, and tools necessary to advance within the western academic system can be strengthened. We argue that whilst such programs are beneficial to Indigenous women's academic progression, universities need to do more to provide greater access and opportunities for Aboriginal and Torres Strait Islander women to occupy leadership roles which has the potential to translate into meaningful structural reforms that would improve outcomes for Indigenous peoples more broadly.

INDIGENOUS WOMEN IN THE ACADEMY

Indigenous academic and professional staff continue to be underrepresented across all levels of higher education comprising just 0.3% of the entire workforce (Thunig and Jones, 2021). Aboriginal and Torres Strait Islander staff are less likely to be employed in fulltime positions (Coates et al. 2021) with fewer Indigenous academics receiving tenure (51% compared to 58.4% for non-Indigenous staff) (Thunig and Jones, 2021). Lack of ongoing appointments can compromise job security as well as the stability needed to address gaps in higher education. Bunda and colleagues (Bunda et al., 2012) for example have written on how statistics can be misleading, highlighting that while the appointment of 2,000 Indigenous staff nationwide may appear progressive on paper, when the type of appointments are taken into consideration it equates to just 266 fulltime positions.

Indigenous women make-up 69% of the Indigenous higher education workforce (Fredericks et al., 2014), which is in contrast to non-Indigenous appointments where women form just 35% of employees (O'Sullivan, 2019). It needs noting that Indigenous women however are not in the range of areas or in the breath of managerial and senior executive positions in which non-Indigenous women are employed.

The appointments of Indigenous women must be accompanied with pathways and opportunities that progress towards senior leadership positions, which have stagnated in recent times (O'Sullivan 2019). To reach parity with non-Indigenous staff and achieve targets of having 3% of the higher education workforce identify as Aboriginal and/or Torres Strait Islander, outcomes across all sectors of higher education from enrolment, attrition, and the executive, need to be improved. Indigenous students currently form just 1% of the entire HDR cohort (Hutchings et al., 2019). Addressing such gaps requires coordinated responses that address all forms of systemic racism and disadvantage. Racism continues to be a major concern with 66% of respondents to the NATSIHEC report (Buckskin et. al 2018) having experienced racial discrimination.

Within academia, Indigenous scholars are often treated as lesser as if their research offers little benefit to mainstream society and is therefore best placed within areas run by Indigenous people for Indigenous audiences, or in areas that provide a general education for non-Indigenous peoples. In addition, a lot of the work done by Indigenous women goes unrecognised and unnoticed. This is despite their assistance to non-Indigenous peoples who have gained recognition for their work as well as promotions, awards, and fellowships. The work of Indigenous women in these contexts is not always seen as making a valuable contribution to knowledge within the world. Institutional structures are built from upholding colonial sentiments that suggests that a) Aboriginal and Torres Strait Islander people (women especially) are incapable of succeeding or managing to the same degree as non-Indigenous peoples and that b) success should be measured by the degree to which they conform or assimilate to the western structures of the institution. Indigenous women and men therefore commonly occupy lower-level positions where they remain under the watch of non-Indigenous supervisors and managers and do not threaten the white patriarchal sovereignty that has become ingrained within universities' governing structures (Fredericks, 2009; 2011; Moreton-Robinson, 2020; 2021a; 2007; Stewart et al., 2021; Stewart, 2021).

Aboriginal and Torres Strait Islander peoples continue to be exoticised objects and the subject of a paternalistic gaze despite having held leadership positions where they have educated forthcoming generations for centuries before European arrival. Bunda and White (2009: 12) observe how,

Indigenous women were economically independent and played important roles within traditional Aboriginal society. They were acknowledged as the main food providers and primary care-givers and teachers of the children; they practiced healing and contributed to the spiritual lives of their communities.

The success of contemporary Indigenous scholars continues this tradition, whilst the hardships faced and battled by pioneering scholars gave Aboriginal and Torres Strait Islander people basic educational rights and laid the foundation for those who came after (Fredericks and White, 2018). Prior to the 1960s, accessing tertiary education was an unlikely prospect for most Aboriginal and Torres Strait Islander people, yet some pioneers showed the nation that Indigenous women's voices had a legitimate and rightful place in research and education. No longer were these women silent, or as Anzaldua expresses "made to identify with the position of object to someone else's subject" (1990: xxiii). They flipped the gaze and were no longer silent.

Women such as Dr Margret Williams-Weir who was the first Aboriginal person to graduate from an Australia university in 1959 (Kennedy et al., 2019), and Maryann Bin Sallik the first Aboriginal lecturer in 1975 (Bin-Sallik, 2000) showed that Indigenous success within the western academy was possible. Their leadership went on to inspire some of the most prolific contemporary thinkers whose work remains seminal to the scholarship of education and other disciplines today, including Margaret Valadian, Marcia

Langton; Pat O'Shane; Aileen Moreton-Robinson; Tracey Bunda; Bronwyn Fredericks; Eleanor Bourke; Larissa Behrendt; Jill Milroy; Patricia Dudgeon; Helen Milroy, and countless others.

LEADERSHIP AS RESISTANCE

Western understandings of leadership are often associated with conformity and compliance. A leader is seen to enforce the rules, regulations, and expectations of an organisation, society, or group of people. "Good leaders" are envisioned as those who maintain the status quo; do not challenge hegemonic narratives; and champion the collective voice. As universities are inherently western institutions, with its leaders appointed on their capacity to represent the interests of its mostly non-Indigenous stakeholders, framing leadership in such a way is problematic as conforming to western institutional structures that are often deaf to Indigenous voices can ultimately contribute to the disadvantage of Aboriginal and Torres Strait Islander people.

For Indigenous people, leadership necessitates acts of resistance and a *refusal to conform* to the oppressive structures that constrain their promotion, knowledges, and cultures (Hooks, 1990; Simpson, 2007; Bargallie, 2020) and to speak back to them. Distinguished Professor Aileen Moreton-Robinson (2020a) described this as "talkin' up", a term that involves an assertion of Indigeneity on Indigenous peoples' own terms. When Indigenous voices and perspectives are asserted within institutions, Indigenous women and men are often characterised as an "unsettling presence" due to their voices forcing institutions, and those within it, to confront colonial history and the continuing disadvantages faced by Aboriginal and Torres Strait Islander people (Fredericks, 2020; Fredericks et al., 2019; Kinnane et al., 2014; Williamson and Dalal, 2007).

In a settler-society where there continues to be repercussions for talkin' back to the colonial system, both personally and professionally (Bargallie, 2020; Duncan et al., 2022; Coates et al., 2022; Tamer, 2022; Trudgett et al., 2017), asserting one's Indigeneity – particularly within academic and creative writing – takes great courage and leadership (Dudgeon et al., 2017; Fredericks and White, 2013; tebrakunna et al., 2022). The need for Aboriginal and Torres Strait Islander people to constantly push back against the western system where race, gender, and power intersect, however, can be exhausting (Bunda and Gilbey, 2021). Caruso (2021: 76) writes of how,

an identifiable 'point of pain' [for Indigenous academics] is the need to assert our rights under university agreed standards of equity when seeking promotion, or in applying for schemes or programs that will furnish us the time to undertake research and writing, thereby increasing our publications output and providing the foundations for career advancement.

At times, Indigenous women might be asked to contribute to a broader event, edited collection, or grant application because the group is seeking an Indigenous woman or person to make the group appear more inclusive – or because they think it would be appropriate to have an Indigenous person involved. Their inclusion therefore is not necessarily because the non-Indigenous group thinks that an Indigenous woman or people might add rigor or depth to the proposed work. It is more than disappointing when this occurs and when non-Indigenous people fail to modify their behaviours to be culturally inclusive and respectful of Indigenous people.

Indigenous people are always modifying their behaviours when they work with non-Indigenous people, especially within education environments that aren't managed or controlled by them. The neglect of non-Indigenous people to adjust their own behaviours and methodologies so that it may incorporate Indigenous standpoints, or treating Indigenous women as 'tokens', limits the pedagogy, research, and datasets which is detriment to both Indigenous and non-Indigenous peoples. Indigenous women do not want to be tokens or shiny pieces of silver to showcase and use to assist non-Indigenous peoples in furthering their careers, especially when it is off the back of their struggles within systems that continue to contain and restrain them.

Reflecting on her own struggles within the university system – which continues to be a threatening space for many Aboriginal people who are made to feel as anomalies whilst on their own Country (Fredericks, 2020; Leroy-Dyer and Heckenberg, 2022) – Nereda White observed how the university "can be too much to cope with, and the result is often burn-out or drop-out" (White, 2000: 105). In a setting that can be suffocating for many Aboriginal and Torres Strait Islander peoples, overcoming the pressures and demands of studying and working within a predominantly white institution is an achievement in and of itself. Every Indigenous student who, through their commitment and perseverance in completing a tertiary course is a leader.

Regardless of whether resistance to oppressive powers is small and subtle, obvert and highly publicised, or the result of disproving stereotypes, acts of resistance that strive to create better futures for Indigenous people are all inspirational acts of leadership. This is why Indigenous academics continue their fight to improve educational outcomes for Indigenous peoples through their scholarship and advocacy (Fredericks et al., 2019).

IDENTIFYING LEADERS

There is an inclination to look at the top of corporate hierarchical structures to identify an organisations' leader(s), commonly represented by its CEO followed by its line managers. If one were to look at a typical corporate structure of most businesses and institutions in Australia today (including universities), Indigenous people's occupancy of leadership positions would be scarce. In 2015, Trudgett, Page and Sullivan (2017) highlighted that just 18 senior positions were held by Indigenous people across 17 Australian universities, with a further 22 having no Indigenous specific positions within its executive structure. The underrepresentation of Indigenous academics within universities shapes a false and negative perception amongst the wider populous of Indigenous peoples' capabilities – solidifying deficit discourses that present Aboriginal and Torres Strait Islander people as academically inferior or less than non-Indigenous people (Fredericks et al., 2014).

The disparity between Indigenous and non-Indigenous publication outputs in peer-review journals and other mediums further exacerbates the false perception that Indigenous scholarship, Indigenous knowledge, and Indigenous modes of writing and dissemination is subordinate or of lesser quality in comparison to the work of non-Indigenous scholars. There are many factors that contribute to Indigenous women's (and men's) ability to successfully publish their works within academia, including balancing workload; acquiring the skills needed to write in a manner conducive to the Anglocentric expectations of the academy (Foley et al., 2015; Fredericks, 2020; Fredericks et al., 2019; Nakata et al., 2019); an understanding of the publishing process and how to direct writing to where it is most impactful for one's career and community; and confidence in one's writing style (Fredericks et al., 2014).

Moreover, being sidelined by supervisors, editors, editorial boards, disciplinary associations, and fellow academics into publishing in Indigenous journals, or Indigenous special editions of discipline-based journals all has consequences in terms of citations and exposure. As does being asked to constantly contribute to journals across a range of disciplines with respect to providing Indigenous input. While needed by the disciplines, it splits an academic's body of work into fragments away from a core discipline area. This results in the scholar not being seen as strong in the discipline in which they are trained or being characterised as a generalist. In the past this has had consequences for employment and promotion, keynote lectures at seminal conferences, invitations to highly ranked discipline journals, and fellowship status to prestigious academies and societies.

For Indigenous women, who make up 69% of the entire Indigenous workforce in Australian universities (Fredericks et al., 2014) with an incremental increase of 7% yearly (Uink et al., 2021), the situation is even dire. While both Indigenous men and women are underrepresented in leadership positions, Indigenous men, who are fewer in number, continue to be promoted at a much greater rate (Coates et al., 2021). The number of Indigenous peoples' promotion to senior leadership roles has stagnated despite greater representation (Fredericks and White, 2018) and more Indigenous people attaining similar or superior qualifications and experience compared to the wider non-Indigenous population (Fredericks and White, 2018). Nereda White and Fredericks (2018: 248) observed in 2018 how,

To date, we have not seen any Indigenous women achieve roles such as Vice-Chancellor, DVC of International, Development, Student Services, Governance, Research, Academic or Engagement or a Pro Vice-Chancellor of Learning and Teaching, Vocational Education, Research, International Relations, Development, Advancement. Nor no offering to obtain these positions on an "acting" basis.

While there is now two Indigenous men who have progressed to these ranks, this has not happened in other areas despite vacancies in the sector. One was also appointed via a direct appointment by a Vice-Chancellor rather than through recruitment or interview. This is still in contrast to the number of non-Indigenous people who are directly promoted into positions, and who move upwards through several positions with Vice-Chancellor or other executive staff patronage. It is very evident from an exploration of the sector, that non-Indigenous leadership does not offer sponsorship or patronage to Indigenous emerging leaders in the same way. This is despite the value of Indigenous leaders in senior positions within universities, especially in their capacity to mentor and guide Indigenous students (both HDR and undergraduate) and early-career scholars (ECR) (Behrendt et al., 2012; Buckskin et al., 2018) as well as in curriculum development, research, and assisting non-Indigenous staff in re-shaping the university to be better universities for all people (Kuokkanen, 2007).

Mentoring relationships between and amongst Indigenous peers can boost the confidence and skills of ECRs, assisting in capacity building whilst providing Aboriginal and Torres Strait Islander scholars with support in navigating institutions that often remain deaf to Indigenous cultures, knowledges, and lived experiences. For Indigenous peers, mentorship transcends impersonal "working relationships", but rather is informed by relationality and a mutual commitment to culture, community, and place. Indigenous mentors can provide culturally appropriate guidance through building relationships with a shared history and understanding of place, and in doing so safeguard mental health. Pvey, Trudgett, Page, Locke, and Harry (2022) outline some of the defining characteristics of Indigenous mentorship including that they are informed by relatedness; move beyond hierarchy, performability, and completion; can be communal, multiple, and intergenerational; and are focused on investing in human capital. While non-Indigenous people can teach skills on how to work within academia, their positionality within the white institution can impede on their capacity to build trust, rapport, and fully understand the experience of Indigenous scholars. If not done amongst Indigenous peers, mentorship lies in danger of reproducing power imbalances.

Locke et al. (2023b) have noted the frustrations of Indigenous early-career staff not having access to Aboriginal and Torres Strait Islander mentors; having to find new mentors when short term positions conclude; or being made to feel like they are being "left to their own devices". This was also the experience of six (now established) Indigenous scholars: Bronwyn Fredericks, Nereda White, Sandra Phillips, Tracey Bunda, Marlene Longbottom, and Debbie Bargallie. These tiddas write on how having "few role models in higher education can mean that it has been hard to know who to ask in our processes of trying to 'figure-out'", what they term as the "secret academic business" of the university (Fredericks et al., 2019: 87).

A 2018 National Aboriginal and Torres Strait Islander Higher Education Consortium report, entitled the *Accelerating Indigenous Higher Education Consultation Paper,* called for the development of high-level policies and leadership models that would target an increased Indigenous workforce and support career pathways (Buckskin et al., 2018). Reports such as these present leadership as a project of empowerment that incentivises the employment of Indigenous staff through top-down structural reforms that address issues such as institutional racism and improves the monitoring, evaluation, and reporting of outcomes. The *Tiddas* program, which was held approximately a decade before the release of the Buckskin report, aimed to affirm, support, and empower Indigenous women with the confidence and tools needed to navigate and prosper within the university system.

LEADERS SHOWIN' UP, TALKIN' UP, AND PUTTIN' UP

To provide leadership and mentorship to Indigenous women in the academy – so that they may develop and refine writing skills and broaden their academic support networks – four full-day workshops were held in 2007 and 2008. The workshops which were foundational to the careers of many Indigenous female scholars today, were coordinated by Professors Tracey Bunda and Nereda White. A writing workshop that followed the initial *Tiddas* program was conducted by Professors Bronwyn Fredericks and Nereda White. The workshops involved 38 Indigenous women at different stages of their careers and of varying levels of employment. The workshops were entitled *Tiddas Showin' Up, Talkin' Up and Puttin' Up* (Bunda and White, 2009), the writers workshop was known as *Tiddas Writin' Up: Indigenous Women and Educational Leadership.* Each session focused on a component of the western academy integral to building successful academic careers, including learning and teaching; scholarship; university administration and management; and community engagement.

Tiddas was successful due to its ability to draw on the expertise and wisdom of Indigenous women who informed the organisation, governance, and delivery of every aspect of the program. Activities and sessions were guided by the advice of a senior circle of Indigenous woman who were versed in working within the academy. This group was made up of Distinguished Professor Aileen Moreton-Robinson, Professor Wendy Brady, Professor Bronwyn Fredericks, Dr Jackie Huggins, and Ms. Angela Leitch. This group of women provided the leadership necessary to ensure that the topics covered, and the ways in which they were delivered, were framed via a cultural lens relevant and appropriate for its Indigenous participants. The senior group shared their stories of working in the academy and gave "particular attention to the challenges facing a woman's career within the university, sharing knowledge of strategies for advancing for assisting in and promoting their careers and the need to balance life and work" (Bunda and White, 2009: 12).

In addition to the practical skills associated with navigating the academy, workshops provided a safe environment "where people shared, challenged each other and supported each other to write" (Fredericks et al., 2014). Each session was led exclusively by Indigenous women who were able to address and share their experience and assist participants in building their own writing toolkits to help them publish and flourish within the academy. In 2011, a special edition of the *Australian Journal of Indigenous Issues* (Fredericks et al., 2011) showcased the work of the participants of *Tiddas* which demonstrated Indigenous women's leadership and contribution to academic research.

In preparation for this edition, an additional workshop was held that aimed to equip participants with the tools necessary to become leading scholars through writing and publishing. This involved covering topics relating to journal rankings and selecting appropriate journals for publication; skills relating to identifying opportunities to publish and sit on editorial boards; the benefits of collaborative and creative writing and ensuring intellectual property rights are retained; and finally, demystifying the peer-review process (Fredericks and White, 2013). In an academic setting that continues to be characterised by the "publish or perish" mentality, these skills aimed to build participants' confidence and leadership skills in a manner that was attuned and sympathetic to the challenges faced by Aboriginal and Torres Strait Islander people within the academy and in their daily lives.

During the workshops, participants formed relationships and developed strong bonds of trust that created of a safe environment where stories could be shared – some of which rendered participants vulnerable. Through openly sharing their wisdoms and knowledges whilst laughing, crying, and eating together, participants created a space where they nurtured and cared for one another in ways that celebrated their autonomy and agency as proud Indigenous women. It was a space where adversities were voiced and validated, and each found solitude in one another's stories. They did not need to demonstrate their "resilience" despite the disadvantages, oppressions, and challenges they faced. Nor did they have to reconfigure themselves as examples of success, which non-Indigenous people often do in reference to Indigenous people (Guthrie Valaskis, Stout & Grimond, 2009). Individually and collectively, Indigenous women respected the space that was created and reflected their diversity as Indigenous women with an array of cultures, histories, experiences, and varied perspectives. In the introduction to the special edition that showcased the work from these workshops, Fredericks (2011: 5) wrote,

The words of the Indigenous academic women contained within this edited collection are words of power and survival. They are words that contribute to our understandings of Indigenous women academics within Australian higher education and that demonstrate the strength of the intersection of Indigenous, womanhood and academic.

As demonstrated in the *Tiddas* program, Indigenous perspectives of leadership frame it as a collective expression of relationality, reciprocity, and collaboration rather than an individual attribute where competition is centred. Through sharing stories and experiences of hardship and triumphs, women learned from and challenged one another in ways that built confidence. In the sharing and listening to each other women took personal and professional risks that built deeper relationships between each other. They learned how other women had navigated barriers and coped with oppressive systems, and how they could effectively challenge the situations they found themselves in (Kenny & Fraser, 2007).

Through their interactions and collaborations Indigenous women engaged in their own emancipation process (Fredericks et al., 2019).

Participants of the program commented on how it benefited their careers. Amy Clelland, who presented at several conferences shortly after the program, stated that "I still can't believe what the *Tiddas* has done for me not only in my career but personally. I'm so privileged" (A Clelland, personal communication, 14 February 2012). Frances Wyld, who went on to publish journal articles (Wyld, 2011; 2021), book chapters (Nghikefelwa et al., 2022), and reports (Buckskin et al., 2011) commented on how she "found solidarity in other Indigenous woman around the country who had similar experiences. I took this information back to my own university confident in my own abilities, asking for challenges and leadership only to find myself silenced and sent back to the end of the queue" (Wyld, 2010). While Wyld speaks of the benefits of creating a safe environment for Indigenous women, she highlights how this was quickly dismissed by an institution at times unwilling to change. Fredericks also speaks to finding safe spaces to work as a scholar (2011a & b).

LEADERSHIP AS COLLABORATION

During the *Tiddas* program, efforts were made to ensure that participants' academic networks were broadened. Attendees were assigned Indigenous tutors and mentors who guided them through the program and the publishing process at its conclusion. The benefits of having access to senior mentors was advantageous to many of the participants who now find themselves providing leadership to forthcoming generations of Indigenous scholars. Leadership models were established and through their interactions "the core group of Indigenous women participants and those who could be named as senior" modeled "leadership and being inclusive of new participants and those participants who could be named as the younger generation of our communities" (Bunda and White, 2009: 14). In another writing workshop, that built on the foundation of the *Tiddas* program, and was held with Indigenous and non-Indigenous postgraduate students, the collaborative nature of leadership was also emphasised (Brien and Fredericks, 2020). Applying a participatory approach, the workshop aimed to explore,

the ways that collaboration can diminish some of the competitiveness encouraged by the quantitative evaluative measures of the contemporary academy, because it encourages a focus on the productivity achieved when individuals work together to produce a quality output (Brien and Fredericks, 2020: para 15).

For Aboriginal and Torres Strait Islander women, many of whom come to study later in life (Fredericks and White, 2018), leadership extends beyond the limits of their initial appointment within an institution – whether as a student or staff – and requires the balancing of obligations and commitments to family and the wider communities to which they are apart (Oliver et al., 2013; Rochecouste et al., 2017). This "stop start" reality of Indigenous women's educational journey can and does impact their ability to publish their research and be promoted within the existing system (Diezmann and Grieshaber, 2009). Whilst cultural obligations to family and community can place additional pressure on women during studies or work commitments, family and culture also empowers women with lived experiences and knowledge that are beneficial to their capacity to act as mentors and leaders. Many Indigenous educators for example, enter research positions after having been employed within their field for many years.

Indigenous researchers are motivated by their responsibilities to family and improving outcomes in the communities to which they belong and/or live and/or collaborate with. Ethical research is structured around the *needs* and *interests* of communities, governed by cultural protocols (Smith, 2012, Martin, 2008). Such protocols centre on building relationships and trustful partnerships with Indigenous peoples, ensuring respect for place and Country. Within Indigenous-focus research therefore, leadership is less about the expertise and knowledge that a researcher can bestow on others, but rather is based on principles of relationality and reciprocity where parties work together to produce relevant data for mutual benefit. While assumptions that Aboriginal and Torres Strait Islander people "naturally" have the authority to enter Indigenous communities and conduct research, primarily based on their Indigeneity, is misguided, the advantage of having firsthand lived experience with communities must be recognised as an advantage within the institution, especially in matters pertaining to Indigenous advancement and community engagement.

The *Tiddas* program provided a space where women could share their experiences whilst also developing the skills and arsenal needed to navigate difficult, and at times racist spaces in which women are often made to feel culturally unsafe (Fredericks, 2020; Universities Australia, 2022; Brown and Shay, 2021; Plater et al., 2020; Taylor et al., 2019). Within colonial systems that force Indigenous peoples to conform to its western structures, the creation of safe spaces and sites of reflection is important to nurture Indigenous leadership (Fredericks et al., 2011; Leroy-Dyer and Heckenberg, 2022).

NURTURING LEADERSHIP

Leadership requires a skillset that assists a person in their understanding of a task; the context in which the task lies; and their ability to guide the people and resources needed to achieve desired outcomes. Whilst leadership is commonly characterised as a "natural" attribute, it requires nuanced responses that can be taught, acquired, and cultivated. A university (as with many other institutions) is a complex system of interlocking laws, regulations, committees, boards, stakeholder interests etc. Whilst we acknowledge the need for greater representation of Indigenous people in senior leadership positions, this must be paired with capacity building and growing Aboriginal and Torres Strait Islander peoples' skills so that they many navigate the complex bureaucratic terrain (Fredericks et al., 2019).

Indigenous peoples are regularly overlooked for mid-level roles or for acting positions that may transition into leadership appointments or interim positions (Fredericks et al., 2019). This has, despite being employed in academic roles in university for decades, contributed to the fact that we have seen less than a handful of Indigenous academics be promoted to positions such as Dean, Pro Vice-Chancellor (outside an Indigenous related field), Deputy Vice-Chancellor or Vice-President, and none as Vice-Chancellor or President (Fredericks et al., 2019). This is despite the first Pro Vice-Chancellor Indigenous being appointed in 2009 and despite witnessing some non-Indigenous colleagues move from Director or Pro Vice-Chancellor positions through to other senior leadership positions quickly via the patronage of other non-Indigenous senior leaders.

For Indigenous people, Locke, Trudgett, and Page (2022: 12) observe how career trajectories are often "ill considered, ill supported and/or undermined by non-Indigenous academics and the institutions in which they were employed". We are also aware of examples where non-Indigenous people have been appointed to mid-level or senior roles without necessarily having the experience, qualifications, and skills needed. In some cases, positions are not advertised simply because the candidate is known by other non-Indigenous to be a "good fit" for their team. They may have previously worked together, be known through another context, or even been recommended via a non-Indigenous colleague. While non-Indigenous staff might quote their institution's policies and talk publicly about inclusion, equality, equity, diversity, fairness, gender, disability, equal opportunity, and merit – along with reconciliation with Indigenous people – their actions often result in further advantaging non-Indigenous people while disadvantaging Indigenous people. In Australian universities this is mostly done by people of the dominant white culture, serving to bolster white supremacy. This, along with the lack of opportunities for development and career pathways for Indigenous people has resulted in their significant under-representation, despite the increasing number of Indigenous people studying and working in Australian universities.

Greater opportunities for Aboriginal and Torres Strait Islander people to be promoted, trained, and empowered with the skillsets needed to occupy these positions are needed (Coates et al., 2021; Buckskin et al., 2018); as is an ethos that trancends stereotype and institutional bias which envisions Indigenous peoples as being best suited for "Indigenous-related" positions. Moreover, some non-Indigenous people need to "call out" the exclusionary behaviours of their colleagues, institutions, and the sector that results in the further advantaging of non-Indigenous people and disadvantaging of Indigenous people. Failing to do so serves to keep the status quo, despite the talk. In an Indigenous context we ask non-Indigenous people and universities to "walk their talk".

As it stands today, non-Indigenous women continue to benefit from initiatives that seek to address gender disparities within universities and do so without acknowledging the continuing struggle of Indigenous women, or establishing the mechanisms needed to aid their promotion (Moreton-Robinson, 2020a). Moreover, they are more often sponsored and supported by non-Indigenous men to this under the guise of addressing gender inequality within high education. We have witnessed the behaviour within circles of white women and white men, which speaks directly to Moreton-Robinson's work (2020) and bolsters white supremacy while they congratulate themselves on addressing gender inequality. The reality is all they've really done is change which white people are in the deck chairs. These actions all continue to marginalise and oppress Indigenous women. Fredericks and White (2018: 246-7) observe how,

Few non-Indigenous women provide promotion or recruitment opportunities for Indigenous women in ways that enable Indigenous women to move through the ranks of the academy to senior roles and in this way they are complicit in the system that biases Indigenous women and maintains the stratified Indigenous workforce. It also further embeds women from the dominant culture as privileged over and above Indigenous women and participants in the ongoing subjugation of Indigenous women.

While Indigenous controlled spaces such as the one established during *Tiddas* celebrates and empowers Indigenous women's leadership, it is built on the backdrop of institutional racism that fails to recognise the value and contributions made by Aboriginal and Torres Strait Islander scholarship. To begin to address and redress the disparate outcomes in education and employment, universities must demonstrate their own leadership and confront the history of colonialism and its complicity in maintaining the power structures that have silenced Indigenous people (Fredericks and Bargallie, 2016; 2020a; b) whilst simultanously veiling white supremecy within a de-politicised space (Kowal, 2010; Anderson and Riley, 2021). This means exposing "white fragility" (DiAngelo, 2018) and engaging in dialogues that are based on critical race theory (Bargallie, 2020; Delgado and Stefancic, 2023; McLaughlin and Whatman, 2011, Moreton-Robinson, 2020; Bunda, 2014) where non-Indigenous peoples reflect on the behaviours and policies that prevent them from understanding and recognising Indigenous perspectives and sovereignties (Fredericks and Bargallie, 2016; Morrison et al., 2019; Moreton-Robinson, 2020a; 2020b; 2021b; 2007).

In recent times, universities have taken steps by establishing Reconciliation Action Plans (Burt and Gunstone, 2018) and cultural competency training in attempts to increase cultural awareness (Universities Australia, 2020; Kennedy et al., 2019). However, more leadership needs to be initiated by universities to translate these programs into measurable outcomes for Indigenous academics which results in parity between Indigenous and non-Indigenous people and outcomes. Cultural competency can quickly become a tokenistic exercise of white benevolence that superficially publicises an institution's goodwill without taking or demonstrating accountability (Brien and Fredericks 2020). The academic achievements of Indigenous women are often exoticised or displayed as stories of success despite adversity, without a meaningful commitment to address the adversities and institutional racism that Indigenous women face daily. Fredericks and colleagues (2019: 79) write how,

We get angry and frustrated with how 'proud' some university leaders are to have us as Indigenous academic women in their organisations and with the reality of how we are exoticised, and how gender, class and race intersect to work against us in ways that continue to marginalise and oppress us and result in containing us within predominately within Indigenous domains within the higher education sector.

Programs such as *Tiddas* demonstrates self-determination and the value of Indigenous-led solutions to the issues that impact Aboriginal and Torres Strait Islander women's careers, lives, and communities. Leadership within the academy however must not be siloed as "Indigenous research" exclusively for "Indigenous people" (Asher, 2010). There is a tremendous amount of knowledge and wisdom that Aboriginal and Torres Strait Islander people have to offer the nation; knowledge that they are willing to share should the opportunity to occupy a leadership role arise. Fredericks and White (2013: 6) write that universities "that are committed to supporting Indigenous women to develop their academic writing and research skills will be richly rewarded with enhanced cultural knowledge and expertise and invigorated academic scholarship achievements".

Indigenous leadership however will not manifest from organisations and institutions paying "lip service" where Indigenous input and scholarship is treated as tokenistic, a checkbox exercise, or a venture of public relations (Fredericks, 2011). Tokenism and disregard is reflected when university leaders offer acknowledgements of country, and talk the talk of reconciliation, diversity, inclusion, quality, and fairness and then carry out practices that further advantage non-Indigenous people and disadvantages Indigenous people. The capacity for Indigenous peoples to become leaders within senior and executive levels already exists. Universities need to provide the access, training, resources and enact their policies into practices through all levels of governance and their operations. Moreover, they need to drive this as a sector.

CONCLUSION

Drawing on the outcomes of the *Tiddas* program we gain insight into how leadership is envisioned and embodied by Indigenous women in the academy. Whilst definitions of leadership are diverse, within an Indigenous context it is generally characterised by establishing mentoring relationships between peers; building capacity within Indigenous communities; being ethically responsible to communities; creating collaborative networks; embedding Indigenous agency in writing and academic outputs; creating safe spaces for academic pursuits and dialogue; and developing the skills to operate within both Indigenous and non-Indigenous paradigms.

It is encouraging to see that enrolment and completion rates of Aboriginal and Torres Strait Islander tertiary students and staff are increasing in some institutions, but completion and employment rates are far from aligning with the non-Indigenous population. Whilst the numbers of Indigenous academics are reaching a critical mass, it is alarming that Aboriginal and Torres Strait Islanders peoples continue to be shut out of senior leadership positions. As means of shattering the "black glass ceiling" Indigenous women have done what they always have since European arrival – "talkin up" to the system through acts of resistance and the assertion of Indigenous sovereignty. Indigenous women and men have forged their own spaces within the university in which to empower themselves with the skills and confidence needed to take lead of their own career trajectories and engage in research that is of benefit to their careers, families, and communities.

The strength and tenacity of pioneering Indigenous leaders have paved the way for future generations, making it possible for many Indigenous women to enter and success in the academy, despite the institutional racism that remains embedded within much of its governing structures. Programs such as *Tiddas* are woven with the threads created by women such as Margret Williams-Weir, Maryann Bin Sallik, and many more. As the success of Indigenous women today are indebted to women such as these, many current Aboriginal and Torres Strait Islander scholars see themselves as having a moral responsibility to build the leadership capacity amongst emerging generations of Indigenous academics. Despite the exhaustion and heavy toll "talkin back" can have on personal and professional lives, Indigenous women continue to produce exceptional and innovative scholarship, producing research that both illuminates and challenges. More leadership must be initiated by universities and non-Indigenous university leaders to challenge themselves to learn and do better. Moreover, they need to talk less and listen more to Indigenous voices and create the mechanisms and structures that values Indigenous peoples, and Indigenous leadership. They need to do less talking about reconciliation, diversity, inclusion, quality, and fairness and demonstrate reconciliation, diversity, inclusion, quality, and fairness through their actions in relation to Indigenous peoples. This would result in re-shaping universities in Australia (Kuokkanen, 2007), and make them more reflective of the country in which they reside and operate, and the populations they seek to serve. It would in essence make them better Australian universities.

REFERENCES

Anderson, L., & Riley, L. (2021). Crafting safer spaces for teaching about race and intersectionality in Australian Indigenous Studies. *Australian Journal of Indigenous Education*, 50(2), 229–236. https://doi.org/10.1017/jie.2020.8 doi:10.1017/jie.2020.8

Anzaldua, G. (Ed.). (1990). Making Face, Mekaing Soul Haciendo Caras Critical Perspectives by Feminists of Color. Aunt Lute Books.

Asher, N. (2010). How does the postcolonial, feminist academic lead? A perspective from the US South. *International Journal of Leadership in Education*, 13(1), 63–76. https://doi.org/10.1080/13603120903242915 doi:10.1080/13603120903242915

Bargallie, D. (2020). *Unmasking the racial contract: Indigenous voices on racism in the Australian Public Service*. Aboriginal Studies Press.

Behrendt, L., Larkin, S., Griew, R., & Kelly, P. (2012). *Review of higher education access and outcomes for Aboriginal and Torres Strait Islander people*. Department of Industry, Innovation, Science, Research and Tertiary Education.

Bin-Sallik, M. A. (2000). *Aboriginal women by degrees: Their stories of the journey towards academic achievement*. University of Queensland Press.

Brien, D. L. & Fredericks, B. (2020). Collaborative writing to enhance cross-cultural understanding within the Academy. *Writing in Practice: The Journal of Creative Writing Research*, 1, 1-8. Sat.

Brown, C., & Shay, M. (2021). From resilience to wellbeing: Identity-building as an alternative framework for schools' role in promoting children's mental health. *Review of Education*, 9(2), 599–634. https://doi.org/10.1002/rev3.3264 doi:10.1002/rev3.3264

Buckskin, P., Malin, M., Warrior, E., Wyld, F., & Meagher, S. (2011). *Engagement, focus and hope for the future: the Port Augusta Partnerships for Success program*, DKCRC Report. [Online] Available: http://www.nintione.com.au/resource/NintiOneResearchReport_66_PartnershipsforSuccess.pdf

Buckskin, P., Tranthim-Fryer, M., Holt, L., Gili, J., Heath, J., Smith, D., Larkin, S., Ireland, S., Macgibbon, L. & Robertson, K. (2018). *NATSIHEC accelerating Indigenous higher education consultation paper*.

Bunda, T. (2014). *The Relationship Between Indigenous Peoples and the University: Solid or What!* [Doctoral Thesis, University of South Australia].

Bunda, T., Gilbey, K. & Monnapula-Mapesela, M. (2021). Black Warrior Women Scholars Speak. *Reimagining the Academy: Shifting Towards Kindness, Connection, and an Ethics of Care*, 19-27.

Bunda, T., & White, N. (2009). *Final project report: The Australian learning and teaching council leadership for excellence in learning and teaching program: Tiddas Showin' Up, Talkin' Up and Puttin' Up: Indigenous women and educational leadership*. Flinders University and Australian Catholic University. https://ltr.edu.au/resources/grants_leadership_tiddasshowinup_finalreport_apr09_0.pdf

Bunda, T., Zipin, L., & Brennan, M. (2012). Negotiating university 'equity' from Indigenous standpoints: A shaky bridge. *International Journal of Inclusive Education*, 16(9), 941–957. https://doi.org/10.1080/13603116.2010.523907 doi:10.1080/13603116.2010.523907

Burt, A., & Gunstone, A. (2018). Cultural Competency through a Reconciliation Action Plan. *Journal of Australian Indigenous Issues*, 21, 46–58. https://search.informit.org/doi/10.3316/informit.143082604918170

Caruso, J. (2021). Identity: Being Aboriginal in the Academy: 'It's an Identity Thing. In A. Nye & J. Clark (Eds.), Teaching History for the Contemporary World. Springer. https://doi.org/10.1177/0004944120969207 doi:10.1007/978-981-16-0247-4_6

Coates, S. K., Trudgett, M., & Page, S. (2021). Examining Indigenous leadership in the academy: A methodological approach. *Australian Journal of Education*, *65*(1), 84–102. doi:10.1177/0004944120969207

Coates, S. K., Trudgett, M., & Page, S. (2022). Ain't no mountain high enough: Aspirations of Indigenous academics within the academy. *International Journal of Leadership in Education*, •••, 1–15. https://doi.org/10.1080/13603124.2022.2068186 doi:10.1080/13603124.2022.2068186

Delgado, R. & Stefancic, J. (2023). *Critical race theory: An introduction*, NyU press.

Deloria, V. J. (2004). Marginal and submarginal. In D. A. Mihesuah & A. C. Wilson (Eds.), *Indigenizing the academy transforming scholarship and empowering communities*. University of Nebraska Press.

DiAngelo, R. (2018). *White fragility: Why it's so hard for white people to talk about racism*. Beacon Press.

Diezmann, C., & Grieshaber, S. (2009). Understanding the achievements and aspirations of new women professors. A report to Universities Australia. Brisbane: Queensland University of Technology.

Dudgeon, P., Herbert, J., Millroy, J., & Oxenham, D. (Eds.). (2017). *Us Women, Our Ways, Our World*. Magabala Books.

Duncan, A., Dockery, M., Kalsi, J., Loan Vu, L., Mavisakalyan, A., & Salazar, S. (2022). *Woort Koorliny: Australian Indigenous Employment Index 2022*. Minderoo. https://www.minderoo.org/indigenous-employment-index/downloads/

Foley, F., Martin-Chew, L., & Nicoll, F. (2015). *Courting blakness: recalibrating knowledge in the sandstone university*. University of Queensland Press.

Fredericks, B. (2009). The epistemology that maintains white race privilege, power and control of Indigenous studies and Indigenous peoples' participation in universities. *Critical Race and Whiteness Studies*, *5*, 1-12.

Fredericks, B. (2011a). Rock Pools of Critical Thought: Finding a place to think through my higher degree and what. a PhD was all about. *Journal of Australian Indigenous Issues*, *14*(1), 19–31.

Fredericks, B. (2011). 'Universities are not the safe places we would like to think they are but they are getting safer': Indigenous Women Academics in Higher Education. *Journal of Australian Indigenous Issues*, *14*(1), 41–53.

Fredericks, B. (2020). Collaborative Creative Processes That Challenge Us as" Anomaly", and Affirm Our Indigeneity and Enact Our Sovereignty. *M/C Journal,* 23. https://doi.org/10.5204/mcj.1674 doi:10.5204/mcj.1674

Fredericks, B., & Bargallie, D. (2016). 'Which way? Talking culture, talking race': Unpacking an Indigenous cultural competency course. *International Journal of Critical Indigenous Studies*, *9*(1), 3–16. https://doi.org/10.5204/ijcis.v9i1.141 doi:10.5204/ijcis.v9i1.141

Fredericks, B., & Bargallie, D. (2020a). An Indigenous Australian Cultural Competency Course: Talking Culture, Care and Power. In J. Frawley, G. Russell, & J. Sherwood (Eds.), *Cultural Competence and the Higher Education Sector: Perspectives, Policies and Practice*. Springer Publications. doi:10.1007/978-981-15-5362-2_16

Fredericks, B. & Bargallie, D. (2020b). Situating race in cultural competency training: A site of self-revelation. *M/C Journal, 23*. https://doi.org/10.5204/mcj.1660 doi:10.5204/mcj.1660

Fredericks, B., Mills, K., & White, N. (2014). 'I now know I can do this now': Indigenous Women and Writing in the Australian Higher Education Sector. *Text, 18*(1), 1–11. http://dx.doi.org/10.52086/001c.27315 doi:10.52086/001c.27315

Fredericks, B., & White, N. (2013). Making the written word part of our toolbox: Aboriginal and Torres Strait Islander women educators. *Redress, 22*, 7-13. https://search.informit.org/doi/10.3316/ielapa.456398554013227

Fredericks, B., & White, N. (2018). Using bridges made by others as scaffolding and establishing footings for those that follow: Indigenous women in the Academy. *Australian Journal of Education, 62*(3), 243–255. https://doi.org/10.1177/0004944118810017 doi:10.1177/0004944118810017

Fredericks, B., White, N., Phillips, S., Bunda, T., Longbottom, M., & Bargallie, D. (2019). Being Ourselves, Naming Ourselves, Writing Ourselves: Indigenous Australian Women Disrupting What It Is to Be Academic Within the Academy. In L. M. Thomas & A. B. Reinertsen (Eds.), *Academic writing and identity constructions: performativity, space and territory in academic workplaces*. Palgrave Macmillan. doi:10.1007/978-3-030-01674-6_5

Fredericks, B. L., White, N., Bunda, T., & Baker, J. (2011). Demonstrating Indigenous women's educational leadership: Tiddas Showin' Up, Talkin' Up and Puttin' Up! *Journal of Australian Indigenous Issues, 14*, 3–8.

Guthrie Valaskis, G., Stout, M. D., & Grimond, E. (Eds.). (2009). *Restoring the Balance First Nations Women, Community, and Culture*. University of Manitoba Press.

Hooks, B. (1990). Feminist theory: From margin to centre. Boston: South End P.

Hutchings, K., Bainbridge, R., Bodle, K., & Miller, A. (2019). Determinants of attraction, retention and completion for Aboriginal and Torres Strait Islander higher degree research students: A systematic review to inform future research directions. *Research in Higher Education, 60*(2), 245–272. https://doi.org/10.1007/s11162-018-9511-5 doi:10.100711162-018-9511-5

Kennedy, J., Thomas, L., Percy, A., Dean, B., Delahunty, J., Harden-Thew, K., & De Laat, M. (2019). An Aboriginal way towards curriculum reconciliation. *The International Journal for Academic Development, 24*(2), 148–162. https://doi.org/10.1080/1360144X.2019.1593172 doi:10.1080/1360144X.2019.1593172

Kenny, C., & Fraser, T. N. (2012). Living Indigenous Leadership Native Narratives on Building Strong Communities. Vancouver, BC, UBCPress.

Kinnane, S., Wilks, J., Wilson, K., Hughes, T., & Thomas, S. (2014). *'Can't be what you can't see': The transition of Aboriginal and Torres Strait Islander students into higher education – Final Report*, The University of Notre Dame Australia; Southern Cross University; Batchelor Institute of Indigenous Tertiary Education. https://www.notredame.edu.au/__data/assets/pdf_file/0020/2882/SI11-2138-OLT-Final-Report-FINAL-Web.pdf

Kowal, E. (2010). Welcome to country? *Meanjin, 69*, 15-173. https://search.informit.org/doi/pdf/10.3316/informit.076992418852903

Kuokkanen, R. (2007). *Reshaping the University Responsibility, Indigenous Epistemes, and the Logic of the Gift*. UBC Press.

Leroy-Dyer, S., & Heckenberg, S. (2022). The Gap will never close if Aboriginal and Torres Strait Islander students don't feel safe on university campuses. *The Conversation*. https://theconversation.com/the-gap-will-never-close-if-aboriginal-and-torres-strait-islander-students-dont-feel-safe-on-university-campuses-180234

Locke, M., Trudgett, M., & Page, S. (2023a). Australian Indigenous early career researchers: Unicorns, cash cows and performing monkeys. *Race, Ethnicity and Education, 26*(1), 1–17. https://doi.org/10.1080/13613324.2022.2114445 doi:10.1080/13613324.2022.2114445

Locke, M. L., Trudgett, M., & Page, S. (2023b). Building and strengthening Indigenous early career researcher trajectories. *Higher Education Research & Development, 42*(1), 156–170. https://doi.org/10.1080/07294360.2022.2048637 doi:10.1080/07294360.2022.2048637

Martin, K. L. (2008). *Please knock before you enter: Aboriginal regulation of outsiders and the implications for researchers*. Post Pressed.

McLaughlin, J., & Whatman, S. (2011). The potential of critical race theory in decolonizing university curricula. *Asia Pacific Journal of Education, 31*(4), 365–377. https://psycnet.apa.org/doi/10.1080/02188791.2011.621243 doi:10.1080/02188791.2011.621243

Moreton-Robinson, A. (2007). Sovereign subjects: Indigenous sovereignty matters. Crows Nest, N.S.W., Allen & Unwin.

Moreton-Robinson, A. (2020a). *Talkin' up to the white woman: Indigenous women and feminism*. University of Queensland Press.

Moreton-Robinson, A. (2020b). Incommensurable sovereignties: Indigenous ontology matters. Routledge handbook of critical Indigenous studies. Routledge. https://doi.org/10.4324/9780429440229 doi:10.4324/9780429440229-23

Moreton-Robinson, A. (2021a). *Place names, monuments and cannibalism: James Cook and the possessive logics of patriarchal white sovereignty*. [Video] Youtube. AIIS Sperker Series, Cornell University. https://www.youtube.com/watch?v=5L_QMLWcE5k

Moreton-Robinson, A. (2021b). The white possessive: Identity matters in becoming Native, Black and Aboriginal. *Borderlands Journal, 20*(2), 4–29. https://doi.org/10.21307/borderlands-2021-011

Morrison, A., Rigney, L.-I., Hattam, R., & Diplock, A. (2019). *Toward an Australian culturally responsive pedagogy: A narrative review of the literature.* University of South Australia. https://apo.org.au/sites/default/files/resource-files/2019-08/apo-nid262951.pdf

Nakata, M., Nakata, V., Day, A., & Peachey, M. (2019). Closing gaps in Indigenous undergraduate higher education outcomes: Repositioning the role of student support services to improve retention and completion rates. *Australian Journal of Indigenous Education, 48*(1), 1–11. https://doi.org/10.1017/jie.2017.36 doi:10.1017/jie.2017.36

Nghikefelwa, J. M., Wyld, F., & Wisker, G. (2022). Creating and Curating: Three Voices from Namibia, Australia and the UK on Decolonising the Literary-Related Doctorate. Decolonising Curriculum Knowledge. Springer.

O'Sullivan, S. 2019. First Nations' Women in the Academy: Disrupting and Displacing the White Male Gaze. In Crimmins, G. (ed) Strategies for Resisting Sexism in the Academy. Palgrave Studies in Gender and Education. Palgrave Macmillan, Cham. https://doi.org/10.1007/978-3-030-04852-5_7

Oliver, R., Rochecouste, J., Bennell, D., Anderson, R., Cooper, I., Forrest, S., & Exell, M. (2013). Understanding Australian Aboriginal Tertiary Student Needs. *International Journal of Higher Education, 2*(4), 52–64. http://dx.doi.org/10.5430/ijhe.v2n4p52 doi:10.5430/ijhe.v2n4p52

Plater, S., Mooney-Somers, J., Barclay, L., & Boulton, J. (2020). Hitting the white ceiling: Structural racism and Aboriginal and Torres Strait Islander university graduates. *Journal of Sociology (Melbourne, Vic.), 56*(3), 487–504. doi:10.1177/1440783319859656

Povey, R., Trudgett, M., Page, S., Locke, M. L., & Harry, M. (2022). Raising an Indigenous academic community: A strength-based approach to Indigenous early career mentoring in higher education. *Australian Educational Researcher.* https://doi.org/10.1007/s13384-022-00542-3 doi:10.100713384-022-00542-3 PMID:35874034

Rochecouste, J., Oliver, R., Bennell, D., Anderson, R., Cooper, I., & Forrest, S. (2017). Teaching Australian Aboriginal higher education students: What should universities do? *Studies in Higher Education, 42*(11), 2080–2098. https://doi.org/10.1080/03075079.2015.1134474 doi:10.1080/03075079.2015.1134474

Simpson, A. (2007). On ethnographic refusal: Indigeneity, 'voice' and colonial citizenship. *Junctures: the journal for thematic dialogue,* (9), 67-80.

Smith, L. T. (2012). Decolonizing methodologies: research and indigenous peoples, London: Dunedin, Zed Books; Otago University Press.

Stewart, G. T., Macdonald, L., Matapo, J., Fa'avae, D. T. M., Watson, B. K. I., Akiu, R. K., Martin, B., Mika, C., & Sturm, S. (2021). Surviving academic Whiteness: Perspectives from the Pacific. *Educational Philosophy and Theory,* 1–12. https://doi.org/10.1080/00131857.2021.2010542 doi:10.1080/00131857.2021.2010542

Tamer, R. (2022). 'Hugely disappointing': Indigenous employees 'almost entirely absent' from senior leadership, report finds. *SBS News*. https://www.sbs.com.au/news/article/hugely-disappointing-indigenous-employees-almost-entirely-absent-from-senior-leaders hip-report-finds/exaft6rew

Taylor, E. V., Lalovic, A., & Thompson, S. C. (2019). Beyond enrolments: A systematic review exploring the factors affecting the retention of Aboriginal and Torres Strait Islander health students in the tertiary education system. *International Journal for Equity in Health*, *18*(1), 1–19. https://doi.org/10.1186/s12939-019-1038-7 doi:10.118612939-019-1038-7 PMID:31477114

Tekrakunna, E. & Evans, J. (2022). *Indigenous Women's Voices 20 Years on from Linda Tihiwai Smith's Decolonizing Methodologies*. Sydney, Zed Books.

Thunig, A., & Jones, T. (2021). 'Don't make me play house-n*** er': Indigenous academic women treated as 'black performer' within higher education. *Australian Educational Researcher*, *48*(3), 397–417. https://doi.org/10.1007/s13384-020-00405-9 doi:10.100713384-020-00405-9

Trudgett, M., Page, S., & Sullivan, C. (2017). Past, present and future: Acknowledging Indigenous achievement and aspiration in higher education. *HERDSA Review of Higher Education*. https://www.herdsa.org.au/herdsa-review-higher-education-vol-4/29-51

Uink, B., Bennett, R., & Van Den Berg, C. (2021). Factors that enable Australian Aboriginal women's persistence at university: A strengths-based approach. *Higher Education Research & Development*, *40*(1), 178–193. http://dx.doi.org/10.1080/07294360.2020.1852185 doi:10.1080/07294360.2020.1852185

Universities Australia. (2022). *Indigenous Strategy 2022-25*. Canberra, Universities Australia. https://www.universitiesaustralia.edu.au/wp-content/uploads/2022/03/UA-Indigenous-Strategy-2022-25.pdf

White, N. (2000). Creativity is the name of the game. In M. A. Bin-Sallik (Ed.), *Aboriginal women by degrees*. University of Queensland Press.

Williamson, J., & Dalal, P. (2007). Indigenising the curriculum or negotiating the tensions at the cultural interface? Embedding Indigenous perspectives and pedagogies in a university curriculum. *Australian Journal of Indigenous Education*, *36*(S1), 51–58. https://doi.org/10.1017/S1326011100004701 doi:10.1017/S1326011100004701

Wyld, F. (2010). Aboriginal women and leadership in the academy. *Frontline*, *18*, 14-15. https://search.informit.org/doi/pdf/10.3316/informit.577008202566700

Wyld, F. (2011). Writing the ephemeral of culture: storm method [Paper in themed section: Shifting Cultures. *Social Alternatives*, *30*, 40–43. https://search.informit.org/doi/10.3316/ielapa.201109581

Wyld, F. (2021). The land as research participant: A storytelling project on climate change and Indigenous perspectives. *Journal of Australian Indigenous Issues*, *24*, 22–34. https://search.informit.org/doi/10.3316/informit.046669925438109

Chapter 4
Emerging Issues in Gender and Leadership:
Succession Planning and Gender Equality in Australian Universities

Sheree Gregory
Western Sydney University, Australia

ABSTRACT

Diversity, equality, and inclusion in leadership are critical for innovation and Australia's future. Despite considerable changes to the position of women in public life in advanced economies since second wave feminism, the invisibility of women in leadership has persisted. The under-representation of women in senior leadership, including women from culturally diverse backgrounds, remains a major challenge. This chapter presents a qualitative study of succession planning in relation to gender in Australian universities. The author argues for a longer-term focus on diversity, equality, and inclusion in leadership, and non-traditional leadership, in succession planning, to negotiate the glass ceiling and move towards a more equitable future of work in Australian universities. The author discusses prioritising intersectional approaches and practices of inclusion in leadership succession planning and management, to reveal how barriers to career progression in the neoliberal university, for non-traditional leaders can be dismantled and more equitable futures of work can be reimagined.

INTRODUCTION

Diversity, equality and inclusion in leadership are critical for innovation and Australia's future. Despite considerable changes to the role and position of women in public life in advanced economies since the second wave of feminism, the invisibility of women in leadership and decision-making roles has persisted (Acker, 2009). The under-representation of women in senior leadership positions, and barriers to their career progression, including women from culturally and ethnically diverse backgrounds and minorities across a range of sectors, and particularly the higher education in Australia, remains a major concern

DOI: 10.4018/978-1-6684-8257-5.ch004

and challenge. More than three decades of accumulated research findings reveal the persistence of this problem. This chapter canvasses some themes and issues from a qualitative study of succession planning and the experiences of senior leadership in the Australian higher education sector. It argues for a longer-term focus on diversity, equality and inclusion in leadership, and for non-traditional leadership, in succession planning, in the Australian higher education sector. I discuss prioritising intersectional approaches and practices of inclusion in leadership succession planning to reveal how barriers to career progression in the neoliberal university for non-traditional leaders can be dismantled and equitable futures of work reimagined. Moreover, the focus of this chapter on leadership succession planning and gender in Australian universities, is not just to bring women into sight, but to sharpen our way of seeing people – to improve the quality of our attention to diversity, equality and inclusion.

The invisibility of non-traditional leaders, as barriers to an equitable future of work and leadership, are features of Australian universities. There is now acknowledgement that there are many impediments to women's progression to senior positions in Australian universities (Probert, 2004; Huppatz, et al., 2019). Structural and cultural barriers limit women's advancement in universities and participation in decision-making and leadership roles – known as the 'glass ceiling' (Acker, 2009). The glass ceiling is highly problematic due to 'the range of invisible barriers that prevent outsiders from gaining access to organizational power, prestige and status' (Glass & Cook, 2020: 1233). According to the glass ceiling, invisible barriers exist that limit the ascension of women and women with diverse backgrounds and identities into leadership roles at the top of an organisation (Acker, 2009). Acker (2009: 201) points out that Inequality Regimes is also key to understanding 'the ongoing creation of inequalities in work organizations', and that 'All organizations have inequality regimes, defined as loosely interrelated practices, processes, actions, and meanings that results in and maintain class, gender and racial inequalities'.

Research confirms that men and women are unequally distributed throughout the university hierarchy, and this appears to be resilient to change (Probert, 2004). This is due to gender biases, and family responsibilities, which may impact their careers, and sexual harassment and exclusion from networks for leadership (Probert, 2004). These barriers highlight the importance of prioritising the value of gender equality in higher education leadership, while also acknowledging some progress, and the challenges facing higher education leaders and workers. For example, citations for the Workplace Gender Equality Agency Employer of Choice for Gender Equality, and Athena Swan (SAGE) initiatives for diversity, equality and inclusion in higher education since 2015, have highlighted the continued effort to advance gender equality in the workplace.

Gender is important for understanding impediments to leadership. Gender and gender relations play a central role in mediating perceptions and experiences, as well as shaping major life options and outcomes (Acker, 2009; Pocock, 2003). How and why women lag as leaders is not a new problem. Indeed, it has been at the centre of research and policy debates for some decades, wherein gender discrimination is deeply embedded in organisations. Further, gender imbalance in leadership is a critical issue, not least because inequality in leadership and decision-making roles in Australia lag behind other advanced economies. Attention to women's working lives, the barriers to advancement, and the conditions that advantage their peers, point to the intersecting issues of the care penalty, work/family conflict in the workplace and household, gendered masculine perceptions surrounding leadership, and gender roles and norms that sustain unconscious bias.

Stepping down, stepping aside, calling time, handing over the reins or a sudden and unexpected change in leader is often big news and challenging for an organisation, leadership and its stakeholders. It is often one of the biggest events in a leader's personal leadership journey. Succession planning is key for effective leadership, and is a term more commonly understood in the economic and business literature among large, wealthy family firms (Gilding et al., 2015). It is known as leadership of talent management and widely recognised in the family business literature, as '... the most important issue that most family firms face' (Handler, 1994 in Harvester et al., 1997: 373). It is a replacement strategy or plan for when a leader suddenly departs (for e.g., due to death, illness, unplanned resignation, among others). 'For a family business to outlive its founder, it must experience succession' (Harvester et al., 1997: 373). It is 'pivotal to business continuity, but is often fraught with tension and indefinitely postponed' (Gilding et al., 2015: 299). In the context of higher education, succession planning and management can make a significant contribution to the capacity to retain intellectual and knowledge capital (McMurray et al., 2012).

This chapter presents an overview of themes and findings from a qualitative study of succession planning from the perspective of senior leaders in Australian universities, in relation to gender. I argue for a longer-term view and initiatives of diversity, equality and inclusion to negotiate a more equitable future of work and leadership in the higher education sector. In this chapter, I ask:

- What do we know about leadership succession planning in universities?
- What, if anything, can succession planning, practices and processes, and problems, tell us about diversity, equality and inclusion in leadership?
- How do leaders negotiate their exit or entrance in leadership roles?
- What barriers to leadership exist for women, and how can obstacles be managed?
- How is power and status sustained or limited?

These questions and issues have implications for individuals, organisations, leadership and Human Resource management policies in higher education. This chapter is divided into four sections. First, I review the literature on leadership succession planning in the Australian higher education sector. Second, I discuss the conceptual background to the study of the under-representation of women in leadership, which aims to frame the findings. In this section, I outline the gendered organisation of academic careers, and the hierarchy of leadership roles within 39 Australian universities. Third, I introduce the study, method and respondents. I then outline some succession planning experiences of senior leaders from qualitative interview data, highlighting the uncertainty, lack of planning, and informal processes for leadership succession planning and management. I canvass some themes and issues and argue for a move beyond current debates of the glass ceiling (Acker, 2009), to develop a framework that emphasises gender as an organising principle and system, the value of diversity, equality and inclusion for a more equitable future of work. The discussion and conclusion summarises the implications of these findings and considers ways forward.

Gender Matters: Leadership Succession Planning in Universities

There has been significant change in universities over the past four decades, which have led to them becoming more entrepreneurial and innovative in order to be sustainable and competitive (McMurray et al., 2012). Executive leaders within universities have engaged in succession planning to varying degrees as a way to manage leadership and future uncertainty. However, succession planning has been a tool and process originating from family businesses and firms, and typically implemented and studied in sectors outside of universities.

Several reviews of succession planning among executive leadership at universities, internationally and external to Australia have indicated a lack of planning, implementing and managing (Ishak et al., 2016) as key issues. There is previously no known qualitative study specifically on succession planning in higher education in Australia, in relation to gender. There has been limited succession planning research conducted in the Australian higher education sector utilising a qualitative approach, and that is not-discipline specific. A review of literature using the ProQuest Central database identified 17 full-text peer-reviewed articles for the search terms 'Succession Planning and Higher Education' (scoping 'All dates'), none of which reported on data from Australia. A review of literature using search terms 'Succession Planning and Educational Leadership' (the same database and scope), identified 18 full-text peer-reviewed articles, consisting of studies conducted in the US, and Asia. Moreover, a review of literature utilising the Google Scholar search engine identified one grey literature report of a study published in the first decade of the twenty-first-century, by the Carrick Institute (Scott et al., 2008) drawing primarily on quantitative online survey data, and forums or workshops in Australia. Scott et al's., (2008) research is focused broadly on wide-ranging aspects of academic leadership, of which succession planning was a finding. Succession planning is often not mentioned other than in outline based around a crisis of academic leadership. Moreover, succession planning in relation to gender and leadership within universities is under-researched.

Existing studies of succession planning in higher education in Australia range from specific faculties (McMurray et al., 2012), academic libraries (McCarthy, 2005), to workforce planning and leadership issues generally (Drew, 2010; Coates & Goedegebuure, 2012). Recent analyses from the United Kingdom, United States, and Asia, are based largely on quantitative methods and linked to succession planning and leadership deficiencies (Cavanaugh, 2017; Ishak et al., 2016; Klein & Salk, 2013; Caleresco, 2013). These studies provide effective snap-shots of succession planning in higher education.

Effective executive decisions and initiatives to lead, manage, and plan their future university workforce, and develop leaders and leadership teams through funding uncertainty and competition for resources on a global basis, are critical for success (McFarland, et al., 2017). The ageing of the baby boomer population creates increased demand for leadership development, and high-performing staff at universities. Whether it is via internationalisation strategies, building research capacity by attracting academics with proven high-quality track-records of research excellence, and nurturing and investing early in academics' careers – university leaders and executive teams develop clear road maps for the future using common strategic planning processes, however, there is limited clarity around succession planning in relation to gender.

Succession planning is one process to manage uncertainty in the future, and is difficult for leaders to openly discuss. Succession planning is characterised as a crisis of leadership in higher education (Scott et al., 2008; Ishak & Kamil, 2016). Non-formalised succession planning strategies, a lack of succession planning and understanding of best practice can result in confusion around leadership, a leadership gap, problems in knowledge transfer (Calereso, 2013). There is ongoing gender imbalance in research and leadership despite gender initiatives for career interruptions. It is acknowledged that approximately twice as many men than women were awarded a Discovery Early Career Researcher Award, Future and Laurete Fellowships in Australia, between the years 2012 and 2015 (Adkins & Dever, 2015). Moreover, the pressures that many 'non-traditional leaders experience likely contribute to a significant talent drain' (Glass & Cook, 2020: 1246), which can have implications for a loss of innovation, creativity and problem-solving capabilities.

Across the Australian higher education sector, women continue to be under-represented in Vice Chancellor positions (Redmond et al., 2017) and remain concentrated at the bottom of the academic hierarchy (Probert, 2004). At the national level, workforce participation data compiled by Universities Australia in 2016 (Table 1: Women in Higher Education workforce in Australia, 2016) shows that most professional staff employed in higher education are women, and more women are employed at the lower levels of academic positions (Lecturer and Senior Lecturer positions) than professorial positions (Level D and E) in universities in Australia.

Table 1. Women in higher education workforce in Australia, 2016

Proportion of women professional and academic staff in universities within Australia	2016
Women in Professional staff positions: ● All professional staff positions ● Senior professional at HEW level 10 and above	66.3% 48.7%
Women in Academic staff positions: ● All academic staff positions ● Senior academic staff at Level D ● Senior academic staff at Level E and above	45.2% 37.2% 27.3%

Source: Universities Australia, '2016 elected inter-institutional gender equity statistics', August 2017, p. 4'.

Data on higher education staff numbers from 2017 to 2018 (Table 2: Participation in Level D, E and above (combined) by gender, 2017 - 2018) show women continue to be under-represented in senior academic positions at Levels D and above, across 39 universities in Australia (in 2018). These senior levels represent the foundation for senior leadership. This data, from Universities Australia, shows university hierarchy by gender.

Table 2. Participation in level D, E and above (combined) by gender, 2017 - 2018

Gender	2017	2018
Female	5,151 (32%)	5,200 (34%)
Male	10,768 (68%)	10,149 (66%)
Total	15,919	15,349

Source: Data from Australian Govt. Department of Education, 'Higher education staff numbers', 2018.

Despite gender equality policy initiatives in higher education, the number of women in senior academic positions in Australia has not significantly increased since 2016. These outcomes were reflected in interviews where reported that to some extent, the current gender imbalance is also shaped by decisions made by grant-funding bodies, which impact research-intensive universities.

This chapter discusses some of the factors that shape and explain contemporary issues surrounding succession planning and the experience of senior leaders in relation to gender in higher education. A theoretical understanding of gender relations highlights the unlikelihood of choosing inequality and invisibility. The moral dimensions of paid work and family life are important to consider to better understand inequality in the social practice of gender relations in leadership. The gendered dimensions of inequality will be discussed in the following section, as an approach to understanding the persistence of experiences and outcomes of invisibility and under-representation of women and non-traditional leaders. The conceptual background argues for the value of thinking tools: 'gender order' and 'work/family regimes' to understand and conceptualise the insights from industry.

Mapping the Conceptual and Theoretical Framework for Understanding Leadership Succession Planning in Australian Universities in Relation to Gender

Australian scholars Connell (2005, 2002), Pocock (2003), and Probert (2004) demonstrate the significance of a gender order and gender relations as power dynamics shaping employment outcomes. Pocock points out that an Australian work-care order is influenced by a balance of forces between managers and workers, the nature and role of the state, and gender order (2003: 34). Probert (2004) highlights the household as a missing key factor in gendered academic careers and women's under-representation in university leadership. International theorists, Hochschild (1989), and Williams (2000) unpack gender and the household as factors shaping a sustained gender inequality.

Conceptually, we need to look to a range of factors to explain gender inequality in the workplace. Leadership decisions about succession planning are enacted in a context where gender orders and power relations exist and are always under construction (Connell, 1987; Pocock, 2003). These power dynamics are inherent in and structure our social relations, the gender order, gender regime, and gendered relations reflect dominant structures of power and group interests (Connell, 1987: 117). Individuals make decisions and behave within the social context of culture, institutions and established norm and values (Pocock, 2003). Pocock's conceptualisation of work–care regimes connects with Acker's (2009) inequality regimes, and comprises the three elements of values, institutions and preferences, which 'at any time or place, work/care outcomes or arrangements are the consequences of the established order and specific embodiment in a work/care regime' (Pocock, 2003: 35).

Probert (2004) and Morehead (2003) both argue for the importance of gender structuring the workplace and household, and how women's employment cannot be isolated from their unpaid work responsibilities. Moreover, unequal gender division of labour in the household determine women's participation in the workforce. These dynamics shape women's under-representation in leadership and barriers to career progression. Moreover, Hochschild (1989) makes the point that looking at the workplace is only half the picture, the other factor that shapes experiences and outcomes occurs in the household, and in particular, the second shift of caring responsibilities and demands that fall largely to women.

Williams' (2000) concept of the 'ideal worker' norm also describes the gendered construction of careers, leadership and workplaces, and women's under-representation. The ideal worker norm is part of the domesticity ideology where an employee working full-time and long hours including overtime if necessary, unencumbered by family responsibilities, almost always has the support of a full-time partner in the household to take care of family and domestic obligations. While there are an increasing number of women today who perform as ideal workers, they are perceived negatively and as deviant if their commitment to caring for children and family life comes second to career (Drago et al. 2006), or if they reject family role responsibilities. An expression of a commitment to caring and family life may be viewed as an indication that the worker will not perform like an ideal worker (Drago, et al., 2006; Drago, et al., 2005). Moreover, the social expectation that women perform as (ideal) carers, (Williams' refers to the 'marginalised carer' norm) limits their capacity as ideal workers. The marginalised carer and care penalty are conceptually relevant in analyses of gender inequality in the workplace.

Part-time and flexible work are offered to both men and women in the workplace to balance paid work and family responsibilities. However, women are more likely to adjust their employment hours around family and care responsibilities (reflected consistently in the high rate of women's part-time work status in national labour force data). Part-time management and leadership roles are often viewed as unviable or counter to business needs, highlighting the covert and overt resistance to flexible work and family friendly practices, which mirrors a deeply embedded, gendered organisation of employment and working-time norms (Charlesworth & Cartwright 2007: 5).

The gender order, gender regimes, gender relations in the household, work/care regimes, ideal worker and care penalty, and the glass ceiling offer a set of thinking tools as background to better understand gender inequality in the workplace and leadership. The concepts frame and contextualise the study of leadership succession planning in universities in relation to gender. They offer an attempt to challenge the social construction of gender roles and norms in relation to leadership that needs to be questioned and reimagined. Other conceptual tools help to understand leadership succession planning in universities in relation to gender, such as uncertainty (in the succession process), continuity (of leadership), and the social dynamics and networks of leaders. The first two concepts (uncertainty and continuity) are documented in the literature on succession planning (Gilding et al., 2015; 2011). The uncertainty, lag and inconsistency in the implementation of a formal succession plan approaches by university leadership, and the importance of leadership capability and continuity are understood among leaders in higher education. The social dynamics and networks of leaders points to how leadership is relational and emphasises the need for better understanding gendered and inclusive social relations.

Next, I introduce the study of leadership succession planning in relation to gender. The research aimed to identify the barriers to women's participation in executive successor roles in universities, as well as the strategies for more effective talent identification for women to take up successor roles, ineffective practices, and to deepen understandings of internal versus external leadership dimensions. The study comprised qualitative interviews with leaders of universities, from the position of Dean to the most senior leadership team and Vice Chancellor, representing the current hierarchy in Australian universities. In order to find out what happens in universities in relation to succession planning, Human Resource departments, senior executive management groups, the office of Vice Chancellors, Deputy and Pro Vice Chancellors, and Deans of public and private universities were contacted.

Method and Participants

A qualitative methodology was utilised in the study, comprising 15 interviews with leaders of universities from the position of Dean to the most senior leadership team and Vice Chancellor, reflecting the hierarchy and structure of leadership across the 39 universities in Australia. Data were collected in 2018 and 2019 across Australia (five states in total). In order to find out what happens in universities in succession planning, Human Resource departments, senior executive management groups, the office of Vice Chancellors, Deputy and Pro Vice Chancellors, and Deans of public and private universities were contacted. Over 70 letters of invitation were sent to university leadership across Australia.

Qualitative methodology and interview technique are useful for asking about leader's plans, lived-experiences, decisions, behaviour and motivations. University senior executive are directly involved in succession planning, and their first-hand account provide an insider perspective (Weick, 1995, 1993, 1985), critical to understanding university approaches to succession management. It is also useful to be able to access what meaning they attribute to their practices and experiences, including finding out what their hopes and concerns may be (Hammersley, 1992). These interests clarify why qualitative research is of value (Crotty, 1998). It enables an approach to key research questions similar to the way Minichiello et al. (1995) highlight capturing meaning, definition, and description of phenomena. The value of qualitative research, according to Bryman (2004), is that it allows researchers to see through the eyes of participants, obtain descriptive details about context, and explore phenomena under question.

Participants

A mix of male and female participants in a range of senior positions were interviewed. Most interviews were conducted in person, with the remainder in teleconference, and one in email. The participants were selected based on their leadership position. The interviews collected data on size of university, size of leadership team, male to female ratio in leadership team, succession planning in higher education experiences, how universities approach succession planning, decision-making experiences, succession planning processes and practices, uncertainties and barriers to succession planning, when succession does not work, and approaches to gender equality in leadership. Table Three shows that a roughly even number of male and female participants took part in interviews (seven males and eight females). Of the six participants holding professional (or non-academic) senior leadership positions (such as Chief Financial Officer, Human Resources Director or Human Resources Executive Director, among others), five were female. Of the three participants holding Vice Chancellor positions, one was female.

Table 3. Position characteristics of participants in the study

Position	Number
Vice Chancellor	3
Pro Vice Chancellor	4
Chief Financial Officer	1
Executive Director / VP	5
Dean / Executive Dean	3
Total	*16

*Denotes one participant in two roles

I recorded each interview with the permission of the participant, made brief field notes (hand written) and transcribed each interview via a professional service for verbatim transcribing. I read the transcripts and I then immersed myself in them to develop a summary document of preliminary themes and findings. I used what Morse and Richards (2002) describe as pattern analysis, which involves looking for and describing patterns within the data. The following is a discussion of key themes from the research.

Findings

1. Lack of succession planning, and keeping gender on the agenda

Emerging Issues in Gender and Leadership

A primary theme running through the interviews was the lack of formal succession planning within the higher education sector. Succession planning is a relatively new, ad hoc, an unevenly and inconsistently developed practice, with limited understanding across universities in Australia today. However, it is a practice that leaders are concerned with, and developing interest. Interview findings highlighted that it was important to advocate for keeping gender on the leadership agenda. For example, a leader must advocate for female candidates within recruitment pools. Without the advocacy work of a current leader, the inclusion of women candidates may be absent. This sustains the practice of non-traditional leaders as hidden, invisible, and in the background. Moreover, leaders were aware of inequality within university processes that relate to leadership succession management, such as internal promotion. One participant commented that women wait longer than men to apply for promotion and that promotion of women to leadership is slow.

2. Succession planning strategies, practices and approaches

A range of formal and informal succession planning practices were reported during interviews. These included, from informal conversations about career planning and development, coaching, shadowing, participation in programs and networks, acting in short-term leadership roles, to 360-degree diagnostics, executive remuneration frameworks, to gender equity frameworks, and nine-box or grid talent assessment tools. Some leaders implement bold and innovative succession planning practices via their own systems aligned with capacity building, workforce and developing a culture, and utilise frameworks from industry to build detailed succession planning charts. Most leaders recognised their inclusion in a past succession planning process, being groomed for a potential role of successor at some point in their careers.

Various strategies and effective practices enable women's participation in leadership in higher education. Some reported by leaders included: prioritising of gender equality in messaging and recruitment practices from the top-down, wherein leaders explicitly communicate the 'need' for more women to be included in a recruitment pool; inclusive workplace culture and strong messaging about inclusive workplace culture practices; 'keeping the door-open' to previous external applicants to widen the pool of potential candidates; and, developing formal leadership training implemented internally.

Universities undertake a range of approaches to succession planning and management. These include from Human Resource training and development, performance management programs and approaches, discipline-specific programs and initiatives, they are critical role-specific only and may therefore not plan for all roles that require leadership succession management, require a balance professional and academic staff leadership capabilities, and utilise a confidential approach. Most leaders are proactive in initiating succession planning in their areas and teams with a focus on balancing both a future vision of their work domains and disciplines (collective) and their own replacement (individual). Some higher education leaders reflected that new approaches are most effective in succession planning and management, rather than keeping on with past practices. For example, identifying future potential leaders, followed by working out what to do to retain and develop leaders in order to grow internal bench strength. The latter would result in new processes and conversations that look and feel different to past processes. Moreover, as part of the succession process, there is work to do around succession management and the management of perceptions upon new appointments.

3. Barriers

A range of barriers to succession planning in relation to gender, were discussed by participants. These included, a limited range of strategic Human Resource Management tools at the disposal of universities that corporates may have access to, not developing a shared vision, a lack of support from Human Resources function, time limitations of Human Resource departments (unable to devote sufficient time to succession planning outside of the work of university), not determining the future strategic focus, the intention of potential successors contrasting with incumbent's intentions, and the challenge of forecasting and a future vision. It was clear that there needs to be, appropriate expertise to be thinking about talent, top-down support from the Vice Chancellor, thoughtful engagement and early development of succession planning, incentive for succession planning and management, and combined with a focus on cultivating effective practices.

DISCUSSION AND CONCLUSION

Inclusive leadership is critical to innovation and Australia's future, yet the under-representation of women in leadership roles in higher education is a key issue (Redmond et al., 2017). Studies on succession planning in higher education in Australia and effective practices are relatively new. Attention in future research is required on how leaders manage succession and leadership change, and developing strategies for an inclusive leadership ecosystem in higher education.

Initiatives to support women as successors and foster inclusion practices in leadership in higher education in the future, could include: succession planning and management frameworks and tools that promote and encourage gender balanced leadership and pipeline improvement, regular reviews and evaluations of gender balance of the most senior group and academic pipeline, targets or quotas for achieving gender balance at the most senior group and academic pipeline as a self-sustaining approach, and short-term leadership appointments as part of talent development. A range of approaches and practices could include: from incentivising evidence-based succession planning, developing and implementing succession planning programs led and supported by advisory groups or committees comprising organisational leadership succession diagnosis, and Human Resource audit of the number and equality-diversity ratio of leaders eligible for retirement. The early identification of the critical roles for succession, potential leaders, and gaps in knowledge and training would assist in the succession planning process. Moreover leaders could be further encouraged to engage with reliable frameworks and tools, underpinned by strategic action plans, milestones and timelines, and to communicate more openly about succession planning. The secrecy of succession may contribute to the ad hoc and inconsistent planning, as well as uncertainty.

Initiatives for gender inclusion succession planning that emphasise 'early' action, may include: welcoming gender quotas and identifying early female potential successors, anticipating vacancies and designing protocols when positions are unable to fulfil diversity, equality and inclusion gaps. Resourcing needs to be prioritised, as well as time and support, for example, the allocation of a succession planning committees comprised of Human Resource specialists to support and assist in promotion and encouragement among discipline leaders to commence thinking early about internal leadership capabilities, needs, and gaps. An increase in early interest and participation of leadership in succession planning, and trust and transparency in relation to gender should be fostered. Openness in communication and relationships of trust are essential for supporting smooth transitions and enabling successors to get off to a good start. Succession planning in relation to gender provides opportunities to implement and review diversity, equality and inclusion policies and practices to ensure they are effective and suitable for the future.

REFERENCES

Acker, J. (2009). From glass ceiling to inequality regimes. *Sociologie du Travail, 51*(2), 199-217.

Adkins, L., & Dever, M., (2015) It's not about the women: gender equality in research. *Australian Feminist Studies, 30*(85), 217-220.

Advance Higher Education: Leadership Education for Higher Education UK. (2019). *Succession Management Tools and Case Studies.* https://www.lfhe.ac.uk/en/research-resources/resource-hub/succession-management/tools/index.cfm

Australian Govt. (2018). List of Australian Universities. *Study in Australia.* https://www.studyinaustralia.gov.au/english/australian-education/universities-and-higher-education/list-of-australian-universities)

Australian Govt. Department of Education. (2018). Higher education staff numbers for 2018. Canberra. https://docs.education.gov.au/node/51701)

Bryman, A. (2004). *Social Research Methods* (2nd ed.). Oxford University Press.

Calareso, J. P. (2013). 'Succession Planning: A Key to Ensuring Leadership' (Feature Article). *Planning for Higher Education Journal, 41*(3), 27–33.

Cavanaugh, J. C. (2017). Who Will Lead? The Success of Succession Planning. *Journal of Management Policy and Practice, 18*(2), 22–27.

Charlesworth, S., & Cartwright, S. (2007). Part-time Work: Policy, Practice and Resistance in a Manufacturing Organisation. In Fastenau, M., Branigan, L., Douglas, K., and Marshall, H., with Cartwright, S., (Eds), Women and Work 2007: Current RMIT University Research, 5-19. RMIT Publishing, Melbourne.

Chief Executive Women. (2017), *Chief Executive Women: Senior Executive Census 2017.* Chief Executive Women. https://cew.org.au/wp-content/uploads/CEW-Executive-Census-2017.pdf

Coates, H., & Goedegebuure, L. (2012). Recasting the Academic Workforce: Why, the Attractiveness of the Academic Profession Needs to be Increased and Eight Possible Strategies for how to go about this from an Australian Perspective. *Higher Education, 64*(6), 875–889. doi:10.100710734-012-9534-3

Connell, R. W. (1987). *Gender and Power: Society, The Person and Sexual Politics.* Allen and Unwin.

Connell, R. W. (2002). *Gender.* Polity Press.

Connell, R. W. (2005). A Really Good Husband: Work/Life Balance, Gender Equity and Social Change. *The Australian Journal of Social Issues, 40*(3), 369–383. doi:10.1002/j.1839-4655.2005.tb00978.x

Crotty, M. (1998). *The Foundations of Social Research: Meaning and Perspective in the Research Process.* Allen and Unwin.

Drago, R., Colbeck, C., Stauffer, K., Pirretti, A., Burkum, K., Faziolo, J., Lazzaro, G., & Habasevich, T. (2006). The Avoidance Bias Against Caregiving: The Case of Academic Faculty. *The American Behavioral Scientist*, *49*(9), 1222–1247. doi:10.1177/0002764206286387

Drago, R., Tseng, Y. P., & Wooden, M. (2004). *Family Structure, Usual and Preferred Working Hours, and Egalitarianism in Australia*, 1-38. Melbourne Institute.

Drago, R., Tseng, Y. P., & Wooden, M. (2005). Usual and Preferred Working Hours in Couple Households. *Journal of Family Studies*, *11*(1), 46–61. doi:10.5172/jfs.327.11.1.46

Drew, G. (2010). Issues and Challenges in higher Educational Leadership. *Australian Educational Researcher*, *37*(3), 57–76. doi:10.1007/BF03216930

Gilding, M., Gregory, S., & Cosson, B. (2011). A Typology of Motives of Family Business Succession Planning. *The Australian Sociological Association Conference*. ASA.

Gilding, M., Gregory, S., & Cosson, B. (2015). Motives and Outcomes in Family Business Succession Planning. *Entrepreneurship Theory and Practice*, *39*(2), 299–312. doi:10.1111/etap.12040

Glass, C., & Cook, A. (2020). Performative contortions: How White women and people of colour navigate elite leadership roles. *Gender, Work and Organization*, *27*(6), 1232–1252. doi:10.1111/gwao.12463

Hammersley, M. (1992). Deconstructing the Qualitative–Quantitative Divide. In J. Brannen (Ed.), *Mixing Methods: Qualitative and Quantitative Research* (pp. 39–55). Avebury.

Handler, W. (1994). Succession in family business: A review of the literature. *Family Business Review*, *7*(2), 133–157. doi:10.1111/j.1741-6248.1994.00133.x

Harvester, P., Davis, P., & Lyden, J. (1997). Succession Planning in Family Business: The Impact of Owner Gender. *Family Business Review*, *10*(4), 373–396. doi:10.1111/j.1741-6248.1997.00373.x

Hochschild, A. R. (1989). *The Second-Shift: Working Parents and the Revolution at Home*. Viking Penguin.

Huppatz, K., Sang, N., & Napier, J. (2019). 'If you put pressure on yourself to produce then that's your responsibility': Mothers' experiences of maternity leave and flexible work in the neoliberal university. *Gender, Work and Organization*, *6*(6), 772–788. doi:10.1111/gwao.12314

Ishak, A. K., & Mustafa Kamil, B. A. (2016). Succession Planning at Higher Education Institutions: Leadership Style, Career Development and Knowledge Management Practices as its Predictors. *International Review of Management and Marketing*, *6*(S7), 214–220.

Klein, M. F., & Salk, R. J. (2013). Presidential Succession Planning: A Qualitative Study in Private Higher Education. *Journal of Leadership & Organizational Studies*, *20*(3), 335–345. doi:10.1177/1548051813483836

McCarthy, J. (2005). Planning a Future Workforce: An Australian Perspective. *New Review of Academic Librarianship*, *11*(1), 41–56. doi:10.1080/13614530500417669

McMurray, A. M., Henly, D., Chaboyer, W., Clapton, J., Lizzio, A., & Temi, M. (2012). Leadership Succession Management in a University Health Faculty. *Journal of Higher Education Policy and Management*, *34*(4), 365–376. doi:10.1080/1360080X.2012.689198

Minichello, V., Aroni, R., Timewell, E., & Alexander, L. (1995), In-depth Interviewing: Principles, Techniques, Analysis, Second Edn., Longman, Frenches Forrest.

Morehead, A. (2003), *How Employed Mothers Allocate Time for Work and Family: A New Framework*, [Ph.D. thesis, The University of Sydney, Sydney].

Morse, J. M., & Richards, L. (2002). *Readme First for a User's Guide to Qualitative Methods*. Sage.

Munro, A. (2016). *Practical Succession Management: How to Future-Proof Your Organisation*. Routledge.

Pocock, B. (2003). *The Work/Life Collision: What Work is doing to Australians and What to Do about It*. The Federation Press.

Probert, B. (2004). If Only it Were a Glass Ceiling: Gendered Academic Careers. In S. Charlesworth & M. Fastenau (Eds.), *Women and Work: Current RMIT University Research* (pp. 7–26). RMIT Publishing.

Redmond, P., Gutke, H., Galligan, L., Howard, A., & Newman, T. (2017). Becoming a female leader in higher education: Investigations from a regional university. *Gender and Education, 29*(3), 332–351. doi:10.1080/09540253.2016.1156063

Scott, G., Bell, S., Coates, H., & Grebennikov, L. (2010). Australian higher education leaders in times of change: The role of Pro Vice-Chancellor and Deputy Vice-Chancellor. *Journal of Higher Education Policy and Management, 32*(4), 401–418. doi:10.1080/1360080X.2010.491113

Scott, G., Coates, H., & Anderson, M. (2008). *Learning Leaders in Times of Change: Academic Leadership Capabilities for Australian Higher Education*. Carrick Institute. https://research.acer.edu.au/higher_education/3

Strachan, G., Peetz, D., Whitehouse, G., Bailey, J., Broadbent, K., May, R., Troup, C., & Nesic, M. (2016), *Women, careers and universities: Where to from here?* Centre for Work, Organisation and Wellbeing, Griffith University. https://www.griffith.edu.au/__data/assets/pdf_file/0023/88124/UA-FINAL-Report-Digital-4-April-2016.pdf

Universities Australia. (2017). *2016 Selected Inter-Institutional Gender Equity Statistics*. Canberra.

Weick, K. E. (1985). Cosmos vs. Chaos: Sense and Nonsense in Electronic Contexts. *Organizational Dynamics, 14*(2), 51–64. doi:10.1016/0090-2616(85)90036-1

Weick, K. E. (1993). Collapse of Sensemaking in Organizations: The Mann Gulch Disaster. *Administrative Science Quarterly, 38*(4), 628–652. doi:10.2307/2393339

Weick, K. E. (1995). *Sensemaking in Organizations*. Sage.

Williams, J. (2000). *Unbending Gender: Why Family & Work Conflict and What to Do About it*. Oxford University Press.

Section 3
Leadership in an Organisational Context

While identification and development of effective leaders is of prime concern in contemporary organizations, context is an important factor that influences leadership styles and leader effectiveness. This section discusses leadership in the organisational context. Linking the issues of gender that is discussed in the previous chapter, the first chapter examines the underrepresentation of women in school leadership positions in India and the United States. The next chapter explored integrated framework for leadership in higher education in Australia, incorporating three major domains, e.g., behaviors, mindsets, and skills. The next chapter discusses the challenges faced by trade unions in the contemporary work environment and emphasized the importance of cohesion, unity, and solidarity, supported by pragmatic, and ethical leadership.

Chapter 5
Women in School Leadership in India and the United States:
Realities, Complexities, and Future Directions

Adity Saxena
Woxsen University, India

Monique Darrisaw Akil
Uniondale Union Free School District, USA

Pavani Ayinampudi
Telangana Social Welfare Residential Educational Institutions Society, India

ABSTRACT

Women's representation in school leadership positions in India, and of Black women in the United States, remains unexplored. This chapter addresses the realities and complexities of women leaders in school education and develops a narrative based on current trends and anticipated challenges for the future. Existing research in educational leadership in schools, case studies, and interviews tend to focus on developing a coherent understanding of the topic. The representation of women in the school, from teachers to leaders, is an inverted pyramid. This chapter aims to provide an overview of how women school leaders from India and the USA manage crises, navigate politics, establish policies and budgets, and where the constraints lie at the school board and family level. Finally, using the grounded theory framework, the authors will present a pattern of women's leadership similarities, differences, and uniqueness in the context of both countries.

"Just like moons and like suns,

DOI: 10.4018/978-1-6684-8257-5.ch005

With the certainty of tides

Just like hopes springing high,

Still, I'll rise."

Maya Angelous

INTRODUCTION

Leadership is a critical aspect of human society, and its significance transcends race, gender, or cultural background. However, despite the strides in advancing gender equality in leadership positions, women's representation in leadership roles remains low.

This book chapter explores the intersection of gender and leadership in two distinct contexts: black women in the United States and women leaders in Indian Schools in the backdrop of a Residential Educational Society from Telangana State in India. Specifically, the chapter examines the particular difficulties women encounter in these situations and how they get around them to become effective leaders.

Drawing on empirical research and relevant literature, this chapter provides insights into the experiences of these two groups of women, highlighting the strategies they employ to achieve success in leadership roles. Ultimately, this chapter aims to contribute to the literature on gender and leadership and inform policymakers, organizations, and individuals on ways to promote gender equality in leadership.

The chapter begins with examining the data that demonstrates the gaps between men and women in leadership and specifically men versus Black women in leadership in the United States followed by review of literature to examine the probable causes for the identified gaps.

The chapter concludes with a presentation of case studies of a Black woman school superintendent and female school principals in the Indian school system in order to provide context to the research that highlights the lived experience of these leaders. These case studies enable us to go beyond the data to find out how Black and Indian women have overcome discrimination, barriers by relying on mentors, informal and formal networks and spirituality to move forward.

Spillane (2004) stated that the "education system" is a complex construct, so research is crucial in improving educational leadership roles to identify the best practices for managing their schools and staff. For instance, research can provide insights into effective communication strategies, team-building, and conflict-resolution techniques, all of which are critical to the success of a school.

Let us understand the importance of this discussion in the school leadership context. This research has wide-reaching implications for both male and female students. The absence of women of color leaders in educational institutions denies these systems the input and critical perspectives from individuals who can lead and support improvement efforts at every level. Additionally, these gaps in leadership negatively reinforce messages of secondary status among women of color in society.

The absence of women of color in educational leadership roles is a complex issue less documented and discussed in academic research and practice (Herring, 2007). There has been a lack of research on the barriers facing Black women and Indian women in educational leadership. This chapter hopes to add to the existing research and foster a discussion on the experiences of Black and Indian women in school leadership. Women of color, including Black, Latina, and Indigenous women, face significant barriers to accessing educational leadership positions.

One significant barrier is the need for more representation in the pipeline to leadership roles. Women of color are underrepresented in teaching positions, which is often seen as a stepping stone to leadership roles. Fewer women of color can gain the experience and skills necessary to move into educational leadership positions (The University of Texas, n.d.). Another way to improve the current percentage of representation is by creating alternate/non-traditional avenues to reach leadership positions.

In addition, women of color face systemic barriers in the education system that perpetuate inequality and limit their access to leadership positions. These barriers include implicit biases, racism, and sexism (Bernal, et. al., 2017), which can affect hiring and promotion decisions. Stereotypes about leadership, such as the idea that leaders should be male and white, can also make it harder for women of color to be considered for leadership roles.

Furthermore, women of color may face additional challenges once they are in leadership positions. They may experience isolation, lack of support from colleagues, and heightened scrutiny and pressure to prove themselves. These challenges can make it difficult for women of color to succeed and advance in leadership roles.

Addressing the absence of women of color in educational leadership roles requires systemic change. Strategies to increase diversity and equity in educational leadership include targeted recruitment (Brown, 2014) and professional development programs, mentoring (Peters, 2010) and networking opportunities. It is essential to create a more inclusive and supportive environment for women of color in education to ensure they have the same opportunities to excel as their male and white counterparts.

A Global View on Women's Leadership in Schools

Many studies advocate that in most countries, women do not hold a proportionately large share of senior leadership and management positions, despite the fact that women tend to be numerically predominate in the teaching profession internationally. Msila (2013) noted that in South Africa, there has been a conscious effort to address the past and present inequalities by ensuring that women are employed in positions of management and leadership in schools. Today, women are in charge of many well-run schools in South Africa. The study's findings also shed light on the fact that, in spite of stereotypes and frequently misconstrued presumptions made by society, there are very few differences in leadership skills between men and women.

Coleman (2005) studied the effects of gender among secondary school principals in England on a large-scale survey. The study came to the conclusion that gender is frequently ignored as a background factor in studies of leadership in education, and that this disparity raises issues of social justice in a 'pluralistic society'.

The authors of Coloring outside the lines: Mentoring women into school leadership discussed two contemporary issues with educational administration in the context of three US states: Maryland, Virginia, and Washington (Gardiner, Enomoto, & Grogan, 2000).

"Dominant culture of educational administration is androcentric, meaning informed by white, male norms," (Gardiner, et al., 2000, p. 1).

Given that women are still viewed as newcomers to the field of educational leadership, many studies have advocated mentoring as a tool to transform leadership for both women's and men's career success. However, the authors of this book support their argument that mentoring is frequently promoted without due consideration by citing a number of studies. (Gardiner et. al., 2000 referred Roche 1979; Schmidt & Wolfe 1980, 45; Lively et. Al. 1992; Bizzari 1995; Didion 1995; Stevens 1995).

When women do receive mentoring, it is often "debilitating rather than empowering," according to Johnsrud (1991), who makes the point that mentoring is rare for women. The authors investigate possibilities for transformation and change toward new forms of mentoring, as opposed to doing away with it altogether.

In the context of ongoing change in the educational systems as schools are being reformed and restructured, Sachs and Blackmore (1998) provide an illustration of the emotional exhaustion of the women leaders in the primary and secondary schools in Queensland, Australia. Women School leaders' emotional expression often includes expectations around how leaders should express or suppress their emotions, what emotions are considered appropriate or inappropriate in specific situations, and how emotions are managed and regulated in the workplace. The authors argue that understanding and acknowledging these emotional rules and contextual factors are essential for effectively supporting and developing education leaders.

A principal stated a recent incident in which a parent reprimanded her in front of a student who was about to be suspended from school. In the words of the parent,

"Why should Johnny listen to you, you are only a woman, he doesn't like women," (Sachs & Blackmore, 1998, p. 267).

Mythili (2017) attempts to examine the representation of women in leadership positions in schools by using all India and state-level secondary data analysis. According to the findings, women are underrepresented in three of the four school leadership positions in all school categories. The underrepresentation of women in school leadership is caused by a number of factors, including:

a) Nearly 60% of school categories lack designated leadership positions, and those managed by acting (Head Masters/Mistress) HMs can be reinstated as teachers at any time as evidence of systemic dysfunction.
b) Sociocultural traditions ingrained in the hegemony are the cause of the underrepresentation of women in positions of leadership in schools.
c) Women are discouraged from taking on leadership roles, among other things, by a lack of family support, other social pressures, and a culture that despises or rejects the competitive nature of leadership roles.

Navigating Leadership Role in Indian School Education System: Unique Challenges of Women Leaders—Case Study from Telangana Social Welfare Residential Educational Institutions Society (TSWREIS), India

Here we focus on female school leaders from the Telangana Social Welfare Residential Educational Institutions Society (TSWREIS) to comprehend the journey of a school leader in the context of India.

Many of the school principals interviewed for this study belong to the marginalized communities and hence their leadership journey overlaps the gender and caste factors.

Note: The views and opinions expressed by the participants of the study are solely those of the individuals and do not necessarily reflect the views of the organization that the participant is affiliated to i.e., TSWREIS.

From these case studies, the authors attempt to discuss the challenges faced by female school leaders from TSWREIS, India, such as gender discrimination, family support, and access of resources. It also looks at the strategies used by female school leaders to overcome these challenges, such as networking, mentoring, and creating a supportive environment.

TSWREIS: An Overview of the Organization Background and Structure

The Telangana Social Welfare Residential Educational Institutions Society (TSWREIS) is a complete grant-in-aid society under the Scheduled Caste Development Department, Ministry of Social Welfare, Government of Telangana, India. It was established in the year 1984 with the objective of providing quality education to the socially and economically backward sections of the society.

The TSWREI Society runs a network of 268 educational institutions offering education from Grade 5 to Post graduation. Along with regular academics, the TSWREI Society offers a plethora of extra-curricular and co-curricular programs to the students, vocational training, upskilling programs (technical and life skills), specialized academies to nurture the budding athletes by providing expert coaches and special training, etc. to name a few. It also provides vocational training and skill development programs to the students (Government of Telangana Social Welfare Residential Educational Institutions Society, n.d.).

Out of the 268 institutions, 30 are residential degree colleges that offer undergraduate courses in more than 27 subjects, exclusively for the marginalized young women (Karunakar, 2019).

The TSWREI Society has been working with the noble aim of providing quality education to the needy and deprived children on par with the other advantaged children. The Society has been sailing along the path of glory for the previous three decades, and this depth is shown in how the Society is outperforming other public and Government organisations in terms of academics, sports, mountaineering, communication skills, etc. Along with providing children with a high-quality education, the Society is working hard to foster an environment that will help them develop the confidence, leadership, and communication skills they need to face the challenges of the 21st century.

The school principals in these institutions are expected to uphold the highest education standards and ensure that the students are provided with a safe and secure learning environment. The principals must also ensure that the students have the necessary resources, essential guidance and support to help them develop their skills and knowledge and reach their full potential.

TSWREIS STRUCTURE

The Secretary, usually an officer from the Indian Administrative Service (IAS) is the organization's Apex Authority, with complete financial and administrative autonomy. However, being a government organization, certain proposals and approvals like recruitment of permanent staff, and major financial decisions will require approval from the State Government's Ministry of Finance.

The Additional Secretary works alongside the Secretary and oversees the finance and establishment verticals.

A Joint Secretary is in charge of a particular vertical across all the institutions. For example, school academics, diet and amenities provided, secondary education, higher education, and so on.

Regional Coordinators (RCOs) are regional officers who oversee the administration of schools/colleges in a specific region. Each RCO is responsible for 10 to 17 schools, depending on the region of jurisdiction. There is no autonomy at this level, but they are kept in the loop for all academic and administrative activities, which adds another layer of monitoring to ensure smooth functioning.

The principal is in charge of the school. There is very limited administrative autonomy, particularly when it comes to recruitment and limited independence with respect to finance. The academic regulation is also centralized with the guidelines coming from the Head Office to the schools and the principal's responsibility is mostly restricted to the implementation of these policies and programs. This system is adopted to maintain uniform standards across the 268 institutions.

Indian school education is based on the 10+2 system, which is followed by most schools in India. The 10+2 system consists of 10 years of schooling, followed by two years of higher secondary education. The 10 years of schooling is divided into five years of primary education, three years of middle school, and two years of high school.

Establishing Context

Prior to beginning this cross-cultural discussion about the barriers facing Black women and Indian women in leadership it is important to establish the definition of the terms and words used throughout the chapter. The term "Black women" is used to refer to non-white women of African descent, regardless of national origin, living and working in the United States. This term encompasses women from the English-speaking or French-speaking Caribbean, Central or South America and the continent of Africa who identify as Black (Pulse, 2019). This frame is very important as opposed to the more generic term, "women of color" which can be used to refer to Latina women, Asian women, Indigenous women and women of mixed races. The authors contend that while women of all races face barriers based on gender, anti-black racism compounds the challenges that Black women face in their quest to leadership roles.

The authors will also discuss the impact of the caste system in India and the role it plays in shaping the trajectory of women leaders in India.

The caste system in India is a system of social stratification that has existed for centuries. The caste system is divided into four main categories: Brahmin, Kshatriya, Vaishya, and Shudra (Pruthi, 2004). Each of these categories is further divided into numerous sub-castes. The caste system has been a source of social and economic inequality in India and has been the subject of much debate and criticism.

The Scheduled Tribes (ST) and Scheduled Caste (SC) emerged from the Indian caste system as a result of the Indian Constitution of 1950 (Ghurye, 1980). The Constitution of India recognized the Scheduled Tribes and Scheduled Caste as socially and economically disadvantaged groups, and provided them with special rights and privileges. This was done in order to ensure that these groups had access to education, employment, and other opportunities that were previously denied to them. The Scheduled Tribes and Scheduled Caste are also guaranteed representation in government and other public institutions.

When presenting the context of school superintendents in the United States, the authors discuss the role of chief executive officer of the school system who is responsible for the overall direction of the school district, manages the district's finances and reports to a locally elected board of trustees.

In Indian context, the challenges faced by women leaders in different levels of hierarchy from School principal to the Joint Secretary cadre in the TSWREIS system is used as the background to develop the narrative and draw conclusions.

Insights from Statistics

There is a persistent gender gap in school district leadership roles. While the majority of teachers across the United States are women (74%), leadership positions are still overwhelmingly held by men ("Teacher Demographics and statistics in the US," n.d.). The gap for Black women is even wider. In New York State only 27% of all superintendents are women and fewer than 3% of all superintendents (outside of New York City) are Black women ("School Superintendent Demographics and Statistics in the US," (n.d.). Less than 2% of all superintendents in the United States are African-American women (Webb, 2022).

The number of female school teachers in India has surpassed that of male counterparts for the first time, according to the Unified 2019-20 District Information System for Education Plus (UDISE+) report. Compared to 2018-19, the number of instructors employed in K–12 institutions increased by 2.72 percent in 2019–20. In 2019–20, 96.87 lakh teachers worked in the field of education, an increase of 2.57 lakhs from the figures for 2018–19. In addition, 49.15 lakh were female teachers, while 47.71 lakh were male teachers (Ministry of Education, 2021). According to the UNESCO Institute for Statistics in Primary Education, 55% of teachers are female.

The educational reforms of the 1990s provided an opportunity to reduce or eliminate barriers to women and minorities being appointed as principals and Superintendents. However, the gender gap in school leadership remains visible in the Indian context.

From Whence We Came

A Brief Summary of the History of Women in School Leadership in Both Contexts

We will explore what the literature says about the systemic barriers that prevent Black women and Indian women from being selected for the chief executive role in school systems. One systemic issue is the problem of the pipeline. ***(Concrete vs. glass ceiling discussion) Black women sometimes have a lack of access to formal mentoring or professional networks where one can be "tapped" for leadership opportunities. Leaders are more likely to ascend to the superintendency from the position of a secondary principal. More women principals are likely to be found in the elementary schools where they may tend to focus more on curriculum than the operational and facilities experiences that school boards tend to prioritize when looking for a Superintendent. Additionally, there are gendered expectations around school and district leadership that make it less likely for Boards of Education and search firms to promote qualified women to leadership roles.

Furthermore, for Black women, there are socially ingrained biases that negatively impact selection such as negative perceptions of likability or credibility based on culture, language and sometimes even skin tone. In addition to general bias, Black women of darker skin tones may be subject to additional bias based on their skin color referred to as colorism, *"skin tone bias, an insidious form of bias that impacts women of darker skin tones across ethnicities and race," (Tulshyan, 2023).*

In the Indian context, as mentioned in the data section, considering the job role and societal bias, many women take up the teaching profession. Unfortunately, this representation is not seen at the leadership level and even in cases of representation, the women leaders are often limited to academic regulation with very little to no hold on the finance and other administration roles of the institution.

Case Studies: "And Still We Rise"

The purpose of the case study section of this work is to explore the protective factors and survival strategies utilized by women of color and Indian women school leaders who have beat the odds to achieve the leadership role. These case studies will not only throw light on the challenges faced but also illustrate the importance of formal and informal networks, mentors, affinity groups, allies and co-conspirators, pipeline programs, self-care, faith and spirituality,

One of our case studies will focus on the work and career of an African-American woman who has served as superintendent in various districts in New York since 2008. Authors will tell her story in hopes that can uncover some common threads between her experiences and that of other women of color in leadership. Similar case studies of women educational leaders in India need to be conducted in order to further understand how gender plays a critical role in determining one's path to leadership in a K-12 educational setting.

Dr. Deborah Wortham: African-American Superintendent in Long Island, New York

Dr. Deborah Wortham, who identifies herself as a Black woman, is currently the Superintendent of the Roosevelt School District in Long Island, New York. Dr. Wortham describes her route to the superintendence as traditional. She started her career as a classroom teacher, she spent 18 years in the classroom as a teacher and then she became an assistant principal in the largest elementary school in the country at that time where she served for two years. Following her tenure as an assistant principal, she was appointed as an elementary school principal, central office director, area superintendent and then superintendent. Dr Wortham served as an assistant superintendent for 24 high schools in Baltimore, Maryland and she has been a superintendent in four different school districts; two in Pennsylvania, one in Baltimore and two different districts in New York State. She has served as a superintendent for 15 years. She has always worked in the lowest performing schools and districts because she believed that that is the work she has been called to do, as a turnaround leader. She believes that in order to improve student achievement, one has to have a district-wide vision for instruction and work to improve the school atmosphere both physically and culturally. She says that she leads with a growth mindset and with a belief in efficacy, the philosophy she attributes to her longevity as a district superintendent and educational leader.

When discussing her ascendency to the superintendency, she has experienced some challenges but she has also benefited from support and mentoring. Along her journey she has been tapped by supervisors to take on promotional opportunities. Some of the challenges she has faced have related to gender as well as stereotypes for women of color. She has experienced inequities in relation to salary, benefits and what she referred to as "overall respect." She noted that in one of her central administrative posts she received significantly less compensation than her male predecessor's contract as well as less favorable perks. Additionally, she noted that the road to the top job hasn't been an easy one. She applied five times before landing her first superintendent job. Dr. Wortham's experience is affirmed by the data which shows that women spend longer in central office roles and enter the superintendency.

"Being an African American female and aspiring to be superintendent means you can and will indeed make great achievements, but not without barriers. The path is not direct, but the journey is yours to travel," (W. Deborah, personal communication, January 14, 2023).

Balancing Work and Family

As a woman in leadership, she has also had to balance family expectations and the demands of her job. Some of her promotions required moving to other states within the country. In order to accept one job which was an hour away from her home, her husband drove over an hour each weekend to meet her. She says that her time with family is a priority and even though the superintendency is a job that can be all encompassing she is strategic about managing her schedule in a way that allows for her to spend quality time with her family. Dr. Wortham was fortunate to have the support of her family in the pursuit of a leadership role. The superintendency is an extremely demanding position.

"The hours are punishing school board politics can be brutal, and public scrutiny is intense," (Superville, 2016).

The long hours that superintendents are required to work can definitely have a negative impact on family life. Between Board meetings, school and community events and managing crises, a superintendent's schedule can be quite unpredictable which means that a partner or spouse would have to assume more responsibilities in terms of childcare or domestic duties. One aspiring Black woman superintendent shared with the author, Dr. Monique Darrisaw-Akil about how the demands on her job were presenting a challenge in her marriage. Although her husband initially supported her career goals, once she took on an assistant superintendent role which required her to be away from her children and her home for a long period of time, he expressed concerns. She stated that she had to re-assess her priorities as a result and is currently unsure if she will still continue to work towards becoming a superintendent at this point. Lack of support from a spouse can thwart attempts at advancement to a CEO role. Although male superintendents have the same time demands placed on them as female superintendents, there is a societal expectation that women will support their husband's career by managing household duties and being the primary parent responsible for childcare even while maintaining jobs outside of the home. While this dilemma isn't present in every household, as evidenced by Dr. Wortham's experience, the fact that many women face this challenge can have an impact on their decision to pursue the superintendent positions.

When discussing how she has combated the challenges of being a Black woman in leadership Dr. Wortham talks a great deal about the impact of faith on her leadership journey and on her life. "I absolutely walk by faith." She is a member of the Christian faith and she is a practicing minister. Faith is one of the survival tools she uses to cope with the stresses of the job, the microaggressions, and the countless decisions she has to make every day. She attributes her success not only to her credentials, but also to the goodness of God. She said that every level of her life has been guided by God's favor. She believes that she was continuously elevated and with the goal of how she can help more students.

Like many Black women, Dr. Wortham feels compelled to help others. There is a familiar African-American quote that says to whom much is given, much is required. This quote is used in the African-American community to instill the value of communalism (Hammond, 2018) and the duty of those who have achieved a measure of success to help others in their community who have not been as fortunate. Dr. Wortham says that she believes that she is at her best when she is helping and developing others (Rosenberg, 2013). She is invested in growing other leaders. Her advice to new leaders is to focus on the practice, not the position. She says, "Try to do good work in whatever position you have. It's the practice, not the position."

The importance of representation in school and district leadership is an area in need of further study. Research conducted by John Hopkins University found that a Black student having at least one Black teacher in third through fifth grade reduced a Black student's probability of dropping out of school by 29 percent (Will, 2017). There is no comparable study on the impact of Black superintendents have on Black student achievement but there is a belief among Black leaders that their presence has an impact on students' beliefs about their own futures. Dr. Wortham said when she was hired as a superintendent a Black student walked up to her and said she couldn't believe that the Board hired an African-American. Dr. Wortham is very aware of the impact that her presence and appearance have on her students. She said young people need to see nappy hair (tightly coiled African-American hair) and they need to see leaders who wear natural hair in the workplace. She said that our young people need to see women of color sitting at the head and in fact everybody needs to see people of color in leadership.

Case Studies of Female School Leaders in TSWREIS

Smt. Kamidi. Pramodha- Grade-1 Principal, Telangana Social Welfare Residential Educational Society, Chitkul, Sangareddy district, India

The Path to Becoming a School Leader

K. Pramodha, who is currently employed as a school principal in the Chitkul, Sangareddy district, took the conventional path to that position. After completing her B. Ed., she began working as a teacher. Prior to joining TSWREIS, Ms. Pramodha worked with several private schools, degree colleges, and intermediate colleges. She started working for the society from 2013 and her first posting was in Karimnagar district which was far from her hometown Hyderabad where her family is settled.

Principal of a School in a Socioeconomically Underdeveloped District

She held a distinctive leadership position as a school principal in the framework of the Karimnagar district. Working in Karimnagar was challenging as the district then lacked good infrastructure, funding, access to quality education and healthcare when compared to the district of Hyderabad where Ms. Pramodha comes from.

On the other hand, Ms K. Pramodha's role as a principal in society differs concerning private and public schools. Students come from the less affluent parts of society, and all institutions are residential. The majority of the students are first-generation learners. Nonetheless, a lot of society's instructors also come from deprived origins.

Gender, Geography, and Unorthodox Thinking are all Significant Challenges as Principal

Some of her difficulties have been brought on by her gender, the school's location, and the neighborhood's conventional attitudes. When she first assumed the position of principal, she was experiencing issues with one male instructor who had been in charge of the principal for three years before her appointment. He used to engage in unethical practices, frequently speaking with the locals and students to create a conspiracy against K. Pramodha. He often called the local press & media to complain about trivial issues, and other common problems that are not exclusive to the school but common for all the district inhabitants.

He attempted to mislead the health supervisor of the school, which would only make things more difficult for her. Given the delicate health concerns, the principal should proceed cautiously. Due to the school's rural location, the hospital was far from the school. In this context, she referred to an incident in which she took a girl student who was seriously ill to the hospital—25 KM away—with the help of just one of the school's staff.

Building Trust Among the Stakeholders in the School Through Leadership

Over time, K. Pramodha acquired school stakeholders' trust by going above and beyond to assist the students and spending more time with the teachers. By listening to the students, she established a respectful dialogue with them. In addition to focusing on enhancing the school's infrastructure, she gave students confidence by assisting them in improving their English communication abilities. By taking into account the students' socioeconomic status and the fact that the school is located in a rural area, she shows leadership strategy in both of her decisions.

She wanted to upgrade the facilities, including adding a computer lab and generators for backup power. The school principal's most significant issue at TSWREIS is dealing with the parents. The parent committee is critical to the school. While dealing with the parents, particularly the males, the principal must be highly cautious.

Parents have an important role as stakeholders in the Society school. However, dealing with the students' fathers might be difficult for the female principals in the system because most of the students come from disadvantaged and marginalized groups. Because of the biases that have been entrenched in them since childhood and in their communities, they can occasionally be reluctant to accept criticism from female principals. Hence, TSWREIS is extremely different from public schools in this regard, the principals must carefully handle communication with the parents while also taking into account the parents' varied experiences.

Juggling the Demands of Motherhood With the Huge Expectations of a Residential School Principal

The conflict between motherhood and the high expectations of a principal's role in a residential school can be challenging to navigate. On the one hand, a residential school principal is expected to be a leader, role model, and mentor for the students. They must also be able to ensure the safety, health, and well-being of the students in their care.

K. Pramodha, a mother of two young boys, discussed the challenges she faced balancing family and her role as a school administrator. At the beginning of her employment, she tried to keep the home under control by making phone calls and making one day-long visit every ten days. Her husband helped her accomplish this. Despite this, her two sons' academic performance suffered after she started working as a principal in the Karimnagar district. Upon her brief return home after a long absence, she often felt like an outsider in her own home.

Further she stated that, 'we need to sacrifice, either we can take care of the family or devote to the role of the principal'. We must be accessible round-the-clock for residential school students especially when dealing with marginalized sections. Their parents leave their students in the schools with a sense of belief on the Society's management and the teachers. We must take the job only if we are committed to it, else we have to leave it.'

"I am working for 600 children without looking at my two children," (P. Kamidi, personal communication, January 31, 2023).

Being Recognized and Valued as a Female School Leader

The Secretary sent K. Pramodha four commendation letters in recognition of her accomplishments as a principal. When she transferred from her previous school, she claimed that the teachers and students still looked forward to seeing her. The Secretary appreciated her initiatives and also recommended others to follow.

SMT. UPPALA VANISRI, PRINCIPAL, RAM REDDY GUDEM SCHOOL, TSWREIS

The Path to Becoming a School Administrator

Before being chosen for the role of principal, U. Vanisri worked as a teacher during the first part of her career. She has spent 30 years as a teacher and 5 years as a principal. Throughout her time as a teacher, she used to be annoyed and upset by the situation where teachers were given very little chance to contribute to the overall running of the school. She seized the opportunity when she was given the chance to lead the school as a principal and improved the learning environment for the students and instructors. She enhanced the quality of education, promoted stronger ties between the teachers and the students, and put better processes into place for the administration of the school as a whole. Her experience helped her manage the role better and being empathetic towards her teachers.

She emphasized that she had never experienced discrimination as a woman leader but admitted that at the beginning of her leadership position, the school's stakeholders—parents, students, and teachers—had some reservations about her leadership abilities and used to put those reservations to the test. As time went on, however, they grew more confident.

She expressed her job satisfaction by saying,

"Whatever I am doing I am happy for that and only answerable to me," (V. Uppala, personal communication, January 31, 2023).

Negotiation With her Spouse to Keep Working at her Desired Profession in Education

She had a lot of help navigating and balancing her personal and professional lives from her spouse and his family. Her professional commitments, which include night shifts and long hours at the residential school, were expressed to the neighborhood by her children with the same kind of support she has received from the other family members.

According to the Indian family system and marriage customs, the groom's parents significantly influence the choice of their job role, posting, etc. As she began her teaching job before getting married, she was able to explain to her future husband and family how passionate she is about her work before getting married and to make it obvious that she will never leave her job in favour of taking care of the family.

U. Vanisri concurred with K. Pramodha that leading the Society's school is indeed very different from leading other public and private institutions. Residential schools in society educate students from marginalized communities. Hence, the difficulty of managing parents and children, comprehending the complexity of the school system, the cognitive component of the students, and dealing with social difficulties require more dedication and passion from the principals.

While passionate about her school principal work, she shared her concerns about not having enough time to spend with her family.

Women School Leaders' Unique Style of Leadership

According to U. Vanisri, when a female principal is in charge, the school environment is more organized, the students are given greater attention, and it feels more like a family. Female principals are more cautious and concerned about everything, including their students' health and education.

In general, men and women have significantly distinct problem-solving styles. Women in leadership positions handled it sensitively and convinced those who spoke up because they are accustomed to convincing their husbands, children, and other family members and use the same rhetorical strategies at work by explaining "why they are doing this, how they are doing this, and for whom they are doing this" for any task they take up in their work life or in this case at the school.

She stated while explaining her leadership style,

"My teachers said that I do not allow even the slightest opportunity for them to escape their responsibilities. My students on the school campus trust me greatly because they know they can knock on my door at any time and share with me. Parents also trust me, so they do not visit the school to inquire about their child.," (V. Uppala, personal communication, January 31, 2023).

She Once Considered Quitting

U. Vanisri expressed her worries about the current level of education, particularly the teachers' casual attitude. Only 10% of instructors, according to her, are passionate about what they do. She believes that a school teacher must have a passion for inspiring students to learn and lead a good life. At one time in her career as a leader, she considered quitting, but she ultimately opted to keep going since she loves her work. Because of her strong leadership style, teachers have complained against her. Her colleagues believe she just pays attention to the students and overlooks the welfare of the faculty. But according to

U. Vanisri, teachers are adults who are informed and aware of the TSWREIS system and though at times it gets difficult it is their duty to go that extra mile for their students if they ever need it.

Towards the conclusion of the conversation, she remembered her school days and the motivating teachers. She said she was influenced by her outstanding teachers and chose to become a teacher as a profession.

She concluded by quoting Swami Vivekananda,

"We should be thankful to the people who give us the opportunity to do service," (V. Uppala, personal communication, January 31, 2023)

Smt. Kambhampati Sarada, Joint Secretary (Academic) TSWREIS

K. Sarada joined the society in 1995 as a Telugu instructor before becoming principal in 2008, Regional Coordinator (RCO) in 2019, and Joint Secretary in 2021. She has 25 years of experience and has never experienced caste- or gender-related discrimination.

She has also appreciated her spouse's contribution to the advancement of her career for helping her manage their two girls and for assisting her in pursuing her profession.

"My husband is my success story," (S. Kambhampati, personal communication, January 31, 2023).

Gender Aspect and Paradigm Shift in School Leadership With Roots in the Indian Family System

She has discussed on the changing paradigm of school leadership and the function of the teachers in the school as a Joint Secretary. K. Sarada expressed her concerns about the fact that only 10 to 20 percent of teachers and principals had the passion and ability to influence a larger audience.

She said that while female principals are sincere and uphold moral values, they lack the command necessary for leadership. As a result, they face disregard from their own teachers. Many principals need to develop their leadership skills. She also brought up one systemic issue: sometimes, teachers may make complaints about hard-working principals. Women leaders are more compassionate, courteous, and caring towards the school and better at handling problems. Male and female principals differ in their levels of patience.

She draws the upbringing of girls in the Indian family structure as one of the influencing factors of leadership attributes of women. Girls in majority of the Indian families are subjected to lot of societal pressure and are expected to behave or take only a specific path, be it professional or personal aspects. As a result, this early education significantly influences the operation approach of many female Principals, whether consciously or unintentionally. They are soft, respectful, caring about the school and have better problem-solving abilities.

She also mentioned that in her tenure, she witnessed many women teachers not opting for their promotion as they have to relocate and move far away from their homes. Sometimes, this pressure of being with the family is to an extent that the female teachers or leaders opt voluntary retirement from their services to care for their families.

MALE SCHOOL LEADERS' PERSPECTIVES ON FEMALE SCHOOL LEADERS

Mr. T. Anjaiah, Principal, Nalgonda District, TSWREIS

Mr. T. Anjaiah worked as an in-charge principal in both boys' and girls' schools for seven years after being hired as a post-graduate English teacher in 1995. Then, based on an interview and merit, he was promoted to Principal. He received the State's Best Principal Award. He comes from a marginalised community like his students and is a first-generation learner in his family.

During the interview, he admitted that in the start of his leadership career, the principals who belonged to the higher class discriminated him based on caste. Even in rare instances, his upper caste subordinate teachers also resisted following his orders. But as his career progressed, he worked hard to overcome those biases.

"Some people still think they are superior because of their birth in a certain family and caste," (T. Anjaiah, personal communication, January 31, 2023).

He served as the girl's school's male principal, allowing him to read about female teachers and comprehend their thought processes. He categorized female teachers into two groups: those who always believed that males were superior to women and those who believed that men always dominated women.

Female leaders from underrepresented groups experienced double inferiority because, on the one hand, they were from a marginalized community and, on the other, were viewed as women who were automatically less than men from a young age. Consequently, those individuals still carry their prejudice when they get to the position of leadership.

As a result, when these female teachers were promoted to leadership roles, they lacked the personality necessary to guide the team and demonstrate the power of leadership, or they harassed their male colleagues.

He stated that the school system grants equal authority to both male and female principals to issue a memo and inform the higher authority, so encouraging newly promoted female school leaders to exercise their power. He also addressed the disrespectful conduct of the male teachers towards the female principals.

He also told the success story of a female principal who, despite beginning her career with a sense of inferiority, eventually became the best Principal within five or six years and advanced to the Regional Coordinator (RCO) level. She has acted as a role model to many leaders over the years.

Indian and Black Women in Leadership: Similarities and Differences

The main difference between a female school principal in India and a black female school leader in the United States is the cultural context in which they operate.

In India, the school principal is likely to be perceived as someone who is expected to maintain traditional values and uphold established social norms. The school principal may also be expected to lead the community and serve as a bridge between the school and the local district.

Black woman school superintendents in the United States will likely bring different experiences and perspectives. She may be expected to be a role model for students of color and to bring a greater awareness of racial and cultural diversity to the school. The black woman leader may also be expected to be a leader in addressing social justice issues in the school and community.

A school superintendent's authority varies from state to state in the United States, but general terms, they are in charge of overseeing the daily operations of a school system, including staff management, hiring, budgeting, curriculum development and implementation, and student achievement. They may also be in charge of creating policy, resolving employee disputes, and speaking on behalf of the school district in the neighborhood.

Although gender bias is integral to every leadership position, more female teachers are recently applying for leadership positions in India. Several women hold leadership positions in the Telangana Tribal Welfare Residential Educational Institutions Society (TTWREIS) and the Telangana Social Welfare Residential Educational Institutions Society (TSWREIS). Finally, Indian society too is gradually accepting female leadership in the education, corporate and political sphere. There is an increase in the number of women-led initiatives and organizations. All of these initiatives and policies, as well as the changing attitudes of society, are working towards reducing gender bias in leadership roles and creating more equal opportunities for women and men to excel in their respective fields.

Limited influence: Female school principals may not have the same level of influence over decision-making as their male counterparts. This is mostly the result of the societal setup and expectations rather than individual capacities.

Social stigma: Female school principals may face social stigma from their peers, students, and parents. This can lead to a lack of respect and support, as well as a lack of confidence in their ability to lead effectively.

CONCLUSION

This chapter has explored the unique experiences of women in school leadership in India, and the United States, revealing the complexities of gender roles, the influence of cultural expectations, and the challenges faced by the black woman school Superintendents and female school Principals in Telangana Social Welfare Residential Educational Institutions Society (TSWREIS), India.

Number of Female School Leaders in India and the USA

Black woman school superintendents are very less in number and often they experience gender biases in terms of recruitment, promotion and pay scale.

"In these United States, persons of color represent 10.9% of the nation's teachers, 12.3% of the nation's principals, but only 2.2% of the nation's superintendents. Women and persons of color, nevertheless, go largely underrepresented as superintendents," (Brown, 2014, as cited in Alston, 2005. p. 675).

In order to improve the representation of Black woman school superintendents it is important to address systemic issues that contribute to their lack of representation. This entails putting into practice procedures that support inclusive hiring and promotion as well as offering equal compensation for equal effort. Therefore, it should be a top focus to address both unconscious and explicit biases. This can be accomplished through diversity and inclusion training for administrators and educators as well as leadership development programmes for prospective superintendents. Finally, it's critical to foster a supportive climate for Black female superintendents and give them the tools they need to succeed in their positions.

In the TSWREIS schools, women outnumber men in positions of leadership. Hence, there is no issue with the proportion of women in leadership positions (Women teachers in Indian schools outnumber men in 2019-20, 2021). Many of the school administrators are from scheduled castes (SC), but majority of female school Principals stated that they never experienced caste- or gender-based discrimination. Their challenges are the structural, personal, emotional, and balancing family and career. The situation at TSWREIS may not be extrapolated as the 'status quo' nevertheless it would serve as a good model to understand the operations of a gender-equitable ecosystem.

Women Leaders Negotiate Work-Family Responsibilities and Support System

Family support for Black woman school superintendents to balance personal and professional life is an area that needs much attention. Compared to the "younger" generation, women in the "older" generation felt more obligated to put their families first. For child care and household support, Black woman school leaders relied on their extended women's "kinship ties," whereas White administrators mostly looked for marital support (Loder, 2005).

TSWREIS's female school Principals acknowledged the existing support system, like their spouses and family members providing additional help with childcare or household tasks to balance their responsibilities (Chaudhuri, Park, & Kim, 2019). Nonetheless, many feel that with their long work hours and extended absence from the home, they are unable to fulfil their duties as a mother and wife.

It is true that many female school teachers may choose not to pursue leadership positions due to various reasons, such as family commitments, social stigmas, or the challenges of working in localities far from home. In addition, working in rural areas can pose additional challenges for female school leaders, including limited access to medical facilities and difficulties in establishing trust with students and parents due to more scrutiny and skepticism from community members and parents who may hold traditional ideas about leadership and gender roles.

These findings cannot be generalized due to the diversity of India's educational system. In the context of TSWREIS, many observations are unique. The results may not necessarily be applicable to other educational contexts. The roles of school principals are highly complex in the broader Indian setting due to issues with gender, hierarchy, systemic issues, and family systems and diverse socio-economic and cultural contexts across the nation.

Male Principals' Perspectives

The authors interviewed male principals to learn about their perspectives on being a school principal. Surprisingly, both male and female school leaders mentioned the same kinds of work challenges, such as long work hours, being away from the family for an extended period, and being unable to attend family social gatherings due to the high commitment required to serve as a principal of a residential school and the limited opportunity for taking longer leaves.

Freedom in Making Financial Decision

The power of school principals to make financial decisions is not gender-specific and largely depends on the institution's nature and policy framework. Typically, a school principal's decision-making authority is constrained by the funds provided by the school board or other Governing body. Any decisions made must receive their approval before being put into effect. Principals may occasionally be granted the right to approve certain expenses up to a specific amount without seeking board or governing body approval. In other situations, all financial choices need to be approved by the board or governing body.

The authority of black women school superintendents to make financial decisions in the United States varies based on the particular school district and the regulations that apply to that district. The school superintendent is ultimately responsible for making financial decisions, such as budgeting and purchasing decisions (Mason, 2016). The ability of school superintendents to make financial decisions may also be restricted or limited by state regulations.

In the framework of this study, school principals in TSWREIS are less free to make financial decisions than school superintendents in the United States. There is no gender-based biases in the financial decisions and remuneration levels of the TSWREIS school principals.

The Problem-Solving and Navigation Approach of Female School Administrators

Female school leaders foster collaboration and cooperation across gender lines. Leadership-focused behaviours that combine with gender perceptions give them ways to go around the educational system's inertia while fostering community trust and a love for children (Mythili, 2019) and encouraging open communication and dialogue with colleagues and stakeholders.

The study's participants argued that it is unlikely that male and female school administrators have equivalent problem-solving skills. Also, research has shown that male and female school administrators adopt different strategies (Izgar, 2008). Whereas women frequently choose a more collaborative and participatory attitude, men typically adopt a more task-oriented process. While women prefer to trust on the expertise of their team members when making decisions, males typically base their conclusions on their own experiences and knowledge (Noppe et. al., 2013). Female school leaders' love and dedication to their families, as well as how they have been negotiating in their personal lives, are reflected in their leadership style at the schools when dealing with the students, staff and other stakeholders.

Female School Administrators in India & USA: Policy Implications

The gender balance of village leadership had significantly changed since 1993, when India introduced gender quotas for elected positions on village councils (Gram Panchayats), according to several research findings. Female elected rural and municipality leaders in India increased from 5% in 1992 to over 40% by 2000 (Kaul & Sahni, 2009; Duflo & Topalova, 2004).

Governments and organisations have found it challenging to adopt gender-neutral and inclusive policies in the Indian educational system due to the complexity of the social structure and the country's large and diverse population.

With about half of all students in India being female, the country has achieved considerable progress in boosting women's participation in education. However, women are still underrepresented in leadership roles in schools. The underrepresentation of women in school leadership significantly impacts India's gender equality and educational standards.

Even in the case of a developed country like the USA, underrepresentation of women in leadership roles at schools is a persistent problem. To provide equitable opportunity for all, the gender gap in school leadership must be addressed because it has important policy implications.

This study presents a few policy recommendations for American black women administrators and Indian school administrators.

- **Increase awareness:** Conveying the significance of gender diversity in school leadership is the first step. Working with educators and school boards, policymakers should emphasize the advantages of having women in leadership positions, such as better academic results, higher teacher retention, and greater parental involvement.
- **Set targets:** Establish goals for increasing the number of women in leadership roles at the school level, and devise a system for tracking the progress. Targets should be ambitious but realistic and based on a comprehensive study of the actual circumstances.
- **Build capacity:** Offering training and development opportunities will help women who want to hold leadership roles strengthen their leadership abilities. Training in disciplines like financial management, strategic planning, and people management is part of this.
- **Remove barriers:** Aware of and addressing the policies and practices obstructing women from holding leadership positions. This covers problems including prejudice, lack of networking opportunities, and cultural biases.
- **Encourage mentorship:** It is important to encourage women who have achieved success in leadership roles in schools to mentor prospective female leaders. Women who want to succeed in their jobs can benefit greatly from mentoring because it can offer them excellent advice, support, and networking opportunities.
- Provide incentives: Policymakers could provide financial or other incentives to schools that meet gender diversity goals in order to encourage them to boost the representation of women in leadership roles.
- Targeted recruiting and retention initiatives for women in school leadership positions are a necessary policy implication. This may entail developing mentoring and leadership development programmes expressly for women as well as providing incentives and support for female candidates for leadership positions.
- We observe the gender roles evolving over time but in majority of communities, women still hold a key role in family responsibilities. While appreciating the cultural contexts, it is important to educate young boys and men on creating support system within the household that can give an incredible push to the women leaders, as evident from the case studies.

In conclusion, increasing the representation of women in school leadership positions in India and black women in the USA is crucial for promoting gender equality and improving the quality of education. By more women participating in the policy decision, raising awareness, setting targets, building capacity, removing barriers, encouraging mentorship, and providing incentives, policymakers can take steps towards achieving this goal.

Since school is the first organized community system that an individual is exposed to (after family), it is important that gender equity starts from school so that we raise future citizens who appreciate gender diversity and understand gender equity.

The interviews revealed a range of original findings from the voices of the female leaders who participated in the study. However, the literature research, policy analysis, and statistical analysis also drew attention to numerous omissions and silences, such as the lack of statistics that take gender into account or attention to gender issues in higher education policy.

Going forward, it is essential to continue to explore the various contexts in which women are leading in schools, to identify strategies to support female school leaders and to create more equitable and inclusive school cultures in different kinds of schools—primary/secondary, urban/rural, state/private and so on.

To conclude, it is evident that women bring their unique capabilities like empathy, compassion, dedication to work etc. to their role as a school leader and encouraging more women leaders is vital to create a sustainable and equitable education system. However, despite the progress made in recent years, women leaders still face challenges such as gender bias, societal norms, and lack of support. To overcome these challenges, creating a conducive environment that encourages and supports women leaders to excel in their roles is crucial.

REFERENCES

Alston, J. (2005). Tempered radicals and servant leaders: Black females persevering in the superintendency. *Educational Administration Quarterly*, *41*(4), 675–688. doi:10.1177/0013161X04274275

Bernal, C., Monosov, N., Stencler, A., Lajoie, A., Raigoza, A., & Akhavan, N. (2017). Gender Bias within the Superintendency: A Comparative Study. *Journal of School Administration Research and Development*, *2*(1), 42–52. doi:10.32674/jsard.v2i1.1925

Brown, A. R. (2014). The recruitment and retention of African American women as public school superintendents. *Journal of Black Studies*, *45*(6), 573–593. doi:10.1177/0021934714542157

Chaudhuri, S., Park, S., & Kim, S. (2019). The changing landscape of women's leadership in India and Korea from cultural and generational perspectives. *Human Resource Development Review*, *18*(1), 16–46. doi:10.1177/1534484318809753

Coleman, M. (2005). Gender and Secondary School Leadership. *International Studies in Educational Administration*, *33*(2).

Duflo, E., & Topalova, P. (2004). *Unappreciated service: Performance, perceptions, and women leaders in India. Manuscript.* Department of Economics, Massachusetts Institute of Technology.

Gardiner, M. E., Enomoto, E., & Grogan, M. (2000). *Coloring outside the lines: Mentoring women into school leadership.* Suny Press.

Ghurye, G. S. (1980). *The scheduled tribes of India.* Transaction Publishers.

Government of Telangana Social Welfare Residential Educational Institutions Society (TSWREIS). (n.d.). *Homepage.* TSWREIS. https://www.tswreis.ac.in/

Hammond, Z. (2018). Culturally Responsive Teaching Puts Rigor at the Center: Q&A with Zaretta Hammond. *Learning Professional*, *39*(5), 40–43.

Herring, L. N. (2007). *First African-American female school superintendent in Georgia: Reflections from the field to the forefront.* Georgia Southern University.

Izgar, H. (2008). Headteachers' leadership Behavior And Problem-Solving Skills: A Comparative Study. *Social Behavior and Personality*, *36*(4), 535–548. doi:10.2224bp.2008.36.4.535

Johnsrud, L. K. (1991). Mentoring between academic women: The capacity for interdependence. *Initiatives*, *54*(3), 7–17.

Karunakar, B. (2019). Telangana Social Welfare Residential Educational Institutions Society: Programs and Facilities Available for Students Empowerment. *Educational Quest-An International Journal of Education and Applied Social Sciences*, *10*(3), 125–133. doi:10.30954/2230-7311.3.2019.2

Kaul, S., & Sahni, S. (2009). Study on the participation of women in Panchayati Raj Institution. *Studies on Home and Community Science*, *3*(1), 29–38. doi:10.1080/09737189.2009.11885273

Loder, T. L. (2005). Women administrators negotiate work-family conflicts in changing times: An intergenerational perspective. *Educational Administration Quarterly*, *41*(5), 741–776. doi:10.1177/0013161X04273847

Mason, P. A. (2016). *The lived experiences of African American female superintendents* [Doctoral dissertation, Ohio University].

Ministry of Education. (2021). *Union Education Minister releases Report on United District Information System for Education Plus (UDISE+) 2019-20*. Ministry of Education. https://pib.gov.in/PressReleasePage.aspx?PRID=1731860

Msila, V. (2013). Obstacles and opportunities in women school leadership: A literature study. *International Journal of Educational Sciences*, *5*(4), 463–470. doi:10.1080/09751122.2013.11890108

Mythili, N. (2017). Representation of women in school leadership positions in India. *NUEPA Occasional Paper, 51*.

Mythili, N. (2019). Quest for success: Ladder of school leadership of women in India. *Social Change*, *49*(1), 114–131. doi:10.1177/0049085718821748

Noppe, R., Yager, S., Webb, C., & Sheng, B. (2013). Decision-Making and Problem-Solving Practices of Superintendents Confronted by District Dilemmas. *The International Journal of Educational Leadership Preparation*, *8*(1), 103–120.

Peters, A. (2010). Elements of successful mentoring of a female school leader. *Leadership and Policy in Schools*, *9*(1), 108–129. doi:10.1080/15700760903026755

Pruthi, R. K. (Ed.). (2004). *Indian caste system*. Discovery Publishing House.

Pulse. (2019). *Who is a 'woman of colour'?* [post]. LinkedIn. https://www.linkedin.com/pulse/who-woman-colour-winitha-michelle-bonney/

Rosenberg, M. (2013, April 29). *Leaning in? Women superintendents making mark in public education*. New York State School Board Association. https://www.nyssba.org/news/2013/04/26/on-board-online-april-29-2013/leaning-in-women-superintendents-making-mark-in-public-education/

Sachs, J., & Blackmore, J. (1998). You never show you can't cope: Women in school leadership roles managing their emotions. *Gender and Education*, *10*(3), 265–279. doi:10.1080/09540259820899

School Superintendent Demographics And Statistics In The US. (n.d.). Zippia. https://www.zippia.com/school-superintendent-jobs/demographics/

Spillane, J. P. (2004). Educational leadership. *Educational Evaluation and Policy Analysis, 26*(2), 169–172. doi:10.3102/01623737026002169

Superville, D. R. (2016, Dec 30). *Few women run the nation's school districts. Why?* PBS News Hours. https://www.pbs.org/newshour/education/women-run-nations-school-districts

Teacher Demographics And Statistics In The US. (n.d.). Zippia. https://www.zippia.com/teacher-jobs/demographics/

The University of Texas. (n.d.). *The Impact of Gender on the Role of Superintendent*. UTPB. https://online.utpb.edu/about-us/articles/education/the-impact-of-gender-on-the-role-of-superintendent/

Tulshyan, R. (2023, April 07). *How Colorism Affects Women at Work*. Harvard Business Review. https://hbr.org/2023/04/how-colorism-affects-women-at-work

Webb, T. D. (2022). *Where are all the African-American Women Superintendents in California, Oregon, and Washington State?* [Doctoral dissertation, University of the Pacific].

Will, M. (2017). Study: Black students more likely to graduate if they have one black teacher. *Education Week*.

Money Control. (2021). *Women teachers in Indian schools outnumber men in 2019-20*. Money Control. https://www.moneycontrol.com/. https://www.moneycontrol.com/news/india/women-teachers-in-indian-schools-outnumber-men-in-2019-20-shows-udise-report-7124421.html

ADDITIONAL READING

Central Board of Secondary Education. (2020). In Persuit of Excellence: A Handbook for Principals. The Secretary, Central Board of Secondary Education, Shiksha Kendra.

Deshpande, M. S. (2010). History of the Indian caste system and its impact on India today. *SSIR*. https://ssir.org/articles/entry/the_concrete_ceiling

Flandro, C. (2023). Madam Superintendent: More women are becoming education leaders but are still underrepresented. *Idahoednews*. https://www.idahoednews.org/news/madame-superintendent-more-women-are-becoming-education-leaders-but-are-still-underrepresented/

Mythili, N. (2019). Legitimisation of women school leaders in India. *Contemporary Education Dialogue, 16*(1), 54–83. doi:10.1177/0973184918804396

National Portal of India. (n.d.). *Policy*. NPI. https://www.india.gov.in/my-government/documents/policy

Organizational Structure. (n.d.). TSWREIS. https://www.tswreis.ac.in/organizationStructure.php

Sreeradha, B. (2018). *Women leaders are still missing at top institutes.* https://economictimes.indiatimes.com/. https://economictimes.indiatimes.com/news/company/corporate-trends/women-leaders-are-still-missing-at-top-institutes/articleshow/67317300.cms?from=mdr

THOMAS. G. E. (2020). *Where Are All the Women Superintendents?* aasa.org. https://aasa.org/school-administratorarticle.aspx?id=14492

KEY TERMS AND DEFINITIONS

School Administrator: A administrator in school could be a Principal, Vice Principal, Dean, Head of Department, or other administrative roles.

Mentoring: mentoring is a process of providing guidance and support to someone, usually a person or someone with less experience, in order to support that person to grow/ perform better/ solve problem.

Spirituality: Developing a sense of our inner potential, realising our interconnectedness with others, and establishing a connection to something more than ourselves are all spiritual practises. Meditation, prayer, yoga, mindfulness, and contemplation are a few examples of the disciplines that can be used. It's frequently regarded as a means to find serenity while expressing love and respect for life.

Swami Vivekananda: He was an Indian Hindu monk who was a philosopher, writer, religious instructor, and the chief devotee of the Indian mystic Ramakrishna.

Race: Race is a social construct that is used to categorize people based on physical and cultural characteristics such as skin color, ancestry, language, and nationality. Race is not determined by any scientific or biological measure and is instead based on societal perceptions and social norms.

Sexism: sexism is bias or discrimination based on gender. It is an oppressive practice that favours one gender over the other, reinforces stereotypes, and objects to the other gender.

Chapter 6
An Integrated Framework for Leadership:
The Case of Higher Education

Narayan Tiwari
Crown Institute of Higher Education, Australia

Wayne Fallon
https://orcid.org/0000-0001-5091-6824
Western Sydney University, Australia

Jayne Bye
Western Sydney University, Australia

ABSTRACT

In the turbulent and volatile operating environment of Australia's higher education sector, leadership is critical in responding to institutional challenges. This chapter presents a dynamic integrated framework for leadership that can support leaders in these institutions and, potentially, other organisations as well. The chapter describes the outcomes of a Delphi study that sought to uncover areas of consensus about leadership, among leaders and academics across the sector. The study revealed 15 distinct elements of leadership, and these were found to fall into three separate but interrelated groups or domains of leadership: behaviours, mindsets, and skills. Together, these domains are claimed to provide an appropriate and practical representation of effective leadership in higher education. The dynamic integration of these domains and elements of leadership into an interrelated tripartite arrangement, a framework for leadership, is argued to represent a new approach to understanding the leadership phenomenon.

INTRODUCTION

Leadership is a confounding and complex phenomenon, often marked by a confusing and sometimes contradictory myriad of different theories and diverse explanations (Mant, 2010). A single universal

DOI: 10.4018/978-1-6684-8257-5.ch006

explanation of leadership remains elusive, not least because its complexity and confusion can be tempered, or even tainted, by subjective elements of what is claimed as leadership (Ingram & Cangemi, 2012). Leadership is nonetheless crucial for the success of large and complex organisations like higher education institutions (HEIs) generally, and universities more specifically (Fitzmaurice, 2013). Leading and managing these institutions effectively often requires distinct understandings and unique skills due to their complicated missions, dynamics, structures and values (Ekman et al., 2018). In the uncertain and volatile operating environments of contemporary higher education (HE), leadership usually plays a critical role in ensuring prompt, effective and agile responses to changes in the sector. Leadership becomes an intense topic of analysis in such situations (Lacy et al., 2017, Betts, 2022).

Using a Delphi study of Australian HEIs as the context, this chapter presents a dynamic integrated Framework for Leadership that can support leadership functions in higher education institutions and, potentially, other organisations. The chapter describes the outcomes of the study that sought consensus among leaders and followers of HEIs, from across the sector. The study focused on the challenges of leadership in turbulent operating environments, without concentrating on any particular type of turbulence. Encompassing leadership mindsets, skills and behaviours, the resultant Framework for Leadership discussed in this chapter represents the distillation and analysis of the data from the Delphi study.

The chapter first details the characteristics of turbulence in contemporary higher education operating environments. It then discusses the challenges of leading in these environments and details the key outcomes of the Delphi study that led to the development of the Framework for Leadership. The elements of the Framework are then explained. The chapter concludes by contemplating the applications of the Framework in contemporary settings. The premise of this chapter, and the Framework more particularly, is that leaders need to be able to strategically integrate a variety of different leadership aspects and elements into their practice (Benmira & Agboola, 2021; Jones et al., 2012) if they are to optimise their leadership capacities.

COMPLEXITY OF LEADERSHIP IN HIGHER EDUCATION

Most of Australia's 42 universities are public institutions, with only 5 private universities. While there is a larger number of non-university higher education providers (NUHEPs) in Australia, mostly operating as private for-profit institutions, these account for only 10% of student enrolments, though the number of enrolments at NUHEPs is slated to increase (TEQSA, 2019). Public universities were generally established with a traditional collegial leadership model, but later moved to a more contemporary managerialist model due to the significant impact of neoliberalism on the sector since the 1980s. The overtly profit-driven non-university higher education providers, on the other hand, were established more explicitly in a prevailing commercially focused economic environment and had thus generally adopted a corporate managerialist model (Bryman, 2007). Perhaps understandably, therefore, leadership practices can differ significantly between institutions.

Not only is leadership in HE claimed to be unique relative to other organisations (Jarrett & Newton, 2020), but leadership itself is also often ambiguous and contested (Juntrasook, 2014). This points to the depth and breadth of challenges faced by HE leaders. Institutions operate in multifaceted environments which are often influenced by a range of different and sometimes conflicting factors. These can include a vast array of issues including, for example, advances in technology, globalisation and intensive institutional competition driven to some extent by student demands and expectations which can have resultant impacts on the academic workforce.

Another factor that adds further complexity to leadership in HE is the variety of stakeholders across the sector. These include students, faculty members, professional staff, regulatory bodies, government and, increasingly, industry partners and employers. HE leaders would generally be expected to consider the needs of all stakeholders, often calling for variable and varying approaches to leading and managing (Sathye, 2004). This heightened intricacy around leadership in HE (Kezar & Holcombe, 2017) indicates that institutions will often need to adjust their operations to remain aligned with their continuously shifting operating environments. In addition, there is a growing complexity in what might be considered the core business of higher education, as institutions turn their attention to international enrolments, offshore-focused transnational education, micro-credentials and executive education, as well as industry-supported in addition to government-funded research.

Kenny (2009) argues that contemporary HEIs are unable to operate effectively as businesses because they need flexible and responsive leadership approaches that are inclusive of frontline academics, in addition to the full range of stakeholder perspectives. However, there is a view that academics, as a key stakeholder group in HEIs, often do not feel part of the decision-making process in institutions (Ndu & Anagbogu, 2007). This may be because the hierarchical leadership structures widely adopted by HEIs are usually too rigid and inflexible to be inclusive (Jones et al., 2012) or to effectively meet the needs of academics who are at times considered more difficult to lead than other public servants (Deem, 2004). Hierarchical managerialism, largely practiced in HEIs, has also increased the gap between academics and management by diminishing academic autonomy (Jones et al., 2012) as faculty seem to experience less academic freedom (Bentley et al., 2013). It is claimed that academics increasingly work in environments where they are told what to teach, how to teach, what research to conduct and where to publish (Burnes et al., 2014). This has been argued to create tensions in institutions.

However, confidence in leadership approaches that rely heavily on hierarchical structures has diminished (Jones et al., 2014), with a sense that contemporary HEIs may be driven to consider discarding the predominantly hierarchical managerial structures in favour of more collaborative and participative approaches to leadership (Jones et al., 2012). The nature and scope of change in HE suggests a need for a more considered or reflective approach to leadership, beyond managerialism, to take account of the vast and varied range of complex interests and trends.

Turbulent Operating Environments of Higher Education

Turbulence occurs when changes are unexpected, uncertain and volatile (Danneels & Sethi, 2011). Such environments can exist in any industry and in almost any situation. Digitisation, technology and climate change, for example, contribute to turbulent operating environments in many industries, with the future of work changing considerably as younger generations enter the workplace with more demanding expectations and, since the COVID-19 pandemic, as employees argue for more flexible working conditions.

Most HEIs have experienced significant turbulence as a result of an apparently endless stream of changes, especially in the last two decades (Croucher & Lacy, 2020). The turbulence in the sector has therefore significantly impacted institutions and how they are led and managed (Hassan et al., 2018). The following discussion identifies and discusses six key characteristics of the turbulence in the sector, indicating some of the challenges leaders are often called upon to navigate. These challenges involve managing tensions between managerialism and collegial approaches to leading and managing, keeping pace with changing technologies and new education delivery methods, confronting intense institutional competition, responding to changing student expectations, handling difficult workforce issues and managing institutional reorganisations.

Managing Tensions Between Managerialism and Collegiality

Academics and to a lesser extent other stakeholders in the sector might generally be thought to support collegial approaches to leadership, with a concern that managerialism has the potential to impede the primary purpose of universities to deliver quality education. This sentiment is consistent with critics of managerialism in HE (Klikauer, 2013). However, a contrary view is that a corporate-style hierarchical approach can be essential for managing risk and making difficult decisions in a fiscally constrained environment (Fullan & Scott, 2009). Also, traditional collegial leadership practices have been argued to be insufficient for and incompatible with generating the strategic direction of a contemporary institution because, with less accountable structures, collegiality has the potential to allow individual imperatives to take precedence over institutional goals (Shattock, 2010). Collegial decision-making can also restrict innovation and change (Fullan & Scott, 2009) and, in times of uncertainty, that approach can inhibit leaders who may be required to make difficult decisions quickly. For these reasons, it is said, collegial decision-making may not always be possible in higher education.

Tight (2014) suggested that a balance of managerialist and collegial approaches is needed to effectively and strategically lead and manage contemporary HEIs. This is because both have a role to play, as leading and managing in difficult times can require managerial directions as well as collegial practices. However, achieving the necessary balance can be challenging because it may not always be apparent when and how collegial components should be incorporated and when more hierarchical managerialist approaches are needed.

Keeping Pace With Changing Technologies and New Delivery Models

Following the sector's relatively comfortable history with innovative education delivery models such as blended learning and work integrated learning, the COVID-19 pandemic and the sector's subsequent urgent responses to generative artificial intelligence platforms have highlighted the importance of modern technology in delivering higher education. Technology extended and enhanced delivery and student engagement models, with moves to deliver new opportunities for learners in the form of short courses such as undergraduate and postgraduate sub-degree programs, micro-credentials and executive programs. During the early stage of the COVID-19 pandemic institutions were encouraged and incentivised to develop their capabilities to deliver courses online, even to offshore students (Croucher & Lacy, 2020). These developments have had a lasting impact on traditional attitudes to delivery and modes of student engagement, creating challenges for institutions and their leaders as they work to keep pace with fast-changing technologies and new delivery models demanded by new generations of learners.

Confronting Intense Competition

Before the COVID-19 pandemic approximately one-quarter of enrolments at Australian universities were international students (TEQSA, 2019). This raised concerns that any downturn in the international education market could cause financial stress for institutions, given the high levels of revenue derived from that market (Powell, 2018). The ongoing impact of the pandemic meant institutions needed to diversify their courses, expand their sources of students, and adapt and diversify flexible modes of delivery such as hybrid, online, offline and blended approaches, to cater for the growing demands of the onshore and offshore markets. The competition for both domestic and international students became more strident (Calderon, 2020). This was in addition to changes to the competitive landscape where traditional competitor nations for international students, such as the United States and United Kingdom, were joined by Canada, China, Singapore, Hong Kong and Malaysia in competing for the international student market (Ernst & Young, 2018). Higher education leaders have therefore been called upon to strategically manage the multifaceted increased competition in the sector to ensure institutional sustainability.

Responding to Changing Student Expectations

Fast-changing technological innovations have heightened the expectations of new generations of students whose needs and demands shift with their increased mobility in a globalised and digitally connected world. Students can sometimes expect to switch seamlessly between on-campus, blended and online modes of study, creating an increased need for institutions to be more flexible and provide a choice of study options and opportunities. This is compounded by new players in higher education, in addition to the now established Massive Open Online Course (MOOC) providers. The new niche providers, often representing non-traditional competitors in higher education, include hi-tech or tech-driven corporations and industry associations which offer a selection of industry-aligned, employment-focused short courses that often concentrate on the workplace skills and attributes demanded by employers. As learners opt for these alternative non-traditional, but credible, cheaper and more flexible offerings (Dewar, 2017; Eassom, 2016), higher education institutions and their leaders are challenged to realistically cater for these shifting and diverse needs and wants of what is their traditional client base.

Handling Difficult Workforce Issues

Connell (2019) has claimed that almost two-thirds of undergraduate teaching is performed by casual academics, usually under insecure work conditions. By their status, they have limited leadership opportunities, and the high ratio of casual to permanent faculty has increased the administrative workload for permanent academics, resulting in workload intensification and less scope to be involved in leadership activities. This can contribute to academic staff feeling left out of institutional decision-making (Crawford & Germov, 2015) and, by limiting leadership succession planning, the practice fails to recognise the leadership potential of early- and mid-career academics and researchers (Loomes et al., 2019).

The issue of casualisation involves consideration of the perspectives of a range of stakeholders, including institutions, academics and, in some cases, unions. For this reason, perhaps, industrial relations conflicts in the higher education sector are not uncommon. With a history of strong involvement and influence from the relevant unions, both the Fair Work Commission and the courts have been called upon in recent years to adjudicate on disputes between institutions and academics. Issues have involved an institution's ability to dismiss an academic for misconduct (ABC, 2019), a university's right to terminate an enterprise agreement (Patty, 2017) and claims of "wage theft" as casual academics are not adequately paid for work performed (Cahill, 2020). It has been argued that changes in the higher education workplace are needed (Coleman, 2019; Lacy et al., 2017), with claims that the prevailing industrial awards inhibit institutional flexibility and therefore impede institutions and leaders from driving change in challenging times.

Managing Institutional Reorganisations, Mergers, and Alliances

Institutional reorganisations have been claimed to be a familiar or even routine feature of higher education (Davis, 2021; Dewar 2017). During the early years of the COVID-19 pandemic, for example, many institutions streamlined teaching programs and introduced academic redundancy strategies, often in response to the decline in international student numbers (Garnder et al., 2020). Against a backdrop of unstable government funding, the sector has also experienced a history of campus closures and relocations (Davis, 2017), campus realignments among institutions (Ernst & Young, 2018), organisational alliances for research and teaching efficiencies (Davis, 2017), and even proposals for university mergers (Hare, 2022). A sense of the long-term unsettling in the sector can perhaps be gained from the somewhat extreme speculation about the existence of only ten higher education institutions worldwide by 2070 (Watters, 2013). These types of strategic and operational challenges for institutional leaders become even more pronounced against the already turbulent milieu of higher education in Australia.

Leading in an Era of Uncertainty

In many organisational contexts, the nature of uncertainty can be both multi-layered and inter-connected, requiring a flexible, dynamic, open and responsive approach to leadership (Bennett, 2017). However, such approaches to leadership are said to be rare in the higher education sector, where managerialist approaches to leadership dominate (Connell, 2019). Decisions are often made by a select few in the upper hierarchy of the institution, with little involvement from other workers (Tight, 2014). This is despite the well-established critiques of managerialist approaches in higher education (eg, Klikauer, 2013) which call for better attention to long-held academic ideals of collaboration and collegiality. Nonetheless, even though managerialism has been recognised as somewhat ineffective and inflexible in times of change (Coleman, 2019), more collaborative and participative approaches to leadership, which centre on consensus, are also limited as potential solutions for the challenges facing contemporary HE leaders (Sahlin, 2012).

Among calls for systemic change to the Australian higher education sector (Betts, 2022; Ernst & Young, 2018), researchers and commentators have pointed to the need for fundamental changes to the way institutions are led and managed (Sims, 2020). Specifically, the calls are for a more relational approach to leadership, to incorporate more collaborative and participative perspectives that can accommodate dynamic interrelationships between leaders and followers (Davis & Jones, 2014). Such process-based relationships recognise the perspectives of both leaders and followers as integral to contemporary leadership, which is thus characterised as a process in which all workers in the institution work together to accomplish common goals (Komives et al., 2007).

The research on which this chapter is based involved a mixed method study of Australia's university and non-university higher education sector, to understand the level of consensus among institutional leaders and frontline academics about leadership challenges and approaches. After two rounds of a Delphi survey, the data indicated a more relational approach was a fundamental necessity for leaders to address the challenges pervading the sector. The data also indicated that focusing on just one aspect of leadership was unlikely to adequately deal with the complexities of the challenges faced by institutional leaders. These findings informed the premise of this chapter, that neither managerialist nor collegial approaches to leadership are alone sufficient in volatile and turbulent operating environments. Aligning with other research (eg, Benmira & Agboola, 2021; Jones et al., 2012), the data highlights the importance of leaders integrating a variety of different leadership aspects and elements into their practice.

Outcomes of the Delphi Study: The Elements of Leadership

While the Delphi approach can trace its origins to attempts at finding consensus among experts about forecasting the future and establishing a chronology of technological events and to judge when events might occur, the Delphi method of research has more recently been successfully designed for and adopted in business research (Weaver & Timothy 1971; Brady, 2005; Green, 2014). The Delphi approach to data collection and analysis is now well recognised as a legitimate and useful tool in understanding business and management issues (Holey et al., 2007; Giannarou & Zervas, 2014; Olsen et al., 2021). In this study of leadership in HE, the Delphi data showed several areas of agreement among leaders and academics around key aspects of leadership. In the analysis of the data, 15 distinct, yet interrelated, elements of leadership were distilled from the consensus among leaders and academics. These elements of leadership are outlined below.

1. Resilience

This is the capacity of leaders to adapt successfully to turbulence that could represent threats to the institution (Walker, 2019). Resilient leaders are able to create a strong institutional culture that has the capacity to pivot and adapt to sudden upheavals in the operating environment (Patterson et al., 2009). The Delphi data indicated resilience could entail leaders showing optimism and being innovative and responsive, and encouraging innovation in finding new avenues for addressing challenges in higher education.

2. Inclusiveness

Being inclusive is the capacity of leaders to genuinely consider followers' contributions and to facilitate meaningful team interactions. According to Komives et al. (2007), to be inclusive, institutional leaders need to know themselves and others, be open to differences and value all perspectives. While the Delphi data highlighted the importance of inclusiveness and consultation, tokenistic approaches to consultation have the potential to infuriate academics and create further tensions. Also, collegial leadership approaches which are supportive and inclusive can be more effective in an uncertain environment.

3. Transparency

This is defined as leaders being open and communicative, and recognising the importance of trust (Jongbloed et al., 2018). The data suggested transparency can be established from developing relationships with and being supportive of followers, showing trust and confidence in them, and from trying to understand their issues, appreciate their ideas and recognising their contributions. The Delphi data indicated the need for leaders to build transparency and trust to help counter the perceived culture of secrecy in the sector, fuelled to some extent by the increased surveillance of academics by leaders (see also Connell, 2019) and by the tokenistic approach to consultation.

An Integrated Framework for Leadership

4. Accountability

This anticipates that leaders should be answerable for their decisions, and that they lay down and follow procedural paths for all to follow (Stensaker & Harvey, 2010). The Delphi data suggested that having greater accountability systems and processes in place are instrumental in transforming the way leaders lead, manage and motivate teams (see also Worrall, 2013). Accountability can also extend to explicit and implicit demands and expectations from governments and the general public, particularly in the case of public institutions. Also, the appointment of short-term leaders who often focus on short-term gains was widely perceived as lacking accountability: such 'short-termism' in the sector creates tensions, participants said, at least by eroding long-term institutional visions.

5. Flexibility

Flexibility enables HE leaders to understand the changing, even challenging, environment and adapt their approaches to respond to a myriad of different situations (Bryman, 2007). The Delphi data highlighted the need for leaders to be able to capitalise on evolving trends in the sector, and to continually align and realign available resources with objectives. This can require a balanced approach, according to participants, when it may be necessary for leaders to draw on aspects of both collegiality and managerialism at different times.

6. Entrepreneurial

Entrepreneurialism can be understood to turn challenges into opportunities which, in the HE context, can create social and economic value for the institution. The entrepreneurial element of leadership has been argued to be vital for innovation and growth (Secundo et al., 2015). While it has been suggested that higher education institutions are often resistant to change (Dyer & Dyer, 2017), the Delphi data indicated leaders require entrepreneurial thinking to be able to understand how to turn turbulence in the sector into opportunities for their institutions.

7. Collaborative

The collaborative element of leadership requires leaders to manage relationships with others both within and outside the organisation. Collaborative thinking generally relies on interpersonal capabilities such as emotional intelligence, respect, authenticity, honesty, flexibility, listening, accountability, and the ability to deal with conflict (Paxton & Van, 2015). Participants in the study noted that contemporary leaders need to think as collaborators to promote and establish a participative culture in their institutions. Specifically, collaborative thinking enables collegial practices that can promote effective succession planning, which was generally seen by participants to be a problem in the sector.

8. Visionary

While the visionary element of leadership generally involves formulating a long-term vision for the institution (Maidique & Hiller, 2018), the data indicated that visionary thinking can also enable innovation and creativity, and can assist leaders to counter the "short-termism" which participants had identified.

There was a sense that senior leaders were often not inclined to implement long-term plans, but tended to focus on their own short-term key performance indicators. Having visionary leaders can allow institutions to focus on promoting their long-term sustainability. Given the calls for systemic change in higher education (Connell, 2019), visionary thinking from leaders was considered essential for developing and communicating future possibilities for institutions and the sector.

9. Reflective

Reflective leaders focus on managing the self, respecting the past, and critically reviewing the past to formulate future practice (Gosling & Mintzberg, 2003). Such thoughtful thinking is at the core of the reflective element of leadership (Butler, 2006). The data indicated that leaders can be required to act boldly or to make extraordinary decisions during uncertain times, and this can be taken to support the need for a reflective capability among leaders. They need to be active listeners, open to change, with the ability to recognise and acknowledge followers' concerns and feelings.

10. Action-oriented

Especially when managing complex and changing contexts, leaders are generally required to combine reflection (thoughtful thinking) with action (practical doing). A blend of action and reflection is thus necessary (Butler, 2006). Leaders and academics in the study agreed that the rigid systems in many higher education institutions, particularly in public universities, are generally resistant to change, and this can be understood to emphasise the importance of action-oriented thinking in higher education leadership.

11. Interpersonal

Interpersonal capabilities of leaders include emotional intelligence, listening and communication skills, and the ability to influence others (Mencl et al., 2016). The Delphi data suggested that effective communication can be vital in maintaining a collegial environment. Other interpersonal capabilities include understanding followers' needs, teamwork, the capacity to motivate others, maintaining trusting relationships, winning the trust of others, and establishing and maintaining networks.

12. Advocacy

The advocacy element refers to a leader's ability to persuade others to support that leader's point of view (Crawford et al., 2014). The data suggested that a leader's advocacy capabilities need to be exercised both within and outside the institution. Advocacy is important in persuading and motivating others in the institution, especially when dealing with the sector's workforce issues. In addition, faced with constantly changing HE policy settings, reduced funding and increased accountability measures, the advocacy element of leadership is important in dealing with government and regulatory bodies. While Zaglas (2021) highlighted the importance of the advocacy role in HE leadership, the Delphi research data indicated that there are increased pressures on HE leaders to establish a negotiating culture within their institutions and with external stakeholders.

13. Strategic

Being strategic encompasses the ability to anticipate challenges, adapt in changing environments, deal with complexity and uncertainty, and to be visionary and flexible in response to change (Marshall, 2006). Leadership in contemporary HE demands strategic vision, especially in times of change (Lacy et al., 2017). According to the Delphi data the strategic element of leadership is important in managing staffing issues and ensuring the financial success of the institution (see also Simon & Lacava, 2008). Such capabilities can contribute to leaders identifying potential opportunities, as well as understanding and interpreting external environments that can influence the success of the institution.

14. Business-oriented

The business-oriented element of leadership includes the ability to manage resources efficiently in a constrained environment (Mumford et al., 2007), to be less risk-averse and to be entrepreneurial. The Delphi data indicated that HE leaders need a balance of business experience as well as sector knowledge, which also suggests the importance of business management capabilities.

15. Facilitative

The facilitative element of leadership emphasises the need for leaders to be participative and inclusive, and to be able to create environments that allow others to lead and be more effective (Mrig & Sanaghan, 2017). Higher education leaders need to be effective facilitators to engender genuine consultation processes in the institution. The data indicated that poor facilitation by leaders can inhibit inclusivity and can create tensions between leaders and academics which can then impede collegiality. To support the importance of the facilitative element of leadership, the Delphi data also suggested that hard managerial practices may not be effective in the HE context as academics seem less responsive to that approach.

A Dynamic Integrated Framework for Leadership

By drawing on the Delphi data from higher education leaders and academics, and incorporating insights from the literature on these topics, the 15 elements of leadership uncovered in the analysis were found to fall into three separate but interrelated groups. These groups are referred to as domains of leadership, namely behaviours, mindsets and skills. Each of these three domains were found to consist of five of the elements of leadership, as outlined in Table 1.

Together, these behaviours, mindsets and skills, as the three domains of leadership, are argued to provide an appropriate and practical representation of the necessary elements of effective leadership in higher education. A dynamic integration of these elements of leadership in this way can be understood to inform an interrelated tripartite arrangement, which arguably represents a new approach to understanding leadership. Figure 1 depicts the interrelated tripartite arrangement of these three domains, and of the 15 identified elements of leadership. The tripartite arrangement is argued to show how the three domains are interconnected, and the suggestion is that, depending on the context, leaders may need to draw on any combination of elements from each of these domains to lead and manage in any situation.

Table 1. Domains and elements of leadership

BEHAVIOURS	MINDSETS	SKILLS
Resilience	Entrepreneurial	Interpersonal
Inclusiveness	Collaborative	Advocacy
Transparency	Visionary	Strategic
Accountability	Reflective	Business-oriented
Flexibility	Action-oriented	Facilitative

Figure 1. Dynamic integrated framework for leadership

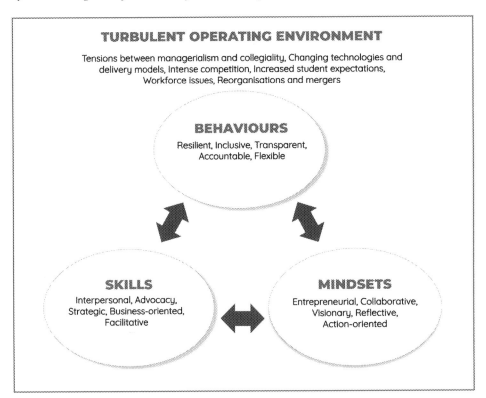

In this dynamic and integrated Framework, leadership behaviours, mindsets and skills influence each other. The bidirectional arrows in the Framework emphasise the interconnected relationships between the domains, and the influential but still independent dynamic nature of these domains point to how any change can influence or be influenced by the other domains. This responsiveness allows for flexibility in the behaviours, mindsets and skills that might be put into action by any leader in any situation, according to the context. In any given situation, leaders may therefore use different combinations of the elements to address the situation. In this way, the various elements that make up the domains of leadership behaviours, mindsets and skills flexibly equip leaders with a range of responses that can support them

An Integrated Framework for Leadership

to effectively and strategically consider, or reflect on, how to best respond to and manage turbulence in their institution and in the wider context of higher education.

The dynamic integrated Framework for Leadership is claimed to offer an appropriate and useful mechanism for achieving the type of leadership response considered necessary in turbulent environments. The Framework thus provides a new way of thinking about, understanding and enacting leadership in contemporary contexts which require a wider repertoire of solutions than managerialism or even collegial approaches to leadership have traditionally offered.

The interrelated and dynamic arrangement of the domains recognises leadership to be a complex, vibrant, interactive process, consistent with the views of Winkler (2010). The Framework also recognises that future leadership approaches may need to integrate a variety of different aspects of leadership, because simplistically focusing on one aspect is unlikely to effectively address the full complexity of the leadership phenomenon.

To understand the integrated nature of the relationship between the domains, leadership behaviours, for example, can be understood to be guided, influenced and promoted by leadership mindsets; and the mindsets, in turn, can help to develop and enhance appropriate leadership skills. Likewise, skills can continuously refine leaders' mindsets and behaviours, and enable them to respond to changeable circumstances flexibly and effectively. Similarly, leadership skills can influence leadership behaviours (Hopp & Pruschak, 2020) and leadership mindsets equip leaders to tackle complex leadership challenges (Jeanes, 2021) while leadership behaviours can be determined by situational aspects, encompassing the context which could include followers, as well as the internal and external environments (Winkler, 2010). The suggestion here is that leadership in a contemporary HE context requires leaders to develop a sense of enacting or engaging a combination of leadership behaviours, mindsets and skills.

The importance of leadership behaviours, mindsets and skills is recognised in the wider literature (Jeanes, 2021; Winkler, 2010). At present, however, no model or framework for leadership explicitly integrates multiple aspects of leadership such as the behaviour, mindset and skill domains identified in this research. Accordingly, this practical tripartite Framework that encompasses the behaviours, mindsets and skills is claimed to offer an innovative approach to leadership practices in higher education.

The interrelated aspect of the domains is argued to convey the agility that is required of leaders in leading and managing in turbulent times. The Framework thus provides a new way of thinking about, understanding and enacting leadership. The dynamic integrated nature of the Framework responds to the need for a new approach to leadership and outlines an appropriate and useful mechanism for achieving the type of leadership response considered necessary in contemporary contexts. The nature and severity of the turbulence in the HE sector has presented significant challenges for institutions and their leaders, and this suggests a need to rethink current leadership practices, a need that is recognised in the wider literature (Sims, 2020; Remenyi et al., 2020).

The Delphi data pointed to ongoing change as a fundamental phenomenon of higher education: that continual process of change can therefore offer leaders a useful structure for working with academics to address the challenges in the sector. This would seem to resonate with many contemporary leadership theories that conceptualise leadership as a process of dynamic interactions between leaders and followers (Winkler, 2010). The Framework for Leadership accordingly includes key aspects of behavioural, situational and contemporary theories relevant to informing the future of leadership in higher education. In this Framework, the leadership behaviours, mindsets and skills can be interpreted as coalescing or merging into an enduring process to support the ongoing work of leaders.

Application of the Framework for Leadership

The broader significance of this Framework is its capacity to recognise the changing context of higher education and the variable nature of the turbulence that impacts the sector. Arguably, the Framework has the potential to support leaders with strategies to navigate challenges and tensions in day-to-day operations, including those created by, for example, the managerialism versus collegiality dichotomy. The Framework could help to overcome what is seen as the impasse between these two approaches which, according to the Delphi data is often overly dichotomised. By dynamically adopting different combinations of elements in the behaviour, mindset and skill domains, the Framework also responds to the call in the literature for an integrated approach to leadership that can be adapted to different situations.

The flexibility and responsiveness of the Framework anticipates the need for leaders to be flexible in their attitude, and recognises the potential benefits and trade-offs of both the collegial and managerialist approaches. The Framework thereby provides ways for leaders to proactively respond to specific situations and to work with and through issues, as appropriate to the context. Not only does the Framework exemplify the flexible nature of leadership that is required in contemporary contexts, but it also conveys a sense of how leadership needs to integrate and work across different imperatives, rather than taking an either/or approach. The Framework thereby reflects leadership that employs multiple approaches to best address any issue in its context.

REFERENCES

ABC. (2019). James Cook University marine scientist Peter Ridd's sacking 'unlawful', court rules. *ABC News*. https://www.abc.net.au/news/2019-04-16/jcu-scientist-peter-ridd-sacking-unlawful-federal-court-judgment/11021554

Benmira, S., & Agboola, M. (2021). Evolution of leadership theory. *BMJ Leader*, 5(1).

Bennett, K. (2017). *Living and Leading Through Uncertainty: Developing Leaders' Capability for Uncertainty*. KR Publishing.

Bentley, P. J., Coates, H., Dobson, I. R., Goedegebuure, L., & Meek, V. L. (2013). Academic job satisfaction from an international comparative perspective: factors associated with satisfaction across 12 countries. In *Job Satisfaction Round the Academic World* (pp. 239–262). Springer. doi:10.1007/978-94-007-5434-8_13

Betts, M. (2022). *The New Leadership Agenda: Pandemic Perspectives from Global Universities*. Taylor & Francis. doi:10.4324/9781003346135

Brady, S. R. (2015). Utilizing and adapting the Delphi method for use in qualitative research. *International Journal of Qualitative Methods*, 14(5), 1609406915621381. doi:10.1177/1609406915621381

Bryman, A. (2007). Effective leadership in higher education: A literature review. *Studies in Higher Education*, 32(6), 693–710. doi:10.1080/03075070701685114

Burnes, B., Wend, P., & By, R. T. (2014). The changing face of English universities: Reinventing collegiality for the twenty-first century. *Studies in Higher Education*, *39*(6), 905–926. doi:10.1080/03075079.2012.754858

Butler, M.J. (2006). 'Thinking Creatively About Learning–The Reflective Mindset', *Aston Business School: Good Practice Guide in Learning and Teaching, Thinking Creatively about Learning*, *3*, 31-7.

Cahill, D. (2020). Wage theft is core university business. *Advocate: Journal of the National Tertiary Education Union*, *27*(3), 28–29.

Calderon, A. (2020). What will follow the international student boom? Future directions for Australian higher education. *Australian Universities Review*, *62*(1), 18–25.

Coleman, W. O. (2019). *Campus Meltdown: The Deepening Crisis in Australian Universities*. Connor Court Publishing.

Connell, R. (2019). *The Good University: What Universities Actually Do and Why it's Time for Radical Change*. Zed Books.

Crawford, E. R., Arnold, N. W., & Brown, A. (2014). From preservice leaders to advocacy leaders: Exploring intersections in standards for advocacy in educational leadership and school counselling. *International Journal of Leadership in Education*, *17*(4), 481–502. doi:10.1080/13603124.2014.931467

Crawford, T., & Germov, J. (2015). Using Workforce Strategy to Address Academic Casualisation: A University of Newcastle Case Study. *Journal of Higher Education Policy and Management*, *37*(5), 534–544. doi:10.1080/1360080X.2015.1079394

Croucher, G., & Lacy, W. B. (2020). Perspectives of Australian higher education leadership: Convergent or divergent views and implications for the future? *Journal of Higher Education Policy and Management*, *42*(4), 516–529. doi:10.1080/1360080X.2020.1783594

Danneels, E., & Sethi, R. (2011). 'New product exploration under environmental turbulence'. *Organization Science*, *22*(4), 1026–1039. doi:10.1287/orsc.1100.0572

Davis, G. (2017). *The Australian Idea of a University*. Melbourne University Press.

Davis, H., & Jones, S. (2014). The work of leadership in higher education management. *Journal of Higher Education Policy and Management*, *36*(4), 367–370. doi:10.1080/1360080X.2014.916463

Davis, I. (2021). University mergers: tough option for hard times. *Campus Morning Mail*.

Deem, R. (2004). The knowledge worker, the manager-academic and the contemporary UK university: New and old forms of public management? *Financial Accountability & Management*, *20*(2), 107–128. doi:10.1111/j.1468-0408.2004.00189.x

Dewar, J. (2017). *Bold Thinking Series: The Future of Universities*. La Trobe University. https://www.latrobe.edu.au/nest/tag/bold-thinking-series/>

Dyer, G., & Dyer, M. (2017). 'Strategic leadership for sustainability by higher education: The American College & University Presidents' Climate Commitment'. *Journal of Cleaner Production*, *140*, 111–116. doi:10.1016/j.jclepro.2015.08.077

Eassom, S. (2016). Futureproof conference. *Campus Review.* <https://www.campusreview.com.au/futureproof2016-presentations/>

Ekman, M., Lindgren, M., & Packendorff, J. (2018). Universities need leadership, academics need management: Discursive tensions and voids in the deregulation of Swedish higher education legislation. *Higher Education, 75*(2), 299–321. doi:10.100710734-017-0140-2

Ernst & Young. (2018). *Can the Universities of Today Lead Learning for Tomorrow? The University of the Future.* E&Y. <https://cdn.ey.com/echannel/au/en/industries/government---public-sector/ey-university-of-the-future-2030/EY-university-of-the-future-2030.pdf>

Fitzmaurice, M. (2013). Constructing professional identity as a new academic: A moral endeavour. *Studies in Higher Education, 38*(4), 613–622. doi:10.1080/03075079.2011.594501

Fullan, M., & Scott, G. (2009). *Turnaround Leadership for Higher Education.* Jossey-Bass.

Garnder, L., Kafka, A. C., & Carlson, S. (2020). Financial Strategies for Crisis and Beyond. Chronicle of Higher Education.

Giannarou, L., & Zervas, E. (2014). Using Delphi technique to build consensus in practice. [IJBSAM]. *International Journal of Business Science and Applied Management, 9*(2), 65–82.

Gosling, J., & Mintzberg, H. (2003). The five minds of a manager. *Harvard Business Review, 81*(11), 54–63. PMID:14619151

Green, R. A. (2014). The Delphi technique in educational research. *SAGE Open, 4*(2), 2158244014529773. doi:10.1177/2158244014529773

Hare, J. (2022). How SA's merger will create a 'university of the future'. *Australian Financial Review.*

Hassan, A., Gallear, D., & Sivarajah, U. (2018). Critical factors affecting leadership: a higher education context. *Transforming Government: People, Process, and Policy, 12*(1), 110–130.

Holey, E. A., Feeley, J. L., Dixon, J., & Whittaker, V. J. (2007). An exploration of the use of simple statistics to measure consensus and stability in Delphi studies. *BMC Medical Research Methodology, 7*(1), 1–10. doi:10.1186/1471-2288-7-52 PMID:18045508

Hopp, C., & Pruschak, G. (2020). Is there such a thing as leadership skill? – A replication and extension of the relationship between high school leadership positions and later-life earnings. *The Leadership Quarterly*, 101475. doi:10.1016/j.leaqua.2020.101475

Ingram, J., & Cangemi, J. (2012). Emotions, emotional intelligence and leadership: A brief, pragmatic perspective. *Education, 132*(4).

Jarrett, K., & Newton, S. (Eds.). (2020). *The Practice of Leadership in Higher Education: Real-world Perspectives on Becoming, Being and Leaving.* Routledge. doi:10.4324/9780367823849

Jeanes, E. (2021). A meeting of mind(sets). Integrating the pedagogy and andragogy of mindsets for leadership development. *Thinking Skills and Creativity, 39*, 100758. doi:10.1016/j.tsc.2020.100758

Jones, S., Hadgraft, R., Harvey, M., Lefoe, G. & Ryland, K. (2014). *Evidence-based Benchmarking Framework for a Distributed Leadership Approach to Capacity Building in Learning and Teaching*, Office for Learning and Teaching, University of Wollongong.

Jones, S., Lefoe, G., Harvey, M., & Ryland, K. (2012). Distributed leadership: A collaborative framework for academics, executives and professionals in higher education. *Journal of Higher Education Policy and Management*, *34*(1), 67–78. doi:10.1080/1360080X.2012.642334

Jongbloed, B., Vossensteyn, H., van Vught, F., & Westerheijden, D. F. (2018). Transparency in higher education: the emergence of a new perspective on higher education governance. In A. Curaj, L. Deca, & R. Pricopie (Eds.), *European Higher Education Area: The Impact of Past and Future Policies* (pp. 441–454). Springer. doi:10.1007/978-3-319-77407-7_27

Juntrasook, A. (2014). "You do not have to be the boss to be a leader": Contested meanings of leadership in higher education. *Higher Education Research & Development*, *33*(1), 19–31. doi:10.1080/07294360.2013.864610

Kenny, J. D. (2009). Managing a modern university: Is it time for a rethink? *Higher Education Research & Development*, *28*(6), 629–642. doi:10.1080/07294360903206934

Kezar, A. J., & Holcombe, E. M. (2017). *Shared Leadership in Higher Education: Important Lessons from Research and Practice*. American Council on Education.

Klikauer, T. (2013). *Managerialism: A Critique of an Ideology*. Palgrave Macmillan. doi:10.1057/9781137334275

Komives, S. R., Lucas, N., & McMahon, T. R. (2007). *Exploring Leadership: For College Students Who Want to Make a Difference*. John Wiley & Sons.

Lacy, W., Croucher, G., Brett, A., & Mueller, R. (2017). *Australian Universities at a Crossroads: Insights from their Leaders and Implications for the Future*. Melbourne Centre for the Study of Higher Education and Berkeley Centre for Studies in Higher Education.

Loomes, S., Owens, A., & McCarthy, G. (2019). Patterns of recruitment of academic leaders to Australian universities and implications for the future of higher education. *Journal of Higher Education Policy and Management*, *41*(2), 137–152. doi:10.1080/1360080X.2019.1565296

Maidique, M. A., & Hiller, N. J. (2018). The mindsets of a leader. *MIT Sloan Management Review*, *59*(4), 76–81.

Mant, A. (2010). Why "leadership" is so difficult - and elusive. *The International Journal of Leadership in Public Services*, *6*(1), 18–24. doi:10.5042/ijlps.2010.0271

Marshall, S. J. (2006). Issues in the development of leadership for learning and teaching in higher education. In *Leadership for Excellence in Learning and Teaching Program additional reading*. Carrick Institute for Learning and Teaching in Higher Education.

Mencl, J., Wefald, A. J., & van Ittersum, K. W. (2016). Transformational leader attributes: Interpersonal skills, engagement, and well-being. *Leadership and Organization Development Journal*, *37*(5), 635–657. doi:10.1108/LODJ-09-2014-0178

Mrig, A., & Sanaghan, P. (2017). *'The skills future higher-ed leaders need to succeed'*, Academic Impressions. CR Mrig Company.

Mumford, T. V., Campion, M. A., & Morgeson, F. P. (2007). The leadership skills strataplex: Leadership skill requirements across organizational levels. *The Leadership Quarterly, 18*(2), 154–166. doi:10.1016/j.leaqua.2007.01.005

Ndu, A. A., & Anagbogu, M. A. (2007). Framework for effective management of universities in the 21st century. In J. B. Babalola & B. O. Emunemu (Eds.), *Issues in Higher Education: Research Evidence from Sub-Saharan Africa*. Bolabay Publications.

Olsen, A. A., Wolcott, M. D., Haines, S. T., Janke, K. K., & McLaughlin, J. E. (2021). How to use the Delphi method to aid in decision making and build consensus in pharmacy education. *Currents in Pharmacy Teaching & Learning, 13*(10), 1376–1385. doi:10.1016/j.cptl.2021.07.018 PMID:34521535

Patterson, J. L., Goens, G. A., & Reed, D. E. (2009). *Resilient Leadership for Turbulent Times: A Guide to Thriving in the Face of Adversity*. R&L Education.

Patty, A. (2017). Landmark enterprise agreement decision gives universities "nuclear" option. *Sydney Morning Herald*. <https://www.smh.com.au/business/workplace/landmark-enterprise-agreement-decision-gives-universities-nuclear-option-20170830-gy6zie.html>

Paxton, D., & Van Stralen, S. (2015). Developing collaborative and innovative leadership: Practices for fostering a new mindset. *Journal of Leadership Education, 14*(4), 11–25. doi:10.12806/V14/I4/I1

Powell, S. (2018). Risks to international student market: Austrade. *The Australian*. https://www.theaustralian.com.au/higher-education/risks-to-international-student-market-austrade/news-story/adfe42ce4b8673a5d8074266db17d3d1>

Remenyi, D., Grant, K. A., & Singh, S. (2020). *The University of the Future Responding to COVID-19* (2nd ed.). ACPIL Reading.

Sahlin, K. (2012). The interplay of organizing models in higher education: what room is there for collegiality in universities characterized by bounded autonomy? In *Managing Reform in Universities* (pp. 198–221). Springer. doi:10.1057/9781137284297_11

Sathye, M. (2004). Leadership in higher education: A qualitative study. *Forum Qualitative Sozialforschung / Forum: Qualitative. Social Research, 5*(3). > doi:10.17169/fqs-5.3.571

Secundo, G., Vecchio, P. D., & Passiante, G. (2015). Creating innovative entrepreneurial mindsets as a lever for knowledge-based regional development. *International Journal of Knowledge-Based Development, 6*(4), 276–298. doi:10.1504/IJKBD.2015.074301

Shattock, M. (2010). Entrepreneurialism and organizational change in higher education. In *Entrepreneurialism in Universities and the Knowledge economy: Diversification and Organizational Change in European Higher Education* (pp. 1–8). Open University Press.

Simon, A., & Lacava, G. (2008). The relationship of strategic thinking and strategic capabilities to success in a sample of Australia's top 500 ASX companies. *Academy of Taiwan Business Management Review*, *4*(1), 1–9.

Sims, M. (2020). *Bullshit Towers: Neoliberalism and Managerialism in Universities in Australia*. Peter Lang Academic Publishers. doi:10.3726/b16811

Stensaker, B., & Harvey, L. (2010). *Accountability in Higher Education: Global Perspectives on Trust and Power*. Routledge. doi:10.4324/9780203846162

Tertiary Education Quality and Standards Agency (TEQSA). (2019). *Statistics Report on TEQSA Registered Higher Education Providers*. TEQSA. https://files.eric.ed.gov/fulltext/ED602734.pdf

Tight, M. (2014). Collegiality and managerialism: A false dichotomy? Evidence from the higher education literature. *Tertiary Education and Management*, *20*(4), 294–306. doi:10.1080/13583883.2014.956788

Walker, B. (2019). *Finding Resilience: Change and Uncertainty in Nature and Society*. CSIRO Publishing.

Watters, A. (2013). A Future with Only 10 Universities. *Hack Education*. <http://hackeducation.com/2013/10/15/minding-the-future-openva>

Weaver, W. (1971). Timothy. The Delphi forecasting method. *Phi Delta Kappan*, *52*(5), 267–271.

Winkler, I. (2010). *Contemporary Leadership Theories: Enhancing the Understanding of the Complexity, Subjectivity and Dynamic of Leadership*. Springer.

Worrall, D. (2013). *Accountability Leadership: How Great Leaders Build a High-Performance Culture of Accountability and Responsibility*. The Accountability Code.

Zaglas, W. (2021). Changes to leadership, advocacy on the card for Universities Australia. *Campus Review*. <https://viewer.joomag.com/campus-review-vol-31-issue-04-april-2021/0906343001620084026?short&>

Chapter 7
Trade Union Leadership and Sustainability in the Contemporary World of Work

Adekunle Tinuoye
https://orcid.org/0000-0002-7500-8619
Micheal Imoudu National Institute for Labour Studies, Nigeria

ABSTRACT

The industrial revolution resulted in a conflict of interest between the employer and employee and the emergence of trade unions. By contributing to harmonizing workplace interests, formulating rules governing workplace relations, and protecting workers' rights and welfare, the imprimatur of trade unions are manifest in every facet of global socio-economic and political progress. However, certain developments, practices, and trends have served to weaken the labor movement and brought to the fore germane questions about the utility of trade unions; and it is against this background, that the ethos of unity, cohesion, and solidarity and backed by sound, pragmatic, and ethical leadership should be utilized in their quest to continue to organize, mobilize, and strategize to champion the cause of the working class. Therefore, this chapter would focus on the above themes and proffer leadership strategies for the continued relevance of trade unions as institutions for servicing worker needs in eras of uncertainty.

INTRODUCTION

Workers have a long history of enduring diverse forms of oppression and embarking on various struggles against employers. Prior to the Industrial revolution, there was mass penurization, emasculation and exploitation of workers, but the industrial revolution resulted in the emergence of trade unions as means of ensuring workers obtain a decent share of labor gains and dismantling the instruments of subjugation. ILO (2005) argued that trade unionism is a means for workers to liberate themselves from poverty and social exclusion and further affirmed that the formation of unions was a reaction against the mechanisms of pauperization, notably: low pay, long working hours, child labour and generally appalling working conditions. The description of workers as the engine room of national economies, cornerstone of eco-

DOI: 10.4018/978-1-6684-8257-5.ch007

nomic growth and pivots of sustainable development (UN, 2020 ;MGI, 2016; ILO, 2015; OECD 2014) means that nations, economies, sectors and organizations cannot accomplish goals without adequately, structurally and productively optimizing their workforce. Labour efficiency and output is vital to achieving rapid and sustained socio-economic and political transformation, citizenry prosperity, national competitiveness and economic growth. This also underpins the linkage between skills, education, competences, aptitude and the enhancement of productive capacities.(Pologeorgis, 2022; GIZ, 2021 ;Smith et al. 2016; UNDP, 2015). Furthermore, the importance of Labour underscored the establishment of the International Labour Organization as the first specialized agency of the United Nations in 1919 designed to advance socio-economic justice through standards aimed at ensuring accessible, productive, and sustainable work in conditions of freedom, equity, security and dignity. Also in recognizing and empowering trade unions as associations meant to protect and advance workers rights and interests, the Declaration on Fundamental Principles and Rights at Wor*k* was made at the 86th session of the International Labour Conference at Geneva in 1988 placing great emphasis on the rights of workers to associate freely and bargain collectively as a fundamental policy.

According to Solidarity Center(2023,) unions are a fundamental element of a free and democratic society whose importance extends beyond the workplace—workers who are economically secure are better able to contribute to their communities, and the issues unions address at the workplace often are closely connected with overall societal and community concerns Thus, according to Svensson (2015), the trade union movement has morphed into one of the world's largest social movement which has played and is playing crucial roles in global social, economic and democratic progress. Trade unions have become the platform through which workers uphold their dignity, maintain their rights and enhance their living and working conditions by seeking a fair share of workplace productivity gains. So whether coming together to create strong voices, seeking to contribute to harmonizing workplace interests and formulating rules governing workplace relations and campaigning against unfair pay, discrimination, or sexual harassment (McNicholas, 2018), workers rely on their ability to join together whether informally or in formal litigation to remedy violations of workplace protections.

Trade unionism is based on the core values of equal opportunities, social solidarity and employment security for workers because unions everywhere share the same goals of meeting the needs of working people. This has been critical in stimulating union struggles, cohesion and unity. Oxfam (2018) pointed out that by forming a counterbalance to the power of wealth, organized workers have been central to the creation of more equal and more democratic societies. Trade unions are also actively involved in the 2030 agenda. ITUC (2017) attested that through their everyday work on upholding freedom of association, social dialogue and collective bargaining, on promoting decent work, social protection and the rights of working people, trade unions are instrumental to the achievement of the Sustainable Development Goals. In a genuine bid to address emerging workplace issues, the International Labour Organization's Centenary Declaration on the Future of work in June 2019 emphasized the key roles of social partners to join forces towards developing a world of work free from violence and harassment; encouraging the growth of strong and representative social partner organizations; promoting workers' rights as a key element for the attainment of inclusive and sustainable growth, with a focus on freedom of association and the effective recognition of the right to collective bargaining as enabling rights and creating effective workplace cooperation as a tool to ensure safe and productive workplaces that respects collective bargaining and its outcomes, and does not undermine the role of trade unions.

Trade unions regarded as the last bulwark for the protection of workers interests are facing debilitating experiences like erosion of membership base, financial incapacitation, temporary cessation of activities and assaults on freedom of association and collective bargaining which constitute obstacles to their effectiveness as espoused by the International Trade Union Confederation in its 2021 Global Rights Index. This and the impacts of COVID 19 Pandemic on trade unions and workers brings to the fore germane questions concerning the leadership, sustainability, relevance and utility of trade unions in the face of relentless onslaught from multiple quarters. Therefore, this chapter would focus on the utilization of the trade union ethos of unity, cohesion and solidarity backed by sound, pragmatic and ethical leadership as strategies to further organize, mobilize and champion the welfare and interests of workers and non-workers in the society during crisis periods. The chapter would conclude by proffering leadership strategies for the continued relevance of trade unions as institutions for servicing worker needs in eras of uncertainty.

TRADE UNION CHALLENGES, ISSUES AND PROBLEMS

Trade unions everywhere are facing perilous times everywhere against the backdrop of inclement workplaces, harsh economic conditions, and profit oriented employers worsened by the socio-economic, psychological and political impacts of COVID-19 (ILO, 2022: ILO,2021a: IMF, 2021: Kniffin, Narayanan,, Anseel et al, 2021, UNDP, 2021: Alicott et al,2020: Berchin, & Guerra, 2020)., Most unions that were virtually struggling to establish and sustain programs to fulfill the personal and collective aspirations of their members had to confront the numerous challenges posed by the pandemic. Prior to the pandemic, majorities of the world's workers were already living on the margins of extreme difficulties and fragile contexts characterized by economic recession and rising cost of basic goods and services, inequality; breakdown of key institutions; widespread insecurity and political unpredictability. The COVID-19 pandemic and its drawbacks (Mahler et al, 2020, ILO, 2021b) made it essential for rapid and qualitative trade union response and coordination since the categories of people mostly exposed to risks of infection are workers and most likely trade union members, This was evinced by its disproportionate impact on a broad range of workers in sectors like health, tourism, hospitality, transportation, food, grocery and delivery via loss of livelihoods, inadequacy of protection coverage, vulnerabilities and high burdens. The fact that pre-existing inequalities made workers less able to cope with the impacts of the pandemic makes it mandatory for trade unions to engage in "instant bargaining" in order to win specific COVID-19 protections such as extra paid sick and family leave time, an end to disciplinary attendance/absentee policies, temporary closure of workplaces (Lessen & Pratt, 2020).

The employer's penchant for placing profit above all other considerations and in the process aiding the systematic abuse of workers' rights and minimization of workers on an unimaginable scale is a recurring workplace feature. Orback (2015) believed that when capital moves freely, wages are dumped, working conditions worsens and production is located where it is cheapest and at the expense of working conditions. Oxfam (2018) averred that large multinationals reduce costs by outsourcing production to smaller businesses that employ informal labour, pay workers lower wages, and provide less secure work which enables them (multinationals) to circumvent labour and social protection legislations. Cunniah (2013) said in the world of globalized supply chains, employers seek to do away with their responsibilities in the name of "flexibility" and "competitiveness" and governments have all but given up on the objective of full and decent employment. Then, Boggs (2002) added that the overriding objective of the neo-liberal market model is to serve the interests of property owners and shareholders and that any obstacle to its capacity to do that - regulation, controls, trade unions, taxation, public ownership, etc are unjustified and should be removed. The cumulative implications of all these is that working people face economic struggles with limited job opportunities, stagnant wages, discrimination, and continuing barriers to self-organization (Mantsios 2015). In response, Thakker(2023) gave a very measured response when he declared that after all unionization and labour struggles are direct mechanisms to better accomplish racial and social equality; the ability for people to afford to live happy and dignified lives is inherently tied to their ability to enjoy fundamental social and civil rights within those lives, too. The most surprising aspect of the entire scenario is that eventually the major beneficiary of worker productivity and trade union activities are the business owners and employers in terms of huge turnovers, profits and share dividends.

But today the stakes are so high for workers globally. The prevalent economic recession, demographic changes, corporate policies, work practices, and government regulations have practically pummeled trade unions into near submission, almost silenced them and excluded them from salient discourses. The decline of manufacturing jobs, the rise of non-standard and flexible work and the persistence and growth of the informal economy, coupled with changes in employment regulations and behavior and the limitation and violation of trade union rights have caused unionization rates to fall in most countries worldwide(Visser, 2019) Again, global trends like demographic shifts rising role of technology and the globalization of value chains are not only altering the nature of work, jobs and skills set of workers, but have also affected the nature of trade unions. Workplace parties routinely flout labour legislations and statutory regulations (which are mostly devoid of effective deterrents and adequate sanctions against potential offenders.) with undisguised impunity and linked with this is the growing futility of regulatory and institutional frameworks that organize and govern industrial relations and labour market practices. Ewing and Hardy (2014) seemed to describe the travails of the average worker when they asserted that the deterioration of pay and conditions for workers is of course a symptom of the great cruelty at the heart of modern society. Trade union leaders and workers need to fully grasp the fact that business owners are neither philanthropists nor charitable organizations and cost cutting measures are part and parcel of organizational survival strategies during eras of crises and gloom.

During the pandemic, the industry witnessed an assortment of employer responses like salary cuts, reduction in hours of work, permanent downsizing, allowances reduction, compulsory leaves, temporary layoffs etc across sectors. This situation led to workers being firmly rooted at the bottom of the global economic food chain and the heightened instability of work that typifies labour relations in the contemporary world of work. This served to add urgency to the calls for the renewal of a viable, dynamic and effective labor movement. In the not too distant future, as the dynamics of work and the world of work continue to experience changes and forces such as organizational behavior, migration, economic changes, global trade and commerce, political undercurrents etc shapes the future of work, trade unions will encounter enormous challenges in terms of articulating, defending and protecting workers rights, interests and positions and devising more effective mobilizing, research and development, advocacy, social dialogue, organizing, public diplomacy, sensitization, awareness raising and global outreach campaigns, initiatives and strategies to remain relevance. Other critical areas include how to promote decent work and a human-centred future of work that can enable workers accomplish their full potentials as equal and active members of society, ensure respect of labour rights and obligations, promote social dialogue and ratification and effective implementation of applicable UN declarations and ILO conventions, promote access to social protection and security, strengthen humane terms and conditions of employment in global supply chains and attain gender equality at work. Therefore, key issues to examine are would the goals and mandates of trade unions change? Are trade unions going to alter their structures and modus operandi? how would trade unions enable workers get their appropriate dues and benefits and defend their rights and interests?, will the trade union movement modify their traditional tactics and strategies and can trade unions morph into different forms or continue to exist in its current form all in a bid to cope with emerging trends and future developments.

TRADE UNION SOLIDARITY AND COHESIVENESS

Union solidarity is a key element of Trade unionism (Olurode & Gaskia, 2022: Cotton, 2015;Burrows 2014; Williams & Uticensis 2013). Solidarity which is at the core of union culture is focused on enhancing human worth and dignity regardless of diversity. It occurs when union members share common values and goals and work together with and for themselves to advance collective interests. To Green (2019), what makes unions work is the solidarity of its members — that collective desire to fight together for something greater. Solidarity is a key union maxim which literarily translates to an injury to one member is an injury to others or what affects one member affects others. It is vital to building strong and effective unions by sustaining workers struggles, typifying union resilience and revitalizing hopes of union triumphs and victories In this era of almost total decline in the quantity of manufacturing jobs, widespread use of subcontracting and outsourcing, growth of the platform economy and the attendant decline in global unionization rates, solidarity is central to trade union rejuvenation – by feeling the pulse of their members, being in tune with their needs, having an idea of their aspirations and purposefully working towards actualizing them. ILO (2007) also articulated that building solidarity was one of the six main goals of union education and a veritable tool in strengthening trade unions as a relevant stakeholder in shaping the 'new unstable workforce' in the emerging world of work.

The basis of solidarity in this context is that workers without distinction must have the rights to join and form trade unions and to enter into collective bargaining over their terms and conditions at work. Solidarity adds value to open, free and cooperative trade unions that ensure the ability of workers to exercise their rights to freedom of association and engage in collective bargaining is optimized and maximized. LRS/NSF (2022) observed that solidarity is about shared power and that sharing decision-making gives everyone the opportunity to be heard. They further noted that this opens the space for everyone to offer resources, actions and commitment at both individual and organizational levels. Ubuntu Age (2012) said Africans have a thing called ubuntu which is part of the gifts that Africa has given to the world. They noted that it stresses the essence of being human, embraces caring about others and being willing to go the extra mile for the sake of another. In sync with this, Oyewunmi & Oyewunmi ((2017) talked about more mutual support, friendship, understanding amongst workers to facilitate more informal dialogue and change perspectives and lives. Solidarity helps to create and maintain economically viable, democratically inclined and united labour organizations by building worker political awareness about the essence of partnering and collaborating to serve collective interests. Inculcating the value of union solidarity in union members, employees and leaders is very critical to organizing and developing the trade union as a movement that can advance the welfare and wellbeing of workers and non workers and their families during diverse periods.

To attain the union objective of becoming an effective tool for workers to escape poverty, exploitation and the violation of their basic human dignity (ILO 2005) requires a great deal of cohesiveness in terms of enhancing union capacity to strategically represent members, engage in fruitful dialogues, build fluid structures and organize new members..The union lay trinity - liberty, equality and fraternity are at the heart of fostering cohesion which is indispensable to promoting union vibrancy, virility and growth. An effective approach to building union cohesion is by highlighting the essence of conscientious and active union membership participation in activities like attending meetings, advocacy on behalf of the union, supporting union actions, partaking in campaigns and paying union dues. These combine together to enhance worker commitment, boost financial sustainability, increase union visibility and promote union virility.

Cohesiveness is linked with unity, structures, consistency and harmony and also helps to engender the pervasiveness of a sense of belonging among trade unions members.. An ensample of cohesiveness via the presence of dedicated, knowledgeable and versatile leaders and members maintaining a united front is vital to articulating and meeting worker interests. Ensuring fairness, equality of opportunities and treatment at work requires robust synergistic management-union-state engagements which can only be facilitated by unions that are cohesive and united. Thus union cohesion enables union leaders, employees, volunteers and members to be on the same page, do not work at cross purposes, join forces to promote common good and work mutually to formulate actionable initiatives to achieve union vision and mission objectives. Jones (2021) noted that if employees are going to be fully on board with company's strategy and direction, they need to know its plans and paths to achieve those goals. A vital role of a good leader is to communicate the company's mission, vision, and strategy, so that everyone understands how they fit into the bigger picture because people who know exactly how their contributions are valued are more likely to fully participate. When union members are carried along, fully understand union direction and key into it they will be more motivated to partner with the union leadership to work for union progress and sustainability.

To develop the right ideological common ground, build unanimity and ensure the realization of collective interests requires steady interactions, consultation and consensus building between trade union leaders and members. Trade union unity is vital to the growth of the labour movement (Andre .2016, 2022 Otobo 2017; COSATU. 2015) by strengthening trade union power, galvanizing members to identify strongly with the union and focusing on attaining union objectives. For instance, one of the biggest challenges facing the Nigerian labour movement today is maintaining a sense of common purpose and minimizing the propensity to splinter or divide against the milieu of ethnic, religious and political differences. Similarly important to building the desired union unity and cohesion is reassurance and reinforcement through exchanges between union leaders and workers that all members are equally important and their wellbeing will be equally championed. This is very important in promoting a heightened sense of belonging, improving participation and increasing interaction and understanding between and among union stakeholders.

In some countries, informal sector workers who constitute the bulk of workers continue to be excluded from the mainstream of trade unionism. In agreeing with this and pontificating that unions were too detached from the new world of work, Roache (2017) said we (unions) got to get closer to the people who are facing the challenges, day in day out. He added that [This is] the organizing that we should have been doing for many years, and some of us have not been doing. Social partners must reiterate like the ILO that working people are not commodities to be bought and sold like goods on stock markets, but are human beings with social, economic and political aspirations for their lives at work, at home and in the society. The good news is that trade unions throughout the world most especially in developing countries have steadily begun to champion the rights of unprotected workers such as mechanics, quarry operators, cattle dealers, fashion designers, tailors, tricycle riders, motorcycle riders, tipper drivers etc, However trade unions should channel more resources and efforts to shoring up protections for unorganized workers through advocacy and lobbying to ensure that the current labour legislations and associated national policies capture their distinct interests.

TRADE UNION LEADERSHIP SKILLS AND QUALITIES

The nature of workplaces has changed considerably. In those days, trade unions thrived in the traditional era of employment dominated mainly by white collared, middle, crafts related, public sector, production and manufacturing and skilled and semi skilled jobs in the industry. But the gradual dominance of non standard forms of employment, shift to service sector, emergence of automation and incipience of artificial intelligence has led to the predominance of workers and work with unstable or precarious jobs. This situation calls for the emergence of a different perspective of hands on, foresighted and pragmatic trade union leadership that can effectively understand, decipher and proffer appropriate responses to emerging developments. At this stage in the world of work, the author agrees with the view of Gumbrell-McCormick and Hyman (2021) that union effectiveness requires 'the capacity to interpret, decipher, sustain, and redefine the demands of the represented so as to evoke the broadest possible consensus and approval and that these functions of leadership are a prerequisite for participative democracy to deliver beneficial results.. Traditionally, UM and CWL (2014) said leadership has been conceptualized as an individual skill associated with the display of specific behaviors (i.e., leadership styles) aimed at increasing organizational performance. In particular, leaders chart the way forward, devise policies, shape organizational culture and model behavior for employees. These are critical actions that can either make or mar any enterprise's continued existence and standing in the world of work. What can hardly be disputed is the vital role that leadership plays in employee and organizational failure or success. So depending on the type of leadership exhibited and the quality of the interactions between leaders and followers, leadership can engender either positive or negative outcomes for organizational success (Boyles, 2023: Monzani & Van Dyck, 2021: Haslam Reicher & Platow,2021: Cameron, 2021).

Leadership provides strategic directions to accomplish unions' mission and vision objectives. Visionary and versatile leaders always add value to trade union sustainability and development by infusing ideas, ideals and ideologies and maintaining the appropriate union consciousness and principles. Trade union leaders need to acquire relevant proactive analytical, innovative and networking skills and techniques (Mauku, 2022: Tinuoye, 2023) in addition to having a comprehensive grasp of union, employer, member and industrial sector strengths, weaknesses, opportunities and threats .These wealth of skills, knowledge and information are important to enable trade union leaders to critically actualize strengths, mitigate weaknesses, grasp workplace dynamics, understand emerging trends, decipher their impacts on unions, explore emerging socio-economic and political forces that shape the global and national operating environment and develop veritable strategic plans of action that will enable the trade unions respond to the challenges of the future world of work.

As new developments unfold in the world of work, **trade unions leadership must be pragmatic enough to continuously devise,, adjust, review, monitor and consolidate pro worker agenda, initiatives, programmes and policies at all levels**. This is very crucial to enable trade unions maintain their representative strength and future legitimacy as the voice of organized labour and ensure the sustainability of its core values of democracy, peace, social justice, equality and solidarity. To embody the tenets of trade unionism, union leaders should be imbued with strong moral courage and integrity to fruitfully safeguard the interests of the world's workers. They are also expected to deploy all their resources, skills and efforts to uphold workers rights, contribute to workplace progress and prevent needless employer-employee conflicts. Tinuoye(2023) added that trade unions whose leaders are altruistically, ideologically, assiduously and tenaciously committed to protecting, advancing, championing and defending members' interests have future prospects of sustained relevance both within and outside the workplace, successfully mobilizing and optimizing resources and shaping society socially, economically and politically.

Workers are the major assets of Trade unions (Waronwant, 2023: Miles, 2021), thus union leadership are expected to devote maximal attention on workers, channel adequate resources on satisfying workers, revolve policies and initiatives around workers and keep workers together as a strong united team. Jones(2021) noted that leaders have .enormous power to make lives (and work) better for employees. Trade unionism is all about improving workers welfare. So when unions focus on core activities and policies such as advancing social justice, defending work based rights, enhancing economic power, engendering labour standards and fighting worker exploitation etc, their members will be in high spirits to pass vote of confidence on, have implicit and explicit trust in and be inspired and motivated by their union and union leadership. The utility of effective trade union leadership is felt through the array of socio-economic and psychological benefits they attract to and enjoyed by working and non working class people and their families.

Industrial democracy is the basis for united and effective trade union associations. Effective leadership is a key element of independent, sustainable, inclusive and democratic trade unions. Such trade unions are built on representation, transparency, accountability, participation and consultation which provide platforms for members to voice concerns, engage leaders, influence policies, monitor decisions and sanction infractions. Lucio and Holder (2020) explained that how we work, what purpose we work for, and what conditions we work in are all questions linked to the questions of democracy and participation, with trade unions normally being at the forefront of these issues through extending the principles of democracy into work in some form or another. Trade union leadership should safeguard and improve existing union democratic systems, norms and ethos by respecting worker dignity and equality, emphasizing on the rule of law, abiding by the tenets of union constitution, promoting meaningful participation of workers in all spheres and focusing on the actualization of workers needs.

Defending the interests of workers and obtaining decent wages and terms and conditions of work for workers in this era is neither a tea party nor stroll in the park/ How far the unions can go in successfully pushing the agenda of workers depends on **the determination, confidence persistency, assertiveness, resilience, boldness and courage of trade union leaders**. These are personal qualities that trade union leaders should have for them to surmount the multitude of challenges and obstacles existing all over today's word of work. Some employers go the whole hog to deploy and unleash an array of underhand tactics, strategies, weapons and to undermine and destabilize (ICIR, 2022: Lafer & Loustaunau, 2020, IndustriALL Global Union, 2018, Alberta Federation of Labour, 2017) the union with the major goal of weakening the capacity of the union as an organization to fight for the rights and dignity of workers. Even landmines have already been laid on the path of union leaders by the state and some workers. Trade union leadership entails a lot of hard work, patience, endurance, dedication, discomfort and sacrifices, Unionists aspiring to union positions must be specialist in marathon and long distance races, instead of being experts in sprints and hurdles

MANAGERIAL IMPLICATIONS OF TRADE UNIONISM AND TRADE UNION LEADERSHIP

The nature, importance and implications of managerial leadership in the context of the private, public, and voluntary sectors have attracted much attention in recent years. In the workplace, trade union leaders and leadership have wide ranging implications on labour management relations, organizational harmony and productivity. For instance, union leadership styles may impact either negatively or positively on union members and their attitude to work and relationships with employers, Even the commitment, participation and loyalty of trade union members may be eroded by unhealthy decisions, policies and behaviours of union leadership. Similarly, certain actions, positions and statements by union leaders could also mar or mar cooperation and partnership with managers by creating obstacles for labour peace and relations leading to union-management acrimony.

The array of changes in the workplace that trade unions are seeking to confront could also be a source of union-management clashes if not properly managed. Also emerging trade union practices that are at variance with management interests and vice versa could harbour mixed implications for management relations. The differences in the goals , roles and interests of management, workers and unions and their convergence could lead to the eruption of conflict, disagreement and disputes in the workplace, Therefore, trade union leaders and managers should be aware that conflict are normal expression of dissatisfaction which are endemic in workplaces and that conflicts are not necessarily disruptive, but can be galvanized to engineer positive change. But this would require harmonization, discussions, dialogue and bargaining between both parties to manage and prevent conflicts and stop them from escalating to the extent of causing grievous harm to the industry.

The workplace should be seen as an integrated and harmonious whole working towards a common purpose that requires some elements of mutuality. Parties need some form of understanding in this regard and build some form of consensus in their expectations and interactions. The idea of paternalism is belongs to the past, trade unions are now viewed as representatives of workers and even in some context, workers can voluntary opt out of trade union membership, So trade unions are essential associations that should operate legally, responsively and responsibly and part a play in decision-making within the workplace.. Again, trade unions must respect the boundaries of management prerogatives and emphasize that the loyalties of workers should be solely to the organization. Consequently, the role of management would lean less towards dominating and controlling and more toward persuading and coordinating. Managers' attitudes and perceptions must be slanted more towards harmony than conflict and the realization that respect for universally recognized labour rights afforded to all workers are linked with sustainable development. The trade union leadership challenge is how to build an agenda to deepen labour-management relations, extend representation and services to members and reinforce the status and position of the union in the future of work. Changing this reality requires fashioning and utilizing strategies that stresses mutuality, shared prosperity, partnership and bipartism between and among management, trade unions leadership and workers.

RECOMMENDATIONS

Leadership Strategies to Achieve Trade Union Unity, Effectiveness, and Cohesion

There is a linkage between membership appreciation and involvement in the decision-making process and higher interest, satisfaction and support (Silla, Gracias, & Peiró, 2020:Valverde-Moreno, Torres-Jimenez,& Lucia-Casademunt, 2020: Dirisu, Worlu, Osibanjo, Salau et al, 2018: Hollyns, 2017: Nazir, & Islam,2017) .Creating a more inclusive labour movement in these very uncertain times has become

Trade Union Leadership and Sustainability in the Contemporary World of Work

very salient. Inclusiveness is at the heart of trade unionism, so it is essential to integrate the contributions of members into union plans, programmes and policies. Trade union leadership can achieve this by stimulating membership involvement in union activities, attracting more women and youths into the union fold, educating workers and the general public about the significance of trade unionism, showing laudable examples and creating opportunities for members to discuss their issues. Incorporating worker's inputs and contributions enriches union policy initiatives and increases union policy influencing abilities. Trade unions are most effective when workers are fully represented, thus the onus is on union leaders to constantly interface with their members before taking crucial decisions or formulating policies that affect them.

Trade Union Leaders are in office to selflessly serve workers. Servant leadership emphasizes leadership as service, focusing on the development of followers and progress of the organization (,Kourteva, 2021: Ebong, Osezua, Oghise & Oki,2020: Gotsis & Griman,2016: Amah, 2019). The reasons for occupying either appointed or elected union positions should be to selflessly serve the union and its members. Therefore, union leaders are expected to offer quality representation, be sensitive to the feelings of their members and do all within their abilities to advance union growth and worker development. The Union is not a one man show, it is a collectivity and the leaders should espouse this ideal. To serve diligently requires keen interest in and listening deeply to what union members think, what they feel and what they want. This demands hard work and perseverance as advocated by Jones (2021) that when you put in the time and effort to be a good leader at work, you' will notice signs of increased employee motivation all around, even when you are not there to directly supervise.

Good leadership inspires individual and collective accountability, responsibility and responsiveness between and among workers. In other words, the presence good leadership at work galvanizes on and off the job performance. Present threats to trade unionism make the commitment and doggedness of trade union leadership a veritable antidote in these times. Therefore, union leaders must take the tasks of charting purposeful paths and developing feasible plans of action to meet member needs very seriously. The actualization of enterprise objectives especially for a trade union is a function of result oriented leadership. Members can only be united and supportive of a union that makes considerable gains and records immense achievements for them. Unions desirous of achieving their mandates must have purposeful, dedicated and effective leadership at the helm of their affairs. The worth of trade union leadership can only be appreciated through the prism of victories and wins for workers during and in the course of union struggles.

The existence of the union is predicated on boosting workers welfare, therefore union leaders need to have this notion at the back of their minds and proceed to lead their members responsively. This would simultaneously motivate and spur membership interest. Indeed (2022) and Jones (2021) drew a linkage between leadership and motivation. Indeed (2022) stressed that motivation within leadership can produce a dedicated and focused workforce. They noted that when leaders motivate employees, the employees often feel engaged and retain interest in work and that motivation is an essential aspect of achieving success by providing many benefits that facilitate successful leadership and organizational growth. Jones (2021) pointed out that Leadership is the link and bridge between organizational values and actions. He added that employees look to leaders to see that the company is serious about its values and when they see that managers are delivering on company values, they will be motivated to promote those values. . On the other hand, leaders who consistently bring positivity to their teams are more likely to spread positivity among employees and improve morale and motivation. A major cause of antipathy towards unions is the narcissistic, over bearing nature and self-indulgent conduct of some union leaders which have fuelled several intra and inter union conflicts that are antithetical to union unity, cohesion and solidarity. Trade union leaders throughout the globe must exhibit great restraint and caution to manage their conduct and comport in office.

Union leaders should not only follow the letter, but also the spirit of equality, solidarity and fraternity. Union leaders should seek to maintain open door policies, shun preferential treatment and avoid creating caucuses within caucuses. Unions thrive when its leaders show understanding, compassion and concern and treat their members equally. Leadership can build cohesive unions by passing clear messages through actions and words that openly demonstrate that nobody either leader or member is bigger than others, nobody is beyond making mistakes and nobody is larger than life. To engender the desired solidarity in the union, leaders must be able to obtain genuine trust and confidence of members through good relations and evidence of working for the good of the entire union and not the interests of special groups.

The union power dynamics and configuration should be designed or structured to ensure that only selfless unionists occupy full time paid union positions and aspire to the top echelon of union elective positions. Members should ensure that unionists with the pedigree, consciousness and experience emerge and are voted as executives. They should be ideological grounded and competent people who will be guided by union precepts and ethos for overall union and worker progress. Let union leaders, who can stand for, by and with workers continuously channel their heart, energy and efforts towards the struggle for the creation of fair work places and systems that can help workers restore their dignity, self actualize and improve their quality of life.. Importantly, trade unions must find an intricate balance between exercising control, power, decision making and authority by the rank and file members, the paid union officials and the elected /appointed union executives.

Organizing is central to union and worker progress.(Kochan & Liebman, 2022: Pazzanese, 2022: Muttaqa, 2021,) Organizing is the lifeblood of any union(Corona, 2022)..The power of trade unions is in their numerically strength which guarantees them a say and voice in workplace issues. Hence, they must continuously, tenaciously, consistently and strategically organize. Corona(2022) noted that unions cannot grow without organizing,. He added that because workers membership makes unions strong, the more members the unions have, the more work they can control. Trade unions that either stop or pay scant attention to organizing are firmly on the highway to extinction and atrophy. As a matter of urgency, unions need to develop specific programmes to reach out to and organize diverse groups of workers ranging from physically challenged, domestic, informal, migrant, organized private sector, marginalized, special needs, deep sea port to export processing zones workers .For instance, workers in private hospitals, secondary schools, primary schools, universities, polytechnics, colleges of education and other allied tertiary institutions in Nigeria rarely exercise the rights to freedom of association, organize and bargain collectively. Some stakeholders have asserted that the present check off regime seems to have blinded union leaders to the burning need to embark on aggressive membership drives.. The necessity for unions to organize the unorganized is reiterated by O'Connor (2017) who espoused that the labour movement risks obsolescence if it does not reverse decline in membership. With this in place, unions are bound to be stronger, more formidable and more financially viable.

Trade unions as a matter of strategy should up their ante in terms of contributing to national socio-economic and political policy dialogues and also proffering credible alternative solutions to salient national issues especially those that have direct bearing on the lives of workers. In most developing countries, trade unions need to enhance their capacities to design actionable policy positions or roadmaps to cope with and respond to unfavorable labour legislations, adverse socio-economic policies, instability in government policies, highly competitive global market, transnationalisation of enterprises etc.. With the new normal brought about by COVID- 19 already in full gear, (Stahl, 2022: Clayton, 2021:Neely, 2021: Sneader^& Simghai, 2021) trade unions leaders must brace up and brainstorm on the way forward for the movement, The labor movement should also show concrete action and commitment to capitalize on their massive membership base and solidarity to create viable alternative political platforms for workers.. Visser(2019) called on trade unions to regain their vitality and youthfulness, find ways to expand beyond their current membership base and succeed in organizing parts of the 'new unstable workforce' in the digital economy.

Lastly, the labour movement should both enhance and institutionalize dialogue and actions and build stronger strategic bridges and alliances with independent civil society, including grassroots organizations, human rights institutions, independent media associations, academics, pro women groups,, legal professionals, faith-based actors, nongovernmental organizations, professional associations, student bodies, and market based organizations etc on areas of mutual interests for collective national progress. The author would also seek for more structured, cooperative and productive engagements between the trade union movement, state actors, international bodies, developmental partner and business community.

FUTURE RESEARCH DIRECTIONS: TRADE UNIONS AND SYSTEMIC CHANGES IN THE WORLD OF WORK AND SOCIETY

An assortment of issues, problems and trends have repeatedly affected the world of work in recent decades These developments signpost the enormous nature of the diverse challenges that trade unions face at the course of advancing germane workplace issues and delivering services to workers One of the most profound was the Covid-19 pandemic and its diverse negative implications on workers, work,, work organizations, societies and nations, The aftermath of the Covid-19 crisis was the popular desire in workplaces across different parts of the globe for more rights, better dignity, stronger voices, more say and better wages to ensure decent living and a sustainable future for working class and their families

The political responses and policy narratives related to work and employment has been largely anti-labor, serving the interests of the powerful and leaving many behind. The problems associated with labour migration are manifold and the world requires concerted actions to tackle the environmental and social consequences of climate change. Majorities of workers suffer socio-economic and political hardships and uncertainty for the future. There is an imperative for the expansion and strengthening of democratic mechanisms, social dialogue and consensus-building dynamics, at all levels which is particularly challenging in the present context that has seen trade unions struggle to remain relevant in very inclement operating environments.

As a result of these trends driven by internal and external factors that negatively impact on \workers rights, standard and quality of life, the trade union movement must concentrate on organizing, mobilizing and related actions for extending the frontiers of social justice and common good everywhere. How can trade unions sustain organizing and mobilizing in the current clime of democracy to drive the much needed changes in the world of work? .How can the trade union movement be resolute, cohesive and tenacious in its struggles under the present uncertain context?.What are the factors that can support the creation of social change in workplaces and society that the trade unions have been so adept at? .What lessons can be gleaned from trade union's past triumphs and how can they be utilized in future struggles?, What skills, capacities, resources and infrastructures do trade unions require to systematically attain its goals and objectives in the contemporary world of work? .The above are key areas of future research that can arise from this work.

CONCLUSION

Fostering organizational performance, productivity and prosperity entails the harmonization of objectives, interests and purposes between management, workers, and trade unions through an array and web of relations and interactions. This is to enable parties join forces, work together, build consensus, anticipate disagreements and resolve disputes. The joint participation of union leadership and organizational management in workplace decision making stabilizes labour management relations and balances the scale of workplace power configuration. Union leadership should recognize the existence of Management interests and exhibit qualities that would encompass the willingness and ability to negotiate mutually acceptable and agreed compromises. However, reputation and integrity matters greatly in the labour movement and struggles. Once it is impugned, it exposes trade union leaders to odium and disapproval.. Apart from the overt lack of confidence by members, agents of the management and the state also capitalize on this to tar union leaders and display open and undisguised disdain for unions.. So trade union leaders must refrain from acts that are inimical to both union and worker advancement

Trade union leadership need to utilize union strength and resources with the goal of engendering fair and equitable workplace power sharing, positively influencing the direction of union power and aiding the distribution of influence to support the attainment of union struggles Also, employers and managements should constructively and consistently strive to engage trade unions during and in the course of optimally utilizing the four M's – men, materials, money and machines) for the purpose of production and achieving enterprise goals.

Effective union leaders and leaderships have serious managerial implications. In the spirit of solidarity, equality, fraternity, the union must be preserved as an open society where the views, rights and welfare of workers are treated equally and adequately protected. Building membership, promoting unity and strengthening internal cohesion and solidarity are essential to equipping the union to prevent the grandiose pauperization and haemorrhaging of workers and act as effective counterforce to the power of capitalists, political elites, corporate hawks and business owners .Trade unions are agents and instruments of social change, therefore sustaining them as catalyst for change, sphere of influence and vehicle for development requires a total reinvigoration and re-inculcation of union ethos and organizing workers to once again exercise power to recreate a world of work that can really work for al. It engenders union leaders to be aware of the immense challenges ahead and brace up and recommit themselves to the onerous task of fighting for all workers, partnering with managers and moving the union forward regardless of the odds. Finally, to create equitable, prosperous and productive workplaces that promotes collective prosperity requires social actors- workers and their representatives and employers and their associations to partner and work together.

REFERENCES

Alberta Federation of Labour. (2017) *Poisoning the Well: What the records tells us about Employer intimidation during union certification plans in Alberta*. Alberta FOL. https://d3n8a8pro7vhmx.cloudfront.net/afl/pages/156/attachments/original/1496781613/Poisoning_the_Well.pdf?1496781613

Allcott, H., Boxell, L., Conway, J., Ferguson, B., Gentzkow, M., & Goldman, B. (2020). *Economic and Health Impacts of Social Distancing Policies During the Coronavirus Pandemic*. SSRN. https://papers.ssrn.com/sol3/papers.cfm?abstract_id=3610422

Andre, M. H. (2016, April). *Trade Union Unity is key for the labour movement (Paper Presentation)*. The 2nd Quadrennial Congress of Trade Union Congress of Swaziland (TUCOSWA), Swaziland. http://www.ilo.org/global/docs/WCMS_466851/lang--en/index.htm

Andre, M. H. (2022). *Preface Trade Union Revitalization: Organizing new forms of work including platform workers*. International Labour Office.

Berchin, I. I., & de Andrade Guerra, J. B. S. O. (2020). Effects of the coronavirus disease 2019 (COVID-19) outbreak on sustainable development and future perspectives. *Res. Globalization, 2*, 1–5. doi:10.1016/j.resglo.2020.100014

Bogg, D. (2002) *Trade Unions Maintaining Relevance in the 21st Century*, (Paper Presentation). The IRN Conference. Irish Congress of Trade Unions.https://www.ictu.ie/press/2002/02/21/trade-unions-maintaining-relevance-in-the-21st-century/

Boyle, M. (2023, January 24) Organizational Leadership: What is it and why it is important. *HBS*. https://online.hbs.edu/blog/post/what-is-organizational-leadership

Burrow, S. (2014) *Challenges and opportunities for Trade unions in 2014*. ILO. www.Ilo.org/actrav/media-center/news/WCMS_234541/lang-en/index.htm

Cameron, K. (2021). *Positively Energizing Leadership: Virtuous Actions and Relationships that create High Performance*. Berrett-Koehler Publishers.

Clayton, J. (2021). *Remote working: Is Big Tech going off work from home?* BBC. https://www.bbc.com/news/technology-56614285

Corona, R. (2022) *Organizing: The Lifeblood of Our Union*. IBEW. https://www.ibew11.org/2022/03/organizing-the-lifeblood-of-our-union/

COSATU. (2015, 13 July) *Unity and Cohesion of COSATU* (Draft Discussion Document). The Congress of South African Trade Unions Special National Congress, Johannesburg, South Africa. http://www.cosatu.org.za/show.php?ID=10655

Cotton, E. (2016) *A matter of principles: the psychodynamics of solidarity in trade unions.* http://eprints.lse.ac.uk/74363/1/blogs.lse.ac.ukA%20matter%20of%20principles%20the%20psychodynamics%20of%20solidarity%20in%20trade%20unions,pdf

Cunniah, D. (2013) Foreword. *Meeting the Challenge of Precarious Work: A Workers' Agenda*. ILO. www.Ilo.org/wcmsp5/groups/public/-ed_dialogue/actrav/documents/publicatiions/wcms 216282pdf.

Dirisu, J., Worlu, R., Osibanjo, A., Salau, O., Borishade, T., Meninwa, S., & Atolagbe, T. (2018). An integrated dataset on organisational culture, job satisfaction and performance in the hospitality industry. *Data in Brief, 19*, 317–321. doi:10.1016/j.dib.2018.04.137 PMID:29892652

Ebong, I. B., Osezua, O., Ogbise, I. F., & Oki, M. (2020). Leadership Challenges and Labour Performance in Organizations. A Study of Nigeria Labour Congress (NLC) (2015-2019) EPRA *International Journal of Research and Development (IJRD)* 5 (9)63-71

Ewing, K & Hendy, J., (2014) Foreword. *Trade Unions and Economic Inequality*. Institute of Employment Research and Centre for Labour and Social Studies.

GIZ. (2021) *Economic Development and Employment.* GIZ. https://www.giz.de/en/ourservices/economic_development_and_employment.html

Gotsis, G., & Grimani, K. (2016). The role of Servant Leadership in Fostering Inclusive Organizations. *Journal of Management Development, 35*(9), 985–1010. doi:10.1108/JMD-07-2015-0095

Green, K. (2019, February 26). *Unions Must Promote Diversity and Inclusion to Maintain Solidarity.* Union Track. https://uniontrack.com/blog/union-diversity-inclusion

Gumbrell-McCormick, R., & Hyman, R. (2019). Democracy in trade unions, democracy through trade unions? *Economic and Industrial Democracy, 40*(1), 91–110. doi:10.1177/0143831X18780327

Haslam, S. A., Reicher, S. D., & Platow, M. J. (2021). *The New Psychology of Leadership: Identity, Influence and Power* (2nd ed.). Psychology Press.

Hollyns, B. A. (2017). Levels of Participation in Decision Making as Correlates of Job Satisfaction and Morale of Teachers in Public Senior Secondary Schools in Delta State *Global Journal of Management and Business Research. Administrative Management, 17*(1), 83–96.

ICIR. (2022, September, 22). *Nigerian government watches as Chinese companies violate labour laws, workers' rights.* International Center For Investigative Reports Report. https://www.icirnigeria.org/nigerian-government-watches-as-chinese-companies-violate-labour-laws-workers-rights/

ILO. (2005, October). *The Role of Trade Unions in the Global Economy and the Fight against Poverty.* The International Workers' Symposium on "Fight Poverty – Organize" Summary and Conclusion, Geneva, Switzerland http://www.ilo.org/wcmsp5/groups/public/@ed_dialogue/@actrav/documents/meetingdocument/wcms_111312.pdf

ILO. (2007, October) *The role of trade unions in workers' education: The key to trade union capacity building* [Paper presentation]. The International Workers' Symposium Geneva, Switzerland. http://actrav-courses.itcilo.org/en/a3-58346/a3-58346-resources/background-paper-ilo-we-symposium.pdf

ILO. (2015). *Decent Work Country Diagnostics - Technical Guidelines to draft the Diagnostics Report.* ILO.

ILO. (2021a). *A Global Trend Analysis on the Roles of Trade Unions in times of COVID-19: A summary of findings.* ILO. http://search.ilo.org/wcmsp5/groups/public/---ed_dialogue/---actrav/documents/ publication/ wcms_767226.pdf

ILO. (2021b). *Global call to action: for a human-centred recovery from the COVID-19 crisis that is inclusive, sustainable and resilient.* ILO. https://www.ilo.org/wcmsp5/groups/public/@ed_norm/@relconf/documents/meetingdocument/wcms_806092.pdf

ILO. (2022). *ILO Monitor on the world of work. Tenth edition Multiple crises threaten the global labour market recovery.* ILO. https://www.ilo.org/wcmsp5/groups/public/---dgreports/---dcomm/---publ/documents/briefingnote/wcms_859255.pdf

IMF. (2021). *World Economic Outlook Report, October.* Washington, DC: International Monetary Fund Indeed Editorial Team. https://uk.indeed.com/career-advice/career-development/why-is-motivation-important-in-leadership

IndustriALL Global Union. (2018) Report of Shell Nigeria Fact Funding Mission. IGU. https://www.industriall-union.org/industriall-investigation-uncovers-exploitation-of-shell-workers-in-nigeria

ITUC. (2017). *International Trade Union Confederation 2017 Global Polls.* ITUC.

ITUC. (2021). *International Trade Union Confederation 2021 Global Rights Index.* ITUC.

Jones, S. (2021). *Inspire Leadership and Motivation in the Workplace.* Confie. https://www.confie.com/insights/leadershipand-motivation-in-the-workplace/

Kniffin, K. M., Narayanan, J., Anseel, F., Antonakis, J., Ashford, S. P., Bakker, A. B., Bamberger, P., Bapuji, H., Bhave, D. P., Choi, V. K., Creary, S. J., Demerouti, E., Flynn, F. J., Gelfand, M. J., Greer, L. L., Johns, G., Kesebir, S., Klein, P. G., Lee, S. Y., & Vugt, M. (2021). COVID-19 and the workplace: Implications, issues, and insights for future research and action. *The American Psychologist, 76*(1), 63–77. doi:10.1037/amp0000716 PMID:32772537

Kochan, T., & Liebman, W. (2022, September 16). *America is seeing a historical surge in workers organizing. Here is how to sustain it.* WBUR. https://www.wbur.org/cognoscenti/2022/09/05/worker-organizing-labor-day-thomas-kochan-wilma-liebman

Kourteva, S. (2021, March 29). Have You Heard Of Servant Leadership? *Forbes.* https://www.forbes.com/sites/forbeseq/2021/03/29/have-you-heard-of-servant-leadership/?sh=7fed643e38 b7

Labour Research Services & National Skills Fund. (2022). *Strategies for inspire, organize and represent workers: The negotiators guide* LRS. https://www.lrs.org.za/wp-content/uploads/2022 /02/The-Negotiators-Guide_Chapter_3_Thinking-about-solidarity-and-coalitions.pdf

Lafer, G., & Loustaunau, L. (2020, July 23). *Fear at work An inside account of how employers threaten, intimidate, and harass workers to stop them from exercising their right to collective bargaining.* EPI. https://www.epi.org/publication/fear-at-work-how-employers-scare-workers-out-of-unionizing/

Lessin, N., & Pratt, D. (2020, April 18). *Organizing on Health and Safety in the face of the Coronavirus.* [Paper presentation]. The Labor Notes Virtual.

Mahler, D. (2020). *The impact of COVID-19 (Coronavirus) on global poverty: Why Sub-Saharan Africa might be the region hardest hit (blog).* World Bank Group, Washington D.C., https://blogs.worldbank.org/opendata/impact-covid-19-coronavirus-global-poverty-why-sub saharan-africa-might-be-region-hardest

Mantsios, G. (2015). Through the Looking-Glass of History: A New Vision for Labor Education. *Journal of Labor and Society*, 18(4), 555–573.

Mauku, M. (2022) *Leadership Qualities in Trade Unions.* [Paper presentation]. Leadership Workshop of the Organization of Trade Unions (NOTU), Maria Flo, Masaka, Uganda. https://ugandajournalistsunion.com/news/2022/06/22/leadership-qualities-in-trade-unionism

McKinsey Global Institute. (2016) *Digital Globalization: The new era of Global Inflows.* McKinsey. https://www.mckinsey.com/~/media/mckinsey/business%20functions/mckinsey%20digital/our%20insights/digital%20globalization%20the%20new%20era%20of%20global%20flows/mgi-digital-globalization-full-report.ashx

McNicholas, C. (2018, May 22). Supreme Court deals significant blows to workers rights. *Economic Policy Institute Newsletter.*

Miles, A. (2020, September 16). *What are Unions and Why are they important.* Heddels. https://www.heddels.com/2020/09/what-are-unions-and-why-are-they-important/

Monzani, L., & Van Dick, R. (2021). Positive Leadership in Organizations. In J. M. Peiro (Ed.), *Oxford Research Encyclopedia of Psychology* (pp. 1–37). Oxford University Press.

Muttaqa, Y. A. (2021). *Working Conditions and Collective Representation of Uber and Bolt Digital Platform Drivers in Nigeria.* Global Labour University (GLU) Working Papers.

Neeley, T. (2021). *Remote work revolution.* Harper Collins Publishers.

O'Connor, S. (2017, September 17). *Trade Unions strive to stay relevant by wooing the young.* FT. https://www.ft.com/content/3f6e9d7c-98bb-11e7-a652-cde3f882dd7b

OECD. (2014). *Job Creation and Local Economic Development*. OECD Publishing. doi:10.1787/9789264215009-

Olurode, O., & Gaskia, J. (2022, May 1). *Nigerian workers should unite and take over power in 2023*. [Press Statement]. The Peoples Alternative Political Movement in commemoration of the 2022 International Workers' Day, Abuja, Nigeria. https://www.vanguardngr.com/2022/05/workers-day-movement-urges-workers-to-unite-take-over-power-in-2023

Orback, J. (2015). The World Needs Union Political Cooperation. In T. Svensson, K. Thapper, & M. Nilsson (Eds.), *How to run a Trade Union: Trade Union Handbook* (pp. 40–41). The Olof Palme International Center.

Otobo, D. (2017, January). *Labour unity and Trade Union governance*. [Paper presentation]. Ilorin, Kwara State, Nigeria. https://www.dailytrust.com.ng/news/opinion/labour-unity-and-trade-union-governance/180917 .html, .

Oyewunmi, O.A, & Oyewunmi, A.E. (2017). Nigeria's Public University System: Are Trade Unions Still Viable. *Asia Pacific Journal of Academic Research in Social Sciences* (2)1-7.

Oxfam. (2018). *Reward work, Not wealth*. Oxfam Briefing Paper. https://www.oxfam.org/sites/www.oxfam.org/files/file_attachments/bp-reward-work-not-wealth-220118-en.pdf

Pazzanese, C. (2022, April 7). Will the message sent by Amazon workers turn into a movement? *Harvard Gazette*. https://news.harvard.edu/gazette/story/2022/04/the-future-of-labor-unions-according-to-harvard-economist/

Pologeorgis, N. A. (2022). *Employability, the Labour Force and the Economy*. Investiopedia. https://www.investopedia.com/articles/economics/12/employability-labor-force-economy.asp

Roache, P. (2017, September 17) *Trade Unions strive to stay relevant by wooing the young*. FT. https://www.ft.com/content/3f6e9d7c-98bb-11e7-a652-cde3f882dd7b

Sanches, W. (2018). Welcome to the Global Worker. *The Global Worker*, *1*(4), 2.

Silla, I., Gracia, F. J., & Peiró, J. M. (2020). Upward voice: Participative decision making, trust in leadership and safety climate matter. *Sustainability (Basel)*, *12*(9), 36–72. doi:10.3390u12093672

Smith, W. C., Sakiko, I., Baker, D. P., & Cheng, M. (2016). Education, health, and labor force supply: Broadening human capital for national development in Malawi. *Cogent Education*, *3*(1), 1. doi:10.1080/2331186X.2016.1149041

Sneader, K., & Singhal, S. (2021, January, 4). *The next normal arrives: The trends that will define 2021 – and beyond*. McKinsey. https://www.mckinsey.com/featured-insights/leadership/the-next-normal-arrives-trends-that-will-define-2021-and-beyond#/

Solidarity Center. (2023). *Trade Union Strengthening*. Solidarity Center. https://www.solidaritycenter.org/what-we-do/trade-union-strengthening/

Stahl, A. (2022, January 22). Workforce trends are changing as we are embrace a new normal in 2022. *Forbes*. https://www.forbes.com/sites/ashleystahl/2022/01/24/workforce-trends-are-changing-as-we-embrace-a-new-normal-in-2022/?sh =19bc2e8c2848

Svensson, T. (2015) *How to run a Trade union*: Trade union handbook. Stockholm: Olof Palme International center.

Thakker, P. (2023, March). Workers of Color Made up 100% OF Union. *Growth, 2022*. https://newrepublic.com/post/171375/workers-color-union-growth-2022

Tinuoye, T. A. (2023, January 30). *Redefining Trade Union practices in a Post Pandemic and Future World of work*, [Paper presentation]. The National Workshop on Trade Union Leadership Development, Ilorin, Nigeria. https://www.harisingh.com/Ubuntu/Age.htm

UNDP. (2015). Human Development Report 2015: Work for Human Development. New York: United Nations Development Programme

UNDP. (2021). *The impact of COVID-19 on Business Enterprises in Nigeria*. UNDP. https://www.undp.org/sites/g/files/zskgke326/files/migration/ng/The-Impact-of-COVID19-on-Business-Enterprises-in-Nigeria .pdf

Valverde-Moreno, M., Torres-Jimenez, M., & Lucia-Casademunt, A. M. (2020). Participative decision-making amongst employees in a cross-cultural employment setting: Evidence from 31 European countries. *European Journal of Training and Development*, 45(1), 14–35. doi:10.1108/EJTD-10-2019-0184

Visser, J. (2019). *Trade Unions in a balance, ILO/Actrav*. Geneva: ILO

Waronwant. (2023, February 15). *News and Analysis: Ten Reasons Why Unions are Important*. War on Want. https://www.waronwant.org/news-analysis/ten-reasons-why-unions-are-important

Williams, D., & Uticensis, K. (2013, August 20) *Creating a culture of unionism in the South.* Facing South. https://www.facingsouth.org/2013/08/creating-a-culture-of-unionism-in -the-south.html

ADDITIONAL READING

Avdagic, S., & Baccaro, L. (2014). The future of employment relations in advanced capitalism: Inexorable decline? In A. G. W. Wilkinson & R. Deeg (Eds.), *The Oxford Handbook of Employment Relations* (pp. 701–726). Oxford University Press.

Bavik, A. (2020). A systematic review of the servant leadership literature in management and hospitality. *International Journal of Contemporary Hospitality Management*, 32(1), 347–382. doi:10.1108/IJCHM-10-2018-0788

Damachi, U. G. (1992). Industrial Relations and African Development. In T. Fashoyin (Ed.), *Industrial Relations and African Development* (pp. 11–27). South Asian Publishers PVT Ltd.

Dockès, E. (2019). New Trade Union Strategies for New Forms of Employment. *European Labour Law Journal*, *10*(3), 219–228. doi:10.1177/2031952519870061

Fashoyin, T. (1986). Trade Unions and Economic Development in Africa. *International Studies of Management & Organization*, *16*(2), 59–78. https://www.jstor.org/stable/40397040. doi:10.1080/00208825.1986.11656430

Ibsen, C. L., & Tapia, M. (2017). Trade union revitalization: Where are we now? Where to next? *The Journal of Industrial Relations*, *59*(2), 170–191. doi:10.1177/0022185616677558

ILO. (2016). *Non-standard employment around the word. Understanding challenges, shaping prospects*. ILO.

ILO. (2022). *World employment and social outlook: Trends 2021*. ILO.

ITUC. (2021). *Trade Unions and the New normal in the world of work*. African Regional Organization of the International Trade Union Confederation, ITUC-Africa.

Manning, G., & Curtis, K. (2009). *The Art of Leadership* (3rd ed.). McGraw-Hill.

Orr, C. A. (1966). Trade Unionism in Colonial Africa. *The Journal of Modern African Studies*, *4*(1), 65–81. doi:10.1017/S0022278X00012970

Ulrich, D., & Ulrich, W. (2010). *The why of work: How great leaders build abundant organizations that win*. McGraw-Hill.

KEY TERMS AND DEFINITIONS

Dialogue: The processes involved in the peaceful resolution of issues, problems and or conflicts through discussions between and among contending or disputing parties.

Innovation: The utilization of additional advances in knowledge and newly acquired skills to ensure the effective performance and completion of a task.

Labor Laws: The aspect of law that deals with regulating employment relationships and setting out terms of engagement between social partners.

Leadership: The art of leading, managing and administering an organization in order to achieve and attain set goals through an array of methods.

Production: The process whereby a firm turns economic inputs like labor, machinery, and raw materials into outputs like goods and services used by consumers.

Technological Change: A combination of invention—advances in knowledge—and innovation.

Trade Union: A group of wages earners that join forces or come together to form an association to protect their common interests and positions.

Wages: Income earned from work and or other production activities which facilitates decent standard and or quality of life.

Work: The deployment of materials, finance, and manpower resources to perform a task, role or function.

Workers' Rights: These are diverse protections by law and rules covering several, but defined aspects which individuals are entitled to by virtue of being workers.

Section 4
Leadership, Work–Life Conflict, Wellbeing, and Happiness

In today's volatile, uncertain, complex, and ambiguous global environment, organisations are increasingly recognising the importance of employee well-being and, their work-life conflict and happiness and the effect of leadership on these issues. The first chapter in this section examines the factors contributing to happiness of academics and proposes a framework for institutional happiness for building sustainable universities. The next chapter explores the effect of ethical leadership on employee well-being in an organisational context. And the third chapter examined the role of effective leadership in enhancing employee performance and retention while promoting employee work-life balance.

Chapter 8
Leading With Happiness:
The Institutional Happiness Framework for Higher Education Leaders

Palak Verma
Amity University, Noida, India

Nitin Arora
Amity University, Noida, India

Ezaz Ahmed
Columbia College, USA

ABSTRACT

This study investigates the changes in leaders' perspectives towards framing new educational policies supporting sustainable empowerment of academicians via focusing on happiness and well-being. The objectives of this study are (1) to explore various factors influencing academicians' happiness post-pandemic, (2) to propose various guidelines for educational leaders to support future policy formulation, and (3) to develop an institutional happiness framework for building sustainable universities. Based on interviews with university professors, a qualitative methodology is being utilized where themes are extracted using NVIVO. The study highlights various factors contributing towards enhancing academicians' happiness (i.e., academic freedom, work-life balance, workload management, annual academic retreats, ex-student appreciation rewards, mindfulness in research). The proposed institutional happiness model can be used to enhance research practices, teaching patterns, community service awareness, and innovation, which positively contribute towards achieving SDG 3, SDG 4, and SDG 9.

1. INTRODUCTION

One of the worst global pandemics in recorded history, coronavirus-19, had a significant effect on the academic sector, causing widespread changes in how education sector operates. The Covid-19 epidemic served as an impetus for this paradigm change, and it occurred irrespective of whether the communities

DOI: 10.4018/978-1-6684-8257-5.ch008

were already established, in the course of development, or underdeveloped. There have been numerous natural and man-made disasters in India's past, but this is the first time in our country's history that the education system has had to undertake a complete 180-degree shift. Due to recent events, the information sharing industry and its players have undergone substantial changes (Doyumaç et al., 2020). Previous works of literature did not foresee the rapid rate at which teaching and learning methods were changing. Although the pandemic hampered efforts to disseminate information, it also presented an unexpected window of opportunity (Han, 2021) to advance toward the Sustainable Development Goals for Education, set by the United Nations in 2030.

Knowledge sharing in India has been propelled in large part by developments in IT and IT-enabled services (Crisolo, 2018). The impact of the education sector on the global economy has grown as a result of digitalization and modernisation. On the other side, the ambiance that the pandemic produced served as a wake-up call to university personnel about the significance of maintaining emotional steadiness and awareness in their work. Recent research has shown that teachers' ability to inspire hope and enthusiasm in their students is crucial, and this has led some to propose introducing "happiness courses" into the educational system (Rodowicz et al., 2020). Happy educators build happy students. Therefore, the new dimension of employee happiness and well-being has emerged as a powerful force in the effort to establish Sustainable Universities alongside technology up-skilling. There has been an enormous change in perspective on the value of happiness at work during the past few decades. Happiness was previously not a major focus in the study of organizational behaviour, but this has changed with the rise of positive psychology and a subsequent focus on employee satisfaction.

Academic Leaders may cultivate a happy and healthy workplace by putting an emphasis on aspects like employee engagement, healthy relationships, and a good and encouraging culture. This is good for the employees individually, and it also helps the institution as a whole (Fisher, 2010a). The COVID-19 pandemic has had a profound impact on the education sector, forcing educational leaders to make tough decisions in order to ensure both immediate survival and long-term growth and development. Initially, many academics were hesitant to adopt the new technology-based models of knowledge exchange, due to health concerns and changes in teaching patterns. Additionally, the blurring of personal and professional boundaries, coupled with an expanded scope of work, has led to increased stress levels among educators. Effective leadership has been identified as a key driver for transforming the education system (Gyang, 2020). Educational leadership is a community-based process that influences and guides individuals to work voluntarily towards achieving common goals in educational institutions (Matthew, 2017). Educational leaders are now prioritizing the well-being of educators and are developing policies that promote a more supportive and balanced environment, with the aim of building sustainable universities. During the pandemic, some of the major leadership styles adopted by academic leaders are authentic leadership, servant leadership, leader-member exchange (LMX), situational leadership, distributed leadership, and ineffective forms of leadership (Lalani et al., 2021).

The COVID-19 pandemic has brought about significant changes in the education sector, including a paradigm shift in the teaching and learning process. As a result, educational leaders have had to make difficult decisions to ensure the survival, growth, and development of their institutions. A higher degree of transformational leadership indicates better efficiency and satisfaction for employees in the Education sector (Antonopoulou et al., 2021). One of the key challenges faced by the sector is the need to retain emotionally balanced Academicians, which is essential for building sustainable universities and achieving Sustainable Development Goal 4. To address this challenge, a new happiness model is needed to guide the development of policies that support educational leaders in fostering the well-being of their staff. Additionally, this study explores the concept of educational leadership and its role in the context of the paradigm shifts experienced in the education sector during the pandemic. In building sustainable universities, it is essential to consider the needs of various stakeholders, including students, educators, and the wider community. Various studies highlight the impact of pandemic on students, or teachers in schools, but very few research has been undertaken focusing University academicians. This study identifies the research gap highlighting the lack of studies being conducted, focussed on Academicians' wellbeing in the University system.

This study aims to investigate how educational leaders can frame new policies that focus on the happiness and well-being of Academicians, in order to support sustainable empowerment and contribute towards building sustainable universities. Traditionally, universities have focused on retaining knowledgeable educators through monetary benefits, but have often neglected their mental, emotional, and social well-being. However, in the post-COVID scenario, Academicians have become extra mindful of the importance of self-care and well-being in their work life. As one of the most important stakeholders in the education sector, Academicians play a crucial role in building sustainably empowered universities. Therefore, this study seeks to examine changes in leaders' perspectives towards developing new policies that support Academicians' well-being and happiness.

This paper focuses on interviewing University professors and exploring various factors that would positively contribute towards building Sustainable Universities with the perspective of an Academician. Therefore, the objectives of this study are as follows-

1. To explore various factors influencing Academicians' Happiness post-pandemic.
2. To propose various guidelines for educational leaders to support future policy formulation.
3. To develop an institutional Happiness Framework for building Sustainable Universities.

The qualitative approach chosen for this study aims to gain a deep understanding of the impact of the pandemic on Academicians' happiness and well-being. The significance of this study lies in its potential to contribute towards the field of education by introducing new dimensions of well-being and happiness as key factors for sustainable development. The study emphasizes that investing in the well-being of Academicians is not only important for their personal growth but also for the growth of educational institutions.

By establishing the foundational grounds for building sustainable universities, this study proposes a new perspective for educational leaders to focus on Academicians' well-being and happiness as a means of achieving sustainable development goals. With the findings of this study, educational leaders will be able to frame new policies and practices that prioritize the well-being and happiness of Academicians, thus strengthening the foundation of education systems and building a sustainable future.

The rest of the study is organized as follows. Section 2 addresses the Literature exploring Happiness and wellbeing aspects and Post covid scenarios in education sector. Section 3 discusses the method used in detail. Then the findings using the interviews and qualitative approach are presented in section 4. Section 5 provides the studies implications. Finally, the study's conclusion along with suggestions for future study are given in the last section.

2. LITERATURE REVIEW

This section discusses impact of pandemic on the education sector and academicians' happiness. Further it illuminates the research work depicting the role of Educational leadership laying the groundwork for determining the influence of pandemic on various aspects for building sustainable universities.

2.1. Impact of the Pandemic on the Education Sector

The sudden outbreak of the COVID-19 pandemic has shaken the entire world and brought attention to the importance of public health and safety. The resulting uncertainty has deeply impacted every sector on a global level, including the education sector (World Health Organization, 2020, Das, 2020). The pandemic forced the education system to shift from traditional in-person learning to online learning, which became the only ray of hope for the major stakeholders in the education sector (Sharma et al., 2021). Teachers had to upskill and adapt to new teaching methodologies to ensure the continuation of the knowledge exchange process (UNESCO, 2020). National and international academic bodies had to collaborate and incorporate available resources to ensure that students could continue learning (Schneider & Council, 2020). The early stages of the lockdown proved to be a challenge for the education sector, but the crisis has also accelerated the pace of advancement in the education industry (Izumi et al., 2021). In India, the education sector has been impacted to such a great extent, unprecedented in the history of the country, given the numerous natural and man-made disasters it has faced in the past. Despite the challenges, the education sector has risen to the occasion and implemented new strategies to ensure that highly skilled academicians are strongly handling the changes in the education sector.

2.2. Technology Adoption in the Education Sector

In addition, the pandemic has provided an opportunity for educational institutions to re-evaluate their goals and redefine the learning outcomes for students. This has prompted the education sector to shift their focus from traditional knowledge delivery to the development of skills and competencies that are relevant to the rapidly changing job market (Kukulska-Hulme & Traxler, 2021). With the rising use of digital technologies in the education sector, students are encouraged to develop skills that enhance their problem-solving abilities, critical thinking, and creativity (Essa et al., 2020). The integration of new technologies has also provided access to education to individuals who were previously excluded from the formal education system due to financial, geographical, or social barriers (Al Lily et al., 2020). Furthermore, the use of digital technologies in the education sector has also led to the emergence of new teaching methods, such as blended learning and flipped classrooms. These methods encourage student-centered learning and provide a more personalized learning experience (Chen et al., 2021). Teachers have become facilitators of learning rather than mere information providers. The use of multimedia and interactive resources has also made the learning process more engaging and enjoyable for students (Joshi et al., 2020). Overall, the pandemic has led to significant changes in the education sector, forcing educational institutions to adapt and innovate to meet the changing needs of students and academicians. The use of digital technologies has accelerated the growth of the education system and provided opportunities for sustainable development in the field. As we move forward, it is important for educational leaders to continue to prioritize the well-being and happiness of academicians, as they are the backbone of the education sector and critical for building sustainable universities (Toquero, 2020).

2.3. Impact of the Pandemic on Higher Education Leaders Post-Pandemic

The pandemic has significantly impacted academic leaders in various ways from managing the shift to remote learning to maintaining financial stability and ensuring the well-being of faculty, staff, and students. Some of the major impacts of the pandemic on academic leaders comprise of Adoption of online learning, Financial Impact, Mental and emotional wellbeing (Crawford et al., 2020). A critical examination of leadership strategies has been undertaken in educational institutions in various countries during covid times. A research critically examined the measures adopted by educational leaders in Barbados and Canada highlighting the need to have a clear direction, collaboration at work and adoptive leadership styles (Marshall, Roache, & Moody-Marshall, 2020). According to a study in Babes- Bolyai University, Romania, the personal characteristics of academic leaders, decentralization of unity and innovation and reinvention opportunities in the university are the major factor explored for coping with the changes due to the pandemic (Dumulescu & Muţiu, 2021).The US Higher Education institution officials adopted all the servant leadership behaviors to handle the shifts taking place due to the pandemic and the crisis leadership measures were not significantly fruitful (Al-Asfour et al., 2022). The crisis faced by the education sector was outlined by the redressal mechanism of universities and educational leaders. The Turkish faculties spotted the relevance of building trustworthy relationships, better leadership forms and efficient communications as the basis for handling the turbulent environment of the pandemic (Örücü & Kutlugün, 2022). The pandemic impacted Universities up to a great extent pushing towards the need for adopting a wider scope of measures to build leadership strategies based on academicians' needs with the vision to build sustainable universities.

2.4. Academicians' Happiness

Businesses are becoming increasingly aware of the need of cultivating a positive work environment for their employees. Employees who report feeling joyful at work are found to be more invested in their jobs, more likely to go above and beyond in their work, and to get along better with their superiors and co-workers. (Business & For, 2012). In addition, research has connected happiness to positive results including fewer turnover, decreased absenteeism, and more creativity and innovation. (Fisher, 2010). Employee happiness is a crucial factor for any industry, and it has also become a popular research topic in the education sector. Ravina-Ripoll et al. (2019) argue that employee happiness is a critical aspect of job satisfaction, productivity, and retention. A long history of research has shown that employee happiness enhances productivity, including in the education sector (Loury, 2012). Sustainable happiness in the education sector is vital for building a positive relationship with human development and ecological resilience (O'Brien, 2012). The role of educators has evolved from merely delivering lectures to being more involved in institutional decisions. This expanded scope of work highlights the demanding nature of this profession, and yet initiatives supporting educators' happiness are still in their infancy stage (Lomas et al., 2017). Happiness and well-being are becoming significant factors contributing to building high-quality educators. Research has shown that better social connectivity with peers and group activities can enhance educators' happiness (Wessels & Wood, 2019). Employee happiness is a strong motivational factor for organizations as it enhances the market image of the educational institution (de Waal, 2018). Moreover, employee happiness positively mediates between job expectations and organizational goals, suggesting that happy employees are more likely to meet the organization's objectives (Thompson & Bruk-Lee, 2021). The COVID-19 pandemic has made educators more aware of their mental and emotional well-being. Therefore, the above literature highlighting the relevance of employee happiness underscores the need to explore the factors that contribute to educators' happiness, with a vision to attain an educator-focused happiness model. Educator-focused happiness models can help create happier and more productive educators, which can translate into better learning outcomes for students.

2.5. Sustainable Universities

SDG4 aims to provide quality education for all, and the COVID-19 pandemic has highlighted the need for upskilling and reskilling of educators to achieve this goal. Jose and Chacko (2017) suggest that sustainable universities can improve educational governance by promoting collaboration and resource sharing among institutions. Dumitrascu and Ciudin (2015) identify factors such as academic and extracurricular activities, as well as overall university attractiveness, that contribute to building sustainable universities. Universities have a social responsibility to promote sustainable development in their communities, and this can be achieved through community-based leadership models, as suggested by Gyang (2020). Energy management is another key aspect of sustainability in higher education institutions, as it promotes a positive relationship with top management support, stakeholder relationships, and risk management, as noted by Saleh et al. (2020). The incorporation of happiness and well-being concepts at an institutional level can also contribute to building sustainable higher education institutions, according to Munar et al. (2020). However, recent studies show that the pandemic has negatively impacted the work-life balance, positive feelings, and engagement levels of educators, leading to a decrease in their happiness levels (Bhatia & Mohsin, 2020; Arora, 2020). This highlights the need for reskilling and empowerment of educators through technological advancements to improve their overall well-being and contribute positively to the building of sustainable universities.

The above subsections outline the literature related to different aspects of the study. Section 2.1 highlights the impact of the pandemic on the Education sector. Technology adoption is the major paradigm shift which has been adopted due to the pandemic and Academicians had to adopt the changes leading to increased stress and work life imbalance (Section 2.2). This leads to the need for progressive measures to be adopted by educational leaders to improve the emotional and mental wellbeing of academicians by focusing on implementing strategies to improve their happiness (Section 2.3, 2.4). Academicians, being the most important stakeholders in the education sector, play a significant role in the adoption of all the changes arisen due to the pandemic and thus moving towards building sustainably empowered Universities (Section 2.5). Hence there is a massive need to build a framework to guide educational leaders by providing them with an academicians' perspective for building sustainable Universities.

3. METHODOLOGY

In this paper, the focus is on exploring the factors that impact the happiness of academicians and proposing an institutional happiness model for building sustainable universities. To achieve this, recent literature related to the post-COVID-19 educational landscape and the concept of academicians' happiness in sustainable universities has been reviewed. In addition to this, empirical data was collected from the field through open-ended interviews (Grounded Theory) with 15 academicians from universities with a minimum of 8 years and a maximum of 22 years of experience. The interviews were based on a standardized questionnaire developed through pilot testing with 5 university professors. The interviews were conducted face-to-face and over digital communication platforms, and the participants were selected through purposeful sampling. The participants were informed that their interviews would be recorded and that pseudonyms would be used to protect their identities. The interviews centred on understanding the impact of the pandemic on educators and how they adapted to develop various skills for sustainability in the education sector. Each conversation spanned between 30 and 50 minutes, and extra conversations were conducted as follow-ups when respondents had more points to make. Once the interviews were conducted, they were transcribed and further themes were extracted using NVIVO. The thematic analysis of the individual semi-structured interviews provided a solid foundation for the new aspects cropping out in the education sector due to the pandemic (Bhatia & Mohsin, 2020; Arora, 2020).

Based on the information gathered from interviews and previous research, a qualitative proposal based on qualitative analysis is given. The cognitive strategy that is most appropriate for a certain researcher serves as the foundation for qualitative analysis. A single theory may appear crystal clear to someone with a similar cognitive style, while it may be incomprehensible to someone with an entirely different cognitive style. As a result, a Grounded theory is built on diverse viewpoints for different individuals, because a single theory may appear crystal clear to someone with a similar cognitive style (Heath & Cowley, 2004). "Grounded theory" is "a set of systematic inductive procedures for doing qualitative research with the objective of establishing a theory," as stated by Charmaz. "Grounded theory" also refers to "the development of a theory." The term "grounded theory" really refers to two separate ideas: (a) a methodology that is characterized by adaptable methodological strategies, and (b) the findings obtained through the use of this type of research (Charmaz & Liska, 2015). In accordance with the findings of this study, the grounded theory is developed by combining pertinent findings from earlier research with the main data obtained from personal interviews, as was said earlier.

Data Collection

The designation, the institution location, and the courses taken by the academicians are tabulated in Table 1. Pseudo names are being used to protect the identities of the interviewees where P stands for Professor, Asso. P stands for Associate professor and Asiss. P stands for Assistant Professor.

Based on the past literatures and interviews, various statements were extracted. In this section we will explore some of the aspects highlighted by the interviewees by bifurcating among the three objectives being explored in this research work.

4. FINDINGS AND DISCUSSIONS

The first section of the findings will explore themes/factors leading to academicians' Happiness in the post Covid times. Further we propose various guidelines highlighted in the interviews to support educational leaders. Lastly, we propose an institutional Happiness framework for building sustainable universities.

4.1 Academicians' Happiness Post-Pandemic

Happiness is a subjective experience that encompasses various dimensions of wellbeing, including emotional, physical, and social aspects. In the context of educational institutions, the COVID-19 pandemic has led to significant disruptions in the exchange of knowledge and skills. However, with the adoption

Table 1.

SNO.	PSEUDO NAMES	DESIGNATION	INSTITUTION LOCATION/ COURSE
1.	P1	Professor & HOI	Haryana/ Management
2.	P2	Professor	Jaipur/ Management
3.	P3	Professor	Delhi/ Political Science
4.	P4	Professor & HOD	Delhi/ Commerce
5.	P5	Professor	Haryana/ Computer science
6.	P6	Professor	Uttar Pradesh/ Civil engineering
7.	Asso.P1	Associate Professor	Uttar Pradesh/ Management
8.	Asso. P2	Associate Professor	Haryana/ Management
9.	Asso. P3	Associate Professor	Chandigarh/ Management
10.	Asso. P4	Associate Professor	Uttar Pradesh/ Designing
11.	Asso. P5	Associate Professor	Delhi/ Computer science
12.	Asiss. P1	Assistant Professor	Uttar Pradesh/ Mass Communication
13.	Asiss. P2	Assistant Professor & HOD	Haryana/ Commerce
14.	Asiss. P3	Assistant Professor	Chhattisgarh/ English
15.	Asiss. P4	Assistant Professor	Kurukshetra/ Commerce

of various digital platforms and technologies, educators have been able to adapt to the new normal and continue to empower students with the necessary skills for their future success (Bao, 2020). Despite the resilience demonstrated by educators during the pandemic, it is crucial to acknowledge the emotional and mental toll it has taken on them. The pandemic has caused unprecedented levels of stress, anxiety, and grief among educators and students alike. This emotional turmoil can negatively impact the wellbeing and academic performance of students, as well as the job satisfaction and work-life balance of educators (Shen & Slater, 2021). To address these challenges, educational leaders have made significant amendments to policies and practices in the education sector. For instance, community-based leadership models have been proposed to foster collaboration and resource sharing among educational institutions, leading to enhanced governance and more sustainable universities (Gyang, 2020). Additionally, incorporating the concept of happiness at the institutional level can promote positive emotions, reliable relationships, and sustainable growth of higher education institutions (Munar et al., 2020).

The post pandemic has somehow outgrown the pace of development in the education sector. According to P4 "The pandemic accelerated the pace of technical and emotional upskilling in educators. We at our department conducted personal conversations with our faculties to understand their concerns and organised technical as well as happiness workshops for them and as a result, now, our faculties feel more comfortable to talk about their feelings than before COVID times."

On the basis of past literature and interviews following themes /factors have been extracted explaining Academicians' happiness in the post-pandemic phase.

4.1.1. Freedom at Workplace

Academicians need the flexibility to work efficiently. Educators at university level require different levels of freedoms on the basis of their position i.e Assistant Professor, associate Professor and Professor. P1 being the HOI highlights that, "We feel happy when we are accepted for what we are. The organization gives us the environment that we are doing things with full commitment because we have the freedom to implement activities and practices which are relevant for the betterment of the institution. I don't need to manipulate myself because I am being respected for what I am. Here I am taking the initiatives as the person I am and they are working really well for the overall growth of the organization.". Further, Asso P5 added that "a role clarity gives an autonomy to the Educator regarding various engagements like teaching-learning, research practices, clerical works etc. Targets with short time might degrade the quality of work being done. The policies should be build in such away that we as academicians could equally focus on our wellbeing and career growth". Assis P2 expressed "The time bound stay within the campus or indulgence in excessive administrative activities is quit restricting as this time could be used for improving our own research and career prospects. The punch-in and punch-out system restricts our freedom to relax and binds us from further connections with industry or market or community."

4.1.2. Work-Life Balance

Work from home has become the standard (Savić, 2020). The recent pandemic grew an imbalance between the personal and professional lives of an academician. Increased technology dependence led working flexibility from remote locations. The new teaching patterns are still being practiced post-pandemic. An academician feels relaxed when the line of division between personal and professional life are clearly defined. In support of this aspect P3 highlights that " We have a strict culture at our University, NO CALLS AFTER 6PM. This helps us grant equal time to our personal as well as professional spaces." Further, Asso P5 highlights that "managing work from home was difficult during the pandemic, but as a result of this, we are expected to work in an online mode even today. We have to take excessive administrative work to home and work meetings are organized on weekends which impacts our personal spaces. This needs to balance as our responsibility towards our family is equally important as our work."

4.1.3. Workload Management

Teachers faced an increase in their workload during the pandemic which is quite a lot in the post pandemic phase as well, due to the changes that are being adopted for building good quality educators (Adedoyin & Soykan, 2020). P6 pointed out that "We have a lot of pressure for administrative work. The processes for a single approval are very tedious as they are completely centralised. AssisP4 further adds that "we as academicians are happy to take classes, join new courses and adopt new advanced technologies but we are overloaded with extra administrative works." and Assis P2 said "If I am handling my classes and administrative work well, then I am unable to focus on research publications and conference presentations which is very important for my own career as professor." Asso P1 highlights that "The targets are timebound which increases the workload."

4.1.4. Recruitment and Promotion Evaluation Standards

Growth in the education sector is dependent on various factors like, Knowledge level, Research Publications, Research projects and most significantly student results or feedbacks. Evaluation of an academician is not based on an overall qualification or performance of an academicians at workplace. Equal importance to all the tasks performed by an academician is relevant while hiring or promoting them.

P2 highlights that " In developed countries liker the US has a strong education policy which states that for gaining a teaching position at a university, a doctorate or a post-doctoral degree is a pre-requisite. Her in Indian educational systems, anyone can enter the academic world and increase the competition for people who have been working hard in the education sector. So, the Indian education system should frame fixed policies for entry and growth in the education system and its actual implementation is necessary". Further, Asso P3 points out that "Research publication is now one of the most important criteria for promotions. But we handle teaching as well as a great load of administrative work which leaves us with less time for research. If I am handle the administrative work well, why is that not being accounted as a part of my growth and add up to my API scores. And if this administrative work is not important, then why are the academicians burdened with it? It's quite stressful when the contributions towards the institution go unrecognised when at the end of the day, others are being values more because I have 2 publications and the other person has 4" AssisP3 pointed that "Frankly, I feel that the education sector is becoming the new cinema where the flag of nepotism is flying high because the recruitments and the promotions are not being fairly judged. And this leads to unhappiness for those who are actually working hard to sustain here."

4.1.5. Annual Academic Retreats

Apart from Academics, students have various options for stress relief as they have the opportunity to indulge themselves into extra-curricular activities with their friends and form informal bonds with the fellow students. But the stressful life of an academician is now a new concern in post covid times. Academicians need various well-being trainings and stress busting sessions with their peers so as to re-energise them at workplace. A common finding is that a better social connectivity with the peers along with some group activities enhances educators happiness. (Wessels & Wood, 2019). Asso P4 shared that "We as academicians are under a lot of stress and sometimes even, we feel like we could be a part of some activity which is for our wellbeing. Some group activities or games with our peers would help us build strong bonds and improve our willingness to take new initiatives with collaborations". Further Assis P1 adds "Universities should organize Annual academic meets and maybe also build stress relieving zones for educators. Various activities like meditation, physical fitness, yoga, etc. could be organized for us and I feel that this would help us connect better with the institution."

4.1.6. Ex-Student Appreciation Rewards

In conversation with all the Interviewees, they were asked to share any such incident in their life when they felt really happy that they were an educator. A new perspective came out of this study was the sense of fulfilment as a reward which an academician gains when their students come back to them after they are successful and owe their success to their teachers. Every academician related their experience with their students emotional connectivity with them. P5 stated an experience "I am having an experience of 28 years and in this time frame I feel the happiest when my students who have passed out, come back to meet me and express their gratitude to me for helping them. One of my students cleared a top-level government exam and he came with a box of sweets and celebrated his achievement with me. A job as an academician is very stressful today, but this feeling that I get feels like a reward to me". Further, Asso2 stated that "One of my students got a placement in his dream company, and she came to meet me and thanked me for the guidance and support. I feel this reward gives me a level of happiness that

I can't express". Asso P4 said "An Academician is not someone who just has to teach classes. We have to connect to the students as now our roles have changed to a facilitator. I feel we as educators, find our happiness in our students' success".

4.1.7. Mindfulness in Research

Research is one of the most relevant aspect of an academicians' growth. Research has become the general basis for addressing the limitations faced by employees. According to a recent study, faculties are willing to participate in significant research projects, which helps them enhance their productivity at the workplace (Arora, 2020). This growing interest in research is because of the new aspects emerging in every field and the research publications help academicians as well as universities to grow their matrices. P1 shared that "New research methodologies and software are being developed which are being used in the university. Faculties are trained for such software and this help academicians upskill themselves and improve their research practices". AssoP2, Asso P4, Assis P3 and P2 stated that "Research publications are a must for our growth. Assis P4 further added that, "Being a part of research projects help me gain knowledge regarding various research methods and what are the new developments in my field of study".

We were able to obtain the word cloud in Figure 1 using NVivo.

Figure 1. Themes extracted from interviews

4.2. Guidelines for Educational Leaders in Policy Formulation

On the basis of interviews, we propose relevant guidelines to educational leaders to redirect their policies towards educators' interests with a goal of building quality educators.

4.2.1. Educational institutions need to build educator friendly policies granting them an environment where they are capable of taking decisions about as their own working patterns. This could be done by clearly defining roles for each academician and granting them an autonomy to decide their plan of action to complete those roles.

4.2.2. Fixed working hours need to be maintained for academicians so as to mark a clear distinction between personal and professional life.

4.2.3. Educational leaders should equally balance out the workload among various academicians and build a separate department for undertaking all the administrative work. Appropriate time should be allocated to academicians so that they could balance their regular tasks along with the extra work. This will reduce stress and improve their mental health.

4.2.4. On a Macro level, fixed rules regarding education levels, experiences and entry into academia needs to be framed and implemented for recruitment and promotion of academicians.

4.2.5. While recruitment and promotions, appropriate weightage should be assigned to each and every contribution of an academician towards the educational institution which includes- Administrative work, research projects, community involvement, industrial connections, student counselling, etc.

4.2.6. Measures need to be taken focusing mental and emotional wellbeing of academicians like Stress relief zones need to be a part of the university infrastructure, personal problem addressal system needs to be set-up, annual retreats for academicians should be organized so as to improve their personal connectivity with their workplace.

4.2.7. Regular research and wellbeing workshops should be organized so as to upskill and reskill educators on personal as well as professional grounds.

4.3. Institutional happiness Framework

Figure 2 portrays the institutional Happiness framework that highlights various factors that positively contribute towards increasing Institutional Happiness framework.

Figure 2. Institutional happiness framework

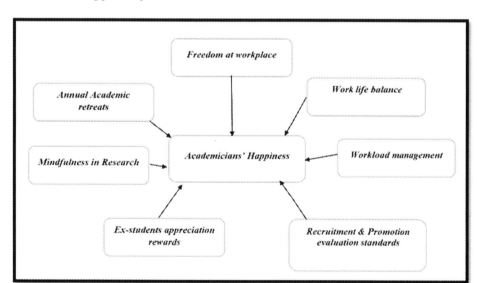

5. IMPLICATIONS

5.1. Policy Implications

This paper identifies various dimensions of pandemic on the Academicians in the education sector. The outcomes of this research are strongly applicable to the present policies framed and adopted by

Educators in the universities. The present study proposes that Academicians well-being is one of the most important concerns in post-pandemic phase. Policies defining clarity in roles for educators helps them manage their work efficiently. Further well-defined workload and work timings help academicians balance their personal and professional lives. The paper suggests that the educational leaders need to frame and implement clear policies for recruitment and promotions of academicians so as to wave off the unnecessary competitions and building well skilled educators. All these changes in the policies would help build sustainably empowered academicians (SDG 4). Frequent informal meets or building stress relieving zones for educators would positively contribute towards building efficient Universities (SDG 9). Universities should invest on taking innovative measures to advance the educators and prepare them in advance for any adversities or further shifts in teaching patterns. Lastly Proper managerial policies should be made for building good industrial relations and educators need to estimate their own skill sets and keep on advancing their technical and emotional aspects. All these aspects would enhance Academicians Happiness thus leading to building sustainable Universities.

5.2. Theoretical Implications

This study provides theoretical understanding by identifying how pandemic has impacted academicians in the university system. The findings show that the pandemic has accelerated the pace of technology adoption in education sector along with a rise in consciousness among Educators. Happiness is one of the major factors heading a university towards achieving sustainability. Research trainings and newly adopted Tech-based teaching patterns have accelerated the pace of upskilling and reskilling of academicians which directly contributes towards a step in achieving the SDG4 (4.4). The newly acquired balanced skills comprising of technological skills and emotional and mental management skills which also helps in supply of qualified academicians to the education sector (4C). Freedom in working patterns and several stress relief programs would strongly support academicians to build a better connectivity with the University. A good working environment with healthy connections with students and peers motivates educators to move ahead and undertake innovative measures. Building technologically equipped infrastructures at universities positively contributes to encouraging innovation and substantially increasing the number of research and development practices (9.5).

The following figure represents the type (Direct or indirect) of impact of accelerated Academicians' happiness on various sustainable development goals.

6. CONCLUSION

The recent pandemic has acted as a catalyst to strengthen the basis of advancement in the education sector which has helped the educational leaders to understand the role of academicians in the successful growth and development of universities. The expanded roles of educators increased their stress levels due to which in the post pandemic phase, Academicians happiness has cropped-up as one of the most significant factors in the adoption of upgraded patterns of work and smooth functioning of Universities. The COVID-19 pandemic has highlighted the importance of mental and emotional well-being for employees in all sectors, including education. The study shows that the pandemic has acted as a wake-up call for the education sectors, as it has illuminated the significance of consciousness and emotional wellbeing in the context of digital development. Academicians' upskilling and reskilling can be used

Figure 3. Direct and indirect contribution towards achievement of SDGs
Note: The figure is generated via using SDG Impact Assessment Tool

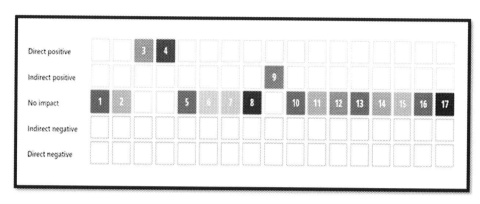

to enhance research practices, teaching patterns, community service awareness and Innovation which positively contributes towards achieving SDG 3, SDG 4 and SDG 9. The study explores and highlights various factors contributing towards enhancing academicians' happiness i.e. Academic freedom, Work life balance, Workload management, Annual Academic retreats, Ex-students appreciation rewards, Mindfulness in Research. Academic Freedom helps academicians feel more empowered in the decision making and improves their commitment towards the University. Further, a well balanced personal and professional life of academicians helps them improve their mental wellbeing and a stress-free mindset. Annual academic meets with fellow academicians, wellbeing training, yoga and meditation sessions and other fun activities arranged for educators help them release their stress and improve their productivity. Arranging for reunion events inviting old students helps academicians meet their students and build a strong sense of accomplishment within themselves by observing their success. Lastly, research trainings and support strongly helps academicians improve there publications and ultimately accelerates their academic growth. The various propositions are highlighted to support educational leaders during policy formulations. Educational leaders may create long-lasting institutions with the support of the Institutional Happiness Framework. The Institutional happiness model strongly supports the educational leaders with an academicians' perspective to build Sustainable Universities, further recommending measures measures to improve academicians' happiness and satisfaction.

7. SCOPE OF FUTURE RESEARCH

The study can be extended by building questionnaires for each factor and collecting quantitative data from a larger sample to check the relevance of Institutional happiness framework. Further, more interviews could be conducted in various geographical areas so as to check for any geographical differences in the responses. New factors could be explored by interviewing different stakeholders in the education sector.

REFERENCES

Adedoyin, O. B., & Soykan, E. (2020). Covid-19 pandemic and online learning: The challenges and opportunities. *Interactive Learning Environments*, 1–13. doi:10.1080/10494820.2020.1813180

Al-Asfour, A., Charkasova, A., Rajasekar, J., & Kentiba, E. (2022). Servant leadership behaviors and the level of readiness to covid-19 pandemic: Evidence from USA higher education institutions. *International Journal of Leadership in Education*, 1–18. doi:10.1080/13603124.2022.2108505

Al Lily, A. E., Ismail, A. F., Abunasser, F. M., & Alhajhoj Alqahtani, R. H. (2020). Distance education as a response to pandemics: Coronavirus and Arab culture. *Technology in Society*, *63*, 101317. doi:10.1016/j.techsoc.2020.101317 PMID:32836570

Antonopoulou, H., Halkiopoulos, C., Barlou, O., & Beligiannis, G. N. (2021). Transformational leadership and digital skills in higher education institutes: During the covid-19 pandemic. *Emerging Science Journal*, *5*(1), 1–15. doi:10.28991/esj-2021-01252

Arora, R. G. (2020). *Happiness among higher education academicians: A demographic analysis*. Academic Press.

Bao, W. (2020). COVID-19 and online teaching in higher education: A case study of Peking University. *Human Behavior and Emerging Technologies*, *2*(2), 113–115. doi:10.1002/hbe2.191 PMID:32510042

Chen, Y., Liu, Y., Zhang, Y., Li, Z., & Zhou, T. (2021). The Effect of Fear of the COVID-19 on Depression Among Chinese Outbound Students Studying Online in China Amid the COVID-19 Pandemic Period: The Role of Resilience and Social Support. *Frontiers in Psychology*, *12*, 750011. doi:10.3389/fpsyg.2021.750011 PMID:34721231

Crawford, J., Henderson, K. B., Rudolph, J., Malkawi, B., Glowatz, M., Burton, R., Magni, P. A., & Lam, S. (2020). COVID-19 : 20 countries' higher education intra-period digital pedagogy responses. *Journal of Applied Learning & Teaching*, *3*(1), 1–20.

Crisolo, N. A. (2018). *Sharpening Education through the Use of Information and Communications Technology*. Online Submission.

Dumulescu, D., & Muţiu, A. I. (2021). Academic Leadership in the Time of COVID-19—Experiences and Perspectives. *Frontiers in Psychology*, *12*, 12. doi:10.3389/fpsyg.2021.648344 PMID:33959076

Fisher, C. D. (2010). Happiness at Work. *International Journal of Management Reviews*, *12*(4), 384–412. doi:10.1111/j.1468-2370.2009.00270.x

Gyang, E. B. (2020). Community-based leadership and sustainable development in higher education. *Journal of Leadership, Accountability and Ethics*, *17*(3), 34–43.

Han, J. L. & S. H. (2021). *The Future of Service Post-COVID-19 Pandemic: Rapid Adoption of Digital Service Technology*. Springer.

Izumi, T., Sukhwani, V., Surjan, A., & Shaw, R. (2021). Managing and responding to pandemics in higher educational institutions: initial learning from COVID-19. *International Journal of Disaster Resilience in the Built Environment*, *12*(1), 51-66.

Joshi, A., Vinay, M., & Bhaskar, P. (2020). Online Teaching amidst COVID-19 in India: An Outlook. *Asian Journal of Distance Education*, *15*(2), 105–111. doi:10.5281/zenodo.4294477

Kukulska-Hulme, A. (2021). Reflections on research questions in mobile assisted language learning. *Journal of China Computer-Assisted Language Learning*, *1*(1), 28–46. doi:10.1515/jccall-2021-2002

Lalani, K., Crawford, J., & Butler-Henderson, K. (2021). Academic leadership during COVID-19 in higher education: Technology adoption and adaptation for online learning during a pandemic. *International Journal of Leadership in Education*, 1–17. doi:10.1080/13603124.2021.1988716

Marshall, J., Roache, D., & Moody-Marshall, R. (2020). Crisis Leadership: A Critical Examination of Educational Leadership in Higher Education in the Midst of the COVID-19 Pandemic. *International Studies in Educational Administration, 48*(3), 30-37.

Munar, A. M., Nadal, J. R., & Gairal-Casadó, R. (2020). A happiness model for the sustainable university. *Sustainability*, *12*(12), 4874.

Örücü, D., & Kutlugün, H. E. (2022). *Navigating the Covid 19 Turbulence in Higher Education: Evidence from Turkish Faculty Members.* Research in Educational Administration & Leadership.

Rodowicz, C. M., Morris, L., Sidman, C. L., & Beyer, K. (2020). The impact of an online happiness course on subjective happiness among college students. *Building Healthy Academic Communities Journal*, *4*(1), 69–81. doi:10.18061/bhac.v4i1.7086

Savić, D. (2020). COVID-19 and work from home: Digital transformation of the workforce. *Grey Journal*, *16*(2), 101–104.

Shen, P., & Slater, P. (2021). The Effect of Occupational Stress and Coping Strategies on Mental Health and Emotional Well-Being among University Academic Staff during the COVID-19 Outbreak. *International Education Studies*, *14*(3), 82–95. doi:10.5539/ies.v14n3p82

Wessels, E., & Wood, L. (2019). Fostering teachers' experiences of well-being: A participatory action learning and action research approach. *South African Journal of Education*, *39*(1), 1–10. doi:10.15700aje.v39n1a1619

Chapter 9
Ethical Leadership and Its Impact on Employee Well-Being:
A Study Based in Manufacturing Firms

Reshma Shrivastava
Amity University, Raipur, India

Imran Nadeem Siddiqui
Amity University, Raipur, India

Gazala Yasmin Ashraf
Amity University, Raipur, India

ABSTRACT

Though ethical leadership and the well-being of employees have been important topics of discussion for research in recent years, just a few studies have looked at the impact of ethical leadership on employee well-being. This chapter aims to examine the effect of ethical leadership on the well-being of employees in the manufacturing firm and to examine the mediating role of employee engagement. The purposive sampling method was used to collect the data through a structured questionnaire, and a total of 264 responses were collected, which were analyzed on Smart PLS version 3.3.2. The findings suggest that there exists a strong correlation between EL and EWB. Also, there is a strong mediation of EE on the relationship between EE and EWB. The theory builds upon and suggests a strong mediating relationship between EL and EWB when EE acts as a mediator. The finding also suggests that the employees can be engaged in an organization to improve performance through EL.

INTRODUCTION

Leadership is an important part of managing a company well. Is leadership important? Yes, it is. Just as the leader regulates the followers same as the behavior of followers regulates. There are many great leaders who actually run their companies better by having better or better outcome situations for people.

DOI: 10.4018/978-1-6684-8257-5.ch009

Ethical Leadership and Its Impact on Employee Well-Being

Company executives and bosses and the market raise concerns about their employees, by all means, to motivate, raise awareness and determine their juniors. Business practices have played an important role in businesses for decades (Khuwaja et al., 2020; Van Vugt & von Rueden, 2020). Therefore, the basic job of management is to keep your followers happy. Herzberg states that in his motivational principles, there are elements of motivators within the organization. In addition to motivation, they can also be hygienic factors. He states that front runners need to be more motivated to persuade their followers. Therefore, the Present study specializes in the questions in this survey. How to generate employee involvement through proper ethical management. According to various studies, transformative leaders have alternative employees within the organization, but ethical leaders generally tend to be replaced within the company. An effective leadership directive or participative leadership both affects the functionality of the organisation. (Van Vugt & von Rueden, 2020). Ethical leadership helps create ethical behavior within an organization. Due to the fact that ethical leaders are attractive and effective leaders who intrigue and maintain their followers (Brown & Trevino, 2006). Ethical management results from a mixture of traits and behaviors consisting of honesty and demonstrating excessive ethical standards, and thoughtful and honest behavior by staff (Brown et al., 2005). Ethical management is part of socialization, and ethical bosses create bilaterally beneficial scenarios that allow them to improve their employees' emotions. This makes employees feel bad (Sharif & Scandura, 2014). Proper management of a company is ethical. Management (Sharif & Scandura, 2014) Ethical management influences the organizational care of staff, thereby enhancing their involvement in the workplace (Ilyas et al., 2020). Leadership and employee involvement have attracted great hobbies for all teachers and practitioners. Many of the hobbies in the region are largely based entirely on certain implicit claims that the involvement of all managers and employees is related to the overall efficiency of the organization. Leadership patterns and employee involvement are important precursors to the joy of doing things and dedication. (Shakeel et al., 2019) identify and address previous research spaces related to ethical management, employee well-being, and hyperlinks between ethical management and employee end results is aimed at. Adnan (2019) concludes that integrity loosens employee connections in ethical management (Adnan, 2019). Ethical management can be interpreted as a behavioral version that teaches managers to develop more ethical leaders (Banks et al., 2020). Ethical management can be interpreted as a form of behavior that teaches managers how to do it (Bedi et al., 2016). Large families under ethical control and various attitudes and behavioral variables have direct and indirect benefits to which ethical management is potentially important to people and businesses. From the various studies, it has been found that the study has focused mainly on ethical leadership and well-being. Many studies have also been conducted on Ethical leadership and employee well-being. How ethical leadership leads to employee engagement is the focal point of the study. The study takes employee engagement as a mediator between ethical leadership and employee well-being. The purpose of the study will be to examine the impact of Ethical leadership style on Employee Well being. The major objective is to find the impact of Ethical leadership on Employee well being with respect to employees in manufacturing sector. The study tries to analyze ethical leadership style and how it impacts employee engagement, by creating employee well being. The data has been analysed using regression analysis. The effects of the contemporary observation exhibit that ethical management affords motivational energy for expertise sharing among personnel. Moreover, the serial mediation consequences of subjective properly-being and social media enhance expertise sharing via way of means of the induction of ethical values (Bhati, 2020).

Ashraf and Siddiqui (2020) states that in today's organization the role of employee engagement is an important phenomenon for the retention of employees. Employee well-being though it does not mediate between Employee engagement and employee retention it is important for motivation.

Citizens' behavior, fear of characteristics, negative emotions or neuroticism can also affect the relationship between ethical leadership and the well-being of employees in the workplace (Fu et al., 2020). Therefore, ethical leadership has been found to make employees afraid of the citizenship of the organization, which reduces their well-being in the workplace. The fear of employees' recognition of an organization's citizenship is an intermediary for ethical leadership to negatively impact workplace well-being and play a full role in mediating. When employees demonstrate organized civic behavior, their motive for organizational interest mitigates the relationship between fear of organized citizenship and workplace well-being. The higher an individual's motivation for an organization's interests, the less adverse effects of an organization's citizenship anxiety on well-being at work.

Review of Literature and Hypothesis Formulation

Ethical Leadership

Ethical leadership is a broader perspective when compared to different management patterns depending on the situation. According to Brown and Treviño (2006), ethical leaders attribute justice and duty to their staff. It is the ethical leaders who influence the outcome of HR. Brown etc., 2005. To expand the ethical and beneficial environment, tremendous codes of conduct, guidelines, rules, and managerial behavior in dealing with others are important. Honest front runners will improve the overall staff performance. Mitonga- Monga (2018) and Joplin et al. (2021) state that involvement can be low in situations of low ethical control. It is ethical management that influences the engagement of paintings. Leadership has a significant commitment to employee involvement (Li et al., 2021).

Ethical Leadership and Wellbeing of Employees

The effects of the contemporary observation exhibit that ethical management affords motivational energy for expertise sharing among personnel. Additionally, the serial mediation effects of subjective well-being and social media facilitate knowledge transfer by inducing ethical ideals (Bhati, 2020). Ashraf and Siddiqui (2020) state that in today's organization, the role of employee engagement is an important phenomenon for the retention of employees. The well-being of the employee though does not mediate between Employee engagement and employee retention, but it is important for motivation.

Citizens' conduct, fear of certain qualities, negative emotions, or neuroticism may all affect the link between ethical leadership and employee well-being (Fu et al., 2020). As a result, ethical leadership has been shown to instill fear among workers about the organization's citizenship, therefore diminishing their workplace wellbeing. The fear of employees' recognition of an organization's citizenship is an intermediary for ethical leadership to negatively impact workplace wellbeing and play a full role in mediating. When employees demonstrate organized civic behavior, their motive for organizational interest mitigates the relationship between fear of organized citizenship and workplace wellbeing. The greater an individual's motivation for an organization's interests leads to fewer adverse effects of an organization's citizenship anxiety on wellbeing at work. The research demonstrates the beneficial impact of effective leadership on the work-related welfare of subordinates in a variety of Western civilization scenarios, as identified by their subordinates. This research demonstrates that subordinates who seem to have a noble boss have a greater level of confidence in their superiors, which results in increased work engagement, job satisfaction, and work-related consequences (Hendriks et al., 2020). The results suggest that organizations that aim to promote the well-being of the employee can greatly benefit from good leadership and stimulating their awareness (Khatri & Gupta, 2019). The focus of the study was to develop an overall measure that focused not only on individual wellbeing but also on social situations and work experience. For example, well-healthy employees can perform their duties better. This is in contrast to a sick employee who affects his performance and thus his general wellbeing. In addition, employee adaptability and positive and positive behavior in the workplace help individuals better adapt to the company's workplace culture, which results in better outcomes and well-being of employees.

Ethical leaders have an impact on each worker's task pleasure and psychological properly-being in particular methods (Fu et al., 2020). By stimulating emotions of mental possession on the part of personnel, ethical leaders might also additionally beautify task pleasure. Second, ethical management ought to have a significant courting with structured variables (affective dedication and task pleasure); ethical management is effective in improving personnel's task pleasure stage and dedication to their enterprise, which additionally indicates that ethical management function is vital in imparting right tenet via way of means of which personnel sense greater recommended to contain their paintings (Qing et al., 2019; Abbas & Tan OweeKowang, 2020)

Following numerous scandals in various sectors such as the oil and banking sectors as a result of unethical behavior by organizational leaders, the world is becoming more focused on and conscious of ethics and ethical leadership (Brown & Treviño, 2006; Waqas et al., 2021). Many business organizations are lacking in ethical leadership (Hassan, Wright, & Yukl, 2014; Zheng et al., 2015). Such incidents show that the unethical behavior of top management, no matter how completely its rules and regulations are followed, may not be enough to save the organization from collapse (Liu et al., 2013). Therefore aside from sports, politicians, and business executives, Ethical Leadership is gaining popularity among the general population, the media, and even members of the international community these days (Eisenbeiss & van Knippenberg, 2015).

Ethical leaders are those who refrain from harming others and engage in behaviors that benefit others (Kanungo, 2001) and who are normatively accepted through personal and interpersonal relationships. Show and encourage subordinates to take such actions in an appropriate manner: communication, strengthening, and decision making (Brown, Treviño, & Harrison, 2005). Ethics are woven throughout leaders' behaviors, attitudes, and beliefs to show their dedication to the cause (Khuntia & Suar, 2004). Ethical leaders provide a positive example for those who follow them, apart from this, they not only provide moral direction but also hold their followers accountable for their right and wrong actions by communicating their moral principles and desires in a straightforward manner (Brown & Treviño, 2006; Iqbal et al., 2020). Leadership that is based on 'right beliefs' and 'strong character' sets moral models for their followers and can persevere in the face of hardship. Having a healthy body, mind, and social life have long been seen as essential components of total happiness (Sharma, Kong, & Kingshott, 2016). "Wellbeing" refers to the absence of negative emotions, such as dread or anxiety (or any combination thereof), in one's state of mind (Diener, Sandvik, & Pavot, 2009), described as a multidimensional entity that encompasses not only the physical but also the spiritual and emotional aspects of the individual (Sharma, Kong & Kingshott, 2016).

According to the World Bank, a resource is a combination of product, people's characteristics, conditions, or energy and is considered essential in itself to be evaluated or guided to achievement and to conserve valuable resources (Hobfoll, 2001). Employees can use EL to access additional resources. According to the previous paragraph, ethical leaders are morally honest people who help colleagues, provide safety nets, and encourage employees in the face of difficulties. Staff gain from their leader's guidance, compassion, and empathetic support. Well-being may be expected to be achieved in the long term via the usage of ethical Leadership (Sarwar et al., 2020). Workers motivated by favorable treatment are obliged to perform and behave better at work (Brown & Mitchell, n.d.). The ethical behavior of the leaders elevates employee job satisfaction which is a crucial factor in the well-being of employees (Koh & Boo, 2001). Therefore, as a supplement to Employee Well Being, ethical leaders should now support workers, defend them from injustice, or organize employment resources.

Ethical Leadership and Employee Engagement

Having a strong connection between the manager and the employee is a key ingredient in the recipe for employee engagement and retention (Kompaso & Sridevi, 2010). When it comes to laying out the strategic narrative, the leadership's job is to make sure that everyone understands it and can see how it is influenced by everyone else. A leader needs to deal with mistakes made by their subordinates while also allowing them to express their own opinions. According to studies, leaders that are successful in increasing employee Engagement have five key skills: alignment, inclusiveness, mentorship, team development, and developing trust. The management should build effective and efficient techniques to identify what workers desire or prospective incentives and grow the employee's job satisfaction inside a business. In addition, workers will be more engaged if managers are more open about the organization's processes and procedures. This will develop integrity amongst leaders and followers. Leaders will tell what has to be done and whatnot, and in the same manner, the employees will follow leaders.

Ethical leadership is linked to workers' willingness to tell their bosses when things go wrong. In addition, Butcher (1997) argues that leaders cannot overlook the obligations and duties of the people they are leading to develop an ethical role model. Ethical bosses are noted for creating an environment that encourages their employees to achieve their objectives and behave ethically (Mayer, Kuenzi, Greenbaum, Bardes, & Salvador, 2009, pp. 1-13). Because of this, people are happier and more engaged at work when they are led by ethical leaders (Brown et al., 2005). Individuals in management roles, such as executive managers and department heads, should be scrutinized for their leadership and management styles to guarantee the well-being of workers (Schulze, 2006, p. 322, cited in Venter, 1998). Brown and Treviño (2006) argue that leaders become more appealing and believable as ethical role models when their workers see them as both moral individuals and ethical leaders. Furthermore, according to Heres and Lasthuizen (2013), ethical leadership affects the connection between the leader, his or her team, and the whole company (p. 96). Ethical leadership builds confidence in both the leader and his or her employees (De Hoogh & Den Hartog, 2008). Employees are involved in the decision-making process as well as their well-being and growth, as stated by Engelbrecht, Heine, and Mahembe (2014; p. 3, quoted in Zhu, May, & Avolio, 2004, pp. 16-26). According to Kalshoven and Boon (2012), ethical leadership communicates favorably to the well-being of an employee by providing such work resources as role descriptions or open support (p. 60).

Employee Engagement and Wellbeing of Employees

Both well-being of employees and employee engagement provides a competitive edge to the organizations by enhancing productivity, efficiency, and organizations performance (Duran & Sanchez, 2021). Employee engagement is a state of mind marked by enthusiasm, devotion, and concentration linked to work. Engaged refers to a more permanent and widespread effective–cognitive state that is not centered on any single item, event, person, or activity, rather than a transient and specific one. Engagement (Schaufeli et al., 2002; Duran & Sanchez, 2021). According to past research, elevated levels of employee physical & psychological health are connected with the achievement of many essential organizational outcomes connected with high-performing firms, such as high levels of employee engagement. It seems to have sufficient theoretical backing and empirical data to support the premise that the well-being of an employee is essential to sustaining sustainable levels of employee engagement (Marin-Garcia, Bonavia, & Losilla, 2020). An increase in the allocation of psychological resources (such as the well-being of employees) benefits workers with greater levels of engagement (He, Morrison, & Zhang, 2019). If companies are concerned about their employees and are concentrating on their wellbeing, employees will, in turn, exhibit positive engagement with the organizations in which they work. (Rasool et al., 2021)

According to empirical research, the psychological environment of the company and the environment in which employees work are important and have a great impact on the excellent performance and behavior of the workplace. As a result, there is a strong positive relationship between organizational health and employee involvement. The relationship between employee involvement and organizational health is also related to organizational performance. This has to do with how well an organization achieves its goals and how well it works in achieving those goals (Lindell & Brandt, 2000). Alternatively, workplaces designed to drive the growth of employee involvement, such as energy, engagement, and effectiveness, improve the well-being of employees and productivity (Leiter & Maslach, 2003). From a bidirectional perspective, the well-being of an employee is critical for achieving and maintaining high levels of employee engagement (Robertson & Cooper, 2010).

Research Methodology

Both primary and secondary methods have been used in this research. Data was gathered in the primary research using a questionnaire created in Google Forms. Respondents were given a Google form to fill out the questionnaire. In Table 1, all the constructs taken for the study have been presented.

The population of the study was employees working in the banking sector. They are the employees working in manufacturing firm of Chhattisgarh. Data collection took almost two to three months. The questionnaire was made, and respondents were supposed to fill the form in google forms. Purposive sampling was employed, and a total of 264 responses were collected.

Data Analysis

The demographic profile of the respondents is given in Table 2 out of the total respondents of 264, 15 percent were females, and 85 percent were male employees. In the above study, 35 percent of respondents were in the age group of 21 to 30, 49 percent were in the age group of 31 to 40 years, and 15 percent were in the age group of 41 to 50 years.

Table 1. Construct derived

Construct	Item Code	Item	Questionnaire	Supporting Literature
Ethical Leadership Style					
Ethical Leadership	EL1	5 items	*Show strong concern for ethical and moral values*	(ELQ) Yukl et al. 2013
	EL2		*Am fair and unbiased when assigning tasks to members*	Shakeel et al. 2020
	EL3		*Insist on doing what is fair and ethical even when it is not easy*	(ELQ) Yukl et al. 2013
	EL4		*Regard honesty and integrity as important personal values*	Brown et al. 2005
	EL5		*Opposе the use of unethical practices to increase performance*	Shakeel et al. 2020
Employee Well Being	EWB 1	3	"I enjoy my work	Pooja Khatri and Pragya Gupta 2019
	EWB 2		I take advantage of opportunities to learn new skills at work	Pooja Khatri and Pragya Gupta 2019
	EWB 3		"I am comfortable with the amount of challenge in my work	Pooja Khatri and Pragya Gupta 2019
Employee Engagement	EE1	3	My leader has good qualty of leadership	AnrushaBhana and Sachin Suknunan (2019).
	EE2		My leader makes organizational goals clear	AnrushaBhana and Sachin Suknunan (2019).
	EE3		My leader creates conducive environment for work engagement	AnrushaBhana and Sachin Suknunan (2019).
	EE4	2	My leader trusts me always	AnrushaBhana and Sachin Suknunan (2019).
	EE5		My leader supports me always	AnrushaBhana and Sachin Suknunan (2019).

Table 2. Respondents profile

Demographic Variable	Category	Frequency	Percentage
Age	21-30	93	35%
	31-40	130	50%
	41-50	41	15%
Gender	Male	222	85%
	Female	42	15%

For the present study, the proposed conceptual model is presented in Figure 1. The model suggests a relationship between ethical leadership and wellbeing of employee, and employee engagement mediated the variables. There are five statements for ethical leadership, five statements for employee engagement, and three statements for wellbeing of employee . Some statements were omitted from the study because their r value was less than 0.70, indicating that they were likely to have the same meaning.

Figure 1. Proposed conceptual model

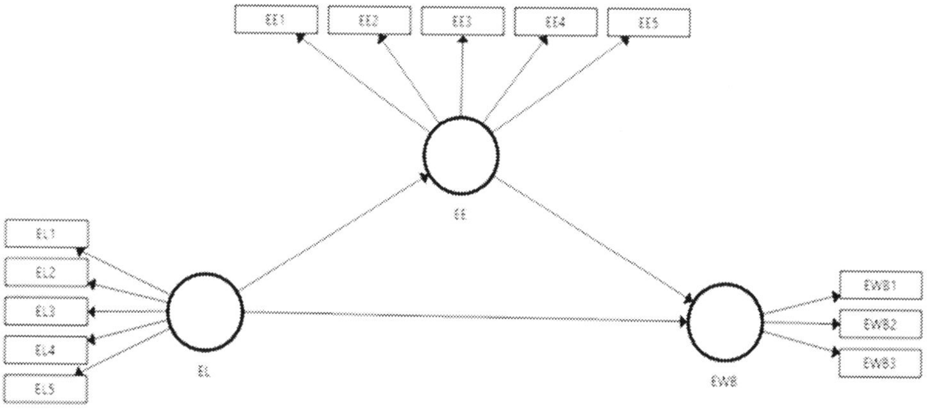

Assessment of Model and Its Measurement

In the model assessment, there are first-order constructs and second-order constructs. In the study, both constructs have been used. In the first-order construct, the variable was analyzed, and all the constructs taken are reflective in nature. Reliability and validity testing has been done to analyze the data through smart pls or PLS-SEM (Ringle et al., 2015); it followed the procedure in two stages has been done systematically to get the result. Anderson and Gerbing (1988).

The first step in the measurement model assessment was to check the convergent validity and composite reliability of the model. Table 3 shows the values of factor loadings, composite reliability (CR), average variance extracted (AVE), Cronbach`s alpha, and DillionGoldstein's rho (rho_A). The factor loading of all items was above 0.7. CR and rho_A values of the constructs were more than the threshold value of 0.7; internal reliability was achieved in the model. Another reliability measure is Cronbach's alpha value, where a value of more than 0.7 represents excellent reliability. The results of the measurement model evaluation show that the reliability criteria are met because the alpha values for all configurations were above the threshold of 0.7. An AVE value greater than 0.5 showed the convergent validity of the composition (Hair et al., 2017). Looking at the results in Table 3 it can be concluded that convergent validity was achieved for the constructs in this study.

After assessing the convergent validity of the composition, the next step was to check the discriminative validity for which two criteria, the Fornell-Larcker criterion and the heterotrait-monotrait ratio (HTMT) of the correlation were proposed. According to the first criterion of discriminative validity proposed by Fornell and Larcker (1981), the square root of the Average Variance value of a configuration must be higher than the correlation coefficient between that configuration and the other configurations in the model. The results of the discriminant validity assessment shown in Table 4 and Table 5 show that the discriminant validity was achieved because the criteria proposed by Fornell and Larcker (1981) and HTMT ratio were met by all components.

Previous bibliographic researchers have shown Henseler et al. (2015)'s HTMT approach. (2015) is superior to the Fornell-Larcker criteria for assessing the validity of discrimination because the HTMT approach has been shown to achieve better sensitivity and specificity (Xia & Chengb, 2017; Rasoolimanesh et al., 2019). According to the HTMT standard, all calculated values of the composition must

Table 3. Measurement model assessment results

	Items	Type	Loadings/Weights	Cronbach's Alpha	rho_A	Composite Reliability	Average Variance Extracted (AVE)
Ethical Leadership	EL1	Reflective	0.874	0.944	0.945	0.957	0.818
	EL2		0.899				
	EL3		0.889				
	EL4		0.924				
	EL5		0.933				
Employee Well Being	EWB1	Reflective	0.836	0.787	0.826	0.872	0.695
	EWB2		0.806				
	EWB3		0.859				
Employee Engagement	EE1	Reflective	0.887	0.924	0.933	0.943	0.769
	EE2		0.899				
	EE3		0.926				
	EE4		0.913				
	EE5		0.748				

Source: Calculated by the author

be less than 0.9 to achieve the validity of the discrimination (Gold et al., 2001; Henseler et al., 2015; Voorhees et al., 2016.). The discriminant validity through HTMT Criterion is above 0.9 so to satisfy the Discriminant validity Confidence interval for a lower band and a higher band has been done at 2.5% minimum and 97.5% maximum band, the data value given in Table 6 proves the discriminant validity. In the present model, reliability and validity have been proved as given in Table 5.

From Figure 2, it is evident that Ethical leadership do not impact the dependent variable well-being of employee significantly the value is 0.142 which is very low. But when employee engagement is acting as a mediator then the indirect relation increases to 0.761 which shows a significant rise in the value

Table 4. Discriminant validity assessment (Fornell-Larcker criterion)

	Employee Engagement	Employee Well Being	Ethical Leadership
Employee Engagement	0.877		
Employee Well Being	0.827	0.834	
Ethical Leadership	0.461	0.493	0.904

Source: Calculated by the author

Table 5. Discriminant validity assessment (HTMT criterion)

	Employee Engagement	Employee Well Being	Ethical Leadership
Employee Engagement			
Employee Well Being	0.927		
Ethical Leadership	0.490	0.564	

Source: Calculated by the author

Table 6. Confidence intervals

	Original Sample (O)	Sample Mean (M)	2.5%	97.5%
Employee Engagement -> Employee Well Being	0.761	0.765	0.714	0.812
Ethical Leadership -> Employee Engagement	0.461	0.461	0.343	0.576
Ethical Leadership -> Employee Well Being	0.142	0.143	0.078	0.211

Source: Calculated by the author

of the dependent variable well-being of an employee due to the independent variable, which is ethical leadership.

All the factors of Employee Engagement and Ethical Leadership has a significant impact on the dependent variable as shown by the path coefficient. The P value indicates independent variable ethical leadership plays a significant role in determining the wellbeing of the employee.

Managerial Implications

In the paper, the framework proposes that ethical leadership has an impact on well-being of employee, and employee engagement activities as a mediator. This framework act as a key to motivating the employees in the organization. Ethical leadership has an impact on the wellbeing of employees but when employee engagement is the mediator, then the relationship is increased. Ethical leadership is found to influence employees in the organization. What is there in the organization which matters in the workplace? When a leader is ethical in his approach than employee engagement increases, and there is well-being among the employees. The result contributes to the literature which focuses on well-being and ethical leadership relationship. Employee engagement is a force that drives the employees wellbeing. Condition of well-being is the mental and physical wellbeing of the employee, which matters a lot in motivating the employees to a large extent. The objective of the study was to find the relationship between Ethical leadership and wellbeing of employee and ethical leadership and employee engagement.

Figure 2. Structural model with R square

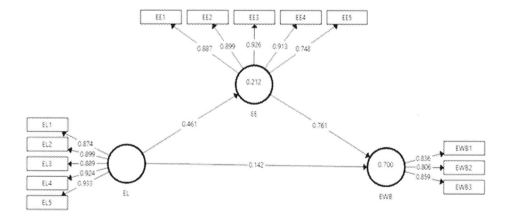

Table 7. Hypothesis testing results

	Original Sample (O)	Sample Mean (M)	Standard Deviation (STDEV)	T Statistics (IO/STDEVI)	P Values	Result
Employee Engagement -> Employee Well Being	0.761	0.765	0.025	30.115	0.000	Supported
Ethical Leadership -> Employee Engagement	0.461	0.461	0.060	7.709	0.000	Supported
Ethical Leadership -> Employee Well Being	0.142	0.143	0.033	4.257	0.000	Supported

Source: Author's Calculation

CONCLUSION

Thus in the study, we conclude that the objective has been served fully. Mainly the first objective was to find the impact of ethical leadership on wellbeing of employee which has been proved by the researcher but it was found that when employee engagement mediates the relationship between ethical leadership and wellbeing of employee, then the dependent variable gets impacted significantly. In general, in organizations employees plays a vital part in the organization. Their wellbeing and engagement mean a lot for the organization so in that aspect ethical leadership can play a very important role. Ethical leadership style focuses on managing the company and, above all, managing the employees. What is ethical leadership governing without biases, maintaining equity in the organization.

REFERENCES

Abbas, A.Tan Owee Kowang. (2020). Impact of Ethical Leadership and Islamic Work Ethics on Employee Commitment and Job Satisfaction. *Journal of Research in Psychology*, *2*(2), 47–58. doi:10.31580/jrp.v2i2.1601

Alam, I., Kartar Singh, J. S., & Islam, M. U. (2021). Does supportive supervisor complements the effect of ethical leadership on employee engagement? *Cogent Business and Management*, *8*(1), 1978371. Advance online publication. doi:10.1080/23311975.2021.1978371

Ashfaq, F., Abid, G., & Ilyas, S. (2021). Impact of ethical leadership on employee engagement: Role of self-efficacy and organizational commitment. *European Journal of Investigation in Health, Psychology and Education*, *11*(3), 962–974. doi:10.3390/ejihpe11030071 PMID:34563084

Ashraf, T., & Siddiqui, D. A. (2020). The Impact of Employee Engagement on Employee Retention: The Role of Psychological Capital, Control at Work, General Wellbeing and Job Satisfaction. *Human Resource Research*, *4*(1), 67. doi:10.5296/hrr.v4i1.16477

Bedi, A., Alpaslan, C. M., & Green, S. (2016). A meta-analytic review of ethical leadership outcomes and moderators. *Journal of Business Ethics*, *139*(3), 517–536. doi:10.100710551-015-2625-1

Bhatti, M. H., Akram, U., Bhatti, M. H., Rasool, H., & Su, X. (2020). Unraveling the effects of ethical leadership on knowledge sharing: The mediating roles of subjective wellbeing and social media in the hotel industry. *Sustainability, 12*(8333).

Brown, M. E., & Treviño, L. K. (2006). Ethical leadership: A review and future directions. *The Leadership Quarterly, 17*(6), 595–616. doi:10.1016/j.leaqua.2006.10.004

Brown, M. E., Treviño, L. K., & Harrison, D. A. (2005). Ethical leadership: A social learning perspective for construct development and testing. *Organizational Behavior and Human Decision Processes, 97*(2), 117–134. doi:10.1016/j.obhdp.2005.03.002

Diener, E., Sandvik, E., & Pavot, W. (2009). *Happiness is the Frequency, Not the Intensity, of Positive Versus Negative Affect*. doi:10.1007/978-90-481-2354-4_10

Duran, M., & Sanchez, J. (2021). Employee Engagement and Wellbeing in Times of COVID-19 : A Proposal of the 5Cs Model. *International Journal of Environmental Research and Public Health, 18*(5470), 2–15. PMID:34065338

Eisenbeiss, S. A., & van Knippenberg, D. (2015). On ethical leadership impact: The role of follower mindfulness and moral emotions. *Journal of Organizational Behavior, 36*(2), 182–195. doi:10.1002/job.1968

Fornell, C., & Larcker, D. F. (1981). Evaluating structural equation models with unobservable variables and measurement error. *JMR, Journal of Marketing Research, 18*(1), 39–50. doi:10.1177/002224378101800104

Fu, J., Long, Y., He, Q., & Liu, Y. (2020). Can Ethical Leadership Improve Employees' Well-Being at Work? Another Side of Ethical Leadership Based on Organizational Citizenship Anxiety. *Frontiers in Psychology, 11*, 1478. Advance online publication. doi:10.3389/fpsyg.2020.01478 PMID:32848973

Fu, J., Long, Y., He, Q., & Liu, Y. (2020). Can Ethical Leadership Improve Employees' Wellbeing at Work? Another Side of Ethical Leadership Based on Organizational Citizenship Anxiety. *Frontiers in Psychology, 11*(July), 1–13. doi:10.3389/fpsyg.2020.01478 PMID:32848973

Gold, A. H., Malhotra, A., & Segars, A. H. (2001). Knowledge management: An organizational capabilities perspective. *Journal of Management Information Systems, 18*(1), 185–214. doi:10.1080/07421222.2001.11045669

Hair, J. F. Jr, Hult, G. T. M., Ringle, C., & Sarstedt, M. (2016). *A primer on partial least squares structural equation modeling (PLS-SEM)*. Sage Publications.

Hassan, S., Wright, B. E., & Yukl, G. (2014). Does Ethical Leadership Matter in Government? Effects on Organizational Commitment, Absenteeism, and Willingness to Report Ethical Problems. *Public Administration Review, 74*(3), 333–343. doi:10.1111/puar.12216

Hendriks, M., Burger, M., Rijsenbilt, A., Pleeging, E., & Commandeur, H. (2020). Virtuous leadership: A source of wellbeing of employee and trust. *Management Research Review, 43*(8), 951–970. doi:10.1108/MRR-07-2019-0326

Henseler, J., Ringle, C. M., & Sarstedt, M. (2015). A new criterion for assessing discriminant validity in variance-based structural equation modelling. *Journal of the Academy of Marketing Science*, *43*(1), 115–135. doi:10.100711747-014-0403-8

Hobfoll, S. E. (2001). The influence of culture, community, and the nested-self in the stress process: Advancing conservation of resources theory. *Applied Psychology*, *50*(3), 337–421. doi:10.1111/1464-0597.00062

Ilyas, S., Abid, G., & Ashfaq, F. (2020). Ethical leadership in sustainable organizations: The moderating role of general self-efficacy and the mediating role of organizational trust. *Sustainable Production and Consumption*, *22*, 195–204. doi:10.1016/j.spc.2020.03.003

Iqbal, Z. A. (2020). Ethical Leadership and Innovative Work Behavior: The Mediating Role of Individual Attributes. *Journal of Open Innovation: Technology, Market, and Complexity, 6*(3), 68. . doi:10.3390/joitmc6030068

Joplin, T., Greenbaum, R. L., Wallace, J. C., & Edwards, B. D. (2021). Employee entitlement, engagement, and performance: The moderating effect of ethical leadership. *Journal of Business Ethics*, *168*(4), 813–826. doi:10.100710551-019-04246-0

Kaffashpoor, A., & Sadeghian, S. (2020). The effect of ethical leadership on subjective wellbeing, given the moderator job satisfaction (a case study of private hospitals in mashhad). *BMC Nursing*, *19*(1), 111. Advance online publication. doi:10.118612912-020-00496-w PMID:33292181

Kanungo, N. R. (2001). Ethical values of transactional and transformational leaders. *Canadian Journal of Administrative Sciences*. Available at: http://search.proquest.com/docview/204887568?accountid=10344 %5Cnhttp://sfx.unilinc.edu.au:9003/csu?url_ver=Z39.88-2004&r ft_val_fmt=info:ofi/fmt:kev:mtx:journal&genre=article&sid=Pr oQ:ProQ%3Aabiglobal&atitle=Ethical+values+of+transactional+a nd+transformati

Khatri, P., & Gupta, P. (2019). Development and validation of wellbeing of employee scale – a formative measurement model. *International Journal of Workplace Health Management*, *12*(5), 352–368. doi:10.1108/IJWHM-12-2018-0161

Khuntia, R., & Suar, D. (2004). A Scale to Assess Ethical Leadership of Indian Private and Public Sector Managers. *Journal of Business Ethics, 49*(1), 13–26. . doi:10.1023/B:BUSI.0000013853.80287.da

Koh, H. C., & Boo, E. H. Y. (2001). The link between organizational ethics and job satisfaction: A study of managers in singapore. *Journal of Business Ethics*, *29*(4), 309–324. doi:10.1023/A:1010741519818

Kompaso, S. M., & Sridevi, M. S. (2010). Employee Engagement: The Key to Improving Performance. *International Journal of Business and Management*, *5*(12), p89. doi:10.5539/ijbm.v5n12p89

Leiter, M. P., & Maslach, C. (2003). *Areas of worklife: A structured approach to organizational predictors of job burnout* (Vol. 3). Research in Occupational Stress and Well Being. doi:10.1016/S1479-3555(03)03003-8

Lindell, M. K., & Brandt, C. J. (2000). Climate quality and climate consensus as mediators of the relationship between organizational antecedents and outcomes. *The Journal of Applied Psychology*, *85*(3), 331–348. doi:10.1037/0021-9010.85.3.331 PMID:10900809

Liu, J., Kwan, H. K., Fu, P. P., & Mao, Y. (2013). Ethical leadership and job performance in China: The roles of workplace friendships and traditionality. *Journal of Occupational and Organizational Psychology*, *86*(4), 564–584. doi:10.1111/joop.12027

Marin-Garcia, J. A., Bonavia, T., & Losilla, J. M. (2020). 'Changes in the association between european workers' employment conditions and wellbeing of employee in 2005, 2010 and 2015'. *International Journal of Environmental Research and Public Health*, *17*(3), 15–22. doi:10.3390/ijerph17031048 PMID:32046002

Mitonga-Monga, J. (2018). Ethical climate influences on employee commitment through job satisfaction in a transport sector industry. *Journal of Psychology in Africa*, *28*(1), 15–20. doi:10.1080/14330237.2018.1426710

Qing, M., Asif, M., Hussain, A., & Jameel, A. (2020). Exploring the impact of ethical leadership on job satisfaction and organizational commitment in public sector organizations: The mediating role of psychological empowerment. *Review of Managerial Science*, *14*(6), 1405–1432. doi:10.100711846-019-00340-9

Rasool, S. F., Wang, M., Tang, M., Saeed, A., & Iqbal, J. (2021). How toxic workplace environment effects the employee engagement: The mediating role of organizational support and wellbeing of employee. *International Journal of Environmental Research and Public Health*, *18*(5), 1–17. doi:10.3390/ijerph18052294 PMID:33652564

Ren, S., & Chadee, D. (2017). Ethical leadership, self-efficacy and job satisfaction in china: The moderating role of guanxi. *Personnel Review*, *46*(2), 371–388. doi:10.1108/PR-08-2015-0226

Ringle, C. M., Wende, S., & Becker, J. M. (2015). *SmartPLS 3*. www.smartpls.com

Robertson, I. T., & Cooper, C. L. (2010). Full engagement: The integration of employee engagement and psychological wellbeing. *Leadership and Organization Development Journal*, *31*(4), 324–336. doi:10.1108/01437731011043348

Ruiz-Palomino, P., Ruiz-Amaya, C., & Knörr, H. (2011). Employee organizational citizenship behaviour: The direct and indirect impact of ethical leadership. *Canadian Journal of Administrative Sciences*, *28*(3), 244–258. doi:10.1002/cjas.221

Sarwar, H., Ishaq, M. I., Amin, A., & Ahmed, R. (2020). 'Ethical leadership, work engagement, employees' wellbeing, and performance: A cross-cultural comparison'. *Journal of Sustainable Tourism*, *28*(12), 2008–2026. doi:10.1080/09669582.2020.1788039

Schaufeli, W. B. (2002). The Measurement of Engagement and Burnout: A Two Sample Confirmatory Factor Analytic Approach. *Journal of Happiness Studies*, *3*(1), 71–92. . doi:10.1023/A:1015630930326

Shakeel, F., Kruyen, P. M., & Van Thiel, S. (2019). Ethical leadership as process: A conceptual proposition. *Public Integrity*, *21*(6), 613–624. doi:10.1080/10999922.2019.1606544

Sharif, M. M., & Scandura, T. A. (2014). Moral identity: Linking ethical leadership to follower decision making. Advances in authentic and ethical leadership. *Research Management*, *10*, 155–190.

Sharma, P., Kong, T. T. C., & Kingshott, R. P. J. (2016). Internal service quality as a driver of employee satisfaction, commitment and performance – exploring the focal role of wellbeing of employee. *Journal of Service Management*, *27*(5), 773–797. doi:10.1108/JOSM-10-2015-0294

Van Vugt, M., & von Rueden, C. R. (2020). From genes to minds to cultures: Evolutionary approaches to leadership. *The Leadership Quarterly*, *31*(2), 101404. doi:10.1016/j.leaqua.2020.101404

Waqas, M., & ... 2021). Impact of ethical leadership on wellbeing of employee: The mediating role of job satisfaction and employee voice. *Middle East J. of Management*, *1*(1), 1. doi:10.1504/MEJM.2022.122577

Xia, E. A. C., & Cheng, K. T. G. (2017). The determinants of purchase intention on counterfeit sportswear. *Journal of Applied Structural Equation Modeling*, *1*(1), 13–26. doi:10.47263/JASEM.1(1)03

Zheng, D., Witt, L. A., Waite, E., David, E. M., van Driel, M., McDonald, D. P., Callison, K. R., & Crepeau, L. J. (2015). Effects of ethical leadership on emotional exhaustion in high moral intensity situations. *The Leadership Quarterly*, *26*(5), 732–748. doi:10.1016/j.leaqua.2015.01.006

Chapter 10
The Basic Strategy of Leadership Landscape:
Employee Retention and Work-Life Balance

Sonali Malewar
Marketing Department, Sri Balaji University, Pune, India

Shilpi Gupta
https://orcid.org/0000-0003-4382-3616
Amity Business School, Amity University, Raipur, India

ABSTRACT

Leadership comportment has a substantial influence on employee behavior, performance, and welfare. The existing theory and research on leadership performance has mainly focused on employee performance, but both terminologies have expanded a lot of magnitude in the present era of the business world. The leaders of the team construct and communicate a vision or an aim that they want the team to accomplish, and the leaders motivate the team to accomplish that goal by explaining the benefits of doing so. The leaders provide their team members with assistance and guidance so that they may make progress toward completing their duties. The present study explains in a theoretical but very interactive way how effective leadership can help boost the performance of employees and sequentially helps the organization recognize its quality employees and tap their efficiencies for the long term through employee retention. Previous research has discovered the influence of several factors on employee well-being to inform the practice to enhance workplace results for both employees and employers.

INTRODUCTION

Leadership is the process of influence and reflects a more complex phenomenon beyond an individual actor (Renko et al, 2015). The ability to inspire others to join in on a shared vision and work together to find and capitalize on opportunities to produce strategic value is a hallmark of effective leadership. Passion, foresight, concentration, and the ability to motivate people are all necessary leadership qualities.

DOI: 10.4018/978-1-6684-8257-5.ch010

Figure 1.

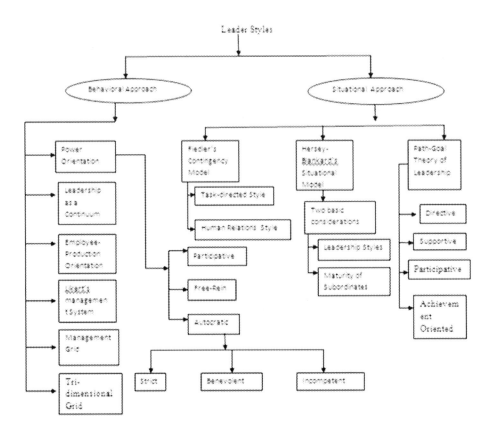

All of these are necessary for effective entrepreneurial leadership, and so are a particular frame of mind and set of abilities that enable leaders to spot, cultivate, and seize fresh possibilities for their businesses. Leadership ability to maintain creativity and flexibility in the face of rapid change and ambiguity.

It is common for managers to underestimate the extent to which the culture of the organization can have an impact on the company's bottom line. How managers motivate direct subordinates, gather and use information, make choices, manage change efforts, and handle crises all have an impact on the climate of the organization, which in turn is influenced by the leadership style of those managers. There are essentially six different kinds of leadership. Each one is founded on a unique set of emotional intelligence skills, functions most effectively in a specific set of circumstances, and modifies the atmosphere of the workplace in a unique set of ways.

Leadership experts provide guidance that is derived from inferences, experiences, and instincts. There are instances when the admonition is spot on, and there are other occasions when it is not.

Leadership Styles

The behavioral approach of leadership has further classification as mentioned below-

People-Oriented Leaders

People-oriented leaders teach their followers to satisfy consumers, bosses, and employees. Because of their interpersonal communication and networking skills, these leaders can build enduring relationships and motivate their staff. They regularly enhance team ties and inspire team members to excel. These leaders encourage teamwork, celebrate others' successes, monitor and evaluate their teams' growth, and help team members improve. According to research, interpersonally oriented leaders that treat subordinates with respect and kindness are often regarded favorably. Similarly, a substantial body of research on leadership has repeatedly demonstrated the favorable effects of a focus on people on outcomes such as work satisfaction, perceived leader efficiency, and performance (Tyler & Blader, 2000, 2002; Yukl, 2012).

Task-Oriented Leaders

Task-oriented executives set goals and achieve organizational objectives because they prioritize task execution over people management. These leaders thrive in well-organized, authoritative surroundings. They prioritize project outcomes over day-to-day development and progress. Task-oriented leaders start projects, organize company processes, clarify stakeholder instructions, and gather data. The extent to which target leaders are viewed as competent in task-related leadership activities such as managing a financial transaction, ensuring the quality of manufactured goods, or raising profits is diminished by their focus on people (Gartzia, & Baniandrés, 2016; Engelbert & Wallgren, 2016).

Participative Leaders

With the rapid changes in the competitive business environment, it has become increasingly difficult for organizational leaders to make timely and effective judgments on their own, which has led to the active participation of employees in organizational decision-making today (Peng et al., 2021). Participative leaders involve everyone in decision-making. These executives prioritize effective communication, cooperation, and feedback to boost project productivity (Cheng et al., 2021). They assign work based on team members' skills and shortcomings to maximize efficiency. Leaders see and hear everyone and consider their comments using this leadership style. Participative leaders may facilitate and coordinate team meetings, ask for constructive comments, implement improvements, and delegate duties to team members for efficiency.

Status-Quo Leaders

Status-quo leaders boost productivity and employee satisfaction. These leaders mix timely work with team assistance and encouragement. Status-quo executives seek to stick with proven organizational procedures and mechanisms. Inspiring leaders encourage subordinates to voice their viewpoints, promote collaborative decision-making, and foster information sharing and teamwork (Burke et al., 2006; Sharma & Kirkman, 2015). Experience guides them more than future vision. Status-quo executives distribute duties equitably, ask for progress updates, enforce corporate policies fairly, and respond to positive and negative comments neutrally.

Indifferent Leaders

Indifferent leaders may not actively contribute to the organization's process but watch their team's performance. Scholars have underlined that the cultural values and conventions of a society have a significant impact on the leadership style of organizational managers, and that the recognized personal traits of effective leaders vary from country to country (Moan and Hetland, 2012; Sabri, 2012).These leaders value individual success over teamwork. This leadership style usually lacks teamwork. Team productivity may suffer under such leaders. Indifferent leaders avoid team questions, procrastinate essential work, assign undesired responsibilities to staff, and protect their interests.

Dictatorial Leaders

Dictatorial leaders prioritize results over team well-being. Autocratic leadership is frequently viewed as detrimental to team morale and effectiveness (De Hoogh et al., 2015; Foels et al., 2000). Leaders may also pressure workers to perform well in difficult conditions. Dictatorial CEOs can produce high-quality achievements, but their negative behavior may increase staff turnover. Dictatorial executives create harsh deadlines, dismiss excuses, avoid team criticism, and prioritize short-term goals over employee well-being.

Country Club Leaders

Country club leaders value employee satisfaction. The leader of the country club has a high regard for people and a low regard for output. Without regard for production, the leader seeks to maintain a pleasant environment (Oberer & Erkollar, 2018). These executives believe a well-cared-for team performs better. Country club leaders inspire trust, confidence, and loyalty in their staff since the work environment supports their professional progress. Some country club leaders forgo productivity to increase team morale and performance. Such leaders respond positively to team member comments, prioritize employee well-being, protect employee rights and interests, and support team member decisions.

Paternalistic Leaders

Parent-child leadership describes this style. Goal-oriented but flexible paternalistic leaders focus on results. Although there are numerous conceptualizations of paternalistic leadership, academics have claimed that paternalistic leadership is comprised of three essential leadership styles: authoritarianism, kindness, and moral leadership (Pellegrini & Scandura, 2008; Bedi, 2020). Leaders establish lofty targets and reward achievers. Paternalistic leaders recognize their team members' talents and may help them succeed professionally. Paternalistic bosses often reward staff for their performance, ignore feedback, provide promising employees leadership and development opportunities, and make all decisions.

LITERATURE REVIEW

Harvard Business Review focused that leadership should be Compassionate. Compassion creates a stronger trust and bond between employees and leaders. Compassionate leaders are perceived as more competent and focused. The Wise Compassion Leadership Matrix (stresses leading subordinates to

Figure 2.
Source: Rasmus Hougaard

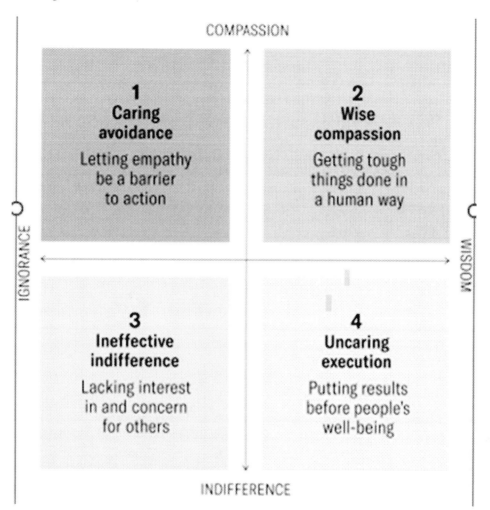

do difficult things humanly. It is concluded that wise compassionate – leaders deliver the best results. Leadership styles are not fixed but vary with the need and situation. It is a flexible mode of matching organizational objectives with self and subordinate goals.

General Leadership

Leadership is essentially a process in which one individual or sometimes a small group of individuals influences the efforts of others toward the achievement of goals in a given set of circumstances (Cole, 2005). Leadership is generally considered a social phenomenon whose foundation is based on the openness of communication between employees and employers with the interaction of the external and internal environment.

Leadership and Employee Retention

The concept of leadership was originally developed in folk psychology to explain the factor of social influence on groups (Jaskaran & Sri-Guru, 2014).

Leadership and Work-Life Balance

According to the Gallup Engagement Index, many employees feel disengaged from their jobs and dislike them (Gallup, 2014). In line with this reasoning, research has established supervisory support (Kossek et al., 2011; McCarthy et al., 2013) and role modeling (Koch and Binnewies, 2015) as antecedents to employees' positive work-life experiences. The mediation effects of work-life balance provide us with greater knowledge and insight into the process by which employees may become engaged. It also extends the outcomes linked to greater work-life balance beyond job satisfaction and well-being outcomes (Haar, 2013; Haar et al., 2014).

Leadership With Organizational Performance

Evidence abounds on the positive correlation between charismatic leadership and enhanced organizational performance (Conger, Kanungo, and Menon, 2000).

Leadership With Power Orientation

The decisive force guiding top-level managers is the organizational strategic decisions and the flow of direction.

Covin and Slevin (2002) argued that managers should endeavor to promote an entrepreneurial dominant logic within the firm. Related to entrepreneurial risk-taking, Kreiser, Marino, and Weaver (2002) argued that risk-taking has long been associated with conceptions of the entrepreneur. McClelland (1961) posited that entrepreneurs tend to be more willing to engage in risk-taking behaviors than non-entrepreneurs.

It is considered that managers with high individual entrepreneurial orientation, have a positive force on the individual as well as organizational performance.

Structural Power Structural power refers to the ability of an individual to influence behavior and/or decision-making based on his/ her hierarchical, or legitimate, positioning within the firm (Astley and Sachdeva 1984; Dailey and Johnson 1997; French, Raven, and Cartwright 1959; Hambrick 1981). Research in entrepreneurial orientation continues to represent a fruitful area of study (Rauch et al. 2009).

GRID AS A MODEL OF LEADERSHIP CULTURE

"Grid" was originally developed by Robert Blake and Jane Mouton between 1958 and 1960 and was first published in 1964 (Blake and Mouton 1964). Haar et al. (2014) noted the importance of addressing the workplace culture – and this might be particularly prevalent if an organization has one predicated on long exhaustive work hours.

Leadership as a Culture

Some research has invoked leadership practices as an important facet or determinant of culture. Ichikawa (1993) refers to leadership as a form of culture, although the cultural context is more societal than organizational. Freeman and Boeker (1984) state that the forms of authority used within organizations and the interactions between individuals and the organization represent an important facet of culture.

DISCUSSIONS

The last two decades have observed a shift in focus from the trait-based theory of leadership to the behavioral-based theory of leadership. But despite the many established theories of leadership, the human traits of the leader along with his skills are the most influential and ethical part of a leader.

The introductory model indicates that the landscape of leadership has many dimensions.

The dimension of transformational and entrepreneurial leadership took a backstage with a focus on understandable, relational conversational, and a strong bond between the employee and employer in the workplace. In the last decade, leadership became synonymous with serving society with the purpose of the growth of subordinates and society.

Work-Life balance is a hot topic in the present scenario especially post covid as employees in the middle age group especially in the age group of 30-50 prioritize managerial support, candid HR policies, recognition of their achievements, and a chance of personal growth along with organizational development as their prime focus. An insensitive and rigid leader decreases the productivity of the employees negatively impacting the work-life balance of the subordinate. The relationship between employer and employee can be strengthened by keeping in view the contrasting talents and working styles of generational differences and their value system. The working HR policies need to be more supportive and congenial fine tuning the goals of the organization with employee welfare. The limitation lies in the extent of support perceived by the employees as satisfactory.

There are a total of six components that make up a healthy work-life balance, including The term Technology Management refers to the process of maximizing the benefits that technology can bring to society. In recent decades, both the variety of technologies being produced and their rate of emergence have expanded, as is widely acknowledged. As a result, the responsibilities of leaders are expanding. As technology goals shift over time, the function will likely continue to evolve. The dynamic business environment, which aims to facilitate technology management by identifying certain situational priorities, is also indicative of the increasing complexity of the function.

Change management refers to methods used to facilitate personal or organizational transformation. "Leadership" refers to the ability of an individual or group to effect positive change within an organization. Leaders are recognized as "Champions of Change" because the top management of any business is responsible for sustaining the process of change and ensuring the organization's operational dependability.

Self-management refers to using one's initiative to pursue goals, while time management refers to maximizing output. Successful leaders blend four facets of their lives: happiness, prosperity, significance, and legacy. To realize one's leadership potential, self-management of leadership development must attend to and engage in all of these realms or spheres of life.

Stress Management involves striking a balance between professional and personal concerns. Exposure to emotion regulation and self-leadership tactics may help employees not only manage their current pressures more successfully but also acquire coping abilities that will enable them to survive the stresses of their future professions.

The term Leisure Management refers to the practice of prioritizing rest alongside one's other commitments, as many of us tend to do when we're busy at work. One could also argue that individuals, families, the lonely, the elderly, the disabled, and the impoverished need opportunity to experience the pleasures of leisure. Leaders feel that this type of encounter can improve their quality of life. Leisure and recreation must put the individual first. It is not just about structures and amenities when it comes to the development and management of leisure, but also about human rights, dignity, and the individuality of the individual. Leisure management is contested from this perspective, and this thread, however fragile, connects discussions on principles, planning, and management.

The other dimension reveals the belief that men and women come from separate planets and therefore their styles of leading are different inherently and are pervasive in popular culture; however, the research suggests that there are no substantial gender disparities in leadership roles. Essentially, the findings of studies conducted on the relationship between gender and leadership over the past two decades continue to be mostly inconsistent. In recent years, there has been an increased emphasis placed on leadership that is transformational as opposed to transactional, as well as leadership that is genuine. There is evidence that lends credence to the concept that men and women are fundamentally distinct, such as the observation that women tend to be somewhat more democratic, participatory, and inclusive. There has been a significant amount of study devoted to analyzing the differences and similarities between masculine and feminine leadership styles. This approach frequently equates male leadership styles with instrumental, agentic, or transactional qualities, while female leadership styles are associated with more communal qualities, nurturing, and people-oriented. These qualities are either considered to be incongruent with idealized leadership attributes, or they are viewed as being more conducive to female leadership styles.

CONCLUSION

The framework of positive psychology has been proven to be the trending theory conducive to the present work-life balance culture with the thread of leadership. The positive frame of the leaders with subordinates builds a culture of commitment in the organization. Increasing empathy with the directive style takes into consideration the individual's consideration for reframing the style of work and encouraging multiple role demands of the organization. The enrichment impact of optimistic management helps in tackling demanding roles and being compassionate for the role demands. There is a widespread belief that conceptions of leadership have received cultural approval. Research on leadership has shown that different cultures often have very different notions and perceptions about what behaviors contribute to outstanding leadership; different leadership prototypes; and differences in leadership style as perceived by male and female subordinates. This means that leadership and related behavioral values need to be understood within a given cultural context. It has been suggested that disparities in leadership styles are due more to differences in country culture than they are to differences in gender.

Moreover, it would appear that leadership either mitigates or amplifies the potentially detrimental impacts of organizational stresses on one's ability to maintain a healthy work-life balance. When employees believe that they are effective and content in the numerous roles that they are required to play, they have a better perception of the degree to which their personal and professional lives are in harmony with one another. It is assumed that authentic leaders can support their own and others' work-life balance by reference to three primary characteristics: self-reflective abilities, moral principles, and individual development through interpersonal attention.

Finally, it is depicted that leaders and managers that cultivate relationships based on trust, respect work-life balance, and treat their employees as unique persons are viewed as more ethical than those who do not. Additionally, when individuals who lack the necessary management abilities are placed in positions of leadership or management, they are viewed as unscrupulous.

IMPLICATIONS

The implication of the subject spreads its wings to HRM professionals in ideal work engagement of employees which forms an integral component of organizational growth and focus. A greater work-life balance achieved by employees results in exploring work allocation and fulfilling work demands and achievement of organizational objectives.

FUTURE SCOPE

The scope of the study can be extended to build a component of trust and provide freedom and positivity resulting in work-life balance. Many external climate-associated factors can be included in the relationship between leadership with work-life balance. The leadership styles can be explored to predict the work-life balance and work engagement of employees.

REFERENCES

Astley, W. G., & Sachdeva, P. (1984). Structural sources of intraorganizational power: A theoretical synthesis. *Academy of Management Review*, *9*(1), 104–113.

Bedi, A. (2020). A meta-analytic review of paternalistic leadership. *Applied Psychology*, *69*(3), 960–1008. doi:10.1111/apps.12186

Blake, R. R., Mouton, J. S., Barnes, L. B., & Greiner, L. E. (1964). Breakthrough in Organization Development. *Harvard Business Review*, *42*(6), 133–155.

Burke, C. S., Stagl, K. C., Klein, C., Goodwin, G. F., Salas, E., & Halpin, S. M. (2006). What type of leadership behaviors are functional in teams? A meta-analysis. *The Leadership Quarterly*, *17*(3), 288–307. doi:10.1016/j.leaqua.2006.02.007

Chang, Y. Y., Chang, C. Y., Chen, Y. C. K., Seih, Y. T., & Chang, S. Y. (2021). Participative leadership and unit performance: Evidence for intermediate linkages. *Knowledge Management Research and Practice*, *19*(3), 355–369. doi:10.1080/14778238.2020.1755208

Cole, G. A. (2005). *Organizational Behaviour*. TJ International.

Conger, J. A., Kanungo, R. N., & Menon, S. T. (2000). *Charismatic Leadership: The Elusive Factor in Organizational Effectiveness*. Jossey-Bass.

Covin, J., & Slevin, D. (2002). The entrepreneurial imperatives of strategic leadership. In M. A. Hitt, R. D. Ireland, S. M. Camp, & D. L. Sexton (Eds.), *Strategic entrepreneurship: Creating a new mindset* (pp. 309–327). Blackwell Publishers.

Daily, C. M., & Johnson, J. L. (1997). Sources of CEO power and firm financial performance: A longitudinal assessment. *Journal of Management, 23*(2), 97–118. doi:10.1177/014920639702300201

De Hoogh, A. H., Greer, L. L., & Den Hartog, D. N. (2015). Diabolical dictators or capable commanders? An investigation of the differential effects of autocratic leadership on team performance. *The Leadership Quarterly, 26*(5), 687–701. doi:10.1016/j.leaqua.2015.01.001

Engelbert, B., & Wallgren, L. G. (2016). The origins of task-and people-oriented leadership styles: Remains from early attachment security and influences during childhood and adolescence. *SAGE Open, 6*(2). doi:10.1177/2158244016649012

Foels, R., Driskell, J. E., Mullen, B., & Salas, E. (2000). The effects of democratic leadership on group member satisfaction: An integration. *Small Group Research, 31*(6), 676–701. doi:10.1177/104649640003100603

Freeman, J., & Boeker, W. (1984). The Ecological Analysis of Strategy. *California Management Review, 26*(3), 73–86. doi:10.2307/41165081

French, J., Raven, B., & Cartwright, D. (1959). *Studies in social power*. The University of Michigan, Institute for Social Research.

Gallup. (2014). *Gallup Engagement Index*. https://www.gallup.com/strategicconsulting/158162/gallup-engagement-index.aspx

Gartzia, L., & Baniandrés, J. (2016). Are people-oriented leaders perceived as less effective in task performance? Surprising results from two experimental studies. *Journal of Business Research, 69*(2), 508–516. doi:10.1016/j.jbusres.2015.05.008

Haar, J. M. (2013). Testing a new measure of work-life balance: A study of parent and non-parent employees from New Zealand. *International Journal of Human Resource Management, 24*(17), 3305–3324. doi:10.1080/09585192.2013.775175

Haar, J. M., Russo, M., Sune, A., & Ollier-Malaterre, A. (2014). Outcomes of work-life balance on job satisfaction, life satisfaction and mental health: A study across seven cultures. *Journal of Vocational Behavior, 85*(3), 361–373. doi:10.1016/j.jvb.2014.08.010

Hambrick, D. C. (1981). Environment, strategy, and power within top management teams. *Administrative Science Quarterly, 26*(2), 253–276. doi:10.2307/2392472 PMID:10251673

Hougaard, R., Carter, J., & Hobson, N. (2020). Compassionate leadership is necessary—but not sufficient. *Harvard Business Review*. https://hbr. org/2020/12/compassionate-leadership-is-necessary-but-not-sufficient

Ichikawa, A. (1993). Leadership as a Form of Culture: It's Present and Future States in Japan. *International Review of Strategic Management, 4*, 155–170.

Jaskaran, S. D., & Sri-Guru, G. S. (2014). Participative leadership and employee job well-being: perceived co-worker support as a boundary condition. *Journal of Psychological Science*, (4), 873.

Koch, A. R., & Binnewies, C. (2015). Setting a good example: Supervisors as work-life-friendly role models within the context of boundary management. *Journal of Occupational Health Psychology*, *20*(1), 82–92. doi:10.1037/a0037890 PMID:25198308

Kossek, E. E., Pichler, S., Bodner, T., & Hammer, L. B. (2011). Workplace social support and work–family conflict: A meta-analysis clarifying the influence of general and work– family-specific supervisor and organizational support. *Personnel Psychology*, *64*(2), 289–313. doi:10.1111/j.1744-6570.2011.01211.x PMID:21691415

Kreiser, P. M., Marino, L. D., & Weaver, K. M. (2002). Assessing the psychometric properties of the entrepreneurial orientation scale: A multi-country analysis. *Entrepreneurship Theory and Practice*, *26*(4), 71–94. doi:10.1177/104225870202600405

McCarthy, A., Cleveland, J. N., Hunter, S., Darcy, C., & Grady, G. (2013). Employee work–life balance outcomes in Ireland: A multilevel investigation of supervisory support and perceived organizational support. *International Journal of Human Resource Management*, *24*(6), 1257–1276. doi:10.1080/09585192.2012.709189

McClelland, D. C. (1961). *The achieving society*. Van Nostrand. doi:10.1037/14359-000

Moan, K., & Hetland, H. (2012). Are leadership preferences universally endorsed or culturally contingent. *Scandinavian Journal of Organizational Psychology*, *4*(1), 5–22.

Nair, P., & Malewar, S. (2013). Effective leadership-employee retention-work life balance: A cyclical continuum. *IOSR Journal of Business and Management*, *10*(3), 80–86. doi:10.9790/487X-1038086

Oberer, B., & Erkollar, A. (2018). Leadership 4.0: Digital leaders in the age of industry 4.0. *International journal of organizational leadership*.

Pellegrini, E. K., & Scandura, T. A. (2008). Paternalistic leadership: A review and agenda for future research. *Journal of Management*, *34*(3), 566–593. doi:10.1177/0149206308316063

Rauch, A., Wiklund, J., Lumpkin, G. T., & Frese, M. (2009). Entrepreneurial orientation and business performance: An assessment of past research and suggestions for the future. *Entrepreneurship Theory and Practice*, *33*(3), 761–787. doi:10.1111/j.1540-6520.2009.00308.x

Renko, M., El Tarabishy, A., Carsrud, A. L., & Brännback, M. (2015). Understanding and measuring entrepreneurial leadership style. *Journal of Small Business Management*, *53*(1), 54–74. doi:10.1111/jsbm.12086

Sabri, H. A. (2012). Re-examination of Hofstede's work value orientations on perceived leadership styles in Jordan. *International Journal of Commerce and Management*, *22*(3), 202–218. doi:10.1108/10569211211260292

Sharma, P. N., & Kirkman, B. L. (2015). Leveraging leaders: A literature review and future lines of inquiry for empowering leadership research. *Group & Organization Management*, *40*(2), 193–237. doi:10.1177/1059601115574906

Tyler, T. R., & Blader, S. L. (2000). *Cooperation in Groups: Procedural Justice*. Social Identity, and Behavioral Engagement.

Tyler, T. R., & Blader, S. L. (2002). The influence of status judgments in hierarchical groups: Comparing autonomous and comparative judgments about status. *Organizational Behavior and Human Decision Processes*, 89(1), 813–838. doi:10.1016/S0749-5978(02)00031-6

Yukl, G. (2012). Effective leadership behavior: What we know and what questions need more attention. *The Academy of Management Perspectives*, 26(4), 66–85. doi:10.5465/amp.2012.0088

Section 5
Dark Side of Leadership

While traditional leadership literature looked at leadership in terms of a positive virtue and charismatic attributes among leaders, the contemporary leadership literature also examines the negative aspects of different leadership styles and attributes. The first chapter in this section provides solutions for reducing toxicity in the work environment while introducing the concept of destructive leadership styles associated with personality disorders. The next chapter examined the relationship between dark triad personality traits such as narcissism, psychopathy, and Machiavellianism and their impact on effective leadership outcomes. The authors argued that dark leadership traits positively correlate with capabilities in leaders during crisis.

Chapter 11
The Dark Side of Leadership

Bhawna Gaur
Amity University, Dubai, UAE

ABSTRACT

Personality traits favored by situational factors may lead to destructive tendencies in a good leader. For example, CEOs such as Larry Page of Google, Lloyd Blankfein of Goldman Sachs, Mark Zuckerberg of Facebook, and Elon Musk of Tesla have exhibited a shift from constructive to destructive leadership style due to situational or environmental factors. Destructive or dark leadership style is associated with personality traits such as narcissism, Machiavellianism, and psychopathy. This chapter introduces the concept of personality disorders that might threaten the effectiveness of an individual as a leader. It will further discuss the factors that contribute to the development of destructive personalities and different types of destructive personalities. This chapter will identify the role of followers and environment that provide legitimacy for immoral actions. It will provide solutions to improve leadership practices to reduce toxicity in the work environment and create a positive workplace.

INTRODUCTION

In the recent past, the corporate environment has become more dynamic and complex, emphasizing the responsibility of leaders to take control of the situation and guide the team members to achieve the organizational goals. Visionary leaders like Bill Gates (Microsoft), Steve Jobs (Apple Inc.), Mark Zuckerberg (Facebook), Howard Schultz (Starbucks), and Jeff Bezos (Amazon.com) have successfully led their firms through substantial transitions for noteworthy accomplishments. Researchers typically emphasize the positive side of successful leaders and have underlined the ideal traits and behaviors of these leaders. However, recent studies have highlighted the destructive or dark side of leadership and its impact on followers and companies. The catastrophic failure of companies like WorldCom, Enron, and Lehman Bros., have highlighted the threats associated with dark leadership styles. Though some academics contend that leadership is by definition a positive force and that the idea of dark or negative leadership is an oxymoron.

DOI: 10.4018/978-1-6684-8257-5.ch011

Definition of Dark Leadership

Over a period of time several definitions of leadership have been proposed. Bentz (1985) analyzed factors related to personality traits responsible for the failure of executives at Sears and Roebuck. He summarized them as

- Poor interpersonal relationship skills
- Lack of competence to achieve business objectives
- Failure to build an effective team and
- Issues with change management.

Conger (1990) studied dark leadership from the construct of charismatic leadership and its pitfalls. He studied some famous leaders and concluded that charismatic leaders displayed traits that distinguished them from managers. However, he also identified that these same traits that made a leader successful under certain circumstances can prove destructive for the organization. He also emphasized that charismatic executives sometimes face issues with strategic vision, interpersonal skills, and general management practices.

Hogan et al. (1990) identified three categories of bad managers. The first is the High Likeability Floater- an individual who is popular but is not a very good leader. Their performance is therefore rarely questioned. The second category is Hommes de Ressentiment- these managers create an impression of being endearing, charismatic, and intelligent, but are often filled with animosity, bitterness, and a desire for vengeance. The third category is narcissists- they want to feel entitled and privileged and have no qualms about asking for special treatment, advantages, and favors. Although all these individuals might initially appear quite endearing, they actually have a darker side.

According to Einarsen et al., (2002) destructive or dark leadership is defined as "the systematic and repeated behavior by a leader, supervisor or manager that violates the legitimate interest of the organization by undermining and/or sabotaging the organization's goals, tasks, resources, and effectiveness and/or the motivation, well-being or job satisfaction of subordinates". This definition has proposed that dark leadership can fall under the domain of destructive behaviors directed at subordinates and destructive behaviors directed at organizations. Destructive leadership behaviors directed at subordinates were coined as "bullies", "derailed leaders", "abusive supervisors", "petty tyrants", "health threatening leader", "intolerant bosses" and "psychopaths". An abusive leader or supervisor as defined by Hornstein (1996) is, "one whose primary objective is the control of others, and such control is achieved through methods that create fear and intimidation." Tepper (2000) defines "abusive supervision" as "subordinates' perceptions of the extent to which supervisors engage in the sustained display of hostile verbal and nonverbal behaviors, excluding physical contact." According to Ashforth (1994) a petty tyrant is, "someone who utilizes their power and authority oppressively, arbitrarily, and possibly vindictively." The term "health threatening leader," coined by Kile (1990), refers to a leader "whose behavior toward subordinates is such that the subordinates develop ill health and link these health problems to the leader's behavior."

Lipman-Blumen (2005) and McCall & Lombardo (1983) have identified destructive leadership behaviors as ones directed against organizational goals. "Toxic leaders" according to Lipman-Blumen are, "leaders who operate without integrity by dissembling and indulging in many other dishonorable behaviors," such as "corruption, hypocrisy, sabotage and manipulation, as well as other miscellaneous unethical, unlawful, and criminal conduct." In addition, Kellerman (2004) notes that leaders may engage in corruption by deceiving, stealing, or otherwise prioritizing their own interests over those of the organization. Leadership coaching consultant Semann & Slattery (2009) defined dark leadership as, "an ongoing pattern of behavior exhibited by a leader that results in overall negative organizational outcomes based on the interactions between the leader, follower and the environment." Thus the leader's selfish interests and misuse of authority can have a negative impact on employee morale and corporate goals.

Hence Dark or Destructive Leadership can be defined as, "behaviors that reflect the poor interpersonal skills of managers due to their selfish interests, and hinder them from developing an effective team, to get support for their strategic vision, leading to negative organizational outcomes."

The above discussion leads to the following characteristics of dark leaders:

1. Leaders exhibit poor interpersonal skills, thus relying on dominance, coercion, and manipulation for attaining organizational goals.
2. Dark leaders have a narrow functional orientation.
3. The leader prioritizes his needs over those of the larger social community.
4. Destructive leaders have a negative impact on the employees' work-life balance and often deviate from the organization's goals.
5. Other than destructive leadership behaviors, susceptible followers and a supportive work environment also play a very important role in negative organizational outcomes.
6. Dark leadership behavior is seldom entirely destructive. Most of the time, circumstances determine whether the results are good or bad.

Personality Traits and Their Impact on Leadership Effectiveness

Leadership is the ability to guide others, in maximizing their efforts to achieve results. Even though there is no set formula to succeed in a leadership position, some personality traits are commonly associated with successful leaders. These traits referred to as 'socially desirable personality traits' or 'bright traits' are responsible for leadership effectiveness in most of the situations. However, these same traits may be counterproductive in certain circumstances or with followers who do not see them as important for group existence. Thus, these traits have a paradoxical quality. Similarly 'socially undesirable traits' or 'dark traits' that are expected to lower leadership effectiveness in general, can actually enhance group survival and fitness in certain circumstances. Countervailing effects of bright and dark traits also depend on the intensity of leaders' trait disposition. For example, while moderate levels of a bright trait, such as extraversion, are desirable and useful for leader and group effectiveness, extreme cases of extraversion, which include risk-taking and a self-serving quest for adventure, may endanger the group as a whole. In the following section, we will discuss the bright and dark traits of leadership and their possible positive and negative implications in certain situations.

Bright Traits

1. **Conscientiousness:** They are responsible, well-organized, diligent team players, exhibiting integrity and persistence in the attainment of organizational goals. They have a strong sense of direction, are detailed-oriented, and are polite in most interpersonal interactions. They define role expectations for their subordinates and promote a fair and ethical work culture in the organization. They plan their work and time schedules. Such leaders give more emphasis on policies, procedures, and

processes. Being self-disciplined they are morally driven to meet the deadlines and complete the work as per the given schedule (Salgado, 2002; Hogan & Hogan, 2001).

Dark Side of This Trait: Though conscientious leaders are perceived to be charismatic and inspirational, they might at times resist change and delay the decision–making process in absence of sufficient evidence to support their preferences. This could lead to poor organizational results, missed business opportunities, less innovation in the organization, risk avoidance, and underutilization of organizational resources. Highly conscientious leaders emerge as perfectionists, uncompromising on work schedules, and critical of their team's performance. They might experience stress during turbulent times or market situations and when the deadlines are not met as planned (Bono & Judge, 2004).

2. **Extraversion:** Extraverts are sociable, assertive, energetic, friendly, and optimistic individuals. They express positive emotions and are considered as 'people's persons' drawing energy from the outside world. They exhibit behaviors consistent with the transformational style of leadership. They are impulsive individuals who believe in completing a task, rather than pondering or thinking about it. They are ambitious and interested in improving their social standing. They work hard to achieve power and get rewards. They express more positive emotions and have many friends and admirers (Hogan et. al., 1994).

Dark Side of This Trait: An excessive extravert individual has a tendency to overestimate their capabilities and behave in grandiose ways to be the center of attention. They rarely encourage input and feedback from subordinates and colleagues and try to alienate employees who want to share their credit and achievements. At times they engage in shallow discussions with employees and in the process fail to provide a strategic focus to the followers. Extraverted leaders may make hasty investment and acquisition decisions and if the returns on such investments are not in line with their aggressive schedules, they might reverse the decision (Hogan & Hogan, 2001).

3. **Agreeableness:** Agreeable leaders are trustworthy, cooperative, inclusive, and gentle. They tend to avoid conflicts and promote cooperation among team members. As such, agreeable leaders are empathetic when giving critical feedback and encourage a supportive and friendly work environment. They are interested in the well-being of others, are conscious of an employee's psychological needs, and pay attention to a subordinate's job satisfaction and growth in the organization. Agreeable individuals have an idealized influence on others due to their trustworthy and cooperative nature (Bono & Judge, 2004).

Dark Side of This Trait: Highly agreeable leaders tend to avoid interpersonal conflicts and often make decisions that can attain the broadest level of approval from everyone involved. Such leaders generally give lenient performance ratings to the employees, which deprives them and the organization of honest appraisal of their work. It might adversely affect the promotion and compensation decisions and lead to biases. Positions that call for complacent acquiescence to the status quo may be best suited for agreeable leaders that adopt a non-confrontational attitude. The two possible outcomes of the transformational leadership pattern, radical process innovations and progressive gains in organizational policy, may therefore be unlikely to be proposed by highly likable leaders (Bernardin et. al., 2000).

4. **Emotional Stability:** Leaders who are emotionally stable are calm, composed, consistent in their emotional displays, and less likely to be affected by unpleasant feelings like tension, worry, or resentment. Emotionally stable individuals enjoy their job, resist impulses, adapt to change and are not easily disheartened by setbacks. Such leaders have a positive outlook on life and circumstances, remain calm in moments of crisis, and bounce back quickly from failures (Salgado, 2002).

    Dark Side of This Trait: Leaders with high levels of emotional stability might be characterized as reserved, disinterested, unexpressive, and unemotional by their followers. Followers of such leaders have repeatedly reported lower levels of job satisfaction and trust, and higher absenteeism and turnover intentions. Such leaders may withhold their honest evaluations of certain employees, leaving these employees unsure of their position in the team. In that spirit, these leaders may hurt the employees, who thrive on regular interactions with their supervisors, and measure their job satisfaction based on the feedback given from their supervisors. They may experience difficulty in getting followers support in adverse situations that demand strong reactions from both leaders and followers (Cable & Judge, 2003).

5. **Openness to Experience:** Such individuals are curious, creative, imaginative and resourceful lateral thinkers. These open-minded leaders can easily cope with organizational change. Like transformational leaders they have an inspirational appeal and promote critical thinking and innovation, to challenge the conventional wisdom on critical issues in the organization (Bono & Judge, 2004).

    Dark Side of This Trait: Individuals scoring high on this trait are characterized as nonconformists, who are considered to be a potential hazard for conventional work settings, as they are easily distracted by abstract ideas, implementing strategies that can jeopardize the long-term plans of an organization. Followers of such leaders might get frustrated with the leader's inability to articulate a specific viewpoint on crucial subjects. As a result, even though these leaders are imaginative and bright, they risk alienating followers who require direct and honest guidance. Leaders who are prone to analytical and abstract thought will probably jeopardize a group's chances of success or survival in situations that call for swift and decisive action (Erdheim et. al., 2006).

6. **Core Self-Evaluations (CSE):** It is a personality trait that comprises of four elements: locus of control, neuroticism, self-esteem, and self-efficacy. These traits are highly correlated with each other and share similar patterns of correlation with organizational outcomes such as employee satisfaction and performance, task motivation, and goal-setting behavior. Strategies incorporating innovation and product differentiation are related to CEOs who have an internal [locus of control] (i.e., feel in charge of their fortunes). High core self-evaluation scores among CEOs are linked to easier and quicker strategic decision-making processes, high-risk initiatives, and organizational persistence in accomplishing challenging goals. The degree to which people value and like themselves is measured by their level of self-esteem. Low self-esteem makes people more dependent on outside forces, as well as more prone to seek out other people's favor and follow their rules and suggestions. Efficiency, also known as generalized self-efficacy, is a crucial psychological term that expresses assurance in our capacity to achieve in particular circumstances. The way a person approaches and completes goals, projects, and obstacles can be significantly influenced by their perception of their own self-efficacy (Judge et. al., 1997).

Dark Side of This Trait: Core self-evaluations leads to self-assessment of one's potential in the world. Extremely positive self-assessments of oneself can have the same negative repercussions as narcissism and hubris. This hyper-CSE personality will reflect the overconfidence of a hubris and self-love of a narcissist. CEOs with hyper-CSE will make strategies that serve their interest, rather than those beneficial for the organization. Though hyper-CSE shares some traits of narcissism and hubris, they cannot be entirely reflective of these personality traits. CSEs personality is distinct, as it does not reflect excessive pride or self-confidence of hubris, or exploitation of a narcissist (Simon & Houghton, 2003).

7. **Intelligence:** Cognitive ability or Intelligence is regarded as an important trait possessed by all leaders (Sternberg & Ruzgis, 1994). Intelligence is linked to success in every aspect of an individual's life. Intelligent leaders have the competence of handling diverse organizational functions, critical decision-making, and developing creative solutions for complex problems (Hernstein & Murray, 1994).

Dark Side of This Trait: The emergence of leaders and their effectiveness are both positively correlated with intelligence. However, if a leader's Intelligent Quotient (IQ) is much higher than the IQ of group members he will be treated as an outsider to the group, which will adversely affect his effectiveness within the group. Groups with a high IQ will be more receptive to an intellectual leader than groups with low IQs. Highly intellectual leaders might show disinterest in simple day-to-day issues that require little or no cognitive intervention. At times these leaders become so occupied with solving difficult problems and analyzing alternatives that they tend to ignore situations demanding quick and decisive action (Stogdill, 1948; Goldberg et al., 2006).

8. **Charisma:** The core tenet of charismatic leadership theory is that a leader's ability to persuade followers often transcends the formal and legal power structures of a group or organization and instead depends on the leader's charm, persuasiveness, and communication skills. Charismatic leaders can influence followers by outlining a compelling vision for the future, encouraging adherence to organizational goals, and fostering a sense of self-efficacy. Numerous empirical studies have found that charismatic leaders can inspire high levels of performance and commitment among followers (Shamir et al., 1993).

Dark Side of This Trait: In some rare circumstances, a charismatic leader might abuse their position and power to further their own interests and gain a personal advantage while taking advantage of their susceptible followers. These followers show blind allegiance and passive obedience to a leader's vision. Charismatic leaders are likely to emerge in situations when a society experiences drastic changes in the social structure. Charismatic leaders inspire long-lasting commitments from their followers by articulating a vision of change that embodies shared values and promises for a better future. As the followers are drawn to the leader's charisma, they tend to discount any information that contradicts their leader's vision. Due to this reason, these followers are more susceptible to manipulation and exploitation by their leader, who misuses the power bestowed upon him by the submissive followers. Charismatic leaders are skilled at delivering powerful speeches using stories and situations, to distract followers from considering unpleasant facts (Conger, 1990).

Dark Traits

1. **Narcissism:** Narcissistic individuals have an exaggerated view of themselves and show signs of strong self-obsession and self-love. They believe that they are exceptional and deserve praise, love, and attention. Narcissists often see others as inferior to themselves, lack empathy, and manipulate conversations to reflect their own preferences and accomplishments. They are insensitive, hostile, and lack interpersonal skills. Narcissistic leaders have a self-serving bias when interpreting information and making decisions that are beneficial to their reputation. Integrity and evaluations of interpersonal effectiveness were adversely correlated with narcissism. Narcissistic managers tend to dominate and take advantage of their humble counterparts, allocating scarce organizational resources to themselves. As a result, these leaders leave a negative impression on subordinates and followers, resulting in lower job satisfaction and motivation, and higher turnover intentions (Rosenthal & Pittinsky, 2006).

   Bright Side of This Trait: Narcissist are assertive individuals who can take challenging decisions at the time of crisis. They are mentally tough individuals who can control their emotions during setbacks and challenges. Narcissist score high on emotional intelligence, mental resilience, and self-confidence. Their inflated self-view acts as a buffer against stress and depression. Their infectious self-confidence helps them to draw attention in any surrounding. Most successful leaders have shown high levels of egotism and self-esteem, two positive traits of a narcissistic personality. While narcissists have an ongoing need for admiration and approval, social approval (associated with transactional and transformational styles of leadership) has been identified as a motive for gaining support in political and social processes. Narcissism is known for strategic dynamism and is positively related to corporate acquisitions. Last but not least, narcissistic leaders choose bold and aggressive behaviors that are likely to highlight their leadership and vision (Morf et al., 2000).

2. **Hubris:** Hubris leaders have an inflated sense of self-worth, excessive pride, self-confidence, and a misconception about their influence in the world. These individuals make more positive assessments of their aptitude, ability, and accomplishments than any logically valid objective appraisal would otherwise imply. They have a defensive approach in the face of most forms of constructive criticism and generally raise doubt about the competence of the evaluator and the evaluation technique. Hubristic leaders tend to neglect conflicting views and negative judgments from subordinates. Hubris CEOs often pay higher premiums during corporate acquisitions as they believe in their ability to achieve success. This attitude is against rational decision-making and might lead to lower corporate valuations and market performance. Compared to Narcissism this trait is mostly triggered by positional power and overestimation of one's capabilities based on certain events (Hayward & Hambrick, 1997).

   Bright Side of This Trait: Hubris leaders depict high self-esteem and self-worth. They are attractive and dominate group discussions, openly sharing their thoughts on issues. Hubris leaders spend more time on research and development when starting a new venture or launching a new product. As they are bold and confident they have the ability to inspire their stakeholders to trust the organization's vision, policies and procedures. In difficult situations Hubris leaders instill confidence and commitment among their followers and peers (Hayward et. al., 2006).

The Dark Side of Leadership

3. **Social Dominance:** Dominant personalities give an impression that they are more competent in comparison to others even when they are not. This behavior supports their journey as a leader and helps them to claim important authoritative positions in their career. They can dominate conversations and use pressure tactics to get things done as per their requirements. They often use fear to manipulate and dictate terms to their subordinates and followers. Such individuals and leaders are detrimental to the organic growth of an organization (Mann, 1959; Anderson & Kilduff, 2009)

Bright Side of This Trait: Dominant leaders are overconfident individuals who believe and controlling and manipulating others. Followers who lack social skills, and score low on self-worth are easily susceptible to such leaders. These leaders can in long run kill the creativity and initiative-seeking capabilities of their followers and of an organization as a whole (Hare et. al., 1997).

4. **Machiavellianism:** This trait is named after a 16th-century author Niccolo Machiavelli, author of the book 'The Prince'. Through the story, Machiavelli has recommended manipulation and persuasion as the prime means to get social and political power. Leaders described as Machiavellian are dominant, politically driven, and influential. They persuade their followers and subordinates by using impression management tactics, for doing things for the leader's benefit. Under Machiavellian supervision, the intrinsic value of work is lost because these leaders emphasize on maximizing opportunities for achieving their goals rather than following protocols or work ethics. Machiavellian individuals follow an authoritarian style of leadership and use their power to abuse their subordinates (McHoskey, 1999; Goldberg, 1999).

Bright Side of This Trait: Machiavellian leaders are strategic decision-makers and are able to manipulate authorities in both corporate and governmental organizations. High Machiavellian leaders show charisma and are highly capable of handling structured and unstructured tasks. They make use of impression management tactics to build strategic political alliances within and outside the organization, which can increase their influence in large social and political networks. Machiavellian leaders have proved to be successful presidents, with great political understanding (Bass, 1990; Yukl, 2002).

Dark Leadership Styles

On the basis of the various studies conducted by researchers following styles of dark or toxic leaders have been identified in the organizations:

1. **Petty Tyranny:** One who abuses power over others is known as a petty tyrant. This type of leadership style develops as a result of managerial failures and breaches in corporate morality. According to preliminary empirical research, tyrant behaviors include being arbitrary and self-aggrandizing, demeaning others, resolving conflicts by force, discouraging initiative, and using non-contingent punishment. This dark leader has a nasty and violent disposition. In most situations, these leaders work towards their selfish motives rather than taking the organization's interests or performance into account. They force their employees to work in a stressful isolated environment, fostering unhealthy work culture. Organizations having a petty tyrant, suffer from a lack of employee commitment and high labor turnover rates (Ashforth, 1994).

2. **Bully Leadership:** This style of leadership develops when bureaucratic and authoritarian leadership philosophies are used oppressively toward the subordinates. Bullying leads to an oppressive organizational culture where employees feel reluctant to take the initiative and assume responsibility. These leaders inflict fear among employees to satisfy their own hidden agendas (Kets de Vries, 1994).

3. **Narcissistic Leadership:** As discussed earlier in dark personality traits, a narcissistic personality is a confident, self-centered individual. Sigmund Freud (1921) named the narcissistic personality after a mythical Greek hero 'Narcissus'. Narcissus became obsessed with himself and his reflection which eventually became the reason for his death (Maccoby, 2000). Many powerful leaders have narcissistic personalities. Narcissistic behavior is dangerous because the individual becomes more important than the organization. The leader lacks confidence and is thus envious of their successful subordinates. They have a strong desire to be appreciated and strive for top positions in organizations. True teamwork, a critical component of a high-performing organization, is seriously threatened by the internalized narcissistic image. Narcissists devote all of their energy to defending their own beliefs rather than encouraging others to do the same.

4. **Paranoid Leadership:** This leadership is characterized by excessive worry, anxiety, and depression (Johns et al., 2004). Paranoid leaders, rarely trust anyone and try to take complete control over organizational resources to discourage others from taking initiative. Filled with fear and jealousy they become hypersensitive to others' actions and attach subjective motives to people's intentions. They create rigid structures to maintain their position and power. Employees exhibit passive attitudes in this negative work culture. These leaders are highly insecure and try to suppress everyone who can be a possible threat to their established power relationship. They are extremely wary and guarded in their interactions with fellow colleagues, family members, and friends. They try to maintain a safe distance in relationships to guard their authority and leadership (Gillaspie, 2009).

5. **Toxic Leadership:** Another form of destructive leadership style characterized by power abuse, favoritism, bullying, jealousy, and biases Yavaş (2016). Toxic leaders reward toxic team members and co-workers who share a similar thought process. They are protective of followers who show unquestioned loyalty. Employees who have differing views are kept away from important meetings and effective roles within the organization (Uygur and Gümüştekin, 2019). He imbibes a feeling of resentment and jealousy in his subordinates. (Reed, 2004). They engage in dysfunctional behaviors such as gossiping and withholding important information, to achieve their desired goals.

6. **Emotionally Dependent Leadership:** These leaders score low on emotional intelligence and self-confidence. Emotionally unstable leaders struggle to get the trust and respect of followers and co-workers. The emotionally unstable CEO puts a personal spin on all of the business operations and draws unfavorable conclusions from them. These managers exert performance pressure on their staff members and blame them for unfavorable consequences (Ballı & Çakıcı, 2019). Vulnerable leaders always aspire to leave the toxic work environment created by them as a result of demotivated employees and deteriorated organizational structure (Gillaspie, 2009).

7. **Passive Aggressive Leadership:** These managers appear casual to their subordinates while hiding more serious issues from them. They regularly find ways to dismiss the employee's ideas without providing a serious justification for their disagreement. Passive-aggressive leadership grapples with uncertainty and accuses others of their mistakes. They criticize their subordinates for unfavorable results, imposing ambiguous workplace regulations (McIntosh and Rima, 1997)

8. **Unethical Leadership:** These leaders do not follow the norms of society and resort to actions that are considered immoral and/or illegal. They also encourage their followers to act unethically and make processes that favor their selfish motives. Unethical leaders destroy the culture of an organization, giving rise to distrust and fear in the work environment. Employee motivation and job performance will drop owing to the unethical practices of a leader. Such leaders shatter an employee's confidence on their superiors and in the organization, resulting in high turnover rates and weak organizational culture (Erdem, 2015).
9. **Abusive Leaders:** These leaders have a negative orientation and believe in using force and abuse to get things done. Such individuals have a negative impact on the work culture, employee motivation, job satisfaction, and organizational commitment. The leader uses rude and harsh words with his subordinates, uses gestures to demean them, and threatens them with job loss. Managers practicing this leadership style lack confidence in their employees and find abuse the only solution to control them to get the work done (Tepper, 2000).
    - **Hubristic Leadership:** As discussed earlier individuals hubris leaders have excessive self-confidence and self-belief, are greedy, arrogant, and lack moral standards. Hubris leaders do not value their employee's ideas and impose decisions based on their understanding of the situation (Özgüzel & Taş, 2016; Uysal & Çelik, 2018; Bektaş 2016). Jeffrey Skilling, former CEO of Enron, was convicted of securities fraud for his role in the company's financial collapse (Eichenwald, 2005).

THE TOXIC TRIANGLE: ROLE OF FOLLOWERS AND ENVIRONMENT

Dark leaders cannot exist without the support of a conducive environment and susceptible followers (Padilla et. al., 2007), highlighted the relationship between leaders, followers, and environment using a 'toxic triangle' (Figure 1). Followers of destructive leaders equally contribute to negative organizational outcomes by following unethical practices to meet their personal goals. For example, in Enron, the followers received rewards in the form of bonuses which further encouraged their fraudulent behavior. Along with susceptible followers, environmental factors such as structural instability, poor cultural values, perceived mismanagement of social or economic conditions, and absence of institutionalization are the breeding grounds for dark leadership.

The elements of the toxic triangle are discussed below:

Destructive Leaders: The first component of this triangle analyses factors contributing to destructive leadership styles like charisma, personalized use of power, narcissism, negative life themes, and an ideology of hate.

1. **Charisma:** One of the most important traits of a leader is charisma, which is used to influence others and make them behave to achieve personal gain e.g., Hitler, Stalin, and Mussolini (Conger, 1990; Howell & Avolio, 1992 and O'Connor et al., 1995). However, not all charismatic leaders are destructive. Evidence supports that charismatic presidents are more successful in achieving results and implementing change than non-charismatic leaders e.g., U.S. President Barack Obama (House, Spangler, & Woycke, 1991). Charismatic leaders are visionary, energetic, and have great presentation skills. (Conger, 1990; Conger & Kanungo, 1987; Gardner & Avolio, 1998). Charismatic leaders achieve goals and entice followers by selling a vision for the future (Yukl, 1999). Though

Figure 1. Elements of the toxic triangle

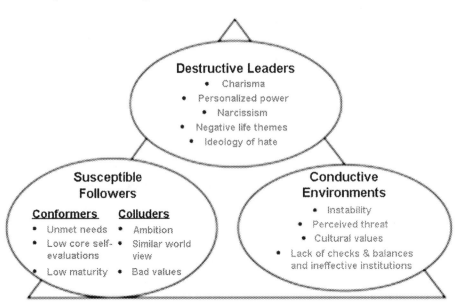

there is a difference in how this vision is perceived by constructive and destructive charismatic leaders. Destructive leaders have a negative vision of the world where survival depends on domination and manipulation (O'Connor et al., 1995). Constructive leaders on the other hand offer a vision beneficial to social institutions (House & Howell, 1992). Constructive charismatic leaders like John Kennedy and Martin Luther King, Jr. had exceptional presentation skills (Burns, 1978; Harvey, 2001). Similarly, destructive charismatic leaders like Hitler and Mussolini demonstrated exceptional rhetorical skills (Pardo Llada, 1988; Redlich, 1999). Both constructive and destructive charismatic leaders require huge stamina and persistence (a form of personal energy) to execute their agendas and face their rivals (Gardner, 1996; Padilla, 2005; Viney, 1999).

2. **Personalized Need for Power:** McClelland's research (1975) suggests that both constructive and destructive charismatic leaders strive to gain power. Power is used by constructive leaders to serve others whereas the same power is used by destructive leaders to impose their goals and dominate others (Conger, 1990; Howell & Avolio, 1992).

3. **Narcissism:** Narcissistic leaders are charismatic and have a strong sense of personalized power. (American Psychiatric Association, 2000 and Rosenthal & Pittinsky, 2006). Autocratic and aggressive leaders like Saddam Hussein and Stalin abused power and demanded unquestioning obedience from their followers (Conger, 1990; Maccoby, 2000 and Sankowsky, 1995). Narcissistic leaders like Hitler used their power to exploit the followers and country's resources to dangerous vulnerability (Paul Kennedy, 1987). Narcissists business leaders make ambitious acquisitions in unrelated sectors, at times paying more than the market value to acquire them (Hayward & Hambrick, 1997 and Malmendier & Tate, 2005).

4. **Negative Life Themes:** According to O'Connor et al. (1995) dark leadership behaviors are associated with negative life experiences. Mostly their negative life stories are related to early life experiences. These leaders have had exploitative adults who have abused them or their family members (Hare, 1993; Katz, 1997; Vaillant, 1977). Josef Stalin's had a traumatic childhood, characterized

by a cruel father. His father was an alcoholic and used to beat him and his mother (Montefiore, 2004). These experiences made him as cruel as his father. Similarly Castro, Hitler and Mussolini also had negative childhood experiences (Raffy, 2004; Redlich, 1999). Leaders who have had a traumatic childhood generally have a destructive image of the world and become indifferent and insensitive to others' situations.

5. **Ideology of Hate:** Destructive leaders have a very negative view of the world. Their childhood experiences have led them to an extreme ideology of hate, in a way that their self-hatred has turned to vanquishing rivals and destroying enemies (Freud, 1966; Cramer, 2000; Garmezy & Masten, 1994 and Vaillant, 1977). As discussed earlier Stalin had a traumatic childhood because of his father. His anger and resentment instilled hatred for powerful people as they reminded him of his father. Eventually, Stalin became a destructive leader engaging in violent acts against fellow Russians and cabinet members. He was a merciless and cruel Russian leader (Montefiore, 2004). Destructive business leaders also view the world in a hateful manner. Wall Street Journal article discussed the intimidating culture of Enron (Raghavan, 2002).

All the factors mentioned above are required for a destructive leader to be successful. A single factor might not be insufficient for a leader to be categorized as destructive. For example, individuals having an ideology of hate and an innate need for power but lack the charisma to drive their followers' behavior will not be able to get the desired results. Similarly, leaders with good rhetorical skills but with socialized motives and positive worldviews are less likely to be destructive. Though these factors are necessary for the proper execution of the dark side of leadership, they are not sufficient. At times the same leaders are not very successful in gaining power with a certain set of followers. Hence it is important to study the contribution of followers and environment to dark leadership personalities.

Susceptible Followers: Followers are the ones who determine and accept the authority and power of a leader (Barnard 1938; Graen & Uhl-Bien, 1995) Those followers who accept the destructive activities of their leaders and support the dark side of leadership do so to satisfy their need for identity, security, safety and social order in an uncertain world. (Kellerman, 2004 and Lipman-Blumen, 2005). Some individuals have a natural tendency to obey authority figures (Milgram, 1974), imitate high-profile leaders (Baharody & Stoneman, 1985), and follow group norms (Asch, 1951). Weierter (1997) identified different types of susceptible followers one who shared the leaders' vision and one who lack clarity on self-concept. Kellerman (2004) defined them as acolytes (true believers of a leader's actions) and bystanders (accepted destructive activities). Followers can be categorized as (i) conformers and (ii) colluders. Conformers follow the leaders out of fear whereas colluders are highly ambitious individuals who follow their leaders to advance their personal agendas. Conformers are characterized as individuals with low self-esteem, low self-efficacy, low psychological maturity, and an external locus of control who are easily susceptible to destructive leaders. While Colluders are characterized as greedy and selfish individuals, who share similar beliefs and traits as that of destructive leaders (Higgins, 1997).

1. **Unmet Basic Needs:** As established by Maslow (1954) and Burns (1978) individuals have a hierarchy of needs. These needs were divided into lower-order and higher-order needs. Until and unless the basic order needs are satisfied, the individuals will not rise to the higher order needs. This holds true for both leaders and followers. Destructive leaders tap into these basic needs of individuals to establish their supremacy. After the global economic depression of the 1930s and World War I, citizens of Italy, Germany, and Russia, were in a poor state and dealt with poverty and starvation,

which set the ground for the rise of Dark leaders like Mussolini, Hitler and Stalin (Arendt, 1951; Tuchman, 1984). In the present world, impoverished countries like Central and West Africa and some parts of South America are ruled by corrupt governments. It is known that individuals in poverty and fear are more easily controlled. When people lack basic necessities and security, they may be more likely to accept extreme ideologies and follow leaders who promise to meet those needs. Additionally, feelings of isolation and loneliness can make people more susceptible to the promises of a strong leader who offers a sense of community and belonging.

2. **Negative Core Self-Evaluations:** CSEs are categorized as the basic elements on the basis of which individuals assess themselves (Judge & Bono, 2001 and Judge et. al., 1997). These core self-evaluations are linked to job satisfaction, motivation, and performance. Researchers have highlighted that individuals with negative CSE scores are more susceptible to dark leaders (Luthans et al., 1998).

3. **Low Maturity:** Individuals with low maturity, as indicated by factors such as ego development, moral reasoning, and self-concept, are more likely to conform to authority and participate in destructive actions. According to Freud (1921), in a crowd, people's sense of morality collapses and they may follow the leader blindly, even if it leads to immoral behavior. This is supported by research, such as Milgram's work (1963, 1974), which suggests that conformist individuals are at risk of harming others. Kohlberg's theory of moral development also states that people who respect rules may still engage in immoral behavior when it is sanctioned by authority (Kohlberg, 1969). Erikson's (1959) developmental theory posits that maturity involves forming a clear sense of self, which can prevent individuals from identifying with destructive leaders and internalizing their values. This vulnerability is especially pronounced in young people, as seen in groups such as the Hitler Youth, Mao's Red Guard, or the Manson family. Followers with low maturity levels admit to a destructive leader's vision and indulge in destructive acts, transforming a confirmer to a colluder (Hoffer, 1951; Kets de Vries, 1989; Weierter, 1997).

4. **Ambition:** Destructive leaders have negative ambitions and their actions can bring disastrous results for the organization. In such organizations, employees who are confirmers or colluders will prosper as they either conform to a leader's ambition or they fulfill their own agenda following the leader's strategies. (Offerman, 2004; McClelland, 1975 and Kellerman, 2004). This was seen in Nazi Germany, where officials competed to please Hitler and implement policies that resulted in the Holocaust (Adams & Balfour, 1998 and Browning, 1989). These dynamics are not unique to Nazi Germany and can be seen in other organizations, such as Enron, where ambitious individuals may collude to profit at the expense of others (McLean & Elkind 2005 and Kellerman, 2004).

5. **Congruent Values and Beliefs:** Followers whose values and beliefs align with those of a destructive leader are more likely to support their vision (Lord & Brown, 2004). Studies have shown that greater similarity between the values and beliefs of leaders and followers leads to greater follower commitment and support (Jung & Avolio, 2000 and Meglino et. al., 1989). When followers see leaders as similar to themselves, they become emotionally attached to the leader and are motivated to follow and support them (Shamir et al., 1993). This in turn will have a positive impact on followers' self-esteem and self-efficacy (Weierter, 1997).

6. **Unsocialized Values:** Individuals who are greedy and selfish, are more likely to support destructive leaders (Hogan, 2006). Ambitious individuals who lack socialization skills are more likely to follow a destructive leader, as these leaders can help them to achieve their goals (McClelland, 1975).

Conducive Environments: Environment or situation is critical to the proper execution of leadership activities. Some factors in a leader's environment can have a negative impact on the leadership. Leadership scholars should take into account the environmental context when analyzing leadership.

1. **Instability:** Instability can provide an opportunity for leaders to gain power and take unilateral decisions (Bass, 1985; Conger & Kanungo, 1987 and Burns, 1978). This centralized decision-making might be difficult to reverse (Kipnis, 1972). Destructive leaders utilize such situations to take control of the systems and execute their power to meet their selfish agendas (Simonton, 1988; Cell, 1974 and Conger & Kanungo, 1998).
2. **Perceived Threat:** Perception of an imminent threat, whether it be mistreatment, economic struggles, or a company facing bankruptcy, can make people accept dominant leaders. Researchers have highlighted that threat draws followers to charismatic leaders, as they believe that such leaders will bring some transformation to normalize the situation and save them (Solomon et. al., 1991). Studies have also proved that objective threats are not necessary, only the perception of a threat is enough for leaders to strengthen their power and motivate followers. (Landau et al., 2004)
3. **Cultural Values:** "Dark leaders" are more likely to emerge in cultures that follow collectivism, uncertainty avoidance, and have high power distance. Societies that fear uncertainty are driven toward strong leaders. Such societies are ruled by dictators who provide structures, make rules and find easy solutions to their complex problems (Hofstede, 1991 and Luthans et al., 1998). Collectivist cultures prefer strong leaders to restore group dynamics. High power-distance cultures, especially those with low educational levels and large disparities in wealth distribution, create a conducive environment for authoritative leaders (Hofstede, 1991).
4. **Absence of Checks and Balances and Institutionalization:** The lack of checks and balances and well-established institutions in an organization or nation can lead to the consolidation of power in a single leader or group, which can be detrimental. Strong institutions, such as government bodies, can prevent the abuse of power by creating countervailing centers of power (Hamilton et. al., 2000). In organizations, independent oversight can be established through independent boards (Gandossy & Sonnenfeldt, 2004). This concept is similar to the idea of "presidentialism" in political science (Zakaria, 1997). Destructive leaders are less likely to succeed in stable systems with strong institutions and proper checks and balances on power and control.

The case of Fidel Castro, the Cuban dictator is analyzed below, to illustrate the dynamics of the toxic triangle.

Castro and Cuba: An Illustration of the Toxic Triangle

Castro, 'The Destructive Leader': Castro was one of the longest-serving dictators in modern history. As a teenager, he was intelligent, energetic, courageous, had a gifted memory of courage, and had a talent for self-promotion. In his early 20s, Castro became a strong opponent of Fulgencio Batista, a Cuban dictator. At the end of 1958, Castro was successful to overthrow the dictator. Castro, 32 years of age extended his control with his followers. Castro was a charismatic, bold, and ruthless young man who was able to attract equally ruthless supporters. He had a fractious relationship with his father and a difficult upbringing in several foster homes. He was ridiculed by his schoolmates for his rural upbringing. (Geyer, 1991; Ros, 2003; Pardo Llada, 1976, Quirk, 1993 and Raffy, 2004), Castro's narcissism and exhibitionism were evident through his grandiose actions, such as sending troops to parts of Africa and Central America, his unwillingness to admit to any mistakes, as well as his lavish lifestyle. Castro's ideology of hatred towards the United States was evident in the statements given by his wives and mistresses (Fuentes, 2004).

Cubans, 'The Susceptible Followers': Cubans were susceptible to following Fidel Castro because of the promises of escape from poverty that he made to two groups of people. The first group was supporters and revolutionaries who supported his vision and would gain power through his leadership. The second group was the rural people and uneducated urban poor citizens who were attracted to the promise of a better life. However, it is debatable to what extent these groups actually benefited from the Castro regime. A third group, the professional middle class, initially supported the revolution but withdrew their support eventually when it was evident that democracy and elections were not on Castro's mind. Many of them fled to the US and Europe during the 1960s, which further consolidated Castro's control by reducing the potential number of dissidents (Latell, 2005; Montaner, 1983, 1999; Pardo Llada, 1988; Thomas, 1998 and Triay, 1999).

Cuba's Propitious Environment: The environment in Cuba prior to Castro's rise to power was characterized by political dysfunction, economic prosperity, and income inequalities, political instability, corrupt institutions, and a culture of presidentialism. This made the population open to a revolution. After coming to power, Castro and his followers replaced the democratic and social institutions with powerful surveillance systems to control dissent. They were also fostering social insecurity by frequently spreading the news about a potential threat from the US invaders or the return of fled Cubans who would reclaim their homes and property (Quirk, 1993).

Destructive Outcomes: An autocratic ruler supported by susceptible followers, and an unresponsive government led to a revolution that was initially praised by leftist thinkers as a model of freedom and economic justice to safeguard human rights. However, freedom came at a great cost to human rights. The overall consequences of Fidel Castro's regime have been an economic disaster. He is estimated to be worth nearly $1 billion, while the Cuban citizens were starved and faced poverty, poor health conditions, low telephone service, and limited electric power generation. Many have fled the country and would continue to do so if given the opportunity. The decline in well-being is not due to economic sanctions by the US but the malpractices of the government and its dysfunctional economy (DePalma, 2006; Matthews, 1961; Kroll, 2006 and Fontova, 2005).

Fidel Castro's leadership as a dictator in Cuba was the result of his personal characteristics, the followers who supported him, and the historical context in which he rose to power.

Interventions to Mitigate Negative Outcomes

To effectively address negative leadership outcomes, it is important to take a systemic approach that considers interventions aimed at elements in all three domains: leaders, followers, and context. By considering interventions at different levels, organizations can address destructive leadership processes more effectively and sustainably.

Leader-Level interventions

Shifting Behavior: Personal coaching to target specific behaviors and channel the desire for personalized power into pro-social actions.

Suppressing Influence: It is important to limit and channel the power of leaders for the betterment of the organization and society. Several assessment tools can be used while deciding on the promotion decisions for leaders to screen out destructive leaders.

Severing Ties: Removing individuals from the organization if their behavioral transgressions are particularly egregious, as they can "spoil the whole barrel" and cause destruction to the organization.

Follower-Level Interventions

At this follower level, three types of interventions could be implemented to (1) shift follower behavior; (2) suppress their susceptibility to dark leaders; or (3) sever ties with followers who have been negatively impacted by dark leaders. First, shifting follower behavior could be achieved through training programs aimed at increasing emotional intelligence, which has been linked to a reduction in susceptibility to dark leaders (Barling et al., 1996). Additionally, providing followers with education on dark leadership traits and how to recognize them can help to increase their awareness and ability to protect themselves from negative impacts. Second, to suppress followers' susceptibility to dark leaders organizations should create a culture that does not tolerate abusive behavior and provides support and resources for victims of dark leadership. This can include implementing and enforcing strict codes of conduct, providing a confidential reporting mechanism, and providing support for employees who have been negatively impacted. Third, if a follower has been negatively impacted by a dark leader, severing ties with the dark leader and providing support for the follower to transition to a new team or position within the organization may be necessary.

Organizational-Level Interventions

Interventions should aim at (1) shifting the organizational culture and climate; (2) suppressing the conditions that allow for dark leadership to thrive; or (3) severing ties with external organizations that enable dark leadership. First, shifting the organizational culture and climate to one that values transparency, ethical behavior, and employee well-being can create an environment that is less conducive to dark leadership. This can include implementing a code of conduct, promoting a culture of open communication, and providing employee training on ethical behavior. Second, suppressing the conditions that allow for dark leadership to thrive can include conducting regular reviews of organizational policies and procedures to identify and address any structural issues that may be contributing to dark leadership. Third, severing ties with external organizations that enable dark leadership can include conducting regular reviews of organizational partnerships and severing ties with organizations that have a history of promoting dark leadership or unethical behavior.

Transforming dark traits is a challenge not only for the leaders but for the whole organization. Alan Goldman suggested that it is important to address the psychological and emotional toxicity of dark leaders to bring transformation. He argues that most of the highly productive leaders have exhibited some form of toxic qualities to become successful. Hence organizations should implement interventions to reduce toxicity and utilize the bright side of the dark traits for organizational benefit (Goldman, 2009b).

CONCLUSION

Most of the literature available on leadership discusses the traits and styles of a successful business leader. However, these traits considered bright traits also have a dark side attached to them which if given a conducive environment can lead to dark tendencies in a leader. It is also important to highlight that susceptible followers also play a very important role in the development and execution of dark leadership styles. Not all dark leaders are bad for the organization. Some dark leaders were successful in bringing good results for the organization in times of distress or in the short run. In the modern world, dark leadership is assessed in terms of organizational outcomes and employee performance. Some organizations accept these leadership styles if these dark leaders can bring success to the organization. However, in the long run, dark leadership behaviors can lower employee morale and job satisfaction, decrease organizational performance, and cause employee stress and burnout which in turn can give rise to suicidal tendencies in employees, increased employee turnover, lawsuits, stakeholder dissatisfaction, and can also impact the goodwill of the organization.

In today's competitive world, it is important to identify destructive behaviors to ensure the smooth functioning of organizations. It will help in reducing the training, maintenance, and survival cost of such individuals. It will further reduce conflicts in the organizations and help in making a progressive environment for the organization. Dark traits should be screened at the time of hiring employees, so that accurate decisions are made when selecting talented individuals for the organization Organizations should build a culture of openness and trust, implement fair policies, and take regular employee feedback to ensure that the organizational environment does not give rise to destructive tendencies in employees.

REFERENCES

Adams, G. B., & Balfour, D. L. (1998). *Unmasking administrative evil*. Sage. doi:10.4135/9781452231525

American Psychiatric Association. (2000). *Diagnostic and statistical manual of mental disorders* (4th ed.). Author.

Anderson, C., & Kilduff, G. J. (2009). Why do dominant personalities attain influence in face-to-face groups? The competence-signaling effects of trait dominance. *Journal of Personality and Social Psychology*, 96(2), 491–503. doi:10.1037/a0014201 PMID:19159145

Arendt, H. (1951). *The origins of totalitarianism*. Harcourt, Brace and Co.

Argyris, C. (1998). Empowerment: The emperor's new clothes. *Harvard Business Review*, 76, 98–105. PMID:10179657

Asch, S. (1951). Effects of group pressure upon the modification and distortion of judgments. In H. Guetzkow (Ed.), *Groups, leadership, and men* (pp. 117–190). Carnegie Press.

Ashforth, B. (1994). Petty tyranny in organizations. *Human Relations*, 47(7), 755–778. doi:10.1177/001872679404700701

Baharody, G., & Stoneman, Z. (1985). Peer imitation: An examination of status and competence hypotheses. *The Journal of Genetic Psychology*, 146(2), 161–170. doi:10.1080/00221325.1985.9914443

Ballı, E., & Çakıcı, A. (2019). Karanlık Liderlik: Otel İşletmelerinde Bir Araştırma. *Turkish Studies*, *14*(2), 155–173. doi:10.7827/TurkishStudies.14775

Bandura, A. (1986). *Social foundations of thought and action: A social cognitive theory*. Prentice–Hall.

Barnard, C. I. (1938). *The functions of the executive*. Harvard University Press.

Bass, B. M. (1985). *Leadership and performance beyond expectations*. Free Press.

Bass, B. M. (1990). *Bass and Stogdill's handbook of leadership. Theory, Research and Managerial Applications* (Vol. 3). The Free Press.

Bektaş, Ç. (2016). Liderlik yaklaşımları ve modern liderden beklentiler. *Selçuk Üniversitesi Akşehir Meslek Yüksekokulu Sosyal Bilimler Dergisi*, *2*(7), 43–53.

Bentz, V. (1985, August). *A view from the top: A thirty year perspective of research devoted to the discovery, description, and prediction of executive behavior*. Paper presented at the 93rd annual convention of the american psychological association, Los Angeles, CA.

Bernardin, H. J., Cooke, D. K., & Villanova, P. (2000). Conscientiousness and agreeableness as predictors of rating leniency. *The Journal of Applied Psychology*, *85*(2), 232–236. doi:10.1037/0021-9010.85.2.232 PMID:10783539

Bono, J. E., & Judge, T. A. (2004). Personality and transformational and transactional leadership: A meta-analysis. *The Journal of Applied Psychology*, *89*(5), 901–910. doi:10.1037/0021-9010.89.5.901 PMID:15506869

Browning, C. (1989). The decision concerning the final solution. In F. Furet (Ed.), *Unanswered questions: Nazi Germany and the genocide of the Jews* (pp. 96–118). Schocken.

Burke, R. J. (2006). Why leaders fail. Exploring the dark side. In R. J. Burke & C. L. Cooper (Eds.), *Inspiring leaders*. Routledge. doi:10.4324/9780203013199-25

Burns, J. (1978). *Leadership*. Harper & Row.

Byrne, D. (1971). *The attraction paradigm*. Academic Press.

Cable, D. M., & Judge, T. A. (2003). Managers' upward influence tactic strategies: The role of manager personality and supervisor leadership style. *Journal of Organizational Behavior*, *24*(2), 197–214. doi:10.1002/job.183

Cell, C. (1974). Charismatic heads of state: The social context. *Behavior Science Research*, *9*(4), 255–305. doi:10.1177/106939717400900401

Cohen, F., Solomon, S., Maxfield, M., Pyszczynski, T., & Greenberg, J. (2004). Fatal attraction: The effects of mortality salience on evaluations of charismatic, task-oriented, and relationship-oriented leaders. *Psychological Science*, *15*(12), 846–851. doi:10.1111/j.0956-7976.2004.00765.x PMID:15563330

Conger, J. (1990). The dark side of leadership. *Organizational Dynamics*, *19*(2), 44–55. doi:10.1016/0090-2616(90)90070-6

Conger, J., & Kanungo, R. (1987). Toward a behavioral theory of charismatic leadership in organizational settings. *Academy of Management Review*, *12*(4), 637–647. doi:10.2307/258069

Conger, J., & Kanungo, R. (1988). The empowerment process: Integrating theory and practice. *Academy of Management Review*, *13*(3), 471–482. doi:10.2307/258093

Conger, J., & Kanungo, R. (1998). *Charismatic leadership in organizations*. Sage. doi:10.4135/9781452204932

Cramer, P. (2000). Defense mechanisms in psychology today: Further processes for adaptation. *The American Psychologist*, *55*(6), 637–646. doi:10.1037/0003-066X.55.6.637 PMID:10892206

DePalma, A. (2006). *The man who invented Fidel: Castro, Cuba, and Herbert L. Matthews of the New York times*. PublicAffairs.

Eichenwald, K. (2005). *Conspiracy of Fools: A True Story*. Broadway Books.

Einarsen, S., Skogstad, A., Aasland, M. S., & Løseth, A. M. S. B. (2002). Destruktivt lederskap: Årsaker og konsekvenser (Causes and consequences of destructive leadership). In A. Skogstad & S. Einarsen (Eds.), *Ledelse på godt og vondt. Effektivitet og trivsel* (pp. 233–254). Fagbokforlaget.

Erdem, A. R. (2015). Eğitim yönetim etiği ve eğitim yönetiminde etik liderliğin kritiği. *Akademik Sosyal Araştırmalar Dergisi*, *3*(10), 1–15.

Erdheim, J., Wang, M., & Zickar, M. J. (2006). Linking the Big Five personality constructs to organizational commitment. *Personality and Individual Differences*, *41*(5), 959–970. doi:10.1016/j.paid.2006.04.005

Erikson, E. H. (1959). *Identity and the life cycle*. International Universities Press.

Finkelstein, S., & Hambrick, D. C. (1990). Top-management-team tenure and organizational outcomes: The moderating role of managerial discretion. *Administrative Science Quarterly*, *35*(3), 484–503. doi:10.2307/2393314

Fontova, H. (2005). *Fidel: Hollywood's favorite tyrant*. Regnery Publishing.

Freud, A. (1966). *The ego and the mechanisms of defense*. International Universities Press.

Freud, S. (1921). *Group psychology and the analysis of the ego*. Hogarth Press.

Fuentes, N. (2004). *La autobiografía de Fidel Castro: I. El paraíso de los otros*. Barcelona: Ediciones Destino.

Gandossy, R., & Sonnenfeld, J. A. (2004). Leadership and governance from the inside out. John Wiley & Sons.

Gardner, H. (1996). *Leading minds: An anatomy of leadership*. Basic Books.

Gardner, W., & Avolio, B. (1998). The charismatic relationship: A dramaturgical perspective. *Academy of Management Review*, *23*(1), 32–58. doi:10.2307/259098

Garmezy, N., & Masten, A. (1994). Chronic adversities. In M. Rutter, L. H. Taylor, & E. Taylor (Eds.), *Child and adolescent psychiatry* (3rd ed., pp. 191–208). Blackwell Scientific Publications.

Gersick, C. J., & Hackman, J. R. (1990). Habitual routines in task-performing groups. *Organizational Behavior and Human Decision Processes*, *47*(1), 65–97. doi:10.1016/0749-5978(90)90047-D PMID:11538273

Geyer, G. (1991). *Guerrilla prince: The untold story of Fidel Castro*. Little, Brown and Company.

Gillaspie, S. M. (2009). *The Impact of Dark Leadership on Organizational Commitment and Turnover*. Emporia State University.

Goldberg, L. R. (1999). A broad-bandwidth, public-domain, personality inventory measuring the lower-level facets of several five-factor models. In I. Mervielde, I. J. Deary, F. De Fruyt, & F. Ostendorf (Eds.), *Personality psychology in Europe* (Vol. 7, pp. 7–28). Tilburg University Press.

Goldberg, L. R., Johnson, J. A., Eber, H. W., Hogan, R., Ashton, M. C., Cloninger, C. R., & Gough, H. G. (2006). The International Personality Item Pool and the future of public domain personality measures. *Journal of Research in Personality*, *40*(1), 84–96. doi:10.1016/j.jrp.2005.08.007

Goldman, A. (2009b). Transforming Toxic Leaders. Stanford Business Books.

Graen, G. B., & Uhl-Bien, M. (1995). Development of leader–member exchange (LMX) theory of leadership over 25 years: Applying a multi-level domain perspective. *The Leadership Quarterly*, *6*, 219–247. doi:10.1016/1048-9843(95)90036-5

Hambrick, D., & Abrahamson, C. (1995). Assessing the amount of managerial discretion in different industries: A multi-method approach. *Academy of Management Journal*, *38*(5), 1427–1441. doi:10.2307/256864

Hamilton, A., Jay, J., & Madison, J. (2000). *The federalist*. Random House.

Hare, A. P., Koenigs, R. J., & Hare, S. E. (1997). Perceptions of observed and model values of male and female managers. *Journal of Organizational Behavior*, *18*(5), 437–447. doi:10.1002/(SICI)1099-1379(199709)18:5<437::AID-JOB806>3.0.CO;2-0

Hare, R. (1993). *Without conscience: The disturbing world of the psychopaths among us*. Simon & Schuster.

Harter, S. (1990). Causes, correlates, and the functional role of global self-worth: A life span perspective. In R. J. Sternberg & J. Kolligan Jr. (Eds.), Competence considered (pp. 67–97). Yale University Press.

Harvey, A. (2001). A dramaturgical analysis of charismatic leader discourse. *Journal of Organizational Change Management*, *14*(3), 253–265. doi:10.1108/09534810110394877

Hayward, M. L. A., & Hambrick, D. C. (1997). Explaining the premiums paid for large acquisitions: Evidence of CEO hubris. *Administrative Science Quarterly*, *42*(1), 103–127. doi:10.2307/2393810

Hayward, M. L. A., Shepherd, D. A., & Griffin, D. (2006). A hubris theory of entrepreneurship. *Management Science*, *52*(2), 160–172. doi:10.1287/mnsc.1050.0483

Hernstein, R. J., & Murray, C. (1994). *The bell curve: Intelligence and class structure in American Life*. Free Press.

Higgins, E. T. (1997). Beyond pleasure and pain. *The American Psychologist*, *52*(12), 1280–1300. doi:10.1037/0003-066X.52.12.1280 PMID:9414606

Hoffer, E. (1951). *The true believer: Thoughts on the nature of mass movements*. Harper & Row.

Hofstede, G. (1991). *Cultures and organizations: Software of the mind*. McGraw–Hill.

Hogan, R., Curphy, G. J., & Hogan, J. (1994). What we know about leadership: Effectiveness and personality. *The American Psychologist, 49*(6), 493–504. doi:10.1037/0003-066X.49.6.493 PMID:8042818

Hogan, R., & Hogan, J. (2001). Assessing leadership: A view from the dark side. *International Journal of Selection and Assessment, 9*(1&2), 12–51. doi:10.1111/1468-2389.00162

Hogan, R., Raskin, R., & Fazzini, D. (1990). The dark side of charisma. In K. Clark & M. Clark (Eds.), Measures of leadership (pp. 343–354). Academic Press.

Hornstein, H. A. (1996). *Brutal Bosses and their pray*. Riverhead Books.

House, R. J., Spangler, W. D., & Woycke, J. (1991). Personality and charisma in the U.S. presidency: A psychological theory of leader effectiveness. *Administrative Science Quarterly, 36*(3), 364–396. doi:10.2307/2393201

Howell, J. M., & Avolio, B. J. (1992). The ethics of charismatic leadership: Submission or liberation? *The Academy of Management Executive, 6*, 43–54.

Janis, I., & Mann, L. (1977). *Decision making: A psychological analysis of conflict, choice, and commitment*. Free University Press.

Johns, L., Cannon, M., Singleton, N., Murray, R., Farrell, M., Brugha, T., & Meltzer, H. (2004). Prevalence and correlates of self-reported psychotic symptoms in the British population. *The British Journal of Psychiatry, 185*(4), 298–305. doi:10.1192/bjp.185.4.298 PMID:15458989

Judge, T., & Bono, J. (2001). Relationship of core self-evaluations traits-self-esteem, generalized self-efficacy, locus of control, and emotional stability—with job satisfaction and job performance: A meta-analysis. *The Journal of Applied Psychology, 86*(1), 80–92. doi:10.1037/0021-9010.86.1.80 PMID:11302235

Judge, T. A., Colbert, A. E., & Ilies, R. (2004). Intelligence and leadership: A quantitative review and test of theoretical propositions. *The Journal of Applied Psychology, 89*(3), 542–552. doi:10.1037/0021-9010.89.3.542 PMID:15161411

Judge, T. A., LePine, J. A., & Rich, B. L. (2006). The narcissistic personality: Relationship with inflated self-ratings of leadership and with task and contextual performance. *The Journal of Applied Psychology, 91*, 762–776. doi:10.1037/0021-9010.91.4.762 PMID:16834504

Judge, T. A., Locke, L. A., & Durham, C. C. (1997). The dispositional causes of job satisfaction: A core evaluations approach. *Research in Organizational Behavior, 19*, 151–188.

Judge, T. A., Piccolo, R. F., & Kosalka, T. (2009). The bright and dark sides of leader traits: A review and theoretical extension of the leader trait paradigm. *The Leadership Quarterly, 20*(6), 855–875. doi:10.1016/j.leaqua.2009.09.004

Jung, D. I., & Avolio, B. J. (2000). Opening the black box: An experimental investigation of the mediating effects of trust and value congruence on transformational and transactional leadership. *Journal of Organizational Behavior, 21*(8), 949–964. doi:10.1002/1099-1379(200012)21:8<949::AID-JOB64>3.0.CO;2-F

Kaiser, R. B., & Hogan, R. (2007). The dark side of discretion: Leader personality and organizational decline. In R. Hooijberg, J. Hunt, J. Antonakis, & K. Boal (Eds.), *Being there even when you are not: Leading through strategy, systems and structures, Monographs in leadership and management* (Vol. 4, pp. 177–197). Elsevier Science. doi:10.1016/S1479-3571(07)04009-6

Katz, M. (1997). *On playing a poor hand well: Insights from the lives of those who have overcome childhood risks and adversities.* W.W. Norton & Company.

Kellerman, B. (2004). *Bad leadership. What it is, how it happens, why it matters.* Harvard Business School Press.

Kellman, H. C., & Hamilton, V. L. (1989). *Crimes of obedience: Toward a social psychology of authority and responsibility.* Yale University Press.

Kennedy, P. (1987). *The rise and fall of the great powers: Economic change and military conflict from 1500 to 2000.* Random House.

Kets de Vries, M. (1989). *Prisoners of leadership.* John Wiley & Sons.

Kets de Vries, M. (2006). The spirit of despotism: Understanding the tyrant within. *Human Relations*, *59*(2), 195–220. doi:10.1177/0018726706062732

Kets de Vries, M. F. (1994). The Leadership Mystique. *The Academy of Management Perspectives*, *8*(3), 73–89. doi:10.5465/ame.1994.9503101181

Kile, S. M. (1990). *Helsefarleg leierskap (Health endangering leadership).* Universitetet i Bergen.

Kipnis, D. (1972). Does power corrupt? *Journal of Personality and Social Psychology*, *24*(1), 33–41. doi:10.1037/h0033390 PMID:5079552

Kohlberg, L. (1969). Stage and sequence: The cognitive developmental approach to socialization. In D. Goslin (Ed.), *Handbook of socialization theory and research* (pp. 347–480). Rand McNally.

Kornai, J. (1995). *Highway and byways: Studies on reform and post-communist transition.* The MIT Press.

Kroll, L. (2006). Fortunes of kings, queens and dictators: A look at the world's wealthiest leaders. *Forbes*. Retrieved December 15, 2006, from https://www.forbes.com/billionaires/2006/05/04/rich-kings-Ed ictators_cz_lk_0504royals.html

Landau, M. J., Solomon, S., Arndt, J., Greenberg, J., Pyszczynski, T., & Miller, C. (2004). Deliver us from evil: The effects of mortality salience and reminders of 9/11 on support for President George W. Bush. *Personality and Social Psychology Bulletin*, *30*(9), 1136–1150. doi:10.1177/0146167204267988 PMID:15359017

Latell, B. (2005). *After Fidel: The inside story of Castro's regime and Cuba's next leader.* Palgrave MacMillan.

LeBreton, J. M., Shiverdecker, L. K., & Grimaldi, E. M. (2018). The Dark Triad and workplace behavior. *Annual Review of Organizational Psychology and Organizational Behavior*, *5*(1), 387–414. doi:10.1146/annurev-orgpsych-032117-104451

Linz, J. (1994). *The failure of presidential democracy.* Johns Hopkins University Press. doi:10.56021/9780801846397

Lipman-Blumen, J. (2005). *The allure of toxic leaders. Why we follow destructive bosses and corrupt politicians — and how we can survive them.* Oxford University Press.

Lord, R. G., & Brown, D. G. (2004). *Leadership processes and follower self-identity.* Lawrence Erlbaum Associates.

Luthans, F., Peterson, S. J., & Ibrayeva, E. (1998). The potential for the "dark side" of leadership in post-communist countries. *Journal of World Business, 33*(2), 185–201. doi:10.1016/S1090-9516(98)90005-0

Maccoby, M. (2000). Narcissistic leaders: The incredible pros, the inevitable cons. *Harvard Business Review, 78,* 68–77.

Mainwaring, S., & Scully, T. (1995). Party systems in Latin America. In S. Mainwaring & T. Scully (Eds.), *Building democratic institutions: Party systems in Latin America* (pp. 1–34). Stanford University Press.

Malmendier, U., & Tate, G. (2005). CEO overconfidence and corporate investment. *The Journal of Finance, 60*(6), 2661–2700. doi:10.1111/j.1540-6261.2005.00813.x

Mann, R. D. (1959). A review of the relationships between personality and performance in small groups. *Psychological Bulletin, 56*(4), 241–270. doi:10.1037/h0044587

Maslow, A. (1954). *Motivation and personality.* Harper.

Matthews, H. (1961). *The Cuban story.* G. Braziller.

McCall, M. W. J., & Lombardo, M. M. (1983). *Off the track: Why and how successful executives get derailed.* Greensboro: Center for Creative Leadership Report No. 21.

McClelland, D. C. (1975). *Power: The inner experience.* Irvington.

McHoskey, J. W. (1999). Machiavellianism, intrinsic versus extrinsic goals, and social interest: A self-determination theory analysis. *Motivation and Emotion, 23*(4), 267–283. doi:10.1023/A:1021338809469

McIntosh, G. L., & Rima, S. D. (1997). *Overcoming the Darkside of Leadership.* Baker Books.

McLean, B., & Elkind, P. (2005). *The smartest guys in the room.* Penguin.

Meglino, B. M., Ravlin, E. C., & Adkins, C. L. (1989). A work values approach to corporate culture: A field test of the value congruence process and its relationship to individual outcomes. *The Journal of Applied Psychology, 74*(3), 424–432. doi:10.1037/0021-9010.74.3.424

Milgram, S. (1963). Behavioral study of obedience. *Journal of Abnormal and Social Psychology, 67*(4), 371–378. doi:10.1037/h0040525 PMID:14049516

Milgram, S. (1974). *Obedience to authority.* Harper & Row.

Montaner, C. (1983). *Fidel Castro y la revolución Cubana* (2nd ed.). Editorial Playor.

Montaner, C. (1999). *Viaje al corazón de Cuba.* Plaza & Janes Editores.

Montefiore, S. (2004). *Stalin: The court of the red tsar*. Knopf.

Morf, C. C., Weir, C., & Davidov, M. (2000). Narcissism and intrinsic motivation: The role of goal congruence. *Journal of Experimental Social Psychology, 36*(4), 424–438. doi:10.1006/jesp.1999.1421

O'Connor, J., Mumford, M., Clifton, T., Gessner, T., & Connelly, M. (1995). Charismatic leaders and destructiveness: An historiometric study. *The Leadership Quarterly, 6*(4), 529–555. doi:10.1016/1048-9843(95)90026-8

Offerman, L. (2004). When followers become toxic. *Harvard Business Review, 84*, 54–60. PMID:14723177

Özgüzel, S., & Taş, S. (2016). Hubris Sendromuna Yakalanan Yöneticilerde Çocukluktaki Aile İçi İletişimin Etkisinin İncelenmesi. *Yüzyılda Eğitim Ve Toplum Eğitim Bilimleri Ve Sosyal Araştırmalar Dergisi, 5*(13).

Padilla, A. (2005). *Portraits in leadership: Six extraordinary university presidents*. Praeger Publishers.

Padilla, A., Hogan, R., & Kaiser, R. B. (2007). The toxic triangle: Destructive leaders, susceptible followers, and conducive environments. *The Leadership Quarterly, 18*(3), 176–194. doi:10.1016/j.leaqua.2007.03.001

Padilla, A., Hogan, R., & Kaiser, R. B. (2007). The Toxic Triangle: Destructive Leaders, Susceptible Followers, and Conducive Environments. *The Leadership Quarterly, 18*(3), 176–194. doi:10.1016/j.leaqua.2007.03.001

Pardo Llada, J. (1976). *Fidel: De los Jesuitas al Moncada*. Plaza & Janes Editores.

Pardo Llada, J. (1988). *Fidel y el "Ché."*. Plaza & Janes Editores.

Quirk, R. (1993). *Fidel Castro*. W. W. Norton.

Raffy, S. (2004). *Castro, el desleal* (P. G. Crespo, Trans.). Santillana Ediciones.

Raghavan, A. (2002). Full speed ahead: How Enron bosses created a culture of pushing limits. *The Wall Street Journal*, p. A1.

Redlich, F. (1999). *Hitler: Diagnosis of a destructive prophet*. Oxford University Press.

Reed, G. E. (2004). Toxic Leadership. *Military Review, 84*(4), 67–71.

Ros, E. (2003). *Fidel Castro y el gatillo alegre: Sus años universitarios*. Ediciones Universal.

Rosenthal, S. A., & Pittinsky, T. L. (2006). Narcissistic leadership. *The Leadership Quarterly, 17*(6), 617–633. doi:10.1016/j.leaqua.2006.10.005

Rotter, J. B. (1966). Generalized expectancies for internal versus external control of reinforcement. *Psychological Monographs, 80*(1).

Salgado, J. (2002). The Big Five personality dimensions and counterproductive behaviors. *International Journal of Selection and Assessment, 10*(1&2), 117–125. doi:10.1111/1468-2389.00198

Sankowsky, D. (1995). The charismatic leader as a narcissist: Understanding the abuse of power. *Organizational Dynamics, 23*(4), 57–71. doi:10.1016/0090-2616(95)90017-9

Schmidt, F. L., & Hunter, J. E. (2000). Select on intelligence. In E. A. Locke (Ed.), *Handbook of principles of organizational behavior* (pp. 3–14). Blackwell.

Shamir, B., Arthur, M., & House, R. (1994). The rhetoric of charismatic leaders: A theoretical extension, a case study, and implications for research. *The Leadership Quarterly*, 5(1), 25–42. doi:10.1016/1048-9843(94)90004-3

Shamir, B., House, R. J., & Arthur, M. B. (1993). The motivational effects of charismatic leadership: A self-concept based theory. *Organization Science*, 4(4), 577–594. doi:10.1287/orsc.4.4.577

Simonton, D. (1988). Presidential style: Personality, biography, and performance. *Journal of Personality and Social Psychology*, 55(6), 928–936. doi:10.1037/0022-3514.55.6.928

Slattery, C. (2009). The Dark Side of Leadership. In S. Slattery (Ed.). Semann & Slattery.

Solomon, S., Greenberg, J., & Pyszczynski, T. (1991). A terror management theory of social behavior: The psychological functions of self-esteem and cultural worldviews. In M. Zanna (Ed.), Advances in experimental social psychology (Vol. 24, pp. 93–159). Academic Press. doi:10.1016/S0065-2601(08)60328-7

Sternberg, R. J., & Ruzgis, P. (1994). *Personality and intelligence*. Cambridge University Press.

Stogdill, R. M. (1948). Personal factors associated with leadership: A survey of the literature. *The Journal of Psychology*, 25(1), 35–71. doi:10.1080/00223980.1948.9917362 PMID:18901913

Tepper, B. J. (2000). Consequences of abusive supervision. *Academy of Management Journal*, 43(2), 178–190. doi:10.2307/1556375

Thomas, H. (1998). *Cuba or the pursuit of freedom*. Plenum Press.

Triay, V. (1999). *Fleeing Castro: Operation Pedro Pan and the Cuban children's program*. University of Florida Press.

Tuchman, B. (1984). *The march of folly: From Troy to Vietnam*. Alfred A. Knopf.

Uygur, A., & Gümüştekin, K. (2019). Karanlık Liderliğin Alt Boyutlarının İncelenmesi. *International Social Sciences Studies Journal*, 5(35), 2552–2562. doi:10.26449ssj.1492

Uysal, Ş. A., & Çelik, R. (2018). Sağlık meslek gruplarında hubris sendromunun varlığına ilişkin keşfedici bir çalışma. *Uluslararası İktisadi Ve İdari İncelemeler*, 17, 103-118.

Vaillant, G. (1977). *Adaptation to life*. Little-Brown.

Viney, J. (1999). *Drive: What makes a leader in business and beyond*. Bloomsbury Publishing.

Vroom, B., & Jago, A. (1974). Decision making as a social process: Normative and descriptive models of leader behavior. *Decision Sciences*, 5(4), 743–769. doi:10.1111/j.1540-5915.1974.tb00651.x

Weierter, S. (1997). Who wants to play "Follow the Leader?" A theory of charismatic relationships based on routinized charisma and follower characteristics. *The Leadership Quarterly*, 8(2), 171–193. doi:10.1016/S1048-9843(97)90015-1

Yavaş, A. (2016). Sectoral Differences in the Perception of Toxic Leadership. *Procedia: Social and Behavioral Sciences, 229,* 267–276. doi:10.1016/j.sbspro.2016.07.137

Yukl, G. (2002). *Leadership in organizations* (5th ed.). Prentice Hall.

Yukl, G. A. (1999). An evaluation of conceptual weaknesses in transformational and charismatic leadership theories. *The Leadership Quarterly, 10*(2), 285–305. doi:10.1016/S1048-9843(99)00013-2

Zakaria, F. (1997). The rise of illiberal democracy. *Foreign Affairs, 76*(6), 22–43. doi:10.2307/20048274

KEY TERMS AND DEFINITIONS

Agreeableness: Agreeableness is a personality trait that refers to the tendency to be cooperative, empathetic, and compassionate. Individuals who are high in agreeableness tend to be friendly, kind, and considerate of others. They are also less likely to be critical or argumentative.

Conscientiousness: Conscientiousness is a personality trait that refers to the tendency to be organized, reliable, and responsible. Individuals high in conscientiousness are often described as hardworking, dependable, and disciplined.

Dark Leadership: Dark leadership is a term used to describe leaders who engage in unethical or immoral behaviors. These behaviors can include manipulation, deceit, exploitation, and abuse of power. Dark leaders may also be characterized by a lack of empathy, a lack of accountability, and a tendency to prioritize their own interests over those of their followers or the organization they lead.

Extraversion: Extraversion is a personality trait that refers to the tendency to be outgoing, sociable, and assertive. Individuals who are high in extraversion tend to be outgoing, energetic, and enjoy the company of others. Extraversion is also one of the five broad dimensions of personality in the "Big Five" personality theory.

Hubris: Hubris is a term used to describe excessive pride or self-confidence, often accompanied by a lack of humility and a disregard for the consequences of one's actions. Hubris can manifest in various forms, and it is considered a negative trait as it can lead to poor judgment and negative outcomes.

Machiavellianism: Machiavellianism is a personality trait that is characterized by the use of manipulation and deceit to achieve one's goals. They tend to view other people as mere instruments to achieve their goals and lack empathy and moral principles.

Narcissism: Narcissism is a personality disorder characterized by excessive self-importance, a lack of empathy for others, and a constant need for admiration and validation. Narcissistic individuals may have an inflated sense of their own abilities and accomplishments and may believe that they are special or unique.

Chapter 12
Positive Impact of Leaders' Dark Triad Personality Traits in Uncertain Times

Gunjan Mishra
ITM University, Raipur, India

Shaivi Shrivastava
Amity University, Raipur, India

Mrityunjay Bandhopadhyay
Amity University, Raipur, India

Navisha Bajaj
Amity University, Raipur, India

Sakshi Mishra
Institute of Public Health, India

Tarannum Sarwar Dani
Jain University (Deemed), India

ABSTRACT

The effectiveness of a leader is determined by their leadership skills. Although each leader has their own distinct style, there are a few commonly known forms of leadership, including transformational, transactional, democratic, servant, and charismatic authority leadership. Contrarily, the dark triad, which includes the personality traits of narcissism, psychopathy, and Machiavellianism, is a dark personality trait. Even though these characteristics of dark triad can cause personality disorders, they somehow improve a leader's ability in a crisis. Secondary data have been gathered through a variety of techniques to support the former mentioned statement. According to the findings, dark traits are positively correlated with effective leadership outcomes and crisis management and decision making, in whole or in part.

DOI: 10.4018/978-1-6684-8257-5.ch012

Positive Impact of Leaders' Dark Triad Personality Traits in Uncertain Times

INTRODUCTION

Leadership research has traditionally focused on positive traits in leaders, effective leadership approaches, and positive outcomes. When discussing leadership styles, transactional leadership is regarded as one of the best for the next generation. The gap between a leader and the genuine interest of their followers may be bigger the more charming and impressive a leader may be. Differently defined as insincere, tyrannical, exploitative, restricting, ineffective, laissez-faire, and involving both active and passive avoidance of leadership obligations, "negative" leadership has been used to describe a variety of behaviours.

But within the field of leadership studies, every study pointing to the dark side is met by a chorus of voices that present leaders as saints, commanders, architects (redesigning society), pedagogues (teaching appropriate behaviours) and physicians (healing-stricken organizations). These metaphors are frequently used by leaders themselves, who are determined to portray themselves as essential for human flourishing.

Nowadays, results are common. More than at any other period in recent memory, established institutions, political parties, and business leaders are devalued. The notion of leadership has gone wrong. The heroic leadership myths that were so prevalent for so long are now being scrutinised by people who go well beyond "the usual suspects" on the left. Therefore, challenging conceptions of leadership gave an idealised view of leadership—a magic mirror that is sparing with the facts. It is time to catch up with reality.

The main objective of this chapter includes why dark personality traits are necessary in times of crisis management for a good leader. This Chapter includes an introduction to dark personality traits with the help of the dark triad theory, the role of a leader during a crisis and the importance of dark traits for a good leader.

LEADERSHIP

When working in a group, a clash of interests and conflicts are bound to happen. To resolve the conflict and find the middle ground, a decision-making figure is required. That figure is usually the "leader" of the group. The leader is not only the peacekeeper or decision-maker of the group, but he is also the motivator and the supportive person who helps the group member achieve their target.

According to the author, Leadership is a leader's ability to help his/her team or group move towards and achieve the goal smoothly. Leadership is said to be an innate ability but it can also be learned and practised. Leadership is a continuous process as a leader must look after the needs and goals of his team members all the time and he must also help them make progress.

To be a good leader, the individual must possess some leadership qualities.

Quality of a Good Leader

A leader must be able to understand the goals and problems of the team he is leading. The following qualities are required to be able to lead a group.

1. A leader should be an active listener. He should make his team members feel heard and included.
2. He should have good motivational skills. He should understand his team members' goals and motivate them to achieve them.

3. A leader should have a high level of self-confidence, if he lacks self-confidence then he won't be able to provide confidence to his followers.
4. A leader must possess good social skills. He should be friendly and approachable so that, his team members can comfortably share their concerns or goals with him.
5. A leader must have good communication skills. He should be a good speaker to help people understand their roles.
6. The leader must acquire competence and knowledge to influence and instruct his team.

Different Styles of Leadership

As an individual have different and unique personalities, leaders have different leadership styles. Some of the commonly known leadership styles are as follows.

1. **Autocratic Leadership:** This type of leadership is also known as authoritative leadership and it is like dictatorship as the leader, who uses this type of leadership holds full power or control over his teammates and takes all the decisions by himself. The leader wants his teammate to follow his instructions without any questions. This type of leadership is encouraged when quick solutions are required. But the followers might feel frustrated and unheard.
2. **Democratic Leadership:** This is also known as participative leadership. In this type of leadership, the leader takes decisions with his teammates after having thorough discussions with them. The group members are free to take initiative and generate creative ideas. This type of leadership might be time-consuming, but it generates great results and satisfaction among the members of the group. The work or decision made through teamwork is always satisfactory and gives out quality results.
3. **Transactional Leadership:** This is also known as managerial leadership, and it only focuses on the organisational work. The leader and group's relation are only based on the work and reward/punishment. The leader tries to generate good outcomes from his team through the rewards and if an individual is unable to mean their goal, then they get punished. This method is good for motivating the group members, but it lacks in creating a good leader-follower relationship.
4. **Laissez-Faire Leadership:** In this leadership style, the leader does not lead the group. The leader only works as a link between the subordinate and supervisor. He provides the information and the job to be done. The rest is done by the team itself. This either leads to great outcomes by the team as they are the decision-makers, or it can lead to procrastination as they have no guidance or motivation.
5. **Transformational Leadership:** This type of leadership helps an individual to transform themselves so that they can achieve their goals. The leader influences and encourages his team members to transform themselves into their ideal form and strive to reach their goals. Even though this is a time-consuming process, it gives out great outcomes.

Leadership Theories

1. **Transactional Theory of Leadership:** This theory of leadership states that the leader and followers' relationship is only based on motivation through reward and punishment. They do not share any bond or connection. The group members are motivated to achieve their targets in the given time so that they can be rewarded and avoid punishment (Weber, 1947).

2. **Transformational Theory of Leadership:** This theory states that the leader and the follower connection or bond is based on the leader's ability to motivate and encourage the followers or the group members to transform into their better or ideal selves. The leader tries to increase the team's self-confidence by helping them achieve their target or goal in an ideal manner (Burns, 1978).
3. **Contingency Theory of Leadership:** This theory states that the leader should have the ability to adapt to different situations. The leader should be versatile and should be able to use different leadership techniques in different situations. This also helps leaders become more knowledgeable and skilled (Fielder, 1964).

PERSONALITY

The word "personality" comes from the Latin word *persona* which denotes mask. People frequently use the words personality, temperament, and character interchangeably. However, in the scientific realm of psychology, these terms have different meanings. It is far broader than a trait, attribute, or characteristic because it includes physical and psychological components. Personality refers to more stable patterns of behaviour, beliefs, and emotions. According to Allport (1937), personality is a dynamic arrangement within an individual of those psychophysical processes that govern his or her distinctive adaptation to his or her environment.

Personality, as a complex construct, cannot be fully defined in terms of a single physiological function, genetics, culture, or social learning. When describing personality, all possible elements and their intricate interrelationship must be considered. As a result, no single theory can fully explain complex human behaviour, nor does it indicate that any theory is valid or incorrect; rather, each idea adds to our understanding of human personality.

Following are the few major approaches that successfully describe human personality:

- **Psychodynamic Theories:** Personality is explained by these theories in terms of early childhood experiences, unconscious drives, needs and motives that drive human behaviours. These ideas include those advanced by psychologists and psychiatrists like Sigmund Freud, Alfred Adler, Karen Horney, and others.
- **Trait Theories:** The trait approach views personality in terms of several traits. These are the fundamental components of human personalities. Traits are distinctive behavioural patterns that are relatively stable and resistant to modification. The trait approach incorporates theories advanced by Allport, Cattell, and Eysenck, among others. Many psychometric tools that measure these traits are based on these theories.
- **Humanistic and Learning Theories:** The humanistic perspective of human personality has a more positive outlook than other approaches. It believes that men are fundamentally virtuous and have an innate propensity for self-growth and self-realization. Behavioural theories, on the other hand, explain human behaviour using principles such as classical conditioning, operant conditioning, observational learning, and so on.
- **Biological Theories:** There are many biological explanations for human personality. These theories tend to explain individual personality differences as a result of different brain structures and their functions. Although certain associations have been found in various research studies, causation could not be established.

Dark Triad Personality

The concept of "dark triad personality" is relatively new in the study of psychology. The term "Dark triad personality" was first coined by Paulhus and Williams (2002) who tried to describe subclinical dark personality traits namely: narcissism, Machiavellianism, and Psychopathy. The terms "narcissism and psychopathy" have roots in psychiatric literature, but it is not the same as clinical conditions of narcissistic personality disorder or antisocial personality disorder which are considered personality disorders as per DSM-V. The aforementioned characteristics that are used in organizational contexts don't significantly affect a person's functioning in their social, professional, or other spheres. These traits can be thought of as existing on a continuum and may vary in intensity from person to person.

Machiavellianism

The personality trait of Machiavellianism has been named after Nicolo Machiavelli. Niccol Machiavelli, an Italian Renaissance statesman and political philosopher who served as the secretary of the Florentine republic, was born in Florence, Italy, on May 3, 1469, and died there on June 21, 1527 (Mansfield, 2023). The concept of Machiavellianism was initially introduced by Christe and Gies (1970) which is characterized by People who are high on Machiavellianism traits and are very cunning manipulators. Although they are frequently perceived in society as skilled liars, their deception frequently goes much deeper. Machiavellians are said to engage in strategic, long-term social manipulation (Paulhus, 2014). Individuals with high levels of this attribute share some traits. To begin with, they typically have a more negative view of others. Everyone in society is only concerned with what is best for them. They usually use deceptive techniques to persuade others to fulfil their demands. They don't think twice about acting unethically (Christie & Gies, 1970). Machiavellians are pessimistic, tactical people who believe that interpersonal manipulation is the key to success in life (Furnham et al., 2013). They are cruel and cold-hearted, and their ultimate focus is to earn money, power, and fame. Unlike psychopathy and narcissism, the construct of Machiavellianism does not exist separately as a personality disorder in psychiatry or clinical psychology.

There is a positive side to this personality trait. People who score high on Machiavellianism do have some advantage over those who score low on Machiavellianism, as evident from a study that showed that high Machs were more likely to be promoted to leadership roles than low Machs, and organisations led by high Machs performed better than those headed by low Machs (Geis, 1968). However, high Mach individuals became less central to the group's communication network and generated fewer administrative ideas when the time came to solve an issue through collaboration. (Oksenberg, 1968). High Machs individuals give off the impression of being successful manipulators; they are resistant to having their attitudes altered and have an efficient task-oriented approach. A potential to function successfully as a leader in task-oriented groups is indicated by the presence of these characteristics, as well as the individual's propensity to assert dominance in the context of a group setting (Drory & Gluskinos, 1980).

Psychopathy

When we hear the term "psychopathy," an image of a serial killer may spring to mind. The term "psychopath" refers to someone callous, emotionally frigid, or who disregards social norms. It is frequently used interchangeably with antisocial personality disorder, a psychiatric condition characterized by a lack of remorse, a lack of empathy, and other criminal inclinations visible during childhood and adolescence (American Psychiatric Association, 2013). The presence of psychopathy features does not always imply the presence of antisocial personality disorder. Furthermore, most of us may exhibit some or all of the characteristics of psychopathy to varying degrees, which is not enough different from normal behaviour to be deemed a condition. Subclinical psychopathy, which refers to persons who display many of the traits of psychopathy except for some of the more severe antisocial tendencies, is commonly discussed in the context of leadership and organization. Moreover, there is little to no qualitative distinction between psychopathy and subclinical psychopathy; their shared traits are essentially the same (Thomas, 2006).

Psychopathy has been conceptualized in a variety of ways throughout history. The idea was first presented in the work of Cleckley (1941), who defined various characteristics of psychopathy. These include a lack of anxiety or fear, a superficial charm, egotism, a lack of remorse, difficulty to create strong bonds with others, poor impulse control, etc. As previously stated, these characteristics can be thought of as existing on a spectrum, with one end reflecting the lack of all psychopathic tendencies and the other showing the presence of all such qualities with full intensity. People who fall somewhere between these two extremes are thought to exhibit subclinical psychopathic qualities, which allow them to be charming, lack empathy to some extent, and are less likely to be dysfunctional in stressful situations due to the existence of low levels of neurotic symptoms. Some scholars have suggested that some of the above key features can be useful in certain contexts, such as the business world, in contrast to the generally held belief that psychopathy is inevitably maladaptive (Lilienfeld, 1994; Lykken, 1995). Having a predisposition towards subclinical psychopathic traits can be advantageous for leaders as it enables them to remain calm and collected in terms of crisis. This lack of nervousness and distress can aid in proper reasoning and sound decision-making needed for effective crisis management.

Narcissism

Like Machiavellianism and psychopathy, Narcissism is the third component of the dark triad (Paulhus and Williams, 2002). The personality trait of narcissism is defined by an exaggerated sense of self, or by a person having a very high level of self-esteem. Many people get confused between narcissism and narcissistic personality disorder. Despite some overlap, both are distinct. One might assume that narcissism exists on a continuum, similar to psychopathy. Although narcissistic tendencies may be present in many people, they can only be classified as a disorder if they significantly impede a person's capacity for daily living (American Psychiatric Association, 2013). On the other hand, People with subclinical narcissism may feel superior to others and are more likely to be very, self-centred, grandiose, manipulative, or even charming, traits that may be advantageous if leaders have them to some extent. Moreover, People's perceptions of leaders are most frequently linked with dominance, confidence, strong self-esteem, and extraversion. Surprisingly, narcissistic people suit this boss picture pretty well (Czarna & Nevicka, 2019). However, People who exhibit narcissistic tendencies are not all going to benefit in the same way. Narcissistic people have a variety of personality characteristics, each of which can play a role in determining whether they are successful or unproductive as leaders. These characteristics range from charm, daring vision, drive to succeed, and risk-taking to possible negative characteristics like lack of compassion and sympathy, abuse, egocentrism, animosity, and unethical inclinations (Czarna & Nevicka, 2019). According to the findings of some researchers, there are circumstances in which narcissism can be advantageous not only to the narcissistic individual but also to the organization as a whole (Chatterjee & Hambrick, 2007). Narcissism is even considered to be more adaptive as compared to the other two components of the dark triad (Rauthmann, 2012). Although the three originated in different ways, Machiavellianism, psychopathy, and narcissism have significant overlap. They all share common traits of selfishness, emotional coldness and manipulation (Paulhus & Williams, 2002).

Figure 1 is an illustration of the dark triad personality trait.

Figure 1.
Note: Dark triad personality type from "A Survey on Human and Personality Vulnerability Assessment in Cyber-security: Challenges, Approaches, and Open Issues" by Papatsaroucha et al. (2021)

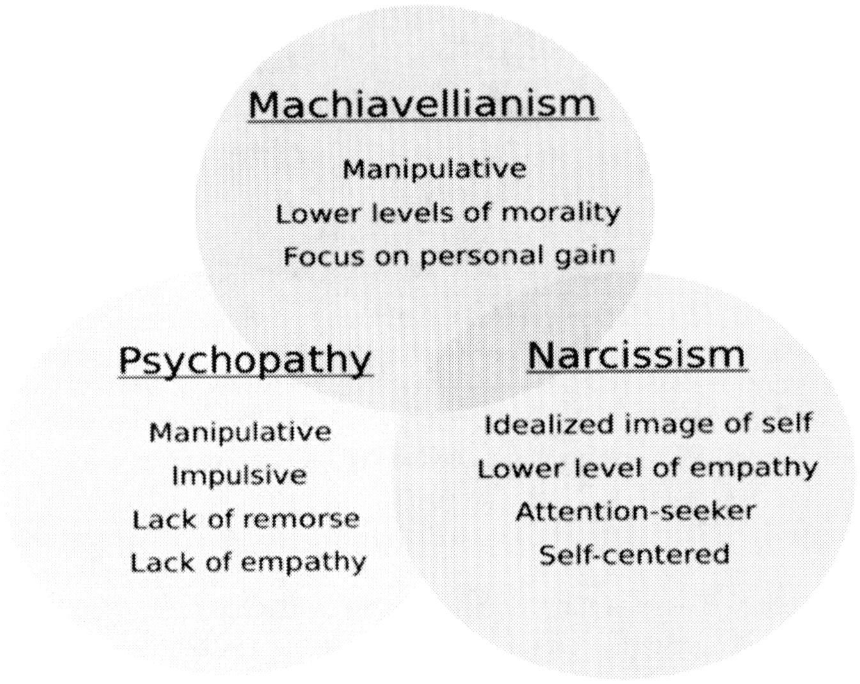

Machiavellianism
Manipulative
Lower levels of morality
Focus on personal gain

Psychopathy
Manipulative
Impulsive
Lack of remorse
Lack of empathy

Narcissism
Idealized image of self
Lower level of empathy
Attention-seeker
Self-centered

THE DARK TRIAD AND LEADERSHIP EFFECTIVENESS

Existing research on leadership effectiveness and dark triad personality focuses far too much on the negative outcomes associated with such leaders, such as job dissatisfaction, organizational dysfunction, losses, and inaction. Even though there are numerous negative consequences associated with leaders who have dark personality traits, as many other studies suggest, having a dark triad personality does indeed have a positive impact on leadership outcomes. The dark triad characteristics might be effective in organizational and leadership jobs. Despite numerous studies showing that psychopathy, Machiavellianism or narcissism is maladaptive, certain studies have revealed the major benefits of these traits. Smith-Lilienfild (2013) found that leaders who score high on subclinical psychopathy are more likely to be intelligent, self-confident, extroverted, and non-neurotic. They have an excellent communication style. The above characteristics are a few of the characteristics of a great leader. Landay et al. (2019) found a positive correlation between psychopathy and leadership effectiveness, up to a certain point after which it becomes negatively correlated. Leaders who show narcissistic traits are often perceived as haughty, dominant, and authoritarian. They are competent leaders who become active in group settings (Nevicka et al, 2011). They are even more charismatic, motivating and visionary (Rosenthal & Pittinsky, 2006). Higher-ranking leaders have higher scores on all three dimensions of the dark triad personality, as reported by both the leaders themselves and their subordinates (Diller et al., 2021).

Some studies suggest that these characteristics may be associated with specific forms of creativity. One of the most recent meta-analyses revealed a modest but significant relationship between creativity and dark triad personality traits (Lebuda et al., 2021). Innovative ideas and solutions can undoubtedly be advantageous in a leadership role. As leaders who are able to think creatively and generate novel solutions to problems may be more effective at attaining their objectives and fostering organisational success.

The connection between the dark triad characteristics and the Big Five psychological traits is one way in which they may be connected with domain of creativity (Jonason et al., 2010). Previous study has connected the Big Five traits to creativity (McCrae, 1987). Narcissism, for example, has been found to be favorably linked with domain-general creativity (Furnham et al., 2013), that can be utilized across multiple areas or situations. This could be because narcissistic people have a lot of confidence, boldness, and self-esteem, which allows them to produce and communicate innovative ideas more effectively.

The motive for attaining a leadership position is mostly driven by a narcissistic temperament and a desire for social supremacy. Therefore, it is not strange if someone appears in one's mind right away, especially those CEOs who receive the highest salary because they also have the highest narcissism scores. All three of the dark triad personality traits are found in positions of authority. Many of the characteristics of a prototype leader, such as charm, self-confidence, strength, and vitality, are exhibited by narcissistic leaders. They also have a drive for power, employ social dominance and manipulating techniques, and share traits with Machiavellian and psychopathic types. They are outgoing, skilled at leading conversations, thrive in groups, and captivate and inspire followers. In addition to having the desire to take leadership positions, dominating personalities are more likely to be promoted or become leaders because they provide the impression of competence. These qualities are necessary for an ideal leader to have to perform well even during times of crisis.

Combination of Dark Triad Traits and Transformational Leadership: Its Positive Outcomes

Hambrick and Mason (1984) developed the upper echelons theory (UET), to illustrate how executives' values, experiences, and personalities play a significant role in organisational decision-making processes and how they affect the strategic decisions that an organisation takes.

Transformational leadership, presented by Bass and Avolio (2004), comprises 4 factors: idealised influence, inspirational motivation, intellectual stimulation, and individualised consideration. According to evolutionary psychologists, dark triad characteristics persisted because they were necessary for people to live and adapt (Pilch, 2020). The dark triad traits have already been linked to a high thirst for power and success as leaders in organisations, according to research (Jonason et al., 2012; Krick et al., 2016).

The traits of the dark triad seem to be more strongly linked to pseudo-transformational leadership, which has great inspiring drive but little idealised influence, intellectual stimulation, and individualised consideration. Pseudo-transformational leaders exhibit self-confidence and power while using manipulation (Machiavellianism), fostering reliance and unconditional allegiance, instilling fear of a leader (psychopathy), and encouraging dependence and terror of others (narcissism) (Barling et al., 2008; Bass

& Steidlmeier, 1999; Christie et al., 2011; Lin et al., 2017). Positive outcomes can depend on charisma, which is the idealised ability of dark leaders to exert their influence quickly. (Christie et al., 2011).

Bass and Avolio's full-range leadership model (1997) identified three key leadership outcomes—satisfaction with leadership, leadership effectiveness, and followers' extra effort. It is assumed that a transformational leader shapes satisfaction (followers are happy with their leader's working techniques), is productive (a leader is viewed as being competent when dealing at different organizational levels) and promotes extra effort (a leader can influence followers to do more than they are expected) (Bass & Avolio, 2004; Bennett, 2009).

Dark personalities are ineffective in organisational settings in the past. This personality type is characterised by a strong desire for wealth, power, and status. There is already some research linking negative personality traits to professional achievement. Since the dark ones frequently succeed in their occupations, there are undoubtedly some professional traits that are worthwhile to learn.

The honesty/humility element of the HEXACO personality model is a major point of overlap for the three dark triad qualities, which show themselves in callous and deceptive interpersonal behaviour as well as self-aggrandizement. It has been hypothesised that people who exhibit high levels of the dark triad traits are motivated to exert dominance through engaging in entrepreneurial action because they find power, control, riches, and admiration to be attractive. (Brownell et al., 2021).

According to a meta-analysis by Brownell et al. (2021), people with high levels of sub-clinical narcissism succeed as entrepreneurs more than their counterparts do. When narcissism and charismatic behaviour are combined, it strengthens friendships, fosters social connections, and supports workers (Campbell and Campbell, 2009; Jonason and Schmitt, 2012). Entrepreneurs with high levels of narcissism are ambitious, highly motivated, tenacious, and extremely entrepreneurial-oriented to achieve their objectives, attain affirmation, and attain power. According to Stockmann et al. (2015), narcissism enhances the team's entrepreneurial self-efficacy and entrepreneurial orientation, which in turn improves business planning performance. It makes sense to assume that the self-centred, self-availing qualities of the dark triad traits and the will to influence that underlies these characteristics have an impact on how social entrepreneurs, or those who exhibit high levels of the dark triad traits, relate to other members of society.

In social identity theory, Fauchart and Gruber (2011) delineated three distinct entrepreneurial identities, Darwinian, Communitarian, and Missionary. It appears plausible that the dark triad features are connected with Darwinian social identity since the underlying social drive of Darwinians is defined by economic self-interest and strengthened by the urge to succeed among the competing firms. Entrepreneurs with high levels of narcissism would develop a Darwinian social identity due to their tendency to advance themselves and their high levels of motivation. Some aspects of entrepreneurial behaviour and its results, such as achievement motivation and opportunity identification, company planning effectiveness, and social network building, are positively impacted by narcissism.

The increasing escalation of corporate and executive authority in today's businesses is a defining characteristic. Coercive control techniques are frequently used to exert this power to enforce conformity. *Coercive persuasion* is the process through which leaders use discursive systems of social control that are challenging and tough for followers to challenge.

Schien's (1961) work on coercion is used to explain how business leaders could create a social environment that directs employees' physical, mental, and emotional resources toward compliance. An effective way to combine strong indoctrination and surveillance is through coercive persuasion. It aims to persuade those who are the target that sincerely adopting the chosen belief systems is completely consistent with their self-interest. This process resembles what has been referred to as *"the Stockholm syndrome"* (Giebels

S.no.	Technique	Manifestation in Modern Organizations
1.	Reference group affiliation	Environmental changes, new entrants and turnover create organizational anxiety. We seek alignment with reference groups to reduce anxiety and increase conformity.
2.	Role modelling	Organizations develop systems of role modelling and mentoring so that members learn appropriate behaviour. We learn from and come to emulate those in positions of power over us as we seek to meet their expectations, which increases conformity.
3.	Peer pressures	Focus on teamworking, shared rewards and shared consequences intensifies peer pressure to conform.
4.	Alignment of identity	Modern workers buy into the firm's strategic vision and shape their behaviours accordingly. Conformity to the vision and values becomes part of our identity.
5.	Performance assessment	Employees are assessed based on their conformity with strategy and practice, including mechanisms such as 360-degree feedback. As individuals, we are expected to conform, and the system is assumed to be correct.
6.	Reward systems	Conformists are rewarded. Dissent, such as whistleblowing or resistance, is punished.
7.	Communication systems	Management and control of communication become central to the organization. Companies exert increased control of stakeholder information and management engagement with stakeholders.
8.	Physical pressure and work life Balance	Members are expected to work longer hours and expend greater effort as a means of demonstrating conformity and commitment. Individuals are expected to demonstrate the fortitude to overcome the physical demands of labour.
9.	Psychological safety	Psychological contracts become invested in expectations of conformity. Mutual support creates both psychological safety and conformity.

et al. 2005), in which abduct victims develop an intrinsic interest in their captors, refuse to be rescued, refuse to testify against them in court, or, as in the case of the heiress-turned-revolutionary Patty Hearst, adopt a new identity consistent with the kidnappers' value systems (Watkins 1976).

Schein identified a variety of conditions that facilitate such outcomes. Such as (1) Reference group affiliation; (2) Organizations developing systems of role modelling and mentoring so that members learn appropriate behaviour; (3) Focus on team working, shared rewards and shared consequences intensifying peer pressure to conform; (4) Modern workers buy into the firm's strategic vision, shape their behaviours accordingly and align their identity with that of the dominant group; (5) The performance of members is assessed based on their conformity with strategy and practice; (6) Conformists are rewarded, while dissent is sanctioned strongly; (7) Management and control of communication become central to the organization; (8) Members are expected to work longer hours and to expend greater effort as a means of demonstrating conformity and commitment, thus coming under intense physical pressure and losing any sense of work-life balance; (9) Psychological safety becomes dependent on conformity. The key points that are rearticulated to manifest in organisations are summarised in Table 1.

Many modern firms now encourage their employees to view their work as more than just a job and to view it as a way of life, a cause, a movement, even "a religion," and eventually, a crusade. Thought reform may appear to be a highly desirable procedure for leaders and managers who want to foster staff commitment rather than merely formal compliance. A key ideological development that supports modern techniques of coercive persuasion is the growing interest in strong corporate cultures and the creation of related "visions."

"Corporate culture" aims to increase management control by invading employees' minds and hearts in an inventive, repressive, and paradoxical way while professing to increase their practical autonomy. Establishing monocultures where decisions are made within a normative framework of fundamental principles that have been developed, or at least approved by management, is the implied goal of the corporate culture. in 2003 (Willmott)

By persuading those in subordinate positions that what is being offered is in their actual best interests, coercive persuasion attempts to avoid the problem of followers' autonomy and opposition. Its message is that individuals should adopt the organisational identity that their leaders have established for them, show ardent dedication to organisational goals, and adopt conformist behaviours that have been formally sanctioned while avoiding any behaviour that may be viewed as "deviant."

SUMMARY

The Current study on the dark triad personality and leadership effectiveness overemphasises the drawbacks of a leader's dark triad traits, such as job discontent, organisational dysfunction, losses, and inaction. Leaders with narcissistic tendencies are frequently seen as arrogant, domineering, and authoritarian. However, narcissistic leaders display many of the traits of the ideal leader, including charisma, self-assurance, power, and vigour. The dark triad traits are already associated with a strong desire for power and success as leaders in organisations. There are some professional skills worth learning.

An important element of overlap for the three dark triad attributes, which manifest as callous and deceitful interpersonal behaviour as well as self-aggrandizement, is the honesty/humility component of the HEXACO personality model. It is reasonable to presume that social entrepreneurs, or people who exhibit high levels of the dark triad traits, react to other members of society differently due to the dark triad traits' self-centred, self-availing features and the drive to influence that underlying these traits. Schein noted circumstances that make coercive persuasion easier. Corporate culture's suggested purpose is to improve management control by infiltrating workers' minds and hearts.

REFERENCES

Allport, G. (1937) Personality: A psychological interpretation. Henry Holt.

Allport, G. W. (1937). *Personality: A psychological interpretation*. Henry Holt.

American Psychiatric Association. (2013). Personality disorders. In Diagnostic and Statistical Manual of Mental Disorders (5th ed.). APA.

Barling, J., Christie, A., & Turner, N. (2008). Pseudo-transformational leadership: Towards the development and test of a model. *Journal of Business Ethics, 81*(4), 851–861. doi:10.100710551-007-9552-8

Bass, B. M., & Avolio, B. J. (1997). Concepts of leadership. In R. P. Vecchio (Ed.), *Leadership: Understanding the dynamics of power and influence in organizations* (2nd ed., pp. 3–22). University of Notre Dame Press.

Bass, B. M., & Steidlmeier, P. (1999). Ethics, character, and authentic transformational leadership behavior. *The Leadership Quarterly, 10*(2), 181–217. doi:10.1016/S1048-9843(99)00016-8

Book, A., Visser, B. A., & Volk, A. A. (2015). Unpacking "evil": Claiming the core of the dark triad. *Personality and Individual Differences, 73*, 29–38. doi:10.1016/j.paid.2014.09.016

Borgholthaus, C. J., White, J. V., & Harms, P. D. (2023). CEO dark personality: A critical review, bibliometric analysis, and research agenda. *Personality and Individual Differences, 201*, 111951. Advance online publication. doi:10.1016/j.paid.2022.111951

Brownell, K. M., McMullen, J. S., & O'Boyle, E. H. Jr. (2021). Fatal attraction: A systematic review and research agenda of the dark triad in entrepreneurship. *Journal of Business Venturing, 36*(3), 106106. doi:10.1016/j.jbusvent.2021.106106

Campbell, W. K., & Campbell, S. M. (2009). On the self-regulatory dynamics created by the peculiar benefits and costs of narcissism: A contextual reinforcement model and examination of leadership. *Self and Identity, 8*(2–3), 214–232. doi:10.1080/15298860802505129

Chatterjee, A., & Hambrick, D. C. (2007). It's all about me: Narcissistic chief executive officers and their effects on company strategy and performance. *Administrative Science Quarterly, 52*(3), 351–386. doi:10.2189/asqu.52.3.351

Christie, A., Barling, J., & Turner, N. (2011). Pseudo-transformational leadership: Model specification and outcomes. *Journal of Applied Social Psychology, 41*(12), 2943–2984. doi:10.1111/j.1559-1816.2011.00858.x

Christie, R., & Geis, F. L. (1970). *Studies in Machiavellianism*. Academic Press.

Cleckley, H. (1941). *The mask of sanity: An attempt to reinterpret the so-called psychopathic personality*. The C. V. Mosby Company.

Czarna, A. Z., & Nevicka, B. (2019). Narcissism and Leadership. Encyclopedia of Personality and Individual Differences, 1–9. doi:10.1007/978-3-319-28099-8_2334-1

Diller, S. J., Czibor, A., Szabó, Z. P., Restás, P., Jonas, E., & Frey, D. (2021, November 19). The positive connection between dark triad traits and leadership levels in self- and other-ratings. *Leadership, Education, Personality. An Interdisciplinary Journal, 3*(2), 117–131. doi:10.136542681-021-00025-6

Drory, A., & Gluskinos, U. M. (1980, February). Machiavellianism and leadership. *The Journal of Applied Psychology, 65*(1), 81–86. doi:10.1037/0021-9010.65.1.81

Fauchart, E., & Gruber, M. (2011). Darwinians, communitarians, and missionaries: The role of founder identity in entrepreneurship. *Academy of Management Journal, 54*(5), 935–957. doi:10.5465/amj.2009.0211

Furnham, A., Hughes, D. J., & Marshall, E. (2013). Creativity, OCD, narcissism, and the Big Five. *Thinking Skills and Creativity, 10*, 91–98. doi:10.1016/j.tsc.2013.05.003

Furnham, A., Richards, S. C., & Paulhus, D. L. (2013). The Dark Triad of personality: A 10-year review. *Social and Personality Psychology Compass, 7*(3), 199–216. doi:10.1111pc3.12018

Gubik, A. S., & Vörös, Z. (2023). Why narcissists may be successful entrepreneurs: The role of entrepreneurial social identity and overwork. *Journal of Business Venturing Insights, 19*, e00364. Advance online publication. doi:10.1016/j.jbvi.2022.e00364

Jonason, P. K., Li, N. P., & Teicher, E. A. (2010). Who is James Bond?: The Dark Triad as an agentic social style. *Individual Differences Research, 8*(2), 111–120.

Jonason, P. K., & Schmitt, D. P. (2012). What have you done for me lately? Friendship-selection in the shadow of the Dark Triad traits. *Evolutionary Psychology, 10*(3), 147470491201000303. doi:10.1177/147470491201000303 PMID:22947669

Landay, K., Harms, P. D., & Credé, M. (2019). Shall we serve the dark lords? A meta-analytic review of psychopathy and leadership. *The Journal of Applied Psychology, 104*(1), 183–196. doi:10.1037/apl0000357 PMID:30321033

Lebuda, I., Figura, B., & Karwowski, M. (2021, June). Creativity and the Dark Triad: A meta-analysis. *Journal of Research in Personality, 92*, 104088. doi:10.1016/j.jrp.2021.104088

Lilienfeld, S. O. (1994). Conceptual problems in the assessment of psychopathy. *Clinical Psychology Review, 14*(1), 17–38. doi:10.1016/0272-7358(94)90046-9

Lin, C. S., Huang, P. C., Chen, S. J., & Huang, L. C. (2017). Pseudo-transformational leadership is in the eyes of the subordinates. *Journal of Business Ethics, 141*(1), 179–190. doi:10.100710551-015-2739-5

Lykken, D. T. (1995). *The antisocial personalities*. Erlbaum.

Mansfield, H. (2023, January 5). Niccolò Machiavelli. *Encyclopedia Britannica*. https://www.britannica.com/biography/Niccolo-Machiavelli

McCrae, R. R. (1987). Creativity, divergent thinking, and openness to experience. *Journal of Personality and Social Psychology, 52*(6), 1258–1265. doi:10.1037/0022-3514.52.6.1258

Nevicka, B., Ten Velden, F. S., De Hoogh, A. H. B., & Van Vianen, A. E. M. (2011). Reality at Odds With Perceptions. *Psychological Science, 22*(10), 1259–1264. doi:10.1177/0956797611417259 PMID:21931153

Oksenberg, L. (1968). *Machiavellianism and organization in five man task oriented groups* [Unpublished doctoral dissertation]. Columbia University.

Papatsaroucha, D., Nikoloudakis, Y., Kefaloukos, I., & Markakis, E. (2021, June 18). *A Survey on Human and Personality Vulnerability Assessment in Cyber-security: Challenges, Approaches. . .* ResearchGate. https://www.researchgate.net/publication/352558956_A_Survey_on_Human_and_Personality_Vulnerability_Assessment_in_Cyber-s ecurity_Challenges_Approaches_and_Open_Issues

Paulhus, D. L. (2014). Toward a Taxonomy of Dark Personalities. *Current Directions in Psychological Science, 23*(6), 421–426. doi:10.1177/0963721414547737

Paulhus, D. L., & Williams, K. M. (2002). The Dark Triad of personality: Narcissism, Machiavellianism and psychopathy. *Journal of Research in Personality*, *36*(6), 556–563. doi:10.1016/S0092-6566(02)00505-6

Rauthmann, J. F. (2012). The Dark Triad and interpersonal perception: Similarities and differences in the social consequences of narcissism, Machiavellianism, and psychopathy. *Social Psychological & Personality Science*, *3*(4), 487–496. doi:10.1177/1948550611427608

Rosenthal, S. A., & Pittinsky, T. L. (2006). Narcissistic leadership. *The Leadership Quarterly*, *17*(6), 617–633. doi:10.1016/j.leaqua.2006.10.005

Schein, E. (1961). Coercive Persuasion: A Sociopsychological Analysis of the "Brainwashing" if American Civilian Prisoners by the Chinese Communists. Norton.

Smith, S. F., & Lilienfeld, S. O. (2013). Psychopathy in the workplace: The knowns and unknowns. *Aggression and Violent Behavior*, *18*(2), 204–218. doi:10.1016/j.avb.2012.11.007

Stelmokienė, A., & Vadvilavičius, T. (2022). Can dark triad traits in leaders be associated with positive outcomes of transformational leadership: Cultural differences [Mogu li se osobine tamne trijade kod vođa povezati s pozitivnim ishodima transformacijskoga vodstva: Kulturne razlike]. *Psihologijske Teme*, *31*(3), 521–543. doi:10.31820/pt.31.3.3

Thomas, J. C., Segal, D. L., Lebreton, J., Binning, J., & Adorno, A. (2006). *Subclinical Psychopaths* (Vol. 1). John Wiley & Sons, Inc.

Willmott, H. (2003). Renewing strength: Corporate culture revisited. *M@n@gement*, *6*(3), 73-87.

Section 6
Emerging Leadership Concepts

The recent COVID-19 pandemic environment revealed the importance of leadership in leading organisations in uncertain and volatile environment. Furthermore, in the face of the organizational challenges brought by the digital revolution, globalisation, and other socioeconomic changes in the word undoubtedly affected future leadership. Hence the first topic in this section explores the challenges of leading in a volatile, uncertain, complex, and ambiguous global environment, while the second discusses the impact of digitization on leadership in small and medium enterprises (SMEs), followed by a chapter examining e-leadership concepts, competencies, and challenges in the era of digital transformation and remote work. The next chapter would investigate business students' understanding of the challenges and preferences in virtual and remote work settings and their perceptions of virtual leadership skills. The last chapter of this section analyses transformational and transactional leadership styles among leaders during the COVID-19 pandemic.

Chapter 13
Leadership in a VUCA World

Bhavika Bindra
Amity University, Noida, India

Shikha Kapoor
Amity University, Noida, India

ABSTRACT

This chapter expands on all of the preceding material by focusing on a leader's capacity to formulate and convey leadership in uncertain times. As the world has become "VUCA"—volatile, unpredictable, complex, and ambiguous—there are no hard and fast rules for operating enterprises in the 2020s. The hierarchical organization paradigm is dead in the VUCA environment, and other models are developing, but there is no dominant model that works for everyone. New times necessitate new regulations, but there is no universal norm that applies to every sector and scenario. Leaders have been walking a tightrope for the last two years, attempting to maintain stability while coping with a disruptive and unpredictable pandemic, failing to hire despite a 15-year high in talent shortages, and revising policies to suit employee expectations for more flexibility at work. Multiple waves of coronavirus variations have put executives in a difficult position: trying to comfort and focus people in the face of ongoing uncertainty while having no idea what will happen next.

INTRODUCTION

VUCA leadership is defined as the capacity to move and react to changes in the corporate environment with focused, rapid, and agile actions. VUCA is continuous and dynamic; things might be pretty obvious one moment and then quickly alter due to oddities, adjacencies, and disruptors the next. Leaders now, it could be said, are in the midst of a prolonged era of growing VUCA. VUCA aspects are not new and have existed for a long time, but the modern society has magnified them. Leaders have more challenges as a result of globalisation, immediate communication, and innovative ecosystems. Management approaches based on command and control look stiff, inflexible, and fragile. There are different types of Leadership styles such as- Transformational leadership: Leadership that tends to make supervisors or followers conscious of the significance of one 's jobs and success of the wellbeing of the organisation

DOI: 10.4018/978-1-6684-8257-5.ch013

along with their very own requirements for their own professional growth and advancement and intend to motivate and lead colleagues to work incredibly hard for the success of the organization. Increasing followers' motivation via leaders' connection and engagement processes (Northouse, 2010). Transactional leadership: Transactional leadership focuses and stresses the completion and accomplishment of assigned tasks on hand. This style of leader fosters and maintains harmonious workplace relationships by promising rewards for excellent performance (Dessler and Starke, 2004). Laissez-faire leadership: Unlike transactional and transformational leadership, laissez-faire leadership seems to be a passive type of leadership. This style of leader often offers his or her believers or workers entire autonomy to make important decisions or accomplish tasks as they see appropriate and suitable (Robbins et al., 2010). According to Hamidifar (2010), executives that use this leadership style typically do not care and show little thought or concern for difficulties that develop in the workplace.

There are strategies for leading through difficult times such as prefer bravery before comfort: Humans are predisposed as individuals seek stability and safety while minimizing risk and pain. In fact, humans do almost everything to persuade oneself that sticking in their comfort zone is the best option. This is when bravery comes into play. Courage is not the same as fearlessness. Humans can still be afraid of making a tough decision or delivering bad news, but nevertheless discover the inner courage to conquer one's fears, step outside of our comfort bubble. Maintain compassionate transparency: According to McKinsey, more than three-quarters of the C-suite executives polled expect the average employee to return to the office at a certain point for at least three days each week. Simultaneously, over three-quarters of the 5,000 employees polled said they would prefer to work remotely for two or more days each week. It's logical that leaders see their return to the workplace as a good thing. For some, it represents the end of the upheaval, a return to the familiar and manageable. Others may regard it as the ideal answer to the real-world disconnect and exhaustion that comes with working remotely. The key objectives include: –

- To explore the VUCA leadership world.
- To identify the leader leading in uncertain times.

Methodology and Need for the Study

The data has been used through various articles, blogs, journals and from other databases. All the information available on the aforesaid sites has been combined and presented in the chapter. Effective leadership has not only help people comprehend change, but it also prepares them to adopt it and flourish in a constantly changing environment at work. Leaders may direct the business to success in times of VUCA by taking concrete actions to communicate with and assist people through change. VUCA requires you to avoid old, obsolete ways to management, leadership, and day-to-day operations.

BACKGROUND

Leadership: Leadership has always been a hotly debated topic. It piqued the curiosity and interest of several historians, philosophers, academics, and scholars who seek to investigate the genuine significance of leadership (Bass, 1990). According to Burns (1978), leadership is one of the most seen and least understood phenomena on the planet (Awan and Mahmood, 2010). Leadership is a vital and significant aspect in improving organisational success (Riaz and Haider, 2010). Leaders in every business are required to do activities with scarce funds to the highest degree possible in order to retain the firm's competitive advantage and profitability (Riaz and Haider, 2010). Various academics have also cited leadership as one of the most important factors in maintaining and improving an organization's competitive edge over its competitors (Zhu et al., 2005; Rowe, 2001; Riaz and Haider, 2010).

As per Kotter (1999), leading is all about charting a course or generating a view about the future, together with the tactics for bringing about the changes required to realise that goal. Other description of leadership per Bennis and Nanus (1985) and Hamidifar (2010) is "Leadership is an influence connection among followers and leaders to act in such a way to attain a set objective or goals". Thus, leadership is a vital component for the development of any organisation, independent of its kind of operations, profit or charity oriented, private or government related.

Leadership Styles

Transformational leadership: Downton (1973) created the term transformational leadership, which was later acknowledged by Northouse (2010). Since the early 1980s, several studies have focused on transformational leadership as one of the more prominent approaches to leadership (Northouse, 2010). As per Bryman (1992), transformational leadership is one of the "New Leadership" paradigms, which emphasises charismatic and successful leadership characteristics.

- Leadership which tends to make followers or subordinates aware of the importance of their employment and performance to the organization's well-being as well as their own demands for personal career progress and growth, and is capable of motivating followers to work much harder for the organization's benefit (Jones and George, 2004)
- Increasing followers' motivation via leaders' connection and engagement processes (Northouse, 2010)
- A leader who can motivate, inspire, or change his or her people to work hard in order to accomplish outstanding results (Robbins et al., 2010)
- Leaders who can influence subordinates' views and attitudes and motivate people to seek their personal interests for the sake of the organisation (Burns, 1978)

Transformational leaderships are defined as:

In contrast to previous theories on features or attributes or circumstantial methods that concentrated on leadership, this transformational leadership focused on the interaction between leaders and followers. Through charisma, transformational leaders are supposed to create a clear vision and goal, inspire self-esteem, and win trust and respect (Bass, 1990). According to Bass (1990), an effective leadership would encourage his or her employees to move above consciousness for the good of the team, company, and society. Furthermore, this sort of leader will prioritise long-term self-improvement and growth over short-term or immediate requirements.

Transactional Leadership: Transactional leadership focuses on and stresses the fulfilment and accomplishment of assigned tasks. This style of leader fosters and maintains harmonious workplace relationships by promising rewards for excellent performance (Dessler and Starke, 2004).

Positive reinforcement includes favourable comments, praise, and acknowledgment for effective compliance with leaders' instructions and achievement of goals (Riaz and Haider, 2010). Similarly, Avolio et al., (1991) stated that transactional leaders are meant and expected to communicate with their followers on a regular basis, notably to explain work instructions and provide direction in order to execute the assigned task. Any awards received for successfully completing given duties must be communicated to those who are her followers (Hamidifar, 2010).

Laissez-Faire Leadership: Laissez-Faire leadership, in contrast to transformative and transactional leadership, is a passive leadership style. This sort of leader often allows his or her followers or workers entire liberty to make choices or perform tasks in whichever way they consider proper and acceptable (Robbins et al., 2010). It is sometimes viewed as a non-transactional style of leadership in which timely choices are not made and action is delayed, as well as neglecting leadership obligations and non-exercise of power. According to Hamidifar (2010), executives that use this leadership style typically do not care and show little concern for challenges that develop in the workplace.

In its original French expression, laissez-faire alludes to a "hands-off, let things ride" mentality. Laissez-Faire leaders are considered to abdicate responsibility, provide little feedback, take long to make decisions, and are uninterested in assisting followers in meeting their requirements (Northouse, 2010).

Origins of VUCA

The term VUCA was coined by the United States Army War College to represent the more volatile, unpredictable, complex, and ambiguous multilateral environment that came from the Cold War's conclusion (Kinsinger & Walch, 2012). The acronym was not invented till the late 1990s, and it wasn't before the terrorist events of September 11, 2001, also that concept and name gained traction. Strategic business executives later embraced the term VUCA to represent the chaotic, tumultuous, and fast changing corporate setting that has emerged as the "new normal." According to all reports, the disruptive "new normal" in business exists. Many corporate models were outmoded during the 2008-2009 financial crisis, for example, when firms all over the world were thrust into chaotic conditions comparable to those encountered by the military. Simultaneously, significant changes occurred as technical advances such as social media expanded, the world's population continued to increase and age, and worldwide calamities impacted lives, economics, and companies.

VUCA

Volatility is represented by the letter "V" in the VUCA acronym. It refers to the type speed, volume, and extent of change that is not predicted (Sullivan, 2012 January 16). Volatility is turbulence, which is becoming more common than in the past. According to the BCG report, 50% of the most tumultuous financial quarters in the last 30 years have happened since 2002. The study also indicated that financial volatility is becoming more intense and lasting longer compared to the past. Sullivan (2012), October 22nd. Digitization, connectivity, trade liberalisation, global rivalry, and business model innovation are further sources of business turmoil today (Reeves & Love, 2012).

The "U" inside the VUCA abbreviation refers for uncertainty, or the inability to forecast events and circumstances (Kinsinger & Walch, 2012). In these unpredictable times, leaders find it difficult to utilise previous challenges and occurrences as indicators of upcoming results, making forecasting difficult and decision-making tough (Sullivan, 2012 January 16). Since they are unidentified or indeterminate, unstable marketplaces cannot be depended on. A company introducing a product might have an influence on competitors since it affects demand and sales. Uber and Airbnb are two well-known VUCA examples of uncertainty. Airbnb changed the hotel sector by inventing procedures, while Uber changed the cab business by making booking easier. They both had distinct business plans that relied largely on tech to revolutionize the industry.

The "C" in VUCA refers to complexity. As per the HR thought the leader John Sullivan (2012 January 16), there are frequently various & complicated reasons & mitigating factors (both inside and outside the business) involved in an issue. This layer of complexity, along with the instability of transition as well as the scarcity of historical predictors, increases the complexity of making decisions. It also leads to ambiguity, the very last letter in the abbreviation. Sullivan defines ambiguity as "the absence of clarity regarding the meaning of an event" or "the reasons and the 'who, what, where, how, and why' while behind events that are taking place (that) are ambiguous and difficult to establish." (16 January 2012). In the VUCA paradigm, ambiguity is defined as the "inability to appropriately comprehend opportunities and threats before they become fatal," according to Col. Eric G. Kail. 3 December 2010 (Kail). According to Kail, one indication of organisational ambiguity is the dissatisfaction that arises when segmented successes lack to add up to a complete or long-term success.

VUCA Assist Leaders in Uncertain Situations

VUCA leadership has been implemented in a number of organisations to help with anything from management and strategy development to crisis management and catastrophe recovery.

Leaders must deal with more in an uncertain environment, make choices more quickly, and manage enormous volumes of information and linked factors. A VUCA leadership style might help them adjust their perspective from depending on predetermined results to considering all options in a difficult situation.

It assists leaders in preparing for ambiguity and managing the risks that come with it.

It means that leaders are:

- Anticipating market, technical, financial, as well as other developments, possibilities, events, and dangers as much as feasible
- Rising the degree of readiness for change
- The capacity to modify strategic plan for both anticipated and unforeseen change
- The requirement of practising leadership dexterity and employ people efficacious of acclimatising to adapt change
- Creating a company culture that really is grateful and adaptable to modify and ambiguity. A leader who can manage uncertainty while staying loyal to their vision and goal will be a valuable addition to any organisation.

VUCA HAS THE GREATEST IMPACT ON BUSINESSES

1. Myntra

Myntra is a great example of a business that has succeeded in the VUCA Environment. Myntra leaders strategically positioned their company and added value by assisting their clients in regaining and expanding their vision. During the start of COVID, Myntra noticed a market for pyjama shorts and recreational clothes since individuals were operating from home and spending hours glued to their computers. Myntra soon enlisted the help of its clothing suppliers and started producing personal-safety and masks equipment.

2. Amazon

Amazon projected record earnings in July, making it one of the few companies to benefit from the coronavirus epidemic. Amazon has been the default retailer and service for many people even during the COVID outbreak because to its vast selection and low costs. They stockpiled food and household items, then bought office supplies and workout apparatus as the crisis unfolded so they could get acclimated to being indoors.

3. Nykaa

Irrespective Covid-19 issue, that has had a huge influence on physical businesses, Nykaa, a beauty and lifestyle company, believes that online sales would recover faster that retail outlet sales. Skincare, Shampoos and moisturisers were deemed necessary, and Nykaa carried them. Nykaa subsequently decided to update its website to provide these things, and as a result, they completed phase one, recording 10% to 15% of their regular commercial turnover.

4. Urbanic

With a shutdown of the famous online app Shein in India, consumers, particularly females, began to hunt for other retailing brand which is famous that could meet their fashion demands. Urbanic recognised the demands of the Indian fashion industry, & because they already had such fashionable items, they increased their promotion to make themselves apparent to a greater number of their potential clients. Urbanic is now one of India's most popular fashion businesses, and it has recently worked with Flipkart & Myntra to broaden their consumer base.

5. Walmart

Walmart's stated mission and motto summarise the company's main purpose: "We save money to help people live better." During its 50-plus-year history, Walmart has created a strong and loyal client base by remaining true to its mission of offering customers with low daily pricing. Customers know they can expect inexpensive costs when they enter a Walmart store.

Reflections on Leadership in the Time of COVID-19

Even though the COVID-19 epidemic is still in its early stages, it prompts reflection on optimal leadership practises. The epidemic highlights healthcare leadership as hospitals and providers adapt to respond. The phrase "a crisis is a horrible thing to squander" provides incentive to examine leadership approaches, particularly now. COVID-19 is a clear threat, as it's currently being felt throughout the world. Since about now 873 008 persons worldwide have been afflicted, with 43 275 fatalities. Aside from the scientific potential to understand better the viral infection, its epidemiological studies, and ways to avoid and treat COVID-19 illness, there's a clear chance for reflection on ways to result in health coverage during a crisis, document best practises, and globally disseminate these leadership principles.

Even as we approach the pandemic's peak— on day ten of a predicted curriculum that anticipates a high point in forty days have already been numerous learnings on leadership—unique acts from 'big L'

Leadership in a VUCA World

representatives with labelled managerial policies in addition to 'little L' representatives without management labels for whom leadership emerges organically. A crisis like this, in fact, puts conventional leadership practices and preconceptions to the question.

In documenting some great practises that I have observed at my institution, the Cleveland Clinic, I will attempt to define and contextualise these practises via the lens of existing leadership paradigms. The framework of five management commitments proposed by Kouzes and Posner3—challenging the system, inspiring a shared perspective, enabling everyone else to respond, modelling the technique, and stirring the soul an especially pertinent classification. So here is a checklist of leadership actions, an annotation of each with specific examples, and a viewpoint regarding whether these behavioural factors motivate or refute existing leadership concepts.

Be Ardent

Predicting events and developing uncertainty measures has a vital leadership competence throughout the covid epidemic. There appear to be two types of proactivity: proactive behaviour both before and after a crisis has developed. Furthermore, both its existence and absence have shown how crucially important proactivity is. The gap in testing capacity in the US must be filled as soon as possible, as well as the possible scarcity of personal protective equipment, are examples of the repercussions of inactivity.

The US Dept. of Health and Human Services' simulation of a viral pandemic from 2019 is highlighted as a good example of foresight in The New York Times on March 20, 2020. The model predicts that a viral outbreak can nauseate 110 million Americans in four weeks, put 7.7 million people in hospitals, and result in 586 000 deaths. Understanding the individuals, roles, and resources needed when a crisis arises requires such anticipatory behaviour, ideally supported by equal action. As will be discussed more below, the connection with prompt action is essential since conceptualization without action is useless.

Real-time, dynamic modelling is an example of proactivity amid a crisis. My laboratory medicine colleagues at my institution were building COVID-19 testing capabilities from the first signs of sickness. As a consequence, as of March 20, 2020, my institution executed about two-thirds of all positive tests in the US state of Ohio, where local testing capacity was built early. As another example, at the Cleveland Clinic, medical students, respiratory therapists, intensivists, and biomedical engineering colleagues are now creating ideas for a quick-production ventilator in anticipation of a need for ventilators that, in the event of a spike, will outpace supply. Med undergraduates at the Cleveland Clinic Lerner College of Medicine have developed an online resource to assist busy interns, residents, and fellows identify volunteer activities in the spirit of "little l" leadership, which might have a huge impact. Proactivity is abundant. Leadership occurs in a dispersed manner, both by people with leadership credentials and by those without.

The leadership commitment of 'challenging the process' by Kouzes and Posner captures proactivity. The coronavirus pandemic has highlighted the need of identifying the existing state—a predicted scarcity of personal safety equipment, creating models with backup plans and, most importantly, using these forecasts to spur action.

Clarify Governance for the Crisis

Crises put current governance systems to the test and necessitate the establishing new temporary roles. As we plan for and be ready for an influx of affected patients, it has become evident inside the covid crisis, for instance, that supply chain management and purchasing protective gear from new sources, such as the painting and building industries, are priorities. The construction of an "incident command" centre that regularly brings together key leaders, takes decisions in real time based on local expertise, and spreads knowledge of these decisions globally is a crucial step. The institutional objective has been to explain the make-up and organisational structure of this event command staff. The emphasis on the requirement to synchronise internal identifications and on information dissemination demonstrates a dedication to "inspiring a shared vision" and "enabling others to act. The structure of govt allows employees to develop locally while also requiring them to discuss their ideas and actions with the serious incident team.

Act…Quickly

Rapid implementation is essential in times of crisis. Establishing an urgent command post shows that decisions must be made quickly and provides the organisational framework for doing so. Moreover, the experience of developing regional COVID-19 test capabilities during a time when the nation's test capability was limited emphasises the necessity and benefit of acting quickly.

Naturally, taking quick action comes with a sense of urgency, which emphasises Kouzes and Posner's focus on "testing the process." The global solar tally of infected people and the corresponding deaths reflect urgency in the instance of coronavirus, therefore there has historically been no need to declare urgency. Yet, it also reminds us not to over-communicate importance and that information should be targeted to the audience. On March 20, 2020, university students still were congregating on beaches to party over spring break. Research showing that young people are not impervious to the risks of major disease brought on by COVID-19 is now receiving more attention.

Communicate Actively

An effective crisis response is the ideal team endeavour since all of the team's members must be unified in pursuit of a single purpose. Communication is essential for establishing the required alignment. In light of George Bernard Shaw's observation that "the single largest obstacle in transmission is indeed the impression that it has occurred,"6 communications has to be regular, iterative, and employ many distribution platforms.

At my institution, virtual meetings to guarantee communication have quickly expanded, with twice-daily calls from institute chairs and the executive team to the command centre. Also, information is being shared with all important audiences via regular webinars, emails, and other means. The CEO, Dr. Mihaljevic, connects including all 66 000 carers through regularly updated videos. Since the start of our planning (on January 21, 2020), communication has been a top focus in order to unite carers and, through openness and meticulous planning, allay anxiety by providing direction on how we will manage and succeed as a team.

LEADERSHIP QUALITIES FOR THE WORKPLACE AFTER COVID-19

Candor

Candor is unambiguous honesty. Although honesty has long been a key leadership attribute, candour is required at this time. Candor is arguably the strongest antidote to a working atmosphere of worry and cynicism. Even if the news is bad, people react much better to such known than to the unknown, which tends to make them worry more, or, even worse, to misleading half-truths or unrestrained optimism about the future.

Communication That Is Consistently Trustworthy and Fact-Based

While it is commendable that the administration's Coronavirus Working Group has regular briefings, the content and tone of those briefings are equally crucial. The takeaway for CEOs is that fostering a sense of community across firms and reducing workplace anxiety will need regular, consistent reality contacts.

Empathy

Leaders typically wear multiple hats, and once employees return to their jobs, they will surely take on new roles as chief counsellors. Undoubtedly, this tragedy has affected so very many individuals that several professionals will continue to work while they are grieving. Leaders who lack empathy naturally should surround themselves with those who can help them do so. Regrettably, during this time, a few careless, insensitive statements or actions can have severe effects on an organization's inherently vulnerable psyche.

Managing Hybrid Teams

One of the few bright spots of this unintended experiment in remote working is that many businesses have learned they may cut expenses and boost productivity by creating and maintaining a more extensive virtual working infrastructure. Furthermore, teleworking standards are anticipated to improve as more employees become used to not needing to travel and spending extra times with their families.

Flexibility and Adaptability

The majority of authorities couldn't have predicted such a radical mass action weeks before the nation started to shut down. Being an excellent leader in this situation may have meant the distinction among life and death. In the face of extraordinary uncertainty, leaders must resist the urge to Most leaders would not have been able to foresee such a drastic and widespread action months before the country began to shut down. Being the ostrich leader in this situation may have meant choosing between life and death. Leaders must reject the temptation to "stick with a choice" in the face of extreme uncertainty in order to appear resolute. Instead, they must be ready to regularly evaluate new facts, information, and input and alter course as necessary.

SKILLS FOR LEADING THROUGH VUCA

Casting for Vision

Clarifying the organization's core value proposition and how you and your team contribute to it on a daily basis during times of transformation is crucial. Your team is better able to understand the big picture when a shared mission and vision are established and communicated. This shared mission and vision act as a cornerstone to which to turn when everything is shifting.

Preparation

This may be able to anticipate impending change by tracking and analysing trends, competitors, and corporate culture to find patterns and variables that might impact your team and the business. You could start to anticipate situations and take proactive action when this is incorporated into your position.

Flexibility and Adaptability

At times of uncertainty and change, the ability to be flexible and adaptable is a crucial leadership quality. VUCA leadership demands being flexible and going completely against one's yearly plan. VUCA leadership necessitates flexibility and adaptability as new information is acquired, decisions are taken, and opportunities are presented.

Decision-Making

In VUCA leadership, a propensity for action is crucial. It is the ability to make a decision in the face of incomplete information, when you are unable to fully appreciate the complexity and interconnection of a decision taken, and when you could rely on expertise because this choice hasn't been made before. To make the best decision again for project, team, and organisation, leaders must recognise that they are operating in an imperfect environment.

Teamwork and Collaboration

Leaders must participate in unique solutions and thought diversity, which requires engagement from all departments & levels of the business, to create new answers in these exceptional times. Because there are no best practises for dealing with vuca, it is even more important for leaders to foster employee cooperation because everyone needs to come up with original ideas and move quickly when circumstances change.

Customer Orientation

Regardless of your position within the company, putting a consumer focus on how external variables will affect the customer journey at the front of decisions is essential to operating in a vuca environment.

The VUCA Prime

The VUCA framework depicts the external and internal circumstances that are currently influencing enterprises. The VUCA Prime was developed by Bob Johansen, eminent associate at the Center for the Future and author of Leaders Build the Next Generation: 10 Innovative Leadership Abilities for an Uncertain World. The best VUCA leaders, in Johansen's opinion, possess vision, expertise, transparency, and flexibility, which are the "flips" of the VUCA method. In order to understand true leadership in a Dynamic and unpredictable context, leaders may develop a continuum of skills known as the VUCA Prime. HR and people management experts may use the VUCA Framework as a "skills and abilities" paradigm for creating leadership development programmes. As vision is much more crucial under tough circumstances, unpredictability with in VUCA Prime may indeed be combated with vision. By making wise decisions to deal with the turbulence while managing to keep the company's vision in mind, representatives with a strong vision of where they'd like his\her organizations to be in the next three to five years will be better able to weather unpredictable environmental changes, including such recessions or competition in their markets. Knowledge or a leader's ability to halt, look, and listen can help reduce uncertainty. To understand the volatility and manage with insight in a VUCA environment, leaders need to have the capacity to see and listen outside of their specific fields of expertise. Executives must do this through developing and displaying cooperation and collaboration skills, as well as interacting with people at all levels of their company. Complexity may be combated by using clarity, the conscious endeavor to make sense of chaos. In a VUCA workplace, chaos strikes quickly and severely. Leaders can tune into all of the details associated with turmoil may make much better, more accurate business judgements. Vision, understanding, accuracy, and agility are not mutually exclusive in the VUCA prime. Instead, they are interrelated factors that help managers become more effective VUCA leaders. Executives must do this through developing and displaying cooperation and collaboration skills, as well as interacting with people at all levels of their company. Complexity may be combated by using clarity, the conscious endeavor to make sense of chaos. In a VUCA setting, chaos strikes quickly and violently. Leaders that have the ability to focus on every aspect of a crisis may be able to make far wiser, more reliable business decisions. Finally, uncertainty may be mitigated through agility, which is the capacity to communicate across the business and act rapidly to implement solutions (Kinsinger and Walch, 2012). Vision, understanding, accuracy, and quickness are not mutually exclusive in the VUCA prime. Instead, they are interrelated factors that help managers become more effective VUCA leaders.

From Personal Fulfilment to Community Purpose

When senior executives find that individuals in their organisation are dissatisfied, many of them take it personally. They overlook the reality that managers and supervisors have a greater direct effect on the elements that drive employee happiness and are better suited to solve it. The most crucial contribution leaders can make is to utilize their position to foster a deeper sense of purpose inside their department or division as they develop and grow more removed from these activities. A lot of studies demonstrate that when employees can relate the mission of their business to their own purpose, they are happier and more involved at work. Senior leaders are uniquely placed to assist them in this endeavour.

From Engagement to Ownership

Other companies have put in place programmes like free lunches, on-site gyms and care centres, and meditation spaces to demonstrate one's appreciation for their staff. Many of these benefits improve client experiences, they have no impact on the level of employee happiness or engagement.

Instead of depending on benefits, top leaders should prioritise establishing inclusive work cultures in which everybody is given the opportunity to contribute to their maximum potential. Making ensuring governance structures allow for workers to address issues they directly face is the first step. People feel more ownership and are more engaged when they can participate in decisions that directly influence their jobs.

From Visibility to Promotability

An employee's impression of being in a dead-end job or having one is a significant source of unhappiness. Employees typically think top leadership has the power to restart their career when they feel like it has halted. In fact, some people could mistakenly believe that things would go better just because they had the chance to complain to a high-ranking official. Skip-level meetings, when senior executives meet with employees who are several levels below them, exacerbate the issue. CEOs regularly hear from employees about grievances that they are unable to resolve without undermining or obviating the authority of the leaders separating them from the individuals they are dealing with.

Leading effectively in a VUCA world:

- Maintain a clear perspective against which to make decisions, as well as the ability to flex and adapt effectively to fast evolving events.
- Provide clear guidance and consistent message in the face of constantly altering priorities, aided by the adoption of new virtual means of communication when needed.
- Plan for hazards, but don't spend too much time on long-term strategic planning. In reaction to such an uncertain situation, don't immediately depend on prior answers and instead place a higher importance on fresh, temporary ones.
- Consider the larger picture. Make judgements based on intuition as well as analysis.
- Be inquisitive. Uncertain times provide chances for risk-taking. Take use of the opportunity to innovate.
- Promote networks over hierarchies - when we achieve greater degrees of interconnectedness and interdependence, cooperation outperforms competition.
- Leverage diversity - as our connections of stakeholders grow in complexity and scale, be sure to take use of the diverse perspectives and experiences they provide. This will help you prepare for the unexpected.
- Never lose sight of the importance of employee engagement. Give individuals the latitude they need to invent new processes, products, and services while providing strategic guidance.
- Get used to feeling uneasy. Resist the need to cling to obsolete, ineffective processes and behaviors. Take chances and enjoy the journey.

Challenges of a VUCA World

Dealing with the influence of technology is volatile.

Digital discussions in companies are now more crucial than ever before due to the influence, usage, and general ambiguity of technology. While technology boosts efficiency, opens up new opportunities, and extends old ones, it also offers a constant threat to established organisations because of its disruptive tendency.

New communication technologies have had the greatest influence on L&D, continually giving prospects for diversification and scaling. Mobile has radically transformed the way we approach work in just a few years, but its long-term influence and incorporation into the workspace needs to be determined. The futures offered by wearables, virtual, and other emerging technologies are even less clear, making it difficult for L&D to predict when a technological shift would take place and, if it does, how the workforce might benefit.

Uncertainty: Worldwide Skills Shortages

Leadership is a very serious issue inside organisations today, with a predicted shortfall of 40 million high-skilled employees by 2020 (Mckinsey, June 2012), increased competition for top talent, and a developing concern surrounding a lack of future leaders. The first world's ageing population has resulted in a smaller labour pool, while occupations are changing - corporations are unable to go out and simply hire the all-in-one grad, technical, and diverse personnel required to overcome the skills gap.

It is the role of talent, learning and development, and human resources to develop existing workers and new recruits into talent capable of not just filling this hole but also leading a company towards the future. Leadership development is critical to the eventual viability of leading firms in a VUCA environment of speed and unpredictability.

More Regulation Makes Things More Complicated-Complex

Since it causes so much training to be commissioned, industry regulation is a powerful motivator for learning and growth. Even now in latest days, events like as the worldwide financial slowdown have raised the emphasis on safety, risk and increasing regulations, which has an impact on L&D.

Compliance is also being driven by increased openness and visibility of worldwide operations. Not only is worldwide compliance and safety a top priority for multinational corporations, but training program also provides a method of standardising processes on a global scale. While world and industry regulation does not always offer a persistent, significant threat to any one sector of company, it does have an impact on numerous business efforts and decisions.

Ambiguous: Company-Wide Broad-Spectrum Leadership

Leadership communications and skills could no longer be funnelled from the top down; they must permeate deeper and wider across a company, with attributes getting a foothold at all levels. In essence, it is about implementing training that is more effective, results in long-term change, and does not result in a significant increase in the training costs per employee.

By investing in leadership, a company may be able to close the skills gap, manage technology's impact, and advance in the VUCA era. If you want to discover how to develop and sustain tomorrow's leaders while also offering higher-quality leadership to a wider audience, have a look at Chief Strategy Officer Piers Lea's slides from the September webinar "Solving the Leadership Problem" at LEO Learning.

Steps Talent Managers Can Take

Senior faculty member at the Center for Creative Leadership Nick Petrie notes that senior leaders are increasingly of the opinion that traditional leadership development techniques such as on training, work assignments, mentoring, and coaching are having failed to provide them with the abilities they require to thrive in a VUCA environment in a 2011 study titled Future Trends in Leadership Development. In a VUCA world, these slower, more employment learning approaches typically collide with the demands of management since knowledge throughout the organization and learning speed outpace them. HR and people management experts must redefine leadership development attempts to concentrate very little on behavioral skills and more on think abstractly skills and mindsets in order to adapt to the faster-paced VUCA environment. Leadership development should emphasize learning agility, self-awareness, ambiguity comfort, and strategic thinking (Petrie, 2011).

Hiring of Leaders Who Are Agile

According to Horney, Pasmore, and O'Shea (2011), HR and talent management experts should measure agility and complex thinking abilities throughout the selection process by employing a structured interview approach tailored to elicit examples of prior agility on the job.

Development of Existing Leaders to Become Leaders Who Are Agile

Employee development will still involve on-the-job training, work assignments, coaching, and mentoring, but in order to create Dynamic and unpredictable leaders, HR and talent acquisition professionals must concentrate on initiatives that promote flexibility, innovative thinking, collaborative effort, interaction, open mindedness to modify, and other greater critical thinking abilities. To keep up with the pace of change, such programmes must be distributed more quickly.

Create an organizational culture that recognizes and rewards VUCA prime behaviors while retaining agile employees.

In order to succeed in a VUCA environment, organizations need to do more than just hire and develop agile leaders. They also need to create an institutional culture that encourages the right behavior. Experts in human resources and people management can foster creativity, agility, and managed risk-taking to help establish a VUCA culture. Performance management solutions should incorporate the ideals and traits of VUCA Prime. Desired behavior may be rewarded with a variety of incentives, including employment perks, pay increases, promotions, and preferred job assignments. The key to the best rewards schemes in a Vuca world is to be adaptable and fluid, and to offer successful leaders the most appealing awards. Organizational cultures that promote and reward maneuverable leaders may begin to new self, attracting and keeping the type of imaginative and innovative talent that organizations need today. This will also provide companies with an edge in our sector.

Leadership in a VUCA World

Figure 1.
Source: https://www.stageshift.coach/blog/learn-to-c-the-world-anew-the-5-c-s-of-vuca-leadership

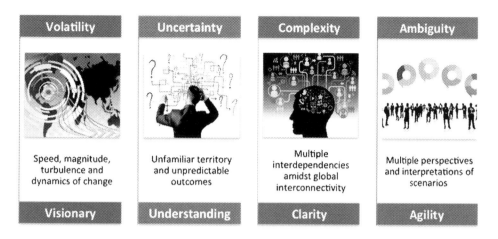

There are five critical practices, or five C's, for becoming a transformative, holistic, strategic, integrative, VUCA-leader.

CURIOSITY

This is to discard conventional ideas of the world functions in favour of the vast potential that life flows through you as you. If someone perceive everything in life as a movie or a mirror, then will soon become aware of the life energy that runs through.

Life happens to us, not to us alone. Life is supposed to educate us self-mastery via the arrival of lessons and blessings so that we can progress to become the greatest person individuals are capable of becoming and contribute to the co-creation of a better world.

COMPASSION

Self-awareness and self-acceptance help to create compassion. This in turn may learn to heal ourselves by understanding that our emotions are a signalling system for previous injuries. Emotional responses to prior trauma hinder cognitive agility.

When individuals' emotions are stimulated, it indicates that a former wound is about to heal. Abuse, betrayal, abandonment, rejection, neglect, deception, or contempt are common causes of this pain. Finding the cause of the initial emotional trauma allows us to repair it with our hearts via understanding and forgiveness. When one is healed, mind is clear, one become quiet, and one achieve the mind's peace.

This method teaches us to have empathy for others and to treat everyone with the awareness that, irrespective of how it looks to us at first glance, we are all trying our best to be the best. This is the step from judgement to comprehension.

CONVICTION

To listen to the most aspirational futures one can imagine, individual must employ our thoughts with concentrated deliberate concentration in the present now to tune our radar to the highest possibilities. Clearly defining an ambitious goal for one's life and organisations improves one's belief that one can live meaningful lives.

Once we have established our radar, get intuitive assistance to achieve visionary results. Routine mental habits activate innovative neurons, which connect new neural connections in our mind. The areas of our brain connected with self-awareness, self-mastery, and higher mental processing actually grow in size and texture with meditation (Joel and Michelle Levey), whereas the amygdala shrinks in size (Matthieu Ricard).

COURAGE

It takes courage to follow an uncharted and uncertain route and navigate it as well you can. Speaking up and becoming a whistle-blower takes courage when the conduct surrounding you exceeds what you believe is fair to others. It takes courage to implement a new approach that contradicts existing practises.

It takes courage to truly listen from of the spirit and to communicate your genuine vulnerable truth. It takes courage to bring out that the findings are not precisely the way they were presented in the mistaken belief that what is not discussed will not be real. Inner spiritual strength supports courage. Kindness and excitement inspire courage.

COLLABORATION

Time and space are both required for collaboration. Collaboration is not the same as collaboration, accommodation. Collaboration is a developing method of consensual developmental enquiry in response to a problem or goal that involves many distinct opinions in the room that are entirely reflective of all participants and a high appreciation for the ideas expressed by each participant. Collaboration is an iterative revelatory process as well. Rather than answers, one should arrive to a collaborative interaction through questions.

BUILD CHARACTER AND CAPACITY

One must first reinvent the structures within which we function in order to make the shift to post-conventional VUCA leadership, as existing processes and systems inhibit our sustainable growth as post-conventional leaders. By utilising an elevating structure such as the Executive Strategic Operating System, we provide tremendous potential for growth from the "outside-in."

Second, one must regard life as a film and a reflection in order to learn through life's lessons and blessings, become consciously aware of our objectives, and be discriminating, truthful, and empathetic in the midst of power dynamics. One has to be the difference we wish for the world, as Gandhi famously said. This is a "inside-out" meditation, judgment, learning, and healing process.

CONCLUSION

The study's goal was to investigate the meaning and styles of leadership, as well as leadership amid uncertainty, in order to find management implications for coping in ever evolving changing environment. The consequences for leadership are not confined to the COVID-19 pandemic, but are broadly applicable to leadership during times of uncertainty in general. This was only an illustration of the context's unpredictability. By embracing VUCA leadership, organisations may remain relevant, achieve long-term success, and maintain the desired level of performance in the midst of uncertainty. Volatility, uncertainty, complexity, and ambiguity are the "new normal" in the workplace of today, and they're fundamentally changing the way businesses operate, yet also the way business executives lead. Leaders no longer require the skills and competences they once did to help their organisations thrive. Corporate executives must now be able to think strategically and critically. HR and people management professionals may help their companies thrive in today's VUCA environment by developing leaders with ambition, understanding, precision, and adaptability to cope with volatility, uncertainty, complexity, and ambiguity.

REFERENCES

Avolio, B. J., Waldman, D. A., & Yammarino, F. J. (1991). Leading in the 1990's: The four I's of transformational leadership. *Journal of European Industrial Training*, *15*(4), 9–16. doi:10.1108/03090599110143366

Awan, M. R., & Mahmood, K. (2010). Relationship among leadership style, organizational culture and employee commitment in university libraries. *Library Management*, *31*(4/5), 253–266. doi:10.1108/01435121011046326

Bass, B. M. (1990). From transactional to transformational leadership: Learning to share the vision. *Organizational Dynamics*, *18*(3), 19–31. doi:10.1016/0090-2616(90)90061-S

Bennett, M. (2021, March 23). Retrieved from Niagara Institute: https://www.niagarainstitute.com/blog/what-is-vuca-leadership

Bennis, W., & Nanus, B. (1985). *Leaders: The Strategies for Taking Charge*. Harper and Row Publishers.

Bryman, A. (1992). *Charisma and Leadership in Organizations*. Sage.

Burns, J. M. (1978). *Leadership*. Harper and Row.

Daft, R. (2010). *New Era of Management* (9th ed.). South-Western Cengage Learning.

Dessler, G., & Starke, F. A. (2004). *Management: Principles and Practices for Tomorrow's Leaders*. Pearson Prentice Hall.

Downton, J. V. (1973). *Rebel Leadership: Commitment and Charisma in a Revolutionary Process*. Free Press.

Hamidifar, F. (2010). A study of the relationship between leadership styles and employee job satisfaction at Islamic Azad University Branches in Tehran, Iran. *AU-GSB e-J.*, *3*, 45-58.

Horney, N., Pasmore, B., & O'Shea, T. (2010). Leadership agility: A business imperative for a VUCA world. *People & Strategy*, *33*, 4.

Jones, G. R., & George, J. M. (2004). *Essentials of Contemporary Management*. McGraw Hill Companies, Inc.

Kalaria, C. (2020). *Leadership — The VUCA perspective*. Retrieved from Medium: https://medium.com/@chiragkalaria/leadership-the-vuca-perspective-9a07aa05193b

Kinsinger, P., & Walch, K. (2012). Living and leading in a VUCA world. Thunderbird University.

Kotter, J. P. (1999). *What Leaders Really Do*. Harvard Business School Press.

Lawrence, K. (2013). *Developing Leaders in a VUCA Environment*. Retrieved from https://emergingrnleader.com/wp-content/uploads/2013/02/developing-leaders-in-a-vuca-environment.pdf

Long & Thean. (2011). *Relationship Between Leadership Style, Job Satisfaction and Employees' Turnover Intention: A Literature Review. Research Journal of Business Management, 5, 91-100.*

Northouse, P. G. (2010). *Leadership: Theory and Practice* (5th ed.). SAGE Publications.

Petrie, N. (2011). *Future trends in leadership development*. Center for Creative Leadership white paper.

Riaz, A., & Haider, M. H. (2010). Role of transformational and transactional leadership on job satisfaction and career satisfaction. *Business and Economic Horizons*, *1*, 29–38. doi:10.15208/beh.2010.05

Robbins, S. P., Decenzo, D. A., & Coulter, M. (2010). *Fundamentals of Management: Essential Concepts and Applications* (7th ed.). Prentice Hall.

Rowe, W. G. (2001). Creating wealth in organizations: The role of strategic leadership. *The Academy of Management Perspectives*, *15*(1), 81–94. doi:10.5465/ame.2001.4251395

StageSHIFT Coaching & Consulting. (2016, May 25). Retrieved from https://www.stageshift.coach/blog/learn-to-c-the-world-anew-the-5-c-s-of-vuca-leadership

Stoller, J. K. (2020). *Reflections on leadership in the time of COVID-19*. BMJ Public Health Emergency Collection. doi:10.1136/leader-2020-000244

Zhu, W., Chew, I. K. H., & Spangler, W. D. (2005). CEO transformational leadership and organizational outcomes: The mediating role of human-capital-enhancing human resource management. *The Leadership Quarterly*, *16*(1), 39–52. doi:10.1016/j.leaqua.2004.06.001

Chapter 14
Future of Leadership:
A Study on Small and Medium Sized Enterprises

Mansi Dudeja
Amity University, Noida, India

Shikha Kapoor
Amity University, Noida, India

ABSTRACT

This chapter discusses how digitization has changed leadership and what it means for leaders. Digitalization has been heralding changes for years, including an increase in remote leadership and the usage of digital communication tools. Small and medium-sized businesses (SMEs) are now faced with the challenge of adjusting to these developments and must deal with significant uncertainties: the key trends that leaders in SMEs should consider, the changes that will affect leadership and how they will alter the behaviours that are essential for success. The experts' predictions for trends include adjustments to organizational structures and workplace practices. Organizationally, businesses will become more flexible and diversified with less emphasis on hierarchies, and they will work more closely together. Big data will have a bigger impact on work, and many jobs will be automated or made simpler by technology.

INTRODUCTION

One of the main topics in the public and academic discourse is the employment of intelligent and connected technology in the workplace and the changes brought about by it (Cascio and Montealegre 2016; Kauffeld and Maier 2020). SMEs are now beginning to alter as a result of digitalization (Hobscheidt et al. 2017). Leaders in production and product development, particularly in SMEs, are crucial to the success of these changes because they serve as a conduit between top management and employees in teams and departments and are in charge of making sure that changes are effectively communicated and executed. Successful leaders play a critical role in the success of workplace transformations brought on by technology (Schlicher et al. 2017).

DOI: 10.4018/978-1-6684-8257-5.ch014

However, in order to carry out their duties, leaders themselves will experience significant change and will require help. This significance of shifting leadership tasks and success-critical leadership behaviours is not yet reflected in leadership research. At the start of this century, neither intelligence nor the interconnection of technology had a part in the leadership study that examined potential changes (e.g., Mumford et al. 2000). The majority of the time, models of common leadership behaviours and activities have not altered for decades (e.g., Fleishman et al. 1991). However, it does not concentrate on the responsibilities and needs of leadership (van Laar et al. 2017, more current study on digital skills and 21st century abilities).

Leaders are important to all types of organizations and play different roles as well as perform various important functions in organization. Nowadays, the purpose of any organizations is to survive and maintain its entity by improving performance. Organizations must always increase their performance to be highly competitive in markets (Arslan & Staub, 2013). Small and Medium Enterprises (SMEs) performance, as a topic, is generating numerous discussion between researchers, practitioner, academics and politicians (Arham, 2014). Previous and to date literature suggest that to achieve good performance of organization, leadership is critically important factor (Boal & Hooijberg, 2001; Choudhary, Akhtar, & Zaheer, 2013; Peterson, Smith, Martorana, & Owens, 2003; Sahin Danisman, 2015; B.-B. P. Uchenwamgbe, 2013; B. Uchenwamgbe, 2013). According to Harms & Creda (2010), leadership is defined as "a process whereby an individual influences a group of individuals to achieve a common goal" (p. 3). To enhance organizational performance, leadership plays a crucial role, therefore, to make the best possible products and services through the best utilization of the available resources, leaders are responsible to the stakeholders of their organizations (Gul, Ahmad, Rehman, Shabir, & Razzaq, 2012). As stated by Hashim, Ahmad, & Zakaria (2012), leaders in the 21st century are faced with an increasingly challenge to lead their organizations effectively. Therefore, leaders must concentrate on developing their effectiveness and use it as a strategic direction to make them apart from their competitors. SMEs are always suffering by severe struggle from globally and inside their industries.

There is sufficient evidence in the literature to suggest that the performance of SMEs is essentially related to the leadership of the leaders (Spinelli, 2006). As Avolio & Yammarino (2013) points out, the activities of the SMEs' leaders relate to leadership, the all-important, driving force of the organization. Leadership is needed to move an organization forward among a changing, competitive landscape by imagining, motivating, organizing, managing and leading employees to a higher level of performance (Tucker & Russell 2004). Consequently, good leadership is required for organizational and team performance (Hogan& Kaiser 2005). Leadership is regarded as effective when it brings positive efficacy of performance, which relates to better organizational performance. Organizational performance, as a result of leadership effectiveness of the leaders, contributes to the firms' success or failure. In summary, the outcomes of leadership as a result of effective leadership influence the satisfaction, work effectiveness and efforts of the employees and leaders in their organizations (Madanchian, Hussein, Noordin, & Taherdoost, 2016a).

LEAD MODEL OF LEADERSHIP

Listening

the capability required of leaders to build intimacy and a sincere relationship with others. Leaders that are able to listen build trust, effectively motivate others via empathy, and pay close attention to the other person.

Executing

a talent required to accomplish difficult tasks, start ambitious projects, and produce outcomes. Leaders foster the organisation and promote progress by setting tough goals.

Analyzing

To accomplish the aims and objectives of the organisation, one must be able to plan, pay attention to detail, evaluate problems in-depth, and lead didactically and methodically. One must also be able to follow procedures, raise a red flag when necessary, and lead coherently.

Dreaming

To find "out of the box" ideas and foster an innovative workplace, leaders must be creative. Leaders must be able to envision the future, drive change, and inspire people to support their goals.

Digitalization in leadership

Production lines and workplace equipment are not the only things that are altered by digitalization, which is defined as the increased adoption of intelligent and linked technology. Additionally, and maybe more significantly, digitalization alters organisational structure, activities, and job needs (Kauffeld and Maier 2020; Mlekus and Maier 2019). These technologies can take the form of intelligent robots that collaborate with staff members (tting et al. 2020) or intelligent software algorithms that decide on candidate selection or shift scheduling (tting and Maier 2018b; Schlicker et al. 2020).

SMEs, however, which often have little time for leadership development (Chadwick et al. 2013, but where leadership quality is essential given the requirement to function under resource constraints, are particularly in need of insights regarding these shifts (Garavan et al. 2016). Therefore, leadership development in SMEs should be in line with both SME strategy and operational environment (Colbert 2004) as well as a plan for potential changes brought about by digitization. We need to understand which significant changes or trends brought on by digitalization will affect leadership in SMEs the most in order to target leadership assistance with precision and be able to proactively educate leaders for impending changes.

Objectives

1. To explore the major trends resulting from digitalization will that will shape future leadership in SMEs

2. To study the change digitalization will bring on future leadership in SMEs
3. To examine the importance of leadership behaviors of future leadership in SMEs due to digitalization.

Small Medium Enterprises (SMEs)

There is no universal definition or criterion for SMEs as they are context dependent and have different definitions for different countries (Abe et al. 2012). Small and Medium Enterprises (SMEs) are perceived as the backbone of any country as they are interlinked with almost every facet of the society and economy. According to Madanchian et al. (2016) SMEs is also viewed as the engine of growth, and catalysts for economic and social transformation in a country. The contributions of SMEs at macro or micro level are the results of successful SMEs managed by effective leaders (Madanchian, Hussein, Noordin, & Taherdoost, 2016b). This is achieved through leadership behaviours or styles of the SMEs' leaders, who have direct influence on their organizational performance, competitive edges and successes (Popa, 2012).

According to SMEs' literatures (e.g. Abu Bakar, Mad, & Abdul Latif, 2006; Arham, 2014; Aris, 2007; Saleh & Ndubisi, 2006; Samad & Hassan, 2007), there is the unique limitations that encountered by SMEs, like having an inadequate employees, lacking resources of finance, lacking experience and background of education and importantly lack of managerial knowledge. Therefore, there are always attempts to understanding the SMEs' performance improvement, these attempts are significant since SMEs is known as one of the vital engines of growth for a country's economy (Kassim & Sulaiman, 2011).

Leadership in SMEs

According to Avolio et al. (2003), leadership has an important role in the development and growth of any organization. The reason for this fact is that the leaders of the organization generally consider all the plans and business decisions, effective and timely decisions considering by the leadership of the organization can have a wide impression on the crucial business results.

In relation with Mumford, Zaccaro, Harding, Jacobs, & Fleishman (2000), leadership becomes more essential when one has to develop and lead adaptive analysis to new or changing situations. Amagoh, 2009; Chen (2013) pointed out that a successful leadership knowledge results from the key elements consist of changing attitudes, personnel development, and improved business and leadership skills.

To drive the success of SMEs, good leadership has been recognized as the key elements (Madanchian et al., 2016b). The literature (Arham, Muenjohn, & Boucher, 2011;Davies, Hides, & Powell, 2002; Razak, 2011), in SMEs shows that insufficient and weak leadership skills are main factors causes failure of SMEs. For that reason, SMEs to guide their firms through all situations either crisis times need to develop their leadership behavior. To avoid organization failure and have good organizational performance, the right leadership behavior is an important element. As Fiedler (1996) approved, due to the leaders contribution to the achievement or failure of an organization, effective leaders are significant.

The response to the challenges faced today by SMEs is only possible through adoption of leadership roles by the various people in charge (Ladzani, 2010). It is important to develop the competences and effectiveness of leadership at various levels, defining mobilizing goals, ensuring the clarity of objectives, building high performance teams, concentrating on developing the best talents, creating a climate favorable to innovation, stimulating permanent learning and creating a culture of value always based on the cohesion of teams and the quality of service provided (Kilpatrick, Cheers, Gilles, & Taylor, 2009).

According to Avolio et al. (2003), still small and medium firms now have a global position. It is important to understand the point that, in this new setting, how leaders face the challenge of working with an ethnically diversified workforce which includes differences in values, traditions, customs and beliefs and what constitutes effective leadership. Some authors (e.g., Anderson, 2009; Andersson & Tell, 2009) found several organizational factors that can influence leadership in SMEs. Nevertheless, according to Short et al. (2002), so far researchers have not reached a consensus about these factors. Therefore, the better the understanding of the leadership's influence on SMEs, the more they can be helped in their growth process. According to a conducted study on the effects of leadership behavior on organization performance in SMEs by Saad et al. (2006), they found out that leadership was an essential factor to successfully implement small manufacturing in SMEs.

On the other hand, and due to the fact that all SMEs are more and more showing to a competitive, dynamic environment full of changes and difficulties, the way they deal with human resources also changes. Nowadays, people are seen as human capital (Youndt, Subramaniam, & Snell, 2004), as an essential part of the organization's success, able to add more or less value to the organization. But for this to happen, the organization has to appreciate them and motivate them to demonstrate their capacities and understand how they can contribute to the firm's good performance. There must be interaction of behavior, which the leader must encourage, and its success depends on the style of leadership. Langowitz & Allen (2010), in a study related to the importance of SME founders, concludes that the leader is the founder and argues that many SME leaders present proactive behavior.

Leadership Tasks and Behaviour Alter as a Result of Digitization

Research interest in behavioural leadership theories, which cover both leadership duties and behaviours, has grown since the turn of the century (Dionne et al. 2014). The taxonomy of leadership tasks (Fleishman et al. 1991) and the LEaD model for success-critical behaviours (Dörr et al. 2012, 2018) are two commonly used models that we introduce in the following in order to analyse changes relating to tasks and behaviour.

Tasks in Leadership

The taxonomy of leadership tasks (Fleishman et al. 1991) outlines four characteristics of leadership duties and was created in an effort to integrate several classification systems. The activities of acquisition (such as acquiring data from many sources), organising and assessment (such as assessing usefulness based on relevance, accuracy, or source), and feedback and control are summarised by information search and structuring (e.g., following up on assignments). The activities of identifying needs and requirements (such as being aware of chances for improvement), planning and coordination (such as scheduling assignments), and information exchange are summarised by the use of information in issue resolution (e.g., exchanging information via various means).

Recruiting, allocation (e.g., allocating individuals in accordance with their qualifications), development (e.g., recognising qualification needs), motivating (e.g., creating a conducive environment), and usage and monitoring responsibilities are all included in managing personnel resources (e.g., dividing workloads). Managing material resources include activities related to procurement and distribution (such as distributing supplies and equipment), upkeep (such as securing finances or maintaining equipment), and use and monitoring (e.g., preparing reports or prescribing how funds will be used)

The growing usage of smart technology may have an impact on some of these duties. Because of the rising usage of Big Data, information search and structuring (particularly acquisition and organisation, but also assessment) may become less common jobs or drastically alter in nature (huge amounts of real time data that are gathered, structured and evaluated by algorithms; e.g., McAfee et al. 2012). Due to an increase in the use of digital and virtual communication technologies like social media, messengers, and video conferencing, some jobs (such providing feedback or communicating) may alter (e.g., Delanoy and Kasztelnik 2020). Others may alter as a result of artificial intelligence (AI) being used to make recommendations or judgments, such as those involving the management of material and human resources (Liem et al. 2018; Itting and Maier, for example).

key Leadership Practises for Success

The LEaD model of leadership behaviour was created in order to condense the most pertinent, resilient, and success-critical leadership behaviours (Dörr et al. 2012, 2018). It illustrates five types of leadership characteristics. Strategy orientation is centred mostly on strategic leadership and relates to identifying market potential, framing future prospects, and accelerating innovation (e.g., Brews and Purohit 2007; Miller and Cardinal 1994). Goal-setting, problem-solving, and outcomes evaluation are all part of results orientation, which is mostly based on task-oriented leadership (e.g., Judge et al. 2004). Employee development is mostly focused on employee orientation and involves mentoring workers, providing feedback, assigning responsibilities, and considering others' opinions (e.g., Judge and Piccolo 2004; Kuoppala et al. 2008). Value orientation is primarily centred on authentic leadership and relates to exuding assurance, radiating honesty, and handling ambiguity (e.g., Avolio and Gardner 2005).

In this situation as well, technology like Big Data and AI may change the meaning of some behaviours (like good communication) or make them less necessary (like assessing results) while making others even more necessary (e.g., implementing changes or coaching employees). Digitalization may potentially result in the creation of new areas of significance in addition to these potential changes in success-critical leadership behaviours. The use of information management and communication technology, as well as ethical and cultural awareness, are some examples of 21st century skills that might be used as examples (Vaikutyt-Pakausk et al. 2018; van Laar et al. 2017, 2018).

Method

Sample

In order to achieve sufficient saturation (Charmaz 2006; Mason 2010), we sampled and analyzed interviews (each around 90–120 min) until new concepts ceased to appear. The final sample consisted of $N = 7$ male experts from regional SMEs; two managing directors, two founders, two heads of human resources, and one head of research and development. The SMEs were from the key production oriented industry branches in this region (such as plant construction and engineering ($n = 3$), metal and electrical industry ($n = 2$), or related service industries ($n = 2$)) with an average of 167.5 employees ($SD = 113.48$; $min = 20$; $max = 350$).

Procedure

We conducted semi structured interviews based on a prospective task analysis (Kato-Beiderwieden et al. 2020). This analysis is based on job analysis methods (e.g., Task Analysis Tool; Koch and Westhoff 2012) that investigates tasks and behavior and additionally allows for a prospective analysis of future jobs. Prior to collecting the data in February 2019, our study was authorized by the university's ethics committee (no. 2019-083).

In the first step, we conducted semi-structured interviews, comprised of questions about trends that will influence leadership in SMEs, about how leadership tasks will change as a result, and descriptions of behavior that is critical for leadership success in the future. Sample questions are "If you look ahead now, which development trends do you foresee concerning future leadership?", "How will usual leadership tasks change in digitalized working environments?", and "How will leadership requirements change through digitalization?" The second step involved the clustering of all trends, examples of changing tasks and qualification, and examples of behavior from the interviews. Following recommendations for job analysis (Koch and Westhoff 2012), these clusters were formed through discussion between two raters (subject matter experts in job analysis) and, in case of tasks and behaviors, matched to dimensions from the above mentioned leadership theories (Dörr et al. 2012; Fleishman et al. 1991). In cases where we could not match clusters to existing dimensions, we created new dimensions (one for new tasks and one for success-critical leadership behavior). In summary, we assigned 71 statements of trends to eight trend dimensions, 86 statements of changing tasks to five task dimensions, and 110 statements of changing success-critical leadership behavior to seven behavior dimensions.

Result

Significant Leadership Trends

Concerning the first study question, experts predict eight main developments that will alter leadership in SMEs. These tendencies might be classified as changes in organisational structures and changes in work design.

Organizational Structure Modifications

Companies will become more agile and diverse structurally, hierarchies will play a smaller role, and companies will collaborate more closely with one another. Experts define agility as more flexibility, shorter product cycles and procedures, the utilisation of agile project teams, and increased work with consumers via platforms. Diversity is defined as the ability to react to the diverse demands of employees by broadening the age range, multidisciplinary collaboration, and globalisation. Leaders must be able to manage multidisciplinary and diverse teams. Experts recognise that the past focus on line management, authority, and work hierarchies in a firm is reducing, while the focus on project teams is expanding.

Workplace Design Modifications

Work in SMEs will become increasingly location-independent, affected by Big Data, and many jobs will be automated or automated. Employees and executives will no longer be tethered to a single location in the future, according to location-independent work. This involves remote leadership (managing work, guiding and influencing job results, and incentive) as well as employee digital coordination (digital exchange, transferring tasks via software, and web meetings). Experts define Big Data's growing importance as the expansion of data gathering, data administration, and data analysis, as well as privacy. The introduction of robotics and support systems, as well as the digitization and automation of processes, are all examples of technology taking over activities (e.g. of business processes or order processing). New technology will lower the number of employees and maybe the amount of leadership jobs. Robots will be employed more in the future, resulting in increased human-robot contact and cooperation. Furthermore, some experts expect that employee personal responsibility (including providing employees greater responsibility and educating them to handle problems on their own) will grow. Other experts believe that personal responsibility of employees will decrease: new technology such as digital support systems may dictate every job step, completely undermining employee autonomy.

Responsibilities for Leadership

It is becoming increasingly vital to know expert areas and departments across the board, recognise interconnecting systems, and operate in an interdisciplinary way in the fields of information usage in problem solving and information search and structure. Routine administrative duties are becoming less common in the management of material resources as assistance is supplied by digital technologies or tasks are shifted to the area of responsibility of employees. Leaders will be held more accountable for outcomes. The most commonly reported change is a clear movement in tasks toward the category managing human resources. The most commonly reported change is a clear shift in chores in favour of the category managing human resources, namely employee development through coaching and responsibility transfer.

Furthermore, analysts regard managing change as a task that will become increasingly important for future leaders. This category includes four tasks: accompanying change, acting flexibly and agilely, speaking freely and clearly, and tolerating failure. These task domains were not previously included in leadership task models.

Leadership Style

Concerning the third study topic, In terms of strategy, it will become increasingly vital to recognise the proper moment for market decisions to be made earlier and more frequently, to foresee future views for digital strategies and cultural changes, and to support not just product innovations but also novel teamwork approaches. The importance of results orientation and unambiguous target agreements remains. Leaders must be able to comprehend basics faster and consider alternative alternatives. Early, clear, and transparent communication, particularly through digital media, as well as the management of change, will become increasingly vital. An openness to the new (e.g., technology, but also cultures) becomes crucial, as does a desire to learn, an understanding of specialisation and technical possibilities, and remaining current on a wide variety of management practises, including the knowledge of how to utilise them intelligently.

Discussion

The changes brought about by digitization will have the most impact on future leadership in SMEs, as well as the implications for leadership duties and behaviour. Concerning our first objective, changes in organisational structures as well as job design. SMEs will become more nimble and diversified structurally, hierarchies will play a less role, and cross-company collaboration will become more widespread. Work in SMEs will become more location-independent and influenced by Big Data, and many tasks will be automated or automated. Concerning our second objective, a clear shift in importance of routine and administrative tasks, such as information search and structuring and managing resources, to the benefit of tasks involving connecting and developing employees. Managing human resources, including employee development through coaching and responsibility transfer, will become more essential, and managing change will emerge as a new work area. Regarding our third objective, which is about changes in success-critical leadership behaviour, leaders in SMEs will need to be more strategy-oriented and focused on clear communication (through various channels), and an openness to the new will emerge as a new area of success-critical behaviour.

Implications for Research and Practice

Leaders play a significant role in the success of technological transformation (Schlicher et al. 2017), especially in SMEs that often struggle more than large firms to embrace new technologies (Lee and Xia 2006). The findings of the current study offer a thorough analysis of the key changes that the digitalization will bring about that will affect leadership in SMEs. Additionally, our examination of how these changes can affect the activities and behaviour of leaders offers important insights into the alignment of well-known leadership models with these impending changes. With regard to the taxonomy of leadership tasks (Fleishman et al. 1991), we could show that the importance of certain tasks clearly shifts from a focus on administrative and routine tasks to development and networking tasks. This insight is in line with other research that showed an overhang of administrative opposed to supportive leadership tasks (Hinrichsen et al. 2021) and a growing importance of relationship-oriented leadership (Schwarzmüller et al. 2018). With regard to changes in the importance of success-critical behaviors (Dörr et al. 2012), this tendency is mirrored by more importance of strategic and communicative behaviors. Concerning both research questions, our results show that digitalization will make change-oriented tasks and behaviors more important that are not included in present models. These results show, that even though a growing body of literature investigates change leadership (Dumas and Beinecke 2018), models of leadership tasks and behavior still need to incorporate this focus.

In order to withstand in times of change and uncertainty, SMEs need a sustainable strategy to prepare their leaders. In order to best support established leaders during these changes and successfully select new leaders, a stronger focus on employee orientation (e.g., empathy), strategy orientation (e.g., decision making), and change management (e.g., openness to change) is needed.

Strengths and Limitations

The prospective investigation of changes in leadership roles and behaviour in SMEs as a result of digitalization is a key strength of this study. To learn about impending changes, this strategy merged the theoretical underpinning of leadership models (Dörr et al. 2012; Fleishman et al. 1991) with the future focus of prospective job analysis (Kato-Beiderwieden et al. 2020). This study does, however, have several flaws. The sample is one of the limitations. Our specialists were managers because we aimed for a strategic perspective on impending developments. Additionally, we only included a smaller sample of managers from particular industrial divisions since we valued in-depth information. Consequently, it may not be possible to generalise leadership to other organisational levels (Bush 2008; Nienaber 2010). Additionally, according to Schwartz (2019), women make up roughly 15% of managers in German SMEs; however, we were unable to recruit one for our sample. Another drawback is that, in contrast to standard job studies, our interview questions were more abstract and less closely related to real behaviour in order to be able to inquire about future duties and requirements. Because of this, future study should build on our understanding by examining a greater variety of male and female leaders at various levels in SMEs, by examining real job holders to develop competence models, and by contrasting leadership in SMEs with low and high levels of digitalization.

CONCLUSION

The increased use of intelligent and connected technology in the workplace will result in significant changes to organisational structure, as well as leadership activities and expectations. These developments provide significant problems to SMEs, not just in terms of selecting new leaders, but also in terms of retaining incumbent leaders. Knowledge of impending changes will encourage the development of leadership research, which will then serve to equip SMEs with the skills needed to tackle these challenges and support their leaders. In conclusion, in the current business environment, it is crucial to understand the leaders of SMEs because of the growing need to comprehend the path to success and the process of establishing sustainable competitive advantages. In other words, SMEs must be able to identify and adopt strategies that allow them to overcome their challenges. (Madanchian et al., 2016). Based on the literature analysis on leadership practises in SMEs in this study, it has been demonstrated that SMEs play a vital role in improving organisational performance through leadership behaviours. In contrast, the results are inconsistent and dubious, and as a result, more work is required to comprehend the function of leadership in SMEs in terms of organisational performance.

REFERENCES

Avolio, B. J., & Gardner, W. L. (2005). Authentic leadership development: Getting to the root of positive forms of leadership. *The Leadership Quarterly, 16*(3), 315–338. doi:10.1016/j.leaqua.2005.03.001

Brews, P., & Purohit, D. (2007). Strategic planning in unstable environments. *Long Range Planning, 40*(1), 64–83. doi:10.1016/j.lrp.2006.12.001

Bush, T. (2008). From management to leadership. *Educational Management Administration & Leadership, 36*(2), 271–288. doi:10.1177/1741143207087777

Cascio, W. F., & Montealegre, R. (2016). How technology is changing work and organizations. *Annual Review of Organizational Psychology and Organizational Behavior, 3*(1), 349–375. doi:10.1146/annurev-orgpsych-041015-062352

Chadwick, C., Way, S. A., Kerr, G., & Thacker, J. W. (2013). Boundary conditions of the high-investment human resource systems-small-firm labour productivity relationship. *Personnel Psychology, 66*(2), 311–343. doi:10.1111/peps.12015

Charmaz, K. (2006). *Constructing grounded theory: A practical guide through qualitative analysis*. SAGE. http://www.loc.gov/catdir/enhancements/fy0657/2005928035-d.html

Colbert, B. A. (2004). The complex resource-based view: Implications for theory and practice in strategic human resource management. *Academy of Management Review*, 29(3), 341–358. doi:10.2307/20159047

Delanoy, N., & Kasztelnik, A. (2020). Business open big data analytics to support innovative leadership and management decision in Canada. *Business Ethics and Leadership*, 4(2), 56–74. doi:10.21272/bel.4(2).56-74.2020

Dionne, S. D., Gupta, A., Sotak, K. L., Shirreffs, K. A., Serban, A., Hao, C., Kim, D. H., & Yammarino, F. J. (2014). A 25-year perspective on levels of analysis in leadership research. *The Leadership Quarterly*, 25(1), 6–35. doi:10.1016/j.leaqua.2013.11.002

Dörr, S. L., Albo, P., & Monastiridis, B. (2018). Digital Leadership – Erfolgreich führen in der digitalen Welt. In S. Grote & R. Goyk (Eds.), *Führungsinstrumente aus dem Silicon Valley: Konzepte und Kompetenzen* (pp. 37–61). Springer. doi:10.1007/978-3-662-54885-1_3

Dörr, S. L., Schmidt-Huber, M., & Maier, G. W. (2012). LEAD® – Entwicklung eines evidenzbasierten Kompetenzmodells erfolgreicher Führung. In S. Grote (Ed.), *Die Zukunft der Führung* (pp. 415–435). Gabler. doi:10.1007/978-3-642-31052-2_22

Dumas, C., & Beinecke, R. H. (2018). Change leadership in the 21st century. *Journal of Organizational Change Management*, 31(4), 867–876. doi:10.1108/JOCM-02-2017-0042

Felfe, J. (2006). Transformationale und charismatische Führung – Stand der Forschung und aktuelle Entwicklungen. *Zeitschrift für Personalpsychologie*, 5(4), 163–176. doi:10.1026/1617-6391.5.4.163

Fleishman, E. A., Mumford, M. D., Zaccaro, S. J., Levin, K. Y., Korotkin, A. L., & Hein, M. B. (1991). Taxonomic efforts in the description of leader behavior: A synthesis and functional interpretation. *The Leadership Quarterly*, 2(4), 245–287. doi:10.1016/1048-9843(91)90016-U

Garavan, T., Watson, S., Carbery, R., & O'Brien, F. (2016). The antecedents of leadership development practices in SMEs: The influence of HRM strategy and practice. *International Small Business Journal*, 34(6), 870–890. doi:10.1177/0266242615594215

Hinrichsen, S., Adrian, B., & Schulz, A. (2021). Approaches to improve shop floor management. In T. Ahram, R. Taiar, K. Langlois, & A. Choplin (Eds.), *Advances in intelligent systems and computing. Human interaction, emerging technologies and future applications III* (Vol. 1253, pp. 415–421). Springer.

Hobscheidt, D., Westermann, T., Dumitrescu, R., Dülme, C., Gausemeier, J., Heppner, H., & Maier, G. W. (2017). Soziotechnische Leistungsbewertung von Unternehmen im Kontext Industrie 4.0. In E. Bodden, F. Dressler, R. Dumitrescu, J. Gausemeier, F. Meyer auf der Heide, C. Scheytt & A. Trächtler (Eds.), *WInTeSys 2017: Wissenschaftsforum Intelligente Technische Systeme*. Verlagsschriftenreihe des Heinz Nixdorf Instituts.

Judge, T. A., & Piccolo, R. F. (2004). Transformational and transactional leadership: A meta-analytic test of their relative validity. *The Journal of Applied Psychology, 89*(5), 755–768. doi:10.1037/0021-9010.89.5.755 PMID:15506858

Judge, T. A., Piccolo, R. F., & Ilies, R. (2004). The forgotten ones? The validity of consideration and initiating structure in leadership research. *The Journal of Applied Psychology, 89*(1), 36–51. doi:10.1037/0021-9010.89.1.36 PMID:14769119

Kato-Beiderwieden, A.-L., Ötting, S., Schlicher, K., Heppner, H., & Maier, G. W. (2020). *Prospektive Kompetenzanalyse (ProKA) – Ein Verfahren zur Einschätzung von zukünftigen Kompetenzveränderungen.* Manuscript submitted for publication.

Kauffeld, S., & Maier, G. W. (2020). Digitalisierte Arbeitswelt. *Gruppe. Interaktion. Organisation. Zeitschrift Für Angewandte Organisationspsychologie, 51*(1), 1–4.

Koch, A., & Westhoff, K. (2012). *Task-Analysis-Tools (TAToo) – Schritt für Schritt Unterstützung zur erfolgreichen Anforderungsanalyse.* Lengerich: Pabst.

Kuoppala, J., Lamminpää, A., Liira, J., & Vainio, H. (2008). Leadership, job well-being, and health effects—A systematic review and a meta-analysis. *Journal of Occupational and Environmental Medicine, 50*(8), 904–915. doi:10.1097/JOM.0b013e31817e918d PMID:18695449

Lee, G., & Xia, W. (2006). Organizational size and IT innovation adoption: A meta-analysis. *Information & Management, 43*(8), 975–985. doi:10.1016/j.im.2006.09.003

Liem, C. C. S., Langer, M., Demetriou, A., Hiemstra, A. M. F., Sukma Wicaksana, A., Born, M. P., & König, C. J. (2018). *Psychology meets machine learning: Interdisciplinary perspectives on algorithmic job candidate screening.* Springer.

Mason, M. (2010). Sample size and saturation in PhD studies using qualitative interviews. *Forum Qualitative Sozialforschung/Forum: Qualitative. Social Research.*

McAfee, A., Brynjolfsson, E., Davenport, T. H., Patil, D. J., & Barton, D. (2012). Big data: The management revolution. *Harvard Business Review, 90*(10), 60–68. PMID:23074865

Miller, C. C., & Cardinal, L. B. (1994). Strategic planning and firm performance: A synthesis of more than two decades of research. *Academy of Management Journal, 37*(6), 1649–1665. doi:10.2307/256804

Mlekus, L., & Maier, G. W. (2019). *Not everyone benefits from technological advancements: Associations with competency requirements and well-being in two occupations.* Manuscript submitted for publication.

Mumford, M. D., Zaccaro, S. J., Harding, F. D., Jacobs, T. O., & Fleishman, E. A. (2000). Leadership skills for a changing world. *The Leadership Quarterly, 11*(1), 11–35. doi:10.1016/S1048-9843(99)00041-7

Nienaber, H. (2010). Conceptualisation of management and leadership. *Management Decision, 48*(5), 661–675. doi:10.1108/00251741011043867

Ötting, S. K., & Maier, G. W. (2018a). The importance of procedural justice in human–machine interactions: Intelligent systems as new decision agents in organizations. *Computers in Human Behavior, 89*, 27–39. doi:10.1016/j.chb.2018.07.022

Ötting, S. K., & Maier, G. W. (2018b). The importance of procedural justice in Human–Machine Interactions: Intelligent systems as new decision agents in organizations. *Computers in Human Behavior, 89,* 27–39. doi:10.1016/j.chb.2018.07.022

Ötting, S. K., Masjutin, L., Steil, J. J., & Maier, G. W. (2020). Let's work together: A meta-analysis on robot design features that enable successful human-robot interaction at work. *Human Factors.* PMID:33176488

Parker, S. K., & Grote, G. (2020). Automation, algorithms, and beyond: Why work design matters more than ever in a digital world. *Applied Psychology.*

Potosky, D., & Lomax, M. W. (2014). Leadership and technology: A love-hate relationship. In M. D. Coovert & L. F. Thompson (Eds.), *SIOP organizational frontiers series. The psychology of workplace technology* (pp. 118–146). Routledge.

Schlicher, K. D., Paruzel, A., Steinmann, B., & Maier, G. W. (2017). Change Management für die Einführung digitaler Arbeitswelten. In G. W. Maier, G. Engels & E. Steffen (Eds.), Handbuch Gestaltung digitaler und vernetzter Arbeitswelten (pp. 1–36). Springer.

Schwartz, M. (2019). *KfW-Mittelstandspanel 2019: Jährliche Analyse zur Struktur und Entwicklungdes Mittelstands in Deutschland.* Frankfurt a.M.

Schwarzmüller, T., Brosi, P., Duman, D., & Welpe, I. M. (2018). How does the digital transformation affect organizations? Key themes of change in work design and leadership. *Management Revu, 29*(2), 114–138.

Vaikutytė-Paškauskė, J., Vaičiukynaitė, J., & Pocius, D. (2018). *Research for CULT committee: Digital skills in the 21st century.* Brussels: European Parliament, Policy Department for Structural and Cohesion Policies.

van Laar, E., van Deursen, A. J. A. M., van Dijk, J. A. G. M., & de Haan, J. (2017). The relation between 21st-century skills and digital skills: A systematic literature review. *Computers in Human Behavior, 72,* 577–588. doi:10.1016/j.chb.2017.03.010

van Laar, E., van Deursen, A. J. A. M., van Dijk, J. A. G. M., & de Haan, J. (2018). 21st-century digital skills instrument aimed at working professionals: Conceptual development and empirical validation. *Telematics and Informatics, 35*(8), 2184–2200. doi:10.1016/j.tele.2018.08.006

Chapter 15
E-Leadership Concepts, Competencies, and Challenges

Siyu Liu
Swinburne University of Technology, Australia

Diana Rajendran
Swinburne University of Technology, Australia

ABSTRACT

The information technology industry is transforming organisations in unprecedented ways. The COVID-19 pandemic has resulted in most organisations having to convert to virtual offices. This transformation has promoted e-leadership in organisations as a means and style of management. To explore e-leadership, this chapter focuses on its concepts, competencies, and challenges. A systematic literature review was conducted involving 331 journal articles, of which 21 were explored in greater depth. The chapter provides a valuable insight into e-leadership practice. It argues that new e-leadership challenges arising from modern ICTs urgently require further research, especially in e-trust, work-life balance, and psychological contracts between management and workers. E-competencies need to be developed together with the ability to manage emotions to overcome challenges in virtual environments that did not exist in the 'face-to-face' world.

INTRODUCTION

Leadership is a dynamic, ever-changing phenomenon (e.g., Silva, 2016), although, for this chapter, the rich history of definitions must be set aside for reasons of space. Moving away from the 'great man' theory and other traditional leadership styles – command-and-control, rules, regulations and boundaries – modern business is all about shared, collective, facilitative and collaborative leadership that embraces freedom of expression and thought. The focus is on outcome and productivity, recognising environmental factors that are important, contingent and situational. This has led to the emergence of e-leadership to meet the challenges of a new technologically mediated management style and the competencies upon which it depends.

DOI: 10.4018/978-1-6684-8257-5.ch015

Objective

This study's objective is to examine e-leadership's competencies and challenges via a systematic literature review. Leadership has always been a hot topic in management, because it is a comprehensive competence for eliciting voluntary support from followers through organisational, executive, decision-making and learning abilities.

BACKGROUND

The critical role of leadership in organisational behaviour is one of the most studied theories in social science (Maheshwari & Yadav, 2020; Day & Antonakis, 2012). Leadership support in organisational behaviours such as performance, organisational competition, strategic direction, and digital transformation is important, because it is not only an ability but also a behavior (Maheshwari & Yadav, 2020). Leading organisational scholars, such as Avolio et al. (2014), posit that the nature of work, its organizing and leadership are changing.

Digitally Mediated Leadership

For cross-border businesses to thrive globally, the leadership style embraced must include extensive reliance on technology. In a digital era characterised by constant, rapid advancement, leaders must elicit synergies from followers through directions and guidance to reshape their organisations. They must themselves possess skills in using technology, understanding its role, implications and potential, and have a high-level capacity to resolve and manage challenges created by the information age. Such digital leadership is an inextricable combination of ICT and leadership (Chang et al., 2022).

Digitally mediated leadership – e-leadership – can be as inspiring as traditional face-to-face leadership. Mainstream technological tools such as artificial intelligence, big data and the cloud influence every aspect of organisations, inevitably changing management. Advanced information technology (AIT) has positively influenced how leaders manage their followers, customers and organisations (Liu et al., 2018). Inevitably most organisations face changes in adapting to this period of high-speed development.

This alternative to traditional leadership was called, in its early days, virtual leadership (Großer & Baumöl, 2017). However, this was replaced by 'electronic leadership' (e-leadership) in the late twentieth century (Esguerra & Contreras, 2016). Avolio et al. (2000) argue that it was a form of traditional leadership but in an information and communication technology (ICT) development context. According to an extensive literature review, e-leadership is a new leadership outcome resulting from the development of ICT and the new work environment it creates under organisational styles. With the continuous development of information and communication technology, the vast majority of organisations have altered the way they conduct business, such as telephone, mail or social media. As a result, virtual teams and e-teams mean that new organisational styles have emerged. Therefore, the connection between leaders and followers has changed due to the emergence of the virtual work environment or home office. Based on this new change, traditional leaders and followers cannot be physically close to one another in the e-environment. The new work environment thus requires a new leadership reform: e-leadership. The framework of logical outcomes leading to e-leadership (Figure 1) demonstrates its differences in the linkage of ICT characteristics, the styles that evolve, and the environment that develops which results in this new leadership.

Figure 1. The e-leadership framework
Source: Adapted from Mohammad (2009)

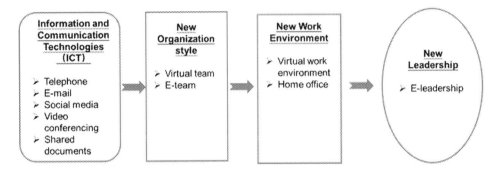

For Avolio et al. (2014), development of e-leadership remained nascent but persistent. A new 'office environment' or 'working from home' has grown rapidly and shows signs of persisting in a post-pandemic age. Hence the effective blending of electronic and traditional methods of communication are far more important for leaders than ever before if they are to achieve effectiveness.

THE CHAPTER METHODOLOGY

Systematic Reviews

A literature review supports systematic collection and synthesis of previous research (Tranfield, Denyer & Smart, 2003), and lays future foundations (Xiao & Watson, 2017). It not only provides comprehensive, valid evidence but also allows comparison of information from evidence reviewed (Snyder, 2019). Xiao and Watson (2017) demonstrate that, as a scientific investigation, a review that is valid, reliable and reproducible can minimize prejudice and support robust conclusions.

Webster and Watson (2002) propose a structured approach to determine reviewable articles: search major journals, browse article abstracts, identify reference articles, and move forward. Mathiassen et al. (2004) expand this to six steps: (1) searching academic databases; (2) selecting articles in ranking journals; (3) choosing articles from content; (4) identifying others from citations; (5) deciding on more articles; and (6) combining steps (3) and (5) to determine relevant topics and delete duplicates.

Review Parameters

Keywords were therefore entered in database "Advanced Search" categories, filtering the search period, language selection, topic category, and author views. Table 1 shows peer-reviewed articles on e-leadership from searching four popular electronic bibliographic databases (EBSCOhost, ProQuest, Scopus,

Table 1. Article identification process and results

Database	No.	No. Selected	No. of Duplicates	No. After Duplicate Removal	No. Included in Qualitative Synthesis
EBSCO	36	20	--	20	10
Scopus	157	25	5	20	6
Web of Science	50	13	2	11	3
ProQuest Central	88	30	6	24	2
	331	88	13	75	21

and Web of Science), allowing for more depth and diversity and to measure impact (Tigre, Curado & Henriques, 2022).

A detailed search of each database was required for screening. Topic keywords searched for were "e-leadership/electronic leadership" using the Boolean operator "OR" between keywords. Keywords must appear in the title or abstract or in a context implying e-leadership, such as 'virtual teams' but for accuracy this chapter also explores management (e-leadership in organisations. The timeframe selected was 2012 to 2022 and the language English. From initial screening there were 331 eligible articles, of which 157 were from the Scopus database and fewest, 36, from EBSCOHost.

After reviewing titles and abstracts, 88 articles were further filtered: 13 were duplicates, meaning 75 remained. After excluding education-related topics, conference reports, and review papers, 32 articles were deemed eligible, then 11 more were excluded as lacking a detailed and clear research methodology, leaving 21 as eligible. In other words, these articles mainly revolve around the analysis of literature-based, conference procedures or case studies. Following the PRISMA framework (Page et al. 2021), these 21 (Figure 2) were eligible for the qualitative synthesis study (Appendix, Table 4).

Distribution of E-Leadership Journals From 2012

Published article numbers showed an upward trend from 2013 to 2014, then stabilized between 2015 and 2018. In 2019, numbers started to rise again, with four published. The COVID-19 outbreak forced people to telework or work from home, hence more scholars focused on practical issues of e-leadership in organisations: ten articles were published between 2020 and 2022, or almost 50% of the number studied.

Thus, scholarly interest in e-leadership research has increased almost annually, and especially after the outbreak of COVID-19, because of the major changes in the method of working – a new global model of work expected to continue even after the pandemic ends (Bouziri et al., 2020; Lambert et al., 2020). E-leadership is a significant trend (Liu et al., 2020), and it is not only this style which will surge ahead but also future research on it.

Country-of-Research Interest

Country-study backgrounds show that the largest proportion of research was conducted in Europe, at 24%. Next is the United States with 14%, and then India, China and Africa all make up 9% of the total. There are a few more cases involving two or four countries studied together; they account for 5% of the

Figure 2. PRISMA flow chart

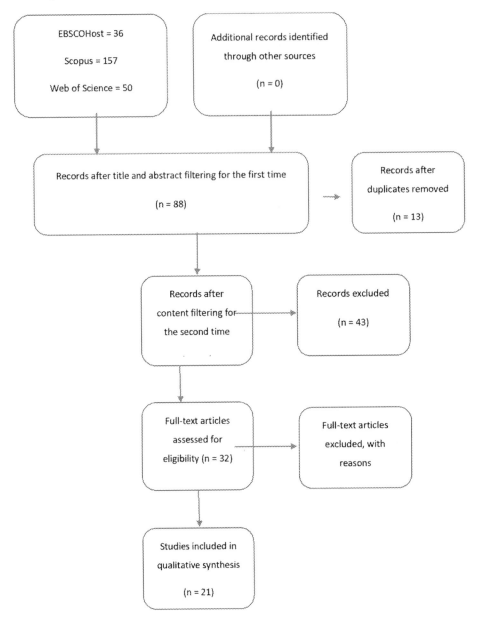

total number, and of these, those involving two countries include Europe and the United States, Europe and Middle Eastern countries, South Korea and the United States, and France and Africa or North Africa. Countries involved in the joint study of four countries include the United States, Europe, Australia and Asia. Canada and Indonesia each accounted for 5% of the total number.

Accordingly, scholars seem more interested in countries in Europe and the United States. McKinsey (2020) analysed the potential for remote work in countries, observing that the United States, an advanced economy, has a workforce that can work remotely for one-third of the time without losing productivity, whereas China and India, emerging economies, show time potential for remote work declining compared with advanced economies. Conversely, the proportion of telecommuting across European countries remained relatively stable before the outbreak of COVID-19, prevalence of telecommuting has been much higher since then (European Commission Science and Knowledge service, 2020). This may be one reason why most scholars prefer to review e-leadership in organisations in advanced economies.

Distribution of Sample Type

The sample type exhibits qualitative, quantitative and mixed methods. More than 60% used a qualitative research methodology; of the others, 33% chose a generally quantitative approach. However, one scholar used the mixed research approach on the topic of e-leadership. From this distribution, the qualitative approach seems to be the most popular research method adopted in our sample.

Statistics of Journal Ranking

The Australian Business Deans Council's (ABDC) Journal Quality List (2022) provides quality rankings for the 21 articles, classified as A*, A, B, and C: three journals were rated A, six were B, and four were C; eight were not rated. Publishers rated A are Emerald Group and Wiley-Blackwell; B are Emerald Group, Springer International Publishing, and Taylor & Francis. Taylor & Francis Online, Emerald Group, Talent First Network (Carleton University); and IGI Global are C-rated. All 21 were published in different journals (Table 5, Appendix).

Qualitative Synthesis

The two themes now explored are the competencies and challenges of e-leadership in organisations.

E-Leadership Competencies

Maduka et al. (2018) summarised the definition of competencies as leader characteristics which demonstrate skills and competencies that impact the effective performance of e-leadership within the professional field. Once e-leaders acquire relevant knowledge, skills and competencies, they can perform tasks or skills with a high level of proficiency and effectiveness. Maduka et al. refer to Kramer's (2005) explanation: unlike traditional leadership, e-leadership competencies required in organisations generally increase. Thus e-competence is one of the key factors that enables e-leadership to develop effectively in an organisation.

In articles from 2019 to 2022, four presented six major electronic competencies: e-communication, e-social skills, e-change management, e-team skills, e-tech 'savvy', and e-trustworthiness. In the development of the information age, e-leadership plays a significant, unique role, because it is one criterion by which a leader can be deemed an effective virtual leader: when effective e-leadership is present, the e-leader is likely to have built accountable teams, developed effective accountability processes, inspired reformation, and built trust virtually (Roman et al., 2019); these elaborate on core competencies based on the six e-competencies (the SEC model) identified by Van Wart et al. in 2017:

Table 2. The six e-competencies of e-leadership

E-Competency	Definition
E-communication	Ability to communicate via ICTs in a clear and organized manner, avoid errors and miscommunication, and not be excessive or detrimental to performance.
E-social	Ability to create a positive work environment and to improve communication and collaboration through various virtual communication methods.
E-change	Ability to manage change initiatives effectively through ICTs.
E-team	Ability to build, motivate, recognize, and hold accountable teams in virtual environments.
E-tech	The leader is technologically savvy and remains current on relevant ICT developments and ICT security-related concerns.
E-trust	Ability when using ICTs to create a sense of trust by being perceived as honest, consistent, and fair.

Source: Roman et al. (2019).

Roman et al. (2019) explain. Since *e-communication competency* takes the form of establishing interconnectedness across geographical distances, including teleworking, it requires "clarity, avoidance of miscommunication and overload, and message delivery". For *e-social competency*, e-leaders need to possess the ability that they can not only provide a positive electronic environment, but also can enhance social connections with electronic communication tools. "*E-Change Management Competency* can involve either change in information technology or restructuring via online environments", mainly involving effective change and restructuring of ICT. In *e-team competency*, many researchers believe that e-team leaders need to do the majority of tasks in virtual teams at the same time, including team-building activities, personal responsiveness, and task management skills: effective e-leaders must have the ability to self-manage, but also inspire positive attitudes and cohesiveness among followers in the virtual team and recognize their work. *E-tech competency* means that e-leaders should possess a high level of competence in mastering multiple ICTs and cybersecurity awareness, "whether through self-learning or training". This also means that effective e-teams are indicated by the means of the information technology base. Finally, they found that *e-trust competency* is vital; it is actively studied by many scholars because it is generally a recognition by e-leaders of the honesty and ethical performance of their team members and will also improve follower morale and thus consolidate stability.

Chaudhary et al. (2022) identified six e-competencies based on Kramer's (2005) seven: "open-mindedness, sensitivity to cultures, dealing with complexity, resilience, creativity, honesty, stable personal life and technical competence". To validate whether six key e-competencies can serve as comprehensive measures for enabling effective e-leadership, Roman et al. (2019) conducted a large-scale N-test with 243 American municipal and county employees, and found e-leadership to be an integrated, multidimensional, emerging concept requiring competencies to support e-leaders in organisations, motivating their reliability and effectiveness. The results illustrated the interdependence between these six: if anyone shows a major failing, this may have a negative impact on e-leaders.

Liu et al. (2020) also addressed competencies, assessing six core e-competencies as the degree of advantage and disadvantage in the practice of competencies via a Qualtrics survey platform in the United States and a telephone survey in South Korea. The numbers surveyed in municipalities and counties in the United States were 96 and 147, respectively; 318 people were surveyed in South Korean cities. The ranking of e-leadership structures was based on the mean scores of respondents (from 4.01 to 3.16 on a 5-point scale). In the six competencies, e-communication had the highest score, 3.66: e-leaders are considered to be the best at e-communication. E-social and e-trust belong to the middle level. E-technology, e-change, and e-team ranked lowest: comparatively, e-leaders were considered either not proficient or relatively inadequate in these three areas.

E-Tech Competency

Wang et al. (2022) agree that the six competencies are interrelated: effective use of e-tech competencies can maximize the effectiveness of communication, and, when e-leaders have the flexibility to master an increasing number of e-tech competencies, they are able to increase effectiveness in bonding, brainstorming and rapid feedback loops. Tan and Antonio (2022) argue that effective e-leaders should possess several technical competencies, including an appreciation of current ICT tools, and the ability to use these tools appropriately in the current environment: a combination of key technical competencies and physical or face-to-face methods can lead to qualified e-leadership. McCann and Kohntopp (2019) agree: the vast majority of organisations worldwide use ICT to solve problems and develop new products or services – electronic technology can not only assist organisations to establish external connections with other enterprises, but also connect with internal organisations and enhance sharing of information.

Meghana and Vijaya (2019) find that e-tech skills are among key skills required for effective e-leadership: "Big data analytics and tools, cloud computing and visualization, mobile app design and development, complex business systems, web development and tools, IT architecture, security skills, ERP systems, and social media" (p. 102), of which social media are considered alternative methods to support or coach the e-leadership process.

Jiang, Luo and Kulemeka (2017) also argue that, if e-leaders can reasonably use social media to connect with virtual teams, this benefits their organisation in completing complex tasks, obtaining real-time information and knowledge, understanding the organisational environment and communicating with internal and external stakeholders. Liu et al. (2018) also emphasize that e-leaders should have the awareness of what different types of ICT can do, because different tools can increase interactivity between e-leaders and followers. Effectiveness of e-leadership can be maximized through e-tech competencies and can also facilitate human resource management: Belitski and Liversage (2019) state that, in small and medium-sized enterprises in developing countries, using information technology, such as mobile applications, the Internet of Things, social media, or other e-tech, can provide the best sense of experience for external customers.

E-leaders therefore need to effectively use e-tech to explain, persuade and gain acceptance inside and outside their organisation (Leduc, Guilbert & Vallery, 2015), because leadership in virtual teams requires e-technology (Appelgren, 2022).

E-Communication Competency

The particularity of e-leadership requires geographically dispersed communication. Torre and Sarti (2020) agree with Fan et al. (2014) that communication actively participates in the change process caused by the new organisational style: it is crucial to strengthen the relationship between leaders and followers by using e-tech. In virtual teams especially, it is even more important to communicate with each other. E-leaders also need to develop new methods of communicating with followers at a distance, which results in the specialisation of communication: when virtual teams involve working in different locations, online video conferencing, intra-organisational email, and instant messaging software replace traditional communication. Hence e-communication competencies are critical to e-leadership.

Elyousfi, Anand and Dalmasso (2021) argue that e-leaders should have effective communication skills in order to influence followers in informal teleconferencing. They should communicate with team members on a regular, detailed and timely basis; effective communication between e-leaders and followers brings advantages to team performance. Given that e-leaders cannot have frequent face-to-face meetings with followers, this may lead to the inability to convey messages accurately (Kashive, Khanna & Powale, 2022), and therefore the quality and skill of electronic communication play a significant role in the flow of information, including accuracy, adequacy, completeness, and credibility of e-communication.

E-Trust Competency

There are seven studies on e-trust competency (Kashive et al., 2022; Rybnikova et al., 2022; Wang et al., 2022; Elyousfi et al., 2021; Torre & Sarti, 2020; Meghana & Vijaya, 2019; Savolainen, 2014) that consistently agree that e-trust is the most critical factor influencing e-leadership. Communication is the foundation of trust, and trust is a necessity because it directly affects performance (Torre & Sarti, 2020; Kashive et al., 2022). There are three stages of developing e-trust: calculative trust, knowledge-based trust, and identification-based trust (Meghana & Vijaya, 2019, p. 103).

Kashive et al. (2022) argue that a competent e-leader can create a positive atmosphere through regular communication, which leads to mutual trust, especially in an environment that lacks one-to-one interactivity (virtual teams). Therefore e-leaders need to encourage the establishment and enhancement of mutual trust (Torre & Sarti, 2020). Rybnikova et al. (2022) similarly argue that e-leaders should be keenly aware of the importance of trust in virtual environments: trust has also been considered a means to help deal with interdependence and interaction between e-leaders and followers facing complexity and uncertainty in the virtual environment.

Savolainen (2014) interviewed individuals in Finnish industries engaged in e-leadership, finding that trust is built through more frequent, shorter contact times. E-trust competencies thus require e-leaders to invest time to build them. Elyousfi et al. (2021) conclude that e-leaders are trust facilitators: trust is "the level of confidence that one individual has in another's competence and his or her willingness to act in a fair, ethical and predictable manner" (p. 511). Wang et al. (2022) also make the point that trust and building trust play a meaningful role for leaders using ICT: trust, as a social and relational structure, can be best developed through the use of e-tech by leaders to achieve a degree of connection with team members; trust in e-leadership is more critical to its impact than in traditional leadership.

Other Competencies

Chaudhary et al. (2022) propose a unique perspective for e-competence and leadership: emotional well-being and emotional intelligence are equally important, because the distance of remote work brings with it multiple intangible psychological and physical harms – isolation, misunderstanding, reduced interpersonal contact, and invisible overtime. Emotional well-being represents positive mental health, so it can lead to distinct effects in terms of job satisfaction, organisational commitment, employee engagement, employee experience and work-life balance. Organisations could achieve and sustain growth during COVID-19 once they were people-centric and concerned about follower well-being. Secondly, emotional intelligence may contribute greatly to e-leader effectiveness in influencing virtual teams for performance, viability and employee satisfaction: e-leaders can use emotions to guide employees to improve decision making and instill a sense of trust and enthusiasm through interpersonal relationships. If e-leaders can use emotional intelligence appropriately to build interpersonal relationships with followers, they are likely to achieve higher job satisfaction and efficiency. Chaudhary et al. (2022) discover that emotional intelligence significantly moderates the link between e-competence and emotional well-being: when emotional intelligence is present in e-leadership, leader e-competence will have a positive impact on follower well-being. Proper emotional management also can lead to leaders dealing more effectively with employee health.

Findings

A qualitative synthesis of the 21 articles confirmed that e-communication, e-tech(nology), e-trust, and emotional management are the basic competencies required for effective e-leadership, while e-trust, the blurring of work and life boundaries and the difficulty of establishing psychological contracts, emerge as particular challenges that e-leaders face. Challenges also include language and interpretation differences, perceived differences during e-communication and cultural differences in virtual worlds. McCann and Kohntopp (2019) argue that countries with high-context cultures – Asia, Saudi Arabia and Southern Europe – are more likely to experience language differences and changes in interpretation than countries with low-context cultures – Switzerland, Germany, the United States or Australia. Context can obstruct effective communication: due to the invisible nature of e-communication, leaders and workers may only perceive what is directly in front of them. For some globalised or transnational organisations, cultural differences between organisations also has an impact. E-communication is also, in practical terms, a challenge to working in and across differing time zones.

Our study provides a valuable insight into the practice of e-leadership in organisations. We suggest that new e-leadership challenges arising from ICTs urgently require further research, especially in e-trust, work-life balance and psychological contracts between management and workers. Four interconnected e-competencies need to be developed quickly and effectively in order for e-leadership to be useful in organisations, and more complex is a need for the ability to manage emotions to overcome challenges in virtual environments that did not seem to exist in the 'face-to-face' world.

E-leadership Challenges

There are challenges for e-leadership (Table 3).

Work-Life Balance

Firstly, from Rybnikova et al. (2022), it is clear use of e-technology has brought convenience to virtual offices yet lack relevant training prevents e-leaders from adequately meeting growing demands for advanced technological knowledge and skills when using e-tech to communicate. The new e-environment brings challenges of intensification and fragmentation of work, but, due to social media platform convenience, e-leaders can contact followers at any time – which, however, may lead to loss of work-life balance. They also demonstrate that e-leadership has led to conflicts with traditional organisational culture, such as "the absence of personal interaction was considered as disrespectful or even embarrassing" (p. 185).

Employees' Dynamic Capabilities

For Luo and Tworek (2022), e-leadership is an enormous challenge in managing and strengthening employees' dynamic capabilities on job performance in crisis situations in order to survive these: if e-leadership does not work to integrate business and information technology systems within an organisation, it will not allow virtual teams to reach their full potential, because, if the e-leader does not have this competence, it will loosen the virtual team and reduce their executive motivation.

The Complexity of Virtual Environments

According to Kashive et al. (2022), given the complexity of virtual environments, understanding the performance of virtual teams and the role of e-leaders in extremely ambiguous environments is difficult: diversity, trust and shared understanding in different physical spaces may face challenges such as confusion, lack of understanding, poor performance, lack of trust, miscommunication and internal conflict – in part due to distance that hinders accurate communication between e-leaders and followers.

Time Zone Impacts, Languages and Cultures, and Work Conflicts

Other challenges, such as working in differing time zones, languages-cultures and work conflicts due to remote work, may adversely affect followers and are not conducive to e-leader effective management (Chaudhary et al., 2022). The emotional intelligence of e-leaders can be a challenge in crisis management, because, if e-leaders lack it, they may not exhibit the emotional stability required to resolve crises or difficulties in the face of high levels of stress.

Complex Human Emotions

Tan and Antonio (2022) also believe that virtual environments change followers' behaviours, feelings, opinions and performance: 'Working from home' has brought with it considerable work, stress and uncertainty. Thus, dealing with complex follower emotions with self-awareness and blind spots is a challenge for e-leaders.

Leadership and ICT Relationship

Wang et al. (2022) point out that the leadership and ICT relationship is a challenge, because e-leaders need to integrate e-tech with traditional meetings to increase efficiency and effectiveness. They need to keep abreast of advanced technologies, adapt to the digital environment to set the right example, and achieve high productivity. Equally importantly, electronic technology also plays a key role in e-leadership and communication patterns, meaning that, once e-leaders have mastered e-tech, they are likely also to build e-trust.

E-Trust

Elyousfi et al. (2021) highlight how virtual teams, as a new form of organisation with more flexibility, lack face-to-face interactivity. Declines in productivity and low performance seen in virtual organisations may be due to problems in the setup, design, management and financial operations of e-leaders. Given that virtual teams lack face-to-face meetings, their lack of trust in each other is detrimental to the cohesiveness of e-teams and may ultimately impact team effectiveness.

Serious Consideration of Cultural Contexts

Liu et al. (2020) find significant differences in perceptions of e-leadership in different countries. Studies mainly focus on seven aspects: e-acceptance, e-adoption, e-substitution, e-preparedness, e-support, e-competencies, and overall leadership. Hence different national cultural contexts present different challenges in e-leadership and innovation. They conclude that national culture can impact e-leadership: from different cultural dimensions; there are differences in broad cultural values, in terms of individualism, uncertainty avoidance, masculinity, long-term orientation, and power distance.

Creating a Culture for E-Leadership

Torre and Sarti (2020) discuss how creating a culture for e-leadership is the core of virtual organisations, including the ability to balance distance and face-to-face relationships, capacity to manage virtual followers, and disseminate new technologies. As technology becomes more pervasive, e-leadership will be inevitable, leading to fewer organisations that do not yet have e-leadership. Thus, when e-leadership is actively considered and widely used, this requires reinforcement of new methods of working, and guiding technological change.

The Role and Importance of E-Competencies for Leadership

Roman et al. (2019)'s six e-competence model presents challenges, although it is relatively reliable and effective in measuring e-leadership and there is no evidence that an e-leader must excel in all six competencies to be effective – yet the absence of one of them has the potential to lead to a decline in long-term leadership effectiveness.

Perceived Fairness and Effectiveness of the Performance Management System

The fairness and effectiveness of the performance management systems are also challenging (Meghana & Vijaya, 2019), because new performance management systems facilitate better financial performance, improved personal performance, and increased engagement. However, "professional isolation, distance monitoring and perceptions about distributive justice" brought about by the virtual environment easily leads followers to experience a series of psychological reactions to e-leadership, such as uncertainty, hidden interdependence and the instability issue of leadership (p. 103). These psychological reactions belong to an invisible agreement: the psychological contract. Once this is hindered, it can result in followers feeling neglected, losing trust, motivation and commitment, which affects performance. Therefore, there is a positive correlation between the fairness and effectiveness of the performance management system and the psychological contract. Meghana and Vijaya also strongly agree that trust is challenging, because e-trust highlights the value of contracts.

As we have observed, challenges in e-leadership include language differences and interpretation differences, and perceived e-communication and cultural differences (high-context versus low-context) in virtual worlds (McCann & Kohntopp, 2019).

Cost of E-Technology

Belitski and Liversage (2019) observe e-technology cost in small and medium-sized enterprises in developing countries: to create new value for their organisations, e-leaders generally need to adopt advanced technologies, but it is difficult to do so in developing countries due to price pressures making it onerous to acquire e-technology.

Expectations From a Single E-Leader to Possess All "Ideal" Leadership Characteristics

In e-leadership, organisations typically expect virtual leaders to meet a broad spectrum of leadership traits and skills, based on organisational culture of adoption: "It includes all virtual communications, AITs that manage knowledge and mine information, technology that enhances decision making, and any technology that affects organisational processes such as artificial intelligence, holograms, "gamification," crowdsourcing, and so on" (Liu et al. 2018, p. 827) – an e-leader needs to possess a vast array of skills and traits in a variety of roles. Yet it is inherently difficult for a single e-leader to possess all "ideal" leadership characteristics.

Occupational and Psychological Well-Being

Jiang, Luo and Kulemeka (2017) find that, when using e-communication, there is enormous work pressure caused by a packed work schedule, increased work responsibilities and strong career motivation. This eventually leads to work-life conflict. Such conflicts can have serious consequences: job burnout, intention to leave, reduced e-trust, satisfaction and commitment. Social media, while bringing convenience to e-leaders, also blur the boundaries between work and life, resulting in negative effects, including longer working hours, increased workload and more pressure.

Workload Intensification

Leduc et al. (2015), too, find that e-technology brings workload challenges, because, in order to complete the demands of the job, e-leaders reinforce and produce goals through the use of e-tech, which may lead to aggravation of workload. Fernandez and Jawadi (2015) focus on absence of face-to-face communication; high-quality relationships in organisations tend to produce positive outcomes, especially in performance; however, working in an electronic space often brings a feeling of isolation, and therefore, this could impact virtual organisations. Finally, the management of cultural diversity and conflict issues likewise has negative consequences for the cohesion of electronic teams.

Communication Problems

As Savolainen (2014) finds, e-leaders are not understood or recognised in the new leadership environment, partly due to the trust issues caused by fewer and less-frequent communications. Enabling personal and personal-like presence through technological devices is a challenge for e-leaders. Lack of face-to-face communication means lack of body language in its entirety, 'missing' gestures, and a less-than-satisfying tone of voice, resulting in communication problems.

E-Trust

Finally, Jawadi's (2014) research interests are also in e-trust management: e-trust leads to several issues for virtuality and interaction between team members and the impact of the development of work habits and communication norms in relationship management. Again, e-trust is an immense challenge.

The 21st century is an era of rapid technological development, with a variety of communication devices becoming common in organisations – such as social media technologies, live video and email communication. As collaborative workplaces are evolving virtually, Brake (2006) spells out that isolation and confusion are two challenges that need to be dealt with, providing practical guidelines on what the e-leader can do to steer clear of these problems by promoting community and clarity (pp. 116-121):

1. Be proactive
2. Apply cultural knowledge
3. Build swift trust
4. Be a problem solver
5. Stay person-centric
6. Stay focused
7. Clarify who and what
8. Establish predictability
9. Communicate context
10. Drive for precision

In essence, this technology-mediated new paradigm of leadership provides many challenges but also opportunities for traditional leaders to re-skill themselves.

Theoretical Framework and Solutions: Behavioral Complexity Theory of Leadership (BCL) and the Pandemic

In order to enable e-leaders to fast-control the dynamic virtual environment, improve follower work performance, and ensure effective development of their organisation, e-leaders need to play different roles in dealing with different challenges. This study draws on the theoretical framework of the behavioral complexity theory of leadership (BCL), which is a combination of cognitive complexity, behavior repertoires, and paradox and contradiction (Kashive et al., 2022). When influential leaders deal with paradoxes and contradictions, they need to simultaneously play multiple and competing roles: an effective leader can deal with challenges that arise in virtual teams through the multiple roles suggested by the

Table 3. E-leadership challenges

No.	Authors	Year	Challenges
1	Rybnikova et al.	2022	Need for suitable training, difficulties in establishing an appropriate work-life balance, and disparities between the traditional organisational culture and digitalization
2	Luo & Tworek	2022	The role of e-leadership in managing and strengthening employees' dynamic capabilities on job performance in crisis situations in order to survive the crisis
3	Kashive et al.	2022	Understanding the performance of virtual teams, role of leaders in an environment of extreme ambiguity and e-trust
4	Chaudhary et al.	2022	Need for developing skills to listen attentively, expressing genuine concern for employees, make themselves more tech-savvy and assume a dynamic role, in the non-physical workspace; contributing to the wellbeing and experience of employees with effective use of technology, communication and change management
5	Tan & Antonio	2022	Dealing with complex human emotions with self-perceptions and blind spots
6	Wang et al.	2022	Leadership and ICT relationship, e-trust
7	Appelgren	2022	——
8	Elyousfi et al.	2021	Setting up, designing, managing and financially operating virtual teams, while leading remotely using technologies, building trusting relationships among team members without personal face-to-face interaction
9	Liu et al.	2020	Serious consideration of cultural contexts
10	Torre & Sarti	2020	Creating a culture of e-leadership
11	Roman et al.	2019	The role and importance of e-competencies for leadership
12	Meghana & Vijaya	2019	Perceived fairness and effectiveness of the performance management system
13	McCann & Kohntopp	2019	Language differences with variations in interpretations; Differences in perceptions during virtual communications in the virtual world
14	Belitski & Liversage	2019	Cost of technology
15	Liu et al.	2018	A single e-leader to possess all "ideal" leadership characteristics
16	Jiang et al.	2017	Occupational and psychological well-being, work-life conflict and social media practices
17	Leduc et al.	2015	Workload intensification
18	Fernandez & Jawadi	2015	Technical issues and relationship management
19	Khouly et al.	2014	Physical distancing, effective communication with followers, using electronic means to motivate followers, and building e-trust
20	Savolainen	2014	Receiving and dealing with emotions; forming overview of subordinates' work situations and circumstances; having personal and personal-like presence
21	Jawadi	2013	The effects of virtuality and interaction between team members and the development of work habits and communication norms in relationship management

Source: Compiled by the authors

BCL. An effective leader thus has the capability to identify needs and adjust behaviours appropriately, choosing the right response role.

The BCL divides leadership roles into two dimensions, internal and external, and eight leadership roles. Internal leadership roles include innovator, broker, producer, and director; external roles include mentor, facilitator, monitor, and coordinator These fully demonstrate the empathy and understanding of the virtual leader for followers or teams. Kashive et al (2022) explain that the mentor role is not only to support and understand followers, but also to build the right relationships to compensate for the distance caused by remote collaboration. When the leader plays the facilitator role, the focus is on promoting cohesion among teams; leaders can use appropriate techniques to resolve disagreements and conflicts based on knowledge sharing. For the monitor role, the leader uses electronic technology to oversee daily tasks and manage team performance. As a coordinator, the leader maintains consistent communication with followers to ensure mission continuity. Faced with external crises, leaders need to play the role of innovators and respond to changes with creative thinking. The broker role means the leader must pay attention to the external environment and stay in touch with it. As a producer, the leader needs to manage time and stress to achieve goals and ultimately increase productivity. A director's job is to clarify expectations and set goals.

Due to the complexity of the global crisis resulting from COVID-19, a model such as the BCL has become especially significant, both in internal and external roles, because it can help organisations address the current crisis by choosing roles that match situations and ultimately resolve challenges.

Building E-Trust

E-trust appears to be a particularly complex challenge for e-leadership and it recurs across seven studies (Savolainen, 2014; Khouly et al., 2014; Jawadi, 2013; Jiang et al., 2017; Elyousfi et al., 2021; Kashive et al., 2022; Wang et al., 2022). E-trust in virtual teams involves members' expectations, acting voluntarily, and working hard on behalf of the team. The e-leader needs to play the roles of mentor, facilitator and coordinator simultaneously to deal with this. This in turn means e-leaders should motivate followers to build e-trust through positive actions and guidance in the context of virtual communication (Elyousfi et al., 2021): for example, using e-tech, such as social media (Khouly et al., 2014) to maintain regular communication with followers, thus creating a positive virtual atmosphere (Kashive et al., 2022). E-trust can also be increased when leaders clearly articulate job goals (Kashive et al., 2022), and through different forms of interaction, openness and information sharing (Savolainen, 2014).

Blurring Boundaries Between Virtual Work and Life

Leduc et al. (2015), Jiang et al. (2017) and Rybnikova et al. (2022) depict a new electronic normalisation of the imbalance between virtual work and life. Based on the convenience of e-tech, it can transform traditional jobs into technology-mediated jobs: remote workers have the flexibility to choose where and when to work. The use of social media in an organisation increases transparency, so e-leaders can achieve better relationships with internal and external constituencies (Jiang et al., 2017). However, as the application of e-technology continues to expand, it may lead to an increase in tasks and longer working hours (Jiang et al., 2017; Rybnikova et al., 2022). In order to avoid such negative consequences, e-leaders must use the role characteristics of mentor and coordinator, and thus apply flexibility in guiding followers' work (Leduc et al., 2015), as well as time management (Meghana & Vijaya, 2019). When followers improve their productivity, they should be rewarded with extra time and energy to fulfill their family responsibilities (Jiang et al., 2017).

Establishing the Psychological Contract

The rapid development of virtual environments has made followers' psychological states more sensitive, based on the influence of uncertainty and stress (Meghana & Vijaya, 2019), especially in the context of the pandemic. Three studies demonstrate the importance of the psychological contract (Fernandez & Jawadi, 2015; Meghana & Vijaya, 2019; Tan & Antonio, 2022). In this case, the e-leader mainly plays the role of mentor, facilitator and coordinator, which develops additional and effective competencies (Tan & Antonio, 2022). For instance, e-leaders should facilitate e-interaction, and demonstrate compassionate leadership by listening to followers (Fernandez & Jawadi, 2015) and ensuring the psychological safety of followers is maintained at the same level as physical health (Tan & Antonio, 2022). It is important that e-leaders maintain a relational psychological contract with followers in order to sustain effective performance management system (Meghana & Vijaya, 2019).

LIMITATIONS

This chapter has limitations. In sample screening, it only focuses on four popular databases, which limits the possibilities of finding more factors influencing effective e-leadership. The selection of academic databases means there may also be some potential bias through missing relevant articles in other literature reviews. In addition, the keywords used in the article search were e-leadership and electronic leadership, which ignore other related keywords such as remote work, virtual, or distance. Therefore, some limitations arise by implication in the main search stage. The review has also not included conference papers, literature reviews, and specific industries. Second, only three competencies were analysed in depth. There is no detailed explanation for other competencies, such as e-change, e-social, and e-team. Moreover, when exploring the challenges of e-leadership, this is only to focus on the parts of the challenges that are most explored in the literature review. However, a comprehensive analysis of e-leadership was not undertaken. This then offers opportunities for further work.

FUTURE RESEARCH DIRECTIONS

In future research, more academic databases, such as Google scholar, or PsycINFO (APA), need to be involved, and the range of selected samples needs to be broader. Future research could include other variables to identify additional facets associated with effective e-leadership. It may not only further explore different contexts, such as different countries, cultures, and time zones, but also select multiple countries to compare factors that affect e-leadership. The six e-capabilities also need to be analysed comprehensively, and other major e-leadership challenges explored. For example, how trust in a virtual environment is promoted through organisational culture and e-leadership could be examined and explored, particularly in cross-cultural settings.

This study explored (albeit unevenly) the e-competencies that e-leaders should master: e-communication, e-social, e-change, e-team, e-tech, e-trust, and emotion management, as well as a series of challenging aspects of attention, including building e-trust, blurring boundaries between virtual work and life, differences in telecommuting hours and cultures in different countries, questioning the fairness and effectiveness of performance management, relationship management in virtual environments, and building psychological contracts. These demonstrated that e-leadership requires the ability to understand and overcome problems in order to be an effective leader in a virtual organisation. Hence there are methods to turn challenges into opportunities to inspire e-leadership effectiveness – among these, e-trust, blurring of work and life boundaries, and difficulty in establishing psychological contracts are the most talked-about by scholars. Therefore, this report has focused on those three aspects.

CONCLUSION

Roles of E-Leaders

The different roles that e-leaders need to play to address challenges that affect e-leadership effectiveness can be explored and resolved through BCL's internal leadership roles. The new e-leadership challenges arising from modern ICTs urgently require further research, especially in e-trust, work-life balance and the psychological contract.

E-tech is used as a mediator to break down the communication barriers imposed by physical distance, thereby enhancing e-interactivity. Secondly, as the foundation of e-leadership, the quality and skill of e-communication, accuracy, integrity and trustworthiness are also key to e-leadership. Thirdly, e-trust may benefit the building of the right relationships. When a higher climate of e-trust is created in virtual organisations, it is conducive to the development of e-leadership. Effective e-leadership builds followers' trust through different forms and frequent interactions. This is because positive mental health can have a positive impact on followers' job satisfaction and engagement. It also requires e-leaders to rely on emotional intelligence to influence their followers. Therefore, understanding the practice of e-leadership in virtual organisations can not only stimulate members to have a positive attitude toward achieving common goals, but also further improve organisational performance.

Practical Implications

There are practical implications. Given how the digital revolution is changing the relationship between leaders and followers (see Van Wart et al., 2019), it is crucial to build a robust body of knowledge on how to lead in virtual environments. This chapter provides further research evidence on the factors that influence effective e-leadership as a new organisational environment, because leadership generated in the virtual work environment has become indispensable. The findings suggest that effective e-leadership can be influenced by actively developing e-competencies to adapt to the new virtual environment. Six key e-competencies can contribute to the effective implementation of e-leadership, each facilitating the others.

Opportunities

Three major challenges are identified in this chapter. When e-leaders have foundational e-competencies, they can turn crises into opportunities by playing a suitable internal role and using the appropriate competencies. Reskilling is important to develop and harness competencies using digital technologies and should also be emphasized where necessary. This chapter thus may not only provide a modest but valuable perspective on the practice of e-leadership, it also has the potential to contribute to knowledge on the transformation of traditional leadership into e-leadership.

REFERENCES

Appelgren, E. (2022). Media management during COVID-19: Behavior of Swedish media leaders in times of crisis. *Journalism Studies, 23*(5-6), 722–739. doi:10.1080/1461670X.2021.1939106

Australian Business Deans Council. (2022). *ABDC Journal Quality List 2022.* https://abdc.edu.au/research/abdc-journal-quality-list/

Avolio, B. J., Kahai, S., & Dodge, G. E. (2000). E-leadership: Implications for theory, research, and practice. *The Leadership Quarterly, 11*(4), 615–668. doi:10.1016/S1048-9843(00)00062-X

Avolio, B. J., Sosik, J. J., Kahai, S. S., & Baker, B. (2014). E-leadership: Re-examining transformations in leadership source and transmission. *The Leadership Quarterly, 25*(1), 105–131. doi:10.1016/j.leaqua.2013.11.003

Belitski, M., & Liversage, B. (2019). E-Leadership in small and medium-sized enterprises in the developing world. *Technology Innovation Management Review, 9*(1), 64–74. doi:10.22215/timreview/1212

Bouziri, H., Smith, D. R., Descatha, A., Dab, W., & Jean, K. (2020). Working from home in the time of Covid-19: How to best preserve occupational health? *Occupational and Environmental Medicine, 77*(7), 509–510. doi:10.1136/oemed-2020-106599 PMID:32354748

Brake, T. (2006). Leading global virtual teams. *Industrial and Commercial Training, 38*(3), 116–121. doi:10.1108/00197850610659364

Chang, C. L., Arisanti, I., Octoyuda, E., & Insan, I. (2022). E-Leadership analysis during pandemic outbreak to enhanced learning in higher education. *TEM Journal, 11*(2), 932–938. doi:10.18421/TEM112-56

Chaudhary, P., Rohtagi, M., Singh, R. K., & Arora, S. (2022). Impact of leader's e-competencies on employees' wellbeing in global virtual teams during COVID-19: The moderating role of emotional intelligence. *Employee Relations, 44*(5), 1042–1057. doi:10.1108/ER-06-2021-0236

Day, D. V., & Antonakis, J. (2012). Leadership: Past, present and future. *The Nature of Leadership, 2*(1), 3–25.

Elyousfi, F., Anand, A., & Dalmasso, A. (2021). Impact of e-leadership and team dynamics on virtual team performance in a public organization. *International Journal of Public Sector Management, 34*(5), 508–528. doi:10.1108/IJPSM-08-2020-0218

Esguerra, G. A., & Contreras, F. (2016). E-leadership, an unavoidable challenge for today's organizations. *Estudios Gerenciales, 32*, 262–268. doi:10.1016/j.estger.2016.08.003

European Commission Science and Knowledge service. (2020). *Science for Policy Briefs: Telework in the EU before and after the COVID-19: Where we were, where we head to.* https://ec.europa.eu

Fernandez, D. B., & Jawadi, N. (2015). Virtual R&D project teams: From e-leadership to performance. *Journal of Applied Business Research, 31*(5), 1693–1708. doi:10.19030/jabr.v31i5.9384

Großer, B., & Baumöl, U. (2017). Why virtual teams work – State of the art. *Procedia Computer Science, 121*, 297–305. doi:10.1016/j.procs.2017.11.041

Jawadi, N. (2013). E-leadership and trust management: Exploring the moderating effects of team virtuality. *International Journal of Technology and Human Interaction, 9*(3), 18–35. doi:10.4018/jthi.2013070102

Jiang, H., Luo, Y., & Kulemeka, O. (2017). Strategic social media use in public relations: Professionals' perceived social media impact, leadership behaviors, and work-life conflict. *International Journal of Strategic Communication, 11*(1), 18–41. doi:10.1080/1553118X.2016.1226842

Kashive, N., Khanna, V. T., & Powale, L. (2022). Virtual team performance: E-leadership roles in the era of COVID-19. *Journal of Management Development, 41*(5), 277–300. doi:10.1108/JMD-05-2021-0151

Khouly, S. E., Ossman, M., Selim, M., & Zaghloul, M. (2014). Impact of e-leadership on leadership styles within the Egyptian government sector. *Competition Forum, 12*(1), 131–140.

Kramer, R. J. (2005). *Developing global leaders: enhancing competencies and accelerating the expatriate experience*. The Conference Board.

Lambert, A., Cayouette-Rembliere, J., Guéraut, E., Le Roux, G., Bonvalet, C., & Girard, V. (2020). How the COVID-19 epidemic changed working conditions in France. *Population et Sociétés, 579*, 1–4.

Leduc, S., Guilbert, L., & Vallery, G. (2015). Impact of ICTs on leadership practices: Representations and actions. *Leadership and Organization Development Journal, 36*(4), 380–395. doi:10.1108/LODJ-07-2013-0090

Liu, C., Ready, D., Roman, A., Van Wart, M., Wang, X., McCarthy, A., & Kim, S. (2018). E-leadership: An empirical study of organizational leaders' virtual communication adoption. *Leadership and Organization Development Journal, 39*(7), 826–843. doi:10.1108/LODJ-10-2017-0297

Liu, C., Van Wart, M., Kim, S., Wang, X., McCarthy, A., & Ready, D. (2020). The effects of national cultures on two technologically advanced countries: The case of e-leadership in South Korea and the United States. *Australian Journal of Public Administration, 79*(3), 298–329. doi:10.1111/1467-8500.12433

Luo, G., & Tworek, K. (2022). E-leadership as a booster of employees' dynamic capabilities influence on job performance. *Scientific Papers of Silesian University of Technology. Organization & Management / Zeszyty Naukowe Politechniki Slaskiej. Seria Organizacji i Zarzadzanie, 155*, 237–248.

Maduka, N. S., Edwards, H., Greenwood, D., Osborne, A., & Babatunde, S. O. (2018). Analysis of competencies for effective virtual team leadership in building successful organisations. *Benchmarking, 25*(2), 696–712. doi:10.1108/BIJ-08-2016-0124

Maheshwari, S. K., & Yadav, J. (2020). Leadership in the digital age: Emerging paradigms and challenges. *International Journal of Business and Globalisation, 26*(3), 220–238. doi:10.1504/IJBG.2020.110950

Mathiassen, L., Saarinen, T., Tuunanen, T., & Rossi, M. (2004). Managing requirements engineering risks: An analysis and synthesis of the literature. *Working Papers on Information Systems, Helsinki School of Economics*, 63.

McCann, J., & Kohntopp, T. (2019). Virtual leadership in organizations: Potential competitive advantage? *S.A.M. Advanced Management Journal, 84*(3), 26–39.

McKinsey Digital. (2020, July 24). *Europe's digital migration during COVID-19: Getting past the broad trends and averages*. McKinsey & Company. https://www.mckinsey.com/business-functions/mckinsey-digital/our-insights/europes-digital-migration-during-covid-19-getting-past-the-broad-trends-and-averages

Meghana, J., & Vijaya, R. (2019). E-leadership, psychological contract and real-time performance management: Remotely working professionals. *SCMS Journal of Indian Management, 16*(3), 101–111.

Mohammad, K. (2009). E-Leadership: The emerging new leadership for the virtual organization. *Journal of Managerial Sciences, 3*(1). At https://www.qurtuba.edu.pk/jms/default_files/JMS/3_1/01_khawaj.pdf

Page, M. J., McKenzie, J. E., Bossuyt, P. M., Boutron, I., Hoffmann, T. C., Mulrow, C. D., Shamseer, L., Tetzlaff, J. M., Akl, E. A., Brennan, S. E., Chou, R., Glanville, J., Grimshaw, J. M., Hróbjartsson, A., Lalu, M. M., Li, T., Loder, E. W., Mayo-Wilson, E., McDonald, S., ... Moher, D. (2021). The PRISMA 2020 statement: An updated guideline for reporting systematic reviews. *Systematic Reviews, 10*(1), 1–11. doi:10.118613643-021-01626-4 PMID:33781348

Roman, A. V., Van Wart, M., Wang, X., Liu, C., Kim, S., & McCarthy, A. (2019). Defining E-leadership as competence in ICT-mediated communications: An exploratory assessment. *Public Administration Review, 79*(6), 853–866. doi:10.1111/puar.12980

Rybnikova, I., Juknevičienė, V., Toleikienė, R., Leach, N., Āboliņa, I., Reinholde, I., & Sillamäe, J. (2022). Digitalisation and e-leadership in local government before COVID-19: Results of an exploratory study. *Forum Scientiae Oeconomia, 10*(2), 173–191.

Savolainen, T. (2014). Trust-building in e-Leadership: A case study of leaders' challenges and skills in technology-mediated interaction. *Journal of Global Business Issues, 8*(2), 45–56.

Silva, A. (2016). What is leadership? *Journal of Business Studies Quarterly, 8*(1), 1–5. PMID:29355200

Snyder, H. (2019). Literature review as a research methodology: An overview and guidelines. *Journal of Business Research, 104*, 333–339. doi:10.1016/j.jbusres.2019.07.039

Tan, R., & Antonio, F. (2022). New insights on employee adaptive performance during the COVID-19 pandemic: Empirical evidence from Indonesia. *Journal of Entrepreneurship. Management and Innovation, 18*(2), 175–206. doi:10.7341/20221826

Tigre, F. B., Curado, C., & Henriques, P. L. (2022). Digital leadership: A bibliometric analysis. *Journal of Leadership & Organizational Studies, 30*(1), 40–70. Advance online publication. doi:10.1177/15480518221123132

Torre, T., & Sarti, D. (2020). The "way" toward e-leadership: Some evidence from the field. *Frontiers in Psychology, 11.* . doi:10.3389/fpsyg.2020.554253

Tranfield, D., Denyer, D., & Smart, P. (2003). Towards a methodology for developing evidence-informed management knowledge by means of systematic review. *British Journal of Management, 14*(3), 207–222. doi:10.1111/1467-8551.00375

Van Wart, M., Roman, A., Wang, X., & Liu, C. (2017). Integrating ICT adoption issues into (e-)leadership theory. *Telematics and Informatics*, *34*(5), 527–537. doi:10.1016/j.tele.2016.11.003

Van Wart, M., Roman, A., Wang, X., Liu, C., Reiter, R., & Klenk, T. (2019). Operationalizing the definition of e-leadership: Identifying the elements of e-leadership. *International Review of Administrative Sciences*, *85*(1), 80–97. doi:10.1177/0020852316681446

Wang, X., Wei, X., Van Wart, M., McCarthy, A., Liu, C., Kim, S., & Ready, D. H. (2022). The role of e-leadership in ICT utilization: A project management perspective. *Information Technology Management*, (February), 1–15. PMID:36311472

Webster, J., & Watson, R. (2002). Analyzing the past to prepare for the future: Writing a literature review. *Management Information Systems Quarterly*, *26*(2), xiii–xxiii.

Xiao, Y., & Watson, M. (2019). Guidance on conducting a systematic literature review. *Journal of Planning Education and Research*, *39*(1), 93–112. doi:10.1177/0739456X17723971

APPENDIX

Table 4. Articles selected

No	Authors	Year of Publication	Title of the Article
1	Rybnikova, I., Juknevičienė, V., Toleikienė, R., Leach, N., Āboliņa, I., Reinholde, I., & Sillamäe, J.	2022	Digitalization and e-leadership in local government before COVID-19: Results of an exploratory study
2	Lou, G., & Tworek, K.	2022	E-leadership as a booster of employees' dynamic capabilities influence on job performance
3	Kashive, N., Khanna, V. T., & Powale, L.	2022	Virtual team performance: E-leadership roles in the era of COVID-19
4	Chaudhary, P., Rohtagi, M., Singh, R. K., & Arora, S.	2022	Impact of leader's e-competencies on employees' wellbeing in global virtual teams during COVID-19: the moderating role of emotional intelligence
5	Tan, R., & Antonio F.	2022	New insights on employee adaptive performance during the COVID-19 pandemic: Empirical evidence from Indonesia
6	Wang, X. H., Wei, X. N., Van Wart M., McCarthy, A., Liu, C., Kim, S., & Ready, D.H.	2022	The role of E-leadership in ICT utilization: A project management perspective
7	Appelgren, E.	2022	Media management during COVID-19: Behavior of Swedish media leaders in times of crisis
8	Elyousfi, F., Anand, A., & Dalmasso, A.	2021	Impact of e-leadership and team dynamics on virtual team performance in a public organization
9	Liu, C., Van Wart, M., Kim, S., Wang, X., McCarthy, A., & Ready, D.	2020	The effects of national cultures on two technologically advanced countries: The case of e-leadership in South Korea and the United States
10	Torre, T., & Sarti, D.	2020	The "way" toward e-leadership: Some evidence from the field
11	Roman, A. V., Van Wart, M., Wang, X., Liu, C., Kim, S., & McCarthy, A.	2019	Defining E-leadership as competence in ICT-mediated communications: An exploratory assessment
12	Meghana, J. & Vijaya, R.	2019	E-leadership, psychological contract and real-time performance management: Remotely working professionals
13	McCann, J., & Kohntopp, T.	2019	Virtual leadership in organizational: Potential competitive advantage?
14	Belitski, M., & Liversage, B.	2019	E-leadership in small and medium-sized enterprises in the developing world
15	Liu, C., Ready, D., Roman, A., Van Wart, M., Wang, X., McCarthy, A., & Kim, S.	2018	E-leadership: An empirical study of organizational leaders' virtual communication adoption
16	Jiang, H., Luo Y., & Kulemeka, O.	2017	Strategic social media use in public relations: Professionals' perceived social media impact, leadership behaviors, and work-life conflict
17	Leduc, S., Guilbert, L., & Vallery, G.	2015	Impact of ICTs on leadership practices: Representations and actions
18	Fernandez, D. B., & Jawadi, N.	2015	Virtual R & D project teams: From e-leadership to performance
19	Khouly, S. E., Ossman, M., Selim, M., & Zaghloul, M.	2014	Impact of E-leadership on leadership styles within the Egyptian government sector
20	Savolainen, T.	2014	Trust-Building in e-leadership: A case study of leaders' challenges and skills in technology-mediated interaction
21	Jawadi, N.	2013	E-leadership and trust management: Exploring the moderating effects of team virtuality

Table 5. Ranking of journals and publishers

Number	Journal Name	Publisher	Ranking
1	Forum Scientiae Oeconomia	Faculty of Applied Sciences of WSB University	Not ranked in ABDC
2	Scientific Papers of Silesian University of Technology. Organization & Management	Taylor & Francis Online	C
3	Journal of Management Development	Emerald Group	C
4	Australian Journal of Public Administration	Wiley-Blackwell Publishing	A
5	The International Journal of Public Sector Management	Emerald Group	B
6	Journal of Employee Relations	Emerald Group	B
7	Journal of Industrial Management & Data Systems	Emerald Group	A
8	Journal of Entrepreneurship, Management and Innovation	http://www.jemi.edu.pl	Not ranked in ABDC
9	Information Technology and Management	Springer International Publishing	B
10	Journal of Public Administration Review	Wiley-Blackwell	A
11	SCMS Journal of Indian Management	The SCMS Group	Not ranked in ABDC
12	Leadership & Organization Development Journal	Emerald Group	B
13	S.A.M. Advanced Management Journal	Society for Advancement of Management, Inc.	Not ranked in ABDC
14	Technology Innovation Management Review	Talent First Network (Carleton University)	C
15	Leadership & Organization Development Journal	Emerald Group	B
16	Competition forum	Indiana: American Society for Competitiveness	Not ranked in ABDC
17	International Journal of Technology and Human Interaction	IGI Global	C
18	International Journal of Strategic Communication	Taylor & Francis	B
19	Journalism Studies	Taylor & Francis	Not ranked in ABDC
20	Journal of Frontiers in Psychology	Frontiers	Not ranked in ABDC
21	Journal of Applied Business Research	Clute Institute	Not ranked in ABDC

Chapter 16
Undergraduate Business Students' Perceptions About Virtual and Remote-Work Leadership Skills

Anas Al-Fattal
https://orcid.org/0000-0001-9736-7439
University of Minnesota, Crookston, USA

Eddie G. Walker II
https://orcid.org/0000-0002-5647-9562
University of Minnesota, Crookston, USA

Rachel Lundbohm
https://orcid.org/0000-0003-4494-8381
University of Minnesota, Crookston, USA

ABSTRACT

With changes introduced to the work environment since the COVID-19 pandemic, an ever-increasing amount of interest has been focused on virtual leadership. This chapter researches the topic of virtual leadership and focuses on investigating business students' perceptions of skills relevant to virtual leadership positions. The chapter presents an empirical exploratory research study conducted through four focus groups with 20 undergraduate business students. The findings reveal business students have a relevant understanding of the differences between traditional and virtual work environments. Socialization and isolation are among the most dominant themes regarding the differences in work modes. The findings also show that business students understand the challenges associated with leading in virtual and remote work settings, and they prefer traditional future leadership positions to avoid such challenges. The study highlights several relevant leadership skills needed according to business students such as communication, the ability to engage, and technological competencies.

DOI: 10.4018/978-1-6684-8257-5.ch016

THE CHANGING CONTEXT

The COVID-19 pandemic has changed the way many employees are working. In the post-COVID environment, 61% of employees who have a workplace outside of their home are choosing to work from home compared to 36% choosing to work from home during the pandemic (Parker et al., 2022). More employees choosing to work from home has created a new challenge related to managing remote and on-site employees. Gupta (2020) outlines the importance of those responsible for making policy (both private and public) to "embrace a remote working future to drive growth" (p. 1). Furthermore, the increasing use of virtual team in business organizations requires business educators to adopt instructional practice that helps students gain skillsets needed in virtual work environments. This qualitative empirical study examines undergraduate business students' perceptions of leadership skills relevant to the virtual and remote-work business environment, especially as it relates to team management. To provide context for this study's research question, trends related to current shifts in required leadership skills are addressed. This discussion leads to the study's aim, purpose, and significance. Further, a review of relevant literature highlights the paucity of similar studies. The chapter then presents and discusses the research methodology and results.

With this voluntary shift towards remote work, more individuals are choosing to work from home through available online channels such as Zoom or Microsoft Teams. Several factors have contributed to this including convenience, time, cost saving, and effectiveness (Caligiuri & De Crieri, 2021). One significant issue to highlight is the overall shift of attitudes regarding the relevance and effectiveness of the remote work modality (Yener, 2022). During the early stages of the pandemic, employers tended to have negative attitudes towards remote work (Pokojski et al., 2022), however, this attitude has become more positive due to the considerable costs savings for employers in terms of space, equipment, costs, and compensation (Licite-Kurbe & Leonovica, 2021).

Leading a team remotely has its challenges and requires relevant skills. According to Mehtab et al. (2017), "It is very difficult for a team leader to control directly every team member's activity due to different geographical location" (p. 184). It is believed that considering current changes and the shift towards acceptable remote work mode, there is an urgent necessity to review and develop theories on leadership. The literature highlights several skills a leader should possess to be successful. Among these are problem-solving (Mumford et al., 2007), decision-making (Ejimabo, 2015), negotiation (Zohar, 2015), and critical thinking (Flores et al., 2012). The literature highlights relevant remote leadership skills, some of which are evident in remote and face-to-face modalities including communication and team-building skills. Nonetheless, it is argued that the significance and relevance of these skills are different between both modes.

Business schools have always paid a considerable amount of attention to developing their students' leadership skills to create future leaders. According to Loucks and Ozgul (2020), "The increasing use of virtual teams in business organizations calls on business education to adopt instructional practices that help students gain an appropriate set of professional skills in order to work in virtual teams" (p. 656). Some have criticized higher educational institutions for not being proactive in developing their goals and courses to cope with market changes, demand, and employability skills requirements (e.g., Bellei and Cabalin (2013), Gleason (2018), and Zaitseva and Goncharova (2020). Rohs et al. (2015) suggest that higher education institutions should be sensitive to continuous market changes and periodically review their programs' core competencies. For example, with universities adapting to online learning during the pandemic, the speed at which professors had to adapt did not always result in a positive experience for the student. In one study, the student's lack of experience using technologies such as Zoom as well as the perceived difficulty professors faced in facilitating student engagement in an online setting were contributing factors to negative perceptions of online learning (Keane et al., 2022).

Higher education students receive minimal training or experiences working in virtual teams or with virtual team leadership while in college yet are often placed in virtual teams early in their careers (Brewer et al., 2015; Fan et al., 2014). Loucks and Ozogul (2020) identified potential ways to integrate virtual team leadership experiences into their courses including integrating coaching when teaching virtual leadership, providing opportunities for peer feedback, and align assessments with the targeted virtual leadership skills being taught (Loucks and Ozogul, 2020). Furthermore, today's higher education students have a variety of experiences leading both in-person and online through their prior educational and work experiences. This is especially true since many students were required to pivot online for school and/or work during the COVID-19 pandemic. Student's prior virtual leadership experiences coupled with the knowledge they are gaining in the classroom have a profound impact on their perceptions of leadership skills necessary for virtual work environments and will have an influence on their ability to lead virtual teams in the future.

It is important to shed light on learners' awareness of remote work leadership skills required in today's complex and changing environment. This study broadens our understanding and knowledge of virtual leadership skills. Results from this study will help develop and update theories on leadership styles and skills and employability skills by discussing how the virtual environment influences the way people (specifically business students) view leadership. The study brings benefits by educating policymakers and program developers at higher education institutions about current market trends and students' preferences and awareness of program requirements. Consequently, this will aid in making their offering more responsive and proactive to market trends and changes. The study also provides benefits to employers and the labor market since developing business students' virtual leadership is among the most relevant employability skills (Loucks & Ozogul, 2020).

It is evident that virtual leadership skills must be taught in higher education institutions to adopt to changing work environments. Therefore, an urgent question to highlight is to what extent have business schools modified their core competencies to accommodate skills required for leaders of remote work environments? Since students have also identified challenges related to facilitating discussions within a virtual environment, it can also be argued that learners' awareness of the significance of virtual and remote work leadership skills is equally relevant. Hence, this study answers the following research question: According to business students, what remote work leadership skills are required to become an effective virtual leader?

Virtual and Remote-Work Leadership Skills

In today's business environment, facilitating online work has become a daily task for many leaders, whether they lead virtual teams that have never met in person or through connecting digitally with coworkers who meet face-to-face regularly (Darics, 2020). Virtual leadership arises from the need to use technology to communicate and collaborate internally and externally and has become a crucial part of the daily work of managers (Cordova-Buiza et al., 2022). Virtual leadership requires the utilization of digital technology to communicate and collaborate with followers in a virtual environment while simultaneously influencing the feelings, attitudes, cognitions, performance, and behavior of followers (Roman et al., 2019; Tuschner et al., 2022, VanWart et al., 2016).

Although virtual leadership pursues the same goal as traditional leadership (Cordova-Buiza et al., 2022), these traits and skill sets are not necessarily transferable to the virtual leadership setting (Cortellazzo et al., 2019; DeRue et al., 2011; Lu et al., 2014; Maduka et al., 2018). It has been suggested that virtual roles are more complicated than traditional leadership roles (Zigurs, 2003; Johnson, 2010). For example, virtual environments are stripped of the information richness available in traditional face-to-face settings (Brake, 2006), and poses unique challenges and requires specific leadership qualities (Cortellazzo et al., 2019; DeRue et al., 2011; Lu et al., 2014; Maduka et al., 2018). Leadership skills and abilities required of virtual leaders include effective communication through appropriate digital technologies, the ability to build teams and develop trust using technology, the ability to demonstrate technology-related expertise (Roman et al., 2019), open-mindedness, flexibility, cultural awareness, the ability to manage complex situations, resiliency, optimism, energy, and honesty (Kramer, 2005). Virtual leaders should also possess specific personality characteristics, cognitive abilities, motives, and competencies (Zaccaro, 2007) to be effective virtual leaders.

Tuschner et al. (2022) identify proximal and distal attributes of virtual leaders that are relevant to be effective. Proximal attributes describe leader traits that are more related to situational behavior and can be trained and learned (Hoffman et al., 2011; Zaccaro, 2007). Distal attributes describe leaders' natural traits, such as personal dispositions and cognitive abilities, that are relatively independent of situational factors. In this regard, Hoffman et al. (2011) indicated that both types of characteristics are correlated with leader effectiveness, implying that while leaders can be born, they can also be made. Proximal skills of effective virtual leaders include the ability to effectively communicate, technological competence, the ability to motivate team members, trust-building capabilities, organizational skills, aptitude coaching, decision-making abilities, change management skills, and the ability to network effectively (Tuschner et al., 2022). Distal characteristics, or natural traits, of virtual leaders include dimensions of personality, cognitive abilities, motives and attitudes, and core beliefs (Tuschner et al., 2022). Other relevant personality characteristics required of virtual leaders include the ability to be adaptable and flexible, (Klus & Müller, 2021; VanWart et al., 2017). Being adaptable and flexible allows virtual leaders to respond instantly to changes occurring in dynamic environments (Klein, 2020). Other important personality traits of virtual leaders include tolerance of ambiguity (Cortellazzo et al., 2019; Shah & Patki, 2020; Wargin & Dobiéy, 2001), courage and ability to take risks, and the ability to make decisions in constantly changing situations (Cortellazzo et al., 2019; Klein, 2020). The following two subsections discuss proximal and distal attributes and skills of virtual leadership found in the literature.

Proximal Attributes

With virtual work still prominent in many industries and educational settings, the ability to communicate effectively is stressed as an important leadership skill. It is especially critical for virtual leaders who are limited to communication through technology and the challenges presented by digital technology (Johnson, 2020; Tuschner et al., 2022). To maintain effective communication, virtual leaders should be transparent (Klein, 2020; Savolainen, 2014) and possess excellent verbal and written communication skills (Kuscu & Arslan, 2016). Virtual leaders should maintain frequent communication and follow-up, while also providing clear direction and goals that team members can understand which is arguably more difficult and more relevant in a virtual setting (Hunsaker & Hunsaker, 2008; Johnson, 2010). A large amount of virtual communication lacks visual cues making listening even more important to understand the content of a message (Byrd, 2019; Hunsaker & Hunsaker, 2008; Mohammad, 2009; Passey, 2014; Ruiller et al.,

2019). It is also imperative to carefully encode messages to avoid the risk of misunderstanding (VanWart et al., 2019), to provide essential timely feedback (Kerfoot, 2010; Loucks & Ozogul, 2020; Maduka et al., 2018), and to be able to hear what cannot be seen (Hunsaker & Hunsaker, 2008; Johnson, 2010).

With the shift to remote work, video conferencing (e.g., Zoom and Microsoft Teams) has been the primary means of connecting with employees and co-workers. Therefore, virtual leaders must possess digital technology skills to overcome communication barriers (Byrd, 2019; Cortellazzo et al., 2019; Zigurs, 2003). Technological acumen enables e-leaders to utilize technology from a cost-benefit perspective and ensure data security and privacy (VanWart et al., 2019). Virtual leaders are also recommended to be able to utilize data analytics to drive organizational progress (Gierlich-Joas et al., 2020; Klein, 2020).

Motivational skills that encourage engagement and commitment from followers are relevant for virtual leaders (Tuschner et al., 2022). Key motivational tactics include providing continual appreciation and recognition of performance through intrinsic and extrinsic awards (Alward & Phelps, 2019; Garcia, 2015; Kuscu & Arslan, 2016; Roy, 2012), empowering team members and offering them more freedom (Klein, 2020; Orte & Dino, 2019), demonstrating that everyone is part of the team (Kuscu & Arslan, 2016), creating a positive relational climate (Torre & Sarti, 2020), facilitating interactions and the exchange of ideas, personalizing the work environment to create a sense of "we" within a virtual team (Kerfoot, 2010), aligning virtual teams around a common goal and purpose (Byrd, 2019; Maduka et al., 2018; Panteli et al., 2019), and allowing team autonomy (Roy, 2012). Another tactic is reported by Ruiller et al. (2019) who found that a sense of team proximity and engagement can be achieved by combining digital communication technologies such as messengers and face-to-face virtual meetings.

Virtual leaders are also advised to gain the trust of followers, especially since physical distance makes relationship-building difficult (Torre & Sarti, 2020). To build trust, these leaders should grant autonomy to their followers and demonstrate care and concern for individuals, (Alward & Phelps, 2019; Norman et al., 2020), be consistent and transparent in their decision-making, create a participative team environment (Gierlich-Joas et al., 2020; Kuscu & Arslan, 2016; Vrana & Singh, 2021), communicate clear expectations, and be accountable for their decisions and actions (Alward & Phelps, 2019). Virtual leaders should utilize situationally appropriate media and technologies (Norman et al., 2020) while attempting to maintain a work-life balance despite the constant access to work through technology (VanWart et al., 2019) to help in building trust. Virtual leaders should also be honest, have integrity and be reliable for followers to find them trustworthy (Norman et al., 2020; VanWart et al., 2017).

Organizational skills are essential to be an effective virtual leader (Tuschner et al., 2022). Specifically, virtual leaders need to establish standard operating procedures for virtual meetings and teamwork (Loucks & Ozogul, 2020; Maduka et al., 2018; Purvanova et al., 2021), set challenging yet realistic goals for their team members (Byrd, 2019; Kerfoot, 2010; Vrana & Singh, 2021), and be proactive in anticipating problems before they occur (Roy, 2012). Due to the lack of traditional in-person interactions and the absence of continuous control, a clearly defined and explicit delegation of tasks is critical (Roy, 2012; Torre & Sarti, 2020).

Virtual leaders are advised to possess coaching skills to encourage workers, ease fears of changes in tasks or positions, and alleviate frustrations caused by a lack of non-verbal communication and technological glitches (Klein, 2020; Klus & Müller, 2021; Roy, 2012). Due to these challenges, virtual leaders should also be able to manage change and be able to plan, monitor, and refine the adoption of digital technologies (VanWart et al., 2019). Virtual leaders should also consider generational differences of employees in terms of their adoption of technology while offering innovative approaches to promote acceptance, embrace change, and encourage innovation (Leeuwen, 2002; Shah & Patki, 2020; Torre & Sarti, 2020).

Distal Attributes

Virtual leaders should also have cognitive abilities including cultural intelligence, social intelligence, general intelligence, and analytical abilities (Cortellazzo et al., 2019; Klein, 2020; Maduka et al., 2018; Norman et al., 2020; Purvanova et al., 2021; Roy, 2012; VanWart et al., 2017). Creativity has also been found to be an important cognitive ability for virtual leaders, allowing e-leaders to meet the organizational challenges of virtual environments with innovative solutions, thereby driving organizational improvements (Klein, 2020; Orte & Dino, 2019).

Within a virtual environment, virtual leaders must possess the appropriate motives, attitudes, and core beliefs necessary to operate effectively in that context. They should be willing to engage in lifelong learning to stay up to date on the latest technologies and trends (Cortellazzo et al., 2019; Klein, 2020; Klus & Müller, 2021), and have a certain level of an entrepreneurial mindset to translate their digital visions into innovative business models and processes (Klein, 2020). Self-confidence and belief in one's ability to lead the virtual team have also been highlighted as relevant (Maduka et al., 2018). It is expected that proximal attributes or skills are identified with greater frequency than distal attributes since they can be trained and are easier to identify than the natural/internal traits of an individual.

Challenges of Virtual Leadership

Being an effective virtual leader comes with a host of challenges as almost all activities are carried out virtually with digital technologies and leaders do not regularly interact face-to-face with followers. Examples of challenges virtual leaders face include ensuring employees are motivated, building relationships and trust, and providing virtual employee training and development programs (Contreras et al., 2020; Machado & Brandão, 2019).

The challenge that comes with managing across different geographical zones, where multiple cultures are present, different rules and regulations exist, and various business processes are applied can be a daunting one for virtual leaders. This diversity creates complexities for virtual leaders as they need to employ different communication and leadership strategies to achieve organizational goals (Mehtab et al., 2017). Another significant challenge for virtual leaders is that they need to balance the virtual demands of their team with their personal life. With followers residing in different time zones, virtual leaders should maintain flexibility with meeting times and modalities. Moreover, since much of the work of virtual leaders is done at home, it can be difficult to achieve a balance between work and family matters (Mehtab et al., 2017).

Methodology

This chapter offers an empirical investigation of business students' perceptions of virtual and remote work leadership. The investigation is underpinned by three research questions: (1) what differences are perceived by business students between virtual and traditional leadership, (2) what skills are relevant for virtual leaders, and (3) what are the possible challenges that face virtual leaders. The nature of the research questions and the originality of the study area suggests a qualitative heuristic exploratory investigation (Creswell & Creswell, 2017; Oppenheim, 2000) by means of focus groups with undergraduate business students from one small public university located in an agricultural region in the Midwest of the US. This study conducted four focus groups (total of 20 students); three were conducted online and one was conducted face-to-face. In recruiting participants, an email was sent to all current business students in the Business Department (n=600). Involvement was encouraged by offering participants a $20 gift card. Twenty students showed interest and were invited to participate. The focus group questions schedule was derived from the literature (Alvani & Charalampous, 2021; Kane et al., 2019; Kiron et al., 2016). Data were analyzed manually following the Miles et al. (2019) method of data reduction, data display, and conclusion drawing and verification. The analysis went simultaneously and separately through two different researchers to create and validate codes to strengthen the results' trustworthiness (Miles et al., 2019).

Data Analysis

The data analysis is structured following the focus group schedule within three distinct sections. After reviewing the participants' profiles, the first section discusses results related to participants' perceptions of the differences between traditional and virtual work environments. The second section presents results about participants' preferences concerning leadership and work environment and the potential perceived challenges. The final section presents results related to skills relevant to leading in a virtual work environment. The section makes use of quotes from the participants to develop the narrative in addressing the research aim and questions.

The study employed a total of twenty participants, with the majority of the participants being in their senior year (n=12). This could have major implications on the data since those students are perceived to be more experienced and have had more business courses (some probably related to leadership). Additionally, these students have more exposure to studying and working in virtual environments, especially since they may have been university students during the time that classes were moved online due to the pandemic. Most of the participants were in their early twenties (n=12). Only four participants were older than 30 years old with at least ten years of professional experience. Seven participants have never had any professional experiences and eight have never had any leadership experience. For those without leadership experience, a lot of references in the focus group discussion were made from their online learning experiences and communications with their instructors or peers.

Traditional and Virtual Environment Differences

When discussing the differences between leading in traditional and virtual work environments, the most dominant theme was socialization versus isolation. Participants believed that working virtually imposed a state of isolation on the workers who might "not feel very much attached to the organization, the team, or even tasks" (FG:3, P:21). Isolation was also related to feelings of loneliness, poor social connections, withdrawal, and low participation. Participants (FG:1 P:3 & P5; FG2: P8, P9, & P10; & FG3: P13, P15, P16; FG4: P17 & P20) mentioned that workers in the virtual environment tend to show low participation in several organizational activities. For those participants, virtual workers might experience lower levels of organizational belonging due to the distance established by this work mode. One interesting theme to emerge in FG2 and FG3 was withdrawal. P10, who had ten years of experience, and had already experienced working virtually mentioned the following, "It is much easier to hide…

you just need turn off your camera and mic and that's it... You don't have to be there at everything being said or participate in every discussion." This was compared to the traditional work environment where a person is "forced to participate and talk" (FG2: P8). Another subtheme to emerge concerning socialization versus isolation was a social relationship. Participants described the virtual environment as poor and lacking human connection.

Working virtually was perceived to be performed only from home where there was a lot of "noise" or "distraction" (FG4: P17) like "family-related duties, TV, or even video games" (FG:1, P:5). These would make it hard for workers to focus on their duties and responsibilities. There was an agreement among all participants that for a worker to succeed in a virtual job, they needed a considerable amount of personal motivation and dedication to avoid "the attraction of being distracted from work duties." P16 expressed serious doubts about the seriousness of virtual work. This participant had already experienced working from home during the pandemic and the participant believed that most people "didn't really work" then.

Another important emerging theme was communication. Participants believed that communication in a virtual work environment was more demanding through available channels, e.g., email messaging and even video conferencing. Communication in a virtual work environment was mentioned to be more time-consuming. This was due to the time needed to formulate email messages, making sure team members read them, and responded promptly. Participants also mentioned ideas related to communication techniques like tone, body language, and facial gestures that were generally lacking in virtual communication.

Virtual Environment Challenges

The second section of the study focused on students' perceptions of possible challenges and preferences of work and leadership modes. Attitudes about work modes were various. Three participants preferred to work fully virtually, and eight preferred to work in a hybrid mode. Nonetheless, when it came to being a leader, all participants preferred the traditional work mode. This unanimous agreement was justified by the participants' awareness that leading virtually could be more demanding and challenging. One participant (P3) said, "I feel more comfortable dealing with people face-to-face... It feels more natural." Another participant (P5) added, "Things lack in virtual work... There are more barriers." Among leadership obstacles imposed in a virtual environment, students believed that it was more difficult to lead by example since team members were not "physically there to observe" their leader (FG1: P1). The "power of human interaction" was also stressed in the four focus groups where this power was "diminished in a virtual environment" (FG1: P6). Another relevant challenge was communication. One participant (FG1: P4) mentioned, "I don't answer text messages and I don't answer emails. I don't want to... because I really can't read them correctly... And the way that I'm going to respond to them would be completely different when I'm in person... I feel like traditional is way easier for me to read people and them to read me."

It was felt that students had certain expectations about their career prospects, and they had planned or envisioned these to be in a traditional work environment. The participants who already had full-time jobs expressed some preference for a hybrid type of leadership position. Their preferences were supported by a few reasons like life-work balance, life stage, focus, and commuting. P10 (FG2) said:

Currently, I get to work from home a couple of days out of the week... I feel like my focus at home is different than my... focus at the office... And a lot of that is for some of the reasons they said, you don't have people just walking by and doing like walk by and distracting you. You can fully focus on what you're working on with fewer distractions than you get in the workplace... But then I still get to go into the work office the other days of the week and get that personal interaction and... time with my coworkers.

P13 added "I think that, like traditional, is good for socialization and everything... Virtual is just very, very convenient... being able to do things on your own time when you can, is really good... for mental health." P16 commented on this saying "there are a lot of pluses for virtual working... I was just saying in a hundred percent work, life balance exists in a virtual world." It is relevant to mention that the five participants (P10, P13, P16, P19, & P20), who preferred a hybrid mode, already had full-time jobs for some years, and a hybrid mode would offer them some relief from the eight-to-five work routine.

Virtual Leadership Skills

The third section of the investigation focused on relevant virtual leadership skills. The data analysis highlighted several skills. The most dominant skill in the discussion was communication. With participants' awareness of the challenges imposed by the virtual work environment related to communication, participants believed that a virtual leader needed to possess exceptional virtual communication competencies. This included video conferencing etiquette, listening, reading, text chatting, and writing emails. On the latter, P7 (FG1) said:

Formatting is really important, especially for emails, because... if you send just a big paragraph, people are less likely to read that than if you have like short bullet points... Under those bullet points, you send like the paragraph, because then people can look at the bullet points of what is going to be discussed, and then they are like, okay, maybe I want to go look at this. It's like you need to get people...direction before sending them into like whatever you're trying to say... I think that really helps people read.

Participants (P3, P5, P8, P9, P13, & P18) also thought that virtual leaders needed to know how and when their teams preferred to communicate. The data showed that virtual leaders also should be able to communicate emotions, attitudes, and tone via written communication. One participant (P9) said, "Sometimes, emails do sound very rude... like if you do not say thank you or greet other people you can feel this is creating a communication gap." Virtual leaders also needed to be skilled in composing communication in an informal style and through informal channels. Multiple participants (n=14) mentioned that they preferred if their virtual leader communicated with them via text messaging. Participants believed that this channel of communication made them feel the messages were less formal and more personalized.

The second important skill found in the data was the ability to engage with others. Since participants understood that the virtual work environment created a sense of isolation and detachment from work and tasks, they believed that a successful virtual leader needed to be highly skilled in engaging team members. Virtual leaders needed to be "proactive and flexible" in redesigning tasks to be "more engaging and relevant" to team members (FG:4: P17). One participant (FG2: P8) said, "it is very hard to really know, understand, and engage with people you've never met... you need to have the knowledge... of how to make things exciting." Reference was made by participants (P3, P4, P12, P16, & P20) on possible strategies a virtual leader could use to get team members to be more engaged, e.g., interactive applications, video conferencing, and online group and team building activities. Some skills related to engaging others were mentioned in the focus group, e.g., motivation, focus, dedication, support, and accountability.

The third important skill was technological competency. In all four focus groups, participants stressed the reliance of virtual work on technology and its relevant applications. All participants believed that a virtual leader should know how to use relevant applications. In FG2, FG3, and FG4, participants (n=9) agreed that a virtual leader was a role model when it came to technology. A virtual leader's technological competency was believed to empower team engagement and commitment. One participant (P16) said, "You are the source and if you're not good with it (technologies), the team members would not care... and disconnect." Participants also believed that a virtual leader should be able to set up technological systems and even provide support to all team members. One participant (P1) said, "having a good grasp on virtual resources that can help in presenting and helping others in the team to present are very important... People still struggle with basic stuff... and would appreciate any support... like sharing screen on Zoom." Several examples of technological support were expected from a virtual leader. Some relevant applications were highlighted in the discussions including Google applications, emails, Zoom, online calendars, spreadsheets, collaborative cloud files, and MS Teams. It was also highlighted that a virtual leader needed to be flexible to learn new applications. One interesting issue to emerge from the data was that participants with professional experience (P10, P13, P14, P16, P19, & P20) showed more awareness of available collaborative applications and platforms.

Several less important skills also emerged from the data including adaptability, time management, organization, empathy, reliability, and establishing connection and trust. On adaptability, participants (n=8) believed that the virtual work environment was in a constant state of change, and leaders needed to be skilled in embracing this change and communicating it to the team members. Concerning time management, participants (n=6) believed it was a relevant skill since working from home could be distracting from work duties. The participants also believed that leaders should be sensitive to the fact that team members might be in different locations of the world with different time zones. Six participants thought that a virtual leader should be very organized with tasks and keep their work files organized, and calendars updated. Four participants thought that empathy was a relevant skill since it would help in understanding and connecting with team members. One participant (P11) said, "You're less inclined to feel about or understand... the team... because you've never met them... you need the ability... to understand that these are people and might have urgencies and stuff."

Discussion

As mentioned earlier, previous researchers have discussed the proximal and distal attributes of effective virtual leaders (Tuschner et al., 2022). When analyzing the results from the business student focus groups, the skills identified mirror many of these attributes. Thus, the results support at least one previous theoretical framework of virtual leadership. The participants were all business students, yet they had different experiences. While some were full-time students with little to no work experience, others were part-time students with full-time jobs (and multiple years of leadership experience). This provided a robust discussion about the similarities and differences between academic and occupational virtual environments. Regardless of the context, many of the participants mentioned similar differences associated with traditional and virtual environments. While there was considerable freedom when working from home, there were also many distractions present that do not exist in the traditional workplace. There was a consensus that communication was more difficult in the virtual environment when compared to the traditional environment. Another challenge mentioned in the virtual environment was the lack of social engagement. The participants within each focus group then discussed the skills necessary to overcome these challenges. Table 2 displays the frequency of each attribute/skill mentioned by each focus group. The frequency with which a skill was mentioned does not reflect the importance placed on said skill.

Table 1. Number of references to different virtual leader attributes/skills by focus group

	Attributes/Skills	Frequencies in Focus Groups (FG)				
		FG1	FG2	FG3	FG4	TOTALS
Proximal	Effective Communication	14	19	25	14	**72**
	Technological Competence	8	13	11	7	**39**
	Motivational	1	5	10	0	**16**
	Trust-Building	0	0	3	5	**8**
	Organizational Skills	4	0	1	8	**13**
	Aptitude Coaching	0	0	1	0	**1**
	Decision-Making	0	0	0	6	**6**
	Change Management	8	8	0	0	**16**
	Networking	0	0	0	0	**0**
Distal	Dimensions of Personality	1	0	5	2	**8**
	Cognitive Abilities	0	1	0	4	**5**
	Individual Motives	0	0	0	0	**0**
	Attitudes	0	0	2	2	**4**
	Core Beliefs	0	0	0	1	**1**

With that said, the proximal skills of communication, engagement, and technological competence were rated as the three most important skills across all four focus groups.

It is no surprise that communication skills emerged as the most important skill for a virtual leader to master. When the context of a face-to-face meeting is not present, there can be a disconnect between what is expected and what the employee thinks is expected if communication is poor. Therefore, emails should be easily read, or video meetings should be conducted to ensure that all team members are clear on what is expected of them. This reinforces VanWart et al.'s (2019) assertion that messages should be carefully encoded to reduce the risk of misunderstandings.

Engagement emerged as the second-most important skill for virtual leaders. This is related to the motivational aspects of leading a team, specifically demonstrating that everyone is a part of the team (Kuscu & Arslan, 2016). Using technological aids that bring virtual teams together can aid in creating a culture of engagement, which results in higher levels of motivation among team members. If team members can connect virtually using conferencing applications like Zoom or Microsoft Teams, then they are more likely to feel a part of the team (even if they cannot meet face-to-face). With motivation being an important part of employees working effectively in a virtual environment, keeping team members engaged is essential. Another challenge to engagement mentioned was leading teams when some members can be spread across multiple time zones. In situations like this, synchronous virtual meetings may not be possible, so leaders must be creative in keeping all members of the team engaged when some may be able to connect virtually and others can only contribute via email or file-sharing (e.g., Google Drive).

Though technological competence emerged as the third most important skill, it is noteworthy that technological competence plays a role in the first two vital skills of a virtual leader. First, participants mentioned that virtual leaders are the facilitators (or source) of the meetings usually through an application like Zoom or Microsoft Teams. If the leader has problems with basic technology (such as connecting all participants to the meeting or sharing the appropriate information for the meeting) then team members will likely lose interest and disengage. This supports previous research that indicates the role of technological competence in overcoming communication barriers (Byrd, 2019; Cortellazzo et al., 2019; Zigurs, 2003). Another aspect of technological competence is keeping up with the relevant software/applications. This helps with communication by making sure all team members have access to the relevant materials. For example, using applications like Google Drive allows people on a team to share many files at once so everyone sees the tasks completed by everyone else. With people able to access all files associated with the tasks at hand, team members can also review and provide feedback to improve the overall product.

While these three skills were rated as the most important, there were some other skills mentioned that helped handle the challenges associated with leading in a virtual environment. These other skills were categorized with the previously mentioned proximal skills. Since COVID-19, the work environment has shifted. Initially, this shift was necessitated by the need to socially distance. Now people have chosen to work from home when given the opportunity (Parker et al., 2022). Even though some of these skills were deemed less important (e.g., adaptability and organizational skills), they were still skills that are necessary for a virtual leader. For example, if a virtual leader has poor organizational skills this can influence their ability to communicate effectively, keep their team engaged (because of a poorly organized meeting), or not have the appropriate technology available.

While this study supports previous research in virtual leadership, there are some limitations. First, this study utilized a group of both on-campus and online students from a Midwestern university. While this could limit the generalizability of the results, the diversity of the participants (age, work experience, modality, and region) mitigates this deficiency. Also, focus groups provide more information by allowing for interaction among the participants and the ability for different points of view to inform the researchers on the topics discussed. Second, focus groups can be difficult to manage and not all participants may engage (Queiros et al., 2017). To prevent this issue, the focus groups were limited in size and the moderator prompted any participant who had not commented on a question to provide input.

CONCLUSION

Even with fewer COVID-19 restrictions, there is still a preference for working in a virtual environment when given the option (Gupta, 2020; Parker et al., 2022). Many participants echoed this preference when asked which environment they would prefer to work (preferring either a virtual or hybrid environment). However, given the challenges associated with leading in a virtual environment, participants indicated their preference to lead in a traditional environment. The results of this qualitative analysis demonstrate important skills necessary to navigate a virtual environment as well as the challenges associated with the virtual environment. Three skills emerged as important for virtual leaders including communication, the ability to engage (or motivate), and technological competence. The relationship among these skills is important to note when examining the effectiveness of virtual leaders. What is also important to note is that acquiring these skills does not happen without appropriate training. The results of this study provide context to guide future training. Whether it is professional development within an individual's place of employment or in a higher education setting, the existence of multiple modalities (i.e., both traditional and virtual environments) will influence how future leaders are trained.

This group of business students demonstrated an awareness of the skills necessary to be an effective virtual leader, which was the purpose of this study. A future direction is to determine how universities, specifically business schools, are developing these skills in their students. In essence, how are they preparing their students to operate effectively in a virtual environment so they can become effective virtual leaders if it is ever necessary to work in a virtual environment? With the growing presence of the virtual environment, universities should follow recommendations like those from Rohs et al. (2015) and evaluate the extent to which their programs prepare their students to operate in both traditional and virtual environments. For example, are assessments of communication skills not only addressing oral communication in a face-to-face setting but also addressing clarity when communicating with team members in a virtual setting? Another skill that should be addressed to prepare people for both traditional and virtual environments is utilizing hands-on learning as a means of engaging with students as well as giving them tools they can use to engage with their team members in multiple environments. Finally, universities can enhance the technological competence of their students by utilizing different modalities for assessments that require different technologies. Addressing how higher education trains future leaders, especially in the business context, will be essential to adapt to the changing market needs following COVID-19.

REFERENCES

Alward, E., & Phelps, Y. (2019). Impactful leadership traits of virtual leaders in higher education. *Online Learning : the Official Journal of the Online Learning Consortium, 23*(3), 72–93. doi:10.24059/olj.v23i3.2113

Avlani, A., & Charalampous, M. (2021). *Exploring the significance of remote leadership competencies in the virtual workplace: A systematic literature review*. Semantic Scholar. doi:10.31124/advance.14781744.v1

Bellei, C., & Cabalin, C. (2013). Chilean student movements: Sustained struggle to transform a market-oriented educational system. *Current Issues in Comparative Education, 15*(2), 108–123.

Brake, T. (2006). Leading global virtual teams. *Industrial and Commercial Training, 38*(3), 116–121. doi:10.1108/00197850610659364

Buiza, F., Aguirre-Parra, P., Garcia-Jimenez, M., & Torres, D. (2021). Corporate social responsibility actions in agribusiness: towards sustainable community development. In *2021 IEEE Sciences and Humanities International Research Conference (SHIRCON)* (pp. 1-4). IEEE. https://doi.org/10.1109/SHIRCON53068.2021.9652243

Byrd, L. (2019). Virtual action learning for virtual leadership development. *Performance Improvement, 58*(8-9), 20–25. doi:10.1002/pfi.21894

Cortellazzo, L., Bruni, E., & Zampieri, R. (2019). The role of leadership in a digitalized world: A review. *Frontiers in Psychology, 10*, 1–21. doi:10.3389/fpsyg.2019.01938 PMID:31507494

Creswell, J., & Creswell, D. (2017). *Research Design: Qualitative, Quantitative, and Mixed Methods Approaches* (5th ed.). SAGE Publishing.

Darics, E. (2020). E-leadership or "how to be boss in instant messaging?" The role of nonverbal communication. *International Journal of Business Communication, 57*(1), 3–29. doi:10.1177/2329488416685068

DasGupta, P. (2011). Literature review: e-leadership. *Emerging Leadership Journeys, 4*(1), 1-36. Retrieved from https://www.regent.edu/acad/global/publications/elj/vol4iss1/home_vol4iss1.htm

DeRue, D., Nahrgang, J., Wellmann, N., & Humphrey, S. (2011). Trait and behavioral theories of leadership: An integration and meta-analytic test of their relative validity. *Personnel Psychology, 64*(1), 7–52. doi:10.1111/j.1744-6570.2010.01201.x

Ejimabo, N. (2015). The influence of decision making in organizational leadership and management activities. *Journal of Entrepreneurship & Organization Management, 4*(2), 2222–2839. doi:10.4172/2169-026X.1000138

Flores, K., Matkin, G., Burbach, M., Quinn, C., & Harding, H. (2012). deficient critical thinking skills among college graduates: Implications for leadership. *Educational Philosophy and Theory, 44*(2), 212–230. doi:10.1111/j.1469-5812.2010.00672.x

Garcia, I. (2015). Emergent leadership: Is e-leadership importance in the quality of virtual education? *RIED: Revista Iberoamericana de Educacion a Distancia, 18*(1). Advance online publication. doi:10.5944/ried.18.1.13798

Gierlich-Joas, M., Hess, T., & Neuburger, R. (2020). more self-organization, more control—Or even both? Inverse transparency as a digital leadership concept. *Business Research, 13*(3), 921–947. doi:10.100740685-020-00130-0

Gleason, N. (2018). *Higher Education in the Era of the Fourth Industrial Revolution*. Springer Nature. doi:10.1007/978-981-13-0194-0

Gupta, A. (2020). *Accelerating Remote Work after COVID-19*. The Center for Growth & Opportunity.

Hoffman, B., Woehr, D., Maldagen-Youngjohn, R., & Lyons, B. (2011). Great man or great myth? A quantitative review of the relationship between individual differences and leader effectiveness. *Journal of Occupational and Organizational Psychology, 84*(2), 347–381. doi:10.1348/096317909X485207

Hunsaker, P., & Hunsaker, J. (2008). Virtual teams: A leader's guide. *Team Performance Management, 14*(1/2), 86–101. doi:10.1108/13527590810860221

Jaffe, R., & Lordan, G. (2020) Five Behavioural Science lessons for managing virtual team meetings. *LSE Business Review*. Available at http://eprints.lse.ac.uk/id/eprint/104808

Johnson, K. (2010). *Virtual Leadership: Required Competencies for Effective Leaders*. Retrieved from https://ecommons.cornell.edu/bitstream/handle/1813/73721/Virtual_Leadership.pdf?sequence=1

Kane, G. C., Phillips, A. N., Copulsky, J., & Andrus, G. (2019). How digital leadership is (n't) different. *MIT Sloan Management Review, 60*(3), 34–39.

Keane, T., Linden, T., Hernandez-Martinez, P., & Molnar, A. (2022). University students' experiences and reflections of technology in their transition to online learning during the global pandemic. *Education Sciences, 12*(7), 453–468. doi:10.3390/educsci12070453

Kerfoot, K. (2010). Listening to see: The key to virtual leadership. *Nursing Economics*, *28*(2), 114. doi:10.1097/00006416-199707000-00008 PMID:20446383

Kiron, D., Kane, G. C., Palmer, D., Phillips, A. N., & Buckley, N. (2016). Aligning the organization for its digital future. *MIT Sloan Management Review*, *58*(1).

Klus, M., & Müller, J. (2021). The digital leader: What one needs to master today's organisational challenges. *Journal of Business Economics*, *91*(8), 1189–1223. doi:10.100711573-021-01040-1

Kramer, R. (2005). *Developing Global Leaders: Enhancing Competencies and Accelerating the Expatriate Experience*. The Conference Board. Retrieved from https://www.conference-board.org/publications/publicationdetail.cfm?publicationid=1058

Kuscu, M., & Arslan, H. (2016). Virtual leadership at distance education teams. *Turkish Online Journal of Distance Education*, *17*(3), 136–156. doi:10.17718/tojde.79230

Licite-Kurbe, L., & Leonovica, R. (2021). Economic benefits of remote work from the employer perspective. In *Proceedings of the 2021 International Conference of Economic Science for Rural Development* (pp. 345-354). 10.22616/ESRD.2021.55.034

Loucks, S., & Ozogul, G. (2020). Preparing business students for a distributed workforce and global business environment: Gaining virtual leadership skills in an authentic context. *TechTrends*, *64*(4), 655–665. doi:10.100711528-020-00513-4

Lu, L., Shen, C., & Williams, D. (2014). Friending your way up the ladder: Connecting massive multiplayer online game behaviors with offline leadership. *Computers in Human Behavior*, *35*, 54–60. doi:10.1016/j.chb.2014.02.013

Maduka, N., Edwards, H., Greenwood, D., Osborne, A., & Babatunde, S. (2018). Analysis of competencies for effective virtual team leadership in building successful organisations. *Benchmarking*, *25*(2), 696–712. doi:10.1108/BIJ-08-2016-0124

Mehtab, K., Rehman, A., Ishfaq, S., & Jamil, R. (2017). Virtual leadership: A review paper. *Mediterranean Journal of Social Sciences*, *8*(4), 183. doi:10.2478/mjss-2018-0089

Miles, M., Huberman, M., & Saldana, J. (2019). *Qualitative Data Analysis: A Methods Sourcebook* (4th ed.). SAGE Publishing.

Mohammad, K. (2009). E-Leadership: The emerging new leadership for the virtual organization. *Journal of Managerial Sciences*, *3*(1).

Mumford, T., Campion, M., & Morgeson, F. (2007). The leadership skills strataplex: Leadership skill requirements across organizational levels. *The Leadership Quarterly*, *18*(2), 154–166. doi:10.1016/j.leaqua.2007.01.005

Norman, S., Avey, J., Larson, M., & Hughes, L. (2020). The development of trust in virtual leader–follower relationships. *Qualitative Research in Organizations and Management*, *15*(3), 279–295. doi:10.1108/QROM-12-2018-1701

Oppenheim, A. (2000). *Questionnaire Design, Interviewing and Attitude Measurement.* Bloomsbury Publishing.

Orte, C., & Dino, M. (2019). Eliciting e-leadership style and trait preference among nurses via conjoint analysis. *Enfermeria Clinica, 29,* 78–80. doi:10.1016/j.enfcli.2018.11.025

Panteli, N., Hjeltnes, T., & Strand, K. (2019). Learning to lead online collaborations: insights from student-based global virtual teams between UK and Norway. *Conference on e-Business, eServices, and e-Society. Springer,* 785–796. 10.1007/978-3-030-29374-1_64

Parker, K., Horowitz, J., & Minkin, R. (2022). *COVID-19 pandemic continues to reshape work in America.* Pew Research Center. Retrieved from https://www.pewresearch.org/social-trends/2022/02/16/covid-19-pandemic-continues-to-reshape-work-in-america/

Philip, J., & Gavrilova Aguilar, M. (2022). Student perceptions of leadership skills necessary for digital transformation. *Journal of Education for Business, 97*(2), 86–98. doi:10.1080/08832323.2021.1890540

Pokojski, Z., Kister, A., & Lipowski, M. (2022). Remote work efficiency from the employers' perspective—What's next? *Sustainability (Basel), 14*(7), 4220. doi:10.3390u14074220

Purvanova, R., Charlier, S., Reeves, C., & Greco, L. (2021). Who emerges into virtual team leadership roles? The role of achievement and ascription antecedents for leadership emergence across the virtuality spectrum. *Journal of Business and Psychology, 36*(4), 713–733. doi:10.100710869-020-09698-0

Queiros, A., Faria, D., & Almeida, F. (2017). Strengths and limitations of qualitative and quantitative research methods. *European Journal of Education Studies, 3*(9), 369–387. doi:10.5281/zenodo.887089

Rohs, M., Vogel, C., & Marks, S. (2015). From supply-driven to demand-oriented academic education: Evidence-based development of study courses to match regional skill shortage with new student groups. *12th PASCAL International Observatory Conference.*

Roman, A., VanWart, M., Wang, X., Liu, C., Kim, S., & McCarthy, A. (2019). Defining e-leadership as competence in ICT-mediated communications: An exploratory assessment. *Public Administration Review, 79*(6), 853–866. doi:10.1111/puar.12980

Roy, S. (2012). Digital mastery: The skills needed for effective virtual leadership. *International Journal of e-Collaboration, 8*(3), 56–66. doi:10.4018/jec.2012070104

Savolainen, T. (2014). Trust-building in e-leadership: A case study of leaders' challenges and skills in technology-mediated interaction. *Journal of Global Business Issues, 8*(2).

Shah, S., & Patki, S. (2020). Getting traditionally rooted Indian leadership to embrace digital leadership: Challenges and way forward with reference to LMX. *Leadership, Education, Personality. An Interdisciplinary Journal, 2*(1), 29–40. doi:10.136542681-020-00013-2

Torre, T., & Sarti, D. (2020). The "Way" toward e-leadership: Some evidence from the field. *Frontiers in Psychology, 11,* 1–14. doi:10.3389/fpsyg.2020.554253 PMID:33262721

VanWart, M., Roman, A., & Pierce, S. (2016). The rise and effect of virtual modalities and functions on organizational leadership: Tracing conceptual boundaries along the e-management and e-leadership continuum. *Transylvanian Review of Administrative Sciences*, *12*(1), 102–122. doi:10.24193/tras.si2021

VanWart, M., Roman, A., Wang, X., & Liu, C. (2017). Integrating ICT adoption issues into (e-) leadership theory. *Telematics and Informatics*, *34*(5), 527–537. doi:10.1016/j.tele.2016.11.003

VanWart, M., Roman, A., Wang, X., & Liu, C. (2019). Operationalizing the definition of e-leadership: Identifying the elements of e-leadership. *International Review of Administrative Sciences*, *85*(1), 80–97. doi:10.1177/0020852316681446

Vrana, J., & Singh, R. (2021). A design thinking perspective. *Journal of Nondestructive Evaluation*, *40*(1), 1–24. doi:10.100710921-020-00735-9 PMID:33424070

Wargin, J., & Dobiéy, D. (2001). E-business and change–managing the change in the digital economy. *Journal of Change Management*, *2*(1), 72–82. doi:10.1080/714042483

Williamson, S., Pearce, A., Dickinson, H., Weeratunga, V., & Bucknall, F. (2021). *Future of Work Literature Review: Emerging Trends and Issues*. Retrieved from https://apo.org.au/node/314497

Yener, H. (2022). Evaluating employee attitudes on working home style during COVID-19 pandemic. *Technium Social Sciences Journal*, *28*, 490–504.

Zaccaro, S. J. (2007). Trait-based perspectives of leadership. *The American Psychologist*, *62*(1), 6–16. doi:10.1037/0003-066X.62.1.6 PMID:17209675

Zaitseva, E., & Goncharova, N. (2020). Planning, design, and management of educational programs. In *ICERI2020 (International Conference of Education, Research, and Innovation)* Proceedings (pp. 796-800). IATED 10.21125/iceri.2020.0235

Zigurs, I. (2003). Leadership in virtual teams: Oxymoron or opportunity? *Organizational Dynamics*, *31*(4), 339–351. doi:10.1016/S0090-2616(02)00132-8

Zohar, I. (2015). "The art of negotiation" leadership skills required for negotiation in time of crisis. *Procedia: Social and Behavioral Sciences*, *209*, 540–548. doi:10.1016/j.sbspro.2015.11.285

Chapter 17
Anglophone Shattered Hopes and Lost Illusions:
Post-Pandemic Political Leadership

Sureyya Yigit
New Vision University, Georgia

ABSTRACT

This chapter investigates within the realm of political communication transformational and transactional leadership during and after the COVID-19 pandemic. It attempts to identify which qualities and styles political leaders need to incorporate in the face of such challenges such as the COVID-19 pandemic. It focuses on the actions taken by Trump, Johnson, Marin, and Ardern within the fields of public health strategies, education, and employment to draw a clear and contrasting portrait of the political landscape regarding trustworthy and resilient leadership.

INTRODUCTION

Courage is grace under pressure. – Ernest Hemingway

In predictions for the future, there are dystopias such as Huxley's Brave New World, where technology allows governments to exercise greater regulation of society, whereby totalitarian states can control how their subjects think and act. Equally, there are utopias penned by philosophers, such as Sir Thomas More's idyllic island life. There are, of course, no guarantees that hope will transform into reality. More often than not, circumstances do not improve markedly.

The second decade of the second millennium was a good illustration of this. In the first months of the year 2020, we witnessed a radical global change. The world as we knew it became unrecognisable. Face-to-face social interactions among citizens were drastically reduced almost everywhere due to the Covid-19 pandemic. At its high point during the spring of 2020, almost two-thirds of the global population lived in mandatory confinement (Bates et al., 2020).

DOI: 10.4018/978-1-6684-8257-5.ch017

This led to the declaration of a state of emergency by numerous States, the closure of external borders, the interruption of face-to-face activity in educational institutions, the closure of factories and entertainment venues, restricted access to all kinds of public spaces, the reduction of physical mobility, the requirement of home confinement, isolation and social distancing to prevent contagion. Populist leaders attempted to turn this crisis into a unique opportunity to elevate their standing and extend their hold on the state apparatus. Thus, an unprecedented event was experienced whereby nation-states transformed themselves into sanitary Leviathans, which even Hobbes probably never imagined, effectively imposing a strict global quarantine. Consequently, through the expedited use of technology, security - especially the surveillance paradigm - has been extended, resurfacing the border as a security artefact through controlling certain mobilities (Csernatoni, 2020). In other words, welcome to the brave new world.

Certainly, global uncertainty has disrupted the foundations of what is established and confronts humanity with new ways of understanding the personal, social, economic, political and cultural. These phenomena imply a systemic crisis that opens new socio-political horizons that may well reinforce the dynamics inherited from the past or may contribute to the change of the world system (Zattoni & Pugliese 2021).

Undoubtedly, many social changes that were already underway have been accelerated, but past practices and structures are also being reproduced. Indeed, in this new context, certain previous dynamics influencing political systems have intensified. For several decades, democratic politics has been characterised by a short-term vision and stark competition for power between candidates to lead the public space and national political institutions, the latest examples of which have been Donald Trump and Boris Johnson.

Two interrelated questions must be asked in the present uncertain and complex world: what features define the socio-political context in which political leadership must function? What qualities and styles do these leaders need to incorporate in the face of such challenges of the Covid-19 pandemic? How have Anglophone political leaders responded to the pandemic? Which type of political leadership has proven more effective in such a crisis and beyond?

This chapter addresses these questions with a strong focus on the phenomenon of political leadership, with a heavy emphasis on political communication. Liberal democracies, face the dilemma of accountability to local citizens in a decision-making process that goes beyond the limits of national politics since various international organisations such as the European Union, United Nations, World Bank, and World Health Organization (WHO) influence and condition the definition of national public policies (Kenwick & Simmons, 2020, Hirschmann, 2021). This research demonstrates how the state sphere has adapted to the globalised world in recent decades. The concept of globalisation and how it contributes to understanding disaster management policies in the current context is analysed. Lastly, there is a brief theoretical review of political leadership and an attempt to conceptualise it from the perspective of the pandemic to understand current political dynamics. Finally, one needs to reflect on the context and qualities of leadership in this new environment.

Methodological Bases of Research

Socio-political concepts condense historical experiences and articulate networks or plots of meaning, which gives it an inevitably multi-faceted character. In a concept, sedimented meanings correspond to different times and circumstances of enunciation, which are put into play in each of its effective uses. From here, one can derive the fundamental characteristic of a concept that can be defined and used precisely because of its ability to transcend its original context and project itself in time (Yigit, 2022). Next, in addition to reviewing the main perspectives and historical uses attributed to the concept of leadership, a definition that transcends the previous contexts in which it has been used is delved into so that it can be useful for understanding leadership processes and politicians in a new world. Thus, the most important debates and theories about the concept must be summarised to reflect on political leadership during and after the Covid-19 pandemic.

Political leadership is a multidisciplinary field of study due to its omnipresent and universal character, having given rise to numerous publications ranging from Blondel to Machiavelli, from Nye to Weber. However, there is no universally accepted definition of leadership nor an agreed definition in the Social Sciences. Thus, leadership is one of human history's most observed and least understood phenomena (Faris & Outcalt, 2001). Leadership is a phenomenon that penetrates practically all human social relations, being the subject of innumerable empirical and theoretical studies, from which the following characteristics emerge: plurality, fragmentation, ambiguity, equivocation and confusion (McMahan & Evans, 2018). Therefore, the definitions of political leadership have increased as studies on the subject have done so (Masciulli, Molchanov & Knight, 2016).

In the post-pandemic context, it is instructive to highlight a dozen significant features: 1) recruit professional experts in the field that have greater experience and knowledge than oneself; 2) listen to the ideas of subordinates; 3) settle important issues directly with relevant colleagues; 4) create a welcoming environment where staff can demonstrate honesty and authenticity and feel comfortable to talk about their weaknesses - to ensure that conflicts do not overflow; 5) establish and cultivate a mission specific to everyone - an overarching goal that oversees daily tasks - as well as a clear vision or mission, renewable and constantly updated for the whole of the government; 6) build an environment that promotes frequent and close interactions between ministries; 7) measure the indicators that are essential; 8) define, prioritise and clearly communicate governmental priorities; 9) foster a culture and develop a mechanism that ensure improvement and positive change; 10) bear in mind that emotional rewards matter more than material rewards; 11) demonstrate integrity through leading by example and commitments; and 12) prepare their organisation to react intelligently in the event of further unforeseen situations. Within such a context, it is also important to remember that diversity is essential for questions of equality and strengthening the governmental ability to solve complex health and related problems and maximise results.

Literature Review

Such a situation corresponds to three basic problems in leadership studies: on the one hand, the multiplicity of disciplines that have addressed the study of this phenomenon in its broadest conception, among which are Anthropology, Political Science, Philosophy, Psychology, Sociology and Organizational Theory. On the other hand, the diversity of approaches conceived for its analysis is the theory of personality traits, behaviourism, positional perspective, situationism-contingent, constructivism and new leadership (Parry & Bryman, 2006). Lastly, a common problem in leadership studies is that keywords with multiple meanings are used without clarifying which meaning the author refers to when s/he uses them, which causes various confusion.

Despite the multiple understandings of the concept, there is a certain consensus in identifying that the main ideas about political leadership come from three perspectives. The first corresponds to the writings of classical thinkers who approach the study of the leader in terms of the "Great Man" and his defining qualities. In this group, we find the following typifications of the leader: the philosopher king (Plato), the prince (Machiavelli), the hero (Carlyle) and the superman (Nietzsche). These studies highlight the subjective-personal dimensions of the leader. The second perspective is represented by thinkers who emphasise the role of situations and contexts in the social production of leadership. This perspective is represented by the invisible hand (Smith), social evolutionism (Spencer), the class struggle (Marx) and the rebellion of the masses (Ortega y Gasset). For Ortega, mass society produces rejection of minorities and leaders due to the learning of the average man that all men are legally equal (Dinnin, 2019). These authors highlight the objective-impersonal conditions in how leaders are formed.

Finally, since the 1940s, it has been about reconciling the two previous perspectives. In this regard, the classic study that fuses the two traditional perspectives was developed by Stogdill and Bass in the so-called relational-interactionist dogma of leadership (Fiedler, 2006). Since Stogdill's work was published, many researchers have recognised the interaction between personal traits and social situations in shaping leaders. In this sense, Hollander elaborated a transactional theory that combines the situational approach with a component of social exchange centred on the reciprocal influences between leader and followers (Hollander, 2013). Likewise, Burns highlighted several aspects of this multidimensional and complex phenomenon: leadership, which is based on conflict, being collective - interaction between leader, followers and society - being resolute and determined, and adopting two basic styles: transformational and transactional (Bass, 1995).

For his part, Tucker conceived political leadership as a process linked to political activity in all those community states where power seeks to legitimise itself (Tucker, 1995). Thus, Tucker identifies leadership with the political sphere and participation in public life, for which he calls for a normative approach to leadership. This approach and its recent developments are relevant to the combination of the leader's characteristics, the values s/he defends and the social scenarios of his actions. More recently, Blondel and Thiébault have highlighted three psychological ties that maintain the leader-follower relationship: political discourse that persuades citizens and party support; the direct leader-citizen relationship through the clientelism, patronage or control of the media; and the reaction of the people to the leaders based on notoriety, popularity and charisma (Blondel & Thiébault, 2010).

All this produces an intense process of leadership personalisation, accompanied by the growing importance of political leaders and their leading role in the media in a presidentialization of politics in systems surrendered and traversed by digital communication tools (Poguntke & Webb, 2005). Effective political communication becomes paramount in a pandemic crisis as the timescale for action is limited (Finset et al., 2020). Effective leader communication informs the public about what is happening during an unprecedented crisis and provides a rationale for implementing policies (Dirani et al., 2020).

Douillet asserts that if the Covid-19 crisis requires a global response, the question of emphasising the local thus makes it possible to understand better how different levels of public action are concretely articulated (Douillet, 2020). Above all, it is at the local level that public policies are implemented and whether their success or failure is at stake. Understanding crisis management from below allows both to understand better the logic of local actors of the first rank, such as mayors and council leaders, to reintegrate into the analysis the constraints they face and to collect elements that will later make it possible to contribute to the evaluation of the public policies implemented.

Through a critical analysis vis-à-vis the long lack of foresight of the international community in the face of the pandemic risk and the responses it deems, Berg believes it to be too indiscriminate and often disproportionate (Berg, 2020). It highlights the serious and lasting consequences of this epidemic, "an economic, social and democratic tsunami", which risks more damage than that sought to be avoided, including morbidity and mortality.

Brown concentrates upon the attraction of history in times of crisis to gain useful lessons from the past to create a base for optimism and provide a perspective on the present by allowing people to see it through the lenses of time and social evolution (Brown, 2021).

Coccia investigates the impact on public health of Italy's first and second waves of COVID-19 (Coccia, 2020). The former had a strong but declining impact on public health with the upcoming summer season, and with the effects of containment measures, the latter had a growing trend of confirmed cases. In contrast, deaths had a stationary trend with a lower impact on public health. Lessons from this can illuminate designing effective policy responses to crisis management such as pandemics.

Dergiades, Milas, Mossialos, et al. assess the quantitative impact of government interventions on deaths related to the COVID-19 outbreak (Dergiades, Milas, Mossialos, et al. 2020). Early state interventions lead to slowing down or reversing the growth rate of deaths. School closures also significantly impacted reducing the growth rate of deaths.

Gao, Yin, Jones, et al. demonstrate patterns of policy interactions; whilst states displayed highly heterogeneous policy attention to COVID-19, there was an evolving policy focus from public health to broader social issues with the World Health Organization's policy documents becoming central to the COVID-19 policy network focusing extensively on scientific literature (Gao, Yin, Jones, et al. 2020).

Buthe, Barcelo, Cheng et al. highlight federal political structures developing effective policies compared to those with unitary political structures finding the former more likely to possess heterogeneity in their policy responses than the latter (Buthe, Barcelo, Cheng, et al. 2020).

Abbasi focuses on protecting civil liberties, finding citizens' clear willingness to renege on civil liberties for better public health conditions (Abbasi, 2020). Second, exposure to health risks is associated with citizens' greater willingness to trade off civil liberties; third, a gradual decline followed by an overall willingness to sacrifice rights and freedom as the pandemic progressed.

Trump's Perilous Pandemic Leadership

In January 2020, President Trump publicly stated that the pandemic was under control, indicating it only related to a single person from China. He praised President Xi for handling the coronavirus and greatly appreciated their efforts and transparency. His National Security Advisor at the time informed him that this would be the biggest national security threat faced so far in his presidency. His Trade Advisor drew attention to the lack of immune protection, or an existing cure would leave millions of Americans in a precarious situation.

In February, Trump claimed that the matter was at hand though privately, he told journalist Bob Woodward that the virus was deadly. Publicly he predicted that by April, it would simply vanish like a miracle that the coronavirus was under control and congratulated himself on his handling. Trump reassured the public that there would be no more cases within a few days as the figures were decreasing remarkably, as what was being faced was just the flu. He prophesized that it would disappear miraculously without providing any scientific evidence.

In March, he shared his conviction that the coronavirus was very mild as hundreds of thousands of Americans were getting better by going to work. Once again, he self-congratulated himself, asking for calm and claiming the disease would disappear. Moreover, he declared that medical experts congratulated him on his knowledge and understanding concerning the coronavirus, that he possessed a natural ability, and that he should have pursued a medical career rather than politics. He stated that he was unconcerned about rising cases as there was a coordinated and fine-tuned plan. Whereas the World Health Organization categorised the coronavirus as a pandemic, Trump reiterated that it would simply go away and that the risk to a vast majority of Americans was very, very low. As the Director of the National Institute of Allergy and Infectious Diseases, Dr Anthony Fauci, told Congress that the health system was failing and not geared to what was needed, Trump rated his own coronavirus response as ten out of ten. He agreed that it was a very contagious virus, but his government had tremendous control over it, and the only thing he could have done better was getting good press. Paradoxically, he declared that he had felt like it was a pandemic long before it was called a pandemic, though he never closed the country for flu and that Americans would be working again by Easter. Unfortunately, the United States became the country with the most confirmed coronavirus cases, which remained the case for the rest of Trump's time in office. He opposed hospital demands for tens of thousands of ventilators. He vented his frustration at the governors of Washington and Michigan, wanting them to appreciate the great job being done. By the end of the month, he accepted that many people were dying, stubbornly hanging on to his belief that it would go away, that people knew it was going away, and that there would be a great victory. On March 30, he made contradictory remarks concerning testing. It was first, declaring that America was testing more than any other nation in the world, that it possessed great tests, and that he had not heard about testing as a problem. Later in the day, he asserted that he had inherited a broken test system, that the whole thing was broken; it was not the flu but something vicious.

In April, Trump's response to governors pleading for medical equipment and ventilators to treat surging coronavirus hospitalisations was that they had insatiable appetites and should have stocked up and be ready long before the crisis hit, suggesting the Federal Government was merely a backup for state governments. He voiced his personal opposition to wearing face masks when greeting foreign dignitaries as the death toll passed 10,000. Quite remarkably, he recommended taking Hydroxychloroquine; which was well worth trying despite not having FDA approval to treat coronavirus. He suggested using a disinfectant that would end the coronavirus in a minute, to research ways to inject to carry out cleansing, whether through ultraviolet or a very powerful light, with the people who knew him considering him the hardest working President in history. At the end of the month, he repeated his mantra that the coronavirus would go away.

In May, he predicted more deaths after which the virus would pass, with or without a vaccine. That the country would return to normal, he rejected nurses' criticisms of medical equipment supply being sporadic as it was not sporadic for many other people. Concerning vaccines, he declared that the disease would go away without a vaccine, alongside testing being overrated. Oddly, it was due to testing; he claimed that America had more cases than other countries as they conducted more testing. Nevertheless, it would go away, and they would not see it again. Trump proclaimed major progress stating that coronavirus numbers were decreasing almost everywhere and that the government had faced the crisis and prevailed. More cases were a badge of honour as it meant American testing was much better. By the end of the month, the death toll passed 100,000, and Trump terminated America's relationship with the World Health Organization.

In June, Trump declared that the coronavirus had at some point gone away and was fading away, dying out as the numbers were starting to improve substantially. Testing had to be slowed down as it was a double-edged sword due to it discovering more cases. He suddenly identified the disease as the ChinaVirus, with the mortality rate dramatically decreasing, being, in fact, one of the lowest in the world, which fake news did not like to dwell upon. In actual fact, with the death toll above 120,000, the U.S. had 4% of the global population but 25% of global coronavirus cases and the second-highest death rate per capita.

Anglophone Shattered Hopes and Lost Illusions

At the very beginning of July, Trump hoped and believed that the coronavirus, at some point, would disappear. He threatened to cut funding to states that did not open schools, disagreeing with the Centre for Disease Control's guidelines for opening schools. Trump revealed that the country had one of the lowest mortality rates in the world, with many cases consisting of young people who would heal in 24 hours. As the U.S. death toll passed 150,000, he referred to Fauci's high approval rating, asking why he himself did not have a high approval rating concerning the virus.

In August, when Fauci suggested America had seen more cases than its European counterparts as it only partially shut down its economy, Trump again reiterated that there were more cases because more were tested. However, everything was under control, asserting that children were almost immune from the disease. By the middle of the month, the country had reported the highest number of COVID-19 deaths in one day since mid-May. He was irate at the Food and Drug Administration revoking Hydroxychloroquine and chloroquine for COVID-19 treatment stating that many in the medical profession disagreed. He accused the deep state at the FDA of making it hard for pharmaceutical firms to find people to test vaccines so that no progress could be made before the presidential election in November. At the end of the month, as the U.S. death toll passed 180,000 and over six million Americans tested positive for the coronavirus, he declared that he had done a great job in Covid but did not get the credit.

The State Under Attack in the New World

For the past half-century, there have been two relevant political phenomena in the world: on the one hand, the democratisation process of many countries in what has been identified as the "third wave" of democratisation; on the other, the nation-state has been subjected to strong influences from the international community that affect its central functions (Skaaning, 2020). Regarding the latter, the monopoly on the use of force has been influenced and transformed by international treaties that affect its sovereignty. Likewise, the accountability of national governments is increasingly oriented not only to voters but also to the supranational institutions of which the state is a part and the financial markets.

However, the development of such world organisations leads to the problem of democratic legitimacy of public policies carried out at the state level, in which broad layers of citizenship are expelled and not recognised in the decision-making process, policies and community life itself, due not only to persistent inequality but also to the social, institutional and technical complexity of socioeconomic processes. Thus, throughout the second decade of the 21st century, citizen proclamations have been seen throughout the Western world, which, in turn, have greatly impacted political behaviour.

Additionally, the ability to provide services and transfer income that contributes to the well-being of citizens and the redistribution of income has been limited due to the need to compete in international markets that demand low taxes, salary moderation and little regulation of the markets, particularly the labour market. Faced with this complex scenario, the dilemma of whether to opt for a "competitive state" or a "welfare state" arises (Habermas, 1995).

States cease becoming universal providers to become catalysts, enablers, protectors, guides, negotiators, mediators and consensus builders. Increasingly, the state is called to link the various actors involved in planning processes, regulation, consultation and decision-making. All of this has led to state political actors needing to be more able to manoeuvre to control the socioeconomic dimension of their territory and more aware of the influence of powerful pressure groups in national states and international organisations (Vaubel, 2006).

Likewise, on the international stage, the fall of the Berlin Wall and the end of the Cold War marked a crucial turning point defined by profound political-institutional, socioeconomic and symbolic-cultural transformations in international relations (Yigit, 2021a). In practice, such transformations have reconfigured local societies, nation-states, and public administrations across the planet. Although states remain the fundamental agents of the national and international political system in this changing scenario, their functions and roles are changing profoundly and rapidly.

Therefore, the way of governing and leading these states and administrations has changed in the past few decades. In addition, the Trump Administration renounced its capacity for world leadership. In parallel, the axis of global power began to shift to Asia, especially China and, to a much lesser extent, to India (Yiğit, 2021b). At the same time, we are witnessing the decline of Western Europe, especially in the southern countries where the Great Recession and the subsequent sovereign debt crisis have had more negative consequences. The Covid-19 pandemic involves important changes in the world system, and we may be at the gates of a new world frontier (Sarkis et al., 2020).

Undoubtedly, the recurring socioeconomic crises, the fiscal crisis of the state, market failures, economic deregulation, bureaucratic state policy, the orientation of public administrations towards the market and the aforementioned international transformations, transnational threats, as well as the growing complexity, diversity, fragmentation and interdependence of local societies —what is commonly conceived as globalisation— are calling for new ways of leading and governing in politics. Furthermore, these new ways of governing and leading must integrate into their agendas the relevance that global public problems acquire in the present world, such as climate change, demographic ageing, sustainable development, change in the energy paradigm, technological innovations, digitalisation of work, global migrations, whose dimensions go beyond the nation-state.

Thus, state-centric government systems based on bureaucratic hierarchy and legal rationality need to be revised and operate from their exclusively national visions. They need the necessary resources to address the problems, challenges and challenges that arise. However, neither are approaches to the market, for example, through privatisation and deregulation. In this way, it is increasingly evident that a new and complex world requires new ways of governing and leading public institutions. There has been a call for a new third way (Navarro, 2020). Added to this are the political deficit of modern, competent, impersonal, well-organised and autonomous states and the crises of legitimacy that liberal-democratic states have suffered for a long time as a consequence of the unfulfilled promises of democracies. In addition, other serious problems afflict polyarchies: political corruption, lack of responses to crises, international security problems, global environmental risks, the rise of populist options, and the excessive power of pressure groups (Boehmke, 2002). Likewise, the public policies developed within the framework of the social welfare state, led by the social democratic parties, have raised great doubts and bitter criticism in recent decades, which has led to the crisis of European social democracy. To illustrate the point, the British Labour Party has been out of power since 2010.

As a recipe to face all these difficulties, the diffusion of the term "good governance" has been produced in recent decades - despite its well-known variety of meanings and diversity of approaches with which its study can be approached - inviting us to reflect on the role of the state and society in public decisions and their interaction in situations in which resources are dispersed where political actors are increasingly interdependent (Yigit, 2021c). Thus, governance is understood as a functional-strategic approach more connected with the finalist and autonomous sense of government action and the development of different strategies of interventionist action. Specifically, governance designates a new governing method that differs from the hierarchical control model, a more cooperative way state and non-state actors participate in mixed public-private networks (Stengel & Baumann, 2017). Thus, among the characteristic notes of governance, the following stand out the interdependence between public, private and voluntary organisations; the relationships and exchange of resources between these agents; interactions based on trust in networks capable of self-organisation and not accountable to the state.

From Globalisation to Crisis Management

Globalisation is a process leading to a single world (Smart, 1994). Due to such processes, from the daily environments where economic, institutional or cultural social practices were developed and circumscribed to the local spheres of the national states, it has gradually passed to other environments of planetary scope. Due to this, the concepts of state and national society lack systemicity; they cannot be considered authentic social systems and, therefore, do not constitute legitimate units of analysis in the Social Sciences (Wallis & Valentinov, 2016). The driving force of the modern social system is the unlimited possibility of capital accumulation beyond national borders. Economic development is not so much that of a state or country but of a world hegemonic power (Wallerstein, 2007).

The process of globalisation must be considered as a context of the changes in which political leadership and government action are developed due to the relevant consequences that this process has on the traditional ability of the State to direct the society and to the transfer of powers to international institutions or those derived from the deregulation of international markets. For this reason, in a globalised society, political leadership and governance processes are not only directed from the state political structure but other structures (international organisations), and agents (multinationals, interest groups, non-governmental organisations) appear strongly, which can be decisive in global governance. Thus, governance, understood as a partial vision of government action, refers to the transformation in the interactions between the state and civil society, emphasising the latter's role and linking it with debates on citizenship in political action.

Therefore, more unusual dynamics are installed with a force that counteracts traditional logic and peremptorily moves us to different scenarios. The reactions to globalisation, market failures, inequalities in the distribution of wealth, deindustrialisation, a relocation that leads to massive unemployment, the plundering of resources, the problems of environmental issues, migratory movements, financial markets, the emptying of the role of the state and its diffuse sovereignty, have led to a questioning of the globalisation process and the pillars of the market system as the most efficient for individuals and societies. In the academic field, studies on mistrust in globalisation and the potential of regulation and compensatory strategies are flourishing, which at the national and transnational level could be shuffled to counteract social scepticism resulting from the growth of inequality, the perception of loss of identity or influence in the global and national security (Marginson, 2021). In addition, especially during the last decade, politics has undergone a great transformation that is reflected in the fact that, although the logic of formal democracy - electoral processes and appeals to citizens - expands more than ever in the discussions politicians and institutions engage in around the world, the democratic recession and the decline of the political sphere become persistent realities.

Recently, populism has been challenging liberal democracy planting its roots in the crisis of representation, especially in the aforementioned crisis of the parties that, together with the limitations of the globalisation of the market discussed above and the social fragmentation produced, become a breeding ground and create opportunities for populist contenders politicise economic insecurities and cultural resentments, in opposition to established traditional politics, giving simple answers to complex problems, using emotion and utilising the confrontation between "us" and "them" (Forgas & Crano, 2021). Modern populism seeks to establish a democratic, but not liberal, order reinforced in:

- A reliance on extraordinary charismatic leadership (witness the espoused styles of leadership demonstrated by Trump and Johnson)
- The relentless strategic pursuit of political polarization (the divisive language and accusations levelled at segments of society by Orban, Bolsanaro, Trump and Johnson provide ample evidence of such an approach, Trump initially expressly refusing to wear a face mask and trying to transform such action into an issue of constitutional freedom)
- A drive to seize control of the state, emasculate liberal institutions, and impose an illiberal constitution (The ATTACK on the U.S. Congress in January 2021, encouraged by Trump, is a vivid example of such behaviour)
- The systematic use of patronage to reward supporters and displace opposition (the dissolution list submitted by Johnson is a dramatic example of such action)

The resurgence of populism and populist leadership have constituted current global dynamics. This was precisely the context of the recent rise of populist leaders such as Donald Trump, Boris Johnson, Marine Le Pen, Viktor Orbán, Matteo Salvini, Jair Bolsonaro, and Giorgia Meloni.

Boris Johnson's Misguided Leadership

When the coronavirus was diagnosed in the United Kingdom, its impact grew progressively worse. Prime Minister Johnson's actions contributed to the worsening of the situation due to his leadership and policy preferences. For a start, Johnson misunderstood the case fatality ratio, the concept of herd immunity, and the risks posed to pensioners.

Johnson's judgment was called into question near the beginning of the crisis, and trust in him and his government was severely rocked in May 2020 when it emerged that his principal adviser had broken the government's COVID guidelines by driving his wife and son to another town nearly 300 miles away while he and his wife possibly had COVID symptoms. This created an uproar nationwide with accusations of double standards as the rest of the country was in a strict lockdown.

The "Test and Trace" programme implemented by the government led to hospitals facing shortages of personal protective equipment (PPE), primarily face masks. Those supplied were of poor quality, and some needed to be fit for purpose. The reason for such a drastic failure can be attributed to decisions made at the governmental level in awarding contracts to supply face masks and PPE to firms that had no prior experience in producing such products.

As the summer approached and the economy slumped, a new programme entitled "Eat Out to Help Out" was introduced. It aimed to encourage the public to go out to restaurants and spend. It turned out to be a disastrous idea as this programme increased new COVID infections. To try and help the economy, many more people suffered from the coronavirus.

At Christmas 2020, another major failure of governance and leadership was witnessed. Rejecting the prevailing scientific consensus and focusing on fringe views, the idea of acquiring herd immunity by natural infection gathered support. He was permitting and encouraging people to socially get together which proved to be a mitigated disaster resulting in thousands of COVID deaths, alongside the widespread emergence of the alpha variant. During the crisis, Johnson promised his government would assist poorer countries with free vaccines. Such pledges to distribute vaccines to lower-income countries did not materialise. By the autumn of 2021, of the promised 100 million doses, less than 10% had been provided.

Lastly, in late 2021 and early 2022, Johnson was repeatedly questioned whether rules had been broken concerning a series of Christmas gatherings held by governmental staff, which he dismissed. When the police investigated this matter, they confirmed that Johnson had broken his rules by attending a party celebrating his birthday. Johnson was issued with and paid a fine alongside his wife and Rishi Sunak, the current prime minister who at the time was serving as Johnson's chancellor.

The coronavirus infected the global supply chains that connect manufacturers and consumers, eroding the international order and emphasising nationalistic responses. The truth is that the foundations of the previous order are shaking, uncertainty and fear are spreading, and the role of leaders is more exposed than ever.

Political Leadership in a New World

This chapter considers an adequate understanding of political leadership supposes observing public leaders as subjects conditioned both by the circumstances of their personal-biographical and social origins and by the socio-historical and political dynamics experienced by them. That is, performing political leadership is much more than the mere occupation of a formal position: leading implies incorporating a set of biographical and social interdependencies in the historically configured political field, seeking results that transcend what is established and, therefore, go beyond the mere administration of current affairs or the management of routine problems. This is how leadership involves addressing difficulties in a contingent context, fighting against resistance to the leader's projects, transforming the existing reality, overcoming political-institutional inertia and inspiring citizens.

Specifically, political leadership consists of interaction-communication between people—political leaders and followers—who build significant links and relations of domination through various symbols such as slogans, speeches, ideologies, programs, and agreements in the socio-political context and social situation in which they find themselves.

In this panorama, political leadership can be conceived as a process developed by agents with various predispositions, motivations and objectives that mobilise, in competition or conflict with others, institutional, political, psychological and other resources, to stimulate, capture the attention and satisfy the wishes of the followers, as well as to try to impose a certain definition of reality in a socio-cultural and political scene, in which, in turn, the defended vision plays a key role by the leader. In sum, political leadership is, in essence, the action carried out around a series of recurring strategic challenges that political leaders and partisans must face, concentrating the work of the political leader on two main tasks: on the one hand, the construction of political identities in order to mobilise certain groups of followers; on the other, promoting and selecting certain public policies linked to said identities.

Thus, leadership is both a product and a producer of the inherited and established interdependencies between leader and followers. This context is potentially in a crisis at present, and through which the first is not always the protagonist or occupies the predominant position, to the extent that the leader can be overwhelmed by the demands of the followers, they have been able to rebel, and the context becomes very uncertain and changing - even becoming the definer of politicians' decisions in times of disaster or crisis as witnessed in recent years. In this way, contexts, followers and leaders are simultaneously important. Therefore, they must be conceived as three equally relevant factors and of equivalent weight in the leadership process, avoiding the mythification of the leaders. The strong leader may well be a socially constructed myth as a consequence of the human need to placate anxiety, uncertainty and fear in the face of unpredictable and unexpected changes since, in such contexts, the leader needs colleagues with political experience who know what they are doing and do not hesitate to express their disagreement with the person to whom they report. However, in scenarios such as the current systemic crisis caused by the Covid-19 pandemic or the 2008 Recession, authoritarian leadership is often requested and perceived as a viable alternative by various social groups convulsed. Thus, Boin warns about the tendency to centralise the decision-making of authoritarian leaders in disasters or systemic crises (Boin, 2019). In any case, whether or not such leaders exist, public opinion is usually interested in them and accepts an authoritarian and technocratic turn embodied in leadership that brings order as a response to chaos or disaster, as seen during the Covid-19 pandemic.

Consequently, the interactions between leaders, followers and contexts have to be analysed as factors of a communication process in which subjective and objective elements have to be considered; the personality reflected in the biography and the socialisation process of the leader, as well as the context or political field in which the leadership tries to institutionalise and legitimise itself before the followers. In this way, every process of political leadership is built on specific, changing or ephemeral circumstances: thus, it has been said that leadership is not static but rather dynamic (Foti, Knee Jr & Backert, 2008). In such circumstances, the leader experiences her/his socialisation process in which s/he apprehends her/his particular way of seeing the world, thinking, saying and doing things. Her/his possible political abilities and, thus, s/he makes her/his imprint in the political field by creating and consolidating the external means—institutions—on which the relationship between leaders and followers is based. Thus, in leadership, charisma plays a key role: the extraordinary qualities attributed to the leader, as well as the personal confidence, passionate dedication and firm belief that the leader inspires in her/his followers (Stone, Russell & Patterson, 2004). For this reason, sentimental and emotional bonds between leaders and followers can be positive or negative, depending on whether the former arouses more or less trust and dedication towards the actions and ideas they display. Such emotional attachments, feelings of attachment or aversion, can become stronger in times of crisis and lead to political polarisation.

Transformational and Transactional Leadership

Regarding the styles of political leadership, as indicated above, transformational leadership has been differentiated from transactional leadership. On the one hand, transactional or negotiation leadership consists of the exchange between leader and followers to approximate reciprocal needs and desires, for example, the exchange of jobs for votes. This leadership pursues values such as sincerity, honesty and responsibility. On the other hand, transformational leadership, in addition to exchanging mutual needs, eliminates followers if necessary since it pursues the achievement of absolute political ideals, even at the cost of eliminating the plurality of the public sphere. This differentiation has been very fruitful in studies on political leadership (Nye, 2013). According to this classification, transformational leadership is oriented towards substantive change processes at critical moments in the political community, such as the political regime change in a state or important transformations within the same regime, such as refounding political parties by their leaders.

For its part, transactional leadership is oriented towards current and operational changes in non-critical situations, such changes being necessary for the functioning of the political community, such as, for example, the reform of the administrative structure of a state to adapt it to socio-political changes. In addition, the difference between the aforementioned leadership styles is given by the relationship produced between the actors who lead and those who are led and how, in turn, such actors are related to socio-political contexts.

Thus, in transformational leadership, the relationship between leaders and followers occurs during great change, establishing a mutual moral commitment between the former and the latter to achieve one or more objectives that imply a substantial change - compared to the previous situation. Therefore, this leadership style appeals to great values such as morals and symbolism that refer to emotion and collective memory, conforming to the vision defended by the leader and strong bonds. Transactional leadership builds a relationship between leaders and followers based on the mutually beneficial exchange of one good—symbolic or material—for another (Sarros & Santora, 2001). Here, the link between those who point the way and those who are willing to follow it is much less intense than in the previous case and, in any case, it is a discontinuous, instrumental link.

Conventionally, transactional leadership is associated with socio-political stability, and transformational leadership is usually associated with great changes and socio-political ruptures. In other words: predictably, in contexts of great change, followers will tend to demand transformational and visionary leaders, while in moments of socio-political stability, followers will prefer transactional and practical leaders. However, at any time, human beings tend to behave by reproducing inherited ideas and practices, adopting reactive and far less proactive actions in the face of transformations.

Specifically, in modern societies, there are constant changes based on which various charismatic leaders emerge. However, many leaders perceived as such are overwhelmed by changing circumstances. There are exceptions to this rule, such as Ardern in New Zealand and Marin in Finland. A fundamental problem of leaders is their adaptation or maladjustment to contextual changes. Moreover therefore, the dilemma of change or die is presented tragically for leadership. This more adaptive, transactional and reformist leadership is often identified with the leadership of women leaders. This new leadership is more consistent with their assigned roles. One can witness the actions taken and the leadership demonstrated by the New Zealand and Finnish prime ministers.

Magical Marin: Finland's Fortune

Finnish prime minister Sanna Marin encouraged a shift from the traditional consensual governmental political control towards local authorities and relevant ministers to tackle the pandemic. The issue of facemasks became a constant feature discussed, especially on social media, becoming a point of trust and distrust that her government could not ignore. Marin, whilst legislating emergency powers, originally shifted control to the central government from regional authorities and municipalities at the beginning of the crisis in the spring of 2020. Later in the autumn, those powers were returned to regional and local authorities resulting in Finnish society and democracy enduring the crisis quite well. The seriousness of the situation was always stressed by several ministers, unveiling cross-sector effects and attempts to seek a solution to the crisis. This demonstrated the strength of the government and legitimated the use of emergency powers legislation.

Overall, Marin's approach and leadership enabled citizens to have confidence in the authorities and mutual communications. During the crisis, participation and confidence were high among those with high levels of education and good health; hence, a positive endorsement by the public contributed to keeping the crisis under control and extending vaccination coverage. Marin enjoyed high standings in terms of openness, transparency, trust and resilience in the face of unprecedented danger, demonstrating strong political will in integrating a strategy encompassing not only public health but education, employment and economic reintegration.

Like Germany and other countries, Finland adopted a "test, track, isolate, and treat" model to control and minimise the damage caused by the pandemic. Unlike Trump and Johnson, Marin tried to maintain low virus reproduction through actions that minimised infection rates and identified spread, sometimes loosening some and others imposing further lockdown measures. Overall, social media, especially Twitter, was a good and effective use to get the government message across to the public.

Marin encouraged and organised all-government parties' press conferences daily to inform the public of governmental actions. The government held press conferences daily. She demonstrated her willingness and preference for a consensus government, including all her ministers from various political parties, to portray a united front to the electorate.

It was in May 2020 that Marin agreed to start planning to lift restrictions; once more, a press conference which included all the government party leaders was held, declaring a new testing and tracing strategy. During the spring of 2020, Marin's all-female government made a powerful representational claim on controlling the pandemic, highlighted by a youthful, multivocal presence in its female-led press conferences. This was another indicator of Marin's inclusive and collaborative leadership focusing on political consensus.

Arduous Ardern: New Zealand Zeal

The New Zealand Covid-19 response has been celebrated as one of the most successful in the world. Prime Minister Ardern put forward an initial elimination strategy aimed at killing or eliminating the virus rather than purely containing it, which later transitioned to a mitigation strategy. The elimination strategy foresaw a complete ban on travel to the country and a strict national lockdown. This policy was successful as New Zealand had more than a hundred days without a single covid case.

Like Marin, she strove for political consensus, making policies in light of emerging scientific evidence, opting for transparency and maximising public communication (Craig, 2021). Ardern was similarly conscious of the need for a comprehensive response to the crisis that rightfully focused on public health and took measures in the realms of the economy and education. The first phase of her leadership witnessed a less severe 18 months of the pandemic until vaccines became widely available. This period was notable for its very low Covid-19 mortality rates; as remarkable as it may sound, life expectancy actually increased.

Ardern's government emphasised that public health was the ultimate priority and policies would primarily focus on that. This reflected her key leadership principles of listening to the scientific community and a strong focus on equal partnership with the Maori. This went hand in hand with her political consensus endeavour. Facing such an unprecedented uncertainty, Ardern was precautionary and aware that there would be a need to create legacy benefits for national healthcare and the public health system. She was aware that pandemics, by nature, are a shared threat; hence framing and effective communication becomes vital resources in combatting the crisis.

Transparency and political consensus were the hallmarks of Ardern's leadership throughout the pandemic. At the initial outset of the crisis, efforts were directed to achieve a multi-party agreement on the response. This was secured, though with the passage of time was lost, and the response became fragmented and politicised. Ardern demonstrated political courage by cutting off her island nation from the outside world, thus severely damaging the tourism industry to ensure the highest levels of public health.

The study of the impact of the gender factor and the concept of leadership is an increasingly explored field, but initially counterintuitive. The leader's image is unconsciously identified, almost immediately, with a male leader. However, despite the underrepresentation of women in leadership roles, both in public opinion and academia, the recurring question remains of what women leaders contribute, whether they have a different, complementary leadership style, or if gender is irrelevant to their performance. For now, there is no consensus on the similarity or differences by gender in the exercise of power: there have been contributions in both directions (Weikart et al. 2007). A calm analysis will be necessary once the Covid-19 crisis has vanished.

Pandemic Political Leadership

Without dwelling on the importance of social capital for governance, which goes beyond the remit of this research, it should be noted that political leadership can be an important factor in promoting greater effectiveness, efficiency and stability in government action in a globalised post Covid-19 world. The personal qualities that public leaders bring to the decision-making process are decisive in determining political results. This is related to the key functions political leadership can perform. First, leaders fulfil the key function of providing direction, impulse or direction to governance structures and networks. From an analytical point of view, this function of political impulse can be divided into two main objectives of leadership: on the one hand, to diagnose and prescribe courses of action; and, on the other, to mobilise and seek support.

Regarding the first objective, the capacity of leadership to identify problems or social demands relevant to the context in order to offer possible responses should be highlighted. The action of the leaders consists of seeking adequate information from the context that provides some keys to define the problems or social demands correctly. Thus, leadership is the art of reducing chaos to impose a simplified definition of a given situation. Regarding the second objective, Tucker (1981) stressed that it would be worth little to adequately define a situation or prescribe adequate courses of action if the leader could not mobilise resources and support meaningfully, which is essential to carry out decisions or projects (Masciulli, Molchanov & Knight, 2016). In other words, building and maintaining a solid "support network" is fundamental in materialising this leadership objective.

The function of political impulse has its maximum expression when the leader faces atypical situations characterised by growing uncertainty and major socio-political changes, such as the loss of relevance of traditional political ideologies, the end of the Cold War, and the crisis of social democracy. In this way, many scholars consider it more appropriate to use political leadership, less so managerial leadership, for those contexts of intense change and instability in which far-reaching decisions must be made (Sancino, 2021).

To the equation of modern political leadership must be added the ability of politicians to respond effectively to changing problems; modern political leaders regularly face traumatic and destabilising events and are expected to deal with them skilfully, relying on experts, in a coordinated manner and being able to communicate with citizens correctly. The truth is that crises also need great leaders to be resolved, with leadership as active or innovative agents capable of responding to current problems and leaders as efficient managers in times of crisis (Tucker, 2017).

The management of emergencies has existed for decades in administrative studies. However, it was not until the attacks on the World Trade Centre in New York on September 11, 2001, that it connected with the political leadership literature. Crisis management has become a defining feature of contemporary governance, and there is an entire literature dealing with the challenges that crises and disasters pose to public leadership (Boin & Hart, 2003). Precisely, part of the literature on crisis management and leadership focuses on these extra-institutional threats and how they - revolutionary movements, terrorism or natural disasters - affect the scrutiny of leadership management and whether this can affect survival. Or re-election in the position of the rulers. The preparations and response a government offers can determine the extent of a disaster. They can also reveal information about the capacity and effectiveness of a leader to govern, making effective leadership visible in times of crisis. There is no consensus concerning whether current crises differ from earlier ones and whether the modern political environment has changed in the last fifteen years. At the same time, modern political leaders retain a great deal of capacity to respond to crises, manage their effects, demonstrate action, and adapt to new decision-making environments, as has been evidenced by Marin and Ardern (Repo, Polsa & Timonen, 2022, McGuire et al., 2020).

Although perhaps too much trust is invested in leadership, other less encouraging visions are also making their way. Especially given President Trump's preposterous claims, the pandemic demonstrated that those in charge did not truly know what they were doing, with many not even pretending they were in charge.

Second, leaders play a prominent role in political communication. Maintaining a fluid communication system by leaders becomes essential for effectively functioning governance networks. Indeed, much of the work of leadership consists of communicating and persuading their team, their competitors, and the rest of those who participate in governance processes.

Third, leaders channel, aggregate, or directly represent social demands and interests. This function derives from the aforementioned collective nature of leadership. The leaders contribute to selecting, articulating and configuring the collective demands to unite the entire community or at least part of it. Thus, leaders become simplifying agents of political reality, embodying and simplifying the representation of demands and interests. However, leaders as agents who simplify political reality contribute to cohesion and polarise the community to the point of causing ruptures and civil conflicts.

For this reason, one can assert that leaders are necessary for polyarchies, but if the citizenry is more interested in personalities than in politics, democracy can face danger. This was witnessed in January 2021 in the United States when President Trump incited his supporters to march on the Capitol, which resulted in armed violence with five deaths, dozens injured and millions of dollars' worth of damage to the building. His speech was extremely controversial and can be seen as evidence of political communication that led to irreparable harm concerning presidential authority, responsibility and the functioning of the American government.

Finally, the leaders fulfil the legitimising function of the new governance processes and, therefore, the new relations between the state and the citizenry. This personalist legitimation, not necessarily charismatic, represents another source of diffuse support for the political system.

Consequently, political leaders such as Trump become symbolic references for citizens immersed in governance and globalisation processes based on their ability to personalise and manipulate collective identities (Choup, 2008). His speeches and actions concerning the death of George Floyd, confederate symbols as well as the death of an American in Charlottesville, Virginia, during a racist clash were further evidence of political communication which were at odds with responsible democratic leadership. In Italy, Matteo Salvini also pursued a strategy of political polarisation in his political communication, specifically focusing on divisive issues and partisan identity, making effective use of social media to attack political opponents (Bordignon, 2020). President Bolsonaro ridiculed the disease in Brazil and expressly opposed social distancing policies whilst attacking China and the medical establishment. His speeches frequently portrayed himself as the only alternative to an imaginary socialist threat posed by his political opponents (Stuenkel, 2021).

Not surprisingly, political leadership throughout history has played the role of holder and manipulator of these collective identities. For this reason, the aforementioned leadership can be considered a powerful antidote against one of the main tensions that governance suffers and often leads to its failure: the blurring of responsibilities. In short, democratic political leadership that exercises the four functions described above could be the agent - not necessarily individual since all leadership has a team; furthermore, in the present circumstances, it would be convenient to implement shared leadership given the growing socio-political complexity - fight against governance without government. In other words, a democratic and shared political leadership that combines such functions leads to responsible governance with clear direction.

CONCLUSION

From the first news in China at the end of 2019 about a new coronavirus which caused rare pneumonia (atypical pneumonia of unknown origin) until the WHO declared it a public health emergency of international importance on January 30, 2020, there was little room for strong and preventive reaction (Eurosurveillance Editorial Team, 2020). Rather, the speed of events and miscalculations - underestimating the threat due to ignorance, complacency or the difficulty of stopping the global machinery and the economic, political, and social logic established - led to the greatest global health crisis of the last hundred years and the questioning of previous ways of life, incompatible with the pandemic (Yiğit, 2021d).

The global spread of Covid-19 - with increasing infections, sick people, and deaths - led the WHO to declare it a pandemic on March 11, 2020 (Cucinotta & Vanelli, 2020). It was not until then that governments began to implement policies systematically. Both were erratic in alleviating community transmission and the cumulative incidence rate. The health crisis became real, and with it, public language and political agendas were transformed. In this way, Covid-19 implies a global rethinking of the political sphere. Likewise, the weaknesses of the political, economic and social systems have been placed on the agenda, as well as the need for leaders and managers to rise to the occasion.

Pandemic and post-pandemic leadership is, above all, adaptive leadership. Citizens expect leaders to be determined in their policies, resilient, human and transparent, who act with vision and who are accountable, able to adapt to the vicissitudes and ups and downs of difficult times, adopting the required public policies. In short, leaders who accept mistakes act by putting citizens at the centre and with a strategic vision, as evidenced by Ardern in New Zealand and Marin in Finland. Thus, in the short and medium term, despite the rampant fragmentation and polarisation, policies focused on protecting health and the battered economy are expected, focusing above all on the most vulnerable people. Johnson put this forward in the United Kingdom through the policy of shielding the most vulnerable during the coronavirus crisis (Sloan et al., 2021).

Strengthening welfare policies and providing essential public services means, after all, guaranteeing human rights and strengthening damaged democracies. The disaffection and disenchantment towards the political, the negative evaluations of the institutions, hit after the economic crisis of 2008, together with the questioning of public leaders intersect with the evaluations of the political responses to the pandemic strictly related to public health –especially the management of confinements, the purchase of medical supplies or the international race for vaccination– in a rarefied climate of great confusion. China and Russia were foremost in highlighting their progress in producing the first vaccines to combat Covid-19 (Zhang & Liu, 2020).

Although political priorities are now oriented towards the public management of the post-pandemic new era, the return to the old normality is becoming illusory. In such a time of historical change, it is essential to pay attention to political leaders to vindicate their role since they are the ones who can guide the electorate towards diverse situations. In this regard, Trump abdicated his responsibility to lead, purposefully searching for ways to polarise the electorate. Johnson, to a certain extent, also fits into this category through his, at best, ignorance of legislation that his government passed, or at worst, wilfully breaking the law and being accused of lying to parliament, which led to him being forced to defend himself before a parliamentary committee in March 2023 (Jenkins, 2023, March 20).

In this sense, the context of the present leadership is characterised, on the one hand, by certain inherited elements, such as the short-term vision of politics as a result of the electoral struggle between antagonistic agents, the resistance and enhancement of policies and national institutions, survival and intensification of socioeconomic inequalities in national societies, the institutional resilience of the nation-state to face systemic crises, the local as an umbrella against interdependencies and the recurrent questioning of the political. On the other hand, there are novel contextual elements such as the recent reconfiguration of the world order, the effects of the Covid-19 pandemic on the process of capitalist globalisation, the emerging problems that it entails and the externalities of the said process during systemic crises; all this crystallised in the possible popular discredit of institutions and leaders. However, in hard times in which systemic crises such as the current one must be managed, the focus is again on the leaders and the expectations about the leadership to come. Hence, it is necessary to reflect on this.

Political leadership in a global society, as the headquarters of the various parts of the world subjected to the social conditions imposed by globalisation, can play a fundamental role in government action. This has become an increasingly complex task, subject to strong tensions and contradictions, because such action cannot be conceived, designed and implemented exclusively from the state's legal-rational, territorial and national interest logic. Although it has not lost its political autonomy and still exercises a major influence on the legitimacy of the public policies that are developed in the sphere of its competence, it must negotiate government action and political decision-making with very diverse agents such as interest groups, multinationals, non-governmental organisations, international organisations due to the complexity, diversity, fragmentation and interdependence that are imposed.

Although transformational and visionary leaders are in demand - both in the process and political results - transactional leaders or negotiators are also necessary due to their recognised ability to reach agreements with the various agents involved in the government's action. Although the media spotlight falls on them, other actors exist, such as leadership teams, private agents and increasingly important non-governmental organisations. Here, the most widely known personalities were Dr Antonio Fauci in the United States as the president's chief medical advisor as well as Professor Chris Whitty, the chief medical officer for England and the U.K. government's chief medical adviser. They were frequently present at the daily press conferences held by their respective political leaders, actively participating in the regular channels of political communication (Koch & Durodié, 2022).

Consequently, in what one can term global society, certain qualities and attributes are required to lead in such a changing, uncertain and volatile scenario. Such qualities try to respond to relevant challenges in government action in the present world: the ability to adapt to changes, integrate uncertainties as central elements in leadership projects and government programs, ability to govern to regulate problems in the medium and long term, avoid short-termism in policies defined as strategic, imagination to be able to think of other possibilities of action different from the conventional ones, ability to understand the situations and perspectives of political adversaries, expanded thinking that enables understanding of the perspectives of agents with political cultures different from the majority, ability to incorporate demands related to global problems into government action, and skills ability to form leadership teams with the above capabilities. This was a major problem for the United Kingdom as the Health Secretary was forced to resign as he broke the law regarding social distancing (Mottram, 2021).

Therefore, based on the arguments developed, it seems probable that government action is guided by democratic and transactional leaders with the ability to reach agreements on the objectives to be developed in the new governance networks and that such leaders do not lose given the challenges, changes and great uncertainties that presently exist. Undoubtedly, in the current scenario, those who intend to influence government action effectively - political leaders and social leaders - should not create more uncertainties with their actions nor offer merely lofty aspirations for change to mobilise partisan supporters but rather take the form of concrete, viable and legitimised projects in the territorial areas that are the object of their action. Johnson and Trump were found wanting regarding this aspect. They failed to demonstrate trust and resilience. Ardern, on the other hand, was highly successful in transitioning from elimination to a mitigation strategy in combatting Covid-19 based on her political will, convictions and integrity.

Thus, a call to prudence in political action is necessary towards cautious and shared political leadership and for the assumption of the corresponding responsibilities by each of the aforementioned agents in their government intervention. Possibly all of this requires the clarification of democratic criteria and values and learning new ways of leading in a globalised society, in which public leaders must dedicate themselves more to asking the right questions than providing supposedly correct answers. In Trump's case he asked irrelevant rhetorical questions with the answers he provided portraying him as perfect. In short, a new and much more complex world implies rethinking the known ways of governing and leading.

Hence the ultimate challenge facing society is finding a way to organise an effective voice to oppose any curtailment or violation of civil rights. The pandemic necessitated a tight technological check by governments on citizens' freedom of manoeuvre and social contact. Arguments were put forth that the brave new world envisaged by Huxley was indeed on the horizon, with the state becoming an all-powerful Leviathan.

The British Labour Party, in its 2022 report on the British constitution, investigated how national recovery and development should take place (Labour Party. 2022, December 05). Its recommendations serve as a summary of the challenges facing contemporary political leadership:

- Restart the economy to create prosperity and opportunity for working people everywhere
- Rebuild trust in politics
- Reunite the country through shared missions and values.

That is indeed a brave new world one can envisage and support.

REFERENCES

Abbasi, K. (2020). The democratic, political, and scientific failures of covid-19. *BMJ, 371*. doi:10.1136/bmj.m4277

Bass, B. M. (1995). Comment: Transformational leadership: Looking at other possible antecedents and consequences. *Journal of Management Inquiry, 4*(3), 293–297. doi:10.1177/105649269543010

Bates, A. E., Primack, R. B., Moraga, P., & Duarte, C. M. (2020). COVID-19 pandemic and associated lockdown as a "Global Human Confinement Experiment" to investigate biodiversity conservation. *Biological Conservation, 248*, 108665. doi:10.1016/j.biocon.2020.108665 PMID:32549587

Berg, N. (2020). The great fear of the year 2020: The coronavirus bug and the great confinement. *Futuribles (Paris, France), 437*, 43–52. doi:10.3917/futur.437.0043

Blondel, J., & Thiébault, J. L. (2010). *Political leadership, parties and citizens*. Routledge.

Boehmke, F. J. (2002). The effect of direct democracy on the size and diversity of state interest group populations. *The Journal of Politics, 64*(3), 827–844. doi:10.1111/0022-3816.00148

Boin, A. (2019). The Transboundary Crisis: Why we are unprepared and the road ahead. *Journal of Contingencies and Crisis Management, 27*(1), 94–99. doi:10.1111/1468-5973.12241

Boin, A., & Hart, P. T. (2003). Public leadership in times of crisis: Mission impossible? *Public Administration Review, 63*(5), 544–553. doi:10.1111/1540-6210.00318

Bordignon, F. (2020). Leader polarisation: Conflict and change in the Italian political system. *South European Society & Politics, 25*(3-4), 285–315. doi:10.1080/13608746.2020.1821464

Brown, T. M. (2021). The COVID-19 Pandemic in Historical Perspective: An AJPH Dossier. *American Journal of Public Health, 111*(3), 402–404. doi:10.2105/AJPH.2020.306136 PMID:33566665

Buthe, T., Barcelo, J., & Cheng, C. (2020). *Patterns of Policy Responses to the COVID-19 Pandemic in Federal vs. Unitary European Democracies. München Hochschule für Politik at the Technical* University of Munich.

Choup, A. M. (2008). The formation and manipulation of collective identity: A framework for analysis. *Social Movement Studies, 7*(2), 191–207. doi:10.1080/14742830802283568

Coccia, M. (2020). *Comparative analysis of the first and second wave of the COVID-19: Is the on-going impact of the second wave on public health stronger than the first one?* Working Paper CocciaLab n. 57/2020. Rome National Research Council of Italy.

Craig, G. (2021). Kindness and control: The political leadership of Jacinda Ardern in the Aotearoa New Zealand COVID-19 media conferences. *Journalism and Media, 2*(2), 288–304. doi:10.3390/journalmedia2020017

Csernatoni, R. (2020). New states of emergency: Normalising techno-surveillance in the time of COVID-19. *Global Affairs, 6*(3), 301–310. doi:10.1080/23340460.2020.1825108

Cucinotta, D., & Vanelli, M. (2020). WHO declares COVID-19 a pandemic. *Acta Biomedica, 91*(1), 157. PMID:32191675

DergiadesT.MilasC.MossialosE. (2020). Effectiveness of Government Policies in Response to the COVID-19 Outbreak. Ssrn doi:10.2139/ssrn.3602004

Dinnin, A. (2019). Ortega y Gasset, Democracy, and the Rule of the People. *Hispanic Research Journal, 20*(6), 548–565. doi:10.1080/14682737.2019.1787612

Dirani, K. M., Abadi, M., Alizadeh, A., Barhate, B., Garza, R. C., Gunasekara, N., Ibrahim, G., & Majzun, Z. (2020). Leadership competencies and the essential role of human resource development in times of crisis: A response to Covid-19 pandemic. *Human Resource Development International, 23*(4), 380–394. doi:10.1080/13678868.2020.1780078

Douillet, A. (2020). To exist in and through the crisis. The management of the health crisis as a means of legitimising the "local". *French Review of Public Administration, 176*, 971–983. doi:10.3917/rfap.176.0129

Eurosurveillance Editorial Team. (2020). Note from the editors: World Health Organization declares novel coronavirus (2019-nCoV) sixth public health emergency of international concern. Eurosurveillance, 25(5), 200131e.

Faris, S. K., & Outcalt, C. L. (2001). The emergence of inclusive, process-oriented leadership. *Developing non-hierarchical leadership on campus: Case studies and best practices in higher education*, 9-18.

Fiedler, F. E. (2006). The contingency model: A theory of leadership effectiveness. *Small groups: Key readings, 369*, 60051-9.

Finset, A., Bosworth, H., Butow, P., Gulbrandsen, P., Hulsman, R. L., Pieterse, A. H., Street, R., Tschoetschel, R., & van Weert, J. (2020). Effective health communication–a key factor in fighting the COVID-19 pandemic. *Patient Education and Counseling, 103*(5), 873–876. doi:10.1016/j.pec.2020.03.027 PMID:32336348

Forgas, J. P., & Crano, W. D. (2021). The psychology of populism: The tribal challenge to liberal democracy. In *The Psychology of Populism* (pp. 1–19). Routledge. doi:10.4324/9781003057680-1

Foti, R. J., Knee, R. E. Jr, & Backert, R. S. (2008). Multi-level implications of framing leadership perceptions as a dynamic process. *The Leadership Quarterly, 19*(2), 178–194. doi:10.1016/j.leaqua.2008.01.007

GaoJ.YinY.JonesB. F. (2020). *Quantifying Policy Responses to a Global Emergency: Insights from the COVID-19 Pandemic*. Northwestern University. https://arxiv.org/abs/2006.13853

Habermas, J. (1995). Paradigms of law. *Cardozo Law Review, 17*, 771.

Hirschmann, G. (2021). The Reassertion of National Sovereignty: A Challenge to International Organizations' Survival? *Security and Human Rights, 31*(1-4), 60–67. doi:10.1163/18750230-bja10003

Hollander, E. P. (2013). Organisational leadership and followership. *Social Psychology at Work: Essays in Honour of Michael Argyle*. https://papers.ssrn.com/sol3/papers.cfm?abstract_id=3692035

Jenkins, S. (2023, March 20). *Of course Boris Johnson is guilty of misleading parliament – stand by for another tory Civil War*. Retrieved March 28, 2023, from https://www.theguardian.com/commentisfree/2023/mar/20/boris-johnson-guilty-midleading-parliament-tory-civil-war-commons

Kenwick, M. R., & Simmons, B. A. (2020). Pandemic response as border politics. *International Organization, 74*(S1), E36–E58. doi:10.1017/S0020818320000363

Koch, N., & Durodié, B. (2022). Scientists advise, ministers decide? The role of scientific expertise in U.K. policymaking during the coronavirus pandemic. *Journal of Risk Research*, *25*(10), 1213–1222. doi:10.1080/13669877.2022.2116083

Labour Party. (2022, December 5). *A New Britain*. Retrieved January 21, 2023, from https://labour.org.uk/page/a-new-britain/

Marginson, S. (2021). *Globalisation: The good, the bad and the ugly*. Working Paper 66, Oxford: Centre for Global Higher Education, University of Oxford.

Masciulli, J., Molchanov, M. A., & Knight, W. A. (2016). Political leadership in context. In *The Ashgate research companion to political leadership* (pp. 23–48). Routledge.

McGuire, D., Cunningham, J. E., Reynolds, K., & Matthews-Smith, G. (2020). Beating the virus: An examination of the crisis communication approach taken by New Zealand Prime Minister Jacinda Ardern during the Covid-19 pandemic. *Human Resource Development International*, *23*(4), 361–379. doi:10.1080/13678868.2020.1779543

McMahan, P., & Evans, J. (2018). Ambiguity and engagement. *American Journal of Sociology*, *124*(3), 860–912. doi:10.1086/701298

Mottram, R. (2021). *Unpaid advisers may seem like a free gift to the government but bring with them issues around access, conflicts of interest, and status*. British Politics and Policy at LSE.

Navarro, V. (2020). Is there a third way? A response to Giddens's The Third Way. In *The Political Economy of Social Inequalities* (pp. 419–428). Routledge. doi:10.4324/9781315231051-25

Nye, J. S. (2013). Presidential leadership and the creation of the American era. In *Presidential Leadership and the Creation of the American Era*. Princeton University Press.

Parry, K., & Bryman, A. (2006). I: 2.1 Leadership in organisations. The SAGE handbook of organisation studies, 5(3), 447-465.

Poguntke, T., & Webb, P. (2005). The presidentialization of politics in democratic societies: A framework for analysis. *The presidentialization of politics: a comparative study of modern democracies*, 1.

Repo, P., Polsa, P., & Timonen, P. (2022). Finnish Response to the First Wave of COVID-19 Accentuated Persuasion. In *Community, Economy and COVID-19: Lessons from Multi-Country Analyses of a Global Pandemic* (pp. 181–203). Springer International Publishing. doi:10.1007/978-3-030-98152-5_9

Sancino, A. (2021). Local political leadership: From managerial performances to leadership hop on social media? *International Journal of Public Leadership*, *17*(3), 283–297. doi:10.1108/IJPL-01-2021-0001

Sarkis, J., Cohen, M. J., Dewick, P., & Schröder, P. (2020). A brave new world: Lessons from the COVID-19 pandemic for transitioning to sustainable supply and production. *Resources, Conservation and Recycling*, *159*, 104894. doi:10.1016/j.resconrec.2020.104894 PMID:32313383

Sarros, J. C., & Santora, J. C. (2001). The transformational-transactional leadership model in practice. *Leadership and Organization Development Journal*, *22*(8), 383–394. doi:10.1108/01437730110410107

Skaaning, S. E. (2020). Waves of autocratization and democratisation: A critical note on conceptualisation and measurement. *Democratization*, *27*(8), 1533–1542. doi:10.1080/13510347.2020.1799194

Sloan, M., Gordon, C., Lever, E., Harwood, R., Bosley, M. A., Pilling, M., Brimicombe, J., Naughton, F., Blane, M., Walia, C., & D'Cruz, D. (2021). COVID-19 and shielding: Experiences of U.K. patients with lupus and related diseases. *Rheumatology Advances in Practice*, *5*(1), rkab003. doi:10.1093/rap/rkab003 PMID:33728396

Smart, B. (1994). Sociology, globalisation and postmodernity: Comments on the "Sociology for one world" thesis. *International Sociology, 9*(2), 149-159.

Stengel, F. A., & Baumann, R. (2017). Non-state actors and foreign policy. In Oxford Research Encyclopedia of Politics. doi:10.1093/acrefore/9780190228637.013.456

Stone, A. G., Russell, R. F., & Patterson, K. (2004). Transformational versus servant leadership: A difference in leader focus. *Leadership and Organization Development Journal*.

Stuenkel, O. (2021, February 17). *Brazil's polarisation and Democratic risks - carnegie endowment for ...* Retrieved March 28, 2023, from https://carnegieendowment.org/2021/02/17/brazil-s-polarization-and-democratic-risks-pub-83783

Tucker, R. C. (1995). *Politics as leadership* (Revised edition). University of Missouri Press.

Tucker, R. C. (2017). The theory of charismatic leadership. In *Leadership Perspectives* (pp. 499–524). Routledge. doi:10.4324/9781315250601-37

Vaubel, R. (2006). Principal-agent problems in international organisations. *The Review of International Organizations*, *1*(2), 125–138. doi:10.100711558-006-8340-z

Wallerstein, I. (2007). Precipitate decline. *Harvard International Review*, *29*(1), 50.

Wallis, S. E., & Valentinov, V. (2016). The imperviance of conceptual systems: Cognitive and moral aspects. *Kybernetes*, *45*(9), 1437–1451. doi:10.1108/K-04-2016-0072

Weikart, L. A., Chen, G., Williams, D. W., & Hromic, H. (2007). The democratic sex: Gender differences and the exercise of power. *Journal of Women, Politics & Policy*, *28*(1), 119–140. doi:10.1300/J501v28n01_06

Yates, K. (2023, March 3). *Did Boris Johnson 'follow the science' on covid? he couldn't even do the maths*. Retrieved March 27, 2023, from https://www.theguardian.com/commentisfree/2023/mar/03/boris-johnson-science-covid-maths-whatapps-advisers

Yigit, S. (2021a). 2021: The geopolitical role of the European Union in the post-cold war order. *IKSAD 7th International Conference on Social Sciences & Humanities Conference Proceedings Book*, 71-98.

Yiğit, S. (2021b). Trump vs China. *The Trade Wars of the USA, China, and the E.U.: The Global Economy in the Age of Populism, 67*.

Yigit, S. (2021c). The Concept of Citizenship and the Democratic State. *Electronic Journal of Social and Strategic Studies, 2*, 5–25.

Yiğit, S. (2021d). The economic and political effects of COVID-19 on the Eurasian Economic Union. *New Normal and New Rules in International Trade, Economics and Marketing*, 35-55.

Yigit, S. (2022). EU-Central Asian Civil Societal Relations: Unrealistic Expectations, Discouraging Results. *Cuadernos Europeos de Deusto*, (5), 149–204. doi:10.18543/ced.2558

Zattoni, A., & Pugliese, A. (2021). Corporate Governance Research in the Wake of a Systemic Crisis: Lessons and Opportunities from the COVID-19 Pandemic. *Journal of Management Studies*, *58*(5), 1405–1410. doi:10.1111/joms.12693

Zhang, L., & Liu, Y. (2020). Potential interventions for novel coronavirus in China: A systematic review. *Journal of Medical Virology*, *92*(5), 479–490. doi:10.1002/jmv.25707 PMID:32052466

Compilation of References

Abbas, A.Tan Owee Kowang. (2020). Impact of Ethical Leadership and Islamic Work Ethics on Employee Commitment and Job Satisfaction. *Journal of Research in Psychology*, 2(2), 47–58. doi:10.31580/jrp.v2i2.1601

Abbasi, K. (2020). The democratic, political, and scientific failures of covid-19. *BMJ, 371*. doi:10.1136/bmj.m4277

ABC. (2019). James Cook University marine scientist Peter Ridd's sacking 'unlawful', court rules. *ABC News*. https://www.abc.net.au/news/2019-04-16/jcu-scientist-peter-ridd-sacking-unlawful-federal-court-judgment/11021554

ABC. (2023). *Managerialism and our obsession with hierarchy*. ABC News. https://www.abc.net.au/radionational/programs/futuretense/managerialism-and-our-obsession-with-hierarchy/101919764

Acker, J. (2009). From glass ceiling to inequality regimes. *Sociologie du Travail*, 51(2), 199-217.

Adams, G. B., & Balfour, D. L. (1998). *Unmasking administrative evil*. Sage. doi:10.4135/9781452231525

Adedoyin, O. B., & Soykan, E. (2020). Covid-19 pandemic and online learning: The challenges and opportunities. *Interactive Learning Environments*, 1–13. doi:10.1080/10494820.2020.1813180

Adkins, L., & Dever, M., (2015) It's not about the women: gender equality in research. *Australian Feminist Studies*, 30(85), 217-220.

Adorno, T., & Horkheimer, M. (1944). *The Culture Industry: Enlightenment as Mass Deception* https://www.marxists.org/reference/archive/adorno/1944/culture-industry.htm

Advance Higher Education: Leadership Education for Higher Education UK. (2019). *Succession Management Tools and Case Studies*. https://www.lfhe.ac.uk/en/research-resources/resource-hub/succession-management/tools/index.cfm

Afonso, P. (2022). A demissão silenciosa (quiet quitting) vai acabar mal. *Observador Jornal Online*. https://observador.pt/opiniao/a-demissao-silenciosa-quiet-quitting-vai-acabar-mal/

Ai, W., Cunningham, W. A., & Lai, M. C. (2022). Reconsidering autistic 'camouflaging' as transactional impression management. *Trends in Cognitive Sciences*, 26(8), 631–645. doi:10.1016/j.tics.2022.05.002 PMID:35641372

Al Lily, A. E., Ismail, A. F., Abunasser, F. M., & Alhajhoj Alqahtani, R. H. (2020). Distance education as a response to pandemics: Coronavirus and Arab culture. *Technology in Society*, 63, 101317. doi:10.1016/j.techsoc.2020.101317 PMID:32836570

Al Mahameed, M., Yates, D., & Gebreiter, F. (2023). Management as Ideology: 'new' managerialism and the corporate university in the period of COVID-19. *Financial Accountability & Management* (https://research.birmingham.ac.uk/en/publications/management-as-ideology-new-managerialism-and-the-corporate-univer.

Alam, I., Kartar Singh, J. S., & Islam, M. U. (2021). Does supportive supervisor complements the effect of ethical leadership on employee engagement? *Cogent Business and Management*, *8*(1), 1978371. Advance online publication. doi:10.1080/23311975.2021.1978371

Al-Asfour, A., Charkasova, A., Rajasekar, J., & Kentiba, E. (2022). Servant leadership behaviors and the level of readiness to covid-19 pandemic: Evidence from USA higher education institutions. *International Journal of Leadership in Education*, 1–18. doi:10.1080/13603124.2022.2108505

Alberta Federation of Labour. (2017) *Poisoning the Well: What the records tells us about Employer intimidation during union certification plans in Alberta.* Alberta FOL. https://d3n8a8pro7vhmx.cloudfront.net/afl/pages/156/attachments/original/1496781613/Poisoning_the_Well.pdf?1496781613

Alemán, A. M. M. (2014). Managerialism as the "new" discursive masculinity in the university. *Feminist Formations*, *26*(2), 107–134. doi:10.1353/ff.2014.0017

Ali, C. (2022). Book Review: Media Capitalism. *TripleC*, *2*(20), 143–146. doi:10.31269/triplec.v20i2.1344

Aljukhadar, M. & Senecal, S. (2022). Targeting the very important buyers VIB: A cluster analysis approach. *Cogent Business & Management*, *9*(1).

Allcott, H., Boxell, L., Conway, J., Ferguson, B., Gentzkow, M., & Goldman, B. (2020). *Economic and Health Impacts of Social Distancing Policies During the Coronavirus Pandemic*. SSRN. https://papers.ssrn.com/sol3/papers.cfm?abstract_id=3610422

Allport, G. (1937) Personality: A psychological interpretation. Henry Holt.

Allport, G. W. (1937). *Personality: A psychological interpretation*. Henry Holt.

Allred, B. B., Snow, C. C., & Miles, R. E. (1996). Characteristics of managerial careers in the 21st century. *The Academy of Management Perspectives*, *10*(4), 17–27. doi:10.5465/ame.1996.3145316

Alston, J. (2005). Tempered radicals and servant leaders: Black females persevering in the superintendency. *Educational Administration Quarterly*, *41*(4), 675–688. doi:10.1177/0013161X04274275

Alward, E., & Phelps, Y. (2019). Impactful leadership traits of virtual leaders in higher education. *Online Learning : the Official Journal of the Online Learning Consortium*, *23*(3), 72–93. doi:10.24059/olj.v23i3.2113

American Psychiatric Association. (2000). *Diagnostic and statistical manual of mental disorders* (4th ed.). Author.

American Psychiatric Association. (2013). Personality disorders. In Diagnostic and Statistical Manual of Mental Disorders (5th ed.). APA.

Anderson, C., & Kilduff, G. J. (2009). Why do dominant personalities attain influence in face-to-face groups? The competence-signaling effects of trait dominance. *Journal of Personality and Social Psychology*, *96*(2), 491–503. doi:10.1037/a0014201 PMID:19159145

Anderson, L., & Riley, L. (2021). Crafting safer spaces for teaching about race and intersectionality in Australian Indigenous Studies. *Australian Journal of Indigenous Education*, *50*(2), 229–236. https://doi.org/10.1017/jie.2020.8 doi:10.1017/jie.2020.8

Compilation of References

Andre, M. H. (2016, April). *Trade Union Unity is key for the labour movement (Paper Presentation)*. The 2nd Quadrennial Congress of Trade Union Congress of Swaziland (TUCOSWA), Swaziland. http://www.ilo.org/global/docs/WCMS_466851/lang--en/index.htm

Andre, M. H. (2022). *Preface Trade Union Revitalization: Organizing new forms of work including platform workers*. International Labour Office.

Antonopoulou, H., Halkiopoulos, C., Barlou, O., & Beligiannis, G. N. (2021). Transformational leadership and digital skills in higher education institutes: During the covid-19 pandemic. *Emerging Science Journal*, *5*(1), 1–15. doi:10.28991/esj-2021-01252

Anzaldua, G. (Ed.). (1990). *Making Face, Mekaing Soul Haciendo Caras Critical Perspectives by Feminists of Color*. Aunt Lute Books.

Appelgren, E. (2022). Media management during COVID-19: Behavior of Swedish media leaders in times of crisis. *Journalism Studies*, *23*(5-6), 722–739. doi:10.1080/1461670X.2021.1939106

Arendt, H. (1951). *The origins of totalitarianism*. Harcourt, Brace and Co.

Argyris, C. (1998). Empowerment: The emperor's new clothes. *Harvard Business Review*, *76*, 98–105. PMID:10179657

Arora, R. G. (2020). *Happiness among higher education academicians: A demographic analysis*. Academic Press.

Asch, S. (1951). Effects of group pressure upon the modification and distortion of judgments. In H. Guetzkow (Ed.), *Groups, leadership, and men* (pp. 117–190). Carnegie Press.

Asher, N. (2010). How does the postcolonial, feminist academic lead? A perspective from the US South. *International Journal of Leadership in Education*, *13*(1), 63–76. https://doi.org/10.1080/13603120903242915 doi:10.1080/13603120903242915

Ashfaq, F., Abid, G., & Ilyas, S. (2021). Impact of ethical leadership on employee engagement: Role of self-efficacy and organizational commitment. *European Journal of Investigation in Health, Psychology and Education*, *11*(3), 962–974. doi:10.3390/ejihpe11030071 PMID:34563084

Ashforth, B. (1994). Petty tyranny in organizations. *Human Relations*, *47*(7), 755–778. doi:10.1177/001872679404700701

Ashraf, T., & Siddiqui, D. A. (2020). The Impact of Employee Engagement on Employee Retention: The Role of Psychological Capital, Control at Work, General Wellbeing and Job Satisfaction. *Human Resource Research*, *4*(1), 67. doi:10.5296/hrr.v4i1.16477

Astley, W. G., & Sachdeva, P. (1984). Structural sources of intraorganizational power: A theoretical synthesis. *Academy of Management Review*, *9*(1), 104–113.

Australian Business Deans Council. (2022). *ABDC Journal Quality List 2022*. https://abdc.edu.au/research/abdc-journal-quality-list/

Australian Govt. (2018). List of Australian Universities. *Study in Australia*. https://www.studyinaustralia.gov.au/english/australian-education/universities-and-higher-education/list-of-australian-universities)

Australian Govt. Department of Education. (2018). Higher education staff numbers for 2018. Canberra. https://docs.education.gov.au/node/51701)

Avlani, A., & Charalampous, M. (2021). *Exploring the significance of remote leadership competencies in the virtual workplace: A systematic literature review.* Semantic Scholar. doi:10.31124/advance.14781744.v1

Avolio, B. J., & Gardner, W. L. (2005). Authentic leadership development: Getting to the root of positive forms of leadership. *The Leadership Quarterly*, *16*(3), 315–338. doi:10.1016/j.leaqua.2005.03.001

Avolio, B. J., Kahai, S., & Dodge, G. E. (2000). E-leadership: Implications for theory, research, and practice. *The Leadership Quarterly*, *11*(4), 615–668. doi:10.1016/S1048-9843(00)00062-X

Avolio, B. J., Sosik, J. J., Kahai, S. S., & Baker, B. (2014). E-leadership: Re-examining transformations in leadership source and transmission. *The Leadership Quarterly*, *25*(1), 105–131. doi:10.1016/j.leaqua.2013.11.003

Avolio, B. J., Waldman, D. A., & Yammarino, F. J. (1991). Leading in the 1990's: The four I's of transformational leadership. *Journal of European Industrial Training*, *15*(4), 9–16. doi:10.1108/03090599110143366

Awan, M. R., & Mahmood, K. (2010). Relationship among leadership style, organizational culture and employee commitment in university libraries. *Library Management*, *31*(4/5), 253–266. doi:10.1108/01435121011046326

Aydın, E., & Azizoglu, O. (2022). *A new term for an existing concept: Quiet Quitting - A self-determination perspective.* V International Congress on Critical Debates in Social Sciences (ICCDSS). https://www.researchgate.net/publication/366530514

Baharody, G., & Stoneman, Z. (1985). Peer imitation: An examination of status and competence hypotheses. *The Journal of Genetic Psychology*, *146*(2), 161–170. doi:10.1080/00221325.1985.9914443

Ballı, E., & Çakıcı, A. (2019). Karanlık Liderlik: Otel İşletmelerinde Bir Araştırma. *Turkish Studies*, *14*(2), 155–173. doi:10.7827/TurkishStudies.14775

Banco de Portugal. (2022). *Taxa de inflação*. Bpstat. https://bpstat.bportugal.pt/conteudos/noticias/1299

Bandura, A. (1986). *Social foundations of thought and action: A social cognitive theory.* Prentice–Hall.

Bao, W. (2020). COVID-19 and online teaching in higher education: A case study of Peking University. *Human Behavior and Emerging Technologies*, *2*(2), 113–115. doi:10.1002/hbe2.191 PMID:32510042

Bargallie, D. (2020). *Unmasking the racial contract: Indigenous voices on racism in the Australian Public Service.* Aboriginal Studies Press.

Barling, J., Christie, A., & Turner, N. (2008). Pseudo-transformational leadership: Towards the development and test of a model. *Journal of Business Ethics*, *81*(4), 851–861. doi:10.100710551-007-9552-8

Barnard, C. I. (1938). *The functions of the executive.* Harvard University Press.

Bass, B. M. (1985). *Leadership and performance beyond expectations.* Free Press.

Bass, B. M. (1990). *Bass and Stogdill's handbook of leadership. Theory, Research and Managerial Applications* (Vol. 3). The Free Press.

Bass, B. M. (1990). From transactional to transformational leadership: Learning to share the vision. *Organizational Dynamics*, *18*(3), 19–31. doi:10.1016/0090-2616(90)90061-S

Bass, B. M. (1995). Comment: Transformational leadership: Looking at other possible antecedents and consequences. *Journal of Management Inquiry*, *4*(3), 293–297. doi:10.1177/105649269543010

Bass, B. M., & Avolio, B. J. (1997). Concepts of leadership. In R. P. Vecchio (Ed.), *Leadership: Understanding the dynamics of power and influence in organizations* (2nd ed., pp. 3–22). University of Notre Dame Press.

Compilation of References

Bass, B. M., & Steidlmeier, P. (1999). Ethics, character, and authentic transformational leadership behavior. *The Leadership Quarterly*, *10*(2), 181–217. doi:10.1016/S1048-9843(99)00016-8

Bates, A. E., Primack, R. B., Moraga, P., & Duarte, C. M. (2020). COVID-19 pandemic and associated lockdown as a "Global Human Confinement Experiment" to investigate biodiversity conservation. *Biological Conservation*, *248*, 108665. doi:10.1016/j.biocon.2020.108665 PMID:32549587

Bauman, Z. (1989). *Modernity and the Holocaust*. Blackwell.

Bedi, A. (2020). A meta-analytic review of paternalistic leadership. *Applied Psychology*, *69*(3), 960–1008. doi:10.1111/apps.12186

Bedi, A., Alpaslan, C. M., & Green, S. (2016). A meta-analytic review of ethical leadership outcomes and moderators. *Journal of Business Ethics*, *139*(3), 517–536. doi:10.100710551-015-2625-1

Behrendt, L., Larkin, S., Griew, R., & Kelly, P. (2012). *Review of higher education access and outcomes for Aboriginal and Torres Strait Islander people*. Department of Industry, Innovation, Science, Research and Tertiary Education.

Bektaş, Ç. (2016). Liderlik yaklaşımları ve modern liderden beklentiler. *Selçuk Üniversitesi Akşehir Meslek Yüksekokulu Sosyal Bilimler Dergisi*, *2*(7), 43–53.

Belitski, M., & Liversage, B. (2019). E-Leadership in small and medium-sized enterprises in the developing world. *Technology Innovation Management Review*, *9*(1), 64–74. doi:10.22215/timreview/1212

Bellei, C., & Cabalin, C. (2013). Chilean student movements: Sustained struggle to transform a market-oriented educational system. *Current Issues in Comparative Education*, *15*(2), 108–123.

Benmira, S., & Agboola, M. (2021). Evolution of leadership theory. *BMJ Leader*, *5*(1).

Bennett, M. (2021, March 23). Retrieved from Niagara Institute: https://www.niagarainstitute.com/blog/what-is-vuca-leadership

Bennett, K. (2017). *Living and Leading Through Uncertainty: Developing Leaders' Capability for Uncertainty*. KR Publishing.

Bennis, W., & Nanus, B. (1985). *Leaders: The Strategies for Taking Charge*. Harper and Row Publishers.

Bentley, P. J., Coates, H., Dobson, I. R., Goedegebuure, L., & Meek, V. L. (2013). Academic job satisfaction from an international comparative perspective: factors associated with satisfaction across 12 countries. In *Job Satisfaction Round the Academic World* (pp. 239–262). Springer. doi:10.1007/978-94-007-5434-8_13

Bentz, V. (1985, August). *A view from the top: A thirty year perspective of research devoted to the discovery, description, and prediction of executive behavior*. Paper presented at the 93rd annual convention of the american psychological association, Los Angeles, CA.

Berchin, I. I., & de Andrade Guerra, J. B. S. O. (2020). Effects of the coronavirus disease 2019 (COVID-19) outbreak on sustainable development and future perspectives. *Res. Globalization*, *2*, 1–5. doi:10.1016/j.resglo.2020.100014

Berg, M. E., & Karlsen, J. T. (2016). A study of coaching leadership style practice in projects. *Management Research Review*, *39*(9), 1122–1142. doi:10.1108/MRR-07-2015-0157

Berg, N. (2020). The great fear of the year 2020: The coronavirus bug and the great confinement. *Futuribles (Paris, France)*, *437*, 43–52. doi:10.3917/futur.437.0043

Bernal, C., Monosov, N., Stencler, A., Lajoie, A., Raigoza, A., & Akhavan, N. (2017). Gender Bias within the Superintendency: A Comparative Study. *Journal of School Administration Research and Development*, *2*(1), 42–52. doi:10.32674/jsard.v2i1.1925

Bernardin, H. J., Cooke, D. K., & Villanova, P. (2000). Conscientiousness and agreeableness as predictors of rating leniency. *The Journal of Applied Psychology*, *85*(2), 232–236. doi:10.1037/0021-9010.85.2.232 PMID:10783539

Betts, M. (2022). *The New Leadership Agenda: Pandemic Perspectives from Global Universities*. Taylor & Francis. doi:10.4324/9781003346135

Bhatti, M. H., Akram, U., Bhatti, M. H., Rasool, H., & Su, X. (2020). Unravelingthe effects of ethical leadership on knowledge sharing: The mediating roles of subjective wellbeing and social media in the hotel industry. *Sustainability*, *12*(8333).

Bin-Sallik, M. A. (2000). *Aboriginal women by degrees: Their stories of the journey towards academic achievement*. University of Queensland Press.

Blake, R. R., Mouton, J. S., Barnes, L. B., & Greiner, L. E. (1964). Breakthrough in Organization Development. *Harvard Business Review*, *42*(6), 133–155.

Blondel, J., & Thiébault, J. L. (2010). *Political leadership, parties and citizens*. Routledge.

Boehmke, F. J. (2002). The effect of direct democracy on the size and diversity of state interest group populations. *The Journal of Politics*, *64*(3), 827–844. doi:10.1111/0022-3816.00148

Bogg, D. (2002) *Trade Unions Maintaining Relevance in the 21st Century*, (Paper Presentation). The IRN Conference. Irish Congress of Trade Unions.https://www.ictu.ie/press/2002/02/21/trade-unions-maintaining-relevance-in-the-21st-century/

Boin, A. (2019). The Transboundary Crisis: Why we are unprepared and the road ahead. *Journal of Contingencies and Crisis Management*, *27*(1), 94–99. doi:10.1111/1468-5973.12241

Boin, A., & Hart, P. T. (2003). Public leadership in times of crisis: Mission impossible? *Public Administration Review*, *63*(5), 544–553. doi:10.1111/1540-6210.00318

Bono, J. E., & Judge, T. A. (2004). Personality and transformational and transactional leadership: A meta-analysis. *The Journal of Applied Psychology*, *89*(5), 901–910. doi:10.1037/0021-9010.89.5.901 PMID:15506869

Book, A., Visser, B. A., & Volk, A. A. (2015). Unpacking "evil": Claiming the core of the dark triad. *Personality and Individual Differences*, *73*, 29–38. doi:10.1016/j.paid.2014.09.016

Bordignon, F. (2020). Leader polarisation: Conflict and change in the Italian political system. *South European Society & Politics*, *25*(3-4), 285–315. doi:10.1080/13608746.2020.1821464

Borgholthaus, C. J., White, J. V., & Harms, P. D. (2023). CEO dark personality: A critical review, bibliometric analysis, and research agenda. *Personality and Individual Differences*, *201*, 111951. Advance online publication. doi:10.1016/j.paid.2022.111951

Bouziri, H., Smith, D. R., Descatha, A., Dab, W., & Jean, K. (2020). Working from home in the time of Covid-19: How to best preserve occupational health? *Occupational and Environmental Medicine*, *77*(7), 509–510. doi:10.1136/oemed-2020-106599 PMID:32354748

Boyle, M. (2023, January 24) Organizational Leadership: What is it and why it is important. *HBS*. https://online.hbs.edu/blog/post/what-is-organizational-leadership

Compilation of References

Brady, S. R. (2015). Utilizing and adapting the Delphi method for use in qualitative research. *International Journal of Qualitative Methods*, *14*(5), 1609406915621381. doi:10.1177/1609406915621381

Brake, T. (2006). Leading global virtual teams. *Industrial and Commercial Training*, *38*(3), 116–121. doi:10.1108/00197850610659364

Brews, P., & Purohit, D. (2007). Strategic planning in unstable environments. *Long Range Planning*, *40*(1), 64–83. doi:10.1016/j.lrp.2006.12.001

Brien, D. L. & Fredericks, B. (2020). Collaborative writing to enhance cross-cultural understanding within the Academy. *Writing in Practice: The Journal of Creative Writing Research*, 1, 1-8. Sat.

Brown, A. R. (2014). The recruitment and retention of African American women as public school superintendents. *Journal of Black Studies*, *45*(6), 573–593. doi:10.1177/0021934714542157

Brown, C., & Shay, M. (2021). From resilience to wellbeing: Identity-building as an alternative framework for schools' role in promoting children's mental health. *Review of Education*, *9*(2), 599–634. https://doi.org/10.1002/rev3.3264 doi:10.1002/rev3.3264

Brownell, K. M., McMullen, J. S., & O'Boyle, E. H. Jr. (2021). Fatal attraction: A systematic review and research agenda of the dark triad in entrepreneurship. *Journal of Business Venturing*, *36*(3), 106106. doi:10.1016/j.jbusvent.2021.106106

Browning, C. (1989). The decision concerning the final solution. In F. Furet (Ed.), *Unanswered questions: Nazi Germany and the genocide of the Jews* (pp. 96–118). Schocken.

Brown, M. E., & Treviño, L. K. (2006). Ethical leadership: A review and future directions. *The Leadership Quarterly*, *17*(6), 595–616. doi:10.1016/j.leaqua.2006.10.004

Brown, M. E., Treviño, L. K., & Harrison, D. A. (2005). Ethical leadership: A social learning perspective for construct development and testing. *Organizational Behavior and Human Decision Processes*, *97*(2), 117–134. doi:10.1016/j.obhdp.2005.03.002

Brown, T. M. (2021). The COVID-19 Pandemic in Historical Perspective: An AJPH Dossier. *American Journal of Public Health*, *111*(3), 402–404. doi:10.2105/AJPH.2020.306136 PMID:33566665

Bryman, A. (1992). *Charisma and Leadership in Organizations*. Sage.

Bryman, A. (2004). *Social Research Methods* (2nd ed.). Oxford University Press.

Bryman, A. (2007). Effective leadership in higher education: A literature review. *Studies in Higher Education*, *32*(6), 693–710. doi:10.1080/03075070701685114

Brzezinski, Z., & Huntington, S. P. (1963). Cincinnatus and the Apparatchik. *World Politics*, *16*(1), 52–78. doi:10.2307/2009251

Buckskin, P., Malin, M., Warrior, E., Wyld, F., & Meagher, S. (2011). *Engagement, focus and hope for the future: the Port Augusta Partnerships for Success program*, DKCRC Report. [Online] Available: http://www.nintione.com.au/resource/NintiOneResearchReport_66_PartnershipsforSuccess.pdf

Buckskin, P., Tranthim-Fryer, M., Holt, L., Gili, J., Heath, J., Smith, D., Larkin, S., Ireland, S., Macgibbon, L. & Robertson, K. (2018). *NATSIHEC accelerating Indigenous higher education consultation paper*.

Buiza, F., Aguirre-Parra, P., Garcia-Jimenez, M., & Torres, D. (2021). Corporate social responsibility actions in agribusiness: towards sustainable community development. In *2021 IEEE Sciences and Humanities International Research Conference (SHIRCON)* (pp. 1-4). IEEE. https://doi.org/10.1109/SHIRCON53068.2021.9652243

Bunda, T. (2014). *The Relationship Between Indigenous Peoples and the University: Solid or What!* [Doctoral Thesis, University of South Australia].

Bunda, T., Gilbey, K. & Monnapula-Mapesela, M. (2021). Black Warrior Women Scholars Speak. *Reimagining the Academy: ShiFting Towards Kindness, Connection, and an Ethics of Care*, 19-27.

Bunda, T., & White, N. (2009). *Final project report: The Australian learning and teaching council leadership for excellence in learning and teaching program: Tiddas Showin' Up, Talkin' Up and Puttin' Up: Indigenous women and educational leadership*. Flinders University and Australian Catholic University. https://ltr.edu.au/resources/grants_leadership_tiddasshowinup_finalreport_apr09_0.pdf

Bunda, T., Zipin, L., & Brennan, M. (2012). Negotiating university 'equity' from Indigenous standpoints: A shaky bridge. *International Journal of Inclusive Education*, *16*(9), 941–957. https://doi.org/10.1080/13603116.2010.523907 doi:10.1080/13603116.2010.523907

Burke, C. S., Stagl, K. C., Klein, C., Goodwin, G. F., Salas, E., & Halpin, S. M. (2006). What type of leadership behaviors are functional in teams? A meta-analysis. *The Leadership Quarterly*, *17*(3), 288–307. doi:10.1016/j.leaqua.2006.02.007

Burke, R. J. (2006). Why leaders fail. Exploring the dark side. In R. J. Burke & C. L. Cooper (Eds.), *Inspiring leaders*. Routledge. doi:10.4324/9780203013199-25

Burnes, B., Wend, P., & By, R. T. (2014). The changing face of English universities: Reinventing collegiality for the twenty-first century. *Studies in Higher Education*, *39*(6), 905–926. doi:10.1080/03075079.2012.754858

Burns, J. (1978). *Leadership*. Harper & Row.

Burrow, S. (2014) *Challenges and opportunities for Trade unions in 2014*. ILO. www.Ilo.org/actrav/media-center/news/WCMS_234541/lang-en/index.htm

Burt, A., & Gunstone, A. (2018). Cultural Competency through a Reconciliation Action Plan. *Journal of Australian Indigenous Issues*, *21*, 46–58. https://search.informit.org/doi/10.3316/informit.143082604918170

Bushee, B., Taylor, D. J., & Zhu, C. 2020. The dark side of investor conferences: Evidence of managerial opportunism. *The Accounting Review* (https://meridian.allenpress.com/accounting-review/article-abstract/doi/10.2308/TAR-2020-0624/487384/The-Dark-Side-of-Investor-Conferences-Evidence-of,

Bush, T. (2008). From management to leadership. *Educational Management Administration & Leadership*, *36*(2), 271–288. doi:10.1177/1741143207087777

Buthe, T., Barcelo, J., & Cheng, C. (2020). *Patterns of Policy Responses to the COVID-19 Pandemic in Federal vs. Unitary European Democracies*. Münich Hochschule für Politik at the Technical University of Munich.

Butler, M.J. (2006). 'Thinking Creatively About Learning–The Reflective Mindset', *Aston Business School: Good Practice Guide in Learning and Teaching, Thinking Creatively about Learning*, *3*, 31-7.

Byrd, L. (2019). Virtual action learning for virtual leadership development. *Performance Improvement*, *58*(8-9), 20–25. doi:10.1002/pfi.21894

Compilation of References

Byrne, D. (1971). *The attraction paradigm*. Academic Press.

Cable, D. M., & Judge, T. A. (2003). Managers' upward influence tactic strategies: The role of manager personality and supervisor leadership style. *Journal of Organizational Behavior*, 24(2), 197–214. doi:10.1002/job.183

Cahill, D. (2020). Wage theft is core university business. *Advocate: Journal of the National Tertiary Education Union*, 27(3), 28–29.

Calareso, J. P. (2013). 'Succession Planning: A Key to Ensuring Leadership' (Feature Article). *Planning for Higher Education Journal*, 41(3), 27–33.

Calderon, A. (2020). What will follow the international student boom? Future directions for Australian higher education. *Australian Universities Review*, 62(1), 18–25.

Cameron, K. (2012). *Positive Leadership: Strategies for Extraordinary Performance*. Berrett-Koehler Publishers.

Cameron, K. (2021). *Positively Energizing Leadership: Virtuous Actions and Relationships that create High Performance*. Berrett-Koehler Publishers.

Camgöz, S. M., & Ekmekci, Ö. T. (2021). *Destructive Leadership and Management Hypocrisy: Advances in Theory and Practice*. Emerald Publishing Limited. doi:10.1108/9781800431805

Campbell, W. K., & Campbell, S. M. (2009). On the self-regulatory dynamics created by the peculiar benefits and costs of narcissism: A contextual reinforcement model and examination of leadership. *Self and Identity*, 8(2–3), 214–232. doi:10.1080/15298860802505129

Caruso, J. (2021). Identity: Being Aboriginal in the Academy: 'It's an Identity Thing. In A. Nye & J. Clark (Eds.), Teaching History for the Contemporary World. Springer. https://doi.org/10.1177/0004944120969207 doi:10.1007/978-981-16-0247-4_6

Cascio, W. F., & Montealegre, R. (2016). How technology is changing work and organizations. *Annual Review of Organizational Psychology and Organizational Behavior*, 3(1), 349–375. doi:10.1146/annurev-orgpsych-041015-062352

Cavanaugh, J. C. (2017). Who Will Lead? The Success of Succession Planning. *Journal of Management Policy and Practice*, 18(2), 22–27.

Cell, C. (1974). Charismatic heads of state: The social context. *Behavior Science Research*, 9(4), 255–305. doi:10.1177/106939717400900401

Chadwick, C., Way, S. A., Kerr, G., & Thacker, J. W. (2013). Boundary conditions of the high-investment human resource systems-small-firm labour productivity relationship. *Personnel Psychology*, 66(2), 311–343. doi:10.1111/peps.12015

Chaiprasit, K., & Santidhiraku, O. (2011). Happiness at Work of Employees in Small and Medium-sized Enterprises, Thailand. *Procedia: Social and Behavioral Sciences*, 25, 189–200. doi:10.1016/j.sbspro.2011.10.540

Chandler, A. D. Jr. (1984). The emergence of managerial capitalism. *Business History Review*, 58(4), 473–503. doi:10.2307/3114162

Chang, C. L., Arisanti, I., Octoyuda, E., & Insan, I. (2022). E-Leadership analysis during pandemic outbreak to enhanced learning in higher education. *TEM Journal*, 11(2), 932–938. doi:10.18421/TEM112-56

Chang, Y. Y., Chang, C. Y., Chen, Y. C. K., Seih, Y. T., & Chang, S. Y. (2021). Participative leadership and unit performance: Evidence for intermediate linkages. *Knowledge Management Research and Practice*, 19(3), 355–369. doi:10.1080/14778238.2020.1755208

Charlesworth, S., & Cartwright, S. (2007). Part-time Work: Policy, Practice and Resistance in a Manufacturing Organisation. In Fastenau, M., Branigan, L., Douglas, K., and Marshall, H., with Cartwright, S., (Eds), Women and Work 2007: Current RMIT University Research, 5-19. RMIT Publishing, Melbourne.

Charmaz, K. (2006). *Constructing grounded theory: A practical guide through qualitative analysis.* SAGE. http://www.loc.gov/catdir/enhancements/fy0657/2005928035-d.html

Chatterjee, A., & Hambrick, D. C. (2007). It's all about me: Narcissistic chief executive officers and their effects on company strategy and performance. *Administrative Science Quarterly*, *52*(3), 351–386. doi:10.2189/asqu.52.3.351

Chaudhary, P., Rohtagi, M., Singh, R. K., & Arora, S. (2022). Impact of leader's e-competencies on employees' wellbeing in global virtual teams during COVID-19: The moderating role of emotional intelligence. *Employee Relations*, *44*(5), 1042–1057. doi:10.1108/ER-06-2021-0236

Chaudhuri, S., Park, S., & Kim, S. (2019). The changing landscape of women's leadership in India and Korea from cultural and generational perspectives. *Human Resource Development Review*, *18*(1), 16–46. doi:10.1177/1534484318809753

Chauvière, M., & Mick, S. S. (2013). The French Sociological Critique of managerialism: Themes and Frameworks. *Critical Sociology*, *39*(1), 139. doi:10.1177/0896920511431501

Chen, Y., Liu, Y., Zhang, Y., Li, Z., & Zhou, T. (2021). The Effect of Fear of the COVID-19 on Depression Among Chinese Outbound Students Studying Online in China Amid the COVID-19 Pandemic Period: The Role of Resilience and Social Support. *Frontiers in Psychology*, *12*, 750011. doi:10.3389/fpsyg.2021.750011 PMID:34721231

Chief Executive Women. (2017), *Chief Executive Women: Senior Executive Census 2017.* Chief Executive Women. https://cew.org.au/wp-content/uploads/CEW-Executive-Census-2017.pdf

Choup, A. M. (2008). The formation and manipulation of collective identity: A framework for analysis. *Social Movement Studies*, *7*(2), 191–207. doi:10.1080/14742830802283568

Christie, A., Barling, J., & Turner, N. (2011). Pseudo-transformational leadership: Model specification and outcomes. *Journal of Applied Social Psychology*, *41*(12), 2943–2984. doi:10.1111/j.1559-1816.2011.00858.x

Christie, R., & Geis, F. L. (1970). *Studies in Machiavellianism*. Academic Press.

Clarke, J., & Newman, J. (1993). The right to manage: A second managerial revolution? *Cultural Studies*, *7*(3), 427–441. doi:10.1080/09502389300490291

Clayton, J. (2021). *Remote working: Is Big Tech going off work from home?* BBC. https://www.bbc.com/news/technology-56614285

Cleckley, H. (1941). *The mask of sanity: An attempt to reinterpret the so-called psychopathic personality.* The C. V. Mosby Company.

Coates, H., & Goedegebuure, L. (2012). Recasting the Academic Workforce: Why, the Attractiveness of the Academic Profession Needs to be Increased and Eight Possible Strategies for how to go about this from an Australian Perspective. *Higher Education*, *64*(6), 875–889. doi:10.100710734-012-9534-3

Coates, S. K., Trudgett, M., & Page, S. (2021). Examining Indigenous leadership in the academy: A methodological approach. *Australian Journal of Education*, *65*(1), 84–102. doi:10.1177/0004944120969207

Compilation of References

Coates, S. K., Trudgett, M., & Page, S. (2022). Ain't no mountain high enough: Aspirations of Indigenous academics within the academy. *International Journal of Leadership in Education*, •••, 1–15. https://doi.org/10.1080/13603124.2022.2068186 doi:10.1080/13603124.2022.2068186

Coccia, M. (2020). *Comparative analysis of the first and second wave of the COVID-19: Is the on-going impact of the second wave on public health stronger than the first one?* Working Paper CocciaLab n. 57/2020. Rome National Research Council of Italy.

Cohen, F., Solomon, S., Maxfield, M., Pyszczynski, T., & Greenberg, J. (2004). Fatal attraction: The effects of mortality salience on evaluations of charismatic, task-oriented, and relationship-oriented leaders. *Psychological Science*, *15*(12), 846–851. doi:10.1111/j.0956-7976.2004.00765.x PMID:15563330

Colbert, B. A. (2004). The complex resource-based view: Implications for theory and practice in strategic human resource management. *Academy of Management Review*, *29*(3), 341–358. doi:10.2307/20159047

Cole, G. A. (2005). *Organizational Behaviour*. TJ International.

Coleman, M. (2005). Gender and Secondary School Leadership. *International Studies in Educational Administration*, *33*(2).

Coleman, W. O. (2019). *Campus Meltdown: The Deepening Crisis in Australian Universities*. Connor Court Publishing.

Conger, J. (1990). The dark side of leadership. *Organizational Dynamics*, *19*(2), 44–55. doi:10.1016/0090-2616(90)90070-6

Conger, J. A., Kanungo, R. N., & Menon, S. T. (2000). *Charismatic Leadership: The Elusive Factor in Organizational Effectiveness*. Jossey-Bass.

Conger, J., & Kanungo, R. (1987). Toward a behavioral theory of charismatic leadership in organizational settings. *Academy of Management Review*, *12*(4), 637–647. doi:10.2307/258069

Conger, J., & Kanungo, R. (1988). The empowerment process: Integrating theory and practice. *Academy of Management Review*, *13*(3), 471–482. doi:10.2307/258093

Conger, J., & Kanungo, R. (1998). *Charismatic leadership in organizations*. Sage. doi:10.4135/9781452204932

Connell, R. (2019). *The Good University: What Universities Actually Do and Why it's Time for Radical Change*. Zed Books.

Connell, R. W. (1987). *Gender and Power: Society, The Person and Sexual Politics*. Allen and Unwin.

Connell, R. W. (2002). *Gender*. Polity Press.

Connell, R. W. (2005). A Really Good Husband: Work/Life Balance, Gender Equity and Social Change. *The Australian Journal of Social Issues*, *40*(3), 369–383. doi:10.1002/j.1839-4655.2005.tb00978.x

Cooke, B. (1999). Writing the left out of management theory: The historiography of the management of change. *Organization*, *6*(1), 81–105. doi:10.1177/135050849961004

Corona, R. (2022) *Organizing: The Lifeblood of Our Union*. IBEW. https://www.ibew11.org/2022/03/organizing-the-lifeblood-of-our-union/

Cortellazzo, L., Bruni, E., & Zampieri, R. (2019). The role of leadership in a digitalized world: A review. *Frontiers in Psychology*, *10*, 1–21. doi:10.3389/fpsyg.2019.01938 PMID:31507494

COSATU. (2015, 13 July) *Unity and Cohesion of COSATU* (Draft Discussion Document). The Congress of South African Trade Unions Special National Congress, Johannesburg, South Africa. http://www.cosatu.org.za/show.php?ID=10655

Cotton, E. (2016) *A matter of principles: the psychodynamics of solidarity in trade unions.* http://eprints.lse.ac.uk/74363/1/blogs.lse.ac.ukA%20matter%20of%20principles%20the%20psychodynamics%20of%20solidarity%20in%20trade%20unions,pdf

Covin, J., & Slevin, D. (2002). The entrepreneurial imperatives of strategic leadership. In M. A. Hitt, R. D. Ireland, S. M. Camp, & D. L. Sexton (Eds.), *Strategic entrepreneurship: Creating a new mindset* (pp. 309–327). Blackwell Publishers.

Craig, G. (2021). Kindness and control: The political leadership of Jacinda Ardern in the Aotearoa New Zealand COVID-19 media conferences. *Journalism and Media*, 2(2), 288–304. doi:10.3390/journalmedia2020017

Cramer, P. (2000). Defense mechanisms in psychology today: Further processes for adaptation. *The American Psychologist*, 55(6), 637–646. doi:10.1037/0003-066X.55.6.637 PMID:10892206

Crawford, E. R., Arnold, N. W., & Brown, A. (2014). From preservice leaders to advocacy leaders: Exploring intersections in standards for advocacy in educational leadership and school counselling. *International Journal of Leadership in Education*, 17(4), 481–502. doi:10.1080/13603124.2014.931467

Crawford, J., Henderson, K. B., Rudolph, J., Malkawi, B., Glowatz, M., Burton, R., Magni, P. A., & Lam, S. (2020). COVID-19 : 20 countries ' higher education intra-period digital pedagogy responses. *Journal of Applied Learning & Teaching*, 3(1), 1–20.

Crawford, T., & Germov, J. (2015). Using Workforce Strategy to Address Academic Casualisation: A University of Newcastle Case Study. *Journal of Higher Education Policy and Management*, 37(5), 534–544. doi:10.1080/1360080X.2015.1079394

Creswell, J., & Creswell, D. (2017). *Research Design: Qualitative, Quantitative, and Mixed Methods Approaches* (5th ed.). SAGE Publishing.

Crisolo, N. A. (2018). *Sharpening Education through the Use of Information and Communications Technology*. Online Submission.

Crotty, M. (1998). *The Foundations of Social Research: Meaning and Perspective in the Research Process*. Allen and Unwin.

Croucher, G., & Lacy, W. B. (2020). Perspectives of Australian higher education leadership: Convergent or divergent views and implications for the future? *Journal of Higher Education Policy and Management*, 42(4), 516–529. doi:10.1080/1360080X.2020.1783594

Csernatoni, R. (2020). New states of emergency: Normalising techno-surveillance in the time of COVID-19. *Global Affairs*, 6(3), 301–310. doi:10.1080/23340460.2020.1825108

Cucinotta, D., & Vanelli, M. (2020). WHO declares COVID-19 a pandemic. *Acta Biomedica*, 91(1), 157. PMID:32191675

Cunniah, D. (2013) Foreword. *Meeting the Challenge of Precarious Work: A Workers' Agenda*. ILO. www.Ilo.org/wcmsp5/groups/public/-ed_dialogue/actrav/documents/publicatiions/wcms 216282pdf.

Czarna, A. Z., & Nevicka, B. (2019). Narcissism and Leadership. *Encyclopedia of Personality and Individual Differences*, 1–9. doi:10.1007/978-3-319-28099-8_2334-1

Daft, R. (2010). *New Era of Management* (9th ed.). South-Western Cengage Learning.

Daily, C. M., & Johnson, J. L. (1997). Sources of CEO power and firm financial performance: A longitudinal assessment. *Journal of Management*, 23(2), 97–118. doi:10.1177/014920639702300201

Compilation of References

Danneels, E., & Sethi, R. (2011). 'New product exploration under environmental turbulence'. *Organization Science*, *22*(4), 1026–1039. doi:10.1287/orsc.1100.0572

Darics, E. (2020). E-leadership or "how to be boss in instant messaging?" The role of nonverbal communication. *International Journal of Business Communication*, *57*(1), 3–29. doi:10.1177/2329488416685068

DasGupta, P. (2011). Literature review: e-leadership. *Emerging Leadership Journeys*, *4*(1), 1-36. Retrieved from https://www.regent.edu/acad/global/publications/elj/vol4iss1/home_vol4iss1.htm

Davis, I. (2021). University mergers: tough option for hard times. *Campus Morning Mail*.

Davis, A. (2017). Sustaining corporate class consciousness across the new liquid managerial elite in Britain. *The British Journal of Sociology*, *68*(2), 234–253. doi:10.1111/1468-4446.12257 PMID:28369838

Davis, G. (2017). *The Australian Idea of a University*. Melbourne University Press.

Davis, H., & Jones, S. (2014). The work of leadership in higher education management. *Journal of Higher Education Policy and Management*, *36*(4), 367–370. doi:10.1080/1360080X.2014.916463

Day, D. V., & Antonakis, J. (2012). Leadership: Past, present and future. *The Nature of Leadership*, *2*(1), 3–25.

De Hoogh, A. H., Greer, L. L., & Den Hartog, D. N. (2015). Diabolical dictators or capable commanders? An investigation of the differential effects of autocratic leadership on team performance. *The Leadership Quarterly*, *26*(5), 687–701. doi:10.1016/j.leaqua.2015.01.001

De Smet, A., Dowling, B., Hancock, B., & Schaninger, B. (2022). The Great Attrition is making hiring harder. Are you searching the right talent pools ? *McKinsey Quarterly, July*.

De Smet, A., Dowling, B., Mugayar-Baldocchi, M., & Schaninger, B. (2021). "Great Attraction" or "Great Attrition"? The choice is yours. *The McKinsey Quarterly*, (September), 1–8. https://www.mckinsey.com/business-functions/people-and-organizational-performance/our-insights/great-attrition-or-great-attraction-the-choice-is-yours

Deem, R. (2004). The knowledge worker, the manager-academic and the contemporary UK university: New and old forms of public management? *Financial Accountability & Management*, *20*(2), 107–128. doi:10.1111/j.1468-0408.2004.00189.x

Delanoy, N., & Kasztelnik, A. (2020). Business open big data analytics to support innovative leadership and management decision in Canada. *Business Ethics and Leadership*, *4*(2), 56–74. doi:10.21272/bel.4(2).56-74.2020

Delgado, R. & Stefancic, J. (2023). *Critical race theory: An introduction*, NyU press.

Deloria, V. J. (2004). Marginal and submarginal. In D. A. Mihesuah & A. C. Wilson (Eds.), *Indigenizing the academy transforming scholarship and empowering communities*. University of Nebraska Press.

DeMarrais, E., Castillo, L. J., & Earle, T. (1996). Ideology, materialization, and power strategies. *Current Anthropology*, *37*(1), 15–31. doi:10.1086/204472

Denning, S. (2020). The quest for genuine business agility. *Strategy and Leadership*, *48*(1), 21–28. doi:10.1108/SL-11-2019-0166

Dent, M., & Barry, J. (2014). New Public Management and the Professions in the UK. In M. Dent, J. Chandler, & J. Barry (Eds.), *Questioning the New Public Management* (p. 8). Routledge.

DePalma, A. (2006). *The man who invented Fidel: Castro, Cuba, and Herbert L. Matthews of the New York times.* PublicAffairs.

DergiadesT.MilasC.MossialosE. (2020). Effectiveness of Government Policies in Response to the COVID-19 Outbreak. Ssrn doi:10.2139/ssrn.3602004

DeRue, D., Nahrgang, J., Wellmann, N., & Humphrey, S. (2011). Trait and behavioral theories of leadership: An integration and meta-analytic test of their relative validity. *Personnel Psychology*, *64*(1), 7–52. doi:10.1111/j.1744-6570.2010.01201.x

Dessler, G., & Starke, F. A. (2004). *Management: Principles and Practices for Tomorrow's Leaders.* Pearson Prentice Hall.

Dewar, J. (2017). *Bold Thinking Series: The Future of Universities.* La Trobe University. https://www.latrobe.edu.au/nest/tag/bold-thinking-series/>

DiAngelo, R. (2018). *White fragility: Why it's so hard for white people to talk about racism.* Beacon Press.

Diener, E., Sandvik, E., & Pavot, W. (2009). *Happiness is the Frequency, Not the Intensity, of Positive Versus Negative Affect.* doi:10.1007/978-90-481-2354-4_10

Diezmann, C., & Grieshaber, S. (2009). Understanding the achievements and aspirations of new women professors. A report to Universities Australia. Brisbane: Queensland University of Technology.

Diller, S. J., Czibor, A., Szabó, Z. P., Restás, P., Jonas, E., & Frey, D. (2021, November 19). The positive connection between dark triad traits and leadership levels in self- and other-ratings. *Leadership, Education, Personality. An Interdisciplinary Journal*, *3*(2), 117–131. doi:10.136542681-021-00025-6

Dinnin, A. (2019). Ortega y Gasset, Democracy, and the Rule of the People. *Hispanic Research Journal*, *20*(6), 548–565. doi:10.1080/14682737.2019.1787612

Dionne, S. D., Gupta, A., Sotak, K. L., Shirreffs, K. A., Serban, A., Hao, C., Kim, D. H., & Yammarino, F. J. (2014). A 25-year perspective on levels of analysis in leadership research. *The Leadership Quarterly*, *25*(1), 6–35. doi:10.1016/j.leaqua.2013.11.002

Dirani, K. M., Abadi, M., Alizadeh, A., Barhate, B., Garza, R. C., Gunasekara, N., Ibrahim, G., & Majzun, Z. (2020). Leadership competencies and the essential role of human resource development in times of crisis: A response to Covid-19 pandemic. *Human Resource Development International*, *23*(4), 380–394. doi:10.1080/13678868.2020.1780078

Dirisu, J., Worlu, R., Osibanjo, A., Salau, O., Borishade, T., Meninwa, S., & Atolagbe, T. (2018). An integrated dataset on organisational culture, job satisfaction and performance in the hospitality industry. *Data in Brief*, *19*, 317–321. doi:10.1016/j.dib.2018.04.137 PMID:29892652

Donaldson, S. I., Lee, J. Y., & Donaldson, S. I. (2019). Evaluating Positive Psychology Interventions at Work: A Systematic Review and Meta-Analysis. *International Journal of Applied Positive Psychology*, *4*(3), 113–134. doi:10.100741042-019-00021-8

Doran, C. (2016). Managerialism: An Ideology and its Evolution. *International Journal of Management. Knowledge and Learning*, *5*(1), 81–97.

Dörr, S. L., Albo, P., & Monastiridis, B. (2018). Digital Leadership – Erfolgreich führen in der digitalen Welt. In S. Grote & R. Goyk (Eds.), *Führungsinstrumente aus dem Silicon Valley: Konzepte und Kompetenzen* (pp. 37–61). Springer. doi:10.1007/978-3-662-54885-1_3

Compilation of References

Dörr, S. L., Schmidt-Huber, M., & Maier, G. W. (2012). LEAD® – Entwicklung eines evidenzbasierten Kompetenzmodells erfolgreicher Führung. In S. Grote (Ed.), *Die Zukunft der Führung* (pp. 415–435). Gabler. doi:10.1007/978-3-642-31052-2_22

Douillet, A. (2020). To exist in and through the crisis. The management of the health crisis as a means of legitimising the "local". *French Review of Public Administration, 176*, 971–983. doi:10.3917/rfap.176.0129

Downton, J. V. (1973). *Rebel Leadership: Commitment and Charisma in a Revolutionary Process.* Free Press.

Drago, R., Tseng, Y. P., & Wooden, M. (2004). *Family Structure, Usual and Preferred Working Hours, and Egalitarianism in Australia,* 1-38. Melbourne Institute.

Drago, R., Colbeck, C., Stauffer, K., Pirretti, A., Burkum, K., Faziolo, J., Lazzaro, G., & Habasevich, T. (2006). The Avoidance Bias Against Caregiving: The Case of Academic Faculty. *The American Behavioral Scientist, 49*(9), 1222–1247. doi:10.1177/0002764206286387

Drago, R., Tseng, Y. P., & Wooden, M. (2005). Usual and Preferred Working Hours in Couple Households. *Journal of Family Studies, 11*(1), 46–61. doi:10.5172/jfs.327.11.1.46

Drew, G. (2010). Issues and Challenges in higher Educational Leadership. *Australian Educational Researcher, 37*(3), 57–76. doi:10.1007/BF03216930

Drory, A., & Gluskinos, U. M. (1980, February). Machiavellianism and leadership. *The Journal of Applied Psychology, 65*(1), 81–86. doi:10.1037/0021-9010.65.1.81

Dudgeon, P., Herbert, J., Millroy, J., & Oxenham, D. (Eds.). (2017). *Us Women, Our Ways, Our World.* Magabala Books.

Duflo, E., & Topalova, P. (2004). *Unappreciated service: Performance, perceptions, and women leaders in India. Manuscript.* Department of Economics, Massachusetts Institute of Technology.

Dumas, C., & Beinecke, R. H. (2018). Change leadership in the 21st century. *Journal of Organizational Change Management, 31*(4), 867–876. doi:10.1108/JOCM-02-2017-0042

Dumulescu, D., & Muţiu, A. I. (2021). Academic Leadership in the Time of COVID-19—Experiences and Perspectives. *Frontiers in Psychology, 12*, 12. doi:10.3389/fpsyg.2021.648344 PMID:33959076

Duncan, A., Dockery, M., Kalsi, J., Loan Vu, L., Mavisakalyan, A., & Salazar, S. (2022). *Woort Koorliny: Australian Indigenous Employment Index 2022.* Minderoo. https://www.minderoo.org/indigenous-employment-index/downloads/

Duran, M., & Sanchez, J. (2021). Employee Engagement and Wellbeing in Times of COVID-19 : A Proposal of the 5Cs Model. *International Journal of Environmental Research and Public Health, 18*(5470), 2–15. PMID:34065338

Dyer, G., & Dyer, M. (2017). 'Strategic leadership for sustainability by higher education: The American College & University Presidents' Climate Commitment'. *Journal of Cleaner Production, 140*, 111–116. doi:10.1016/j.jclepro.2015.08.077

Eagleton-Pierce, M., & Knafo, S. (2020). Introduction: The political economy of managerialism. *Review of International Political Economy, 27*(4), 763–779. doi:10.1080/09692290.2020.1735478

Eassom, S. (2016). Futureproof conference. *Campus Review.* <https://www.campusreview.com.au/futureproof2016-presentations/>

Ebong, I. B., Osezua, O., Ogbise, I. F., & Oki, M. (2020). Leadership Challenges and Labour Performance in Organizations. A Study of Nigeria Labour Congress (NLC) (2015-2019) EPRA *International Journal of Research and Development (IJRD)* 5 (9)63-71

Edwards, R. (1979). *Contested Terrain*. Heinemann.

Egghe, L. (1986). On the 80/20 rule. *Scientometrics*, *10*(1-2), 55–68. doi:10.1007/BF02016860

Eichenwald, K. (2005). *Conspiracy of Fools: A True Story*. Broadway Books.

Einarsen, S., Skogstad, A., Aasland, M. S., & Løseth, A. M. S. B. (2002). Destruktivt lederskap: Årsaker og konsekvenser (Causes and consequences of destructive leadership). In A. Skogstad & S. Einarsen (Eds.), *Ledelse på godt og vondt. Effektivitet og trivsel* (pp. 233–254). Fagbokforlaget.

Eisenbeiss, S. A., & van Knippenberg, D. (2015). On ethical leadership impact: The role of follower mindfulness and moral emotions. *Journal of Organizational Behavior*, *36*(2), 182–195. doi:10.1002/job.1968

Ejimabo, N. (2015). The influence of decision making in organizational leadership and management activities. *Journal of Entrepreneurship & Organization Management*, *4*(2), 2222–2839. doi:10.4172/2169-026X.1000138

Ekman, M., Lindgren, M., & Packendorff, J. (2018). Universities need leadership, academics need management: Discursive tensions and voids in the deregulation of Swedish higher education legislation. *Higher Education*, *75*(2), 299–321. doi:10.100710734-017-0140-2

Elyousfi, F., Anand, A., & Dalmasso, A. (2021). Impact of e-leadership and team dynamics on virtual team performance in a public organization. *International Journal of Public Sector Management*, *34*(5), 508–528. doi:10.1108/IJPSM-08-2020-0218

Engelbert, B., & Wallgren, L. G. (2016). The origins of task-and people-oriented leadership styles: Remains from early attachment security and influences during childhood and adolescence. *SAGE Open*, *6*(2). doi:10.1177/2158244016649012

Enteman, W. F. (1993). *Managerialism: the Emergence of a New Ideology*. University of Wisconsin Press.

Erdem, A. R. (2015). Eğitim yönetim etiği ve eğitim yönetiminde etik liderliğin kritiği. *Akademik Sosyal Araştırmalar Dergisi*, *3*(10), 1–15.

Erdheim, J., Wang, M., & Zickar, M. J. (2006). Linking the Big Five personality constructs to organizational commitment. *Personality and Individual Differences*, *41*(5), 959–970. doi:10.1016/j.paid.2006.04.005

Erikson, E. H. (1959). *Identity and the life cycle*. International Universities Press.

Ernst & Young. (2018). *Can the Universities of Today Lead Learning for Tomorrow? The University of the Future*. E&Y. <https://cdn.ey.com/echannel/au/en/industries/government---public-sector/ey-university-of-the-future-2030/EY-university-of-the-future-2030.pdf>

Esguerra, G. A., & Contreras, F. (2016). E-leadership, an unavoidable challenge for today's organizations. *Estudios Gerenciales*, *32*, 262–268. doi:10.1016/j.estger.2016.08.003

European Commission Science and Knowledge service. (2020). *Science for Policy Briefs: Telework in the EU before and after the COVID-19: Where we were, where we head to*. https://ec.europa.eu

Eurosurveillance Editorial Team. (2020). Note from the editors: World Health Organization declares novel coronavirus (2019-nCoV) sixth public health emergency of international concern. Eurosurveillance, 25(5), 200131e.

Ewing, K & Hendy, J., (2014) Foreword. *Trade Unions and Economic Inequality*. Institute of Employment Research and Centre for Labour and Social Studies.

Ewin, R. E. (1993). Corporate loyalty: Its objects and its grounds. *Journal of Business Ethics*, *12*(5), 387–396. doi:10.1007/BF00882029

Fairlie, P. (2011). Meaningful work, employee engagement, and other key employee outcomes: Implications for human resource development. *Advances in Developing Human Resources*, *13*(4), 508–525. doi:10.1177/1523422311431679

Faris, S. K., & Outcalt, C. L. (2001). The emergence of inclusive, process-oriented leadership. *Developing non-hierarchical leadership on campus: Case studies and best practices in higher education*, 9-18.

Fauchart, E., & Gruber, M. (2011). Darwinians, communitarians, and missionaries: The role of founder identity in entrepreneurship. *Academy of Management Journal*, *54*(5), 935–957. doi:10.5465/amj.2009.0211

Fayol, H. (1916). *Managerialism Industrielle et Generale [Industrial and General managerialism]*. London: Sir I. Pitman & Sons, ltd.

Feldman, D. C., & Weitz, B. A. (1991). From the invisible hand to the gladhand: Understanding a careerist orientation to work. *Human Resource Management*, *30*(2), 237–257. doi:10.1002/hrm.3930300206

Felfe, J. (2006). Transformationale und charismatische Führung – Stand der Forschung und aktuelle Entwicklungen. *Zeitschrift für Personalpsychologie*, *5*(4), 163–176. doi:10.1026/1617-6391.5.4.163

Fernandez, D. B., & Jawadi, N. (2015). Virtual R&D project teams: From e-leadership to performance. *Journal of Applied Business Research*, *31*(5), 1693–1708. doi:10.19030/jabr.v31i5.9384

Fiedler, F. E. (2006). The contingency model: A theory of leadership effectiveness. *Small groups: Key readings*, *369*, 60051-9.

Figueiredo, P., & Fonseca, C. (2022). Leadership and Followership in an Organizational Change Context: Positive leader development: Theoretical model proposal, 161–196.

Figueiredo, P., & Joaquim, A. F. (2022). The impact of artificial intelligence and intergenerational diversity. In F. Ince (Ed.), *Leadership Perspectives on Effective Intergenerational Communication and Management* (p. 28). IGI Global.

Finkelstein, S., & Hambrick, D. C. (1990). Top-management-team tenure and organizational outcomes: The moderating role of managerial discretion. *Administrative Science Quarterly*, *35*(3), 484–503. doi:10.2307/2393314

Finset, A., Bosworth, H., Butow, P., Gulbrandsen, P., Hulsman, R. L., Pieterse, A. H., Street, R., Tschoetschel, R., & van Weert, J. (2020). Effective health communication–a key factor in fighting the COVID-19 pandemic. *Patient Education and Counseling*, *103*(5), 873–876. doi:10.1016/j.pec.2020.03.027 PMID:32336348

Fiorenza, E. S. (1986). Missionaries, Apostles, Coworkers: Romans 16 and the Reconstruction of Women's Early Christian History. *Word & World*, *6*(4), 420–433.

Fisher, C. D. (2010). Happiness at Work. *International Journal of Management Reviews*, *12*(4), 384–412. doi:10.1111/j.1468-2370.2009.00270.x

Fitzmaurice, M. (2013). Constructing professional identity as a new academic: A moral endeavour. *Studies in Higher Education*, *38*(4), 613–622. doi:10.1080/03075079.2011.594501

Fleishman, E. A., Mumford, M. D., Zaccaro, S. J., Levin, K. Y., Korotkin, A. L., & Hein, M. B. (1991). Taxonomic efforts in the description of leader behavior: A synthesis and functional interpretation. *The Leadership Quarterly*, *2*(4), 245–287. doi:10.1016/1048-9843(91)90016-U

Flores, K., Matkin, G., Burbach, M., Quinn, C., & Harding, H. (2012). deficient critical thinking skills among college graduates: Implications for leadership. *Educational Philosophy and Theory*, *44*(2), 212–230. doi:10.1111/j.1469-5812.2010.00672.x

Foels, R., Driskell, J. E., Mullen, B., & Salas, E. (2000). The effects of democratic leadership on group member satisfaction: An integration. *Small Group Research*, *31*(6), 676–701. doi:10.1177/104649640003100603

Foley, F., Martin-Chew, L., & Nicoll, F. (2015). *Courting blakness: recalibrating knowledge in the sandstone university*. University of Queensland Press.

Fontova, H. (2005). *Fidel: Hollywood's favorite tyrant*. Regnery Publishing.

Forgas, J. P., & Crano, W. D. (2021). The psychology of populism: The tribal challenge to liberal democracy. In *The Psychology of Populism* (pp. 1–19). Routledge. doi:10.4324/9781003057680-1

Fornell, C., & Larcker, D. F. (1981). Evaluating structural equation models with unobservable variables and measurement error. *JMR, Journal of Marketing Research*, *18*(1), 39–50. doi:10.1177/002224378101800104

Foti, R. J., Knee, R. E. Jr, & Backert, R. S. (2008). Multi-level implications of framing leadership perceptions as a dynamic process. *The Leadership Quarterly*, *19*(2), 178–194. doi:10.1016/j.leaqua.2008.01.007

Fredericks, B. & Bargallie, D. (2020b). Situating race in cultural competency training: A site of self-revelation. *M/C Journal*, *23*. https://doi.org/10.5204/mcj.1660 doi:10.5204/mcj.1660

Fredericks, B. (2020). Collaborative Creative Processes That Challenge Us as" Anomaly", and Affirm Our Indigeneity and Enact Our Sovereignty. *M/C Journal*, *23*. https://doi.org/10.5204/mcj.1674 doi:10.5204/mcj.1674

Fredericks, B., & White, N. (2013). Making the written word part of our toolbox: Aboriginal and Torres Strait Islander women educators. *Redress*, *22*, 7-13. https://search.informit.org/doi/10.3316/ielapa.456398554013227

Fredericks, B. (2009). The epistemology that maintains white race privilege, power and control of Indigenous studies and Indigenous peoples' participation in universities. *Critical Race and Whiteness Studies*, *5*, 1-12.

Fredericks, B. (2011). 'Universities are not the safe places we would like to think they are but they are getting safer': Indigenous Women Academics in Higher Education. *Journal of Australian Indigenous Issues*, *14*(1), 41–53.

Fredericks, B. (2011a). Rock Pools of Critical Thought: Finding a place to think through my higher degree and what. a PhD was all about. *Journal of Australian Indigenous Issues*, *14*(1), 19–31.

Fredericks, B. L., White, N., Bunda, T., & Baker, J. (2011). Demonstrating Indigenous women's educational leadership: Tiddas Showin'Up, Talkin'Up and Puttin'Up! *Journal of Australian Indigenous Issues*, *14*, 3–8.

Fredericks, B., & Bargallie, D. (2016). 'Which way? Talking culture, talking race': Unpacking an Indigenous cultural competency course. *International Journal of Critical Indigenous Studies*, *9*(1), 3–16. https://doi.org/10.5204/ijcis.v9i1.141 doi:10.5204/ijcis.v9i1.141

Fredericks, B., & Bargallie, D. (2020a). An Indigenous Australian Cultural Competency Course: Talking Culture, Care and Power. In J. Frawley, G. Russell, & J. Sherwood (Eds.), *Cultural Competence and the Higher Education Sector: Perspectives, Policies and Practice*. Springer Publications. doi:10.1007/978-981-15-5362-2_16

Fredericks, B., Mills, K., & White, N. (2014). 'I now know I can do this now': Indigenous Women and Writing in the Australian Higher Education Sector. *Text*, *18*(1), 1–11. http://dx.doi.org/10.52086/001c.27315 doi:10.52086/001c.27315

Fredericks, B., & White, N. (2018). Using bridges made by others as scaffolding and establishing footings for those that follow: Indigenous women in the Academy. *Australian Journal of Education*, *62*(3), 243–255. https://doi.org/10.1177/0004944118810017 doi:10.1177/0004944118810017

Fredericks, B., White, N., Phillips, S., Bunda, T., Longbottom, M., & Bargallie, D. (2019). Being Ourselves, Naming Ourselves, Writing Ourselves: Indigenous Australian Women Disrupting What It Is to Be Academic Within the Academy. In L. M. Thomas & A. B. Reinertsen (Eds.), *Academic writing and identity constructions: performativity, space and territory in academic workplaces*. Palgrave Macmillan. doi:10.1007/978-3-030-01674-6_5

Freeman, J., & Boeker, W. (1984). The Ecological Analysis of Strategy. *California Management Review*, *26*(3), 73–86. doi:10.2307/41165081

French, J., Raven, B., & Cartwright, D. (1959). *Studies in social power*. The University of Michigan, Institute for Social Research.

Freud, A. (1966). *The ego and the mechanisms of defense*. International Universities Press.

Freud, S. (1921). *Group psychology and the analysis of the ego*. Hogarth Press.

Fuentes, N. (2004). *La autobiografía de Fidel Castro: I. El paraíso de los otros*. Barcelona: Ediciones Destino.

Fu, J., Long, Y., He, Q., & Liu, Y. (2020). Can Ethical Leadership Improve Employees' Well-Being at Work? Another Side of Ethical Leadership Based on Organizational Citizenship Anxiety. *Frontiers in Psychology*, *11*, 1478. Advance online publication. doi:10.3389/fpsyg.2020.01478 PMID:32848973

Fullan, M., & Scott, G. (2009). *Turnaround Leadership for Higher Education*. Jossey-Bass.

Furnham, A., Hughes, D. J., & Marshall, E. (2013). Creativity, OCD, narcissism, and the Big Five. *Thinking Skills and Creativity*, *10*, 91–98. doi:10.1016/j.tsc.2013.05.003

Furnham, A., Richards, S. C., & Paulhus, D. L. (2013). The Dark Triad of personality: A 10-year review. *Social and Personality Psychology Compass*, *7*(3), 199–216. doi:10.1111pc3.12018

Gagnon, M. A. (2021). Ghost management as a central feature of accumulation in corporate capitalism: the case of the global pharmaceutical sector. In M. Benquet & T. Bourgeron (Eds.), *Accumulating Capital Today - Contemporary Strategies of Profit and Dispossessive Policies* (pp. 163–177). Routledge. doi:10.4324/9781003089513-15

Gallup. (2014). *Gallup Engagement Index*. https://www.gallup.com/strategicconsulting/158162/gallup-engagement-index.aspx

Gandossy, R., & Sonnenfeld, J. A. (2004). *Leadership and governance from the inside out*. John Wiley & Sons.

GaoJ.YinY.JonesB. F. (2020). *Quantifying Policy Responses to a Global Emergency: Insights from the COVID-19 Pandemic*. Northwestern University. https://arxiv.org/abs/2006.13853

Garavan, T., Watson, S., Carbery, R., & O'Brien, F. (2016). The antecedents of leadership development practices in SMEs: The influence of HRM strategy and practice. *International Small Business Journal*, *34*(6), 870–890. doi:10.1177/0266242615594215

Garcia, I. (2015). Emergent leadership: Is e-leadership importance in the quality of virtual education? *RIED: Revista Iberoamericana de Educacion a Distancia*, *18*(1). Advance online publication. doi:10.5944/ried.18.1.13798

Gardiner, M. E., Enomoto, E., & Grogan, M. (2000). *Coloring outside the lines: Mentoring women into school leadership*. Suny Press.

Gardner, H. (1996). *Leading minds: An anatomy of leadership.* Basic Books.

Gardner, W. L., & Martinko, M. J. (1988). Impression management in organizations. *Journal of Management, 14*(2), 321–338. doi:10.1177/014920638801400210

Gardner, W., & Avolio, B. (1998). The charismatic relationship: A dramaturgical perspective. *Academy of Management Review, 23*(1), 32–58. doi:10.2307/259098

Garmezy, N., & Masten, A. (1994). Chronic adversities. In M. Rutter, L. H. Taylor, & E. Taylor (Eds.), *Child and adolescent psychiatry* (3rd ed., pp. 191–208). Blackwell Scientific Publications.

Garnder, L., Kafka, A. C., & Carlson, S. (2020). Financial Strategies for Crisis and Beyond. Chronicle of Higher Education.

Gartzia, L., & Baniandrés, J. (2016). Are people-oriented leaders perceived as less effective in task performance? Surprising results from two experimental studies. *Journal of Business Research, 69*(2), 508–516. doi:10.1016/j.jbusres.2015.05.008

Gaskell, K. (2017). *Inspired leadership: how you can achieve extraordinary results in business.* John Wiley & Sons.

Gauthier, H. (2015). A Multi-Dimensional Model for Positive Leadership. *Strategic Leadership Review, 5*(1), 6–16. https://slr.scholasticahq.com/article/9-a-multi-dimensional-model-for-positive-leadership

Gersick, C. J., & Hackman, J. R. (1990). Habitual routines in task-performing groups. *Organizational Behavior and Human Decision Processes, 47*(1), 65–97. doi:10.1016/0749-5978(90)90047-D PMID:11538273

Geyer, G. (1991). *Guerrilla prince: The untold story of Fidel Castro.* Little, Brown and Company.

Ghurye, G. S. (1980). *The scheduled tribes of India.* Transaction Publishers.

Giannarou, L., & Zervas, E. (2014). Using Delphi technique to build consensus in practice. [IJBSAM]. *International Journal of Business Science and Applied Management, 9*(2), 65–82.

Gierlich-Joas, M., Hess, T., & Neuburger, R. (2020). more self-organization, more control—Or even both? Inverse transparency as a digital leadership concept. *Business Research, 13*(3), 921–947. doi:10.100740685-020-00130-0

Gilding, M., Gregory, S., & Cosson, B. (2011). A Typology of Motives of Family Business Succession Planning. *The Australian Sociological Association Conference.* ASA.

Gilding, M., Gregory, S., & Cosson, B. (2015). Motives and Outcomes in Family Business Succession Planning. *Entrepreneurship Theory and Practice, 39*(2), 299–312. doi:10.1111/etap.12040

Gillaspie, S. M. (2009). *The İmpact of Dark Leadership on Organizational Commitment and Turnover.* Emporia State University.

GIZ. (2021) *Economic Development and Employment.* GIZ. https://www.giz.de/en/ourservices/economic_development_and_employment.html

Glass, C., & Cook, A. (2020). Performative contortions: How White women and people of colour navigate elite leadership roles. *Gender, Work and Organization, 27*(6), 1232–1252. doi:10.1111/gwao.12463

Gleason, N. (2018). *Higher Education in the Era of the Fourth Industrial Revolution.* Springer Nature. doi:10.1007/978-981-13-0194-0

Gold, A. H., Malhotra, A., & Segars, A. H. (2001). Knowledge management: An organizational capabilities perspective. *Journal of Management Information Systems, 18*(1), 185–214. doi:10.1080/07421222.2001.11045669

Compilation of References

Goldberg, L. R. (1999). A broad-bandwidth, public-domain, personality inventory measuring the lower-level facets of several five-factor models. In I. Mervielde, I. J. Deary, F. De Fruyt, & F. Ostendorf (Eds.), *Personality psychology in Europe* (Vol. 7, pp. 7–28). Tilburg University Press.

Goldberg, L. R., Johnson, J. A., Eber, H. W., Hogan, R., Ashton, M. C., Cloninger, C. R., & Gough, H. G. (2006). The International Personality Item Pool and the future of public domain personality measures. *Journal of Research in Personality*, *40*(1), 84–96. doi:10.1016/j.jrp.2005.08.007

Goldman, A. (2009b). Transforming Toxic Leaders. Stanford Business Books.

Goleman, D. (2000). *Emotional Intelligence & Working With Emotional Intelligence*. Bantam; Reprint edition.

Gosling, J., & Mintzberg, H. (2003). The five minds of a manager. *Harvard Business Review*, *81*(11), 54–63. PMID:14619151

Goswami, B. K., Singh, J., & Goswami, A. (2019). Impact Of High Performance Human Resource Management Practices On Employee Engagement With The Moderating Role Of Ethical Leadership. *International Journal of Advanced Science and Technology*, *28*(19), 331–334. http://sersc.org/journals/index.php/IJAST/article/view/2538

Gotsis, G., & Grimani, K. (2016). The role of Servant Leadership in Fostering Inclusive Organizations. *Journal of Management Development*, *35*(9), 985–1010. doi:10.1108/JMD-07-2015-0095

Government of Telangana Social Welfare Residential Educational Institutions Society (TSWREIS). (n.d.). *Homepage*. TSWREIS. https://www.tswreis.ac.in/

Graeber, D. (2014). Anthropology and the rise of the professional-managerial class. *HAU*, *4*(3), 73–88. doi:10.14318/hau4.3.007

Graen, G. B., & Uhl-Bien, M. (1995). Development of leader–member exchange (LMX) theory of leadership over 25 years: Applying a multi-level domain perspective. *The Leadership Quarterly*, *6*, 219–247. doi:10.1016/1048-9843(95)90036-5

Graham, J. T. (2022). The Quiet Quitting Movement. *Sage HR Blog*. https://blog.sage.hr/the-quiet-quitting-movement/

Green, K. (2019, February 26). *Unions Must Promote Diversity and Inclusion to Maintain Solidarity*. Union Track. https://uniontrack.com/blog/union-diversity-inclusion

Green, R. A. (2014). The Delphi technique in educational research. *SAGE Open*, *4*(2), 2158244014529773. doi:10.1177/2158244014529773

Gregory, P. R. 1991. *Soviet Bureaucratic Behavior*. University of Houston. https://www.ucis.pitt.edu/nceeer/1991-804-13-Gregory.pdf

Grinyer, J., Russell, A., & Collison, D. (1998). Evidence of Managerial Short-termism in the UK. *British Journal of Management*, *9*(1), 13–22. doi:10.1111/1467-8551.00072

Großer, B., & Baumöl, U. (2017). Why virtual teams work – State of the art. *Procedia Computer Science*, *121*, 297–305. doi:10.1016/j.procs.2017.11.041

Gubik, A. S., & Vörös, Z. (2023). Why narcissists may be successful entrepreneurs: The role of entrepreneurial social identity and overwork. *Journal of Business Venturing Insights*, *19*, e00364. Advance online publication. doi:10.1016/j.jbvi.2022.e00364

Gumbrell-McCormick, R., & Hyman, R. (2019). Democracy in trade unions, democracy through trade unions? *Economic and Industrial Democracy*, *40*(1), 91–110. doi:10.1177/0143831X18780327

Gupta, A. (2020). *Accelerating Remote Work after COVID-19*. The Center for Growth & Opportunity.

Gupta, S. (2002). *Corporate capitalism and political philosophy*. Pluto Press.

Guthrie Valaskis, G., Stout, M. D., & Grimond, E. (Eds.). (2009). *Restoring the Balance First Nations Women, Community, and Culture*. University of Manitoba Press.

Gyang, E. B. (2020). Community-based leadership and sustainable development in higher education. *Journal of Leadership, Accountability and Ethics*, *17*(3), 34–43.

Haar, J. M. (2013). Testing a new measure of work-life balance: A study of parent and non-parent employees from New Zealand. *International Journal of Human Resource Management*, *24*(17), 3305–3324. doi:10.1080/09585192.2013.775175

Haar, J. M., Russo, M., Sune, A., & Ollier-Malaterre, A. (2014). Outcomes of work-life balance on job satisfaction, life satisfaction and mental health: A study across seven cultures. *Journal of Vocational Behavior*, *85*(3), 361–373. doi:10.1016/j.jvb.2014.08.010

Habermas, J. (1995). Paradigms of law. *Cardozo Law Review*, *17*, 771.

Haciyakupoglu, G., Hui, J. Y., Suguna, V. S., Leong, D., Bin, M. F., & Rahman, A. (2018). *Countering Fake News A Survey Of Recent Global Initiatives*. S. Rajaratnam School of International Studies. https://think-asia.org/handle/11540/8063

Hair, J. F. Jr, Hult, G. T. M., Ringle, C., & Sarstedt, M. (2016). *A primer on partial least squares structural equation modeling (PLS-SEM)*. Sage Publications.

Hambrick, D. C. (1981). Environment, strategy, and power within top management teams. *Administrative Science Quarterly*, *26*(2), 253–276. doi:10.2307/2392472 PMID:10251673

Hambrick, D., & Abrahamson, C. (1995). Assessing the amount of managerial discretion in different industries: A multi-method approach. *Academy of Management Journal*, *38*(5), 1427–1441. doi:10.2307/256864

Hamidifar, F. (2010). A study of the relationship between leadership styles and employee job satisfaction at Islamic Azad University Branches in Tehran, Iran. *AU-GSB e-J.*, *3*, 45-58.

Hamilton, A., Jay, J., & Madison, J. (2000). *The federalist*. Random House.

Hammersley, M. (1992). Deconstructing the Qualitative–Quantitative Divide. In J. Brannen (Ed.), *Mixing Methods: Qualitative and Quantitative Research* (pp. 39–55). Avebury.

Hammond, Z. (2018). Culturally Responsive Teaching Puts Rigor at the Center: Q&A with Zaretta Hammond. *Learning Professional*, *39*(5), 40–43.

Han, J. L. & S. H. (2021). *The Future of Service Post-COVID-19 Pandemic: Rapid Adoption of Digital Service Technology*. Springer.

Handler, W. (1994). Succession in family business: A review of the literature. *Family Business Review*, *7*(2), 133–157. doi:10.1111/j.1741-6248.1994.00133.x

Hare, A. P., Koenigs, R. J., & Hare, S. E. (1997). Perceptions of observed and model values of male and female managers. *Journal of Organizational Behavior*, *18*(5), 437–447. doi:10.1002/(SICI)1099-1379(199709)18:5<437::AID-JOB806>3.0.CO;2-0

Hare, J. (2022). How SA's merger will create a 'university of the future'. *Australian Financial Review*.

Hare, R. (1993). *Without conscience: The disturbing world of the psychopaths among us*. Simon & Schuster.

Harter, J. (2022). *Is Quiet Quitting Real?* Gallup. https://www.gallup.com/workplace/398306/quiet-quitting-real.aspx

Harter, S. (1990). Causes, correlates, and the functional role of global self-worth: A life span perspective. In R. J. Sternberg & J. Kolligan Jr. (Eds.), Competence considered (pp. 67–97). Yale University Press.

Harvester, P., Davis, P., & Lyden, J. (1997). Succession Planning in Family Business: The Impact of Owner Gender. *Family Business Review*, *10*(4), 373–396. doi:10.1111/j.1741-6248.1997.00373.x

Harvey, A. (2001). A dramaturgical analysis of charismatic leader discourse. *Journal of Organizational Change Management*, *14*(3), 253–265. doi:10.1108/09534810110394877

Haslam, S. A., Reicher, S. D., & Platow, M. J. (2021). *The New Psychology of Leadership: Identity, Influence and Power* (2nd ed.). Psychology Press.

Hassan, A., Gallear, D., & Sivarajah, U. (2018). Critical factors affecting leadership: a higher education context. *Transforming Government: People, Process, and Policy*, *12*(1), 110–130.

Hassan, S., Wright, B. E., & Yukl, G. (2014). Does Ethical Leadership Matter in Government? Effects on Organizational Commitment, Absenteeism, and Willingness to Report Ethical Problems. *Public Administration Review*, *74*(3), 333–343. doi:10.1111/puar.12216

Hatchuel, A., & Segrestin, B. (2019). A century old and still visionary: Fayol's innovative theory of management. *European Management Review*, *16*(2), 399–412. doi:10.1111/emre.12292

Hayward, M. L. A., & Hambrick, D. C. (1997). Explaining the premiums paid for large acquisitions: Evidence of CEO hubris. *Administrative Science Quarterly*, *42*(1), 103–127. doi:10.2307/2393810

Hayward, M. L. A., Shepherd, D. A., & Griffin, D. (2006). A hubris theory of entrepreneurship. *Management Science*, *52*(2), 160–172. doi:10.1287/mnsc.1050.0483

Hendriks, M., Burger, M., Rijsenbilt, A., Pleeging, E., & Commandeur, H. (2020). Virtuous leadership: A source of wellbeing of employee and trust. *Management Research Review*, *43*(8), 951–970. doi:10.1108/MRR-07-2019-0326

Henseler, J., Ringle, C. M., & Sarstedt, M. (2015). A new criterion for assessing discriminant validity in variance-based structural equation modelling. *Journal of the Academy of Marketing Science*, *43*(1), 115–135. doi:10.100711747-014-0403-8

Herman, E. S., & McChesney, R. W. (1997). *The global media: The new missionaries of corporate capitalism*. Cassell.

Hernstein, R. J., & Murray, C. (1994). *The bell curve: Intelligence and class structure in American Life*. Free Press.

Herring, L. N. (2007). *First African-American female school superintendent in Georgia: Reflections from the field to the forefront*. Georgia Southern University.

Higgins, E. T. (1997). Beyond pleasure and pain. *The American Psychologist*, *52*(12), 1280–1300. doi:10.1037/0003-066X.52.12.1280 PMID:9414606

Hinrichsen, S., Adrian, B., & Schulz, A. (2021). Approaches to improve shop floor management. In T. Ahram, R. Taiar, K. Langlois, & A. Choplin (Eds.), *Advances in intelligent systems and computing. Human interaction, emerging technologies and future applications III* (Vol. 1253, pp. 415–421). Springer.

Hirschman, A. (1970). *Exit, Voice, and Loyalty: responses to decline in firms, organizations, and states*. Harvard University Press.

Hirschmann, G. (2021). The Reassertion of National Sovereignty: A Challenge to International Organizations' Survival? *Security and Human Rights*, *31*(1-4), 60–67. doi:10.1163/18750230-bja10003

Hobfoll, S. E. (2001). The influence of culture, community, and the nested-self in the stress process: Advancing conservation of resources theory. *Applied Psychology*, *50*(3), 337–421. doi:10.1111/1464-0597.00062

Hobscheidt, D., Westermann, T., Dumitrescu, R., Dülme, C., Gausemeier, J., Heppner, H., & Maier, G. W. (2017). Soziotechnische Leistungsbewertung von Unternehmen im Kontext Industrie 4.0. In E. Bodden, F. Dressler, R. Dumitrescu, J. Gausemeier, F. Meyer auf der Heide, C. Scheytt & A. Trächtler (Eds.), WInTeSys 2017: Wissenschaftsforum Intelligente Technische Systeme. Verlagsschriftenreihe des Heinz Nixdorf Instituts.

Hochschild, A. R. (1989). *The Second-Shift: Working Parents and the Revolution at Home*. Viking Penguin.

Hoffer, E. (1951). *The true believer: Thoughts on the nature of mass movements*. Harper & Row.

Hoffman, B., Woehr, D., Maldagen-Youngjohn, R., & Lyons, B. (2011). Great man or great myth? A quantitative review of the relationship between individual differences and leader effectiveness. *Journal of Occupational and Organizational Psychology*, *84*(2), 347–381. doi:10.1348/096317909X485207

Hofstede, G. (1991). *Cultures and organizations: Software of the mind*. McGraw-Hill.

Hogan, R., Raskin, R., & Fazzini, D. (1990). The dark side of charisma. In K. Clark & M. Clark (Eds.), Measures of leadership (pp. 343–354). Academic Press.

Hogan, R., Curphy, G. J., & Hogan, J. (1994). What we know about leadership: Effectiveness and personality. *The American Psychologist*, *49*(6), 493–504. doi:10.1037/0003-066X.49.6.493 PMID:8042818

Hogan, R., & Hogan, J. (2001). Assessing leadership: A view from the dark side. *International Journal of Selection and Assessment*, *9*(1&2), 12–51. doi:10.1111/1468-2389.00162

Holey, E. A., Feeley, J. L., Dixon, J., & Whittaker, V. J. (2007). An exploration of the use of simple statistics to measure consensus and stability in Delphi studies. *BMC Medical Research Methodology*, *7*(1), 1–10. doi:10.1186/1471-2288-7-52 PMID:18045508

Hollander, E. P. (2013). Organisational leadership and followership. *Social Psychology at Work: Essays in Honour of Michael Argyle*. https://papers.ssrn.com/sol3/papers.cfm?abstract_id=3692035

Hollyns, B. A. (2017). Levels of Participation in Decision Making as Correlates of Job Satisfaction and Morale of Teachers in Public Senior Secondary Schools in Delta State *Global Journal of Management and Business Research. Administrative Management*, *17*(1), 83–96.

Hooks, B. (1990). Feminist theory: From margin to centre. Boston: South End P.

Hopp, C., & Pruschak, G. (2020). Is there such a thing as leadership skill? – A replication and extension of the relationship between high school leadership positions and later-life earnings. *The Leadership Quarterly*, 101475. doi:10.1016/j.leaqua.2020.101475

Horney, N., Pasmore, B., & O'Shea, T. (2010). Leadership agility: A business imperative for a VUCA world. *People & Strategy*, *33*, 4.

Hornstein, H. A. (1996). *Brutal Bosses and their pray*. Riverhead Books.

Hougaard, R., Carter, J., & Hobson, N. (2020). Compassionate leadership is necessary—but not sufficient. *Harvard Business Review*. https://hbr.org/2020/12/compassionate-leadership-is-necessary-but-not-sufficient

House, R. J., Spangler, W. D., & Woycke, J. (1991). Personality and charisma in the U.S. presidency: A psychological theory of leader effectiveness. *Administrative Science Quarterly*, *36*(3), 364–396. doi:10.2307/2393201

Howell, J. M., & Avolio, B. J. (1992). The ethics of charismatic leadership: Submission or liberation? *The Academy of Management Executive*, *6*, 43–54.

Howington, J. (2022). *Employee Engagement Report: Job Satisfaction and Work Flexibility*. FlexJobs for Employers. https://www.flexjobs.com/employer-blog/employee-engagement-report-job-satisfaction-work-flexibility/

Hoyle, E., & Wallace, M. (2005). *Educational Leadership – Ambiguity, Professionals & managerialism*. Sage. doi:10.4135/9781446220078

Hunsaker, P., & Hunsaker, J. (2008). Virtual teams: A leader's guide. *Team Performance Management*, *14*(1/2), 86–101. doi:10.1108/13527590810860221

Huppatz, K., Sang, N., & Napier, J. (2019). 'If you put pressure on yourself to produce then that's your responsibility': Mothers' experiences of maternity leave and flexible work in the neoliberal university. *Gender, Work and Organization*, *6*(6), 772–788. doi:10.1111/gwao.12314

Hutchings, K., Bainbridge, R., Bodle, K., & Miller, A. (2019). Determinants of attraction, retention and completion for Aboriginal and Torres Strait Islander higher degree research students: A systematic review to inform future research directions. *Research in Higher Education*, *60*(2), 245–272. https://doi.org/10.1007/s11162-018-9511-5 doi:10.100711162-018-9511-5

Ichikawa, A. (1993). Leadership as a Form of Culture: It's Present and Future States in Japan. *International Review of Strategic Management*, *4*, 155–170.

ICIR. (2022, September, 22). *Nigerian government watches as Chinese companies violate labour laws, workers' rights*. International Center For Investigative Reports Report. https://www.icirnigeria.org/nigerian-government-watches-as-chinese-companies-violate-labour-laws-workers-rights/

ILO. (2005, October). *The Role of Trade Unions in the Global Economy and the Fight against Poverty*. The International Workers' Symposium on "Fight Poverty – Organize" Summary and Conclusion, Geneva, Switzerland http://www.ilo.org/wcmsp5/groups/public/@ed_dialogue/@actrav/documents/meetingdocument/wcms_111312.pdf

ILO. (2007, October) *The role of trade unions in workers' education: The key to trade union capacity building* [Paper presentation]. The International Workers' Symposium Geneva, Switzerland. http://actrav-courses.itcilo.org/en/a3-58346/a3-58346-resources/background-paper-ilo-we-symposium.pdf

ILO. (2015). *Decent Work Country Diagnostics - Technical Guidelines to draft the Diagnostics Report*. ILO.

ILO. (2021a). *A Global Trend Analysis on the Roles of Trade Unions in times of COVID-19: A summary of findings*. ILO. http://search.ilo.org/wcmsp5/groups/public/---ed_dialogue/---actrav/documents/ publication/ wcms_767226.pdf

ILO. (2021b). *Global call to action: for a human-centred recovery from the COVID-19 crisis that is inclusive, sustainable and resilient*. ILO. https://www.ilo.org/wcmsp5/groups/public/@ed_norm/@relconf/documents/meetingdocument/wcms_806092.pdf

ILO. (2022). *ILO Monitor on the world of work. Tenth edition Multiple crises threaten the global labour market recovery*. ILO. https://www.ilo.org/wcmsp5/groups/public/---dgreports/---dcomm/---publ/documents/briefingnote/wcms_859255.pdf

Ilyas, S., Abid, G., & Ashfaq, F. (2020). Ethical leadership in sustainable organizations: The moderating role of general self-efficacy and the mediating role of organizational trust. *Sustainable Production and Consumption*, *22*, 195–204. doi:10.1016/j.spc.2020.03.003

IMF. (2021). *World Economic Outlook Report, October*. Washington, DC: International Monetary Fund Indeed Editorial Team. https://uk.indeed.com/career-advice/career-development/why-is-motivation-important-in-leadership

Incentive Research Foundation. (2015). Generations in the Workforce & Marketplace : Preferences in Rewards. *Recognition & Incentives*, (January), 2018.

IndustriALL Global Union. (2018) Report of Shell Nigeria Fact Funding Mission. IGU. https://www.industriall-union.org/industriall-investigation-uncovers-exploitation-of-shell-workers-in-nigeria

Ingram, J., & Cangemi, J. (2012). Emotions, emotional intelligence and leadership: A brief, pragmatic perspective. *Education*, *132*(4).

Ion, C. G. (2015). Husserl, Habermas, and the Lifeworld as the Overall Horizon within Which Individuals Act. *Linguistic and Philosophical Investigations*, (14), 115–120.

Iqbal, Z. A. (2020). Ethical Leadership and Innovative Work Behavior: The Mediating Role of Individual Attributes. *Journal of Open Innovation: Technology, Market, and Complexity*, *6*(3), 68. . doi:10.3390/joitmc6030068

Ishak, A. K., & Mustafa Kamil, B. A. (2016). Succession Planning at Higher Education Institutions: Leadership Style, Career Development and Knowledge Management Practices as its Predictors. *International Review of Management and Marketing*, *6*(S7), 214–220.

ITUC. (2017). *International Trade Union Confederation 2017 Global Polls*. ITUC.

ITUC. (2021). *International Trade Union Confederation 2021 Global Rights Index*. ITUC.

Izgar, H. (2008). Headteachers' leadership Behavior And Problem-Solving Skills: A Comparative Study. *Social Behavior and Personality*, *36*(4), 535–548. doi:10.2224bp.2008.36.4.535

Izumi, T., Sukhwani, V., Surjan, A., & Shaw, R. (2021). Managing and responding to pandemics in higher educational institutions: initial learning from COVID-19. *International Journal of Disaster Resilience in the Built Environment*, *12*(1), 51-66.

Jaffe, R., & Lordan, G. (2020) Five Behavioural Science lessons for managing virtual team meetings. *LSE Business Review*. Available at http://eprints.lse.ac.uk/id/eprint/104808

Jain, A. K., & Sullivan, S. (2019). An examination of the relationship between careerism and organizational commitment, satisfaction, and performance. *Personnel Review*, *49*(9), 1553–1571. doi:10.1108/PR-05-2019-0280

Janis, I., & Mann, L. (1977). *Decision making: A psychological analysis of conflict, choice, and commitment*. Free University Press.

Jaros, S. (2018). Expansive and Focused Concepts of managerialism in CMS. *Tamara, 16*(1-2):1-12.

Jarrett, K., & Newton, S. (Eds.). (2020). *The Practice of Leadership in Higher Education: Real-world Perspectives on Becoming, Being and Leaving*. Routledge. doi:10.4324/9780367823849

Jaskaran, S. D., & Sri-Guru, G. S. (2014). Participative leadership and employee job well-being: perceived co-worker support as a boundary condition. *Journal of Psychological Science*, (4), 873.

Compilation of References

Jawadi, N. (2013). E-leadership and trust management: Exploring the moderating effects of team virtuality. *International Journal of Technology and Human Interaction*, *9*(3), 18–35. doi:10.4018/jthi.2013070102

Jeanes, E. (2021). A meeting of mind(sets). Integrating the pedagogy and andragogy of mindsets for leadership development. *Thinking Skills and Creativity*, *39*, 100758. doi:10.1016/j.tsc.2020.100758

Jenkins, S. (2023, March 20). *Of course Boris Johnson is guilty of misleading parliament – stand by for another tory Civil War*. Retrieved March 28, 2023, from https://www.theguardian.com/commentisfree/2023/mar/20/boris-johnson-guilty-midleading-parliament-tory-civil-war-commons

Jiang, H., Luo, Y., & Kulemeka, O. (2017). Strategic social media use in public relations: Professionals' perceived social media impact, leadership behaviors, and work-life conflict. *International Journal of Strategic Communication*, *11*(1), 18–41. doi:10.1080/1553118X.2016.1226842

Johns, L., Cannon, M., Singleton, N., Murray, R., Farrell, M., Brugha, T., & Meltzer, H. (2004). Prevalence and correlates of self-reported psychotic symptoms in the British population. *The British Journal of Psychiatry*, *185*(4), 298–305. doi:10.1192/bjp.185.4.298 PMID:15458989

Johnson, K. (2010). *Virtual Leadership: Required Competencies for Effective Leaders*. Retrieved from https://ecommons.cornell.edu/bitstream/handle/1813/73721/Virtual_Leadership.pdf?sequence=1

Johnsrud, L. K. (1991). Mentoring between academic women: The capacity for interdependence. *Initiatives*, *54*(3), 7–17.

Jonason, P. K., Li, N. P., & Teicher, E. A. (2010). Who is James Bond?: The Dark Triad as an agentic social style. *Individual Differences Research*, *8*(2), 111–120.

Jonason, P. K., & Schmitt, D. P. (2012). What have you done for me lately? Friendship-selection in the shadow of the Dark Triad traits. *Evolutionary Psychology*, *10*(3), 147470491201000303. doi:10.1177/147470491201000303 PMID:22947669

Jones, S. (2021). *Inspire Leadership and Motivation in the Workplace*. Confie. https://www.confie.com/insights/leadershipand-motivation-in-the-workplace/

Jones, S., Hadgraft, R., Harvey, M., Lefoe, G. & Ryland, K. (2014). *Evidence-based Benchmarking Framework for a Distributed Leadership Approach to Capacity Building in Learning and Teaching*, Office for Learning and Teaching, University of Wollongong.

Jones, G. R., & George, J. M. (2004). *Essentials of Contemporary Management*. McGraw Hill Companies, Inc.

Jones, S., Lefoe, G., Harvey, M., & Ryland, K. (2012). Distributed leadership: A collaborative framework for academics, executives and professionals in higher education. *Journal of Higher Education Policy and Management*, *34*(1), 67–78. doi:10.1080/1360080X.2012.642334

Jongbloed, B., Vossensteyn, H., van Vught, F., & Westerheijden, D. F. (2018). Transparency in higher education: the emergence of a new perspective on higher education governance. In A. Curaj, L. Deca, & R. Pricopie (Eds.), *European Higher Education Area: The Impact of Past and Future Policies* (pp. 441–454). Springer. doi:10.1007/978-3-319-77407-7_27

Joplin, T., Greenbaum, R. L., Wallace, J. C., & Edwards, B. D. (2021). Employee entitlement, engagement, and performance: The moderating effect of ethical leadership. *Journal of Business Ethics*, *168*(4), 813–826. doi:10.100710551-019-04246-0

Joshi, A., Vinay, M., & Bhaskar, P. (2020). Online Teaching amidst COVID-19 in India: An Outlook. *Asian Journal of Distance Education*, *15*(2), 105–111. doi:10.5281/zenodo.4294477

Judge, T. A., Colbert, A. E., & Ilies, R. (2004). Intelligence and leadership: A quantitative review and test of theoretical propositions. *The Journal of Applied Psychology*, *89*(3), 542–552. doi:10.1037/0021-9010.89.3.542 PMID:15161411

Judge, T. A., LePine, J. A., & Rich, B. L. (2006). The narcissistic personality: Relationship with inflated self-ratings of leadership and with task and contextual performance. *The Journal of Applied Psychology*, *91*, 762–776. doi:10.1037/0021-9010.91.4.762 PMID:16834504

Judge, T. A., Locke, L. A., & Durham, C. C. (1997). The dispositional causes of job satisfaction: A core evaluations approach. *Research in Organizational Behavior*, *19*, 151–188.

Judge, T. A., & Piccolo, R. F. (2004). Transformational and transactional leadership: A meta-analytic test of their relative validity. *The Journal of Applied Psychology*, *89*(5), 755–768. doi:10.1037/0021-9010.89.5.755 PMID:15506858

Judge, T. A., Piccolo, R. F., & Ilies, R. (2004). The forgotten ones? The validity of consideration and initiating structure in leadership research. *The Journal of Applied Psychology*, *89*(1), 36–51. doi:10.1037/0021-9010.89.1.36 PMID:14769119

Judge, T. A., Piccolo, R. F., & Kosalka, T. (2009). The bright and dark sides of leader traits: A review and theoretical extension of the leader trait paradigm. *The Leadership Quarterly*, *20*(6), 855–875. doi:10.1016/j.leaqua.2009.09.004

Judge, T., & Bono, J. (2001). Relationship of core self-evaluations traits-self-esteem, generalized self-efficacy, locus of control, and emotional stability—with job satisfaction and job performance: A meta-analysis. *The Journal of Applied Psychology*, *86*(1), 80–92. doi:10.1037/0021-9010.86.1.80 PMID:11302235

Jung, D. I., & Avolio, B. J. (2000). Opening the black box: An experimental investigation of the mediating effects of trust and value congruence on transformational and transactional leadership. *Journal of Organizational Behavior*, *21*(8), 949–964. doi:10.1002/1099-1379(200012)21:8<949::AID-JOB64>3.0.CO;2-F

Juntrasook, A. (2014). "You do not have to be the boss to be a leader": Contested meanings of leadership in higher education. *Higher Education Research & Development*, *33*(1), 19–31. doi:10.1080/07294360.2013.864610

Juusola, K. (2023). Coping with managerialism: Academics' responses to conflicting institutional logics in business schools. *International Journal of Management Education*, *17*(1), 89–107.

Kaffashpoor, A., & Sadeghian, S. (2020). The effect of ethical leadership on subjective wellbeing, given the moderator job satisfaction (a case study of private hospitals in mashhad). *BMC Nursing*, *19*(1), 111. Advance online publication. doi:10.118612912-020-00496-w PMID:33292181

Kaiser, R. B., & Hogan, R. (2007). The dark side of discretion: Leader personality and organizational decline. In R. Hooijberg, J. Hunt, J. Antonakis, & K. Boal (Eds.), *Being there even when you are not: Leading through strategy, systems and structures, Monographs in leadership and management* (Vol. 4, pp. 177–197). Elsevier Science. doi:10.1016/S1479-3571(07)04009-6

Kalaria, C. (2020). *Leadership — The VUCA perspective*. Retrieved from Medium: https://medium.com/@chiragkalaria/leadership-the-vuca-perspective-9a07aa05193b

Kane, G. C., Phillips, A. N., Copulsky, J., & Andrus, G. (2019). How digital leadership is (n't) different. *MIT Sloan Management Review*, *60*(3), 34–39.

Kanungo, N. R. (2001). Ethical values of transactional and transformational leaders. *Canadian Journal of Administrative Sciences*. Available at: http://search.proquest.com/docview/204887568?accountid=10344%5Cnhttp://sfx.unilinc.edu.au:9003/csu?url_ver=Z39.88-2004&r ft_val_fmt=info:ofi/fmt:kev:mtx:journal&genre=article&sid=Pr oQ:ProQ%3Aabiglobal&atitle=Ethical+values+of+transactional+a nd+transformati

Kark, R., & Van Dijk, D. (2019). Keep your head in the clouds and your feet on the ground: A multifocal review of leadership–followership self-regulatory focus. *The Academy of Management Annals*, *13*(2), 509–546. doi:10.5465/annals.2017.0134

Karunakar, B. (2019). Telangana Social Welfare Residential Educational Institutions Society: Programs and Facilities Available for Students Empowerment. *Educational Quest-An International Journal of Education and Applied Social Sciences*, *10*(3), 125–133. doi:10.30954/2230-7311.3.2019.2

Kashive, N., Khanna, V. T., & Powale, L. (2022). Virtual team performance: E-leadership roles in the era of COVID-19. *Journal of Management Development*, *41*(5), 277–300. doi:10.1108/JMD-05-2021-0151

Kato-Beiderwieden, A.-L., Ötting, S., Schlicher, K., Heppner, H., & Maier, G. W. (2020). *Prospektive Kompetenzanalyse (ProKA) – Ein Verfahren zur Einschätzung von zukünftigen Kompetenzveränderungen*. Manuscript submitted for publication.

Katz, M. (1997). *On playing a poor hand well: Insights from the lives of those who have overcome childhood risks and adversities*. W.W. Norton & Company.

Kauffeld, S., & Maier, G. W. (2020). Digitalisierte Arbeitswelt. *Gruppe. Interaktion. Organisation. Zeitschrift Für Angewandte Organisationspsychologie*, *51*(1), 1–4.

Kaul, S., & Sahni, S. (2009). Study on the participation of women in Panchayati Raj Institution. *Studies on Home and Community Science*, *3*(1), 29–38. doi:10.1080/09737189.2009.11885273

Keane, T., Linden, T., Hernandez-Martinez, P., & Molnar, A. (2022). University students' experiences and reflections of technology in their transition to online learning during the global pandemic. *Education Sciences*, *12*(7), 453–468. doi:10.3390/educsci12070453

Kellerman, B. (2004). *Bad leadership. What it is, how it happens, why it matters*. Harvard Business School Press.

Kellman, H. C., & Hamilton, V. L. (1989). *Crimes of obedience: Toward a social psychology of authority and responsibility*. Yale University Press.

Kennedy, J., Thomas, L., Percy, A., Dean, B., Delahunty, J., Harden-Thew, K., & De Laat, M. (2019). An Aboriginal way towards curriculum reconciliation. *The International Journal for Academic Development*, *24*(2), 148–162. https://doi.org/10.1080/1360144X.2019.1593172 doi:10.1080/1360144X.2019.1593172

Kennedy, P. (1987). *The rise and fall of the great powers: Economic change and military conflict from 1500 to 2000*. Random House.

Kenny, C., & Fraser, T. N. (2012). Living Indigenous Leadership Native Narratives on Building Strong Communities. Vancouver, BC, UBCPress.

Kenny, J. D. (2009). Managing a modern university: Is it time for a rethink? *Higher Education Research & Development*, *28*(6), 629–642. doi:10.1080/07294360903206934

Kenwick, M. R., & Simmons, B. A. (2020). Pandemic response as border politics. *International Organization*, *74*(S1), E36–E58. doi:10.1017/S0020818320000363

Kerfoot, K. (2010). Listening to see: The key to virtual leadership. *Nursing Economics*, *28*(2), 114. doi:10.1097/00006416-199707000-00008 PMID:20446383

Kets de Vries, M. F. R., & Korotov, K. (2012). Developing Leaders and Leadership Development. SSRN *Electronic Journal*. doi:10.2139/ssrn.1684001

Kets de Vries, M. (1989). *Prisoners of leadership*. John Wiley & Sons.

Kets de Vries, M. (2006). The spirit of despotism: Understanding the tyrant within. *Human Relations*, *59*(2), 195–220. doi:10.1177/0018726706062732

Kets de Vries, M. F. (1994). The Leadership Mystique. *The Academy of Management Perspectives*, *8*(3), 73–89. doi:10.5465/ame.1994.9503101181

Kezar, A. J., & Holcombe, E. M. (2017). *Shared Leadership in Higher Education: Important Lessons from Research and Practice*. American Council on Education.

Khatri, P., & Gupta, P. (2019). Development and validation of wellbeing of employee scale – a formative measurement model. *International Journal of Workplace Health Management*, *12*(5), 352–368. doi:10.1108/IJWHM-12-2018-0161

Khouly, S. E., Ossman, M., Selim, M., & Zaghloul, M. (2014). Impact of e-leadership on leadership styles within the Egyptian government sector. *Competition Forum*, *12*(1), 131–140.

Khuntia, R., & Suar, D. (2004). A Scale to Assess Ethical Leadership of Indian Private and Public Sector Managers. *Journal of Business Ethics*, *49*(1), 13–26. . doi:10.1023/B:BUSI.0000013853.80287.da

Kile, S. M. (1990). *Helsefarleg leierskap (Health endangering leadership)*. Universitetet i Bergen.

Kinnane, S., Wilks, J., Wilson, K., Hughes, T., & Thomas, S. (2014). 'Can't be what you can't see': The transition of Aboriginal and Torres Strait Islander students into higher education – Final Report, The University of Notre Dame Australia; Southern Cross University; Batchelor Institute of Indigenous Tertiary Education. https://www.notredame.edu.au/__data/assets/pdf_file/0020/2882/SI11-2138-OLT-Final-Report-FINAL-Web.pdf

Kinsinger, P., & Walch, K. (2012). Living and leading in a VUCA world. Thunderbird University.

Kipnis, D. (1972). Does power corrupt? *Journal of Personality and Social Psychology*, *24*(1), 33–41. doi:10.1037/h0033390 PMID:5079552

Kiron, D., Kane, G. C., Palmer, D., Phillips, A. N., & Buckley, N. (2016). Aligning the organization for its digital future. *MIT Sloan Management Review*, *58*(1).

Klein, M. F., & Salk, R. J. (2013). Presidential Succession Planning: A Qualitative Study in Private Higher Education. *Journal of Leadership & Organizational Studies*, *20*(3), 335–345. doi:10.1177/1548051813483836

Klikauer, T. (2013). Managerialism – Critique of an Ideology. Palgrave.

Klikauer, T. 2018. Adorno on ideology: ideology critique and mass consumerism, in: Coban. S. (eds), Media, Ideology and Hegemony. Leiden: Brill. doi:10.1163/9789004364417_006

Klikauer, T., & Tannò, A. (2022). Managerialism. In K. Schedler (Ed.), Elgar Encyclopaedia of Public Management (pp. 340–345). Edward Elgar. doi:10.4337/9781800375499.managerialism

Klikauer, T., & Young, M. (2021). Global Warming's Walking Dead. *Counterpunch*. https://www.counterpunch.org/2021/08/23/global-warmings-walking-dead/

Compilation of References

Klikauer, T. (2007). *Communication and Management at Work*. Palgrave. doi:10.1057/9780230210899

Klikauer, T. (2013). *Managerialism: A Critique of an Ideology*. Palgrave Macmillan. doi:10.1057/9781137334275

Klikauer, T. (2019). A preliminary theory of managerialism as an ideology. *Journal for the Theory of Social Behaviour*, *49*(4), 421–442. doi:10.1111/jtsb.12220

Klikauer, T. (2022). *Media Capitalism*. Palgrave.

Klikauer, T. (2023). *The Language of managerialism*. Palgrave/Springer. doi:10.1007/978-3-031-16379-1

Klug, K., Felfe, J., & Krick, A. (2022). Does Self-Care Make You a Better Leader? A Multisource Study Linking Leader Self-Care to Health-Oriented Leadership, Employee Self-Care, and Health. *International Journal of Environmental Research and Public Health*, *19*(11), 6733. doi:10.3390/ijerph19116733 PMID:35682319

Klus, M., & Müller, J. (2021). The digital leader: What one needs to master today's organisational challenges. *Journal of Business Economics*, *91*(8), 1189–1223. doi:10.100711573-021-01040-1

Kniffin, K. M., Narayanan, J., Anseel, F., Antonakis, J., Ashford, S. P., Bakker, A. B., Bamberger, P., Bapuji, H., Bhave, D. P., Choi, V. K., Creary, S. J., Demerouti, E., Flynn, F. J., Gelfand, M. J., Greer, L. L., Johns, G., Kesebir, S., Klein, P. G., Lee, S. Y., & Vugt, M. (2021). COVID-19 and the workplace: Implications, issues, and insights for future research and action. *The American Psychologist*, *76*(1), 63–77. doi:10.1037/amp0000716 PMID:32772537

Koch, A., & Westhoff, K. (2012). *Task-Analysis-Tools (TAToo) – Schritt für Schritt Unterstützung zur erfolgreichen Anforderungsanalyse*. Lengerich: Pabst.

Koch, A. R., & Binnewies, C. (2015). Setting a good example: Supervisors as work-life-friendly role models within the context of boundary management. *Journal of Occupational Health Psychology*, *20*(1), 82–92. doi:10.1037/a0037890 PMID:25198308

Kochan, T., & Liebman, W. (2022, September 16). *America is seeing a historical surge in workers organizing. Here is how to sustain it*. WBUR. https://www.wbur.org/cognoscenti/2022/09/05/worker-organizing-labor-day-thomas-kochan-wilma-liebman

Koch, N., & Durodié, B. (2022). Scientists advise, ministers decide? The role of scientific expertise in U.K. policymaking during the coronavirus pandemic. *Journal of Risk Research*, *25*(10), 1213–1222. doi:10.1080/13669877.2022.2116083

Koch, R. (2011). *The 80/20 Principle: The Secret of Achieving More with Less: Updated 20th anniversary edition of the productivity and business classic*. Hachette.

Koh, H. C., & Boo, E. H. Y. (2001). The link between organizational ethics and job satisfaction: A study of managers in singapore. *Journal of Business Ethics*, *29*(4), 309–324. doi:10.1023/A:1010741519818

Kohlberg, L. (1969). Stage and sequence: The cognitive developmental approach to socialization. In D. Goslin (Ed.), *Handbook of socialization theory and research* (pp. 347–480). Rand McNally.

Koliousi, P., & Miaouli, N. 2018. *Efficient bargaining versus Right to manage in the era of liberalization*. School of Economic Sciences, Athens University of Economics and Business. https://www.dept.aueb.gr/sites/default/files/wp04-2018-Koliousi-Miaouli-JULY-27.pdf.

Komives, S. R., Lucas, N., & McMahon, T. R. (2007). *Exploring Leadership: For College Students Who Want to Make a Difference*. John Wiley & Sons.

Kompaso, S. M., & Sridevi, M. S. (2010). Employee Engagement: The Key to Improving Performance. *International Journal of Business and Management*, *5*(12), p89. doi:10.5539/ijbm.v5n12p89

Kornai, J. (1995). *Highway and byways: Studies on reform and post-communist transition.* The MIT Press.

Kossek, E. E., Pichler, S., Bodner, T., & Hammer, L. B. (2011). Workplace social support and work–family conflict: A meta-analysis clarifying the influence of general and work– family-specific supervisor and organizational support. *Personnel Psychology, 64*(2), 289–313. doi:10.1111/j.1744-6570.2011.01211.x PMID:21691415

Kotter, J. P. (1999). *What Leaders Really Do.* Harvard Business School Press.

Kourteva, S. (2021, March 29). Have You Heard Of Servant Leadership? *Forbes.* https://www.forbes.com/sites/forbeseq/2021/03/29/have-you-heard-of-servant-leadership/?sh=7fed643e38 b7

Kowal, E. (2010). Welcome to country? *Meanjin, 69*, 15-173. https://search.informit.org/doi/pdf/10.3316/informit.076992418852903

Kramer, R. (2005). *Developing Global Leaders: Enhancing Competencies and Accelerating the Expatriate Experience.* The Conference Board. Retrieved from https://www.conference-board.org/publications/publicationdetail.cfm?publicationid=1058

Kramer, R. J. (2005). *Developing global leaders: enhancing competencies and accelerating the expatriate experience.* The Conference Board.

Kreiser, P. M., Marino, L. D., & Weaver, K. M. (2002). Assessing the psychometric properties of the entrepreneurial orientation scale: A multi-country analysis. *Entrepreneurship Theory and Practice, 26*(4), 71–94. doi:10.1177/104225870202600405

Kroll, L. (2006). Fortunes of kings, queens and dictators: A look at the world's wealthiest leaders. *Forbes.* Retrieved December 15, 2006, from https://www.forbes.com/billionaires/2006/05/04/rich-kings-Edictators_cz_lk_0504royals.html

Kukulska-Hulme, A. (2021). Reflections on research questions in mobile assisted language learning. *Journal of China Computer-Assisted Language Learning, 1*(1), 28–46. doi:10.1515/jccall-2021-2002

Kuokkanen, R. (2007). *Reshaping the University Responsibility, Indigenous Epistemes, and the Logic of the Gift.* UBC Press.

Kuoppala, J., Lamminpää, A., Liira, J., & Vainio, H. (2008). Leadership, job well-being, and health effects—A systematic review and a meta-analysis. *Journal of Occupational and Environmental Medicine, 50*(8), 904–915. doi:10.1097/JOM.0b013e31817e918d PMID:18695449

Kuscu, M., & Arslan, H. (2016). Virtual leadership at distance education teams. *Turkish Online Journal of Distance Education, 17*(3), 136–156. doi:10.17718/tojde.79230

Labour Party. (2022, December 5). *A New Britain.* Retrieved January 21, 2023, from https://labour.org.uk/page/a-new-britain/

Labour Research Services & National Skills Fund. (2022). *Strategies for inspire, organize and represent workers: The negotiators guide* LRS. https://www.lrs.org.za/wp-content/uploads/2022/02/The-Negotiators-Guide_Chapter_3_Thinking-about-solidarity-and-coalitions.pdf

Lacy, W., Croucher, G., Brett, A., & Mueller, R. (2017). *Australian Universities at a Crossroads: Insights from their Leaders and Implications for the Future.* Melbourne Centre for the Study of Higher Education and Berkeley Centre for Studies in Higher Education.

Compilation of References

Lafer, G., & Loustaunau, L. (2020, July 23). *Fear at work An inside account of how employers threaten, intimidate, and harass workers to stop them from exercising their right to collective bargaining.* EPI. https://www.epi.org/publication/fear-at-work-how-employers-scare-workers-out-of-unionizing/

Lalani, K., Crawford, J., & Butler-Henderson, K. (2021). Academic leadership during COVID-19 in higher education: Technology adoption and adaptation for online learning during a pandemic. *International Journal of Leadership in Education*, 1–17. doi:10.1080/13603124.2021.1988716

Lambert, A., Cayouette-Rembliere, J., Guéraut, E., Le Roux, G., Bonvalet, C., & Girard, V. (2020). How the COVID-19 epidemic changed working conditions in France. *Population et Sociétés*, 579, 1–4.

Landau, M. J., Solomon, S., Arndt, J., Greenberg, J., Pyszczynski, T., & Miller, C. (2004). Deliver us from evil: The effects of mortality salience and reminders of 9/11 on support for President George W. Bush. *Personality and Social Psychology Bulletin*, 30(9), 1136–1150. doi:10.1177/0146167204267988 PMID:15359017

Landay, K., Harms, P. D., & Credé, M. (2019). Shall we serve the dark lords? A meta-analytic review of psychopathy and leadership. *The Journal of Applied Psychology*, 104(1), 183–196. doi:10.1037/apl0000357 PMID:30321033

Latell, B. (2005). *After Fidel: The inside story of Castro's regime and Cuba's next leader.* Palgrave MacMillan.

Lawrence, K. (2013). *Developing Leaders in a VUCA Environment.* Retrieved from https://emergingrnleader.com/wp-content/uploads/2013/02/developing-leaders-in-a-vuca-environment.pdf

LeBreton, J. M., Shiverdecker, L. K., & Grimaldi, E. M. (2018). The Dark Triad and workplace behavior. *Annual Review of Organizational Psychology and Organizational Behavior*, 5(1), 387–414. doi:10.1146/annurev-orgpsych-032117-104451

Lebuda, I., Figura, B., & Karwowski, M. (2021, June). Creativity and the Dark Triad: A meta-analysis. *Journal of Research in Personality*, 92, 104088. doi:10.1016/j.jrp.2021.104088

Leduc, S., Guilbert, L., & Vallery, G. (2015). Impact of ICTs on leadership practices: Representations and actions. *Leadership and Organization Development Journal*, 36(4), 380–395. doi:10.1108/LODJ-07-2013-0090

Lee, G., & Xia, W. (2006). Organizational size and IT innovation adoption: A meta-analysis. *Information & Management*, 43(8), 975–985. doi:10.1016/j.im.2006.09.003

Leiter, M. P., & Maslach, C. (2003). *Areas of worklife: A structured approach to organizational predictors of job burnout* (Vol. 3). Research in Occupational Stress and Well Being. doi:10.1016/S1479-3555(03)03003-8

Lepore, J. (2009). Not So Fast - Scientific management started as a way to work. How did it become a way of life? *The New Yorker* (www.newyorker.com).

Leroy-Dyer, S., & Heckenberg, S. (2022). The Gap will never close if Aboriginal and Torres Strait Islander students don't feel safe on university campuses. *The Conversation*. https://theconversation.com/the-gap-will-never-close-if-aboriginal-and-torres-strait-islander-students-dont-feel-safe-on-university-campuses-180234

Lessin, N., & Pratt, D. (2020, April 18). *Organizing on Health and Safety in the face of the Coronavirus.* [Paper presentation]. The Labor Notes Virtual.

Licite-Kurbe, L., & Leonovica, R. (2021). Economic benefits of remote work from the employer perspective. In *Proceedings of the 2021 International Conference of Economic Science for Rural Development* (pp. 345-354). 10.22616/ESRD.2021.55.034

Liem, C. C. S., Langer, M., Demetriou, A., Hiemstra, A. M. F., Sukma Wicaksana, A., Born, M. P., & König, C. J. (2018). *Psychology meets machine learning: Interdisciplinary perspectives on algorithmic job candidate screening.* Springer.

Lilienfeld, S. O. (1994). Conceptual problems in the assessment of psychopathy. *Clinical Psychology Review*, *14*(1), 17–38. doi:10.1016/0272-7358(94)90046-9

Lin, C. S., Huang, P. C., Chen, S. J., & Huang, L. C. (2017). Pseudo-transformational leadership is in the eyes of the subordinates. *Journal of Business Ethics*, *141*(1), 179–190. doi:10.100710551-015-2739-5

Lindell, M. K., & Brandt, C. J. (2000). Climate quality and climate consensus as mediators of the relationship between organizational antecedents and outcomes. *The Journal of Applied Psychology*, *85*(3), 331–348. doi:10.1037/0021-9010.85.3.331 PMID:10900809

Linz, J. (1994). *The failure of presidential democracy.* Johns Hopkins University Press. doi:10.56021/9780801846397

Lipman-Blumen, J. (2005). *The allure of toxic leaders. Why we follow destructive bosses and corrupt politicians — and how we can survive them.* Oxford University Press.

Liu, C., Ready, D., Roman, A., Van Wart, M., Wang, X., McCarthy, A., & Kim, S. (2018). E-leadership: An empirical study of organizational leaders' virtual communication adoption. *Leadership and Organization Development Journal*, *39*(7), 826–843. doi:10.1108/LODJ-10-2017-0297

Liu, C., Van Wart, M., Kim, S., Wang, X., McCarthy, A., & Ready, D. (2020). The effects of national cultures on two technologically advanced countries: The case of e-leadership in South Korea and the United States. *Australian Journal of Public Administration*, *79*(3), 298–329. doi:10.1111/1467-8500.12433

Liu, J., Kwan, H. K., Fu, P. P., & Mao, Y. (2013). Ethical leadership and job performance in China: The roles of workplace friendships and traditionality. *Journal of Occupational and Organizational Psychology*, *86*(4), 564–584. doi:10.1111/joop.12027

Locke, M. L., Trudgett, M., & Page, S. (2023b). Building and strengthening Indigenous early career researcher trajectories. *Higher Education Research & Development*, *42*(1), 156–170. https://doi.org/10.1080/07294360.2022.2048637 doi:10.1080/07294360.2022.2048637

Locke, M., Trudgett, M., & Page, S. (2023a). Australian Indigenous early career researchers: Unicorns, cash cows and performing monkeys. *Race, Ethnicity and Education*, *26*(1), 1–17. https://doi.org/10.1080/13613324.2022.2114445 doi:10.1080/13613324.2022.2114445

Locke, R. R. (1996). *The Collapse of the American Management Mystique.* Oxford University Press. doi:10.1093/acprof:oso/9780198774068.001.0001

Locke, R. R., & Spender, J. C. (2011). *Confronting managerialism: how the Business Elite and their Schools threw our Lives out of Balance.* Zed Books. doi:10.5040/9781350219304

Loder, T. L. (2005). Women administrators negotiate work-family conflicts in changing times: An intergenerational perspective. *Educational Administration Quarterly*, *41*(5), 741–776. doi:10.1177/0013161X04273847

Long & Thean. (2011). *Relationship Between Leadership Style, Job Satisfaction and Employees' Turnover Intention: A Literature Review. Research Journal of Business Management, 5, 91-100.*

Loomes, S., Owens, A., & McCarthy, G. (2019). Patterns of recruitment of academic leaders to Australian universities and implications for the future of higher education. *Journal of Higher Education Policy and Management*, *41*(2), 137–152. doi:10.1080/1360080X.2019.1565296

Lord, R. G., & Brown, D. G. (2004). *Leadership processes and follower self-identity*. Lawrence Erlbaum Associates.

Loucks, S., & Ozogul, G. (2020). Preparing business students for a distributed workforce and global business environment: Gaining virtual leadership skills in an authentic context. *TechTrends*, *64*(4), 655–665. doi:10.100711528-020-00513-4

Lu, L., Shen, C., & Williams, D. (2014). Friending your way up the ladder: Connecting massive multiplayer online game behaviors with offline leadership. *Computers in Human Behavior*, *35*, 54–60. doi:10.1016/j.chb.2014.02.013

Luo, G., & Tworek, K. (2022). E-leadership as a booster of employees' dynamic capabilities influence on job performance. *Scientific Papers of Silesian University of Technology. Organization & Management / Zeszyty Naukowe Politechniki Slaskiej. Seria Organizacji i Zarzadzanie*, *155*, 237–248.

Luthans, F., Peterson, S. J., & Ibrayeva, E. (1998). The potential for the "dark side" of leadership in post-communist countries. *Journal of World Business*, *33*(2), 185–201. doi:10.1016/S1090-9516(98)90005-0

Lykken, D. T. (1995). *The antisocial personalities*. Erlbaum.

Lynn, A. (2017). MacIntyre, managerialism, and Metatheory: Organizational Theory as an Ideology of Control. *Journal of Critical Realism*, *16*(2), 143–162. doi:10.1080/14767430.2017.1282299Magretta, J. (2012). *What Management Is: How it works and why it's everyone's business*. Profile.

Maccoby, M. (2000). Narcissistic leaders: The incredible pros, the inevitable cons. *Harvard Business Review*, *78*, 68–77.

Maduka, N. S., Edwards, H., Greenwood, D., Osborne, A., & Babatunde, S. O. (2018). Analysis of competencies for effective virtual team leadership in building successful organisations. *Benchmarking*, *25*(2), 696–712. doi:10.1108/BIJ-08-2016-0124

Maheshwari, S. K., & Yadav, J. (2020). Leadership in the digital age: Emerging paradigms and challenges. *International Journal of Business and Globalisation*, *26*(3), 220–238. doi:10.1504/IJBG.2020.110950

Mahler, D. (2020). *The impact of COVID-19 (Coronavirus) on global poverty: Why Sub-Saharan Africa might be the region hardest hit (blog)*. World Bank Group, Washington D.C., https://blogs.worldbank.org/opendata/impact-covid-19-coronavirus-global-poverty-why-sub saharan-africa-might-be-region-hardest

Maidique, M. A., & Hiller, N. J. (2018). The mindsets of a leader. *MIT Sloan Management Review*, *59*(4), 76–81.

Mainwaring, S., & Scully, T. (1995). Party systems in Latin America. In S. Mainwaring & T. Scully (Eds.), *Building democratic institutions: Party systems in Latin America* (pp. 1–34). Stanford University Press.

Malmendier, U., & Tate, G. (2005). CEO overconfidence and corporate investment. *The Journal of Finance*, *60*(6), 2661–2700. doi:10.1111/j.1540-6261.2005.00813.x

Mann, R. D. (1959). A review of the relationships between personality and performance in small groups. *Psychological Bulletin*, *56*(4), 241–270. doi:10.1037/h0044587

Mansfield, H. (2023, January 5). Niccolò Machiavelli. *Encyclopedia Britannica*. https://www.britannica.com/biography/Niccolo-Machiavelli

Mant, A. (2010). Why "leadership" is so difficult - and elusive. *The International Journal of Leadership in Public Services*, *6*(1), 18–24. doi:10.5042/ijlps.2010.0271

Mantsios, G. (2015). Through the Looking-Glass of History: A New Vision for Labor Education. *Journal of Labor and Society*, *18*(4), 555–573.

Marginson, S. (2021). *Globalisation: The good, the bad and the ugly.* Working Paper 66, Oxford: Centre for Global Higher Education, University of Oxford.

Marguerat, D. (2002). *The first Christian historian: Writing the'Acts of the Apostles.* Cambridge University Press. doi:10.1017/CBO9780511488061

Marin-Garcia, J. A., Bonavia, T., & Losilla, J. M. (2020). 'Changes in the association between european workers' employment conditions and wellbeing of employee in 2005, 2010 and 2015'. *International Journal of Environmental Research and Public Health, 17*(3), 15–22. doi:10.3390/ijerph17031048 PMID:32046002

Marshall, J., Roache, D., & Moody-Marshall, R. (2020). Crisis Leadership: A Critical Examination of Educational Leadership in Higher Education in the Midst of the COVID-19 Pandemic. *International Studies in Educational Administration, 48*(3), 30-37.

Marshall, S. J. (2006). Issues in the development of leadership for learning and teaching in higher education. In *Leadership for Excellence in Learning and Teaching Program additional reading.* Carrick Institute for Learning and Teaching in Higher Education.

Martin, K. L. (2008). *Please knock before you enter: Aboriginal regulation of outsiders and the implications for researchers.* Post Pressed.

Masciulli, J., Molchanov, M. A., & Knight, W. A. (2016). Political leadership in context. In *The Ashgate research companion to political leadership* (pp. 23–48). Routledge.

Maslow, A. (1954). *Motivation and personality.* Harper.

Mason, P. A. (2016). *The lived experiences of African American female superintendents* [Doctoral dissertation, Ohio University].

Mason, M. (2010). Sample size and saturation in PhD studies using qualitative interviews. *Forum Qualitative Sozialforschung/Forum: Qualitative. Social Research.*

Mathiassen, L., Saarinen, T., Tuunanen, T., & Rossi, M. (2004). Managing requirements engineering risks: An analysis and synthesis of the literature. *Working Papers on Information Systems, Helsinki School of Economics,* 63.

Matthews, H. (1961). *The Cuban story.* G. Braziller.

Mauku, M. (2022) *Leadership Qualities in Trade Unions.* [Paper presentation]. Leadership Workshop of the Organization of Trade Unions (NOTU), Maria Flo, Masaka, Uganda. https://ugandajournalistsunion.com/news/2022/06/22/leadership-qualities-in-trade-unionism

McAfee, A., Brynjolfsson, E., Davenport, T. H., Patil, D. J., & Barton, D. (2012). Big data: The management revolution. *Harvard Business Review, 90*(10), 60–68. PMID:23074865

McCall, M. W. J., & Lombardo, M. M. (1983). *Off the track: Why and how successful executives get derailed.* Greensboro: Center for Creative Leadership Report No. 21.

McCann, J., & Kohntopp, T. (2019). Virtual leadership in organizations: Potential competitive advantage? *S.A.M. Advanced Management Journal, 84*(3), 26–39.

McCann, L. (2017). Killing is our business and business is good: The evolution of war managerialism from body counts to counterinsurgency. *Organization, 24*(4), 491–515. doi:10.1177/1350508417693852

Compilation of References

McCarthy, A., Cleveland, J. N., Hunter, S., Darcy, C., & Grady, G. (2013). Employee work–life balance outcomes in Ireland: A multilevel investigation of supervisory support and perceived organizational support. *International Journal of Human Resource Management*, *24*(6), 1257–1276. doi:10.1080/09585192.2012.709189

McCarthy, J. (2005). Planning a Future Workforce: An Australian Perspective. *New Review of Academic Librarianship*, *11*(1), 41–56. doi:10.1080/13614530500417669

McClelland, D. C. (1961). *The achieving society*. Van Nostrand. doi:10.1037/14359-000

McClelland, D. C. (1975). *Power: The inner experience*. Irvington.

McCrae, R. R. (1987). Creativity, divergent thinking, and openness to experience. *Journal of Personality and Social Psychology*, *52*(6), 1258–1265. doi:10.1037/0022-3514.52.6.1258

McGuire, D., Cunningham, J. E., Reynolds, K., & Matthews-Smith, G. (2020). Beating the virus: An examination of the crisis communication approach taken by New Zealand Prime Minister Jacinda Ardern during the Covid-19 pandemic. *Human Resource Development International*, *23*(4), 361–379. doi:10.1080/13678868.2020.1779543

McHoskey, J. W. (1999). Machiavellianism, intrinsic versus extrinsic goals, and social interest: A self-determination theory analysis. *Motivation and Emotion*, *23*(4), 267–283. doi:10.1023/A:1021338809469

McIntosh, G. L., & Rima, S. D. (1997). *Overcoming the Darkside of Leadership*. Baker Books.

McKinsey Digital. (2020, July 24). *Europe's digital migration during COVID-19: Getting past the broad trends and averages*. McKinsey & Company. https://www.mckinsey.com/business-functions/mckinsey-digital/our-insights/europes-digital-migration-during-covid-19-getting-past-the-broad-trends-and-averages

McKinsey Global Institute. (2016) *Digital Globalization: The new era of Global Inflows*. McKinsey. https://www.mckinsey.com/~/media/mckinsey/business%20functions/mckinsey%20digital/our%20insights/digital%20globalization%20the%20new%20era%20of%20global%20flows/mgi-digital-globalization-full-report.ashx

McLaughlin, J., & Whatman, S. (2011). The potential of critical race theory in decolonizing university curricula. *Asia Pacific Journal of Education*, *31*(4), 365–377. https://psycnet.apa.org/doi/10.1080/02188791.2011.621243 doi:10.1080/02188791.2011.621243

McLean, B., & Elkind, P. (2005). *The smartest guys in the room*. Penguin.

McMahan, P., & Evans, J. (2018). Ambiguity and engagement. *American Journal of Sociology*, *124*(3), 860–912. doi:10.1086/701298

McMurray, A. M., Henly, D., Chaboyer, W., Clapton, J., Lizzio, A., & Temi, M. (2012). Leadership Succession Management in a University Health Faculty. *Journal of Higher Education Policy and Management*, *34*(4), 365–376. doi:10.1080/1360080X.2012.689198

McNicholas, C. (2018, May 22). Supreme Court deals significant blows to workers rights. *Economic Policy Institute Newsletter*.

Meghana, J., & Vijaya, R. (2019). E-leadership, psychological contract and real-time performance management: Remotely working professionals. *SCMS Journal of Indian Management*, *16*(3), 101–111.

Meglino, B. M., Ravlin, E. C., & Adkins, C. L. (1989). A work values approach to corporate culture: A field test of the value congruence process and its relationship to individual outcomes. *The Journal of Applied Psychology, 74*(3), 424–432. doi:10.1037/0021-9010.74.3.424

Mehtab, K., Rehman, A., Ishfaq, S., & Jamil, R. (2017). Virtual leadership: A review paper. *Mediterranean Journal of Social Sciences, 8*(4), 183. doi:10.2478/mjss-2018-0089

Mencl, J., Wefald, A. J., & van Ittersum, K. W. (2016). Transformational leader attributes: Interpersonal skills, engagement, and well-being. *Leadership and Organization Development Journal, 37*(5), 635–657. doi:10.1108/LODJ-09-2014-0178

Micocci, A., & Di Mario, F. (2018). *The fascist nature of neoliberalism.* Routledge.

Miles, A. (2020, September 16). *What are Unions and Why are they important.* Heddels. https://www.heddels.com/2020/09/what-are-unions-and-why-are-they-important/

Miles, M., Huberman, M., & Saldana, J. (2019). *Qualitative Data Analysis: A Methods Sourcebook* (4th ed.). SAGE Publishing.

Milgram, S. (1963). Behavioral study of obedience. *Journal of Abnormal and Social Psychology, 67*(4), 371–378. doi:10.1037/h0040525 PMID:14049516

Milgram, S. (1974). *Obedience to authority.* Harper & Row.

Miller, C. C., & Cardinal, L. B. (1994). Strategic planning and firm performance: A synthesis of more than two decades of research. *Academy of Management Journal, 37*(6), 1649–1665. doi:10.2307/256804

Miller, D. (2008). *A century of spin: how public relations became the cutting edge of corporate power.* Pluto Press.

Minichello, V., Aroni, R., Timewell, E., & Alexander, L. (1995), In-depth Interviewing: Principles, Techniques, Analysis, Second Edn., Longman, Frenches Forrest.

Ministry of Education. (2021). *Union Education Minister releases Report on United District Information System for Education Plus (UDISE+) 2019-20.* Ministry of Education. https://pib.gov.in/PressReleasePage.aspx?PRID=1731860

Mitonga-Monga, J. (2018). Ethical climate influences on employee commitment through job satisfaction in a transport sector industry. *Journal of Psychology in Africa, 28*(1), 15–20. doi:10.1080/14330237.2018.1426710

Mlekus, L., & Maier, G. W. (2019). *Not everyone benefits from technological advancements: Associations with competency requirements and well-being in two occupations.* Manuscript submitted for publication.

Moan, K., & Hetland, H. (2012). Are leadership preferences universally endorsed or culturally contingent. *Scandinavian Journal of Organizational Psychology, 4*(1), 5–22.

Mohammad, K. (2009). E-Leadership: The emerging new leadership for the virtual organization. *Journal of Managerial Sciences, 3*(1). At https://www.qurtuba.edu.pk/jms/default_files/JMS/3_1/01_khawaj.pdf

Mohammad, K. (2009). E-Leadership: The emerging new leadership for the virtual organization. *Journal of Managerial Sciences, 3*(1).

Money Control. (2021). *Women teachers in Indian schools outnumber men in 2019-20.* Money Control. https://www.moneycontrol.com/. https://www.moneycontrol.com/news/india/women-teachers-in-indian-schools-outnumber-men-in-2019-20-shows-udise-report-7124421.html

Compilation of References

Montaner, C. (1983). *Fidel Castro y la revolución Cubana* (2nd ed.). Editorial Playor.

Montaner, C. (1999). *Viaje al corazón de Cuba*. Plaza & Janes Editores.

Montefiore, S. (2004). *Stalin: The court of the red tsar*. Knopf.

Monzani, L., & Van Dick, R. (2021). Positive Leadership in Organizations. In J. M. Peiro (Ed.), *Oxford Research Encyclopedia of Psychology* (pp. 1–37). Oxford University Press.

Morehead, A. (2003), *How Employed Mothers Allocate Time for Work and Family: A New Framework*, [Ph.D. thesis, The University of Sydney, Sydney].

Moreton-Robinson, A. (2007). Sovereign subjects: Indigenous sovereignty matters. Crows Nest, N.S.W., Allen & Unwin.

Moreton-Robinson, A. (2020b). Incommensurable sovereignties: Indigenous ontology matters. Routledge handbook of critical Indigenous studies. Routledge. https://doi.org/10.4324/9780429440229 doi:10.4324/9780429440229-23

Moreton-Robinson, A. (2021a). *Place names, monuments and cannibalism: James Cook and the possessive logics of patriarchal white sovereignty*. [Video] Youtube. AIIS Sperker Series, Cornell University. https://www.youtube.com/watch?v=5L_QMLWcE5k

Moreton-Robinson, A. (2020a). *Talkin' up to the white woman: Indigenous women and feminism*. University of Queensland Press.

Moreton-Robinson, A. (2021b). The white possessive: Identity matters in becoming Native, Black and Aboriginal. *Borderlands Journal*, *20*(2), 4–29. https://doi.org/10.21307/borderlands-2021-011

Morf, C. C., Weir, C., & Davidov, M. (2000). Narcissism and intrinsic motivation: The role of goal congruence. *Journal of Experimental Social Psychology*, *36*(4), 424–438. doi:10.1006/jesp.1999.1421

Morrison, A., Rigney, L.-I., Hattam, R., & Diplock, A. (2019). *Toward an Australian culturally responsive pedagogy: A narrative review of the literature*. University of South Australia. https://apo.org.au/sites/default/files/resource-files/2019-08/apo-nid262951.pdf

Morse, J. M., & Richards, L. (2002). *Readme First for a User's Guide to Qualitative Methods*. Sage.

Mottram, R. (2021). *Unpaid advisers may seem like a free gift to the government but bring with them issues around access, conflicts of interest, and status*. British Politics and Policy at LSE.

Mrig, A., & Sanaghan, P. (2017). *'The skills future higher-ed leaders need to succeed', Academic Impressions*. CR Mrig Company.

Msila, V. (2013). Obstacles and opportunities in women school leadership: A literature study. *International Journal of Educational Sciences*, *5*(4), 463–470. doi:10.1080/09751122.2013.11890108

Mumford, M. D., Zaccaro, S. J., Harding, F. D., Jacobs, T. O., & Fleishman, E. A. (2000). Leadership skills for a changing world. *The Leadership Quarterly*, *11*(1), 11–35. doi:10.1016/S1048-9843(99)00041-7

Mumford, T. V., Campion, M. A., & Morgeson, F. P. (2007). The leadership skills strataplex: Leadership skill requirements across organizational levels. *The Leadership Quarterly*, *18*(2), 154–166. doi:10.1016/j.leaqua.2007.01.005

Munar, A. M., Nadal, J. R., & Gairal-Casadó, R. (2020). A happiness model for the sustainable university. *Sustainability*, *12*(12), 4874.

Munro, A. (2016). *Practical Succession Management: How to Future-Proof Your Organisation*. Routledge.

Muttaqa, Y. A. (2021). *Working Conditions and Collective Representation of Uber and Bolt Digital Platform Drivers in Nigeria.* Global Labour University (GLU) Working Papers.

Mythili, N. (2017). Representation of women in school leadership positions in India. *NUEPA Occasional Paper, 51.*

Mythili, N. (2019). Quest for success: Ladder of school leadership of women in India. *Social Change, 49*(1), 114–131. doi:10.1177/0049085718821748

Nair, P., & Malewar, S. (2013). Effective leadership-employee retention-work life balance: A cyclical continuum. *IOSR Journal of Business and Management, 10*(3), 80–86. doi:10.9790/487X-1038086

Nakata, M., Nakata, V., Day, A., & Peachey, M. (2019). Closing gaps in Indigenous undergraduate higher education outcomes: Repositioning the role of student support services to improve retention and completion rates. *Australian Journal of Indigenous Education, 48*(1), 1–11. https://doi.org/10.1017/jie.2017.36 doi:10.1017/jie.2017.36

Navarro, V. (2020). Is there a third way? A response to Giddens's The Third Way. In *The Political Economy of Social Inequalities* (pp. 419–428). Routledge. doi:10.4324/9781315231051-25

Ndu, A. A., & Anagbogu, M. A. (2007). Framework for effective management of universities in the 21st century. In J. B. Babalola & B. O. Emunemu (Eds.), *Issues in Higher Education: Research Evidence from Sub-Saharan Africa.* Bolabay Publications.

Neeley, T. (2021). *Remote work revolution.* Harper Collins Publishers.

Nevicka, B., Ten Velden, F. S., De Hoogh, A. H. B., & Van Vianen, A. E. M. (2011). Reality at Odds With Perceptions. *Psychological Science, 22*(10), 1259–1264. doi:10.1177/0956797611417259 PMID:21931153

Nghikefelwa, J. M., Wyld, F., & Wisker, G. (2022). Creating and Curating: Three Voices from Namibia, Australia and the UK on Decolonising the Literary-Related Doctorate. Decolonising Curriculum Knowledge. Springer.

Nienaber, H. (2010). Conceptualisation of management and leadership. *Management Decision, 48*(5), 661–675. doi:10.1108/00251741011043867

Niu, Y. (2021). Enlightenment of Positive Psychology on Human Resource Management. *Modern Management Forum, 5*(1), 30. 10.18686/mmf.v5i1.3169

Noe, T. H., & Rebello, M. J. (1996). Asymmetric information, managerial opportunism, financing, and payout policies. *The Journal of Finance, 51*(2), 637–660. doi:10.1111/j.1540-6261.1996.tb02697.x

Noppe, R., Yager, S., Webb, C., & Sheng, B. (2013). Decision-Making and Problem-Solving Practices of Superintendents Confronted by District Dilemmas. *The International Journal of Educational Leadership Preparation, 8*(1), 103–120.

Norman, S., Avey, J., Larson, M., & Hughes, L. (2020). The development of trust in virtual leader–follower relationships. *Qualitative Research in Organizations and Management, 15*(3), 279–295. doi:10.1108/QROM-12-2018-1701

Northouse, P. G. (2010). *Leadership: Theory and Practice* (5th ed.). SAGE Publications.

Nye, J. S. (2013). Presidential leadership and the creation of the American era. In *Presidential Leadership and the Creation of the American Era.* Princeton University Press.

O'Connor, S. (2017, September 17). *Trade Unions strive to stay relevant by wooing the young.* FT. https://www.ft.com/content/3f6e9d7c-98bb-11e7-a652-cde3f882dd7b

O'Connor, J., Mumford, M., Clifton, T., Gessner, T., & Connelly, M. (1995). Charismatic leaders and destructiveness: An historiometric study. *The Leadership Quarterly, 6*(4), 529–555. doi:10.1016/1048-9843(95)90026-8

O'Sullivan, S. 2019. First Nations' Women in the Academy: Disrupting and Displacing the White Male Gaze. In Crimmins, G. (ed) Strategies for Resisting Sexism in the Academy. Palgrave Studies in Gender and Education. Palgrave Macmillan, Cham. https://doi.org/10.1007/978-3-030-04852-5_7

Oberer, B., & Erkollar, A. (2018). Leadership 4.0: Digital leaders in the age of industry 4.0. *International journal of organizational leadership*.

OECD. (2014). *Job Creation and Local Economic Development*. OECD Publishing. doi:10.1787/9789264215009-

OECD. Stat. (2021). *Average annual hours actually worked per worker*. Labour Force Statistics. https://stats.oecd.org/index.aspx?DataSetCode=ANHRS

Offerman, L. (2004). When followers become toxic. *Harvard Business Review*, *84*, 54–60. PMID:14723177

Oksenberg, L. (1968). *Machiavellianism and organization in five man task oriented groups* [Unpublished doctoral dissertation]. Columbia University.

Olckers, C., van Zyl, L., & van der Vaart, L. (2017). *Theoretical Orientations and Practical Applications of Psychological Ownership*, 1–332. doi:10.1007/978-3-319-70247-6

Oleksa-Marewska, K., & Tokar, J. (2022). Facing the Post-Pandemic Challenges: The Role of Leadership Effectiveness in Shaping the Affective Well-Being of Healthcare Providers Working in a Hybrid Work Mode. *International Journal of Environmental Research and Public Health*, *19*(21), 14388. doi:10.3390/ijerph192114388 PMID:36361264

Oliver, R., Rochecouste, J., Bennell, D., Anderson, R., Cooper, I., Forrest, S., & Exell, M. (2013). Understanding Australian Aboriginal Tertiary Student Needs. *International Journal of Higher Education*, *2*(4), 52–64. http://dx.doi.org/10.5430/ijhe.v2n4p52 doi:10.5430/ijhe.v2n4p52

Olsen, A. A., Wolcott, M. D., Haines, S. T., Janke, K. K., & McLaughlin, J. E. (2021). How to use the Delphi method to aid in decision making and build consensus in pharmacy education. *Currents in Pharmacy Teaching & Learning*, *13*(10), 1376–1385. doi:10.1016/j.cptl.2021.07.018 PMID:34521535

Olurode, O., & Gaskia, J. (2022, May 1). *Nigerian workers should unite and take over power in 2023*. [Press Statement]. The Peoples Alternative Political Movement in commemoration of the 2022 International Workers' Day, Abuja, Nigeria. https://www.vanguardngr.com/2022/05/workers-day-movement-urges-workers-to-unite-take-over-power-in-2023

Oppenheim, A. (2000). *Questionnaire Design, Interviewing and Attitude Measurement*. Bloomsbury Publishing.

Orback, J. (2015). The World Needs Union Political Cooperation. In T. Svensson, K. Thapper, & M. Nilsson (Eds.), *How to run a Trade Union: Trade Union Handbook* (pp. 40–41). The Olof Palme International Center.

Orte, C., & Dino, M. (2019). Eliciting e-leadership style and trait preference among nurses via conjoint analysis. *Enfermeria Clinica*, *29*, 78–80. doi:10.1016/j.enfcli.2018.11.025

Örücü, D., & Kutlugün, H. E. (2022). *Navigating the Covid 19 Turbulence in Higher Education: Evidence from Turkish Faculty Members*. Research in Educational Administration & Leadership.

Osula, B., & Ng, E. C. W. (2014). Toward a Collaborative, Transformative Model of Non-Profit Leadership: Some Conceptual Building Blocks. *Administrative Sciences*, *4*(2), 87–104. doi:10.3390/admsci4020087

Otobo, D. (2017, January). *Labour unity and Trade Union governance*. [Paper presentation]. Ilorin, Kwara State, Nigeria. https://www.dailytrust.com.ng/news/opinion/labour-unity-and-trade-union-governance/180917.html, .

Ötting, S. K., & Maier, G. W. (2018a). The importance of procedural justice in human–machine interactions: Intelligent systems as new decision agents in organizations. *Computers in Human Behavior, 89*, 27–39. doi:10.1016/j.chb.2018.07.022

Ötting, S. K., Masjutin, L., Steil, J. J., & Maier, G. W. (2020). Let's work together: A meta-analysis on robot design features that enable successful human-robot interaction at work. *Human Factors*. PMID:33176488

Oxfam. (2018). *Reward work, Not wealth*. Oxfam Briefing Paper. https://www.oxfam.org/sites/www.oxfam.org/files/file_attachments/bp-reward-work-not-wealth-220118-en.pdf

Oyewunmi, O.A, & Oyewunmi, A.E. (2017). Nigeria's Public University System: Are Trade Unions Still Viable. *Asia Pacific Journal of Academic Research in Social Sciences* (2)1-7.

Özgüzel, S., & Taş, S. (2016). Hubris Sendromuna Yakalanan Yöneticilerde Çocukluktaki Aile İçi İletişimin Etkisinin İncelenmesi. *Yüzyılda Eğitim Ve Toplum Eğitim Bilimleri Ve Sosyal Araştırmalar Dergisi, 5*(13).

Padilla, A. (2005). *Portraits in leadership: Six extraordinary university presidents*. Praeger Publishers.

Padilla, A., Hogan, R., & Kaiser, R. B. (2007). The toxic triangle: Destructive leaders, susceptible followers, and conducive environments. *The Leadership Quarterly, 18*(3), 176–194. doi:10.1016/j.leaqua.2007.03.001

Page, M. J., McKenzie, J. E., Bossuyt, P. M., Boutron, I., Hoffmann, T. C., Mulrow, C. D., Shamseer, L., Tetzlaff, J. M., Akl, E. A., Brennan, S. E., Chou, R., Glanville, J., Grimshaw, J. M., Hróbjartsson, A., Lalu, M. M., Li, T., Loder, E. W., Mayo-Wilson, E., McDonald, S., ... Moher, D. (2021). The PRISMA 2020 statement: An updated guideline for reporting systematic reviews. *Systematic Reviews, 10*(1), 1–11. doi:10.118613643-021-01626-4 PMID:33781348

Panteli, N., Hjeltnes, T., & Strand, K. (2019). Learning to lead online collaborations: insights from student-based global virtual teams between UK and Norway. *Conference on e-Business, eServices, and e-Society. Springer*, 785–796. 10.1007/978-3-030-29374-1_64

Papatsaroucha, D., Nikoloudakis, Y., Kefaloukos, I., & Markakis, E. (2021, June 18). *A Survey on Human and Personality Vulnerability Assessment in Cyber-security: Challenges, Approaches. . . ResearchGate*. https://www.researchgate.net/publication/352558956_A_Survey_on_Human_and_Personality_Vulnerability_Assessment_in_Cyber-security_Challenges_Approaches_and_Open_Issues

Pardo Llada, J. (1976). *Fidel: De los Jesuitas al Moncada*. Plaza & Janes Editores.

Pardo Llada, J. (1988). *Fidel y el "Ché."*. Plaza & Janes Editores.

Parker, K., Horowitz, J., & Minkin, R. (2022). *COVID-19 pandemic continues to reshape work in America*. Pew Research Center. Retrieved from https://www.pewresearch.org/social-trends/2022/02/16/covid-19-pandemic-continues-to-reshape-work-in-america/

Parker, M. (2019). Alternatives to Management Ideas. In A. Sturdy, (Eds.), *Oxford Handbook of Management Ideas* (p. 497). Oxford University Press.

Parker, S. K., & Grote, G. (2020). Automation, algorithms, and beyond: Why work design matters more than ever in a digital world. *Applied Psychology*.

Parry, K., & Bryman, A. (2006). I: 2.1 Leadership in organisations. The SAGE handbook of organisation studies, 5(3), 447-465.

Compilation of References

Patterson, J. L., Goens, G. A., & Reed, D. E. (2009). *Resilient Leadership for Turbulent Times: A Guide to Thriving in the Face of Adversity*. R&L Education.

Patty, A. (2017). Landmark enterprise agreement decision gives universities "nuclear" option. *Sydney Morning Herald*. <https://www.smh.com.au/business/workplace/landmark-enterprise-agreement-decision-gives-universities-nuclear-option-20170830-gy6zie.html>

Paulhus, D. L. (2014). Toward a Taxonomy of Dark Personalities. *Current Directions in Psychological Science*, 23(6), 421–426. doi:10.1177/0963721414547737

Paulhus, D. L., & Williams, K. M. (2002). The Dark Triad of personality: Narcissism, Machiavellianism and psychopathy. *Journal of Research in Personality*, 36(6), 556–563. doi:10.1016/S0092-6566(02)00505-6

Paxton, D., & Van Stralen, S. (2015). Developing collaborative and innovative leadership: Practices for fostering a new mindset. *Journal of Leadership Education*, 14(4), 11–25. doi:10.12806/V14/I4/I1

Pazzanese, C. (2022, April 7). Will the message sent by Amazon workers turn into a movement? *Harvard Gazette*. https://news.harvard.edu/gazette/story/2022/04/the-future-of-labor-unions-according-to-harvard-economist/

Pellegrini, E. K., & Scandura, T. A. (2008). Paternalistic leadership: A review and agenda for future research. *Journal of Management*, 34(3), 566–593. doi:10.1177/0149206308316063

Peters, A. (2010). Elements of successful mentoring of a female school leader. *Leadership and Policy in Schools*, 9(1), 108–129. doi:10.1080/15700760903026755

Petrie, N. (2011). *Future trends in leadership development*. Center for Creative Leadership white paper.

Philip, J., & Gavrilova Aguilar, M. (2022). Student perceptions of leadership skills necessary for digital transformation. *Journal of Education for Business*, 97(2), 86–98. doi:10.1080/08832323.2021.1890540

Plachy, R. J., & Smunt, T. L. (2022). Rethinking managership, leadership, followership, and partnership. *Business Horizons*, 65(4), 401–411. doi:10.1016/j.bushor.2021.04.004

Plater, S., Mooney-Somers, J., Barclay, L., & Boulton, J. (2020). Hitting the white ceiling: Structural racism and Aboriginal and Torres Strait Islander university graduates. *Journal of Sociology (Melbourne, Vic.)*, 56(3), 487–504. doi:10.1177/1440783319859656

Pocock, B. (2003). *The Work/Life Collision: What Work is doing to Australians and What to Do about It*. The Federation Press.

Poguntke, T., & Webb, P. (2005). The presidentialization of politics in democratic societies: A framework for analysis. *The presidentialization of politics: a comparative study of modern democracies*, 1.

Pokojski, Z., Kister, A., & Lipowski, M. (2022). Remote work efficiency from the employers' perspective—What's next? *Sustainability (Basel)*, 14(7), 4220. doi:10.3390u14074220

Pollitt, C. (1990). *Managerialism and the public services: the Anglo-American experience*. Basil Blackwell.

Pologeorgis, N. A. (2022). *Employability, the Labour Force and the Economy*. Investiopedia. https://www.investopedia.com/articles/economics/12/employability-labor-force-economy.asp

Potosky, D., & Lomax, M. W. (2014). Leadership and technology: A love-hate relationship. In M. D. Coovert & L. F. Thompson (Eds.), *SIOP organizational frontiers series. The psychology of workplace technology* (pp. 118–146). Routledge.

Povey, R., Trudgett, M., Page, S., Locke, M. L., & Harry, M. (2022). Raising an Indigenous academic community: A strength-based approach to Indigenous early career mentoring in higher education. *Australian Educational Researcher*. https://doi.org/10.1007/s13384-022-00542-3 doi:10.100713384-022-00542-3 PMID:35874034

Powell, S. (2018). Risks to international student market: Austrade. *The Australian*. https://www.theaustralian.com.au/higher-education/risks-to-international-student-market-austrade/news-story/adfe42ce4b8673a5d8074266db17d3d1>

Prasad, S. B. (Ed.). (1968). Managerialism for economic development: essays on India. Martinus Nijhoff. doi:10.1007/978-94-011-7499-2

Probert, B. (2004). If Only it Were a Glass Ceiling: Gendered Academic Careers. In S. Charlesworth & M. Fastenau (Eds.), *Women and Work: Current RMIT University Research* (pp. 7–26). RMIT Publishing.

Pruthi, R. K. (Ed.). (2004). *Indian caste system*. Discovery Publishing House.

Pulse. (2019). *Who is a 'woman of colour'?* [post]. LinkedIn. https://www.linkedin.com/pulse/who-woman-colour-winitha-michelle-bonney/

Purvanova, R., Charlier, S., Reeves, C., & Greco, L. (2021). Who emerges into virtual team leadership roles? The role of achievement and ascription antecedents for leadership emergence across the virtuality spectrum. *Journal of Business and Psychology*, *36*(4), 713–733. doi:10.100710869-020-09698-0

Qing, M., Asif, M., Hussain, A., & Jameel, A. (2020). Exploring the impact of ethical leadership on job satisfaction and organizational commitment in public sector organizations: The mediating role of psychological empowerment. *Review of Managerial Science*, *14*(6), 1405–1432. doi:10.100711846-019-00340-9

Queiros, A., Faria, D., & Almeida, F. (2017). Strengths and limitations of qualitative and quantitative research methods. *European Journal of Education Studies*, *3*(9), 369–387. doi:10.5281/zenodo.887089

Quirk, R. (1993). *Fidel Castro*. W. W. Norton.

Raffy, S. (2004). *Castro, el desleal* (P. G. Crespo, Trans.). Santillana Ediciones.

Raghavan, A. (2002). Full speed ahead: How Enron bosses created a culture of pushing limits. *The Wall Street Journal*, p. A1.

Ramsay, H., Scholarios, D., & Harley, B. (2000). Employees and high-performance work systems: Testing inside the black box. *British Journal of Industrial Relations*, *38*(4), 501–531. doi:10.1111/1467-8543.00178

Rasool, S. F., Wang, M., Tang, M., Saeed, A., & Iqbal, J. (2021). How toxic workplace environment effects the employee engagement: The mediating role of organizational support and wellbeing of employee. *International Journal of Environmental Research and Public Health*, *18*(5), 1–17. doi:10.3390/ijerph18052294 PMID:33652564

Rauch, A., Wiklund, J., Lumpkin, G. T., & Frese, M. (2009). Entrepreneurial orientation and business performance: An assessment of past research and suggestions for the future. *Entrepreneurship Theory and Practice*, *33*(3), 761–787. doi:10.1111/j.1540-6520.2009.00308.x

Rauthmann, J. F. (2012). The Dark Triad and interpersonal perception: Similarities and differences in the social consequences of narcissism, Machiavellianism, and psychopathy. *Social Psychological & Personality Science*, *3*(4), 487–496. doi:10.1177/1948550611427608

Redín, D. M., Meyer, M., & Rego, A. (2023). Positive leadership action framework: Simply doing good and doing well. *Frontiers in Psychology*, *13*(January), 1–14. doi:10.3389/fpsyg.2022.977750 PMID:36687856

Redlich, F. (1999). *Hitler: Diagnosis of a destructive prophet*. Oxford University Press.

Redmond, P., Gutke, H., Galligan, L., Howard, A., & Newman, T. (2017). Becoming a female leader in higher education: Investigations from a regional university. *Gender and Education*, *29*(3), 332–351. doi:10.1080/09540253.2016.1156063

Reed, G. E. (2004). Toxic Leadership. *Military Review*, *84*(4), 67–71.

Remenyi, D., Grant, K. A., & Singh, S. (2020). *The University of the Future Responding to COVID-19* (2nd ed.). ACPIL Reading.

Renko, M., El Tarabishy, A., Carsrud, A. L., & Brännback, M. (2015). Understanding and measuring entrepreneurial leadership style. *Journal of Small Business Management*, *53*(1), 54–74. doi:10.1111/jsbm.12086

Ren, S., & Chadee, D. (2017). Ethical leadership, self-efficacy and job satisfaction in china: The moderating role of guanxi. *Personnel Review*, *46*(2), 371–388. doi:10.1108/PR-08-2015-0226

Repo, P., Polsa, P., & Timonen, P. (2022). Finnish Response to the First Wave of COVID-19 Accentuated Persuasion. In *Community, Economy and COVID-19: Lessons from Multi-Country Analyses of a Global Pandemic* (pp. 181–203). Springer International Publishing. doi:10.1007/978-3-030-98152-5_9

Riaz, A., & Haider, M. H. (2010). Role of transformational and transactional leadership on job satisfaction and career satisfaction. *Business and Economic Horizons*, *1*, 29–38. doi:10.15208/beh.2010.05

Ringle, C. M., Wende, S., & Becker, J. M. (2015). *SmartPLS 3*. www.smartpls.com

Roache, P. (2017, September 17) *Trade Unions strive to stay relevant by wooing the young*. FT. https://www.ft.com/content/3f6e9d7c-98bb-11e7-a652-cde3f882dd7b

Robbins, S. P., Decenzo, D. A., & Coulter, M. (2010). *Fundamentals of Management: Essential Concepts and Applications* (7th ed.). Prentice Hall.

Robertson, I., & Cooper, C. (2011). *Well-being Productivity and Happiness at Work*. Palgrave Macmillan London. doi.org/10.1057/9780230306738

Robertson, I. T., & Cooper, C. L. (2010). Full engagement: The integration of employee engagement and psychological wellbeing. *Leadership and Organization Development Journal*, *31*(4), 324–336. doi:10.1108/01437731011043348

Robison, J. (2021). *What Disruption Reveals About Engaging Millennial Employees*. Gallup. https://www.gallup.com/workplace/328121/disruption-reveals-engaging-millennial-employees.aspx

Rochecouste, J., Oliver, R., Bennell, D., Anderson, R., Cooper, I., & Forrest, S. (2017). Teaching Australian Aboriginal higher education students: What should universities do? *Studies in Higher Education*, *42*(11), 2080–2098. https://doi.org/10.1080/03075079.2015.1134474 doi:10.1080/03075079.2015.1134474

Rodowicz, C. M., Morris, L., Sidman, C. L., & Beyer, K. (2020). The impact of an online happiness course on subjective happiness among college students. *Building Healthy Academic Communities Journal*, *4*(1), 69–81. doi:10.18061/bhac.v4i1.7086

Rohs, M., Vogel, C., & Marks, S. (2015). From supply-driven to demand-oriented academic education: Evidence-based development of study courses to match regional skill shortage with new student groups. *12th PASCAL International Observatory Conference*.

Roman, A. V., Van Wart, M., Wang, X., Liu, C., Kim, S., & McCarthy, A. (2019). Defining E-leadership as competence in ICT-mediated communications: An exploratory assessment. *Public Administration Review*, *79*(6), 853–866. doi:10.1111/puar.12980

Ros, E. (2003). *Fidel Castro y el gatillo alegre: Sus años universitarios*. Ediciones Universal.

Rosenberg, M. (2013, April 29). *Leaning in? Women superintendents making mark in public education*. New York State School Board Association. https://www.nyssba.org/news/2013/04/26/on-board-online-april-29-2013/leaning-in-women-superintendents-making-mark-in-pub
lic-education/

Rosenfeld, P. (1995). *Impression Management in Organisations – Theory, Measures, Practice*. Routledge.

Rosenthal, S. A., & Pittinsky, T. L. (2006). Narcissistic leadership. *The Leadership Quarterly*, *17*(6), 617–633. doi:10.1016/j.leaqua.2006.10.005

Rotter, J. B. (1966). Generalized expectancies for internal versus external control of reinforcement. *Psychological Monographs*, *80*(1).

Rowe, W. G. (2001). Creating wealth in organizations: The role of strategic leadership. *The Academy of Management Perspectives*, *15*(1), 81–94. doi:10.5465/ame.2001.4251395

Roy, S. (2012). Digital mastery: The skills needed for effective virtual leadership. *International Journal of e-Collaboration*, *8*(3), 56–66. doi:10.4018/jec.2012070104

Rudolph, C. W., Katz, I. M., Lavigne, K. N., & Zacher, H. (2017). Job crafting: A meta-analysis of relationships with individual differences, job characteristics, and work outcomes. *Journal of Vocational Behavior*, *102*(314), 112–138. doi:10.1016/j.jvb.2017.05.008

Ruiz-Palomino, P., Ruiz-Amaya, C., & Knörr, H. (2011). Employee organizational citizenship behaviour: The direct and indirect impact of ethical leadership. *Canadian Journal of Administrative Sciences*, *28*(3), 244–258. doi:10.1002/cjas.221

Rybnikova, I., Juknevičienė, V., Toleikienė, R., Leach, N., Āboliņa, I., Reinholde, I., & Sillamäe, J. (2022). Digitalisation and e-leadership in local government before COVID-19: Results of an exploratory study. *Forum Scientiae Oeconomia*, *10*(2), 173–191.

Sabri, H. A. (2012). Re-examination of Hofstede's work value orientations on perceived leadership styles in Jordan. *International Journal of Commerce and Management*, *22*(3), 202–218. doi:10.1108/10569211211260292

Sachs, J., & Blackmore, J. (1998). You never show you can't cope: Women in school leadership roles managing their emotions. *Gender and Education*, *10*(3), 265–279. doi:10.1080/09540259820899

Sahlin, K. (2012). The interplay of organizing models in higher education: what room is there for collegiality in universities characterized by bounded autonomy? In *Managing Reform in Universities* (pp. 198–221). Springer. doi:10.1057/9781137284297_11

Salgado, J. (2002). The Big Five personality dimensions and counterproductive behaviors. *International Journal of Selection and Assessment*, *10*(1&2), 117–125. doi:10.1111/1468-2389.00198

Sanches, W. (2018). Welcome to the Global Worker. *The Global Worker*, *1*(4), 2.

Sancino, A. (2021). Local political leadership: From managerial performances to leadership hop on social media? *International Journal of Public Leadership*, *17*(3), 283–297. doi:10.1108/IJPL-01-2021-0001

Compilation of References

Sankowsky, D. (1995). The charismatic leader as a narcissist: Understanding the abuse of power. *Organizational Dynamics, 23*(4), 57–71. doi:10.1016/0090-2616(95)90017-9

Sarkis, J., Cohen, M. J., Dewick, P., & Schröder, P. (2020). A brave new world: Lessons from the COVID-19 pandemic for transitioning to sustainable supply and production. *Resources, Conservation and Recycling, 159*, 104894. doi:10.1016/j.resconrec.2020.104894 PMID:32313383

Sarros, J. C., & Santora, J. C. (2001). The transformational-transactional leadership model in practice. *Leadership and Organization Development Journal, 22*(8), 383–394. doi:10.1108/01437730110410107

Sarwar, H., Ishaq, M. I., Amin, A., & Ahmed, R. (2020). 'Ethical leadership, work engagement, employees' wellbeing, and performance: A cross-cultural comparison'. *Journal of Sustainable Tourism, 28*(12), 2008–2026. doi:10.1080/09669582.2020.1788039

Sathye, M. (2004). Leadership in higher education: A qualitative study. *Forum Qualitative Sozialforschung / Forum: Qualitative. Social Research, 5*(3). > doi:10.17169/fqs-5.3.571

Savić, D. (2020). COVID-19 and work from home: Digital transformation of the workforce. *Grey Journal, 16*(2), 101–104.

Savolainen, T. (2014). Trust-building in e-Leadership: A case study of leaders' challenges and skills in technology-mediated interaction. *Journal of Global Business Issues, 8*(2), 45–56.

Savolainen, T. (2014). Trust-building in e-leadership: A case study of leaders' challenges and skills in technology-mediated interaction. *Journal of Global Business Issues, 8*(2).

Schaufeli, W. B. (2002). The Measurement of Engagement and Burnout: A Two Sample Confirmatory Factor Analytic Approach. *Journal of Happiness Studies, 3*(1), 71–92. . doi:10.1023/A:1015630930326

Schein, E. (1961). Coercive Persuasion: A Sociopsychological Analysis of the "Brainwashing" if American Civilian Prisoners by the Chinese Communists. Norton.

Schindler, J. (2022). How To Identify And Manage Quiet Quitting. *Forbes.* https://www.forbes.com/sites/forbescoachescouncil/2022/10/28/how-to-identify-and-manage-quiet-quitting/?sh=3f1d95c24c4f

Schlicher, K. D., Paruzel, A., Steinmann, B., & Maier, G. W. (2017). Change Management für die Einführung digitaler Arbeitswelten. In G. W. Maier, G. Engels & E. Steffen (Eds.), Handbuch Gestaltung digitaler und vernetzter Arbeitswelten (pp. 1–36). Springer.

Schmidt, F. L., & Hunter, J. E. (2000). Select on intelligence. In E. A. Locke (Ed.), *Handbook of principles of organizational behavior* (pp. 3–14). Blackwell.

Schmidt, M. (2010). Trabalho e saúde mental na visão da OIT. *Revista Do Tribunal Regional Do Trabalho, 51*(81), 489–526.

School Superintendent Demographics And Statistics In The US. (n.d.). Zippia. https://www.zippia.com/school-superintendent-jobs/demographics/

Schwartz, M. (2019). *KfW-Mittelstandspanel 2019: Jährliche Analyse zur Struktur und Entwicklungdes Mittelstands in Deutschland*. Frankfurt a.M.

Schwarzmüller, T., Brosi, P., Duman, D., & Welpe, I. M. (2018). How does the digital transformation affect organizations? Key themes of change in work design and leadership. *Management Revu, 29*(2), 114–138.

Scott, A. (2018). *How Artificial Intelligence and Intergenerational Diversity Are Creating Anxiety in The Workplace*. Institute for Public Relations. https://instituteforpr.org/how-artificial-intelligence-and-intergenerational-diversity-is-creating-anxiety-in-the-workplace/

Scott, G., Coates, H., & Anderson, M. (2008). *Learning Leaders in Times of Change: Academic Leadership Capabilities for Australian Higher Education*. Carrick Institute. https://research.acer.edu.au/higher_education/3

Scott, D. E., & Scott, S. (2016). Leadership for quality university teaching: How bottom-up academic insights can inform top-down leadership. *Educational Management Administration & Leadership*, 44(3), 511–531. doi:10.1177/1741143214549970

Scott, G., Bell, S., Coates, H., & Grebennikov, L. (2010). Australian higher education leaders in times of change: The role of Pro Vice-Chancellor and Deputy Vice-Chancellor. *Journal of Higher Education Policy and Management*, 32(4), 401–418. doi:10.1080/1360080X.2010.491113

Scott, W. G., & Hart, D. K. (1991). The Exhaustion of managerialism. *Society*, 28(3), 39–48. doi:10.1007/BF02695594

Secundo, G., Vecchio, P. D., & Passiante, G. (2015). Creating innovative entrepreneurial mindsets as a lever for knowledge-based regional development. *International Journal of Knowledge-Based Development*, 6(4), 276–298. doi:10.1504/IJKBD.2015.074301

Seeck, H., Sturdy, A., Boncori, A. L., & Fougère, M. (2020). Ideology in management studies. *International Journal of Management Reviews*, 22(1), 57. doi:10.1111/ijmr.12215

Seligman, M. E., & Csikszentmihaly, M. (2000). Positive Psychology. In American Psychologist Asociation, 55(1), 5–14.

Shah, S., & Patki, S. (2020). Getting traditionally rooted Indian leadership to embrace digital leadership: Challenges and way forward with reference to LMX. *Leadership, Education, Personality. An Interdisciplinary Journal*, 2(1), 29–40. doi:10.136542681-020-00013-2

Shakeel, F., Kruyen, P. M., & Van Thiel, S. (2019). Ethical leadership as process: A conceptual proposition. *Public Integrity*, 21(6), 613–624. doi:10.1080/10999922.2019.1606544

Shamir, B., Arthur, M., & House, R. (1994). The rhetoric of charismatic leaders: A theoretical extension, a case study, and implications for research. *The Leadership Quarterly*, 5(1), 25–42. doi:10.1016/1048-9843(94)90004-3

Shamir, B., House, R. J., & Arthur, M. B. (1993). The motivational effects of charismatic leadership: A self-concept based theory. *Organization Science*, 4(4), 577–594. doi:10.1287/orsc.4.4.577

Sharif, M. M., & Scandura, T. A. (2014). Moral identity: Linking ethical leadership to follower decision making. Advances in authentic and ethical leadership. *Research Management*, 10, 155–190.

Sharma, P. N., & Kirkman, B. L. (2015). Leveraging leaders: A literature review and future lines of inquiry for empowering leadership research. *Group & Organization Management*, 40(2), 193–237. doi:10.1177/1059601115574906

Sharma, P., Kong, T. T. C., & Kingshott, R. P. J. (2016). Internal service quality as a driver of employee satisfaction, commitment and performance – exploring the focal role of wellbeing of employee. *Journal of Service Management*, 27(5), 773–797. doi:10.1108/JOSM-10-2015-0294

Shattock, M. (2010). Entrepreneurialism and organizational change in higher education. In *Entrepreneurialism in Universities and the Knowledge economy: Diversification and Organizational Change in European Higher Education* (pp. 1–8). Open University Press.

Compilation of References

Shen, P., & Slater, P. (2021). The Effect of Occupational Stress and Coping Strategies on Mental Health and Emotional Well-Being among University Academic Staff during the COVID-19 Outbreak. *International Education Studies, 14*(3), 82–95. doi:10.5539/ies.v14n3p82

Shepherd, S. (2018). Managerialism: An ideal type. *Studies in Higher Education, 43*(9), 1668–1678. doi:10.1080/03075079.2017.1281239

Silla, I., Gracia, F. J., & Peiró, J. M. (2020). Upward voice: Participative decision making, trust in leadership and safety climate matter. *Sustainability (Basel), 12*(9), 36–72. doi:10.3390u12093672

Silva, A. (2016). What is leadership? *Journal of Business Studies Quarterly, 8*(1), 1–5. PMID:29355200

Simon, A., & Lacava, G. (2008). The relationship of strategic thinking and strategic capabilities to success in a sample of Australia's top 500 ASX companies. *Academy of Taiwan Business Management Review, 4*(1), 1–9.

Simon, H. A. (1960). *The new science of management decision.* Harper. doi:10.1037/13978-000

Simonton, D. (1988). Presidential style: Personality, biography, and performance. *Journal of Personality and Social Psychology, 55*(6), 928–936. doi:10.1037/0022-3514.55.6.928

Simpson, A. (2007). On ethnographic refusal: Indigeneity, 'voice' and colonial citizenship. *Junctures: the journal for thematic dialogue,* (9), 67-80.

Sims, M. (2020). *Bullshit Towers: Neoliberalism and Managerialism in Universities in Australia.* Peter Lang Academic Publishers. doi:10.3726/b16811

Singh, P., Bala, H., Dey, B. L., & Filieri, R. (2022). Enforced remote working: The impact of digital platform-induced stress and remote working experience on technology exhaustion and subjective wellbeing. *Journal of Business Research, 151*(August 2021), 269–286. doi:10.1016/j.jbusres.2022.07.002

Singh, A., Jha, S., Srivastava, D. K., & Somarajan, A. (2022). Future of work: A systematic literature review and evolution of themes. *Foresight, 24*(1), 99–125. doi:10.1108/FS-09-2020-0093

Skaaning, S. E. (2020). Waves of autocratization and democratisation: A critical note on conceptualisation and measurement. *Democratization, 27*(8), 1533–1542. doi:10.1080/13510347.2020.1799194

Slattery, C. (2009). The Dark Side of Leadership. In S. Slattery (Ed.). Semann & Slattery.

Sloan, M., Gordon, C., Lever, E., Harwood, R., Bosley, M. A., Pilling, M., Brimicombe, J., Naughton, F., Blane, M., Walia, C., & D'Cruz, D. (2021). COVID-19 and shielding: Experiences of U.K. patients with lupus and related diseases. *Rheumatology Advances in Practice, 5*(1), rkab003. doi:10.1093/rap/rkab003 PMID:33728396

Smart, B. (1994). Sociology, globalisation and postmodernity: Comments on the "Sociology for one world" thesis. *International Sociology, 9*(2), 149-159.

Smith, L. T. (2012). Decolonizing methodologies: research and indigenous peoples, London: Dunedin, Zed Books; Otago University Press.

Smith, S. F., & Lilienfeld, S. O. (2013). Psychopathy in the workplace: The knowns and unknowns. *Aggression and Violent Behavior, 18*(2), 204–218. doi:10.1016/j.avb.2012.11.007

Smith, W. C., Sakiko, I., Baker, D. P., & Cheng, M. (2016). Education, health, and labor force supply: Broadening human capital for national development in Malawi. *Cogent Education, 3*(1), 1. doi:10.1080/2331186X.2016.1149041

Sneader, K., & Singhal, S. (2021, January, 4). *The next normal arrives: The trends that will define 2021 – and beyond*. McKinsey. https://www.mckinsey.com/featured-insights/leadership/the-next-normal-arrives-trends-that-will-define-2021-and-beyond#/

Snyder, H. (2019). Literature review as a research methodology: An overview and guidelines. *Journal of Business Research*, *104*, 333–339. doi:10.1016/j.jbusres.2019.07.039

Sohail Butt, R., Wen, X., & Yassir Hussain, R. (2020). Mediated Effect of Employee Job Satisfaction on Employees' Happiness at Work and Analysis of Motivational Factors: Evidence from Telecommunication Sector. *Asian Business Research Journal*, *5*(September), 19–27. doi:10.20448/journal.518.2020.5.19.27

Solidarity Center. (2023). *Trade Union Strengthening*. Solidarity Center. https://www.solidaritycenter.org/what-we-do/trade-union-strengthening/

Solomon, S., Greenberg, J., & Pyszczynski, T. (1991). A terror management theory of social behavior: The psychological functions of self-esteem and cultural worldviews. In M. Zanna (Ed.), Advances in experimental social psychology (Vol. 24, pp. 93–159). Academic Press. doi:10.1016/S0065-2601(08)60328-7

Sood, B. (2021). The Emergence of Managerial Capitalism in Europe, *International Journal of Research in Engineering*. *Science and Management*, *4*(11), 169–177.

Spillane, J. P. (2004). Educational leadership. *Educational Evaluation and Policy Analysis*, *26*(2), 169–172. doi:10.3102/01623737026002169

Spiro, C. (2006). Generation Y in the Workplace. *Defense AT*, *L*(November- December), 16–19.

StageSHIFT Coaching & Consulting. (2016, May 25). Retrieved from https://www.stageshift.coach/blog/learn-to-c-the-world-anew-the-5-c-s-of-vuca-leadership

Stahl, A. (2022). What's Really Happening With Quiet Quitting? *Forbes*. https://www.forbes.com/sites/ashleystahl/2022/11/02/whats-really-happening-with-quiet-quitting/?sh=3d6f676c2ab1

Stahl, A. (2022, January 22). Workforce trends are changing as we are embrace a new normal in 2022. *Forbes*. https://www.forbes.com/sites/ashleystahl/2022/01/24/workforce-trends-are-changing-as-we-embrace-a-new-normal-in-2022/?sh=19bc2e8c2848

Stander, M. W., & Coxen, L. (2017). A Review of the Relationship Between Positive Leadership Styles and Psychological Ownership. In *Theoretical Orientations and Practical Applications of Psychological Ownership*. Springer International Publishing. doi:10.1007/978-3-319-70247-6_3

Stelmokienė, A., & Vadvilavičius, T. (2022). Can dark triad traits in leaders be associated with positive outcomes of transformational leadership: Cultural differences [Mogu li se osobine tamne trijade kod vođa povezati s pozitivnim ishodima transformacijskoga vodstva: Kulturne razlike]. *Psihologijske Teme*, *31*(3), 521–543. doi:10.31820/pt.31.3.3

Stengel, F. A., & Baumann, R. (2017). Non-state actors and foreign policy. In Oxford Research Encyclopedia of Politics. doi:10.1093/acrefore/9780190228637.013.456

Stensaker, B., & Harvey, L. (2010). *Accountability in Higher Education: Global Perspectives on Trust and Power*. Routledge. doi:10.4324/9780203846162

Sternberg, R. J., & Ruzgis, P. (1994). *Personality and intelligence*. Cambridge University Press.

Stewart, G. T., Macdonald, L., Matapo, J., Fa'avae, D. T. M., Watson, B. K. I., Akiu, R. K., Martin, B., Mika, C., & Sturm, S. (2021). Surviving academic Whiteness: Perspectives from the Pacific. *Educational Philosophy and Theory*, 1–12. https://doi.org/10.1080/00131857.2021.2010542 doi:10.1080/00131857.2021.2010542

Stogdill, R. M. (1948). Personal factors associated with leadership: A survey of the literature. *The Journal of Psychology*, *25*(1), 35–71. doi:10.1080/00223980.1948.9917362 PMID:18901913

Stoller, J. K. (2020). *Reflections on leadership in the time of COVID-19*. BMJ Public Health Emergency Collection. doi:10.1136/leader-2020-000244

Stone, A. G., Russell, R. F., & Patterson, K. (2004). Transformational versus servant leadership: A difference in leader focus. *Leadership and Organization Development Journal*.

Strachan, G., Peetz, D., Whitehouse, G., Bailey, J., Broadbent, K., May, R., Troup, C., & Nesic, M. (2016), *Women, careers and universities: Where to from here?* Centre for Work, Organisation and Wellbeing, Griffith University. https://www.griffith.edu.au/__data/assets/pdf_file/0023/88124/UA-FINAL-Report-Digital-4-April-2016.pdf

Stuenkel, O. (2021, February 17). *Brazil's polarisation and Democratic risks - carnegie endowment for ...* Retrieved March 28, 2023, from https://carnegieendowment.org/2021/02/17/brazil-s-polarization-and-democratic-risks-pub-83783

Superville, D. R. (2016, Dec 30). *Few women run the nation's school districts. Why?* PBS News Hours. https://www.pbs.org/newshour/education/women-run-nations-school-districts

Svensson, T. (2015) *How to run a Trade union*: Trade union handbook. Stockholm: Olof Palme International center.

Tamer, R. (2022). 'Hugely disappointing': Indigenous employees 'almost entirely absent' from senior leadership, report finds. *SBS News*. https://www.sbs.com.au/news/article/hugely-disappointing-indigenous-employees-almost-entirely-absent-from-senior-leadership-report-finds/exaft6rew

Tan, R., & Antonio, F. (2022). New insights on employee adaptive performance during the COVID-19 pandemic: Empirical evidence from Indonesia. *Journal of Entrepreneurship. Management and Innovation*, *18*(2), 175–206. doi:10.7341/20221826

Taylor, E. V., Lalovic, A., & Thompson, S. C. (2019). Beyond enrolments: A systematic review exploring the factors affecting the retention of Aboriginal and Torres Strait Islander health students in the tertiary education system. *International Journal for Equity in Health*, *18*(1), 1–19. https://doi.org/10.1186/s12939-019-1038-7 doi:10.118612939-019-1038-7 PMID:31477114

Teacher Demographics And Statistics In The US. (n.d.). Zippia. https://www.zippia.com/teacher-jobs/demographics/

Tekrakunna, E. & Evans, J. (2022). *Indigenous Women's Voices 20 Years on from Linda Tihiwai Smith's Decolonizing Methodologies*. Sydney, Zed Books.

Tepper, B. J. (2000). Consequences of abusive supervision. *Academy of Management Journal*, *43*(2), 178–190. doi:10.2307/1556375

Tertiary Education Quality and Standards Agency (TEQSA). (2019). *Statistics Report on TEQSA Registered Higher Education Providers*. TEQSA. https://files.eric.ed.gov/fulltext/ED602734.pdf

Thakker, P. (2023, March). Workers of Color Made up 100% OF Union. *Growth, 2022*. https://newrepublic.com/post/171375/workers-color-union-growth-2022

The University of Texas. (n.d.). *The Impact of Gender on the Role of Superintendent*. UTPB. https://online.utpb.edu/about-us/articles/education/the-impact-of-gender-on-the-role-of-superintendent/

Thomas, H. (1998). *Cuba or the pursuit of freedom*. Plenum Press.

Thomas, J. C., Segal, D. L., Lebreton, J., Binning, J., & Adorno, A. (2006). *Subclinical Psychopaths* (Vol. 1). John Wiley & Sons, Inc.

Thompson, D. (2022). Quiet Quitting Is a Fake Trend. Why Does It Feel Real? *The Atlantic*. https://www.theatlantic.com/newsletters/archive/2022/09/quiet-quitting-trend-employee-disengagement/671436/

Thunig, A., & Jones, T. (2021). 'Don't make me play house-n*** er': Indigenous academic women treated as 'black performer' within higher education. *Australian Educational Researcher*, *48*(3), 397–417. https://doi.org/10.1007/s13384-020-00405-9 doi:10.100713384-020-00405-9

Tight, M. (2014). Collegiality and managerialism: A false dichotomy? Evidence from the higher education literature. *Tertiary Education and Management*, *20*(4), 294–306. doi:10.1080/13583883.2014.956788

Tigre, F. B., Curado, C., & Henriques, P. L. (2022). Digital leadership: A bibliometric analysis. *Journal of Leadership & Organizational Studies*, *30*(1), 40–70. Advance online publication. doi:10.1177/15480518221123132

Tinuoye, T. A. (2023, January 30). *Redefining Trade Union practices in a Post Pandemic and Future World of work*, [Paper presentation]. The National Workshop on Trade Union Leadership Development, Ilorin, Nigeria. https://www.harisingh.com/Ubuntu/Age.htm

Torre, T., & Sarti, D. (2020). The "way" toward e-leadership: Some evidence from the field. *Frontiers in Psychology*, *11*. . doi:10.3389/fpsyg.2020.554253

Tranfield, D., Denyer, D., & Smart, P. (2003). Towards a methodology for developing evidence-informed management knowledge by means of systematic review. *British Journal of Management*, *14*(3), 207–222. doi:10.1111/1467-8551.00375

Triay, V. (1999). *Fleeing Castro: Operation Pedro Pan and the Cuban children's program*. University of Florida Press.

Trofimov, A., Matviienko, L., Emishyants, O., Tretiakova, Y., Zelenin, V., Andrushchenko, T., & Kotsiuba, H. (2019). Socio-psychological factors of corporate loyalty. *International Journal of Scientific and Technology Research*, *8*(11), 3439–3442.

Trudgett, M., Page, S., & Sullivan, C. (2017). Past, present and future: Acknowledging Indigenous achievement and aspiration in higher education. *HERDSA Review of Higher Education*. https://www.herdsa.org.au/herdsa-review-higher-education-vol-4/29-51

Tuchman, B. (1984). *The march of folly: From Troy to Vietnam*. Alfred A. Knopf.

Tucker, R. C. (1995). *Politics as leadership* (Revised edition). University of Missouri Press.

Tucker, R. C. (2017). The theory of charismatic leadership. In *Leadership Perspectives* (pp. 499–524). Routledge. doi:10.4324/9781315250601-37

Compilation of References

Tulshyan, R. (2023, April 07). *How Colorism Affects Women at Work*. Harvard Business Review. https://hbr.org/2023/04/how-colorism-affects-women-at-work

Tyler, T. R., & Blader, S. L. (2000). *Cooperation in Groups: Procedural Justice*. Social Identity, and Behavioral Engagement.

Tyler, T. R., & Blader, S. L. (2002). The influence of status judgments in hierarchical groups: Comparing autonomous and comparative judgments about status. *Organizational Behavior and Human Decision Processes, 89*(1), 813–838. doi:10.1016/S0749-5978(02)00031-6

Uink, B., Bennett, R., & Van Den Berg, C. (2021). Factors that enable Australian Aboriginal women's persistence at university: A strengths-based approach. *Higher Education Research & Development, 40*(1), 178–193. http://dx.doi.org/10.1080/07294360.2020.1852185 doi:10.1080/07294360.2020.1852185

UNDP. (2015). Human Development Report 2015: Work for Human Development. New York: United Nations Development Programme

UNDP. (2021). *The impact of COVID-19 on Business Enterprises in Nigeria*. UNDP. https://www.undp.org/sites/g/files/zskgke326/files/migration/ng/The-Impact-of-COVID19-on-Business-Enterprises-in-Nigeria.pdf

Universities Australia. (2017). *2016 Selected Inter-Institutional Gender Equity Statistics*. Canberra.

Universities Australia. (2022). *Indigenous Strategy 2022-25*. Canberra, Universities Australia. https://www.universitiesaustralia.edu.au/wp-content/uploads/2022/03/UA-Indigenous-Strategy-2022-25.pdf

Unnu, N. A. A. (2019). Boosting positivity and performance: A case study of organizational coaching. Handbook of Research on Positive Organizational Behavior for Improved Workplace Performance, 34–54. doi:10.4018/978-1-7998-0058-3.ch003

Uygur, A., & Gümüştekin, K. (2019). Karanlık Liderliğin Alt Boyutlarının İncelenmesi. *International Social Sciences Studies Journal, 5*(35), 2552–2562. doi:10.26449ssj.1492

Uysal, Ş. A., & Çelik, R. (2018). Sağlık meslek gruplarında hubris sendromunun varlığına ilişkin keşfedici bir çalışma. *Uluslararası İktisadi Ve İdari İncelemeler, 17*, 103-118.

Vaikutytė-Paškauskė, J., Vaičiukynaitė, J., & Pocius, D. (2018). *Research for CULT committee: Digital skills in the 21st century*. Brussels: European Parliament, Policy Department for Structural and Cohesion Policies.

Vaillant, G. (1977). *Adaptation to life*. Little-Brown.

Valverde-Moreno, M., Torres-Jimenez, M., & Lucia-Casademunt, A. M. (2020). Participative decision-making amongst employees in a cross-cultural employment setting: Evidence from 31 European countries. *European Journal of Training and Development, 45*(1), 14–35. doi:10.1108/EJTD-10-2019-0184

Van Gelderen, M., Kautonen, T., & Fink, M. (2015). From entrepreneurial intentions to actions: Self-control and action-related doubt, fear, and aversion. *Journal of Business Venturing, 30*(5), 655–673. doi:10.1016/j.jbusvent.2015.01.003

van Laar, E., van Deursen, A. J. A. M., van Dijk, J. A. G. M., & de Haan, J. (2017). The relation between 21st-century skills and digital skills: A systematic literature review. *Computers in Human Behavior, 72*, 577–588. doi:10.1016/j.chb.2017.03.010

van Laar, E., van Deursen, A. J. A. M., van Dijk, J. A. G. M., & de Haan, J. (2018). 21st-century digital skills instrument aimed at working professionals: Conceptual development and empirical validation. *Telematics and Informatics*, *35*(8), 2184–2200. doi:10.1016/j.tele.2018.08.006

Van Vugt, M., & von Rueden, C. R. (2020). From genes to minds to cultures: Evolutionary approaches to leadership. *The Leadership Quarterly*, *31*(2), 101404. doi:10.1016/j.leaqua.2020.101404

Van Wart, M., Roman, A., Wang, X., & Liu, C. (2017). Integrating ICT adoption issues into (e-)leadership theory. *Telematics and Informatics*, *34*(5), 527–537. doi:10.1016/j.tele.2016.11.003

Van Wart, M., Roman, A., Wang, X., Liu, C., Reiter, R., & Klenk, T. (2019). Operationalizing the definition of e-leadership: Identifying the elements of e-leadership. *International Review of Administrative Sciences*, *85*(1), 80–97. doi:10.1177/0020852316681446

VanWart, M., Roman, A., & Pierce, S. (2016). The rise and effect of virtual modalities and functions on organizational leadership: Tracing conceptual boundaries along the e-management and e-leadership continuum. *Transylvanian Review of Administrative Sciences*, *12*(1), 102–122. doi:10.24193/tras.si2021

Vaubel, R. (2006). Principal-agent problems in international organisations. *The Review of International Organizations*, *1*(2), 125–138. doi:10.100711558-006-8340-z

Vieira De Faria, R., & Zanotelli De Alvarenga, R. (2021). A Convenção 190 Da Oit E a Proteção À Saúde Mental Dos Trabalhadores. *Ano*, *7*, 1257–1285.

Viney, J. (1999). *Drive: What makes a leader in business and beyond*. Bloomsbury Publishing.

Visser, J. (2019). *Trade Unions in a balance, ILO/Actrav*. Geneva: ILO

Vrana, J., & Singh, R. (2021). A design thinking perspective. *Journal of Nondestructive Evaluation*, *40*(1), 1–24. doi:10.100710921-020-00735-9 PMID:33424070

Vroom, B., & Jago, A. (1974). Decision making as a social process: Normative and descriptive models of leader behavior. *Decision Sciences*, *5*(4), 743–769. doi:10.1111/j.1540-5915.1974.tb00651.x

Walker, B. (2019). *Finding Resilience: Change and Uncertainty in Nature and Society*. CSIRO Publishing.

Wallace-Wells, D. (2017). The Uninhabitable Earth. *NY Mag*. https://nymag.com/.

Wallace-Wells, D. (2019). *The Uninhabitable Earth: life after warming*. Tim Duggan Books.

Wallerstein, I. (2007). Precipitate decline. *Harvard International Review*, *29*(1), 50.

Wallis, S. E., & Valentinov, V. (2016). The impervance of conceptual systems: Cognitive and moral aspects. *Kybernetes*, *45*(9), 1437–1451. doi:10.1108/K-04-2016-0072

Wang, X., Wei, X., Van Wart, M., McCarthy, A., Liu, C., Kim, S., & Ready, D. H. (2022). The role of e-leadership in ICT utilization: A project management perspective. *Information Technology Management*, (February), 1–15. PMID:36311472

Waqas, M., & ... 2021). Impact of ethical leadership on wellbeing of employee: The mediating role of job satisfaction and employee voice. *Middle East J. of Management*, *1*(1), 1. doi:10.1504/MEJM.2022.122577

Wargin, J., & Dobiéy, D. (2001). E-business and change–managing the change in the digital economy. *Journal of Change Management*, *2*(1), 72–82. doi:10.1080/714042483

Compilation of References

Waronwant. (2023, February 15). *News and Analysis: Ten Reasons Why Unions are Important*. War on Want. https://www.waronwant.org/news-analysis/ten-reasons-why-unions-are-important

Watters, A. (2013). A Future with Only 10 Universities. *Hack Education*. <http://hackeducation.com/2013/10/15/minding-the-future-openva>

Weaver, W. (1971). Timothy. The Delphi forecasting method. *Phi Delta Kappan, 52*(5), 267–271.

Webb, T. D. (2022). *Where are all the African-American Women Superintendents in California, Oregon, and Washington State?* [Doctoral dissertation, University of the Pacific].

Webster, J., & Watson, R. (2002). Analyzing the past to prepare for the future: Writing a literature review. *Management Information Systems Quarterly, 26*(2), xiii–xxiii.

Weick, K. E. (1985). Cosmos vs. Chaos: Sense and Nonsense in Electronic Contexts. *Organizational Dynamics, 14*(2), 51–64. doi:10.1016/0090-2616(85)90036-1

Weick, K. E. (1993). Collapse of Sensemaking in Organizations: The Mann Gulch Disaster. *Administrative Science Quarterly, 38*(4), 628–652. doi:10.2307/2393339

Weick, K. E. (1995). *Sensemaking in Organizations*. Sage.

Weierter, S. (1997). Who wants to play "Follow the Leader?" A theory of charismatic relationships based on routinized charisma and follower characteristics. *The Leadership Quarterly, 8*(2), 171–193. doi:10.1016/S1048-9843(97)90015-1

Weikart, L. A., Chen, G., Williams, D. W., & Hromic, H. (2007). The democratic sex: Gender differences and the exercise of power. *Journal of Women, Politics & Policy, 28*(1), 119–140. doi:10.1300/J501v28n01_06

Wessels, E., & Wood, L. (2019). Fostering teachers' experiences of well-being: A participatory action learning and action research approach. *South African Journal of Education, 39*(1), 1–10. doi:10.15700aje.v39n1a1619

White, N. (2000). Creativity is the name of the game. In M. A. Bin-Sallik (Ed.), *Aboriginal women by degrees*. University of Queensland Press.

Williams, D., & Uticensis, K. (2013, August 20) *Creating a culture of unionism in the South*. Facing South. https://www.facingsouth.org/2013/08/creating-a-culture-of-unionism-in-the-south.html

Williams, J. (2000). *Unbending Gender: Why Family & Work Conflict and What to Do About it*. Oxford University Press.

Williamson, S., Pearce, A., Dickinson, H., Weeratunga, V., & Bucknall, F. (2021). *Future of Work Literature Review: Emerging Trends and Issues*. Retrieved from https://apo.org.au/node/314497

Williamson, J., & Dalal, P. (2007). Indigenising the curriculum or negotiating the tensions at the cultural interface? Embedding Indigenous perspectives and pedagogies in a university curriculum. *Australian Journal of Indigenous Education, 36*(S1), 51–58. https://doi.org/10.1017/S1326011100004701 doi:10.1017/S1326011100004701

Will, M. (2017). Study: Black students more likely to graduate if they have one black teacher. *Education Week*.

Willmott, H. (2003). Renewing strength: Corporate culture revisited. *M@n@gement, 6*(3), 73-87.

Windham-Bradstock, C. (2022). Three Solutions To Quiet Quitting. *Forbes*. https://www.forbes.com/sites/forbeshumanresourcescouncil/2022/10/12/three-solutions-to-quiet-quitting/?sh=64327b435f1b

Winkler, I. (2010). *Contemporary Leadership Theories: Enhancing the Understanding of the Complexity, Subjectivity and Dynamic of Leadership*. Springer.

Worrall, D. (2013). *Accountability Leadership: How Great Leaders Build a High-Performance Culture of Accountability and Responsibility*. The Accountability Code.

Wren, D. A., Bedeian, A. G., & Breeze, J. D. (2002). The foundations of Henri Fayol's administrative theory. *Management Decision*, 40(9), 906–918. doi:10.1108/00251740210441108

Wyld, F. (2010). Aboriginal women and leadership in the academy. *Frontline*, 18, 14-15. https://search.informit.org/doi/pdf/10.3316/informit.577008202566700

Wyld, F. (2011). Writing the ephemeral of culture: storm method [Paper in themed section: Shifting Cultures. *Social Alternatives*, 30, 40–43. https://search.informit.org/doi/10.3316/ielapa.201109581

Wyld, F. (2021). The land as research participant: A storytelling project on climate change and Indigenous perspectives. *Journal of Australian Indigenous Issues*, 24, 22–34. https://search.informit.org/doi/10.3316/informit.046669925438109

Xia, E. A. C., & Cheng, K. T. G. (2017). The determinants of purchase intention on counterfeit sportswear. *Journal of Applied Structural Equation Modeling*, 1(1), 13–26. doi:10.47263/JASEM.1(1)03

Xiao, Y., & Watson, M. (2019). Guidance on conducting a systematic literature review. *Journal of Planning Education and Research*, 39(1), 93–112. doi:10.1177/0739456X17723971

Yates, K. (2023, March 3). *Did Boris Johnson 'follow the science' on covid? he couldn't even do the maths*. Retrieved March 27, 2023, from https://www.theguardian.com/commentisfree/2023/mar/03/boris-johnson-science-covid-maths-whatapps-advisers

Yavaş, A. (2016). Sectoral Differences in the Perception of Toxic Leadership. *Procedia: Social and Behavioral Sciences*, 229, 267–276. doi:10.1016/j.sbspro.2016.07.137

Yener, H. (2022). Evaluating employee attitudes on working home style during COVID-19 pandemic. *Technium Social Sciences Journal*, 28, 490–504.

Yigit, S. (2021a). 2021: The geopolitical role of the European Union in the post-cold war order. *IKSAD 7th International Conference on Social Sciences & Humanities Conference Proceedings Book*, 71-98.

Yiğit, S. (2021b). Trump vs China. *The Trade Wars of the USA, China, and the E.U.: The Global Economy in the Age of Populism*, 67.

Yiğit, S. (2021d). The economic and political effects of COVID-19 on the Eurasian Economic Union. *New Normal and New Rules in International Trade, Economics and Marketing*, 35-55.

Yigit, S. (2021c). The Concept of Citizenship and the Democratic State. *Electronic Journal of Social and Strategic Studies*, 2, 5–25.

Yigit, S. (2022). EU-Central Asian Civil Societal Relations: Unrealistic Expectations, Discouraging Results. *Cuadernos Europeos de Deusto*, (5), 149–204. doi:10.18543/ced.2558

Compilation of References

Yukl, G. (2002). *Leadership in organizations* (5th ed.). Prentice Hall.

Yukl, G. (2012). Effective leadership behavior: What we know and what questions need more attention. *The Academy of Management Perspectives*, *26*(4), 66–85. doi:10.5465/amp.2012.0088

Yukl, G. A. (1999). An evaluation of conceptual weaknesses in transformational and charismatic leadership theories. *The Leadership Quarterly*, *10*(2), 285–305. doi:10.1016/S1048-9843(99)00013-2

Zaccaro, S. J. (2007). Trait-based perspectives of leadership. *The American Psychologist*, *62*(1), 6–16. doi:10.1037/0003-066X.62.1.6 PMID:17209675

Zaglas, W. (2021). Changes to leadership, advocacy on the card for Universities Australia. *Campus Review*. <https://viewer.joomag.com/campus-review-vol-31-issue-04-april-2021/0906343001620084026?short&>

Zaitseva, E., & Goncharova, N. (2020). Planning, design, and management of educational programs. In *ICERI2020 (International Conference of Education, Research, and Innovation)* Proceedings (pp. 796-800). IATED 10.21125/iceri.2020.0235

Zakaria, F. (1997). The rise of illiberal democracy. *Foreign Affairs*, *76*(6), 22–43. doi:10.2307/20048274

Zattoni, A., & Pugliese, A. (2021). Corporate Governance Research in the Wake of a Systemic Crisis: Lessons and Opportunities from the COVID-19 Pandemic. *Journal of Management Studies*, *58*(5), 1405–1410. doi:10.1111/joms.12693

Zhang, L., & Liu, Y. (2020). Potential interventions for novel coronavirus in China: A systematic review. *Journal of Medical Virology*, *92*(5), 479–490. doi:10.1002/jmv.25707 PMID:32052466

Zheng, W., Qu, Q., & Yang, B. (2009). *Toward a theory of Organizational Culture Evolution*. Human Resource Development Review. https://www.semanticscholar.org/paper/Toward-a-Theory-of-Organizational-Cultural-Zheng-Qu/ef7901609c74b998aee4c6bcfea3376221c4d554

Zheng, D., Witt, L. A., Waite, E., David, E. M., van Driel, M., McDonald, D. P., Callison, K. R., & Crepeau, L. J. (2015). Effects of ethical leadership on emotional exhaustion in high moral intensity situations. *The Leadership Quarterly*, *26*(5), 732–748. doi:10.1016/j.leaqua.2015.01.006

Zhu, W., Avolio, B. J., & Walumbwa, F. O. (2009). Moderating role of follower characteristics with transformational leadership and follower work engagement. *Group & Organization Management*, *34*(5), 590–619. doi:10.1177/1059601108331242

Zhu, W., Chew, I. K. H., & Spangler, W. D. (2005). CEO transformational leadership and organizational outcomes: The mediating role of human-capital-enhancing human resource management. *The Leadership Quarterly*, *16*(1), 39–52. doi:10.1016/j.leaqua.2004.06.001

Zigurs, I. (2003). Leadership in virtual teams: Oxymoron or opportunity? *Organizational Dynamics*, *31*(4), 339–351. doi:10.1016/S0090-2616(02)00132-8

Zohar, I. (2015). "The art of negotiation" leadership skills required for negotiation in time of crisis. *Procedia: Social and Behavioral Sciences*, *209*, 540–548. doi:10.1016/j.sbspro.2015.11.285

About the Contributors

Ataus Samad is an academic at the Western Sydney University, School of Business. His research interest is leadership and settlement of migrants in regional areas. He published his research findings in reputed peer-reviewed journals besides presenting his research findings at national and international conferences. His publications have been cited in reputed journals, books, conference papers and dissertations by academics from Asia, the Pacific, Europe, North America, Africa and the Middle East. Besides publishing in high-quality peer-reviewed journals, Dr. Samad published two research reports on sustainable employment and settlement of migrants in regional Australia. He also presented his views on contemporary issues in the mainstream media such as the Australian Broadcasting Corporation (ABC) Television, ABC Radio, newspapers in Australia and online media. Dr. Samad was a reviewer for several peer reviewed journals and the Australian and New Zealand Academy of Management (ANZAM) conference. Dr. Ataus Samad is a member of recognized professional bodies such as the AACSB (Association to Advance Collegiate Schools of Business), ANZAM and Western Sydney University Humanitarian and Development Research Initiative (HADRI). Besides his role as an academic, Dr. Samad was a member of the Advisory Panel for the Queensland Government's Minister for Multicultural Affairs (2016-2018) and an advisory panel member and Acting Chair of a not-for-profit organisation Regional Opportunities Australia (ROA, 2018-2020). Currently, he is a member of the Ethnic Communities of New South Wales. He has proven professional experience in leadership roles in multi-disciplinary organisations including the Defence Force and the United Nations (UN).

Ezaz Ahmed is a Professor of Business and Dean of Columbia College's Division of Business, Leadership, and Communication in South Carolina, United States. As a Senior Certified Professional (SCP) accredited by the Society for Human Resource Management (SHRM) and a professional certified member (CAHRI) of the Australian Human Resources Institute (AHRI), Dr. Ahmed possesses extensive expertise in Human Resources and Business disciplines as an academic and researcher. Dr. Ahmed has been a member of the Australian HR Institute's inaugural Research Advisory Panel and chaired the Organizational Behavior stream at the Australian and New Zealand Academy of Management (ANZAM). Before joining Columbia College, Dr. Ahmed held the positions of MBA Program Director and Head of Undergraduate and Graduate Business Programs at Flinders University and Central Queensland University in Australia. Having spent over a decade in Australia as an academic leader, he received the Central Queensland University's Students' Voice Awards for On-Campus and Distance Educator of the Year. Dr. Ahmed has effectively led teams in curriculum evaluation, academic strategy formulation, and accreditation process coordination. He has served as both the chair and a member of various prestigious academic advisory panels and discipline streams within higher education and professional institutions.

About the Contributors

In recent years, Dr. Ahmed's research has concentrated on artificial intelligence in higher education, employee psychological contracts, leadership, the influence of information and communication technology (ICT), the integration of skilled migrants in regional areas, and the development of inclusive employment possibilities for disabled employees. His involvement spans international, national, and industry-based research projects and grants.

Nitin Arora is currently a Rekhi Singh Endowed Professor of Happiness at Amity International Business School, Amity University Uttar Pradesh, Noida India. He is the Head of Amity Rekhi Centre of Excellence for the Science of Happiness. He had graduated from M.S. University, Gujarat– B.E. (Chemical), MBA from IMS, Devi Ahilya University Indore, MP and doctorate (Ph.D) from Universidad Azteca, Chalco, Mexico. He has more than 19 years of rich academic experience with more than 30 research papers in International Journals/Conferences and Two books. He has been awarded recently with Positivity Award in a Conclave organized by Brain Behaviour Research Foundation of India and has been keynote speaker and trainer in various Happiness Conferences and Conclaves organized by Global institutions. He was instrumental in raising endowment fund for 200,000USD. He teaches Science of happiness, Behavioural Sciences, Human Values, and Artificial Intelligence and Human Cognition. He is a Proctor, Editor of Amity Journal of Happiness and Peace and is mentoring 7 PhD scholars. He has served in various capacities in Educational institutions based in Jordan, Bahrain, London, and Singapore.

* * *

Anas Al-Fattal is an Assistant Professor of Marketing at the University of Minnesota, Crookston. He received his master's and Ph.D. degrees from the University of Leeds, UK. He has a wide range of experiences in marketing and education from different parts of the world, including Syria, Oman, Turkey, the UK, and the US. He has worked on several projects on reforming higher education and building capacities in research. The focus of his study and research has been educational management, marketing strategy, applied psychology, consumer behavior (student choice), and cryptocurrency. ORCID ID: 0000-0001-9736-7439.

Pavani Ayinampudi is a life scientist with a Masters and PhD in Animal Biology from one of India's Institutions of Eminence, the University of Hyderabad. With more than seven years of research experience in the field of Animal biology, she joined TSWREIS as a Lecturer and taught Zoology at the undergraduate level. Later, she was assigned the role of Officer on Special Duty (OSD) in the Department of Higher Education and was designated in charge for academics across 30 Residential Degree colleges in Telangana under TSWREIS. During her 2-year tenure as OSD, she played a key role in introducing the B. Pharmacy course, BSc (Hons) in Design and Technology in partnership with NIFT-Hyderabad, BSc Bioinformatics and French as Second language in TSWR Degree Colleges. She also is the coordinator for the international collaborations of TSWREIS with John Hopkins University, Harvard University and other international organizations like Launch Gurls, United Way etc. Faculty lounges, Academic Coordinator System, Digital literacy weeks, centralized time table and higher education trainings were a few of her ideations at TSWREIS. She also is the Convener of the first International Conference of TSWREIS, BioMe '23 that witnessed a delegation of ~800 participants from 3 continents. She is currently working on bringing new national and international partners on board to build the Social Welfare Residential Degree Colleges as Centres for Academic Excellence. Dr. Pavani's vision is to create policies that provide 'quality education for all' which she plans to achieve by working closely with the government and regulatory bodies in education sector. Outside work, she is an avid star gazer and a movie buff.

Navisha Bajaj is currently pursuing her final year Honours programme in Applied Psychology from Amity University Chhattisgarh, Raipur, Her interest area is in Industrial / organizational Psychology.

Mrityunjay Bandyopadhyay is currently pursuing final year Honors programme in Applied Psychology from Amity University Chhattisgarh, Raipur, He has a keen interest in studying leadership types and traits with reference to uncertain times.

Abraham Bradfield is a non-Indigenous research officer with the Office of the Pro-Vice Chancellor (Indigenous Engagement) at the University of Queensland. Grounded in Anthropology, Social Sciences, and critical Indigenous Studies, Abraham applies a cross and transdisciplinary approach to his research to explore themes relating to colonisation, identity, and the intercultural. He remains committed to developing and implementing morally responsible research that challenges colonial power structures and encourages new habits of thought and praxis.

Tracey Bunda is a Ngugi/Wakka Wakka woman and grew up on the lands of the Jagera/Jugera/Yugarapul peoples. Professor Bunda is Professor of Indigenous Education and the current Academic Director of the Aboriginal and Torres Strait Islander Studies Unit, The University of Queensland and convener of the Critical Aboriginal and Torres Strait Islander Studies major in the Bachelor of Arts and Social Sciences.

Jayne Bye is a Senior Lecturer, School of Business, Western Sydney University.

Monique Darrisaw-Akil is the Superintendent of Schools in the Uniondale Union Free School District in Uniondale, New York. She was most recently served as the Assistant Superintendent for Secondary Education, Programs and Policy at the Brentwood School District. She is also the founding principal of the Academy of Urban Planning High School in Brooklyn. Dr. Darrisaw-Akil has over 27 years of experience in public education, 22 of which were in New York City public schools. Dr. Darrisaw-Akil is an experienced leadership coach, curriculum writer, consultant, staff developer and workshop presenter. Her work's focus has been on promoting equity through providing a high-quality education to all students. Dr. Darrisaw- Akil has developed Middle School Literacy Initiatives, College Application Bootcamps, and implemented Restorative Justice programs in school districts in which she worked. Additionally, she has implemented student-centered programs as the Girls, Inc. leadership program, the Friendship Club which promotes friendship between special needs students and their general education peers and as she also established a regionally recognized My Brother's Keeper program which provides mentoring, college and career support and leadership development for young men of color. Dr. Darrisaw-Akil earned a B.A. and M.A. from Brooklyn College, CUNY and a doctorate in Educational Leadership, Management and Policy from Seton Hall University. She is a Trustee for the SUNY Old Westbury Foundation, a member of the National Coalition of 100 Black Women Long Island and a "Big" with Big Brothers Big Sisters, Long Island. She has been a featured speaker for organizations such as the Urban League of Long Island, Coalition of Educating Boys of Color, and the Nation Alliance of Black School Educators.

About the Contributors

She has also been a guest on NPR discussing restorative justice, and has been featured in publications such as Newsday, New York Daily News and US News and World Report.

Wayne Fallon is an Adjunct Fellow, School of Business, Western Sydney University.

Paula Figueiredo has a degree in Economics with a specialization in Human Resources Economics, a Master in Human Resources Management and a PhD in Management. She is currently a professor at higher education institutions, and she has also been the Director of an institution since 2019. Paula has 20 years of experience in the business area with functions of direction, coordination, and consultancy. Throughout her professional experience, she has collaborated on leadership development projects. At the research level, she has developed research on Human Resource Development, more specifically Leadership Development in organizations, with some publications in scientific journals and conferences.

Cristina Nogueira da Fonseca has a degree in Sociology, specializing in Community Psychology, Positive Psychology and Human Resource Management. She is the Founder and Partner of Happytown-Happiness Science Based, the first Portuguese consultant specialized in Corporate Happiness. She is a Teacher and Trainer and is considered one of the references in the area, being a guest speaker at several events.

Bronwyn Fredericks, PhD, is a Professor and the Deputy Vice-Chancellor (Indigenous Engagement) at the University of Queensland. She has over 30 years' experience working with Aboriginal and Torres Strait Islander communities, Indigenous health organisations, NGOs, and Government agencies. Her research, based in the fields of health and education and grounded within the political reality of Indigenous peoples' daily lives, exemplifies her commitment to social justice and improving Indigenous health and education outcomes.

Bhawna Gaur, Ph.D. (Human Resource Management), is an Associate Professor and the Head of Case Centre at Amity University Dubai. She has 19+ years of industry and academic experience in the field of human resource management. Her case studies are published at The Case Centre, (United Kingdom) which have been downloaded by well-known business schools, consulting firms and publishing houses. Through the case studies she has analyzed industry and region-specific issues, such as Women Entrepreneurship, Water scarcity, Absher Initiative, Family business, Sustainability, Expo 2020 and Citizenship policy of UAE among others. Her case studies on corporate leadership have highlighted the strategic perspectives, entrepreneurial styles, regional challenges, and government policies that affect the employment landscape of the Middle Eastern region. Under her able guidance Amity Case Centre has published more than 200 case units representing a broad range of management subjects such as business strategy, marketing, finance, corporate governance, economics, innovation and human resource management, to complement the learning outcomes for courses in Management and Commerce. Along with case studies she has also published several papers in topics related to Human Resource Management, Organization Behavior, People Analytics, Stress Management, Succession Planning and Talent Management.

Shilpi Gupta is an FCWA and her research interests includes Behavioral finance and stock market volatility.

Ana Filipa Vieira Joaquim has a master's degree in Master in teaching Economics and Accounting and is marketing graduate. Currently she is pursuing a PhD in Global Studies. A high school teacher by profession and trainer in several entities. She has participated in many conferences, seminars, and lectures, and has authored and co-authored several articles and book chapters. Her main interests are education, management, and politics. Nowadays her study fields are populism, critical thinking and human skills in labour.

Thomas Klikauer, born half-way between Castle Frankenstein, the place where Johannes Gutenberg invented the printing press, and where Carl Benz invented the motor car, Bremen and Boston (MAs) and Warwick (PhD), teaches MBAs at the SGSM at Western Sydney University, Australia. Among his 870 publications are thirteen books. He lives in the sunny beachside suburb of Coogee in the eastern parts of Sydney, Australia.

Rachel Lundbohm is an Assistant Professor of Management at the University of Minnesota Crookston (UMC). She holds a BS in Marketing from St. Cloud State University, an MBA from the University of North Dakota, and a DBA from Metropolitan State University. Dr. Lundbohm has taught a variety of courses in management, marketing, and entrepreneurship. She has also worked with multiple entrepreneurs and economic development entities through applied research projects, course embedded experiential learning projects, and consulting activities. Her research interests include trends in digital and virtual marketing and management, hybrid learning, learning through simulation, and community engaged scholarship. ORCID ID: 0000-0003-4494-8381.

Sonali Malewar is a Sr. Assistant Professor in the domain of marketing with an experience of 20 years. Her research interests include Consumer behaviour and their consumption pattern.

Gunjan Mishra has received her PhD in Psychology from University of Rajasthan in 2009 and also holds the degree in Management. She has more than 18 years of experience both academic and administrative in various Universities in India. Currently, she is a professor of Psychology in ITM University Raipur. She writes and presents widely in the domain of positive psychology, counseling, social and organizational psychology. She has published extensively in various international and national journals of repute.

Sakshi Mishra holds a degree in dentistry and is currently pursuing Masters in Public Health from Institute of Public Health, Rajasthan University of Health Sciences, Jaipur. She is an avid reader. She has presented papers, posters in various international & national conference of medicine, public health and psychology.

Diana Rajendran, PhD, is a Senior Lecturer in Management at Swinburne School of Business, Law, and Entrepreneurship. Her research is on workforce diversity, migrant workers, leadership and work-life balance.

Adity Saxena holds a Ph.D. in Mass Communication, is a certified design thinker from Virginia University, and is an elected member of the Board of Directors of College Art Association, USA. In addition, she has been part of several global projects as a researcher and advisor, including European

About the Contributors

Union projects like Corporate Storytelling and Designing Life After COVID-19, a project by Harvard School of Public Health. Her recent research project is design thinking for social change, a funded project by Erasmus+. Recently she has been featured in The Academic Woman Magazine, the UK, in Jan-March, 2022 issue. She has over 20+ years of experience in teaching and leadership roles in higher education with an innovative Design Thinking approach. Apart from her academic role, she has been actively involved in students' well-being. As an outcome, in 2019, she was invited to the United States as a Restorative Justice co-facilitator in a school project. Currently, she is the India representative of the RJEd project. Her academic and research interests are primarily in design thinking, gender & education, visual narratives, communication design, social media communication, and development communication. Many of her studies are the result of international collaboration and have been published in international journals. She has served as a resource person on numerous international platforms, including the American Institute of Graphic Arts. Her dream is to create an enjoyable learning space for learners and educators.

Shaivi Shrivastava is currently pursuing her final year Honours programme in Applied Psychology from Amity University Chhattisgarh, Raipur, She has a keen interest in studying personality and her dissertation is focused in the area of dark triad personality traits.

Narayan Tiwari is the Chief Executive Officer, Crown Institute of Higher Education.

Palak Verma is a Research Scholar at Amity College of Commerce and Finance and a member of the Core team of Amity Rekhi Centre of Excellence for Science of Happiness, Amity University, Noida, Uttar Pradesh, India. She is a young Researcher who is establishing herself in Knowledge Creation with a keen interest in Management of Human Resources, Organizational behaviour, Crisis management, Organizational well-being & Happiness, and the Role of Technology Empowerment in the Education Sector. She has been among the Core members in organizing FDPs with Government Institutions like AICTE and the Ministry of Happiness in India. Further, she has coordinated various conferences and Organizational Trainings in the field of Happiness and Well-Being.

Eddie G. Walker II (Ph.D., University of North Dakota) is an Associate Professor of Sport and Recreation Management at the University of Minnesota Crookston. Dr. Walker's research interests include sport ethics, corporate social responsibility, leadership, and psycho-social aspects of sport. ORCID ID: 0000-0002-5647-9562.

Sureyya Yigit is a Professor of Political and International Relations at the School of Politics and Diplomacy, New Vision University, Tbilisi, Georgia. He has been the Senior Consultant to ZDS – Women's Democracy Network Public Fund, Bishkek, Kyrgyz Republic, since 2013.

Index

A

Agreeableness 179, 193, 201
apostles of managerialism 1, 11
Australia 1, 36, 38, 40, 45, 47-50, 52-56, 58-59, 61, 63-67, 72, 92-93, 97, 109, 248, 252, 257
Australian higher education sector 51, 56-58, 97

B

Black Women 69-70, 74-75, 78, 83, 86-87
Bright and Dark traits 176, 178
Business Students Perceptions 272

C

capacity building 41, 45, 63, 107, 125
Cohesion 110-112, 114-115, 118, 120, 122-123, 238, 247, 260, 263, 304
collective bargaining 110-112, 114, 126
Conscientiousness 178, 193, 201
Consensus among leaders and academics 92, 98
corporate apparatchiks 1, 9-13
corporate happiness 21-22, 26, 28
COVID-19 13, 19-20, 22-23, 25, 28, 30, 94-95, 97, 108, 112, 121, 123, 125-126, 128, 132-133, 135-138, 144, 146-147, 159, 222-225, 233-234, 248, 251, 253, 256, 263, 266-268, 272-274, 283-285, 287-293, 295-296, 300, 302-303, 305-312

D

Dark Leadership 176-178, 183, 185-187, 191-192, 195, 201
Dark Leadership Styles 176, 183, 192
Dark Triad 197, 202-203, 206-210, 212-215
Delphi study 92-93, 98
Dialogue 48, 53, 79, 86, 90, 111, 113-114, 118, 121, 124-125, 129

Domains of leadership 92, 101-102

E

E-Competencies 248, 253-254, 257, 259, 264-266
education 16-17, 36-38, 40-43, 46-59, 61-67, 69-75, 78, 80-82, 84, 86-90, 92-101, 103-109, 111, 114, 120, 125-127, 132-141, 143-147, 158, 191, 213, 238, 266, 269, 273-274, 283-289, 301-302, 309-310
Educational Leaders 76, 132-139, 142, 144-145
E-Leadership Challenges 248, 257, 262, 264-265
Elements of leadership 92, 98, 101-102
Employee Engagement 19, 22, 26-27, 31-32, 133, 148-150, 152-154, 156-161, 228, 256
Employee Retention 27, 150, 158, 163, 168
Employee Well-Being 148-150, 163, 166, 191
Ethical Leadership 32, 110, 112, 148-152, 154, 156-162
Europe 3, 17, 190, 195, 251-252, 257, 268, 289, 296
European Union 289-290, 311
Extraversion 178-179, 201, 207

F

Foreign Policy 289, 311

G

Gender 39, 46-47, 53, 55-67, 69-71, 73-76, 79, 82, 84-91, 113, 170, 303, 311
Gender Equality 55-56, 59, 62-63, 65, 69-70, 86-87, 113
Global 1, 4, 6-7, 15-16, 22, 31-32, 58, 71, 104, 109-114, 116-117, 120, 123-127, 132-133, 135, 187, 195, 220, 224, 229, 239, 251, 253, 263, 266-268, 284-287, 289-290, 292, 294, 296-299, 305-311
Globalisation 93, 217, 241, 267, 289-290, 296-297, 304, 306, 310-311

Index

H

Higher education 17, 37-38, 42-43, 47, 49-59, 61-67, 74, 87, 92-101, 103-109, 132, 136-137, 139, 146-147, 266, 273-274, 283-285, 309-310
HRM practices 19
Hubris 181-182, 185, 195, 199-201

I

ideology 1-17, 26, 60, 107, 185, 187, 190
Indigenous Australia 36
Inequalities 56, 71, 110, 112, 190, 297, 306, 310
Inequality 46, 55-56, 59-61, 63, 65, 71, 74, 112, 124, 295, 297
Innovation 49, 55, 58, 64, 95, 98-99, 129, 132, 136, 144-145, 160, 179-180, 220, 238, 240, 246, 259, 266, 268, 277, 288
Institutional Happiness 132, 134, 137-138, 143, 145
International Relations 41, 289, 296
Interventions 31, 190-191, 293, 312

L

Labor Laws 129
leader 2, 9, 13, 19, 25-32, 39-40, 56-57, 61, 63, 67, 72, 76, 78-81, 83, 88-89, 100, 102, 104, 107, 115, 119-120, 148, 152, 157, 165-166, 169, 176-178, 180-181, 183-185, 187-189, 191-192, 195-197, 199-200, 202-206, 208-210, 212, 217-221, 225, 227, 239, 245, 253, 257, 261-263, 265-266, 273-277, 279, 281-286, 291-292, 299-301, 303-304, 308, 311
Leadership 1-2, 5, 11-23, 25-34, 36-51, 54-67, 69, 71-90, 93-96, 98-110, 112, 115-116, 118-120, 122-129, 133-137, 139, 146-152, 154, 156-174, 176-179, 181-187, 189-210, 212-215, 217-223, 225-230, 232-251, 253, 255-256, 258-262, 264-269, 273-275, 277-281, 283-293, 296-311
Leadership SME 235

M

Machiavellianism 176, 183, 198, 201-202, 206-209, 213-215
management 1-5, 7-10, 12-19, 25-26, 29-32, 42, 55, 57, 61, 63-67, 71, 80, 84, 87, 94, 98, 101, 105-109, 118, 122, 124, 128-129, 132, 137, 140, 144-146, 149-152, 158-160, 162, 165, 169-174, 177, 183, 194-197, 200, 202-203, 207, 211-213, 217-218, 221, 223-224, 227, 230, 233-235, 240-249, 251, 253-255, 257-261, 263-264, 266-269, 273, 275, 281, 285-286, 288, 290, 292-293, 297, 299, 303-306, 308-309, 312
managerialism 1-17, 94-95, 97, 99, 103-104, 107, 109
Manufacturing Firm 148, 153
mental health 19-20, 22-23, 30, 41, 49, 143, 147, 172, 256, 265, 280
Mentoring 41, 47, 53, 69, 71-73, 75-76, 87-89, 91, 211, 230, 240
Movement 19-23, 26, 28-30, 32, 110-111, 113-115, 118, 120-123, 127, 211, 242, 308

N

Narcissism 176, 181-182, 185-186, 189, 199, 201-202, 206-210, 213, 215
NVIVO 132, 138, 142

O

Organization 2, 4, 7, 9, 12, 14, 17-18, 25-28, 66, 74, 105, 107, 111, 117-119, 126, 129, 135-136, 140, 148-153, 157-158, 161, 163-164, 166, 168-171, 173, 177-185, 188-189, 191-192, 200-201, 207, 211, 214, 217-219, 225-226, 230, 236, 238-239, 266-268, 278, 281, 285-286, 290, 293-294, 309-311

P

Pandemic 19, 22-23, 94-97, 104, 110, 112-113, 121, 123, 128, 133-140, 143-144, 146-147, 217, 222-223, 233, 251, 261, 264, 266, 268, 272-274, 278-279, 285, 287-294, 296, 300-310, 312
Performance 4, 7-8, 16, 20, 25, 27-28, 31-32, 34, 63, 80, 88, 100, 116, 119, 122-124, 129, 139-140, 148, 150-151, 153, 160-163, 165-166, 168, 171-173, 177, 179-185, 188, 192-193, 196, 198, 200, 210-211, 213, 218-219, 230, 233, 236, 238-239, 244, 246, 249, 253-254, 257-261, 263-268, 274, 276, 284-285, 303
Personality Traits 176-178, 181, 184, 202-203, 206, 208-210, 275, 291
positive psychology 19-20, 25-26, 29, 31-33, 133, 170
Principal 23, 69, 72, 74-76, 78-83, 85, 91, 298
Production 9, 23, 105, 112, 116, 122, 129, 160, 166, 235, 237, 240, 292, 310

R

Race 39, 46-48, 50-52, 69-70, 76, 91, 306
Remote-work 272-274

377

Representatives 110, 118, 122, 223, 227

S

School Administrator 69, 80, 91
School Superintendent 70, 75, 84, 86, 88, 90
Sexism 53, 71, 91
social justice 71, 83, 110, 116-117, 121
Spirituality 70, 76, 91
Succession Planning 55-66, 96, 99
Susceptible Followers 176, 178, 181, 185, 187, 190, 192, 199
Sustainable Universities 132-139, 144-145
Swami Vivekananda 82, 91
Systematic Literature Review 33, 247-249, 269, 284

T

talent management 19, 29, 57, 230
Technological Change 129, 259
Thematic Analysis 138
tiddas 36-37, 42-49, 51
Toxic Triangle 176, 185-186, 189, 199
Trade Union 110-123, 125, 127-129
Trade Unions 110-129
Turbulent environment 136

U

Uncertain Times 100, 118, 202, 217-218, 228

V

Virtual Leadership 249, 267, 272, 274-275, 277, 280-281, 283-287
Virtual Leadership Skills 272, 274, 280, 286
VUCA 217-218, 220-221, 226-230, 232-234

W

Wages 2, 13, 34, 112-113, 117, 121, 129
wellbeing 33, 49, 67, 114-115, 134, 136-141, 143-145, 150-151, 153-154, 157-162, 217, 266
Well-Being 19, 24, 26-28, 33, 79, 107, 132-135, 137, 141, 144, 147-153, 156-157, 159, 163, 166, 168, 173, 177, 179, 190-191, 219, 246, 256-257, 260, 295
Women of Color 70-71, 74, 76, 78
Work 3, 6-8, 10-11, 15-20, 22, 24, 26-33, 37-47, 55-57, 59-67, 76-78, 81, 85, 88, 90, 94-97, 103-105, 110-130, 133-147, 150-153, 158-161, 163, 165-166, 168, 170-171, 173, 176, 178-180, 183-185, 188, 198, 204, 207, 210-211, 217-220, 225, 227-230, 235-236, 241-244, 247, 249, 251-252, 254, 256-258, 260-261, 263-266, 272-281, 283-288, 292-293, 296, 299, 304, 309
Workers 1-3, 5, 7, 9, 13, 20-26, 28-30, 56, 60, 97, 110-128, 130, 150, 152-153, 161, 166, 210-212, 218, 220, 228-229, 240, 248, 257, 263, 276, 278-279
Workers' Rights 110-112, 124, 130
Work-Life Balance 24, 132, 137, 139-140, 163, 168-172, 178, 211, 248, 256-257, 265, 276

Recommended Reference Books

IGI Global's reference books are available in three unique pricing formats:
Print Only, E-Book Only, or Print + E-Book.

Order direct through IGI Global's Online Bookstore at
www.igi-global.com or through your preferred provider.

ISBN: 9781799887096
EISBN: 9781799887119
© 2022; 413 pp.
List Price: US$ **250**

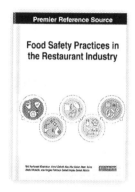

ISBN: 9781799874157
EISBN: 9781799874164
© 2022; 334 pp.
List Price: US$ **240**

ISBN: 9781668440230
EISBN: 9781668440254
© 2022; 320 pp.
List Price: US$ **215**

ISBN: 9781799889502
EISBN: 9781799889526
© 2022; 263 pp.
List Price: US$ **240**

ISBN: 9781799885283
EISBN: 9781799885306
© 2022; 587 pp.
List Price: US$ **360**

ISBN: 9781668455906
EISBN: 9781668455913
© 2022; 2,235 pp.
List Price: US$ **1,865**

Do you want to stay current on the latest research trends, product announcements, news, and special offers?
Join IGI Global's mailing list to receive customized recommendations, exclusive discounts, and more.
Sign up at: **www.igi-global.com/newsletters**.

Publisher of Timely, Peer-Reviewed Inclusive Research Since 1988

www.igi-global.com | Sign up at www.igi-global.com/newsletters | facebook.com/igiglobal | twitter.com/igiglobal | linkedin.com/igiglobal

Ensure Quality Research is Introduced to the Academic Community

Become an Evaluator for IGI Global Authored Book Projects

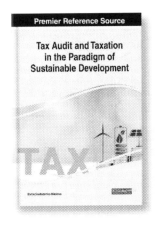   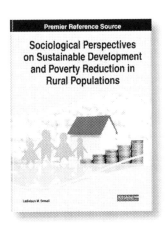

The overall success of an authored book project is dependent on quality and timely manuscript evaluations.

Applications and Inquiries may be sent to:
development@igi-global.com

Applicants must have a doctorate (or equivalent degree) as well as publishing, research, and reviewing experience. Authored Book Evaluators are appointed for one-year terms and are expected to complete at least three evaluations per term. Upon successful completion of this term, evaluators can be considered for an additional term.

If you have a colleague that may be interested in this opportunity, we encourage you to share this information with them.

Easily Identify, Acquire, and Utilize Published Peer-Reviewed Findings in Support of Your Current Research

IGI Global OnDemand

Purchase Individual IGI Global OnDemand Book Chapters and Journal Articles

For More Information:
www.igi-global.com/e-resources/ondemand/

Browse through 150,000+ Articles and Chapters!

Find specific research related to your current studies and projects that have been contributed by international researchers from prestigious institutions, including:

- Accurate and Advanced Search
- Affordably Acquire Research
- Instantly Access Your Content
- Benefit from the InfoSci Platform Features

"It really provides an excellent entry into the research literature of the field. It presents a manageable number of highly relevant sources on topics of interest to a wide range of researchers. The sources are scholarly, but also accessible to 'practitioners'."

- Ms. Lisa Stimatz, MLS, University of North Carolina at Chapel Hill, USA

Interested in Additional Savings?

Subscribe to
IGI Global OnDemand Plus

Learn More

Acquire content from over 128,000+ research-focused book chapters and 33,000+ scholarly journal articles for as low as US$ 5 per article/chapter (original retail price for an article/chapter: US$ 37.50).

7,300+ E-BOOKS. ADVANCED RESEARCH. INCLUSIVE & AFFORDABLE.

IGI Global e-Book Collection

- **Flexible Purchasing Options** (Perpetual, Subscription, EBA, etc.)
- Multi-Year Agreements with **No Price Increases** Guaranteed
- **No Additional Charge** for Multi-User Licensing
- No Maintenance, Hosting, or Archiving Fees
- Continually Enhanced & Innovated **Accessibility Compliance Features** (WCAG)

Handbook of Research on Digital Transformation, Industry Use Cases, and the Impact of Disruptive Technologies
ISBN: 9781799877127
EISBN: 9781799877141

Handbook of Research on New Investigations in Artificial Life, AI, and Machine Learning
ISBN: 9781799886860
EISBN: 9781799886877

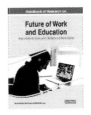

Handbook of Research on Future of Work and Education
ISBN: 9781799882756
EISBN: 9781799882770

Research Anthology on Physical and Intellectual Disabilities in an Inclusive Society (4 Vols.)
ISBN: 9781668435427
EISBN: 9781668435434

Innovative Economic, Social, and Environmental Practices for Progressing Future Sustainability
ISBN: 9781799895909
EISBN: 9781799895923

Applied Guide for Event Study Research in Supply Chain Management
ISBN: 9781799889694
EISBN: 9781799889717

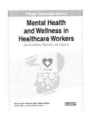

Mental Health and Wellness in Healthcare Workers
ISBN: 9781799888130
EISBN: 9781799888147

Clean Technologies and Sustainable Development in Civil Engineering
ISBN: 9781799898108
EISBN: 9781799898122

Request More Information, or Recommend the IGI Global e-Book Collection to Your Institution's Librarian

For More Information or to Request a Free Trial, Contact IGI Global's e-Collections Team: eresources@igi-global.com | 1-866-342-6657 ext. 100 | 717-533-8845 ext. 100

Are You Ready to Publish Your Research

IGI Global offers book authorship and editorship opportunities across 11 subject areas, including business, computer science, education, science and engineering, social sciences, and more!

Benefits of Publishing with IGI Global:

- Free one-on-one editorial and promotional support.
- Expedited publishing timelines that can take your book from start to finish in less than one (1) year.
- Choose from a variety of formats, including Edited and Authored References, Handbooks of Research, Encyclopedias, and Research Insights.
- Utilize IGI Global's eEditorial Discovery® submission system in support of conducting the submission and double-blind peer review process.
- IGI Global maintains a strict adherence to ethical practices due in part to our full membership with the Committee on Publication Ethics (COPE).
- Indexing potential in prestigious indices such as Scopus®, Web of Science™, PsycINFO®, and ERIC – Education Resources Information Center.
- Ability to connect your ORCID iD to your IGI Global publications.
- Earn honorariums and royalties on your full book publications as well as complimentary content and exclusive discounts.

Join Your Colleagues from Prestigious Institutions, Including:

Learn More at: www.igi-global.com/publish
or Contact IGI Global's Aquisitions Team at: acquisition@igi-global.com

Individual Article & Chapter Downloads
US$ 29.50/each

Easily Identify, Acquire, and Utilize Published Peer-Reviewed Findings in Support of Your Current Research

- Browse Over **170,000+ Articles & Chapters**
- **Accurate & Advanced** Search
- Affordably Acquire **International Research**
- **Instantly Access** Your Content
- Benefit from the *InfoSci® Platform Features*

THE UNIVERSITY of NORTH CAROLINA at CHAPEL HILL

" *It really provides an excellent entry into the research literature of the field. It presents a manageable number of highly relevant sources on topics of interest to a wide range of researchers. The sources are scholarly, but also accessible to 'practitioners'.* "

- Ms. Lisa Stimatz, MLS, University of North Carolina at Chapel Hill, USA

Interested in Additional Savings?

Subscribe to **IGI Global OnDemand *Plus***

Learn More

Acquire content from over 137,000+ research-focused book chapters and 33,000+ scholarly journal articles for as low as US$ 5 per article/chapter (original retail price for an article/chapter: US$ 29.50).

IGI Global Proudly Partners with

Editorial Services

Providing you with High-Quality, Affordable, and Expeditious Editorial Support from Manuscript Development to Publication

Copy Editing & Proofreading

Perfect your research paper before publication. Our expert editors will correct faulty spelling, grammar, punctuation, and word usage.

Scientific & Scholarly Editing

Increase your chances of being published. Our expert editors will aid in strengthening the quality of your research before submission.

Figure, Table, Chart & Equation Conversions

Enhance the visual elements of your research. Let our professional designers produce or correct your figures before final submission.

Journal Recommendation

Save time and money when you rely on our expert journal selectors to provide you with a comprehensive journal recommendation report.

Order now to receive an automatic **10% Academic Discount** on all your editorial needs.

Scan the QR Code to Learn More

Upload Your Manuscript, Select Your Desired Editorial Service, and Receive a Free Instant Quote

Email: customerservice@econtentpro.com

econtentpro.com

Printed in the United States
by Baker & Taylor Publisher Services